T0189426

Lecture Notes in Computer Science 14014

Founding Editors

Gerhard Goos
Juris Hartmanis

The series Lecture Notes in Computer Science (LNCS), including its subseries Lecture Notes in Artificial Intelligence (LNAI) and Lecture Notes in Bioinformatics (LNBI), has established itself as a medium for the publication of new developments in computer science and information technology research, teaching, and education.

LNCS enjoys close cooperation with the computer science R & D community, the series counts many renowned academics among its volume editors and paper authors, and collaborates with prestigious societies. Its mission is to serve this international community by providing an invaluable service, mainly focused on the publication of conference and workshop proceedings and postproceedings. LNCS commenced publication in 1973.

Masaaki Kurosu · Ayako Hashizume
Editors

Human-Computer Interaction

Thematic Area, HCI 2023
Held as Part of the 25th HCI International Conference, HCII 2023
Copenhagen, Denmark, July 23–28, 2023
Proceedings, Part IV

 Springer

Editors
Masaaki Kurosu
The Open University of Japan
Chiba, Japan

Ayako Hashizume
Hosei University
Tokyo, Japan

ISSN 0302-9743 ISSN 1611-3349 (electronic)
Lecture Notes in Computer Science
ISBN 978-3-031-35571-4 ISBN 978-3-031-35572-1 (eBook)
https://doi.org/10.1007/978-3-031-35572-1

This Springer imprint is published by the registered company Springer Nature Switzerland AG
The registered company address is: Gewerbestrasse 11, 6330 Cham, Switzerland

Foreword

Human-computer interaction (HCI) is acquiring an ever-increasing scientific and industrial importance, as well as having more impact on people's everyday lives, as an ever-growing number of human activities are progressively moving from the physical to the digital world. This process, which has been ongoing for some time now, was further accelerated during the acute period of the COVID-19 pandemic. The HCI International (HCII) conference series, held annually, aims to respond to the compelling need to advance the exchange of knowledge and research and development efforts on the human aspects of design and use of computing systems.

The 25th International Conference on Human-Computer Interaction, HCI International 2023 (HCII 2023), was held in the emerging post-pandemic era as a 'hybrid' event at the AC Bella Sky Hotel and Bella Center, Copenhagen, Denmark, during July 23–28, 2023. It incorporated the 21 thematic areas and affiliated conferences listed below.

A total of 7472 individuals from academia, research institutes, industry, and government agencies from 85 countries submitted contributions, and 1578 papers and 396 posters were included in the volumes of the proceedings that were published just before the start of the conference, these are listed below. The contributions thoroughly cover the entire field of human-computer interaction, addressing major advances in knowledge and effective use of computers in a variety of application areas. These papers provide academics, researchers, engineers, scientists, practitioners and students with state-of-the-art information on the most recent advances in HCI.

The HCI International (HCII) conference also offers the option of presenting 'Late Breaking Work', and this applies both for papers and posters, with corresponding volumes of proceedings that will be published after the conference. Full papers will be included in the 'HCII 2023 - Late Breaking Work - Papers' volumes of the proceedings to be published in the Springer LNCS series, while 'Poster Extended Abstracts' will be included as short research papers in the 'HCII 2023 - Late Breaking Work - Posters' volumes to be published in the Springer CCIS series.

I would like to thank the Program Board Chairs and the members of the Program Boards of all thematic areas and affiliated conferences for their contribution towards the high scientific quality and overall success of the HCI International 2023 conference. Their manifold support in terms of paper reviewing (single-blind review process, with a minimum of two reviews per submission), session organization and their willingness to act as goodwill ambassadors for the conference is most highly appreciated.

This conference would not have been possible without the continuous and unwavering support and advice of Gavriel Salvendy, founder, General Chair Emeritus, and Scientific Advisor. For his outstanding efforts, I would like to express my sincere appreciation to Abbas Moallem, Communications Chair and Editor of HCI International News.

July 2023   Constantine Stephanidis

HCI International 2023 Thematic Areas and Affiliated Conferences

Thematic Areas

- HCI: Human-Computer Interaction
- HIMI: Human Interface and the Management of Information

Affiliated Conferences

- EPCE: 20th International Conference on Engineering Psychology and Cognitive Ergonomics
- AC: 17th International Conference on Augmented Cognition
- UAHCI: 17th International Conference on Universal Access in Human-Computer Interaction
- CCD: 15th International Conference on Cross-Cultural Design
- SCSM: 15th International Conference on Social Computing and Social Media
- VAMR: 15th International Conference on Virtual, Augmented and Mixed Reality
- DHM: 14th International Conference on Digital Human Modeling and Applications in Health, Safety, Ergonomics and Risk Management
- DUXU: 12th International Conference on Design, User Experience and Usability
- C&C: 11th International Conference on Culture and Computing
- DAPI: 11th International Conference on Distributed, Ambient and Pervasive Interactions
- HCIBGO: 10th International Conference on HCI in Business, Government and Organizations
- LCT: 10th International Conference on Learning and Collaboration Technologies
- ITAP: 9th International Conference on Human Aspects of IT for the Aged Population
- AIS: 5th International Conference on Adaptive Instructional Systems
- HCI-CPT: 5th International Conference on HCI for Cybersecurity, Privacy and Trust
- HCI-Games: 5th International Conference on HCI in Games
- MobiTAS: 5th International Conference on HCI in Mobility, Transport and Automotive Systems
- AI-HCI: 4th International Conference on Artificial Intelligence in HCI
- MOBILE: 4th International Conference on Design, Operation and Evaluation of Mobile Communications

List of Conference Proceedings Volumes Appearing Before the Conference

47. CCIS 1836, HCI International 2023 Posters - Part V, edited by Constantine Stephanidis, Margherita Antona, Stavroula Ntoa and Gavriel Salvendy

https://2023.hci.international/proceedings

Preface

Human-Computer Interaction is a Thematic Area of the International Conference on Human-Computer Interaction (HCII). The HCI field is today undergoing a wave of significant innovation and breakthroughs towards radically new future forms of interaction. The HCI Thematic Area constitutes a forum for scientific research and innovation in human-computer interaction, addressing challenging and innovative topics in human-computer interaction theory, methodology, and practice, including, for example, novel theoretical approaches to interaction, novel user interface concepts and technologies, novel interaction devices, UI development methods, environments and tools, multimodal user interfaces, human-robot interaction, emotions in HCI, aesthetic issues, HCI and children, evaluation methods and tools, and many others.

The HCI Thematic Area covers four major dimensions, namely theory and methodology, technology, human beings, and societal impact. The following four volumes of the HCII 2023 proceedings reflect these dimensions:

- Human-Computer Interaction (Part I), addressing topics related to design and evaluation methods, techniques and tools, and interaction methods and techniques
- Human-Computer Interaction (Part II), addressing topics related to children-computer interaction, emotions in HCI, and understanding the user experience
- Human-Computer Interaction (Part III), addressing topics related to human-robot interaction, chatbots and voice-based interaction, and interacting in the metaverse
- Human-Computer Interaction (Part IV), addressing topics related to supporting health, quality of life and everyday activities, as well as topics related to HCI for learning, culture, creativity, and societal impact.

Papers of these volumes are included for publication after a minimum of two single-blind reviews from the members of the HCI Program Board or, in some cases, from members of the Program Boards of other affiliated conferences. We would like to thank all of them for their invaluable contribution, support, and efforts.

July 2023

Masaaki Kurosu
Ayako Hashizume

Human-Computer Interaction Thematic Area (HCI 2023)

Program Board Chairs: **Masaaki Kurosu**, *The Open University of Japan, Japan* and **Ayako Hashizume**, *Hosei University, Japan*

Program Board:

- Salah Ahmed, *University of South-Eastern Norway, Norway*
- Valdecir Becker, *Federal University of Paraiba, Brazil*
- Nimish Biloria, *University of Technology Sydney, Australia*
- Zhigang Chen, *Shanghai University, P.R. China*
- C. M. Nadeem Faisal, *National Textile University, Pakistan*
- Yu-Hsiu Hung, *National Cheng Kung University, Taiwan*
- Jun Iio, *Chuo University, Japan*
- Yi Ji, *Guangdong University of Technology, P.R. China*
- Hiroshi Noborio, *Osaka Electro-Communication University, Japan*
- Katsuhiko Onishi, *Osaka Electro-Communication University, Japan*
- Mohammad Shidujaman, *Independent University, Bangladesh, Bangladesh*

The full list with the Program Board Chairs and the members of the Program Boards of all thematic areas and affiliated conferences of HCII2023 is available online at:

http://www.hci.international/board-members-2023.php

HCI International 2024 Conference

The 26th International Conference on Human-Computer Interaction, HCI International 2024, will be held jointly with the affiliated conferences at the Washington Hilton Hotel, Washington, DC, USA, June 29 – July 4, 2024. It will cover a broad spectrum of themes related to Human-Computer Interaction, including theoretical issues, methods, tools, processes, and case studies in HCI design, as well as novel interaction techniques, interfaces, and applications. The proceedings will be published by Springer. More information will be made available on the conference website: http://2024.hci.international/.

General Chair
Prof. Constantine Stephanidis
University of Crete and ICS-FORTH
Heraklion, Crete, Greece
Email: general_chair@hcii2024.org

https://2024.hci.international/

Contents – Part IV

HCI for Learning, Culture, Creativity and Societal Impact

Supporting Health, Quality of Life and Everyday Activities

Design and Performance Analysis of a Smart Bag Reminder System for Parents

Md Farhad Hossain[1,2], Mengru Xue[1,3(✉)] (iD), Yuqi Hu[1,2],
and Mohammad Shidujaman[4] (iD)

[1] Ningbo Research Institute, Zhejiang University, Ningbo, China
{22151447,mengruxue,yuqihu}@zju.edu.cn
[2] School of Software Technology, Zhejiang University, Ningbo, China
[3] College of Computer Science and Technology, Zhejiang University, Hangzhou, China
[4] Independent University, Bangladesh (IUB), Dhaka, Bangladesh
shantothusets@iub.edu.bd

Abstract. The parents of a newborn must pay close attention at all times in order to keep track of the many details involved in caring for their child. When leaving the house with a newborn, it can be difficult for parents to remember and pack all of the necessary items. In this paper, we show a light-feedback reminder bag and a light-sound feedback reminder bag that use a pressure sensor to remind parents when anything is missing from the bag. A user study was conducted with 13 participants (8 fathers and 5 mothers) to understand their experiences with our two reminder bags. The results show that light-sound feedback facilitates parent reminders better than light feedback. This work transfers the attention from babies to new parents in order to help them adjust to their new role with less stress.

Keywords: Smart bag · Reminder system · Pressure sensor · New Parents · Light-sound feedback

1 Introduction

Using baby items and activities in the wrong way can hurt babies, which makes it hard for parents. When it comes time for a family to go, the parents just take the bag and walk out the door, secure in the knowledge that they have everything necessary to meet the baby's requirements. Even though bags are an effective way to keep related objects together, parents often encounter breaks in their memory and overlook an essential item. Bags, in their present iteration, are not particularly effective at communicating their contents. When they look at something, it is not always easy to identify what it is. All of the necessary goods are concealed inside a bag that seems to have nothing inside. Parents are able to glance inside a bag and see what items are inside, but it is impossible to tell what is missing from the bag just by looking into it. Take the diaper bag as an illustration here. This bag stores a variety of items, including new diapers, wipes, a changing pad, lotion, hand sanitizer, snacks, chew toys, a change of clothing, and much more, all in one convenient location [1]. Even if the bag keeps all of the materials together, it is difficult for parents to recall whether or not a necessary item is missing. This may result in a situation that is both humiliating and unpleasant for the parents.

© The Author(s), under exclusive license to Springer Nature Switzerland AG 2023
M. Kurosu and A. Hashizume (Eds.): HCII 2023, LNCS 14014, pp. 3–18, 2023.
https://doi.org/10.1007/978-3-031-35572-1_1

In our previous work, we showed a reminder concept for a smart bag that could be used as a reminder. That design makes use of modular pressure sensors in order to offer lighting feedback if any objects are missing from the bag. The feedback suggests that there is something that ought to be in the bag but is not. In our previous research, the participants wanted to interact with the prototype in order to better comprehend it, but they were unable to do so because of the epidemic. Their comments, which were based on our prototype's video, were evaluated. The previous study was done through an online interview as its primary data collection method, but offline field research was required in order to have a complete understanding of what it is that parents seek. Through our previous studies, we obtained user feedback as well as suggestions and potential problems. The overwhelming majority of those who participated in our previous research suggested that we incorporate sound feedback with the lighting in our subsequent research; they believed this would result in a more innovative outcome. Several participants also suggested that we include the name of the object in the audio feedback so that they pay more attention. In addition, they said that without lighting feedback, only voice command reminders could be used [22].

After analyzing the drawbacks and suggestions from previous research, we came up with the new idea of a Reminder Bag system as a way to assist new parents in their day-to-day lives. This system works by using an Arduino installing a pressure sensor module, an LED light in each of the bag's pockets, and a speaker. Along with the different light feedback from different pockets, the speaker also gives different sound feedback. As soon as the pressure sensor determines that objects have been pushed against it, the light and sound feedback will become active. The bag uses a modular pressure sensor that is readily detachable, and parents can choose the number of pockets that can be utilized. In addition, the audio feedback can be customized according to their preferences, and they can label the front of each pocket with the items they use most often. When using this method, parents' recollection is aided more by the light-sound feedback than it is by the light feedback.

The two main contributions of this research are:

- light-sound feedback facilitates parent reminders better than light feedback.
- Evaluating the previous and current reminder systems in a 13-participant user study.

The remainder of this paper is organized as follows: In the next section, we present related work about reminders, including smart bag reminders with lights and sound feedback. We then proceed to describe the system implementation for the smart bag reminder. Finally, we present the evaluation, results of the evaluation and discuss the feasibility of making reminder systems and the design criteria for making such systems so that new parents' daily lives are easier.

2   Related Work

2.1   Multi-modal Reminders in Various Ways

When it comes to caring for their infant, new parents may find help from a variety of programs, such as an alarm that serves as a reminder of important tasks and can be installed on their mobile devices. This may sometimes result in the application experiencing technical problems. Around the concept of smart bag reminders for various circumstances, several preliminary research and design ideas have begun to emerge. According to the findings of a number of studies, there is a wide variety of different approaches that are referred to as "reminders" that families take in order to successfully juggle the competing demands of their jobs, their families, their homes, and their participation in enrichment activities [1–3]. These approaches are taken by families in order to ensure that they are able to successfully juggle all of these competing responsibilities. It is similar to a spell checker that teaches a child to spell better or an activity pack that teaches them to create routines, and both of these things assist the child in becoming more independent. On the other hand, there is no such thing as a precise idea of a reminder that is capable of reminding the user. In addition, there are a number of additional studies that might serve as a conceptual recall for a variety of locations [4–7]. These investigations also make use of the technique of reminder, and based on what older people stated they desired and required, studies indicate some of the needs and desires of older users for a multi-modal reminder system.

2.2 System of Reminders Using Light and Sound

The Lady Bag is a set of designs for lady's purses that employ LEDs [8], which were designed by academics at Simon Fraser University. One way in which the bag might be used to express oneself is to carry a torch, like the torch bag. Their designs also demonstrated the use of a radio frequency identification (RFID) system, which indicated that the LEDs would be able to work in order to communicate with one another when an item was missing. Having said that, the use of an RFID system does come with a few restrictions [9]. RFID comes with a hefty price tag in the form of an ever-increasing number of potential dangers to users' privacy and security [10]. In particular, radio frequency identification (RFID) tags are often bigger than bar-code labels, and each tag is designed specifically for a particular use mainly due to the fact that the majority of tags are fastened to the inside of the rear cover. Furthermore, when tags are placed within 1/8 of an inch of one another, they may interfere with one another [10]. Several studies have discussed the sound feedback reminder in their studies for different cases, and user studies have revealed that sound feedback can be used in future studies [11, 12]. However, there are no appropriate sound feedback reminder prototypes available at the moment to assist new parents in remembering to bring essential items for their babies.

2.3 Smart Bag Reminder

In our previous work, we presented a smart bag reminder design that uses modular pressure sensors to provide lighting feedback when any items are missing from the bag. The feedback indicates that there is something that should have been in the bag but is not there. Due to the epidemic, our previous research user study was carried out online. Unfortunately, we were unable to carry out any more user research offline, where the participants were unable to engage with our prototype. During the interviews, we demonstrated how our prototype worked by showing a video that simulated the experience of using our smart bag reminder system in real life. This enabled the participants to more easily picture our description of how the system works in our previous work. However, the vast majority of user who participated in the research were satisfied with the previous idea of a smart reminder bag, as well as the fact that they also provided suggestions and drawbacks. The vast majority of the participants in our previous work suggested that we include sound feedback with lighting in our future work; they felt that doing so would make it more innovative. Several participants also proposed that we add the name of the item in the audio feedback so that they pay more attention. Furthermore, they said that without lighting feedback, only voice command reminders could be utilized. Moreover, the previous study was done using an online interview; in order to thoroughly understand user demands, an offline field study was required.

Under the above conditions, previous research by many authors has resulted in the identification of a number of unique reminder ideas, each of which may be implemented via a variety of diverse approaches. Following the research into the advantages and disadvantages of various reminder systems, it was discovered that the majority of the systems do not seem to have a well-defined reminder capable of bringing it to the user's attention in a reliable way. In our previous work, we presented the "light feedback" reminder. We iterate the Reminder Bag system as a means to aid new parents in their everyday lives in a more innovative way [19] after analyzing the drawbacks and suggestions from previous research. In this study, we present a new smart bag reminder approach that combines both sound and light feedback. The feedback indicates that there is something that should have been in the bag that is not there. Our research team believes that "sound-light" feedback is an effective way to remind people in this study based on the findings of past research.

3   Realization of Prototypes

In order to make the lives of new parents easier and save them the anguish of being unable to remember certain things, the purpose of this project is to design a smart bag called the "Reminder Bag" that will remind them to bring essential items for their baby whenever they go out. The remainder of this section will provide a detailed explanation of the smart bag reminder prototype's design process as well as its execution.

3.1   System Design

We placed a high priority on the portability of the reminder system as well as its capacity to provide feedback in real time. Our research team believes that the work that serves perfectly as "bag" is a fantastic example of a media reminder strategy. As a result of its direct nature and the ample room it provides for the installation of sensors, it is the product that is most relevant to the situation. We developed two prototypes (one based on our previous research on light feedback and the other on a new concept of light-sound feedback that we present in this paper as proofs of concept) in order to determine whether or not our idea could actually be put into practice and, at the same time, to demonstrate that our proposition is feasible. In the two different prototypes, we utilized pressure sensors due to their low level of complexity in terms of construction and their high level of long-term reliability, which includes a high level of resistance to impacts, vibrations, and variations in dynamic pressure. This decision was made due to a number of factors, including the following: Circuits are not very complicated and do make it feasible to do measurements with a high degree of accuracy [13]. There is also a linear output with a response time of one millisecond that serves as a quick reminder signal [14]. In our previous study, we just offered light feedback, which can attract the attention of users. In this paper, we present light sound feedback because we believe that combining sound feedback with light will be more effective than light feedback and can attract the attention of users more rapidly. A number of other studies [15–17] have been conducted to give conceptual recall for various areas. We believed that this kind of reminder could be valuable to users.

3.2   Implementation

As our primary starting point, we used a bag that was created specifically for the purpose of transporting the necessities that are required for newborns. In a configuration that has a total of six pockets, there are in total 4 pockets on the inside of the bag, in addition to the two pockets that are located on the outside of the bag.

Light Feedback Prototype. There are four pockets on the inside of the bag and two pockets on the outside of the bag in a six-pocket design, as illustrated in Fig. 1(a, c). We gathered the emitter portion of each pocket in one location and the resister section in another so that we could easily provide electricity. The battery (9 V) served as our power source, with the positive end connected to a resistor and the negative end attached to the transistor's emitter region.

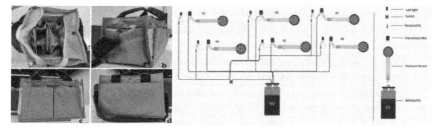

Fig. 1. (a–d) The smart bag reminder design provides lighting feedback, and (e) the technical implementation.

Figure 1(e) is an illustration of the technical implementation that was used in this prototype. At the conclusion of the operation, we put a switch controller (Fig. 1b) in the system so that the user could turn the system on and off whenever they wished. Each pocket has a pressure sensor that is linked to a transistor (C945). A transistor, as it is generally known, is made up of three semiconductor portions known as the emitter, base, and collector, in that order. The transistor's base and collector were connected to the pressure sensor. As a reminder, each pocket has an LED light. This light is divided into two parts: positive and negative. The positive portion is connected to the transistor's base, while the negative portion is connected to the 1 k resistor that we utilized. Each pocket was approached in the same way. The modular pressure sensor unit can be simply added or removed to meet the demands of the user.

Light-Sound Feedback Prototype. The six-pocket design of this bag is identical to the previous design (Fig. 2a, b), with four internal pockets and two external pockets. Inside of each pocket, we installed six pressure sensors.

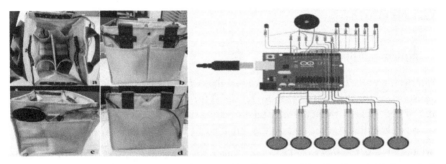

Fig. 2. (a–d) The smart bag reminder design provides light-sound feedback, and (e) the technical implementation.

To serve as a gentle nudge, there is an LED light in each pocket, and a speaker for providing audio feedback has been placed (Fig. 2c), and is connected to each pressure sensor as well as the light. We used six distinct audio tones associated with items that parents bring for their babies as a form of audio feedback. These included a tone of water flowing for water, a tone of a cow mooing for milk, a tone of a diaper zipper opening for diapers, a tone of clothes falling for clothes, a tone of snacks being chewed for snacks, and a tone of tissue being pulled for tissue. According to the findings of our previous studies, these items are frequently carried outdoors with the infant. This served to quickly remind the parents of what they were bringing and needed to take. The audio feedback can be customized to fit the requirements of the parents. The design implementation can be seen in (Fig. 2e). In this phase of the implementation, all resistors of value 220 Ω have been used. All that we've utilized in this implementation that's linked to the Arduino Mega (2560), including all of the components (Fig. 2d). The power supply for this particular installation was a power bank that had a capacity of 5 k amps.

4   Evaluation

The objectives of the user study are to determine whether light-sound feedback is more effective at facilitating parent reminders than simple light feedback, to investigate the efficacy of the Reminder Bag, and to identify potential design avenues for the advancement of intelligent Reminder Bags in the future. Meanwhile, we also conducted an investigation into the user experience by gathering quantitative and qualitative data from follow-up interviews and analyzing them correspondingly.

4.1 Participant

Our work shifted the attention from infants to their new parents in order to make it easier for the latter to adjust to their new roles and reduce the stress associated with the transition. As a result, our attention was being directed at new parents. We went to a local children's park, where a lot of parents would bring their infants to make friends and have fun. We were able to find one father at the Children's Park who was willing to participate when we asked him whether he would be willing to participate in the study, and then we used a method known as 'linear snowball sampling' [18] in order to recruit participants. A total of 13 users were recruited for the study (8 fathers and 5 mothers). These participants were the responsible caregivers for the baby. Everyone who participated provided their written informed consent.

4.2 Setting Up

For the user testing, we have selected a meeting room, and have sent invitations to all of our participants. We developed two prototypes (Fig. 3a and 3b) for the user study that could facilitate the user experience of the design concept. We carried both of our prototypes to the location that we had decided to utilize for user testing.

Fig. 3. (a) Light-feedback reminder bag; (b) Light-sound feedback reminder bag; and (c) Items inside the box.

In addition to that, we carried 15 baby items with us including milk, normal water, a hot water pot, diapers, clothes, tissues, lotion, spray, medicine, toys, juice, biscuits, towels, baby powder, and baby cream, which included items that were often brought out by parents as well as those that were collected through our previous study. We placed all of the items inside a box (Fig. 3c).

4.3 Procedure

We were not given any information about our prototypes prior to the experiment, including how they function or their purpose. We wanted users to be able to understand themselves after using the bag. We directly moved into the experiment. At the beginning of the experiment, we gave the participant a page with the names of six randomly selected items, including medicine, a towel, a hot water pot, a toy, baby powder, and lotion, for 1 min. After that, we gave them a task: They have to pack these six items from that box into the prototype as fast as they can. First, we provided them with a lighting feedback prototype. After that, we provided them with the light-sound feedback prototype for doing the same task with a list of six different items, including water, milk, diapers, cloth, tissue, and biscuits. The order to finish the tasks were counterbalanced. To obtain quantitative data, we record the time and make an observational note of the finished packaging. The task as conducted with each user one by one individually. The objective of this task was to investigate the disparities in packaging that exist between the two prototypes (Fig. 4).

Fig. 4. A father is doing the task with both prototypes (a) light feedback, (b) light-sound feedback, and a mother is doing the task with both prototypes (c) light feedback, (d) light-sound feedback.

Following the completion of the task, we asked them to provide us with their individual responses to our questionnaire and to discuss their experiences with the prototypes in order to gather qualitative data.

4.4 Measurements

Quantitative Data. The quantitative statistics presented in this paper are arranged in the following direction:

i. **Time for each person to finish packaging the six items (by seconds).** During the course of the task, we keep separate records of the times spent packing. In the earlier section, we stated that the purpose of this task was to analyse the differences in packaging that are present between the two prototypes. The amount of time they spent was split according to our light feedback and our light sound feedback. Moreover, we determined the packaging efficiency by calculating the average value {*Average value = sum of data / number of measurements*} [21] of each person's packed items using the light feedback and the light-sound feedback systems.

ii. **Accuracy for each person's packaged items with both prototypes.** During the duration of the task, we kept track of the number of user packs that were correct and the number that made mistakes in accordance with the items that we had provided for the task. We provided them with 15 items, and for each task, we instructed them to pack 6 items depending on those items. Accordingly, we investigated how accurate their remarks appeared. We calculate the accuracy rate of the participants' packaging of the items using light-sound feedback prototypes and light feedback prototypes, respectively.

iii. **Likert scale survey system,** we conducted a Likert scale survey to obtain quantitative results on two smart bag reminders [20]. After the user study procedure ended, we sent the participants a link to an online survey questionnaire with five questions, two of which were repeated for both prototypes to measure how differently they perform in quantitative terms. Last point, which was to see which prototypes participants preferred. We asked them to submit their quantitative feedback about our two prototypes. All of the data that was gathered was placed in a new sheet in Excel, and then calculations were performed using the Likert scale score in accordance with its analysis instructions [20].

Qualitative Data. In order to collect qualitative data, we asked that they discuss their experiences with the prototypes and provide us with their individual replies to the questionnaire that we had given them at the end of the experiment. The questionnaires are below:

- What do you think of the light prototype? Can it help you remember things during packaging? How can it help? Any drawbacks of this design?
- Do you think the design is useful in your real life to remind you while bring your child outdoor? Why?
- What do you think of the light-sound prototype? Can it help you remember things during packaging? How can it help? Any drawbacks of this design?
- Do you think the design is useful in your real life to remind you while bring your child outdoor? Why?
- About this two design, which prototype do you like more? Why?
- Will you use this bag in your daily life? Why?
- Do you have any suggestions for us about the design?

During the course of carrying out the questionnaires, we made it a point to take careful note of any pertinent observations that arose for the purpose of using these notes in the subsequent compilation of qualitative data. In order to explore and collect the information gained from the questionnaire in a comprehensive manner, the data that was obtained from the questionnaire was transcribed through a process known as thematic analysis.

5 Results

5.1 Quantitative Results

Time for Each Person to Finish Packaging the Six Items (by seconds): Table 1 shows an overview of the descriptive data for the time spent by participants, which was divided into seconds based on our light feedback and our light sound feedback.

It took our thirteen participants a combined total of 575 s to package our light-based feedback prototypes. Using the average value method [21], we split this total time spent by participants into their individual totals. It takes each participant an average of 44.23 s to achieve efficiency with our light feedback prototypes. Our thirteen participants required a total of 547 s to package our prototypes with light-sound feedback. With our

Table 1. List of data for each participant's time to finish packaging.

Participants	Light feedback	Light-sound feedback
P1	50 s	44 s
P2	79 s	72 s
P3	36 s	32 s
P4	39 s	35 s
P5	33 s	30 s
P6	39 s	31 s
P7	41 s	37 s
P8	32 s	43 s
P9	39 s	55 s
P10	45 s	37 s
P11	55 s	43 s
P12	49 s	39 s
P13	38 s	49 s

light-sound feedback prototypes, it takes each participant an average of 42.07 s to obtain efficiency. The average time spent comparing light sound feedback and light feedback prototypes was: $(44.23-42.07 = 2.16)$ seconds, which suggests that our light-feedback prototypes took an additional 2.16 s per person.

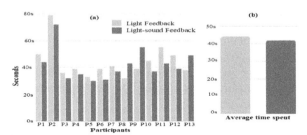

Fig. 5. (a) Time spent comparing the graph between the light sound feedback and light feedback prototypes, and (b) Average time graphs comparing light sound feedback and light feedback prototypes.

Figure 5 illustrates the amount of time spent comparing the graphs of light sound feedback and light feedback prototypes, as well as the average amount of time spent on the graphs of light sound feedback and light feedback prototypes based on the results of our research process.

Accuracy for Each Person's Packaged Items with Both Prototypes: According to Table 2, the accuracy of light feedback prototypes is lower than that of light sound feedback prototypes. This can be seen by comparing the both of prototypes.

Table 2. List of data for each participant's accuracy to finish packaging.

Participants	Light feedback	Light-sound feedback
P1	100%	100%
P2	83%	100%
P3	100%	100%
P4	100%	100%
P5	100%	100%
P6	100%	100%
P7	83%	100%
P8	100%	100%
P9	83%	100%
P10	100%	83%
P11	100%	100%
P12	100%	100%
P13	100%	100%

The overall accuracy graph for each person is shown in Fig. 6.

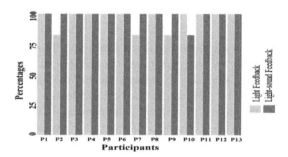

Fig. 6. Data list graph for each participant's accuracy to complete packing.

Likert-Scale Survey System: A Likert-scale survey system was carried out by us so that we could get quantitative findings about both smart bag reminders. After transferring all of the data that had been acquired onto a new sheet in Excel, calculations were carried out using the Likert scale score in accordance with the analysis instructions that came along with it [20]. Table 3 displays the total average score that respondents gave on the Likert scale for the questions that were answered in the online survey.

Questions 1 and 2 in Table 3 concerned light feedback prototypes, while Questions 3 and 4 focused on light sound feedback prototypes. The comparison of light feedback and light-sound feedback resulted in an average score that indicated that the light-sound feedback prototypes performed more effectively than the light feedback prototypes. It

Table 3. The overall average on the Likert scale for the questions in the online survey.

Question No	Online survey Questionnaire	Average Likert scale
1	I think that the light feedback reminder bag helps me remember things during packaging	3.53
2	I believe the light feedback reminder bag will be useful in real life to remind me to take my child outside	3.61
3	I think that the light-sound feedback reminder bag helps me remember things during packaging	4.30
4	I believe the light-sound feedback reminder bag will be useful in real life to remind me to take my child outside	4.23
5	I believe that a light-sound feedback reminder bag facilitates reminders better than a light-feedback reminder bag	4.53

was evidenced by the fact that the light-sound feedback prototypes received a higher score than the light feedback prototypes. According to the Likert scale, the findings of Question 5 are shown in Table 3, which met with a good reception. These results show that a reminder bag with both light and sound feedback was better at helping participants remember than a reminder bag with only light feedback.

5.2   Qualitative Results

User Interview Results on the Light Feedback Prototype: The participants provided us with indications that they enjoyed performing the task that we offered them. Nine of the participants (out of 13) were able to properly identify the bag as a reminder. They said that as they were packing, the light switched on, which drew their attention to what was going on. During the process of packing, light input helped them determine which pockets had previously been filled. This helped speed up the process. The (P8) participant finished the job in the shortest amount of time. (P8) particularly stated that, "*during the packing process, I was simply focused on the light in those pockets that I saw light off, and I realized I hadn't placed an item in them after that I had packaged them.*" The P5 participant also completed the task in the quickest period of time. P5 also mentioned that, "*the packaging time, I was looking in the pocket to see which pocket was free and packed, then my eyes were on the light, and after that, I realized that those pocket pack lights were turned on, but the rest of the pocket were turned off, and then I just filled them.*" These participants (P1, P2, P4 and P11) were unable to determine precisely what it was meant to accomplish. During the nightly packing process, they thought that having this light feedback would make it easier for them to see what was packed inside the bag. When we asked if the lighting could help them remember things while packing, they realized it was a type of lighting reminder. They mentioned that it has the potential to make them more attentive and has the capability of helping them remember items if any are not in the bag pockets during the process of packing. The participants mentioned that in real life, when they take their babies out, they need to carry a lot of items, and sometimes they forget to bring them, so this reminder has the ability to pay them more attention and also remind them if they forget to put items in the bag. (P9) mentioned that, "*during the task, I recognized this light feedback as one form of paying attention that is bringing more attention to packing, and it can assist me in packing if I forget items to pack in real life*". In addition to that, the (P13) participant said, "*I observed a number of reminders in real life that people were utilizing in different ways, but this was the first time I saw this sort of reminder using light feedback without using any other application.*" Overall, the majority of participants expressed contentment with the idea of receiving light feedback. This is shown through the use of positive language. The research assisted us in confirming the idea behind the design and finding problems with it. For example, most of the participants said the light wasn't bright enough, and the wiring connection that we just put in outside is affecting how the technical problems are handled.

User Interview Results on the Light-Sound Feedback Prototype: During the task phase with the light-sound prototypes, the largest number of participants displayed enjoyment through the use of a smile. They realized it was a sound feedback with light, and that when they packaged things, the audio feedback related to the items was delivered when they were packaging, we saw that our sound feedback helped them move more quickly. The greatest majority of participants said that while they were working on the task, receiving sound feedback assisted them in recognizing what they were packing. They didn't have to double-check what they put in the bag since the sound feedback helped them identify the items. The (P13) participant took the second maximum time to finish the task with light-sound feedback prototypes. The (P13) participant mentioned that "*during the task, I was enjoying the audio feedback when I was packaging items, which is the reason I took a little bit.*" A number of the participants reported that they were able to identify the items in the bag with the assistance of the sound feedback that we provided, which allowed them to do so even though they couldn't see what was packed inside the bag. The (P9) participants took the maximum time for the task with light sound feedback. (P9) noted that "*when I heard the sound when I was packing stuff, I was surprised because I did not think it was related to what I packed.*" The participants said that light-sound feedback has the ability to identify them in a unique way while they are packing items and can attract more interest in real life. (P3) noted that "*sometimes I forget to pack items when I take my baby outside; I think utilizing this prototype can focus my attention more on packing since sound feedback is more enticing during the packaging periods, and I thought that using the prototype can help me remember to pack items.*" These prototypes were met with a great deal of enthusiastic support from the participants. The vast majority of participants report that the light-sound feedback enhances their ability to remember important items. In addition to this, a few users have pointed out a few drawbacks with the prototypes. They reported that we made extensive use of wearable connectivity, which can result in a variety of technological issues. Additionally, the sound tone that we offered was of a slightly lower loudness, which may have an impact on users of varying ages.

In general, the light-sound feedback reminder prototypes were preferred by all of the participants above the light feedback reminder prototype. During the task using the light feedback prototype, the participants said that they were provided a view inside the bag to see what they packed since the prototype was unable to determine what was packed. In the light-sound feedback prototype, they didn't have to look inside any of the items that they packed due to the sound feedback, which made packing with sound much easier for them. In addition, participants said that both of the reminder bags can help them remember things in their everyday lives. Some of the participants said they wanted to have one to use in their daily lives to remind them to pack items. They also gave a lot of ideas for how prototypes could be improved for future work.

6 Discussion

Light-sound feedback is a more effective method of facilitating parent reminders than light feedback separately. During the course of the task, the vast majority of our participants remarked that sound is the kind of feedback that is used the most often by individuals. The majority of participants like our light-sound feedback reminder since it is something they are used to hearing in their day-to-day lives and hence is more familiar to them. The sound feedback that we used has the ability to both attract people and make them smile.

In this paper, as a media to convey the idea behind our reminder, we chose to utilize a bag. Researchers from a range of areas have each developed their own unique method for the purpose of serving as a reminder. We have shown our concept of a reminder by utilizing a bag since we believed that if we used any other components, it would provide a more complex challenge for the parents. To remind parents to be there at the appropriate time and place, we chose to utilize bags as our media of communication rather than relying on any other components.

We made use of a pressure sensor module in each of our prototypes. This module can be added or removed at any time by the parents. In addition, the light-sound feedback reminder included six distinct sound tones that were each associated with a specific item. Parents can customize the sound whenever they want. It is an acceptable and useful technique to help new parents take care of their infants in their day-to-day lives by applying reminders to everyday items such as a bag. The two reminder bag prototypes shown in this study each have a total of just six pockets between them. Depending on the person who uses them, bags may come in a wide range of styles. It depends on how many items they have on them at the moment. It is possible that the essentials for two or even three children will need to be carried by them, depending on the number of children for whom they are accountable. They need more space in their bag. Our ideas for a reminder can be implemented with any kind of bag, and it can have as many compartments as the user requires. Therefore, the adaptability of bag types and the use of modular sensing are quite significant.

One of our user categories is made up of individuals who have recently become parents. We design for those who are in charge of caring for the infant, also known as "caregivers". We are all aware that the task of providing care for a newborn does not exclusively fall on the shoulders of the parents, but also on any other adults who are legally responsible for the child, such as the child's grandparents or a babysitter. In actuality, the dynamics of the family will determine the response to the question of who is responsible for caring for the infant.

7 Future Work and Conclusion

Currently, the prototype implementations for the experiment are quite straightforward, and very little care has been given to the design of the interactive prototype. During the user study, participants mentioned that additional wiring concerns can be technical challenges that we incorporated into our prototypes. This may have an effect not only on the effectiveness but also on the user experience of the reminder bag. The prototype needs to be worked on more until it is reliable enough to use every day. The look of the artifact also needs to be polished so that the person using it doesn't feel awkward or embarrassed.

In this paper, we have offered a light-feedback smart bag reminder and a light-sound feedback smart bag reminder for new parents in the hopes of making their day-to-day lives easier and more manageable. According to the quantitative and qualitative results, light-sound feedback facilitates parent reminders better than light feedback. We discussed the system design, functionality, and ramifications of designing reminder systems that can have an effect on the daily lives of new parents.

References

1. Park, S.Y., Zimmerman, J.: Investigating the opportunity for a smart activity bag. In: Proceedings of the SIGCHI Conference on Human Factors in Computing Systems, pp. 2543–2552. Georgia, USA (2010)
2. Zimmerman, J.: Designing for the self: making products that help people become the person they desire to be. In: Proceedings of the SIGCHI Conference on Human Factors in Computing Systems, pp. 395–404. Boston, USA (2009)
3. Lee, M.K., Davidoff, S., Zimmerman, J., Dey, A.K.: Smart bag: managing home and raising children. In: Proceedings of the 2007 Conference on Designing Pleasurable Products and Interfaces, pp. 434–437. Helsinki, Finland (2007)
4. Williamson, J.R., McGee-Lennon, M., Brewster, S.: Designing multimodal reminders for the home: pairing content with presentation. In: Proceedings of the 14th ACM international conference on Multimodal interaction, pp. 445–448. California, USA (2012)
5. Stawarz, K., Cox, A.L., Blandford, A.: Don't forget your pill! Designing effective medication reminder apps that support users' daily routines. In: Proceedings of the SIGCHI Conference on Human Factors in Computing Systems, pp. 2269–2278. Ontario, Canada (2014)
6. Abdul Razak, F.H., Sulo, R., Wan Adnan, W.A.: Elderly mental model of reminder system. In: Proceedings of the 10th Asia Pacific Conference on Computer Human Interaction, pp. 193–200. Shimane, Japan (2012)
7. Hansson, R., Ljungstrand, P.: The reminder bracelet: subtle notification cues for mobile devices. In CHI'00 Extended Abstracts on Human Factors in Computing Systems, pp. 323–324. Hague, Netherlands (2000)
8. LadyBag Project: http://www.ladybag.official.ws/
9. Sheth, D.S., Singh, S., Mathur, P.S., Vydeki, D.: Smart laptop bag with machine learning for activity recognition. In: 2018 Tenth International Conference on Advanced Computing (ICoAC), pp. 164–171. Chennai, India (2018)

10. Marquardt, N., Taylor, A.S., Villar, N., Greenberg, S.: Rethinking RFID: awareness and control for interaction with RFID systems. In: Proceedings of the SIGCHI Conference on Human Factors in Computing Systems, pp. 2307–2316. Georgia, USA (2010)
11. Groß-Vogt, K.: The drinking reminder: prototype of a smart jar. In: Proceedings of the 15th International Conference on Audio Mostly, pp. 257–260. Graz, Austria (2020)
12. Reschke, D., Böhmer, M., Sorg, M.: Tactifloor: design and evaluation of vibration signals for doorway reminder systems. In: Proceedings of the 16th International Conference on Mobile and Ubiquitous Multimedia, pp. 449–455. Stuttgart, Germany (2017)
13. Nanda, G., Cable, A., Bove, V.M., Ho, M., Hoang, H.: bYOB [Build Your Own Bag] a computationally-enhanced modular textile system. In: Proceedings of the 3rd International Conference on Mobile and Ubiquitous Multimedia, pp. 1–4. College Park, Maryland (2004)
14. Minami, K., Kokubo, Y., Maeda, I., Hibino, S.: Real-time feedback of chest compressions using a flexible pressure sensor. Resuscitation **99**, e11–e12, Hibino, Shingo (2016)
15. Kim, S.W., Kim, M.C., Park, S.H., Jin, Y.K., Choi, W.S.: Gate reminder: a design case of a smart reminder. In: Proceedings of the 5th Conference on Designing Interactive Systems: Processes, Practices, Methods, and Techniques, pp. 81–90. Cambridge, MA, USA (2004)
16. Williamson, J.R., McGee-Lennon, M., Freeman, E., Brewster, S.: Designing a smartpen reminder system for older adults. In: CHI 2013 Extended Abstracts on Human Factors in Computing Systems, pp. 73–78. Paris, France (2013)
17. Harjuniemi, E., Häkkilä, J.: Smart handbag for remembering keys. In: Proceedings of the 22nd International Academic Mindtrek Conference, pp. 244–247. Tampere, Finland (2018)
18. Wagner, C., Singer, P., Karimi, F., Pfeffer, J., Strohmaier, M.: Sampling from social networks with attributes. In: Proceedings of the 26th International Conference on World Wide Web, pp. 1181–1190. Perth, Australia (2017)
19. Wang, K.-J., Shidujaman, M., Zheng, C.Y., Thakur, P.: HRIpreneur thinking: strategies towards faster innovation and commercialization of academic HRI research. In: 2019 IEEE International Conference on Advanced Robotics and its Social Impacts (ARSO), pp. 219–226. Beijing (2019)
20. Joshi, A., Kale, S., Chandel, S., Pal, D.K.: Likert scale: Explored and explained. British J. Appl. Sci. Technol. **7**(4) (2015)
21. https://tutorial.math.lamar.edu/classes/calci/avgfcnvalue.aspx
22. Arroyo, D., Guo, Y., Yu, M., Shidujaman, M., Fernandes, R.: Towards the design of a robot for supporting children's attention during long distance learning. In: Wagner, A.R., et al. (eds.) ICSR 2020. LNCS (LNAI), vol. 12483, pp. 332–343. Springer, Cham (2020). https://doi.org/10.1007/978-3-030-62056-1_28

Possibility of Relaxation Level Measurement During Music Listening Using Reverberation Envelope

Nana Kasajima[✉] and Yumi Wakita

Osaka Institute of Technology, Osaka, Japan
m1m22r13@st.oit.ac.jp, yumi.wakita@oit.ac.jp

Abstract. Our lifestyle has changed in recent years due to a massive pandemic. This has put us under great stress. We want to create a relaxing space as a simple way to cope with this stress without having to change the location. Therefore, we researched music and lighting with the aim of providing relaxing spaces that can relieve stress. This paper will first discuss music. We focused on the envelope index (E-value), which has been previously proposed as an indicator of acoustic signal features related to the audibility of reverberation. This index can be used for recordings made in an anechoic room, but is generally used for music with reverberation. We wanted to explore the possibility of E-values as an indicator of relaxing music. Therefore, the E-values of musical pieces were investigated. Furthermore, when participants were asked to listen to musical pieces with different E-values, it was found that those with higher E-values were less relaxing. The E-value may be able to quantify the relationship between musical pieces and relaxation.

Keywords: Reverberation Envelope · Relaxation Degree · Difference of Music Piece · Difference of Playing Method

1 Introduction

People's lives changed when the COVID-19 pandemic prevented them from going out. They had more opportunities to spend all day in their own space at home, and this lifestyle change caused new stresses [1]. So, we aimed to create a room that relieves as much stress as possible. Among the various elements that make up a space, we will focus on music and lighting to explore which of their elements are effective for relaxation. Currently, we are first conducting research on music.

Previous studies have made it clear that music has a psychological effect on people. Generally, slow tempo and relaxing music is believed to give a sense of relaxation. However, there are a variety of factors through which music can affect humans, and we have not yet been able to unify and quantify them [2, 3]. Interestingly, Ronald et al. [4] reported that reverberation affects the emotional characteristics of an instrument. Reverberation has been regarded as an important spatial element, but if it affects musical emotion, there may also be some relationship between reverberation and relaxation. If this relationship can be quantified, it will provide a numerical clarification of the psychological impact of music on humans. Therefore, we focused on the envelope index, which has been proposed as an indicator of the acoustic characteristics of a piece of music related to the audibility of reverberation. We then investigated the possibility that the envelope index can lead to a quantification of the relationship between relaxation and a piece of mus.

2   Reverberation Envelope Index (E-value)

Irimajiri [5] defined the "effective reverberation component" as how much of the rever-beration component of a musical sound can be heard unmasked in a piece of music. The author proposed a method to derive the amount of effective reverberation from the envelope of the musical signal waveform. According to the paper [5], in Zubicker's time characteristic of masking over time (critical curve) [6], pre-masking is not applied when the acoustic signal level increases. In this case, it is assumed that the signal attenuates with a slope of −400 dB as post-masking. Therefore, the left assumption is applied to musical sounds recorded in an anechoic chamber, and the curve is used as the "audio signal envelope." On the other hand, if reverberation is added to this acoustic signal, the reverberation component can be hypothetically described as a curve that decays from the peak of the signal waveform with a slope corresponding to each reverberation time (−20 dB/s for a reverberation time of 3 s). Since it can be thought of only as a virtual decay curve, it is called a "hypothetical reverberation envelope." The energy ratio of the signal envelope (approximately the acoustic signal level) to the hypothetical reverber-ation envelope is defined as the acoustic signal characteristic of the music piece with respect to reverberation hearing, which is the envelope index (E-value). The formula for calculating the envelope index is described in the equation below. In the formula, t is time, δt is segment length, i is segment number, $p_{(t)}$ is the signal waveform, n_1 is the segment number where the signal waveform reached its maximum value, n_2 is the segment number where the signal power of the segment exceeds the decay line power of the segment, and T is the reverberation time:

$$P(i) = \frac{1}{\delta t} \int_{i \cdot \delta t}^{(i+1) \cdot \delta t} p_{(t)}^2 dt \tag{1}$$

$$P_{rev}(i) = P(n_1) \times 10^{\frac{-60 \cdot \delta t}{10 \cdot T}(i - n_1)}$$
$$n_1 \leq i < n_2 \tag{2}$$

$$E_r = 10 log_{10} \left\{ \frac{\sum_{i=1}^{N} P_{rev}(i)}{\sum_{i=1}^{N} p(i)} \right\} (dB) \tag{3}$$

Originally, the E-value was applied to musical pieces recorded in an anechoic cham-ber. The higher the E-value, the more easily the reverberation component is heard. However, we applied this index to musical pieces recorded in a reverberant environ-ment. In this case, the E-value is no longer the amount of effective reverberation, but an index that expresses how much reverberation is heard in a musical piece that already has reverberation. Therefore, when a musical piece has reverberation close to the hypothetical reverberation, the range between the audio signal envelope and the hypothetical reverberation envelope will be closer. Because of this, the E-value will be lower. Conversely, when the musical piece is less likely to contain reverberation, the range between the audio signal envelope and the hypothetical reverberation envelope is further apart. Because of this, the E-value will be higher. Figure 1 shows the relationship between the audio signal envelope and the hypothetical reverberation envelope when the E-value is low and Fig. 2 shows it when the E-value is high.

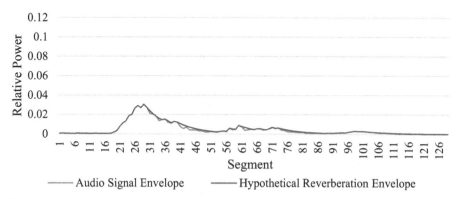

Fig. 1. Relationship between the audio signal envelope and the hypothetical reverberation envelope (E-value is low).

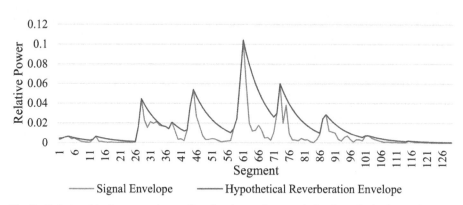

Fig. 2. Relationship between the audio signal envelope and the hypothetical reverberation envelope (E-value is high).

In order to use the above E-value as an indicator of how much reverberation is being heard in a musical piece, the above is based on the assumption that the part of the musical piece that did not assume pre-masking (i.e., the part where the acoustic signal level increases) has no reverberation. So, in Eq. (3), only the part where the audio signal envelope and the hypothetical reverberation envelope diverge was altered to be used in the calculation of the E-value. The altered equation is shown below:

$$E_r = 10log_{10}\left\{\frac{\sum_{i=1}^{N} P_{rev}(i)}{\sum_{i=1}^{N} p(i)}\right\}(P_{rev}(i) \neq P(i))\,(dB) \tag{4}$$

3 Relationship Between the E-value of a Musical Piece and Relaxation

3.1 E-value of a Musical Piece

Several studies have reported on the relationship between impressions of musical pieces and physiological responses to classical music [7, 8]. We selected 11 classical pieces that had already been rated as uplifting or tranquil in papers [7–9] that discussed the impressions that music makes on humans. Tranquil musical pieces were used as relaxing musical pieces in several papers. In addition, the Cello Suite No. 1 BWV1007 Prelude was selected as a source of an uplifting and different pitch compared to the tranquil classical pieces. Table 1 shows the selected musical pieces.

Table 1. Details of the classical pieces used in the E-value calculation.

Impressions	Title of musical piece	Composer	Length
Uplifting or lively	Spring 1st mov. From The Four Seasons	A. Vivaldi	3 min 33 s
	Arrival of the Queen of Sheba	Handel	4 min 58 s
	Cello Suite No.1 BWV1007 Prelude	J. S. Bach	2 min 31 s
	Eine Kleine Nachtmusik 1st mov.	Mozart	5 min 53 s
	Blauen Donau	J. Strauss	7 min 42 s
Tranquil (Relaxing)	Meditation from Theis	Massenet	5 min 6 s
	Adagio for Strings, Violin and Organ in Gm	Albinoni	8 min 23 s
	Air on the G String	J. S. Bach	5 min 1 s
	Canon in D	Pachelbel	4 min 47 s
	Chopin Etude Op.10 No.3	Chopin	4 min 16 s
	Clair de lune	Debussy	4 min 17 s
	Ombra Mai Fu (Largo)	Handel	2 min 49 s

The E-values for each musical piece in Table 1 were compared using Eq. (4). The reverberation time for calculating the hypothetical reverberation envelope was set to 1, 1.5, 2, 2.5, and 3 s, and the segment length was set to 20 ms. Table 2 shows the E-values for each musical piece, and Fig. 1 shows the relationship between the E-values and reverberation time for each musical piece. Table 2 and Fig. 1 show that the E-value tends to be higher for uplifting musical pieces and lower for tranquil musical pieces, although it varies depending on the reverberation time.

Table 2. E-value of each musical piece at each reverberation time.

Title/Reverberation time	1.0[s]	1.5[s]	2.0[s]	2.5[s]	3.0[s]
Spring 1st mov. from The Four Seasons	1.61	1.97	2.29	2.51	2.71
Arrival of the Queen of Sheba	1.41	1.72	1.98	2.20	2.38
Cello Suite No.1 BWV1007 Prelude	1.38	1.56	1.75	1.95	2.10
Eine Kleine Nachtmusik 1st mov.	1.22	1.56	1.82	2.03	2.22
Meditation from Theis	1.19	1.23	1.34	1.44	1.53
Blauen Donau	0.96	1.11	1.27	1.42	1.56
Adagio for Strings, Violin and Organ in Gm	0.85	1.03	1.21	1.39	1.55
Air on the G String	0.74	0.87	1.00	1.13	1.25
Canon in D	0.72	0.87	0.99	1.12	1.23
Chopin Etude Op.10 No.3	0.62	0.83	1.13	1.48	1.80
Clair de lune	0.61	0.73	0.92	1.18	1.47
Ombra Mai Fu (Largo)	0.57	0.73	0.85	0.97	1.13

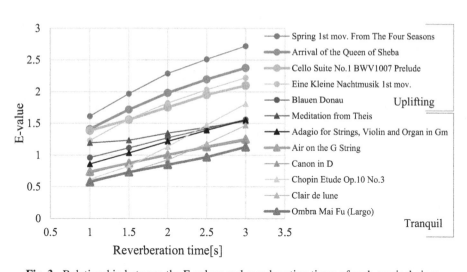

Fig. 3. Relationship between the E-values and reverberation times of each musical piece.

3.2 Relationship Between the Relaxation Degrees and the Classical Music

We chose two uplifting musical pieces (Arrival of the Queen of Sheba and Cello Suite No.1 BWV1007 Prelude) and two tranquil musical pieces (Air on the G String and Ombra Mai Fu) from the selections in Table 1. Then, 12 people were asked to listen to the 4 musical pieces under the conditions described in Table 3. Then, a questionnaire survey was conducted, in which participants rated each musical piece on a five-point scale of "how much they liked it" and "how relaxed they felt during it."

Table 3. Survey conditions.

Listening method	– Speaker (five people)
	– Headset for phones (seven people)
Description of evaluation	– How much did you like this musical piece?
	– How relaxed did you feel listening to this musical piece?
How to evaluate	Does not apply at all (1) to Very applicable (5) on a five-point scale

The results of the questionnaire are shown in Fig. 4. The number below the name of the musical piece in the figure represents the E-value of that piece at a reverberation time of 2 s (details are shown in Table 2). It was found that uplifting musical pieces with high E-values (especially Arrival of the Queen of Sheba) were less relaxing. Furthermore, on the questions about how relaxed you feel, there were significant differences between Arrival of the Queen of Sheba and Ombra Mai Fu, and between Arrival of the Queen of Sheba and Air on the G String.

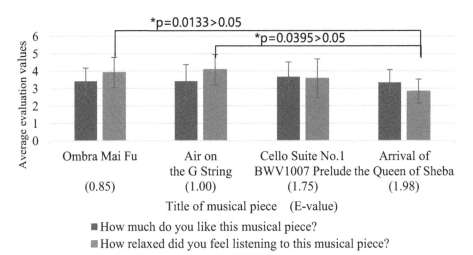

Fig. 4. Relationship between the E-value of a musical piece and the degree of preference and relaxation.

4 Clarification of the Relationship Between Relaxation Degree and E-value

4.1 Relationship Between E-value and Different Playing Methods

The E-value depends on the tempo and the number of instruments played [5]. Therefore, E-values were calculated in the same way as in 3.1, using the same instruments and musical pieces, but with pieces in which only the playing technique was varied. The musical piece performed was Strauss' Pitchcart Polka. There were four playing methods: original, pitchcart, staccato, and legato. The details of each playing method are shown in Table 4.

Table 4. The details of each playing method.

Name of Playing Method	Playing Characteristics
Original	Basically, the same as "pitchcart" (plucking strings with fingers), but with stronger intonation
Pitchcart	Played by plucking the strings with your fingers
Staccato	Played with a bow, cutting off the sound
Legato	Played with a bow without breaking the note

Table 5 shows the E-values for the reverberation times of 1, 1.5, 2, 2.5, and 3 s for each playing method shown in Table 4. The relationship between the E-value and the reverberation time for each playing method is shown in Fig. 5. Table 5 and Fig. 5 show that the E-value of "original" was the highest and that of "legato" was the lowest, regardless of the reverberation time. The E-value was also affected by the playing method. It can be said that the E-value was higher when playing the strings with fingers, and lower when playing with a bow.

Table 5. E-value for each playing method at each reverberation time.

Playing Method/Reverberation Time	1.0[s]	1.5[s]	2.0[s]	2.5[s]	3.0[s]
Original	2.58	3.30	3.71	4.18	4.43
Pitchcart	1.85	2.09	2.57	2.99	3.31
Staccato	0.84	1.35	1.65	2.05	2.36
Legato	0.61	0.80	0.99	1.05	1.25

4.2 Relationship Between the Relaxation Degree and Playing Methods

Similar to 3.2, a questionnaire survey was conducted on the musical pieces in Table 4 to examine preferences and relaxation. The results are shown in Fig. 6. The number below the name of the musical piece in the figure represents the E-value of that piece at a reverberation time of 2 s (details are shown in Table 5). It was found that musical pieces with higher E values played with the fingers tended to be less relaxing than those with lower E values played with the bow.

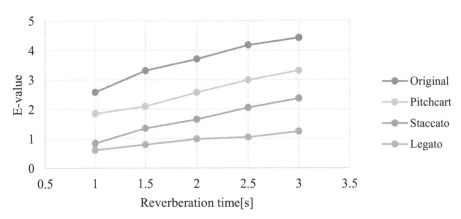

Fig. 5. Relationship between the E-values and reverberation time for each playing method.

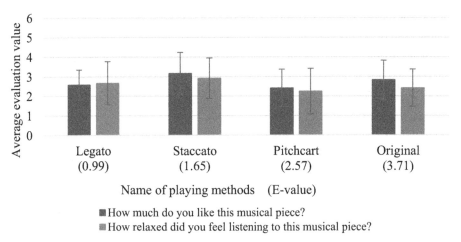

Fig. 6. Relationship between the E-value of playing methods and the degree of preference and relaxation.

4.3 Relationship Between Different Parts of the Same Musical Piece with Different E-values and Relaxation

In 4.1, the E-value was found to be affected by differences in playing method, even for the same musical piece. In other words, the E-value changed as the playing changed within the same musical piece. Therefore, we selected the parts with different E-values within the same musical piece and conducted the same experiment as in 4.1 on them. The musical pieces used were Strauss' Blauen Donau and Mozart's Ah, vous dirai-je, maman. Table 6 shows the playing characteristics of the selected parts and the E-values at 2 s of reverberation time.

Figure 7 shows the results of the questionnaire for the selected parts in Table 6. The number below the name of the musical piece in the figure represents the E-value of that piece at a reverberation time of 2 s (details are shown in Table 6). When compared within

Table 6. The playing characteristics of the selected parts and the E-values at 2 s of reverberation time.

Title	Naming of the selected part	Playing characteristics	E-value
Ah, vous dirai-je, maman	Ah, vous dirai-je, maman A	Lots of repetitive melodies, tranquil	1.10
	Ah, vous dirai-je, maman B	Lots of repetitive melodies, uplifting	1.19
Blauen Donau	Blauen Donau A	Tranquil	1.57
	Blauen Donau B	Uplifting	1.82

the same musical piece, both musical pieces tended to be less relaxing in the parts with higher E-values than in the parts with lower ones. There was a significant difference between A and B for Ah, vous dirai-je, maman. Significant differences were also found between Ah, vous dirai-je, maman A and Blauen Donau B, even when the two musical pieces were not the same. As expected, it was found that musical pieces with higher E-values tended to be less relaxing than those with lower E-values.

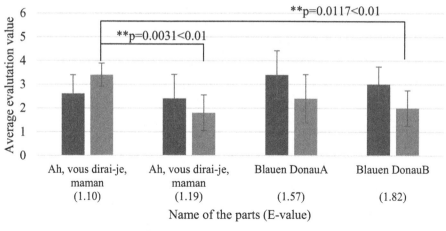

Fig. 7. Relationship between different E-values in the parts with different E-values within the same musical piece and the degree of preference and relaxation.

5 Discussion

The above experiment indicated that the E-value determines how close the reverberation in a musical piece is to the hypothetical reverberation envelope and suggested that the E-value may be correlated with a sense of relaxation. Furthermore, E-values depend on tempo. The slower the tempo of a musical piece, the lower the E-value, and the more people feel relaxed. We believe that the E-value may be an indicator of relaxation, in terms of both tempo and the audibility of reverberation.

In addition, there was a difference in the amount of change in the E-value with reverberation time between musical pieces with a low E-value and those with a high E-value. Figure 8 shows the relationship between the slope of the E-value in Fig. 3 and the E-value at a reverberation time of 2 s. The figure shows that the slope is smaller for musical pieces with low E-values and larger for musical pieces with high E-values for musical pieces selected with reference to the previous paper. This may indicate that musical pieces with low E-values already have a high reverberation component, making it harder for the audio signal envelope and hypothetical reverberation envelope to separate even if the reverberation time is changed. In other words, it may suggest that musical pieces with low E-values are less likely to be affected by reverberation time.

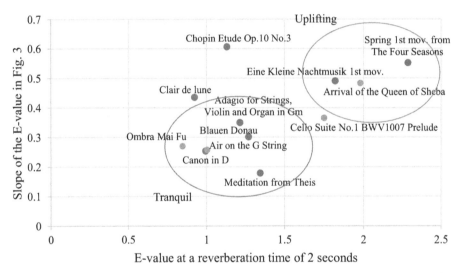

Fig. 8. Relationship between the slope of the E-value in Fig. 3 and the E-value at a reverberation time of 2 s.

6 Conclusions and Future Work

To explore the possibility of E-values as an indicator of relaxing musical pieces, we had the participants listen to musical pieces with different E-values to examine the degree to which they felt relaxed. The results showed that the lower the E-value, the more relaxed one tends to feel. However, there are many factors that can change the E-value. In the future, we would like to explore factors that correlate well with E-values from more musical pieces and clarify their relationship with relaxation. In the future, we will investigate the impact of physiological measurements on physical relaxation and work on lighting to provide a more relaxing environment.

Acknowledgments. Thanks to Dr. Hideo Irimajiri for his guidance and valued cooperation.

References

1. Bhattacharjee, A., Ghosh, T.: COVID-19 pandemic and stress: coping with the new normal. J. Prevent. Health Promot. **3**(1), 30–52. (2022). https://www.ncbi.nlm.nih.gov/pmc/articles/PMC 8855221/
2. Kulinski, J., Ofori, E.K., Visotcky, A., Smith, A., Sparapani, R., Fleg, J.L.: Effects of music on the cardiovascular system. Trends Cardiovascul Med **32**(6), 390–398 (2022). https://www. ncbi.nlm.nih.gov/pmc/articles/PMC8727633/
3. Thoma, M.V., Scholz, U., Ehlert, U., Nater, U.M.: Listening to music and physiological and psychological functioning: the mediating role of emotion regulation and stress reactivity. Psychol Health **27**(2), 227–241 (2012). https://www.researchgate.net/publication/289584257_The_Eff ects_of_Reverberation_on_the_Emotional_Characteristics_of_Musical_Instruments
4. Mo, R., Bin, W., Hoener, A.: The effects of reverberation on the emotional characteristics of musical instruments. J. Audio Eng. Soc. **63**(12), 966–979 (2016). https://www.researchgate. net/publication/289584257_The_Effects_of_Reverberation_on_the_Emotional_Characterist ics_of_Musical_Instruments
5. Irimajiri, H., Iwamiya, S.: Optimal reverberation mixing level of orchestral sounds recorded in an anechoic room. J. Acoust. Soc. Jpn. **69**(5), 215–223 (2013). https://www.jstage.jst.go.jp/ article/jasj/69/5/69_KJ00008612066/_pdf
6. Zwicker, E., Fastl, H.: Phychoacoustics: Facts and Models, 2nd edn., pp. 216–219. Springer, Berlin/Heidelberg/New York (1999)
7. Ebihara, N., Nakajima, M.: Effects of music on stress reduction. J. Facul. Human. **56**, 49–58 (2012). Toyama University. https://www.hmt.u-toyama.ac.jp/uploads/ebihara56.pdf
8. Nakajima, H., Omi, M.: Influence of music listening on state anxiety, feelings and physiological responses. Proc. Japan. Soc. Cogn. Psychol. **2011**, 1 (2011). https://www.jstage.jst.go.jp/article/ cogpsy/2011/0/2011_0_1/_pdf/-char/ja
9. Kumamoto, T., Ota, K.: Design, implementation, and opening to the public of an impression-based music retrieval system. Trans. Japan. Soc. Artific. Intell. AI **21**(3), 310–318 (2006). https://www.jstage.jst.go.jp/article/tjsai/21/3/21_3_310/_pdf/-char/ja

Interaction Design of Wrist Health Prevention Products Based on Persuasive Design and AHP-Entropy Weight Method

Yuna Li and Yongyan Guo[✉]

School of Art Design and Media, East China University of Science and Technology, No. 130, Meilong Road, Xuhui District, Shanghai, People's Republic of China
1340703043@qq.com

Abstract. The development of the Internet has extended a variety of related physical products and changed people's living habits and ways, and the sub-health problems of the wrist are one of the significant health problems caused by this. In order to solve the need to prevent and alleviate wrist health problems, wrist grip ball products occupy a large number of markets. Objective In order to meet the good experience of consumers, obtain effective user perceptual evaluation of online shopping wrist force ball products, so as to improve product design. Methods The original corpus of online comments is constructed from the Jingdong Mall network platform by Python crawler technology, and the obtained data is processed by natural language processing of word segmentation and word vector space, and the data processing results are constructed by users' perceptual evaluation polar words, and the intensity of emotional association is calculated. In order to ensure the accuracy of the extraction of product design features of the wrist force ball, natural language processing will be carried out in combination with the product specification corpus to obtain the core design features mined by online reviews. The core design features extracted are analyzed by user evaluation, and the user perceptual evaluation of wrist force ball products is obtained. Conclusion The emotional association relationship of users in the process of carpal force ball product use, the positive and negative evaluation of each component are obtained, which provides strategies and directions for the improvement design of wrist force ball products, and provides a reference for the research on product design using online review mining.

Keywords: Persuasive design · Wrist health · SOHO family · Gamification

1 Introduction

With the innovation in the era of Internet technology and the post-epidemic social era, the total number of SOHO users is on the rise, and the accompanying user needs are gradually attracting attention. SOHO users refer to the special working group who work at home. Complexity of working environment and freedom of working time bring sub-health problems of SOHO users. According to the sub-health population survey report of iResearch, SOHO population is one of the groups with a high rate of sub-health problems. According to data surveys and industry reports, the main sub-health problems of SOHO users are cervical spine diseases, followed by wrist health problems, such as carpal tunnel syndrome. With the increase in the number of SOHO users, the wrist health demand brought by living time and irregular office is more and more obvious. Therefore, there is a large market demand for products that meet the home office environment, efficient and interesting to alleviate and prevent the wrist health demand.

Persuasion design is a persuasion method based on computer technology. Through the analysis and study of the causes, processes and results of user behaviors, combined with the purpose of user behaviors, strategies can be formulated at each stage to promote users to achieve the purpose of behavior. The purpose is to enable users to complete the target behavior comfortably and efficiently, so as to achieve the role of persuasion. Persuasive design has a remarkable effect in the current situation of computer-dominated products, especially in the direction of medical and health care, which can effectively change users' habitual behavior content. In order to make a full quantitative analysis of the content of the persuasive design strategy constructed, AHP-entropy weight method is combined with the subjective and objective strategy weight assignment analysis to perfect and construct a more accurate persuasive design strategy model, guide the interactive product design practice based on the needs of SOHO users, and provide better product experience for users.

2   Relevant Research Theory and Background

In order to better understand the current status of wrist health prevention products and the status quo of wrist health problems of SOHO users, the preliminary design background and theory were studied and analyzed to provide feasible ideas for the follow-up research and experiment. This chapter is mainly carried out from three aspects: the research background of SOHO wrist health, the research status of persuasion design, and the application research status of AHP-entropy weight method, so as to fully grasp the research status, so as to realize the innovation of research methods and contents.

2.1   Wrist Health Status of SOHO Nationality

SOHO users conduct paperless office for a long time, operate the mouse and keyboard, and their wrists are in repeated and excessive activities for a long time, which is easy to cause "carpal tunnel syndrome" [1]. Usually due to overwork of the wrist and fingers, SOHO users often appear wrist joint pain, hand inflexibility, cramps, swelling, spasms, grip strength and the ability to work together in various parts of the hand is reduced. There are a wide variety of wrist-related health problems. The main treatment methods are surgery and conservative treatment. Conservative treatment includes drug or tool maintenance and training and rehabilitation, etc. This health condition needs to be effectively controlled in the prevention stage. According to a "wrist ball" wrist training product industry data reflect, wrist health problems are common among SOHO users, home living environment causes users to use electronic equipment for a long time irregularly, at home, other wrist work and work at the same time to increase the wrist health burden, In addition, the lack of communication and confusion in the home environment bring a certain psychological burden to SOHO users. SOHO people have the need of wrist health prevention training, special user characteristics need certain psychological experience and entertainment consideration.

In view of the above wrist health prevention, rehabilitation, relief needs, there are some solutions on the market, including wrist ball (prevention training), retractor (rehabilitation training), wrist strap (protection and relief) three main categories, as shown in Fig. 1, among which the sense of experience and entertainment strong wrist ball products. Its product brands include keep, Li Ning, Anta and other sports and fitness brand products, and its price is concentrated around 50–300 yuan. At present, the products on the market can solve the wrist strength and pain training relief, but few focus on the prevention of wrist health problems of the products, and most of the physical products, poor user experience, need to improve the design.

Fig. 1. Existing wrist health products (wrist strap, trainer, wrist ball from left to right)

2.2 Research Status of Persuasive Design Application

Captology is an emerging discipline that studies persuasion technology. It was first proposed by Stanford Professor Fogg in 1996, combining persuasion in psychology with computer interaction technology [2]. At present, the persuasive design method mainly constructs appropriate persuasive design strategy models for different users and behaviors, and provides guidance for design practice, among which the interface and other software products are mostly practiced. For example, Chen Zhaojie et al. built a persuasive design model by observing children's user behaviors and guided the design research of children's learning table [3]. Sun Ningna et al. guided the interface design of middle school English online learning through persuasive design, which effectively improved the learning efficiency and significantly enhanced students' learning interest [4]. In addition, some studies are related to the application of persuasive strategies at different design levels. For example, Lou Shuting et al. studied the application methods of persuasive strategies at the visual representation level and obtained relevant research results on visual persuasion, which made the application of persuasive design more detailed and extensive [5]. After the above data query and literature reading, most of the studies mainly use psychological methods such as questionnaire survey, theoretical analysis, and user interview to conduct the research on the combination of persuasion design and product. The lack of more adequate quantitative analysis methods weakens the convincing degree of persuasion strategy in practical application.

In view of the current research status of persuasion design application methods, this study proposed the combination of AHP-entropy weight and subjective and objective weight analysis method to further quantify the effectiveness of persuasion design strategies, and develop more accurate and effective design practice guidance for wrist health products.

2.3   Research and Application Status of AHP-Entropy Weight Method

Analytic Hierarchy Process (AHP) is a subjective weighting method that combines quantitative and qualitative analysis to make decisions on complex issues. It was put forward by Saaty, an American operational research scientist, in the 1970s. At present, it has been widely used in technology evaluation, correlation analysis, resource allocation and other fields [6]. AHP mainly carries out weight analysis of subjective factors. In order to reduce experimental errors brought by subjective analysis, weight analysis of objective indicators is carried out by combining entropy weight method. The entropy weight method mainly determines the objective weighting method of index weights according to the amount of information provided by the observed values of indicators, which is widely used in the fields of social economy and engineering technology [6]. Ahp-entropy weight method is mostly used in the construction of evaluation models. For example, Liu Dashuai et al. calculated the satisfaction and importance of user demands based on entropy weight method and FKM algorithm, and established a comprehensive evaluation model [6]. Yin Haodong et al. expanded the evaluation of design schemes of EDM cutting machine tools through the index weight analysis of AHP-entropy weight method. The weight coefficient of this method can enhance the effectiveness of expert design strategy. For example, Chen Xiang determined the weight coefficient of various indicators in product design by using entropy weight method, thus improving the effectiveness of expert judgment [7]. In summary, AHP-entropy weight method can effectively carry out quantitative weight analysis of design elements or indicators, and enhance the effectiveness of subjective factors. In this study, there is a lack of quantitative analysis of the effective principles of persuasive design in the persuasive design strategy model. The innovative combination of AHP-entropy weight method and persuasive strategy enhances the effectiveness of persuasive design and provides an optimal approach to design schemes.

2.4   Research Framework and Experimental Process

This study is mainly divided into three parts. The purpose of this study is to get a user-centered design practice of physical interactive wrist health prevention products with good persuasive effect through scientific design strategy guidance. The three main contents are (a) wrist health demand research of SOHO users, (b) model construction of persuasion design strategy, and (c) weight analysis of AHPs-entropy weight method of persuasion strategy scheme. Through the experimental steps of the above three processes, a reasonable wrist health prevention product design scheme is established to guide the design output, and an innovative research method combining persuasive design and AHP-entropy weight method is provided to make the design scheme more effective. The specific research framework is shown in Fig. 2.

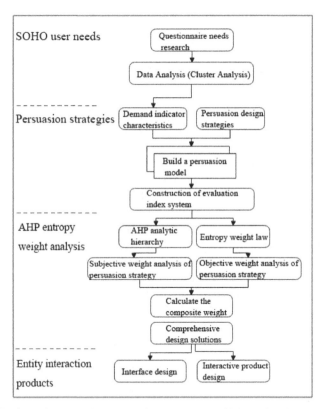

Fig. 2. Main research framework and process (self-drawn by the author)

3   Study on Wrist Health Needs of SOHO Users

The above chapter has conducted a preliminary study on the relationship between the research methods and the content of each part of the research, and explored the current research status. Questionnaire research is mainly delivered to target users through online means, which is a user research method to collect user information and opinions quickly and conveniently. The problems involved are of strong purpose and convenient for quantitative analysis of data. The research takes SOHO special user groups as the object, in order to explore their life needs generated under real office conditions, research questions are designed, and the wrist needs and pain points generated by the current users of this group in the work are found, as well as the cognition of the wrist health of SOHO users and the experience of existing solutions.

3.1   Questionnaire Design

Firstly, a questionnaire was designed for the wrist health of SOHO users, focusing on the age information, occupational attributes, work/life status, physical and mental status, hand work habits/time, sports, entertainment and other contents of the target users. After understanding these basic information, we further investigate whether users have wrist health problems, what pain/discomfort symptoms they have, how to solve them, whether it is effective, etc., aiming to obtain the common wrist health needs of respondents through progressive questions.

In order to further clarify the wrist health needs of users, the questions in the questionnaire are mainly designed from the following aspects:

- SOHO clan user in the age of information and content of the work: age different influences of users on the wrist health training and different symptoms, work content will affect the user wrist causes different health problems.
- user's cognition and perception of wrist health problems: specific users in the state of the health problem before cognitive stage, is one of the key factors of promoting behavior happen next.
- user used in wrist and discomfort: often the habit of hand and wrist will affect users of health behavior, a reflection of discomfort has been clear about the wrist healthy relationship with the user.
- current mitigation strategies (prevention) what/how is the effect: clear user alleviate wrist pain and prevent the wrist disease means, whether has the tendency, provide reference for later design.
- to alleviate the expectations of products: state of the user personal perception subjective estimates of expected products, can provide clustering reference for requirement analysis.
- The questionnaire is mainly divided into the above topics and contains 25 questions in total. It takes about 3 min to fill in. The following part of the questionnaire design content is shown in Fig. 3, which is related to the user's mitigation mode.

19. Have you purchased and used related steamed bun products for your wrist health problems [single selection period].

■   Bought

■   Haven't Bought*

20. Which of the following categories of health products do you purchase fall into [Multiple choice questions]*

■   Sports and fitness Massage

■   Therapy Time reminder

■   Health medicine

■   Entertainment stress

■   Reduction Other

21. Do you insist on using the purchased product [multiple choice question].

■   Yes, it's hot.

■   No, it's not good.

■   Some are used, some don't."

22. What motivates you to purchase and use this product [multiple choice question].

■   Good looking,

■   fun and fun,

■   good fatigue relief effect,

■   simple and convenient to use,

■   wearable,

■   portable,

■   affordable price

23. What makes you abandon this product [multiple choice].

■   Poor fatigue relief T

■   he use process is complicated

■   The learning cost is high, and I can't think of using it When I ask when I use a big flower,

■   I am not used to it,

■   It will aggravate physical fatigue after use

Fig. 3. Part of the questionnaire design content

3.2   Quantitative Analysis of SOHO Users' Wrist Health Needs

This questionnaire is distributed online, and core users fill in the questionnaire for SOHO group, without setting age and gender restrictions. A total of 163 valid questionnaires were collected and forwarded on various platforms, and data sets from the questionnaire survey were collected. The frequency statistics method was used to conduct descriptive statistical analysis on the basic information of participants, as shown in Table 1. The basic information of the participants mainly included age, gender, working style and wrist health, among which the people who perceived the discomfort of wrist health accounted for 73%. Users with such information characteristics were the focus of the follow-up user screening analysis.

Table 1. Descriptive analysis of wrist demand questionnaire of SOHO users

Sample size	163
Gender	79 women/84 men (48%/52%)
Age	20–26 years (32%), 26–35 (54%), >35 years (14%)
How it Works	Computer office (68%), manual work (24%), walking office (8%)
Wrist health	Never unwell (27%), often unwell (38%), occasionally unwell (35%)

(1) Reliability and validity test

In order to ensure the accuracy and effectiveness of the next data study, the reliability and validity analysis of the data results obtained from this questionnaire survey was carried out. Data analysis in this study was conducted in SPSS2022. The test results show that the α coefficient is 0.898, higher than 0.8, as shown in Table 2, indicating that the data obtained by the questionnaire is highly reliable. Bartlett spherical test, as shown in Table 5, showed a significance of less than 0.05, while KMO value was 0.869, higher than 0.8, indicating high data validity (Table 3).

Table 2. Internal consistency Coefficient of questionnaire & KMO and Bartlett test

Cronbach 的 Alpha		**Number of projects**
.898		163
Kaiser-Meyer-Olkin Measure sampling appropriateness		.869
Bartlett Spherical characterization	About chi-square	753.689
	df	74
	Salience	.000

Through the data cluster analysis results of SOHO wrist health products, the demand and pain point problems of wrist health prevention products centered on SOHO users were defined. Based on the clustering results, the persuasion design model was constructed.

Table 3. Clustering center definition naming and secondary factor summary

Definition	Cluster 1	Cluster2	Cluster3	Cluster 4
	Reduce the difficulty of behavior	self-adaptability	Multidimensional perception	Predictability of effect
Secondary correlation factors	Short activity time	Daily behavior	Visual feedback	Effective guidance
	Simple operation mode	Fit the mood	Auditory feedback	Explicit reward
	Action feedback in time	Daily tracking	Tactile feedback	Social sharing

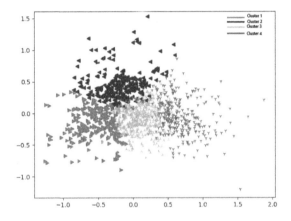

Fig. 4.

4 Construction of Persuasive Design Model for Wrist Health Prevention Products

On the basis of the above research on user needs, combined with the persuasive design method, a user-centered design scheme model is constructed, including a number of persuasive design strategies. First of all, the process analysis of wrist health prevention behavior of SOHO users was carried out, and the user needs of four categories of cluster analysis centers were combined in the behavior diagram, in which the above secondary related factors were used as auxiliary binding points. A behavior stage that can meet both the behavior process of the behavior diagram and the user's needs is obtained. The persuasive design principle is applied in this persuasive behavior stage, so as to build a persuasive design scheme of wrist health prevention products based on the needs of SOHO users.

4.1   Wrist Health Prevention Behavior Counseling Chart

The behavior table proposed by Professor Fogg is another typical theoretical achievement of behavioral persuasion after the FBM model. It is mainly used to locate the types of user behaviors and correspond to different behavioral persuasion strategies according to different behavioral types. In the table, according to the different duration of the behavior, it can be divided into "spot single behavior", "short-term phase behavior" and "long-term continuous behavior". Each behavior can be divided into five stages according to the standard of "starting new behavior", "doing familiar behavior", "increasing behavior intensity", "reducing behavior intensity" and "stopping the existing behavior". By arranging and combining three behavior types and five behavior stages, the user's behavior can be positioned. Based on the content of the above behavior table, this study builds a behavior table model, Fig. 5, which can display the user process, aiming at the wrist health problems of the SOHO family. This behavior table combines Fogg behavior types and constructs behaviors according to the user process of preventing behaviors, which simultaneously satisfies the FBM model relationship between motivation, ability and behavior. Among them, the behavior marked in red is the relevant persuasion behavior of the four clustering centers obtained from the above cluster analysis.

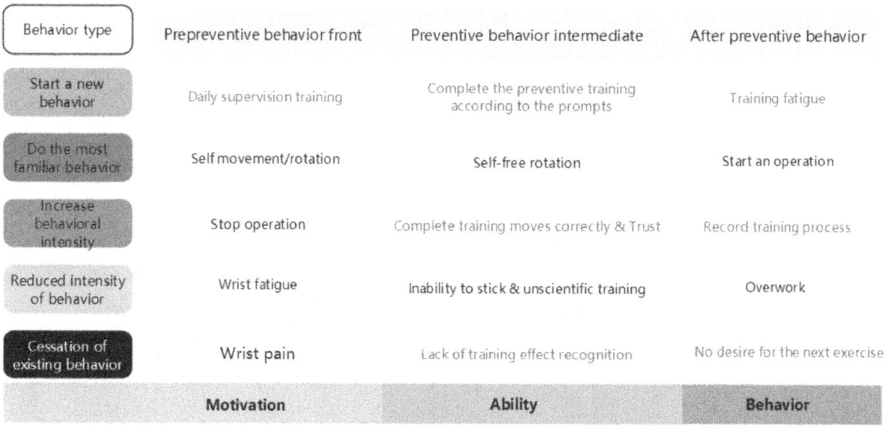

Behavior type	Prepreventive behavior front	Preventive behavior intermediate	After preventive behavior
Start a new behavior	Daily supervision training	Complete the preventive training according to the prompts	Training fatigue
Do the most familiar behavior	Self movement/rotation	Self-free rotation	Start an operation
Increase behavioral intensity	Stop operation	Complete training moves correctly & Trust	Record training process
Reduced intensity of behavior	Wrist fatigue	Inability to stick & unscientific training	Overwork
Cessation of existing behavior	Wrist pain	Lack of training effect recognition	No desire for the next exercise
	Motivation	**Ability**	**Behavior**

Fig. 5. SOHO User Wrist Health Prevention Behavior persuasion Model (drawn by the author)

4.2   Design Scheme of Promoting Behavior Motivation Model

The summary and analysis of the form of behavioral persuasion transformed the above research on the needs of SOHO users into persuasive design behavior, and successfully realized the transformation of user-based design needs. In order to realize the persuasive design behavior obtained from the above summary, combined with the principles of persuasive design, a design factor model was constructed that could promote the above persuasive design behavior. This model shows the motivation model of behavior existence and points out the persuasive design principle of each motivation behavior. According to the user clustering behavior transformation presented in the above behavior table, and combined with the comprehensive motivational persuasion principle model, more accurate persuasion design principle content is screened. The wrist health prevention and persuasion design behaviors of SOHO users mainly include seven contents: "start daily supervision training", "start to complete preventive training according to the prompts", "enhance the correct completion of training actions & trust", "stop the lack of training effect cognition", "start cognitive training fatigue", "enhance the recording of training process", "stop the next exercise without desire". By combining the content of seven persuasive behaviors with the wrist health motivation model combined with the persuasive design principles in Fig. 6, eight relevant persuasive design principles were obtained: "advice and reminder", "reward", "role building", "similarity", "difficulty reduction", "guidance", "self-monitoring", and "social learning".

Since the process of model construction and persuasion principle analysis is mainly qualitative analysis, and the process of quantitative analysis is lacking, the quantitative analysis of design scheme principle is carried out by combining AHP-entropy weight method, so as to obtain the design scheme with weight measurement and better guide the design practice.

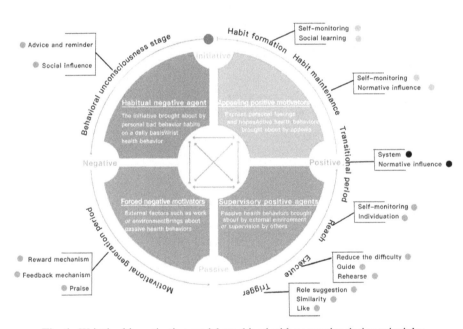

Fig. 6. Wrist health motivation model combined with persuasive design principles

5 AHP- Entropy Weight Method is Used to Analyze the Weight of Persuasion Design Scheme

5.1 Construction of Evaluation Index System

After expert opinions and literature reading, based on the above research, the design scheme of wrist health prevention products for SOHO users is to meet the needs of SOHO users through appropriate persuasive design principles. Therefore, this evaluation index system takes the four types of user needs obtained from cluster analysis as the criterion layer and the corresponding persuasive design principles as the index layer to construct. The construction model has been revised by professional teams for several rounds to ensure its rationality (Fig. 6).

Fig. 7. SOHO wrist health prevention product persuasion design evaluation index system

(1) AHP subjective weight analysis

The AHP method is used to determine the weight of evaluation indicators, which mainly includes four steps: the importance comparison of indicators, the construction of complementary judgment matrix, the establishment of fuzzy consistency matrix and the calculation of the weight value of each indicator [6]. Firstly, 10 experts were invited to compare and score the importance of each evaluation index using the 0–1 evaluation scale, and pairwise elements were used for comparative analysis. In the evaluation method, "0" means none, "0.5" means equal, and "1" means yes. A complementary judgment matrix A was constructed according to the scoring and measurement results of each index, and a fuzzy consistent matrix B was constructed through the complementary judgment matrix. Finally, the AHP weight value Y of each final index was calculated. The calculation methods involved are as follows:

$$A = \left(a_{ij}\right)_{n \times n} = \begin{array}{c} C_1 \\ C_2 \\ \vdots \\ C_n \end{array} \begin{bmatrix} a_{11} & a_{12} & \cdots & a_{1n} \\ a_{21} & a_{22} & \cdots & a_{2n} \\ \vdots & \vdots & \vdots & \vdots \\ a_{n1} & a_{n2} & \cdots & a_{nn} \end{bmatrix} \tag{1}$$

$$\left(b_{ij}\right)_{n \times n} :$$

$$b_{ij} = \sum_{j=1}^{n} a_{ij}$$

$$b_{ij} = \frac{b_i = b_i}{2n} + 0.5 \tag{2}$$

$$Y_j \frac{y_j}{\sum\limits_{j=1}^{n} y_j} \tag{3}$$

According to the above calculation methods, the weight of each element of the evaluation index system was calculated, and the weight results of the wrist health prevention product design scheme for SOHO users were obtained, as shown in Table 4.

Table 4. SOHO group user persuasion design evaluation index weight

Serial number	Evaluation index	Weight number
C1	Advice and reminder	0.191 7
C2	guide	0.068 5
C3	similarity	0.012 5
C4	like	0.191 7
C5	Social influence	0.068 5
C6	Role building	0.019 6
C7	reward	0.460 1
C8	feedback	0.380 6
C9	individuation	0.230 2
C10	self-monitoring	0.460 1
C11	Normative influence	0.019 6

(2) Objective weight analysis of entropy weight method

The entropy weight method is used to determine the weight of the evaluation index, which mainly includes four steps: constructing the original data matrix, normalization processing, calculating the eigenvalue and entropy value, and calculating the weight of the evaluation index. Ten design experts were invited to score each index interpretation card, and the index scoring data was taken as the original data to form matrix D. An example of an explanation card is shown in Fig. 8. The characteristic weight of evaluation value of the ith scheme of the JTH evaluation index is calculated, that is, the specific weight value of the JTH evaluation index in the ith scheme, and the matrix F is obtained. Then the entropy value Ej of the JTH index is calculated. Finally, the objective weight Wj of the index can be calculated from the entropy value of the JTH index. Among them, the calculation formula of each part is as follows:

$$D = \left(d_{ij}\right)_{n \times n} = \begin{bmatrix} d_{11} & d_{12} & \cdots & d_{1n} \\ d_{21} & d_{22} & \cdots & d_{2n} \\ \vdots & \vdots & \vdots & \vdots \\ d_{m1} & d_{m2} & \cdots & d_{mn} \end{bmatrix} \tag{4}$$

$$f_{ij} = \frac{d'_{ij}}{\sum\limits_{j=1}^{n} d'_{ij}} \tag{5}$$

$$E_{\mathrm{j}} = -k \sum_{j=1}^{n} f_{ij} \ln f_{ij} \; k = \frac{1}{\ln n} \tag{6}$$

$$W_j = \frac{1 - E_j}{m - \sum\limits_{j=1}^{m} E_j}, \, 0 \le W_j \le 1, \sum_{j=1}^{m} W_j = 1 \tag{7}$$

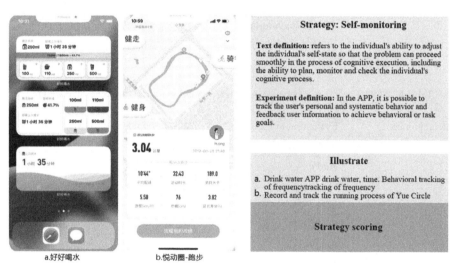

a.好好喝水   b.悦动圈-跑步

Fig. 8. Auxiliary explanatory card for professionals to score evaluation indicators (take C10 self-monitoring as an example)

After the above calculation steps, the objective weight analysis of the design scheme of wrist health prevention products for SOHO users is carried out, and the results are as follows (Table 6):

Table 5. SOHO group user persuasion design evaluation index weight

Serial number	Evaluation index	Weight number
C1	Advice and reminder	0.114 6
C2	guide	0.194 3
C3	similarity	0.112 5
C4	like	0.220 4
C5	Social influence	0.108 2
C6	Role building	0.179 5
C7	reward	0.238 6
C8	feedback	0.193 9
C9	individuation	0.187 2
C10	self-monitoring	0.129 3
C11	Normative influence	0.098 7

Table 6. SOHO group user persuasion design evaluation index comprehensive weight

Serial number	Evaluation index	Weight number	sort
C1	Advice and reminder	0.231 3	5
C2	guide	0.226 1	6
C3	similarity	0.194 2	9
C4	like	0.209 7	8
C5	Social influence	0.156 8	10
C6	Role building	0.213 6	7
C7	reward	0.489 4	1
C8	feedback	0.398 7	2
C9	individuation	0.246 1	4
C10	self-monitoring	0.350 5	3
C11	Normativeinfluence	0.109 7	11

(3) Comprehensive weight analysis

AHP has strong subjectivity when dealing with evaluation indexes, while entropy weight method is mainly based on quantized data and has great objectivity. Therefore, combining AHP and entropy weight method, the weight values calculated respectively are combined to give weight, and the comprehensive weight coefficient of each evaluation index φj is obtained, which can make the experimental results more reasonable. The calculation method is as follows:

$$\phi_j = \frac{Y_j W_j}{\sum\limits_{j=1}^{m} Y_j W_j}, 0 \le \varphi_j \le 1, \sum_{j=1}^{n} \phi_j = 1 \tag{8}$$

In order to obtain more reasonable weight analysis results of evaluation index system, the comprehensive evaluation index weight of wrist health prevention product design scheme for SOHO users was carried out according to the above calculation method. The results are as follows:

In summary, through the weight analysis of persuasive design principles conducted by AHP-entropy weight method, the top 5 persuasive design schemes are rewards, feedback, self-monitoring, personalization, suggestions and reminders. This indicates that rewards and feedback brought by entertainment should be emphasized in the design and research of wrist preventive products for SOHO users, and certain monitoring and tracking functions should be provided to encourage users to conduct recording training and complete self-supervision. Through some suggestions and reminders to prompt users to operate content, personalized design while considering the complexity of the design.

6 Design Evaluation and Practice

The above experimental research provides a basis for the development and research of wrist health prevention products for SOHO users. This design scheme makes full use of the combination of hardware and software technology, takes the weight analysis principle of persuasion design into full consideration in the APP interface design, transforms the principle of persuasion strategy with gamification thinking, and realizes the design requirements of "reward" and "feedback". Rewards and good feedback mechanisms increase how often users use the product and enhance the user experience. Hardware products mainly carry out the interactive realization of the action of software games, and the somatosensory interaction of the hand and wrist. Through the prompts and operations on the software side, the hand strength can be trained in a standardized way, and the training content can be completed through the interaction of hardware products. Hardware products can also cooperate with the software side for feedback of multi-dimensional channels such as sound, lighting and direction to meet user needs.

6.1 Guidelines for the Design of Persuasive Wrist Health Prevention Products APP

Design criteria: The above experimental results and analysis show that the wrist health prevention products have priority in the design, the combination of software APP products and hardware products, better mobilize the enthusiasm of users, enhance participation, improve user experience. The user-centered design and development of preventive product software APP products are carried out, and the summary design hierarchy is shown in Fig. 9. This design level serves as a reference for the design guidance of APP software products.

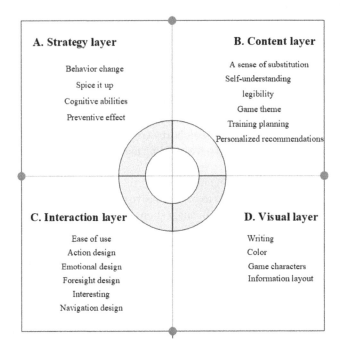

Fig. 9. Guidelines for APP product design

Information architecture: This study sorted out the information architecture of APP software products according to the design guidelines obtained above. As shown in Fig. 10, the main content architecture includes four parts, including "fun training", "theme game", "sound sensing space" and "social circle". APP training content needs to be connected to hardware products through software Bluetooth setting.

Interface design: Set up a small game training mechanism, link to hardware products through game actions, and provide users with various reward mechanisms. During the game, light and sound are interactive through hardware products. With the function of training record diary, it is convenient for users to watch the personal training situation in real time and complete self-monitoring. Provide social sharing function to satisfy users' behavioral persuasion in social learning, social influence and other aspects. The game theme includes "national style games" and "fierce fighting games", and the game actions refer to the knowledge content of medical wrist training, as shown in Fig. 11. This interface has APP mobile terminal and computer web terminal.

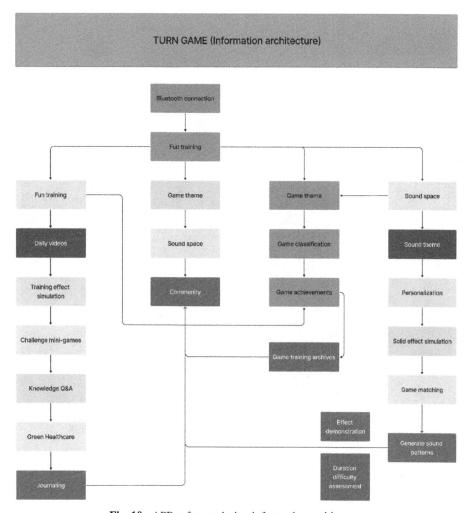

Fig. 10. APP software design information architecture

Description: The theme of the game is to break Bridges with different images as the main line, and different levels have different game scenes. The main content is that users can control the direction and speed of the floating ball through hardware products, and control the jumping and tumbling game by clicking the concave and convex drum.

(2) Hardware product design

Description: Using levitation technology, the overall design modeling intention comes from the Musical Instruments of the drumming band (Fig. 11).

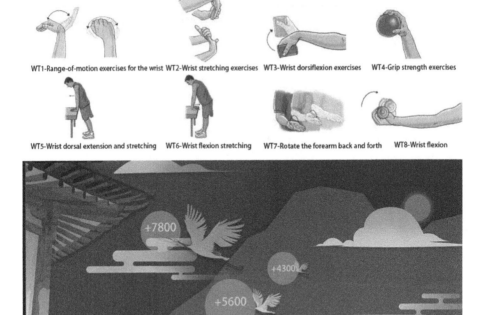

WT1-Range-of-motion exercises for the wrist WT2-Wrist stretching exercises WT3-Wrist dorsiflexion exercises WT4-Grip strength exercises

WT5-Wrist dorsal extension and stretching WT6-Wrist flexion stretching WT7-Rotate the forearm back and forth WT8-Wrist flexion

Fig. 11. Medical wrist training part posture and part of the game interface

Fig. 12. Hardware product renderings

Product application process: Characters jump up and down in left and right directions through the massage protrusion around, the movement direction of the game characters is controlled through the swing of the floating ball above, and the movement speed and distance of the game characters are controlled according to the grip power. The ball above can play voice and music, set lights, create a sound space, and enhance the overall fun experience of training.

7 Conclusion and Prospect

In this study, persuasive design method is used to design interactive products for wrist health prevention of SOHO users. In the research method, AHP-entropy weight method and persuasive design are combined. The research results confirm the effectiveness of AHP-entropy weight method in quantitative analysis of persuasive design content, which can further improve the accuracy of persuasive design. It provides some reference for the research and development of persuasion design. However, due to the small amount of data used in the research, its application scope is limited. Persuasive design strategy is effective in guiding interaction design, but it challenges the further development of persuasive design to serve more precise interaction principles to users. This study effectively improves the accuracy of the implementation of persuasive design by means of more quantitative analysis. In the future, a large number of combined studies are needed to open up greater application prospects for persuasive design.

References

1. Shi, M., Zhang, K.: Research on persuasive design in the prevention of white-collar "carpal tunnel syndrome". Develop. Innov. Mech. Electric. Prod. **32**(6), 3 (2019)
2. Fogg, B.: Persuasive computers: perspectives and research directions. In: Sigchi Conference on Human Factors in Computing Systems, pp. 225–232. ACM Press/Addison-Wesley Publishing Co. (1998)
3. Chen, C., Zheng, K., Liu, X., et al.: Research on the design of intelligent children's study table based on persuasive technology. Furniture Inter. Decorat. (2021)
4. Lou, S., Deng, R., Cao, E.: Research on the visualization method of persuasive design in APP. Pack. Eng. **38**(14), 4 (2017)
5. Liu, D., Yang, Q., Lv, J., et al.: Research on the comprehensive importance of user needs integrating user satisfaction. Acta Photonica Sinica **40**(6), 1137–1143 (2019)
6. Chen, X., Wei, H.: Research on product design scheme evaluation based on structure entropy weight TOPSIS method. J. Graph. **41**(3), 446–452 (2020)

Make It Short: A Pilot Study on an Adaptive Nutrition Tracking App

Martin Lurz[1(✉)], Barbara Prommegger[1], Markus Böhm[2], and Helmut Krcmar[1]

[1] Department of Computer Science, Technical University of Munich, Munich, Germany
martin.lurz@tum.de
[2] Department of Informatics, University of Applied Sciences Landshut, Landshut, Germany

Abstract. Over the years, obesity has been rising. This does not only lead to a higher prevalence of non-communicable diseases that affect the health of an individual, but also high costs for society. Although existing research in the field of mobile health suggests that mobile nutrition tracking applications can be considered a well-accepted and low-cost intervention, current nutrition apps are struggling in multiple areas like time-intense food tracking, incorrect reporting by users, and neglect of aspects such as in variety. For this reason, this study has iteratively developed a mobile app that allows users to decide for themselves how precisely, and therefore, how time-consuming, they want to track their diets. In a final study, it was evaluated how the new tracking method was used, perceived, and accepted by users. Good ratings were observed for usability as well as a large majority of food records accompanied with extensive details.

Keywords: App · User · Behavior · mHealth · Nutrition · Usability · Acceptance

1 Introduction

Obesity has been a main concern of international public health systems for decades. In 2016, over 1.9 billion adults aged 18 years and older were overweight, while 650 million of these adults were obese [1]. Despite various efforts to resolve the health crisis, numbers are still rising, even in countries with high education and, therefore, should be more aware regarding wellness [2]. According to the Robert Koch Institute [3], about two-thirds of men (67%) and half of the women (53%) in Germany are overweight, while a quarter of adults (23% of men and 24% of women) are obese. Besides obesity, an improper diet is also correlated with non-communicable diseases (NCDs) such as cardiovascular diseases (CVDs), certain types of cancer, and diabetes mellitus [4, 5]. About one-third of CVDs are caused by inadequate nutrition [6]. Further studies also show that overweight and obese individuals have significantly higher odds of healthcare utilization and productivity losses than those of normal-weight [7]. To address this progressive trend toward obesity and low-quality diets, many countries developed national food-based dietary guidelines (FBDGs) [8]. However, awareness about FBDGs within a population is mostly low, especially in lower levels of society [9].

M. Kurosu and A. Hashizume (Eds.): HCII 2023, LNCS 14014, pp. 50–66, 2023.
https://doi.org/10.1007/978-3-031-35572-1_4

Along with the growth of the smartphone market, research in the field of mobile applications is experiencing an increase. Research in mobile health (m-health) showed that smartphone apps can be considered both a low-cost and generally well-accepted intervention [10]. However, apps in the health and fitness category have also one common problem: high dropout rates. App usage analytics showed that they tend to lose more than half of their original users after only one month [11], with high dropout rates starting in the first few days [12]. One reason is thought to be the manner in which popular nutrition apps function: most build on so-called nutrition diaries which demand a very precise (mostly exact to the gram) tracking of one's daily diet [13, 14]. However, the process of recording foods and snacks remains burdensome and tedious for end users. According to Chen et al. [15], users of nutrition tracking applications often report a decreasing motivation over time and that the tracking functionality is too time-consuming. Thus, for this research, we designed a nutrition app that allows adaptive nutrition tracking. This should allow users to decide on the degree of precision and, therefore, time investment, every time they enter new information.

Therefore, the question of this study is: *how do users respond to an adaptive approach that allows less detailed tracking?*

To close this research gap, we first present important background knowledge on nutrition assessment and apps, followed by a description of the technical artifact that was specifically developed for this study. Afterwards, the conducted user study is described and the results are shown. Finally, we discuss our results and give an answer to our research question and conclude the findings in this paper.

2 Background

This study combines the fields of nutrition sciences and information systems. In the following, we would like to give a brief insight is provided into the corresponding state of research.

2.1 Food Tracking

Food tracking is a nutritional method derived from food assessment [16]. Its main purpose is to help individuals maintain the diet recommended by their health professionals and general guidelines. Moreover, it gives patients the opportunity to reflect on their eating behaviors. With an overview of their food intake composition, patients are likelier to change bad eating behaviors by discussing them with their health professionals [17]. Traditional food tracking methods include interviews, questionnaires, and paper-based diaries. In many cases, users find traditional methods such as diaries, which are mostly assessed as dietary records, tedious, time-consuming, and burdensome. This in turn discourages people from frequent monitoring [17, 18]. Meanwhile, interviews can be conducted in the form of a food recall or dietary history, while questionnaires in the form of a food frequency questionnaire (FFQ). Each of these assessment methods is used for different purposes. For instance, the 24-h food recall is often used to measure food intake, whereas dietary history is used to understand long-term eating patterns [16].

However, although traditional food tracking methods are simple to utilize and inexpensive, these create many burdens for both patients and health professionals [17]. For example, the 24-h food recall, and the FFQ are both retrospective methods, hence requiring memory recollection of food eaten throughout the day [19]. Consequently, the recording would likely be delayed, enhancing the imprecision, and bias of human memory. Therefore, researchers are looking for methods that make it easier for users to record food intake immediately after a meal, with the data stored in a reliable location which can be easily accessed anywhere [17].

2.2 Nutrition Apps

In recent years, due to proliferating mobile technologies and their universal uptake, the emergence of mHealth has received more attention. Particularly, there are tens of thousands of health and fitness apps, including those which target nutrition and dietary behavior [20]. However, most nutritional and dietary apps generally focus on weight loss and calorie counting, with their titles mainly containing either "calorie" or "weight" as keywords [19]. MyFitnessPal is considered the most popular nutrition-oriented app and had nearly 9 million users in 2014 [20]. Users also like mHealth apps because these provide instant feedback through favorable presentation varieties, mostly in charts and tables [17]. Some even offer motivational or reminder emails related to current diet status and provide a community of users [21].

Despite providing conveniences for people to record their food intake and improve awareness of daily nutrition, there are still challenges that users experience with currently available food tracking apps. One of the most noted challenges are time-consuming food tracking mechanisms [15, 22]. Even if features such as barcode scanning are included, adding nutrition information for home-cooked food remains difficult [15]. These factors are seen as reasons for users not tracking unhealthy meals (underreporting) and thereby lowering their overall motivation to record their diet [23, 24]. Additionally, most individuals poorly gauge portion size for which 49% of errors in energy estimation dietary records is attributed [15].

Although most nutrition apps in the market still depend on user self-reporting and input, there has been an increasing development on the integration of these apps with mobile camera features, visual data capture devices, and natural language processing [19, 20]. Despite its benefits, there are still some concerns about the effectiveness of current nutrition apps since these frequently pay more attention to the quantification of calories, macronutrients, and micronutrients intake. Meanwhile, the most useful available data to practitioners and users alike are the dietary pattern and nutritional intake behavior of different food groups such as fruits, vegetables, or whole grains [20]. Thus, a tool which documents the intake of fruits, vegetables, legumes, and whole grains, as well as the overconsumption of sodium, saturated fats, and added sugar, is needed, especially as the latter group is linked to chronic diseases, including diabetes and hypertension [20].

2.3 Food Guidelines

Following the publication of "Preparation and use of food-based dietary guidelines," consulted by the World Health Organization (WHO) along with the Food and Agriculture Organization (FAO) [25], many countries have developed their own food-based dietary guidelines (FBDGs). FBDGs aim to translate a vast evidence base about relations between foods, diet patterns, and health into specific, culturally appropriate, and actionable recommendations. Subsequently, FBDGs influence consumer behavior, national diet, nutrition, as well as health policies and programs [26]. To have food guidelines be used by the general public, the guides need to convey the concepts of variety, proportionality, and adequacy, that is, moderation, in the dietary recommendations through pictorial images [26]. As such, FBDGs help consumers visualize how a healthy diet should be. Different countries have respective tactics to introduce and promote consumer adaptation of FBDGs. To further enhance the effects of FBDGs, many countries create additional guidelines to assist consumers with portion size as well as not just advise what to consume, but also how often, and in what quantity.

In Germany, there are three FBDGs from the German Nutrition Society (DGE): "10 guidelines of the DGE for a wholesome diet," the three-dimensional (3D) Food Guide Pyramid, and the DGE Nutrition Circle [27]. The standard nutrient-based recommendations are conveyed into FBDGs to inform consumers what a healthy, balanced diet should be composed of. While the "10 guidelines of the DGE for a wholesome diet" and the DGE Nutrition Circle aim directly at consumers, the pyramid model is used only by trained specialists, specifically in nutrition counseling and education [27].

Despite its proven benefits, the DGE FBDGs, and the DGE Nutrition Circle still have not been widely used by the public, more importantly by young people. A study by Bechthold et al. [27] reported that only 14% of the population was familiar with the "10 guidelines of the DGE," and only 10% was familiar with the DGE Nutrition Circle [27].

3   Technical Concept

The main goal is to provide users with a tool which would allow food tracking on different granularity levels while still being able to provide personalized feedback as suggested by Brug et al. [28]. To create a valuable technical artifact, we followed the Design Science Research Approach (DSRA) [29] (see Fig. 1). The DSRA defines three important keystones which need to be considered: knowledge base, environment, and research.

As a start, we defined our *environment* by identifying current challenges in the area of nutrition tracking. The study identified high dropout rates, mainly due to the time-consuming dietary recording mechanism [15, 22], as well as the problem of over-and under-reporting of quantities consumed [30], as major areas for improvement.

Next, the study investigated the existing *knowledge base* in the field of nutrition apps by reviewing published scientific literature. Existing scientific methods of food recording were examined in particular. Additionally, the study evaluated how prior nutrition apps were structured and how they functioned. Finally, existing food guidelines, and their respective approach to rating nutrition were analyzed. During this research, the study identified that most modern solutions do not give attention to consumed quantities of certain food categories such as vegetables or fruits, but rather only calories [20].

Building on the two insight areas of *environment* and *knowledge base*, the study started developing a mobile application which would allow dynamic food tracking based on the time and motivation of its users. The study executed two *Develop/Evaluate Cycles*. In each cycle, a prototype was developed, and subsequently evaluated to gain a better insight into the needs and wishes of potential users.

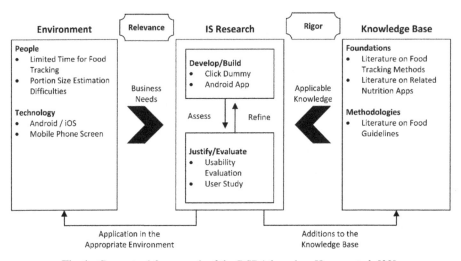

Fig. 1. Conceptual framework of the DSRA based on Hevner et al. [29].

During the first cycle, a click dummy of a potential user interface for food tracking was developed. The goal was to present the first version of the new food-tracking method to potential users so that their opinions could be considered as early as possible in the design process. For the evaluation session, 15 participants in the age range of 18 to 25 years were recruited. First, they had to enter one food record using the click dummy and the think-aloud method [31]. Afterwards, questions regarding usability as well as their opinions and perceptions of the method design were asked.

During the second cycle, a prototype mobile app that incorporates feedback from the first cycle was developed. Afterwards, we conducted a system evaluation in the form of a user study.

3.1 Tracking Approach

The idea in developing an effective food recording method was to divide the food tracking mechanism into multiple steps that allow users to finish tracking at any layer if they were not motivated enough to complete the whole questionnaire right away. Therefore, the tracking feature should be designed in a way that is able to draw a certain level of additional knowledge after each layer.

During the conception phase, different FBDGs were evaluated with regard to their compatibility with the planned tracking approach. For this prototype, it was finally decided to base the assessment tool on the so-called "Nutrition Circle" by the DGE [32]. This German FBDG focuses mainly on the balance of different food categories in daily and weekly food consumption which has been shown to ensure a balanced diet as well as help to significantly reduce the risk for several NCDs [33]. In total, four layers of questions were designed starting with general information to more precise details: food categories (level one), portion size (level two), product categories (level three), and preparation style (level 4).

In the first level, as shown in Fig. 3, users are asked which predefined food categories they consumed. Although the Nutrition Circle guideline does not include alcohol, sweetened beverages, and snacks, these categories were still added to the study approach so that users could keep track of how much unhealthy food intake they consumed throughout the day.

To know if users consumed a proportionate amount of each type of food, the second level of questions request information about portion size. Based on scientific literature, it was expected that users would find this question the most difficult of all three. As it has been shown that users of food tracking applications perceive the usage of scales as tedious, and consumed portion size estimates are especially imprecise when relying on food weights in combination with untrained users [34], the study aimed to incorporate the measurement per hand technique [35] into the application. This method by the Bundeszentrum für Ernährung (BZfE) [35] defines portions through the hand size of the user which eliminates the need to weigh or estimate the weight of food consumed. This should enable users to quickly and accurately track portions.

The third level questions ask users to provide more details about what specific food items they ate in each group. For vegetables and fruits, variety was seen as more important than the specific vegetable or fruit wherein users can simply select the colors of their consumed vegetables and fruits. This reduced the cumbersomeness of unnecessary details about specific names of fruits and vegetables because, for instance, a bowl of salad, or soup usually contains many kinds of vegetables or fruits. The selection of colors was incorporated to determine the variety a user consumes over a certain amount of time since a wide range of colors is considered beneficial [36].

The last level of questions includes cooking methods for each food category. Therefore, the purpose of this method is to remind users about the different levels of healthiness as well as enhance their awareness of other less-caloric cooking methods for the same type of food.

3.2 User Interface

The overall user interface design was aimed to be simple and discrete, but also vibrant enough to encourage the excitement of interacting with the app.

When a new user initially opens the app, an onboarding screen is shown. Since the application incorporates a novel approach to food tracking which users will not be familiar with, even if they used other nutrition apps before, this feature should help familiarize them with the new method. Furthermore, the freedom of choice in tracking frequency and granularity is explained. Afterwards, the user is directed to the home screen (see Fig. 2c) which contains links to all major functionalities of the app. Users can view a summarized rating of their diet based on the food records entered for the day (see Fig. 2a). By selecting longer time ranges at the top of the screen, the user can retrieve feedback on the last week or month.

Furthermore, personalized recommendations according to the underlying Nutrition Circle and entered food records are listed (see Fig. 2b). The feedback section is adaptive to the granularity of user entries. If the user decided to just enter data on the first level questions and accordingly does not state the consumed amounts, the user retrieves recommendations to consume dairy products, vegetables, and fruits daily if not having done so. Furthermore, regarding animal products, the application detects if the user consumed them too often within a month or week and thereby might exceed the recommended amount by the DGE. If the user further specifies the number of portions consumed during tracking, all rules by the DGE which state the recommended amount of each food category are considered within the feedback. Additionally, feedback on variety is given to encourage users to form a healthy and balanced diet.

Clicking on the gear icon at the upper right corner of the home screen opens the screen settings (see Fig. 2d) where users can customize their dietary style. For example, food categories such as meat or dairy products can be removed for vegetarian or vegan users. Additionally, users can switch off a reminder function as well as revisit the onboarding tour. Moreover, a default-on reminder feature was added since notifications have been shown to motivate users to open the app and perform in-app tasks [37, 38]. Finally, by clicking the "Add Record" button on the home screen, users can add a new food record to the app.

Fig. 2. Overview of entered food records per day (a), personalized recommendations based on food records (b), the home screen (c), and app settings (d).

For recording the food type, the first level questions were aimed to fit onto the screen without the need to scroll down (see Fig. 3a). This was possible because the different food categories were structured in a grid layout similar to a smartphone screen display. Each grid square was given a solid background color based on the representative colors of each food category in the Nutrition Circle. To support users in selecting the right categories, users can open an explanation for each category by holding the respective tile. The explanation contains general information about the category as well as examples of associated food products.

This study followed a previous research which suggested that both the button color and placement can be used to nudge users toward choosing a certain option [39]. Therefore, the colors of the buttons were chosen to encourage users to input as many food intake details as possible. After selecting the consumed categories, the user can press the "Next" button to navigate to the following level of the tree or click on the "Save and Exit" button to quit recording. In addition, the "Next" button was prominently placed above the "Save and Exit" button. This design aims to encourage the user toward continuing to answer the questions of the tree without limiting autonomy.

For the portion size selection process, additional toggle buttons were added for partial portions. Furthermore, users can view explanations on the definition of a portion for each food category at the end of the respective box.

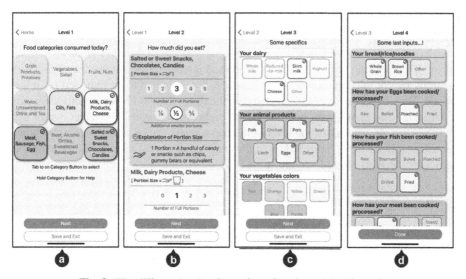

Fig. 3. The different levels of questions: Level one (a) to four (d).

4 Evaluation

For the evaluation of the app, a user study was conducted. This evaluation form was chosen as it allows the investigation of more natural user behavior (i.e. app use) than a controlled observation (e.g. laboratory experiment) would.

4.1 Methodology

The study consisted of four main stages: (1) Recruiting, (2) a pre-questionnaire, (3) an app testing period over seven days, and (4) a post-questionnaire. For recruiting participants, the user study was promoted in the social network accounts of the researchers. Selected participants were at least 18 years old and either owned an Android or iOS device. Participants were first asked to fill out the pre-questionnaire. Afterwards, the seven day testing period started. No assistance was provided except for the installation of the application. Succeeding the usage period, the user was then asked to fill out a post-intervention questionnaire. While the pre-questionnaire included items regarding demographics (age, gender, weight, height, and education), health goals, prior knowledge regarding nutrition apps as well as the perceived importance of health based on the questions of Lau et al. [40], the post-questionnaire contained items to collect user opinion about the app functions. The measurement instruments used included the System Usability Scale (SUS) [41], the User Experience Questionnaire (UEQ) [42], and the Technology Acceptance Model 3 (TAM) [43] as well as open text questions for determining areas of improvement.

4.2 Participants

During the recruiting phase, 25 people expressed interest. However, as not all finished the study by completing the post-questionnaire, 8 people had to be removed from the sample. Thus, the app was evaluated based on the usage data of 17 participants as shown in Table 1. Nine participants were male and eight were female. The mean age of the attendees was 31. The education level of the participants can be considered rather high. The average Body Mass Index (BMI) of the sample group was calculated following the method of the World Health Organization [44].

4.3 Results

During the app usage period, recruited participants opened the mobile application 5.3 times per day (SD = 3.89). Four participants—although not requested—proceeded to use the application after the post-survey, recording further M = 5.75 records one week after study completion.

Within the study period 346 nutrition entries were input by the study participants. Accordingly, every user created 20.35 entries on average with each record taking 1.47 min (SD = 1.14 min) to make. Since the adaptive question tree enables the user to decide on the granularity and frequency of tracking, the number of entries per day and per user varies widely. However, the number of records results in a mean tracking frequency of 2.80 records per day. Overall, ten experiment attendees (62.5%) of the sixteen participants decided to track their nutrition daily. Furthermore, the tracking frequencies for the ten participants who journaled their food intake daily varied in the number of records as observable in Fig. 4.

From a granularity perspective, 342 (98.84%) of the 346 food records were completed by finishing all questions of the adaptive question tree. Accordingly, only four data points were created by submitting the results without answering until the end of the adaptive

Table 1. Measurements of the Recruited Participants

Participants		17
Gender	Male	9 (53%)
	Female	8 (47%)
BMI	Underweight	0
	Normal	13 (76%)
	Overweight	3 (18%)
	Obese	1 (6%)
Used Nutrition Apps Before	Yes	7 (41.2%)
	No	10 (58.8%)
	Mean	Standard Deviation
Age	31	12.1
BMI	21.6	3.7
Importance of Health	15.1	2.7

question tree. Three of these four records were saved after finishing the first level of the question tree and thus, accordingly, not even recording the amount consumed. The fourth incomplete tracking entry was answered up to the third level. Generally, the gathered data points suggest that most of the study attendees (82.4%) journaled their nutrition by always answering all questions.

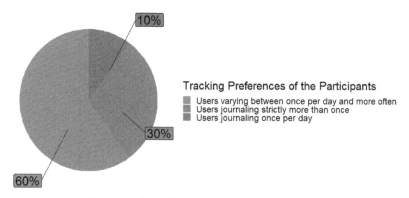

Tracking Preferences of the Participants
- Users varying between once per day and more often
- Users journaling strictly more than once
- Users journaling once per day

Fig. 4. Daily tracking frequencies of participants.

Regarding the included measurement instruments, with an average SUS score of 80 as shown in Table 1, the study results show overall good usability according to the SUS rating scale by Bangor et al. [45]. No major differences were found between male and female participants. Participants with a BMI above 25 perceived the system as slightly more usable (M = 81.25, SD = 7.22). Another difference in the SUS rating can be found between the age groups of the participants. Attendees older than 50 years rated the perceived usability with M = 84.16 (SD = 2.88) whereas the younger participants stated a mean usability score of 77.5 (SD = 5.59).

Answers to the User Experience Questionnaire (UEQ) suggest, according to Laugwitz et al. [46], a nearly perfect perspicuity, a good efficiency, and above-average dependability of the app (see Table 2). The perspicuity is thereby in the range of the ten percent best results and, accordingly, the mobile application was perceived as easily understandable and not complicated or confusing. Overall, the pragmatic quality of the app can be regarded as good. The enjoyable quality of the application was perceived as worse than the task-oriented quality determinants. Novelty was reported as below average. Stimulation was perceived as above average and thus the system might be considered slightly more interesting and motivating than the average UEQ results of other systems. The attractiveness of the app was perceived as good by study attendees. Thus, the overall perceived user experience can be considered as good.

Table 2. Post-questionnaire average results validated by measuring instruments.

Item		(Value Range)	Average	Standard Deviation
SUS		(1–100)	79.9	9.03
UEQ	Attractiveness	(−3–+3)	1.61	
	Perspicuity	(−3–+3)	2.09	
	Efficiency	(−3–+3)	1.76	
	Dependability	(−3–+3)	1.32	
	Stimulation	(−3–+3)	1.25	
	Novelty	(−3–+3)	0.62	
TAM	PU	(1–7)	4.9	1.01
	PEOU	(1–7)	5.8	0.54
	SE	(1–7)	4.3	0.82
	RES	(1–7)	5.4	1.01
	ENJ	(1–7)	4.9	1.25
	OUT	(1–7)	4.7	1.40
	BI	(1–7)	4.4	

Regarding the TAM3 Questionnaire, users rated perceived ease of use (PEOU) best as shown in Table 2, followed by the result for demonstrability (RES). The perceived enjoyment (ENJ) and the perceived usefulness (PU) retrieved average ratings. Overall, the lowest score was reported on perceived self-efficiency (SE) and thus the degree to which individuals feel the need to improve their diet by using the app without any further help from other sources outside of it can be considered as lowest in comparison to other determinants. No major differences could be found between genders except male participants rated the RES (MRES_MALE = 5.72, SDRES_MALE = 0.57) and the perceived output quality (OUT) (MOUT_MALE = 4.93, SDOUT_MALE = 1.51) slightly higher than did the female study attendees (MRES_FEMALE $= 5.03$, SDRES_FEMALE $=$ 1.29, MOUT_FEMALE $= 4.42$, SDOUT_FEMALE $= 1.32$). The group of participants with a BMI greater than 24.9 rated RES and OUT slightly higher than the average, suggesting that the perceived feedback quality was higher and easily reproducible for attendees with a normal BMI. The perceived enjoyment during application usage is also higher for this group (MENJ $= 5.42$, SDENJ $= 1.26$). Furthermore, the reported behavioral intention to use the system is, on average, 0.9 points higher than for system users with a healthy BMI.

To be able to draw meaningful insights regarding areas for improvement, the study evaluated the post-questionnaire open text fields asking for specific problems. Therefore, answers were aggregated, and categorized into eight different categories. As listed in Table 3, major issues included difficulties regarding portion size assessment, problems inputting vegan and vegetarian alternatives such as tofu and soy milk as well as adding several vegetables and fruits such as cauliflower and nuts.

5 Discussion

The average results on the SUS and TAM yield that the application can be considered easy to use while the tested tracking method was perceived as an efficient way to record nutrition. The mean SUS score suggests that the overall usability of the system is comparable to, or even outperforms, several existing nutrition tracking applications in the market and research regarding usability [47].

Although the results on output quality, self-efficiency, and perceived usefulness are above average, the application should be further improved under consideration of these categories. In detail, the usefulness, as a major predictor for the behavior intention toward the usage of the system, has to be further improved as it is currently one of the determinants rated worst by the study attendees. Following the TAM model, the perceived usefulness of the application might thereby be moderated by increasing the application output quality. This coincides with the qualitative findings on the overall application design in which more detailed feedback was requested by four participants within the experimental evaluation, suggesting that the current feedback functionality does not satisfy the needs of all users. Thus, it seems promising to enable the users to retrieve more detailed feedback from the application. For instance, the application can be enabled to track the calorific value and macronutrients of the consumed food. For an implementation of this feature, however, the application has to be connected to a food database in future development that holds detailed nutrition values for all food categories and average nutrition values for each food color under consideration of different cooking methods.

The qualitative results on input-related problems revealed several possible improvements to further increase the usability of the question tree for different food items. Firstly, a future iteration of the prototype should enable users to track most of the existing vegan and vegetarian food alternatives for meat and dairy products. Also, expanding the color selection for fruits and vegetables, with the colors brown, and white, should help people add items such as onions, potatoes, and cauliflower more easily. Furthermore, the explanations on portion sizes might be stated in a more detailed manner for the different products within each category. Finally, it seems considerable to further differentiate

Table 3. Input-related issues with the tested food tracking approach.

Category (Number of Participant Feedback)	Products or Meals
Drinks and Beverages (2)	"Coffee" (P8), "Drinks with very low amounts of sugar, e.g. coffee or juice mixed with water" (P11)
Dairy Products (2)	"Cream" (P4), "Cream, or more dairy products" (P13)
Cooking Methods (1)	"Meat in the oven" (P4)
Vegan and Vegetarian Food Alternatives (2)	"Tofu, Falafel" (P1) "Difficult to track vegan alternatives like for example soy milk" (P10)
Fruits and Vegetables (2)	"Legumes" (P10), "Nuts, Cauliflower" (P7)
Portion Size (3)	"Dishes composed of different ingredients." (P15, P16) "[…]Estimating quantities is difficult, e.g., how many servings is a palm-sized slice of sausage, if an equally-sized slice of meat is a serving?" (P15)
Grain and Potato Products (1)	"in the third layer of the question tree there were very few answer options, e.g. I could not choose potatoes even though the first layer proposed potatoes, I had to choose 'Other' quite often" (P11)
Other (2)	"In general, the available options are very limited and you miss products of every category quite easily" (P17) "It is not possible to retroactively add a record" (P15)

within the category of drinks and beverages. The reported need by participants is the ability to track the difference in consumed beverages such as coffee, fruit juice, and smoothies. These questions may provide users feedback on the amount of alcohol and caffeine consumed. From a research perspective, a possible implementation of feedback regarding alcohol and caffeine can be considered beneficial since high consumption of both ingredients was found to profoundly affect health [48, 49].

Of course, the findings of this study are not without limitations. First, the presented results were drawn from a small sample group. Due to this limited number, no statistical significance could be calculated. Additionally, there was no equal distribution of participants in terms of demographics, thus, the overall level of high education of the sample group should be mentioned. Furthermore, known influencing factors of user studies such as confirmation bias [50] and response bias [51] might apply. Finally, the time frame of seven days until the follow-up questionnaire could only provide a brief insight into app usage behavior, which means that no final statements could be made about long-term behavior.

Regarding the tracking approach, only three participants made use of stopping the tracking early. This might be reasoned by the overall short length of the questions and the digital nudging approach by the button design. As adding the above mentioned elements will result in a larger question tree, more users might consider stopping after their desired granularity level while the perceived efficiency should not be affected by the additional questions. Accordingly, users who requested more detailed feedback on their nutrition might be satisfied without negatively affecting the other users who were already satisfied by the current design of the tracking mechanism.

6   Conclusion and Future Work

Overall, the evaluation of the study shows that the application has good usability and can be considered as easy to use. The usability was especially high for participants older than 50 years, while the perceived enjoyment, and the usage intention were rated highest for participants with a BMI greater than 25. This leads to the conclusion that the app and the underlying food-tracking approach can be considered as easy to use and an efficient way to track nutrition. Additionally, the qualitative findings on both the question tree and the overall application design are synthesized to propose further improvements to the application that would increase its PU. Accordingly, this paper contributes to research in the field of information system design within the field of m-health by evaluating a new approach for nutrition tracking.

For future research, adjusting the first version of the presented food tracking approach to the given feedback is suggested. This includes smaller adjustments such as additional colors for the fruit and vegetable categories as well as a scientific method to translate detailed food tracking into macro-nutrient values such as calories. Since categories such as "Sweet, Snacks, and Chocolate" are quite broad, more questions will have to be added to ensure a reliable calculation. Finally, a larger user study over a longer period should be conducted in order to gain more stable results and statistically significant results. Additionally, this will help gain detailed insights into different subgroups regarding usage behavior over a longer time frame.

References

1. World Health Organization: Obesity and overweight. https://www.who.int/news-room/fact-sheets/detail/obesity-and-overweight. Accessed 23 Dec 2020
2. OECD and European Union: Health at a Glance: Europe 2020. OECD Publishing, Paris (2020)
3. Robert Koch Institute: Overweight and obesity. https://www.rki.de/EN/Content/Health_Monitoring/Main_Topics/Overweight_Obesity/obesity_node.html. Accessed 24 Dec 2020
4. Robertson, A.: Food and health in Europe: a new basis for action. WHO regional publications. European series (2004)
5. Sotos-Prieto, M., et al.: Changes in diet quality scores and risk of cardiovascular disease among US men and women. Circulation **132**(23), 2212–2219 (2015)

6. World Health Organization: Food and health in Europe: a new basis for action (WHO Regional Publications, European Series, No. 96). World Health Organization, Copenhagen, Denmark (2004)
7. Yates, N., et al.: The economic burden of obesity in Germany: results from the population-based KORA studies. Obes. Facts 9(6), 397–409 (2016)
8. Herforth, A., Arimond, M., Álvarez-Sánchez, C., Coates, J., Christianson, K., Muehlhoff, E.: "A Global Review of Food-Based Dietary Guidelines," (in eng). Adv. Nutr. 10(4), 590–605 (2019). https://doi.org/10.1093/advances/nmy130
9. Keller, I., Lang, T.: "Food-based dietary guidelines and implementation: lessons from four countries–Chile, Germany, New Zealand and South Africa," (in eng). Public Health Nutr. 11(8), 867–874 (2008). https://doi.org/10.1017/s1368980007001115
10. Payne, H.E., Lister, C., West, J.H., Bernhardt, J.M.: Behavioral functionality of mobile apps in health interventions: a systematic review of the literature. JMIR Mhealth Uhealth 3(1), e3335 (2015)
11. Perez, S.: Flurry Examines App Loyalty: News & Communication Apps Top Charts, Personalization Apps See High Churn. TechCrunch. https://techcrunch.com/2012/10/22/flurry-examines-app-loyalty-news-communication-apps-top-charts-personalization-apps-see-high-churn/. Accessed 20 Oct 2021
12. Thompson, F.E., Subar, A.F.: Dietary assessment methodology. In: Coulston, A.M., Boushey, C.J., Ferruzzi, M.G., Delahanty, L.M. (eds.) Nutrition in the Prevention and Treatment of Disease, ch. 1, p. 1072. Academic Press (2017)
13. YAZIO: YAZIO Calorie Counter & Intermittent Fasting App. https://play.google.com/store/apps/details?id=com.yazio.android&hl. Accessed 18 Oct 2022
14. MyFitnessPal Inc.: Calorie Counter - MyFitnessPal. https://play.google.com/store/apps/details?id=com.myfitnesspal.android. Accessed 18 Oct 2022
15. Chen, J., Berkman, W., Bardouh, M., Ng, C.Y.K., Allman-Farinelli, M.: The use of a food logging app in the naturalistic setting fails to provide accurate measurements of nutrients and poses usability challenges. Nutrition 57, 208–216 (2019)
16. Luo, Y., Liu, P., Choe, E.K.: Co-Designing food trackers with dietitians: Identifying design opportunities for food tracker customization. In: Proceedings of the 2019 CHI Conference on Human Factors in Computing Systems, pp. 1–13 (2019)
17. Rusin, M., Årsand, E., Hartvigsen, G.: Functionalities and input methods for recording food intake: a systematic review. Int. J. Med. Inform. 82(8), 653–664 (2013)
18. Turner-McGrievy, G.M., Beets, M.W., Moore, J.B., Kaczynski, A.T., Barr-Anderson, D.J., Tate, D.F.: Comparison of traditional versus mobile app self-monitoring of physical activity and dietary intake among overweight adults participating in an mHealth weight loss program. J. Am. Med. Inform. Assoc. 20(3), 513–518 (2013)
19. Franco, R.Z., Fallaize, R., Lovegrove, J.A., Hwang, F.: Popular nutrition-related mobile apps: a feature assessment. JMIR Mhealth Uhealth 4(3), e85 (2016)
20. Hingle, M., Patrick, H.: There are thousands of apps for that: navigating mobile technology for nutrition education and behavior. J. Nutrition Educ. Behav. 48(3), 213–218. e1 (2016)
21. Cox, A.M., McKinney, P., Goodale, P.: Food logging: an information literacy perspective. Aslib J. Inform. Manage. (2017)
22. Lupton, D.: 'I just want it to be done, done, done!' Food tracking apps, affects, and agential capacities. Multimodal Technol. Interact. 2(2), 29 (2018)
23. Cordeiro, F., et al.: Barriers and negative nudges: exploring challenges in food journaling, (in eng). Proc. SIGCHI Conf. Hum. Factor Comput. Syst. 2015, 1159–1162 (2015). https://doi.org/10.1145/2702123.2702155
24. König, L.M., Attig, C., Franke, T., Renner, B.: Barriers to and facilitators for using nutrition apps: systematic review and conceptual framework, (in eng). JMIR Mhealth Uhealth 9(6) (2021). https://doi.org/10.2196/20037

25. Joint, F., Organization, W.H.: Preparation and use of food-based dietary guidelines. World Health Organization (1998)
26. Herforth, A., Arimond, M., Álvarez-Sánchez, C., Coates, J., Christianson, K., Muehlhoff, E.: A global review of food-based dietary guidelines. Adv. Nutr. **10**(4), 590–605 (2019)
27. Bechthold, A., Wendt, I., Laubach, B., Mayerböck, C., Oberritter, H., Nöthlings, U.: Consumers' awareness of food-based dietary guidelines in Germany. Results of a representative survey. Ernahrungs Umschau **64**(7), 112–119 (2017)
28. Brug, J., Glanz, K., Van Assema, P., Kok, G., Van Breukelen, G.J.: The impact of computer-tailored feedback and iterative feedback on fat, fruit, and vegetable intake. Health Educ. Behav. **25**(4), 517–531 (1998)
29. Bichler, M.: Design science in information systems research. Wirtschaftsinformatik **48**(2), 133–135 (2006). https://doi.org/10.1007/s11576-006-0028-8
30. Calvert, C., Cade, J., Barrett, J.H., Woodhouse, A., Group, U.S.: Using cross-check questions to address the problem of mis-reporting of specific food groups on Food Frequency Questionnaires. Eur. J. Clin. Nutri. **51**(10), 708–712 (1997). https://doi.org/10.1038/sj.ejcn.1600480
31. Boren, T., Ramey, J.: Thinking aloud: reconciling theory and practice. IEEE Trans. Prof. Commun. **43**(3), 261–278 (2000)
32. Deutsche Gesellschaft für Ernährung "DGE-Ernährungskreis." https://www.dge.de/ernaehrungspraxis/vollwertige-ernaehrung/ernaehrungskreis/. Accessed 18 Oct 2022
33. Oberritter, H., Schäbethal, K., Von Ruesten, A., Boeing, H.: The DGE nutrition circle—presentation and basis of the food-related recommendations from the German Nutrition Society (DGE). Ernahrungs Umschau **60**(2), 24–29 (2013)
34. Young, L.R., Nestle, M.: Portion sizes in dietary assessment: issues and policy implications. Nutr. Rev. **53**(6), 149–158 (1995)
35. Bundeszentrum für Ernährung (BZfE). Portionsgröße - gemessen mit der eigenen Hand. https://www.bzfe.de/portionsgroesse-gemessen-mit-der-eigenen-hand/. Accessed 18 Oct 2022
36. Minich, D.M.: "A review of the science of colorful, plant-based food and practical strategies for" eating the rainbow. J. Nutrition Metabol. **2019** (2019)
37. Sandborg, J., et al.: Participants' engagement and satisfaction with a smartphone app intended to support healthy weight gain, diet, and physical activity during pregnancy: Qualitative study within the HealthyMoms trial. JMIR Mhealth Uhealth **9**(3), e26159 (2021)
38. Zhao, Z., Arya, A., Orji, R., Chan, G.: Effects of a personalized fitness recommender system using gamification and continuous player modeling: system design and long-term validation study. JMIR Ser. Games **8**(4), e19968 (2020)
39. Utz, C., Degeling, M., Fahl, S., Schaub, F., Holz, T.: (Un) informed consent: studying GDPR consent notices in the field. In: Proceedings of the 2019 ACM SIGSAC Conference on Computer and Communications Security, pp. 973–990 (2019)
40. Lau, R.R., Hartman, K.A., Ware, J.E.: Health as a value: methodological and theoretical considerations. Health Psychol. **5**(1), 25 (1986)
41. Brooke, J.: SUS: a quick and dirty usability scale. In: Jordan, P.W.(ed.) Usability Evaluation in Industry, pp. 189–194 CRC Press (1996)
42. Schrepp, M., Hinderks, A., Thomaschewski, J.: Applying the User Experience Questionnaire (UEQ) in different evaluation scenarios. In: Marcus, A. (ed.) DUXU 2014. LNCS, vol. 8517, pp. 383–392. Springer, Cham (2014). https://doi.org/10.1007/978-3-319-07668-3_37
43. Venkatesh, V., Bala, H.: Technology acceptance model 3 and a research agenda on interventions. Decis. Sci. **39**(2), 273–315 (2008). https://doi.org/10.1111/j.1540-5915.2008.00192.x

44. World Health Organization: A healthy lifestyle - WHO recommendations. https://www.who.int/europe/news-room/fact-sheets/item/a-healthy-lifestyle---who-recommendations. Accessed 3 Feb 2023

45. Bangor, A., Kortum, P., Miller, J.: Determining what individual SUS scores mean: adding an adjective rating scale. J. Usabil. Stud. **4**(3), 114–123 (2009)

46. Laugwitz, B., Held, T., Schrepp, M.: Construction and evaluation of a user experience questionnaire. In: Holzinger, A. (eds.) HCI and Usability for Education and Work. USAB 2008. LNCS, vol. 5298. Springer, Berlin, Heidelberg (2008). https://doi.org/10.1007/978-3-540-89350-9_6

47. Ferrara, G., Kim, J., Lin, S., Hua, J., Seto, E.: A focused review of smartphone diet-tracking apps: usability, functionality, coherence with behavior change theory, and comparative validity of nutrient intake and energy estimates. JMIR Mhealth Uhealth **7**(5), e9232 (2019)

48. Nawrot, P., Jordan, S., Eastwood, J., Rotstein, J., Hugenholtz, A., Feeley, M.: Effects of caffeine on human health. Food Addit. Contam. **20**(1), 1–30 (2003)

49. Room, R., Babor, T., Rehm, J.: Alcohol and public health. Lancet **365**(9458), 519–530 (2005)

50. Oswald, M.E., Grosjean, S.: Confirmation bias. Cognitive Illusions: A Handbook on Fallacies and Biasesi Thinking, Judgement and Memory, vol. 79, p. 83 (2004)

51. Sedgwick, P.: Non-response bias versus response bias. BMJ **348** (2014)

Practicality Aspects of Automatic Fluid Intake Monitoring via Smartwatches

Rainer Lutze[1]([⊠]) and Klemens Waldhör[2]

[1] Dr.-Ing. Rainer Lutze Consulting, Wachtlerhof, Langenzenn, Germany
rainerlutze@lustcon.eu
[2] FOM University of Applied Sciences, Nuremberg, Germany
klemens.waldhoer@fom.de

Abstract. Daily sufficient fluid intake is one of the important conditions of human health. Only an automatic monitoring of a sufficient fluid intake volume fulfills practicality requirements for people especially dependent on such intake, e.g. during specific medical treatment or older people experiencing a diminished sensation of natural thirst. Programmable smartwatch apps can realize such an automatic fluid intake volume monitoring from the morning till night time with sufficient precision impeding dehydration. We present an innovative five aspects approach for a comprehensive analysis of the application area. First, how much fluid volume shall be orally ingested by an individual person? Second, in which way can fluid intake acts reliably be detected from gestures? Third, how can the ingested total volume be automatically estimated? Fourth, in which way can the daily fluid volume already ingested so far be indicated to a smartwatch wearer at a glance and in an intuitive way? Fifth and at last, when and in which situations do advices to the smartwatch wearer to drink a beverage right now meet his/her open mind and eyes? For the necessary machine learning, data mining, and recognition respectively classification process of physiologic activities the applied statistics and artificial intelligence methods will be presented, analyzed and evaluated from a practical perspective.

Keywords: automatic fluid intake monitoring by smartwatches · automatic determination of fluid intake volume · UI aspects of effective fluid intake advices · smartwatches

1 Background and Motivation

Fluid intake is one of the essential activities of animals and humans in order to replenish and balance the body water losses taking place by the physiological processes of those living beings. The necessity of fluid intake is signaled by the sensation of thirst, which starts at a loss of 0,5% of body water. Body water losses of more than 3% cause unnoticeable mental disorientation and cannot be compensated in their effects in less than 16–24 h [1, 2]. Especially for older people, where the natural sensation of thirst is gradually diminishing, dehydration is one of the major risks factors for tumbles and

M. Kurosu and A. Hashizume (Eds.): HCII 2023, LNCS 14014, pp. 67–86, 2023.
https://doi.org/10.1007/978-3-031-35572-1_5

other accidents in daily life. Monitoring the daily fluid volume intake is also of importance for many medical treatments, which are dependent on flushing out given drugs and performed in the kidneys by excretion via urine. This requires a corresponding prior or simultaneous fluid intake (e.g. in oncological chemotherapy) in order to maintain the body water balance.

Only the automatic monitoring of the daily oral fluid intake volume has a chance to ensure sufficient fluid intake in practice. Programmable smartwatches, typically worn from rising in the morning till retiring to bed in night time, are a suitable device to execute such a monitoring over the whole course of the day. They are on duty at home as well as equally on the way. They work perfect if worn on the preferred hand, and even for ambidextrous persons they deliver acceptable results in automatic monitoring of fluid volume intake ([29], see also Sect. 3.3). In contrast to camera based surveillance systems, smartwatches do not presuppose a cost-intensive infrastructure and have no privacy problems. Another alternative for automatic monitoring, intelligent drinking vessels automatically weighing and transmitting their corresponding content, burden users with the necessary logistics of carrying and using them everywhere, which might be stigmatizing in specific social contexts. [8] gives a comprehensive, up-to-date overview of the different applicable technologies of automatic fluid intake monitoring.

2 Prior Work

Automatic fluid intake monitoring by smartwatches bears three fundamental challenges:

I. Recognizing fluid intake acts ("drinking") by arm and hand gestures as one the typical _activities of daily living_ (ADLs, [10]). This concept has been introduced by S. Katz in the scope of assessing care-giving activities. We concentrate in recognizing computational tractable ADLs like fluid intake and how to differentiate it from similar gestures like combing, teeth-brushing, having, yawning. Gesture recognition is typically based on _supervised_ machine learning (ML) of selected positive and negative example gestures.

II. Predicting the amount of fluid ingested, if a drinking act has been recognized. If no volume prediction can be done, monitoring the time periods between fluid intake acts may serve as a remedy, in order avoid excessive time periods without ingesting fluids.

III. Controlling the dialogue with the smartwatch wearer, user, in case of an insufficient _actual_ fluid intake volume in comparison to the necessary individual _nominal_ daily fluid intake amount. Apart from determining this individually different daily amount (see Sect. 3.1), this challenge is primarily an HCI challenges, when and in which contextual situations warnings and advice to the user should be given, so that a given notice is accepted and meets understanding ears, eyes and mind.

Challenge I. has been tackled by the authors and other groups in recent years [11, 12, 14–16, 18, 19]. It has been proven that _artificial neuronal networks (ANN)_ are one of the most effective technologies for ADL recognition by smartwatches [19], comparing _ANN, logistic regression, linear discriminant analysis, K-NN means, support vector machines (SVM), naïve Bayes, decision tree, random forest,_ and _rule induction._ Typically, a F_1 score, the harmonic mean of _precision_ and _recall,_ of more than 95% will be achieved by the best performing recognition algorithms. This score depends on wearing the smartwatch at the preferred arm respectively an informed consent of ambidextrous users to perform drinking with the hand where the smartwatch is worn.

The full extent of relevant ADLs which can be recognized by smartwatch based location analysis and motion analysis is described in [23]. The recognized ADLs are atomic elements within a structured health hazard handling monitoring process [17, 21, 24]. Individual health hazards are described *in a declarative way* by a finite automaton, representing the up-to-date care-giving knowledge. Such a distributed, declarative representation of the care-giving knowledge has decisive advantages for the maintenance of such pragmatic, volatile knowledge by domain experts (see Fig. 2, [17]). But, the different health hazards need to be monitored by the smartwatch simultaneously. These health hazard handling structures also include the communication with the user as further atomic elements (see Fig. 1), in order to giving advice to the smartwatch wearer about appropriate (re)actions in the specific situation [17]. Selecting the right communication requires a suitable prioritization of health hazards [21, 24]. If the user isn't capable to react to a given advice, automatic alerting will follow. The alerting of distant help – and corresponding data transmission: *current geographic position, vital data* – builds on the integrated cellular radio modules typically included in all upfront mainstream smartwatches and allows autonomous communication.

Fig. 1. Samsung Gear S® fluid intake advice (pre-alert, alert), 2016

For challenge II., the complex aspects of determining the individual nominal daily fluid intake amounts will be described in Sect. 3.1. Only very recently, the standard recommendations of 30 ml of daily fluid intake per kg of body weight [1, 2] respectively a minimal total volume of 1500 to 1600 ml for older women/2000 ml for older males

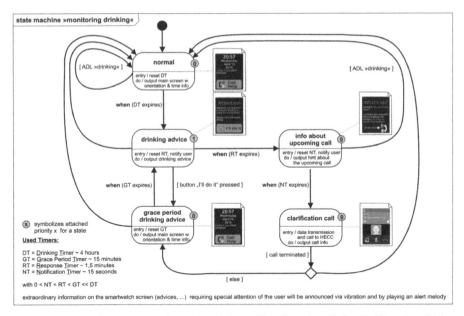

Fig. 2. Declarative representation of health hazard handling for missing fluid intake, 2016

[3–5] have been superseded by a much more detailed calculation incorporating environmental and lifestyle factors in [7]. References [27, 28] and [29] address the problem of automatically estimating the amount of ingested fluid with smartwatch based fluid intake recognition. [27] has proposed a tripartition of the fluid intake ADL in the sequence of three *sub-activities* ([27]: "gesture spotting of *micro-activities*"):

a) *("lifting")* rising the arm, especially the forearm, and rotate the forearm / hand for lifting the drinking vessel to the mouth,
b) *("sipping")* the fluid intake act itself,
c) *("descending")* upending the forearm/hand and lowering the arm for releasing
d) the drinking vessel.

This approach is meanwhile standard and has been extended by [28] by a preceding *"fetching"* sub-activity for gripping the drinking vessel, and a concluding *"releasing"* sub-activity for putting the drinking vessel finally on a stand/table. Although, this enclosing sub-activities sometimes do only demarcate a complete *sequence* of drinking activities and are not specific for each individual drinking activity. It is known that there is no linear correlation between the "sipping" *time* and the ingested *volume*. Individual habits, but also the wide scale of openings of drinking vessels are too different. Unfortunately, the movements of the hand holding the drinking vessel are so minimal during "sipping", that no resilient conclusions can be drawn from these movements [12].

An earlier approach of the authors, as sketched above, instead of predicting the ingested volume and comparing that volume to the recommended individual nominal volume [29], used only the time periods between two recognized fluid intake acts in order to issues advices (pre-alerts) and alerts [19, 22]. This approach elaborates the original proposal of [13], to calculate the current wellbeing of a user based on the *duration* and *distribution* respectively *absence* of typical ADLs over the course of the day. The original wellbeing calculation of [13] has been amended in [22] by the aspects of mobility of the smartwatch user. Such a wellbeing calculation requires i) initial ML by example in an - at least - one week training phase and later ii) ongoing daily adaption of the nominal values characterizing the occurrence of ADLs in the operational use phase of the app.

For challenge III., improving the acceptance of provided advice, the authors have proposed in [25] to use reinforcement ML in order to find out about the situational conditions of accepted advice in the past. This is done during operational use of the app. In essence, the learning algorithm recognizes and clusters the situational conditions, when advices has been accepted by the user and was completely presented to the smartwatch wearer without cancelling or interrupting the advice presentation. Additionally considering the present emotional situation of the user for more empathic and result oriented dialogues would be further very helpful. Unfortunately, this is only partially possible with today's mainstream smartwatches due to their limited sensorial instrumentation [26], especially the absence of skin conductivity and temperature sensors.

3 The Five Aspects of Automatic Fluid Intake Monitoring via Smartwatches

The five central aspects of automatic fluid intake monitoring, applied to the use of smartwatches for this monitoring process, will be presented in the following Sects. 3.1–3.5. Our specific motivation for using smartwatch devices for the monitoring task has been explained in the last paragraph of Sect. 1.

Automatic fluid intake monitoring via smartwatches will be done by customized apps running on those programmable smartwatches, a feature provided by the wide-spread smartwatches from Apple, Google, Samsung and others. These apps can access the built-in sensors of smartwatches, typically: *3D accelerometer, 3D gyro, magnetometer, barometer, heart rate data and GPS position, spatial orientation and speed data.* The smartwatch operating systems often also provide a *step counter* as a synthetic sensor. For short range communication, typically *NFC, bluetooth (BT)* and *wireless LAN (Wi-fi)* are on board for a smartwatch. For long distance communication purposes, at least for the upfront models - also an *integrated cellular radio* for data transmission and telephony is available, including (waterproofed) *microphones* and loudspeaker.

3.1 The Nominal Daily Oral Fluid Intake Volume

Regularly oral fluid intake is necessary to compensate the daily body water losses by urine excretion, insensible transcutaneous evaporation, respiratory water loss, water loss in feces and by sweat. In the total daily water turnover (WT) balance (Fig. 1), the total water intake (TWI) is the sum of fluid intake by drinking water and beverages, eating solid food with preformed water contained, metabolic water generated by the oxidation of carbohydrates, respiratory water uptake (from air humidity) and insensible transcutaneous water uptake. The percentage of preformed water in the consumed solid food strongly depends on the composition of this food respectly diet and may be in the dimension of 20 to 70%. Therefore a deliberate control of daily oral fluid intake by water/beverages is the method of choice to assure a sufficient hydration of the human body.

[1, 2] specify a volume of 30 ml per kg bodyweight per day for the necessary body water intake by drinking and eating for older adults aged 51 and up. The European food Safety Authority (EFSA) specifies a nominal value of 1600 ml for older females, 2000 ml for older males ([3], recommendation 61) of fluid intake, in order to avoid low intake dehydration. A daily fluid intake volume between 1500 ml and 2000 ml for older people is also proposed by [4]. [5] suggests a minimal daily fluid intake of 1600 ml for older adults in order to ensure adequate hydration. However, the daily fluid intake volume must be lower in case of *heart* or *renal insufficiencies* and may be substantially higher in case of exposure to higher temperatures (summer heat) and/or heavy physical activities. Also, fluid loss by *fewer, extreme diarrhea or vomiting* needs to be compensated by increased fluid intake. If the fluid influx and efflux level is balanced in the human body (see Fig. 3), a cessation of excess oral fluid intake is internally managed in the human body by an *swallowing inhibition* controlled by regional brain activities [6].

A more fine-grained approach for calculating the daily WT is presented by Yamada et al. [7], based on an extensive study carried out with 5604 persons in the age range from neonates until 96 years and from 23 low, medium and high developed countries around the world. The study utilized the dilution of the hydrogen isotope deuterium for measuring the WT. By linear regression analysis, the study worked out that WT for adults positively corresponds with age, fat free mass (FFM), physical activity level (PAL) of a person and the air temperature, relative humidity and altitude at the place of residence of as well as the location of the place of residence in a low, medium or high developed, industrial country. Because the body composition is not easily to determine, in the presented WT formula the FFM is approximated by the gender, weight and (binary) athlete status of a person.

For industrial countries, the WT prediction of [7] in ml per day translates into:

$$WT = [1076 * PAL(\%)] + [14.34 * \text{body weight (kg)}] + [394.9 * SEX] + [5.823 * \text{humidity (\%)}] + [1070 * ATHLETE] + [0.4726 * \text{altitude (m)}] - [0.3529 * age^2 \text{(years)}] + [24.78 * age \text{(years)}] - [1.865 * temp^2 \text{(°C)}] - [19.66 * temp \text{(°C)}] - 713.1$$

where PAL = total energy expenditure (mJ) /
basic energy expenditure (mJ),

SEX = 1 for males, = 0 for females,

ATHLETE = 1 for practicing athletes, = 0 otherwise

Example: For 65 year old male, 80 kg of weight, 175 cm of height, with a PAL of 150%, age related a non-practicing athlete, living at a place of residence with an average temp of 18 °C, 50% relative humidity at an altitude of 300 m, the daily water turnover WT estimation will be: **2938** ml. If we consider a 2,5% respiratory and transcutaneous uptake of water within this WT each, plus a 10% metabolic water generation within this WT,

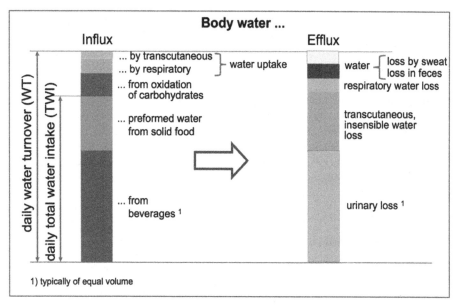

Fig. 3. Daily body water turnover (in accordance with [2, 7])

a total water intake of **2497** ml from fluid and solid food ingestion remains. Assuming a 35% intake of preformed water from solid food (a very conservative estimation, [2], table 2), this results in a residue of **1623** ml necessary daily oral fluid intake by water and/or beverages. This oral fluid intake is about **55 %** of the daily WT. For the same person and at the same location, in *summer time* with 30 °C temperature, the WT increases to **3776** ml and the necessary daily oral fluid intake by water and/or beverages will be **2086** ml.

So, for the purpose of defining the individual nominal oral daily fluid intake volume max_{LI} from water and/or beverages with respect to the total water intake (TWI), and if the total water turnover WT has been determined for the specific personal characteristics of the individuum and its current location, and if finally no deviant meal habits are known for the individuum, we set:

TWI = WT - 2.5% (for respiratory uptake) - 2.5% (for transcutaneous uptake) - 10% (for generated metabolic water)

max_{LI} = TWI − 35% (for preformed water from solid food)

Additionally, a estimation for the total body water volume (TBW) will be necessary, in order to have a threshold for an onset of dehydration. We use the widely accepted anthropometric calculation of Watson, Watson, and Batt [9] based on a study with 458 males and 265 females in liters:

TBW = 2.447 − [0.09516 * age (years)] + [0.1074 * height (cm)] +
[0.3362 * body weight], if SEX = male

= -2.097 + [0.1069 * height (cm)] + [0.2466 * body weight (kg)]
if SEX = female

Example cont.: For our male person from above, the total body water volume resulting from the TBW formula above would be **42** l. This equals to 52,4% of the stated body weight and conforms with the age related, range statements of [1, 2]. The critical 3% threshold of body water loss will be **1260** ml. Further assuming the above calculated 55% replenishment of body water by oral fluid intake via water and/or beverages, this results in a volume of **690** ml, the absence of which has to be reliably detected by our monitoring app.

3.2 Automatic Detection of Fluid Intake Acts

In the last years, a four *phase* methodology [18–20] for data collection, preparation, ML modelling and deployment has been developed by the authors of this paper based on the work of Baldauf [16].

1. *Data collection* phase: In this first phase selected, labeled positive and negative training examples of corresponding fluid intake gestures will be collected by a specific data capturing smartwatch app [18, 23]. In our use case, a ten second recording window was used for each probe and about 300 *positives* samples and 900 *negative* samples of fluid intake gesture have been collected.
2. *Data preparation* phase: The collected data will be standardized to a uniform time grid and cleansed from incomplete samples. About 40 relevant statistical features for each probe will be calculated. The process does not run on a smartwatch, but typically utilizes cloud-based services (e.g. Rapid Miner, Keras).
3. *ML modelling* phase: Based on those probes and features supervised machine learning models are trained. The model chosen will depend on the computational power available for the target smartwatch. A suitable machine learning model ranging from *logistic regression* (for limited power smartwatches) to *ANN* (for the high-end current smartwatches from Apple, Google and Samsung) will be trained. We have focused in further developments and optimizations mainly on ANNs, which after some tuning came up with an accuracy of 99%. The input layer of the ANN are the computed 40 statistical parameters from the aggregated sensors computed in the preceding phase. The output layer of an ANN are i) the recognized ADLs, ii) relevant sub-activities of those ADLs plus iii) a null ADL for any other unknown ADL. Relevant sub-activities of the liquid intake ADL include for example the *lifting* and *descending* of the forearm / hand with the drinking vessel (see Sect. 2).

Our current ANN features LSTM neuron cells ([30], Chap. 7.5) and three hidden layers. The reasons for refining the original shallow, feed-forward ANN [23] with only one hidden layer to LSTM is not only the hardware respectively system support available right now with the Apple *Accelerate* framework [31] for performant and energy efficient vector processing. Specifically, we now can utilize the hardware supported Basic Neural

Network Subroutines (BNNS) package [32] within this framework, whereas originally all neuron cells had to be completely software simulated by array data structures. Originally BNNS supported primarily CNNs, but now also LSTM ANNs are being supported. The decisive *"lifting"* sub-activity (sub-activity a), section 2) is composed of a temporally superimposed *sequence* of *raising – turning – remaining* movements respectively vice-versa for sub-activity *"decending"* (sub-activity c), section 2) We therefore estimate that those movements in their temporal dependencies can best be detected by LSTMs.

The original machine learning platform "Rapid Miner" ([18–20]) has been mean-while replaced by the TensorFlow 2 based Keras [33]. The Keras ML platform selects the attributes for the *artificial neuronal network* (ANN) used for the deployment phase later. The attributes will be passed (and edited) via Apple's CORE ML platform [34] to the Basic Neural Network Support (BNNS) library [32] actually running on the smartwatch.

It is important to state that the decisive factor for the choice of an appropriate ML model is not the best recognition rate (accuracy) at all, but the recognition rate in relation to the energy consumption for the algorithm's execution as long as it does not go below some lower limits (e.g. 95%). And this needs also be seen in connection with the false-positive-rate. We have to ensure at least a daily 16 hour operation period of the smartwatch app without recharging the device's battery. Therefore the model and if an ANN is used esp. The number of the neurons and hidden layers have been chosen very pragmatically with respect to these power requirements.

4. *Deployment phase:* The trained ML models of preceding phase will then be applied for real time monitoring in order to generate predictions. The app comes with a pre-trained, person independent *universal model* for ADL recognition. The input values are computed and prepared as described above for phases 1 to 3. Normally this is done in one second intervals using a 10 s sliding window over the sensor raw data [16, 18, 24]. While ANNs produce high accuracy for producing predictions, a disadvantage is the amount of computation needed. Here more simple models like logistic regression are less computational intensive, but with less accuracy. But a key question is if an accuracy of 99% is always really needed. While in case of a tumble a high accuracy is required, esp. Also preventing false positives, for the fluid intake use case a lower accuracy (95%) is less problematic. One may accept this degradation if one gains several additional hours of smartwatch uptime.

3.3 Automatic Estimation of Fluid Intake Volume

Whereas automatic fluid intake recognition will work in a person independent way, the automatic fluid intake volume estimation builds on an initial, individual configuration of the app and regular (daily) recalculation of nominal values. The personal data (*sex, age, weight, height, athletic status, PAL)* of the smartwatch wearer for WT, TBW will be acquired in an initial setup dialogue of the app. For the daily *temperature* and *humidity* values, in the absence of an *ambient temperature sensor* of the smartwatch, a rough estimation from the present i) *latitude* and *longitude* of location of the smartwatch wearer and ii) season of the year will be made. In reality, this rough estimation may be substantially wrong for extraordinary weather conditions, special location (e.g. death valley) or if the smartwatch wearer stays in an air-conditioned environment. Today, only the *altitude* of the smartwatch wearer's present location can be determined automatically from GPS or a barometric sensor of the smartwatch.

The typical *attachment* time t_α of the smartwatch in the morning and typical time t_Ω of *detachment* of the smartwatch at night will be noticed from the smartwatch wearer on a daily basis and adapted and extrapolated weekly by time-series analysis [22]. These values will be tabulated and may be different for each day of a week in order to adapt to the personal lifestyle. The advantage of a regular adaption via time-series analysis is that it also considers typical seasonal changes over a year. Values t_α, t_Ω will be used for calculating the *individual, typical nominal distribution function* for the total daily fluid intake volume (see below). Thus, these parameters influence the user individual timing of the dehydration notifications in Sect. 3.5.

In the scope of the fluid intake ADL, sub-activity b) *"sipping"* (see definition in Sect. 2) will not be tracked via the LSTM. The motion patterns for gradually inclining the drinking vessel in this phase are so minimal, that no effective recognition rates can be achieved. On the contrary, for performing *"sipping"*, the forearm and hand typically remain nearly motionless for at least a second, which allowed a clear demarcation and training of the separate sub-activities a) *"lifting", c)"descending"* defined in Sect. 2.

Therefore, the recognition of the fluid intake ADL has been constituted by a sequence of a *"lifting"* sub-activity (ending at time t_u) followed by a *"descending"* sub-activity (starting at time t_v) within real time difference $\Delta SIP_{uv} = t_v - t_u$ ($1 \leq \Delta SIP_{uv} \leq 9$ s) between both, which will be rated as the *"sipping"* sub-activity. This additional constraint allowed to reduce *false positives* for the superordinate fluid intake activity below 5%. The ΔSIP_{uv} upper boundary has been acquired from the experiments [29].

The experiments[1] in [29] concluded, that there is no individual, constant *swallowing volume*. The individual, single swallowing volume varies between 10 ml and 40 ml even for the same person and between several persons. It also varies over the course of the day, probably based on changing personal thirst levels. The most relevant factor for the changing swallowing volume was identified in the intake of a *hot* or *cold* beverage[2]. We observed that hot beverages were swallowed typically with 1 to at most 3 swallowing motions. 4 and 5 swallowing motions were used both for (the consecutive intake of no more so) hot and cold beverages (Fig. 4). Cold beverages were typically ingested with 6 and more swallowing motions. The observed *median volume value* M_{HD} for *hot* beverages (coffee, tea) is 17 ml and the median M_{CD} for *cold* beverages (mineral water, soft drinks, ...) is 32 ml. Initially [29], we used these means values M_{HD}, M_{CD} for the individual swallowing volumes: $SW_{HD} := M_{HD}$, $SW_{CD} := M_{CD}$.

---

[1] The experiments where conducted with n = 7 persons in the age group of interest: 50 to 72 years. The test persons agreed, after acquiring ground truth data in phase 1 of the experiment over the course of either a full day or full week, to use the smartwatch in phase 2 of the experiment also for a full day or a full week. Each ingested beverage during the test period had to be time-stamped and recorded, measured or weighed with kitchen scales in order to provide the necessary ground truth. Test persons included as well ambidextrous persons as persons with a predominant, preferred hand.

[2] Ingested fluids included: *cold table and mineral water, soft drinks like apple juice, different flavors of hot tea, various kinds of hot coffee and chocolate*. Alcoholics were not permitted in the experiments.

A second major results from the author's experiments of [29], a fixed *duration of a single swallowing motion time* T_{SW} of about **1.1 s** could be observed for all participants and at all times of the experiments, which comprised an analysis of 937 fluid ingestion acts. Maybe there are few individual differences for the swallowing duration in the order of one or two tenths of seconds, but the precise determination was beyond the scope of the experiments.

This allows a simple rule of three calculation of the ingested volume vol(t) for a recognized *"sipping"* sub-activity starting at time t and with a duration of ΔSIP_{tu}. If no *"sipping"* sub-activity starts at time t, vol(t) has a value of 0. Otherwise, let N_{sw} denote the rounded integer division result of $\Delta SIP_{tu}/T_{SW}$, then

$$\textbf{vol(t)} = N_{sw} * SW_{HD}, \qquad \text{if } N_{sw} \leq 3$$
$$= (SW_{HD} + SW_{CD}) / 2, \qquad \text{if } 3 < N_{sw} < 6$$
$$= N_{sw} * SW_{CD}, \qquad \text{if } N_{sw} \geq 6$$

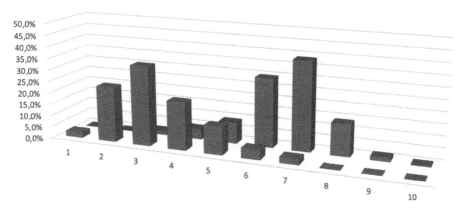

Fig. 4. Distribution of the number of swallows motions for **hot** and **cold** beverages from [29]

The experiment of [29] also disclosed that the discrete distribution function of the *total daily fluid intake volume* for many participants almost has a *linear shape* (Fig. 6). Therefore a *linear distribution* function $F_{LI}(t)$ (Fig. 5) for the nominal total daily fluid intake volume has been used in the monitoring app, possibly different for each day of the week. The argument t is the current time. For the *maximum $F_{LI}(t)$ value* max_{LI}, we choose the calculation of Sect. 3.1 based on the specific water turnover WT at the current location of the smartwatch wearer as a default value. A deviant max_{LI} value can be defined in the app setup dialogue, if prescribed by the smartwatch wearer's physician in case of special medical conditions.

$$F_{LI}(t) = 0, \qquad\qquad\qquad \text{for } t \leq t_\alpha,$$
$$= \max_{LI} * (t - t_\alpha) / (t_\Omega - t_\alpha), \quad \text{for } t_\alpha < t < t_\Omega,$$
$$= \max_{LI}, \qquad\qquad\qquad \text{for } t \geq t_\Omega$$

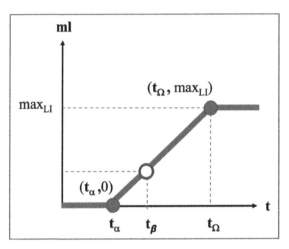

Fig. 5. FLI(t) linear equation through points $(t_\alpha, 0)$ and $(t_\Omega, \max_{LI})$

$\max_{LI}$ will be increased per 45 min of registered continuous intensified physical activity by 15%, if not specifically prescribed by a physician. Intensified physical activity will be registered by considerable physical movement plus increased pulse rate and can be securely detected by the standard smartwatch sensors.

For the definition of the daily total fluid intake estimation function $E_{LI}(t)$ we need the actual attachment time t_β at the considered day, in order to compensate the situation, that the user attaches the smartwatch substantially later than at the typical attachment time t_α. In such a situation, we will assume that the user has already consumed a volume of beverages before attachment time t_β of the smartwatch as described by $F_{LI}(t)$. Then

$$E_{LI}(t) = F_{LI}(t_\beta) + \sum_{u=t_\beta}^{u \leq t} vol(u)$$

A further improvement of the estimation quality for ELI(t) – in refining the approach of [29] – has been be achieved by using *individually calibrated swallowing volumes* SWHD, SWCD for hot and cold beverages instead of the *median swallowing volumes* MHD, MCD stated above. Calibration is performed in the scope of the initial setup dialogue of the monitoring app. The smartwatch wearer is asked to take a typical swallow of a hot and cold beverages consecutively at least 3 times. Before and after each swallow the drinking vessel used has to weighed with kitchens scales. The typical 1g precision of kitchen scales allows directly to conclude the ingested volume (1 g $\approx$ 1 ml with respect to the beverages consumed) from the weight difference after a swallow. The arithmetic mean value for the three swallows of a hot and cold beverage will be utilized bythe

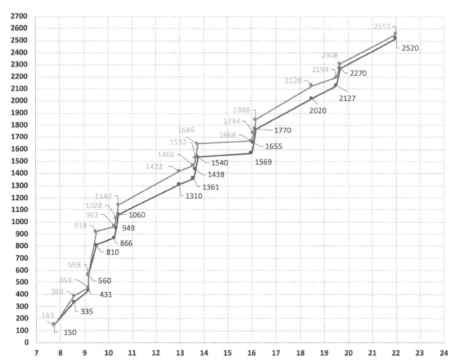

Fig. 6. Estimated fluid intake volume $E_{LI}(t)$ vs. actual fluid intake volume $A_{LI}(t)$ in ml (y-axis), over the hours of a day (x-axis). In this case with a mean percentage error, MPE, of only 6,06%, achieved via individually calibrated swallow volumes of the test person.

monitoring app for SWHD, SWCD. Kitchen scales were also used for providing the necessary ground truth in measuring and calculating the *actual* total daily fluid intake volume ALI(t) during the experiments.

If, for a specific time t of the day, $t_\alpha \le t \le t_\Omega$, the difference $F_{LI}(t) - E_{LI}(t)$ exceeds the threshold of X% (X = 1.5, 2, 3) of the portion of TBW that needs to be replenished by fluid intake from beverages.

$$F_{LI}(t) - E_{LI}(t) > TBW * (TWI / WT) * X\%$$

notifications will be produced (see Sect. 3.5) remembering to ingest a beverage. If the difference exceeds 2% respectively 3% the urgency for the notifications will be stepwise increased. A significant notification will be also issued, if, for a time t, the estimated total fluid intake volume exceeds the expected daily limit,

$$E_{LI}(t) > F_{LI}(t_\Omega)$$

if this limit has been specifically prescribed by a physician. Finally, in [29] it was observed for more than 96% of all fluid intake ADLs, the test persons *used their predominant respectively a preferred hand* within the experiment, even the ambidextrous persons. Our current hypothesis, why this seemingly also holds for ambidextrous persons, argues that for older persons during the course of their life a certain routine partition of activities has been established, e.g. *drinking* and *slender craftwork* typically done with the *left* hand, *writing* with the right hand. The 96% have been achieved after the participants were advised about the consequences of using the opposite hand without the smartwatch app for drinking, namely the lacking consideration of their fluid intake and a following ostensible dehydration.

As a quality measure of our approach we use the *mean percentage error* (MPE), the average volume by which the estimations vol(t) for a recognized fluid intake act at time t differs from the actually ingested volume at that time. Usage of MPE allows to compensate underrun and overrun in estimations over the course of a day. In summary, with the presented optimized approach, a MPE of less than 10% could be achieved for the test persons.

3.4 Informing the Smartwatch Wearer

The Android Wear™ smartwatch OS does allow *continuous background operations* [35] for a monitoring app. In the Apple WatchOS *app lifecycle model* [36], apps are typically permitted only short runtime sessions in foreground or background mode. The apps are kept most of the time in a *suspended* execution state, in order to retain smartwatch battery power. Although, scheduled 30 min extended runtime background activation periods (*"smart alarm" background* sessions) are supported and can be scheduled consecutively for (nearly) continuous operation of the recognition algorithm. The deliberate price for this is a haptic alarm within each activation session, in order to keep the user aware that the monitoring process is operating in the background. Communication from the monitoring app running in the background to the user will be only possible via *complications* and *notifications*.

A specific *complication* integrated the used watch home screen, the *watch face,* provides the smartwatch wearer – always visible and with one glance - with status information about the calculated hydration status. For symbolizing the current hydration status, we use a partially filled glass in the center of a circular gauge [29]. The color and filled portion of the gauge indicates the total oral fluid volume estimation for the specific day (see Fig. 7), optionally also considering the previous day (see discussion in Sect. 4). The glass symbol and gauge will be regularly updated by current data from the background monitoring process.

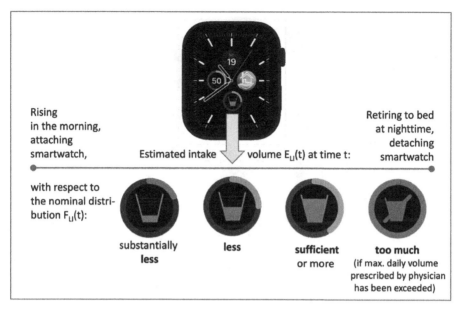

Fig. 7. Complications used indicating the actual hydration status, see [29]

3.5 Giving Advice to the Smartwatch Wearer

A specific *notification* about insufficient fluid intake is automatically issued starting from a TBW loss of 1.5% of the portion that needs to be replenished by oral fluid intake. It includes an advice to drink something right now (Fig. 8) and thus must therefore be presented to the user in situations, where such an advice will be very likely noticed and accepted. Notifications present the actual health situation with respect to the onset of dehydration of the user in a full screen mode and allow corresponding user feedback, primarily to acknowledge respectively agree to the given advice. Technically, a notification issued by the monitoring app will be brought to the smartwatch screen even if issued from a process running in the background of the smartwatch.

From the acceptance perspective for such advices, the complex HCI control answer includes four factors: i) a suitable situation has to be identified, where the user is probably at or nearby a location to really ingest a beverage, and ii) without jeopardizing himself or others, and iii) advice should come upon a user in a low stress respectively emotion state, and last not least, iv) suitable situations may be individually different and thus have to be finally learned from the reaction of the user to fluid intake advices in the past. The techniques we have used to address these four factors include:

- *Location* analysis, is the user currently at home or in the vicinity of his home where there is the opportunity to consume a beverage?
- *Motion* analysis, is the user currently steering a car or driving a bicycle at high speed, so that he would potentially jeopardize himself or others if he would drink right now?
- *Emotion* analysis, is the user currently stressed or high emotional state?

Fig. 8. Apple Watch "long-look" **notification** presentation of the app, if the user looks at his/her smartwatch (Fig. 3, [29]). A mild dehydration of 265 ml is symbolized via beam scales. The user can either react to the notification by his/her intention to drink in the near future, or dismiss the notification at all. (The dismissal option is always possible in the Apple ecosystem).

- *Cluster* analysis, has the user declined or cancelled prior advices for fluid intake right now in a comparable prior situation? Then the advice should not be presented in this situation unless an already onset of dehydration gets dangerous.

Not all analyses done really do require artificial intelligence (AI) technology. Considering an optimal resource efficiency on the wearable device, computationally less expensive algorithms will be sufficient for the following calculations:

- for *location analysis*, the presence of the well-known home wireless network (Wi-Fi) will be sufficient for taking the binary decision of being at home or not. Alternatively and more power demanding, GPS can be used, which only requires geometric calculations.
- For *motion analysis,* the current speed of motion will be reliably delivered by corresponding GPS parameters.
- for regularly adapting the *nominal values of ADLs (duration, frequency)* and *attachment, detachment time of the smartwatch,* we use *time series analysis* [22].
- For *emotion analysis,* currently only the *stress* dimension of emotions can be used in the absence of third-party available, *relative skin temperature* and *skin conductivity* sensors [26]. Stress can be easily concluded from commonly available smartwatch heart rate sensors – or even better: heart rate variability sensors – in the absence of ongoing physical activity of the smartwatch wearer. The latter can also easily be determined on smartwatches.
- for the *learning of situational contexts,* we use agglomerative *clustering* based on a manhattan metric in a four dimensional hypercube of (geographic) location, day of the week, time (grid) of the day, and (moving) speed [25].

4   Discussion

The presented approach is obviously primarily suited for relatively *healthy* persons. The recognition of deteriorated health conditions with consequences on fluid intake like severe *fewer or bleeding, vomiting, diarrhea, ...* is beyond the scope of the current approach. The only parameter which can be specified and prescribed by a physician, and will be considered by our approach, is the maximum nominal daily fluid intake volume max_{LI} in case of *heart insufficiencies* and/or *renal impairment.*

Currently, by default we start the daily hydration calculation with a value of zero, thus assuming that there is *no remaining dehydration* from the previous day. Such a negative starting value for E_{LI} (t_β) can be configured as an option for the app.

The general assumption of a linear distribution function for the nominal oral fluid intake over the course of day could be superseded by a *customized deviant distribution function.* The discrete distribution profile would be sampled during an initial one week training phase of the smartwatch app. Then a continuous distribution would be fitted through the recorded discrete points and the function would be scaled up (or down) in order to reach function value max_{LI} at the detachment time t_Ω by the end of a day.

A more comprehensive location analysis could be performed by a *connected smartwatch* accessing regional points of interest (POIs): is the user currently at a location, where beverages will be available (e.g. gas station, shopping center, downtown, ...)? The data would be computed only on demand (already onset of dehydration) and used only instantly, not recorded and no movement profile would be build-up. But, a cost – benefit analysis still needs to be done, if this really is a requested feature from the user perspective.

A third-party accessible, integrated ambient temperature sensor of a smartwatch will be of substantial value for considering respiratory water loss and water loss by sweat in order to estimate the consequences of ongoing physical activities or exposure to unfavorable climatic conditions. But, such sensors must compensate the effects of the skin temperature and heat emission and will probably work, even when they will be available, only in environments (e.g. indoors), where no isolating clothing is worn.

Loss by sweat can be up to several liters per hour [2] in unfavorable climatic conditions and may be life-threatening. If exposure to extreme climatic conditions is to be expected for the smartwatch wearer (e.g. during an outback tour, climbing/skiing, expedition, ...), the usage of an external, BT linked temperature and humidity sensor worn at the outer cover of the clothing currently is the only available remedy today.

5   Conclusions

The presented five aspects approach allows an comprehensive scope of analysis of the field of application. Progress was achieved in the improved calculation of nominal values and individual calibration of swallowing volumes, resulting in an MPE for the daily oral total fluid intake volume estimation of less than 10%. But, the available sensorial instrumentation of widespread, up-to-date programmable smartwatches is still too narrow. Especially an *ambient temperature sensor* fully integrated in a programmable smartwatch and accessible by third-party smartwatch apps will be invaluable for further quality improvements. From the HCI perspective, the customization of the app, the acceptance and information scope of warnings and advice to the smartwatch wearer is expandable, but require a cost – benefit analysis respectively assessment by the users.

References

1. Hall, J.E., Guyton, A.C.: Textbook on Medical Physiology, 14th edn. Elsevier Publishing Inc., Philadelphia, PA, USA (2020)
2. Köhnke, K.: Water balance and the nutritional importance of water and beverages. Ernährungsumschau **58**(2), 88–94 (2011). (in German). https://www.ernaehrungs-umschau.de/filead min/Ernaehrungs-Umschau/pdfs/pdf_2011/02_11/EU02_2011_088_095.qxd.pdf
3. Volkert, D., Beck, A.M., Cederholm, T., Cruz-Jentoft, A., Goisser, S., et al.: ESPEN guideline on clinical nutrition and hydration in geriatrics. Clin. Nutrition **38**, 10–47 (2018). (Elsevier). https://doi.org/10.1016/j.clnu.2018.05.024
4. Mascot, O., Miranda, J., Santamaría, A.L., Pueyo, E.P., Pascual, A., Butigué, T.: Fluid intake recommendation considering the physiological adaptions of adults over 65 years: a critical review. Nutrients **12**(11), 1–14 (2020). (MDPI). https://doi.org/10.3390/nu12113383
5. Hodgkinson, B., Evans, D., Wood, J.: Maintaining oral hydration in older adults: a systematic review. Int. J. Nurs. Pract. **9**(3), S19–S278 (2003). (J. Wiley & Sons). https://doi.org/10.1046/j.1440-172X.2003.00425.x
6. Saker, P., Farrell, M.J., Egan, G.F., McKinley, M.J., Denton, D.A.: Overdrinking, swallowing inhibition, and regional brain responses prior to swallowing. In: Proceedings of the National Academy of Sciences of the United States of America (PNAS), vol. 113, no. 43, October 10, 2016, pp. 12274–12379 (2016). https://doi.org/10.1073/pnas.1613929113
7. Yamada.Y. et al.: Variation in human water turnover associated with environmental and lifestyle factors. Science **378**(6622), 909–915 (2022). https://doi.org/10.1126/science.abm 8668
8. Cohen, R., Fernie, G., Fekr, A.R.: Fluid intake monitoring systems for the elderly: a review of the literature. Nutrients **13**(6), 1–28 (2021). (MDPI). https://doi.org/10.3390/nu13062092
9. Watson, P.E., Watson, I.D. Batt, R.D.: Total body water volume for adult males and females estimated from simple anthropometric measurements. Am. J. Clin. Nutrition **33**(1), 27–39 (1980). https://doi.org/10.1093/ajcn/33.1.27
10. Katz, S.: Assessing self-maintenance: activities of daily living, mobility, and instrumental activities of daily living. J. Am. Geriatr. Soc. **31**(12), 721–727 (1983)
11. Weiss, G.M., Timko J., Gallagher, C. Yoneda, K., Schreiber A.: Smartwatch-based activity recognition: a machine learning approach. In: IEEE-EMBS International Conference on Biomedical and Health Informatics (BHI), pp. 426–429. Las Vegas, USA (2016). https://doi.org/10.1109/BHI.2016.7455925
12. Amft, O., Bannach, D., Pirkl, G., Kreil, M., Lukowicz, P.: Towards wearable sensing-based assessment of fluid intake. In: 8th IEEE International Conference on Pervasive Computing and Communications Workshop (PERCOM) 2010, pp. 298–303 (2010). https://doi.org/10.1109/PERCOMW.2010.5470653
13. Suryadevara, N.K., Mukhopadhyay, S.C.: Determining wellness through an ambient assisted living environment. IEEE Intell. Syst. **29**(3), 30–37 (2014). https://doi.org/10.1109/MIS.2014.16
14. Wellnitz, A., Wolff, J.P., Haubelt, C., Kirste, T.: Fluid intake recognition using inertial sensors. In: ACM 6th International Workshop on Sensor-based Activity Recognition and Interaction (IOWAR 2019), Berlin, Germany, article no. 4, pp. 1–7 (2019). https://doi.org/10.1145/3361684.3361688
15. Chun, K.S., Sanders, A.B., Adaimi, R., Streeper, N., Conroy, D.E., Thomaz, E.: Towards a generalizable method for detecting fluid intake with wrist-mounted sensors and adaptive segmentation. In: ACM International Conference on Intelligent User Interfaces (IUI 2019), pp. 80–85 (2019).https://doi.org/10.1145/3301275.3302315

16. Baldauf, R.: Mobile Sensor-Based Drinking Detection. FOM University, Research Paper (2015). [in German]
17. Lutze, R., Waldhör, K.: A smartwatch software architecture for health hazard handling for elderly people. In: IEEE International Conference on HealthCare Informatics (ICHI) 2015, pp. 356–361, Dallas, USA (2015). https://doi.org/10.1109/ICHI.2015.50
18. Waldhör, K., Baldauf, R.: Recognizing Trinking ADLs in Real Time using Smartwatches and Data Mining, Rapid Miner Wisdom/Europe Conference, Ljubljana, Slovenia (2015). https://www.researchgate.net/publication/301772482_Recognizing_Drinking_ADLs_in_Real_Time_using_Smartwatches_and_Data_Mining
19. Lutze, R., Baldauf, R., Waldhör, K.: Dehydration prevention and effective support for the elderly by the use of smartwatches. In: 17th IEEE International Conference on E-Health Networking, Application & Services (HealthCom), 14–17 Oct 2015, Boston, USA (2015). https://doi.org/10.1109/HealthCom.2015.7454534
20. Waldhör, K., Lutze, R.: Smartwatch based tumble recognition – a data mining model comparison study. In: 18th IEEE Int. Conference on E-Health, Networking, Application & Services (HealthCom), 14.-16.9.2016, Munich, Germany (2016). https://doi.org/10.1109/HealthCom.2016.7749464
21. Lutze, R., Waldhör, K.: The application architecture of smartwatch apps – analysis, principles of design and organization. In: Mayr, H.C., Pinzger, M. (Hrsg.) INFORMATIK 2016. LNI, vol. P259, ISBN 978-3-88579-653-4, ISSN 1617–5468, pp. 1865–1878. Springer, Bonn (2016). https://cs.emis.de/LNI/Proceedings/Proceedings259/1865.pdf
22. Lutze, R., Waldhör, K.: Integration of stationary and wearable support services for an actively assisted living of elderly people: capabilities, achievements, limitations, prospects—a case study. In: Wichert, R., Mand, B. (eds.) Ambient Assisted Living. ATSC, pp. 3–26. Springer, Cham (2017). https://doi.org/10.1007/978-3-319-52322-4_1
23. Lutze, R., Waldhör, K.: Personal health assistance for elderly people via smartwatch based motion analysis. In: IEEE International Conference on Healthcare Informatics (ICHI), 23–26 Aug 2017, pp. 124–133. Park City, UT, USA (2017). https://doi.org/10.1109/ICHI.2017.79
24. Lutze, R., Waldhör, K.: Model based dialogue control for smartwatches. In: Kurosu, M. (ed.) HCI 2017. LNCS, vol. 10272, pp. 225–239. Springer, Cham (2017). https://doi.org/10.1007/978-3-319-58077-7_18
25. Lutze, R., Waldhör, K.: Improving dialogue design and control for smartwatches by reinforcement learning based behavioral acceptance patterns. In: Kurosu, M. (ed.) HCII 2020. LNCS, vol. 12183, pp. 75–85. Springer, Cham (2020). https://doi.org/10.1007/978-3-030-49065-2_6
26. Lutze, R., Waldhör, K.: Practical suitability of emotion recognition from physiological signals by mainstream smartwatches. In: In: Kurosu, M. (eds.) Human-Computer Interaction. Technological Innovation. HCII 2022, LNCS, vol. 13303, Proceedings Part II, pp. 362–375, Springer (2022). https://doi.org/10.1007/978-3-031-05409-9_28
27. Hamatani, T., Elhamshary, M., Uchiyama, A., Higashino, T.: FluidMeter: gauging the human daily fluid intake using smartwatches. In: ACM Proceedings on Interactive, Mobile, Wearable, Ubiquitous Technologies (IMWUT), vol. 2(3), article no. 113, 1–15 (2018). https://doi.org/10.1145/3264923
28. Huang, H.-Y., Hsieh, C.-Y., Liu, K.-C., Hsu, S.J.-P., Chan, C.-T.: Fluid intake monitoring system using a wearable inertial sensor for fluid intake management. Sensors **20**(22), 1–17 (2020). https://doi.org/10.3390/s20226682
29. Lutze, R.: Practicality of automatic monitoring sufficient fluid intake for older people. In: IEEE 10th International Conference on Healthcare Informatics (ICHI), June 11–14, pp. 330–336. Rochester, MN, USA (2022). https://doi.org/10.1109/ICHI54592.2022.00054
30. Aggarwal, C.C.: Neural Network and Deep Learning – A Textbook. Springer International Publishing 2018, Springer, Cham, Switzerland

31. NN: Accelerate. Developer Information, Apple Inc. https://developer.apple.com/documentation/accelerate. Retrieved 6 Jan 2023

32. NN: Basic Neural Network Subroutines (BNNS). Developer Information, Apple Inc. https://developer.apple.com/documentation/accelerate/bnns. Retrieved 6 Jan 2023

33. NN: Keras Deep Learning Framework. https://keras.io/. Retrieved 6 Jan 2023

34. NN: Core ML – Integrate Machine Learning Models Into Your App. Developer Information, Apple Inc. https://developer.apple.com/documentation/coreml. Retrieved 6 Jan 2023

35. NN: Guide to Background Work. Android Developers. Google Inc. https://developer.android.com/guide/background. Retrieved 6 Jan 2023

36. NN: Working with the watchOS App Life Cycle. Developer Information, Apple Inc. https://developer.apple.com/documentation/watchkit/wkextensiondelegate/working_with_the_watchos_app_life_cycle. Retrieved 6 Jan 2023

Temperature Prediction Model for Advanced Renal Function Preservation in Partial Nephrectomy

Toshihiro Magaribuchi[1], Akihiro Hamada[1], Kimihiko Masui[1], Ryosuke Yasue[2], Masanao Koeda[2], and Atsuro Sawada[1(✉)]

[1] Department of Urology, Graduate School of Medicine, Kyoto University, Kyoto, Japan
atsuro7@kuhp.kyoto-u.ac.jp
[2] Department of Human Information Engineering, Okayama Prefectural University, Okayama, Japan

Abstract. The standard procedure for small renal cell carcinoma is a partial nephrectomy. In this procedure, renal blood flow is interrupted during tumor resection to control bleeding. It is known that cooling the kidney (cold ischemia) during this procedure reduces postoperative deterioration of renal function. The optimal deep renal temperature for cold ischemia is about 20 °C. However, the only method for measuring the deep renal temperature is an invasive needle puncture with a thermocouple. In the past, we have used thermal imaging cameras to simulate intraoperative tissue heat conduction and quantify heat diffusion in biological tissues. We will apply this experience to establish a simple, noninvasive method for measuring deep kidney temperature by creating a formula model to predict deep kidney temperature from the kidney surface temperature using a thermal imaging camera. In this study, we develop a temperature prediction model that can predict the deep kidney temperature from the surface temperature of the kidney measured with a thermal imaging camera. Using pig kidneys, we measure the temperature change when the kidneys are cooled. And we estimate the thermal diffusivity of the kidneys by comparing the actual temperature change data with the results of 3D unsteady heat conduction simulation. At this point, we have already estimated the thermal diffusivity of the kidney using sliced pig kidney sections. In the future, we plan to collect data more similar to actual surgery using whole pig kidneys and improve the heat conduction equation.

Keywords: Partial nephrectomy · Cold ischemia · Temperature prediction model

1 Introduction

Partial nephrectomy is now established as the standard treatment for small renal cancer. In partial nephrectomy, only the tumor and surrounding tissue are removed, thus preserving renal function after surgery. Renal ischemia is commonly used to temporarily block blood flow to the kidney to control bleeding during tumor resection. However, renal ischemia is associated with renal dysfunction. Ice slush is placed around the kidney during renal

M. Kurosu and A. Hashizume (Eds.): HCII 2023, LNCS 14014, pp. 87–95, 2023.
https://doi.org/10.1007/978-3-031-35572-1_6

ischemia to cool the kidney (cold ischemia) to prevent renal dysfunction. Cold ischemia has been reported to be effective in preserving renal function in the postoperative period when the duration of ischemia time is prolonged [1].

The appropriate deep renal temperature for the preservation of renal function is approximately 20 °C, and it has been confirmed that cold ischemia in open human abdominal surgery can cool the kidney to 20 °C in approximately 10 min [2]. At present, the only reported method for measuring deep renal temperature is the invasive method of puncturing the kidney with a needle-type thermocouple. Therefore, when cold ischemia is performed in surgery, the surgeon only waits 5–10 min after the start of cooling without measuring the deep renal temperature. However, the rate at which the kidneys are cooled is affected by the thickness of the perirenal fat tissue and the extent of the kidney exposure, so the time required for adequate renal cooling varies markedly from case to case, ranging from 3–20 min [3]. This case-to-case difference is important because excessive or inadequate cooling can adversely affect postoperative renal function.

In a previous study, we reported on a 2D thermal diffusion model based on thermographic measurements of thermal diffusion in liver tissue. This allowed them to successfully quantify thermal damage inside biological tissue caused by electrocautery using heat conduction simulation [4]. We came up with the idea that noninvasive prediction of deep kidney temperatures would be possible by applying the methods used in this study to quantify thermal damage inside living tissue using thermal diffusion measurement with a thermal imaging camera and thermal conduction simulation.

In this research, we propose a non-invasive method for deep kidney temperature measurement, which predicts the deep kidney temperature by estimating the thermal diffusivity from the temperature data of a needle thermocouple and a 3-dimensional unsteady heat conduction simulation.

2 Implicit Solution of the Heat Conduction Equation

In this research, the three-dimensional unsteady heat conduction equation:

$$\frac{\partial T}{\partial t} = \alpha \left(\frac{\partial^2 T}{\partial x^2} + \frac{\partial^2 T}{\partial y^2} + \frac{\partial^2 T}{\partial z^2} \right) \tag{1}$$

is discretized by the implicit Gauss-Seidel method into equation:

$$\frac{T^n_{x,y,z} + C_x + C_y + C_z}{1 + 2\alpha \Delta t (\frac{1}{\Delta x^2} + \frac{1}{\Delta y^2} + \frac{1}{\Delta z^2})} \tag{2}$$

Simulations are performed using this equation. In this equation,

$$C_x = \frac{\Delta t \times \alpha}{\Delta x^2} \left(T^{n+1}_{x-1,y,z} + T^{n+1}_{x+1,y,z} \right) \tag{3}$$

$$C_y = \frac{\Delta t \times \alpha}{\Delta y^2} \left(T^{n+1}_{x,y-1,z} + T^{n+1}_{x,y+1,z} \right) \tag{4}$$

$$C_z = \frac{\Delta t \times \alpha}{\Delta z^2} \left(T^{n+1}_{x,y,z-1} + T^{n+1}_{x,y,z+1} \right) \tag{5}$$

T represents temperature, x, y, and z are coordinates, and α is thermal diffusivity.

3   Cooling of Pig Kidney and Measurement of Temperature Change

To estimate deep temperature using heat conduction simulation, renal temperature data during cold ischemia is required as original data. In this research, an experimental device was constructed to measure renal temperature changes during cooling (see Fig. 1). This device is fabricated with a 3D printer (Snapmaker2.0 F250), and a needle thermocouple can be vertically punctured and fixed at the specified position on a renal section. The puncture position was set at the center of the cooling surface of the porcine kidney section as the origin, with $(x, y, z) = (0, 0, 3)$ for 1ch, $(0, 0, 6)$ for 2ch, $(0, 0, 9)$ for 3ch, and $(0, -3, 6)$ for 4ch, for a total of 4 needle thermocouples for measurement (see Fig. 3). To suppress external temperature changes, the kidney sections were covered with Styrofoam and the space between them and the experimental device was filled with Styrofoam. Ice was placed on the upper surface of the kidney to reproduce cooling by an ice slush, while the lower portion was in contact with air. Pig kidney slices were used for cooling, one with renal capsule and the other without renal capsule, and temperature data were measured four times by taking two samples from each specimen. Pig kidney sections were removed and cut into cubes of approximately 10 mm per side, and measurements were started when the temperature was stable. Four seconds after the start of temperature measurement, ice was placed on top of the experimental device as shown in Fig. 2 to start cooling, and was maintained until the end of the measurement. In this experiment, 88598AZ EB needle thermocouples were used. Temperature data was output every second for each channel. The temperature measurement data for 10 min is shown in Fig. 4.

Fig. 1. Experimental device to measure renal temperature changes.

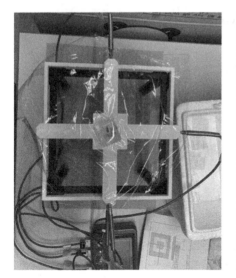

Fig. 2. Ice was placed on top of the experimental device.

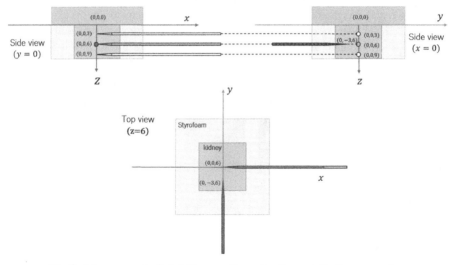

Fig. 3. Measurement of pig kidney section using four needle thermocouples.

4 Comparison of Simulated Data and Measured Data

4.1 Calculation of Thermal Diffusivity

By comparing the measured temperature data with the simulated temperature prediction data, an estimate of the thermal diffusivity was calculated for the temperature data in cooling the pig kidney shown in Fig. 4. The object of this simulation was a cube shape with 10 mm per side, similar to the pig kidney section, and Δx, Δy, and Δz were set to 0.1, respectively.

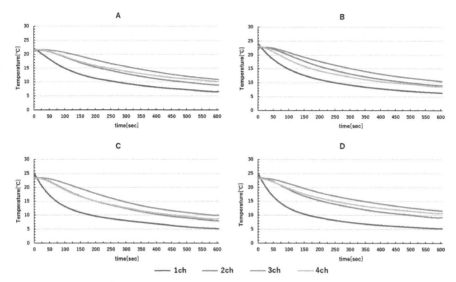

Fig. 4. Temperature change during kidney cooling. Kidney with renal capsule (A and B) kidney without renal capsule (C and D)

4.2 Difference Value Between Simulated and Measured Data

The initial temperature at each point was the initial temperature at the start of measurement with a needle thermocouple in the original data. Assuming that the organ was being cooled with ice, the temperature distribution was calculated when the upper surface of the object was continuously cooled to 0 °C from the start to the end of the simulation with $\Delta t = 0.1$s. The simulation time was 600 s. The thermal diffusivity was changed in the range of 0.0005 to 0.003 cm^2/s in 0.0001 cm^2/s increments based on the estimates obtained by the authors' previous study, and temperature data were generated. The estimated value in this study refers to the thermal diffusivity with the smallest temperature difference from the original data. Python 3 was used for the simulations. For each thermal diffusivity, Fig. 5 shows the results of comparing the difference every 0.1 s between the temperature data from the theoretical needle thermocouple and the temperature data from the simulation. The average of the differential temperature data values in 1ch to 3ch was calculated as the differential value for each thermal diffusivity. The measured temperature data was every 1 s, and since it was used to measure to one decimal place, the measured data was approximated by a polynomial equation with a seventh order function, and the data was every 0.1 s. The values were close to those of the original data. Comparing the measured original data and the simulated temperature data, the simulated temperature data showed a more rapid decrease in temperature.

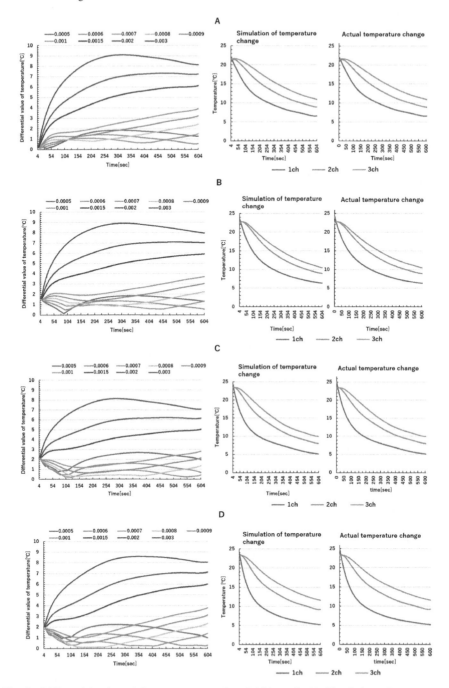

Fig. 5. Differential value of the temperature of each kidney (Left). Simulation of temperature change (Center). Actual temperature change (Right). Kidney with renal capsule (A and B). Kidney without renal capsule (C and D)

5   Future Plans

5.1   Measurement of Temperature Change During Kidney Cooling Using Whole Pig Kidney

Accurate deep temperature evaluation is difficult based on the thermal diffusivity of pig kidney sections alone since kidney cooling includes the effects of the area of the kidney surface being cooled, the surrounding air, urinary tract tissue, and adipose tissue. Therefore, it is necessary to modify the thermal diffusivity and model based on temperature changes in the whole pig kidney. A needle thermocouple is punctured into a pig kidney at a depth of 1cm from the renal surface to measure temperature. This depth of puncture allows measurement of deep renal temperature [5] (see Fig. 6). The pig kidney is cooled with an ice slush, and when the deep renal temperature reaches 20 °C, the ice slush is removed and the renal surface temperature is measured with a thermal imaging camera to confirm the relationship with the deep temperature (see Fig. 7). The thermal diffusivity and model are modified so that the surface and deep temperature results are consistent with the simulation results.

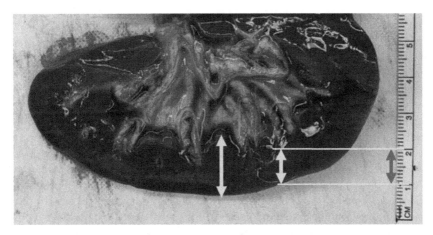

Fig. 6. Depth for proper measurement of the deep temperature of pig kidney parenchyma.

5.2   Measurement of Temperature Change Using a Living Pig Kidney.

In vivo, the response to renal cooling is expected differently depending on blood flow and surrounding organs in contact with the kidney, so modification of the temperature prediction using living animal data is necessary. Temperature measurements are made after reproducing renal cold ischemia in open surgery. The rest of the flow is the same as in 5-1.

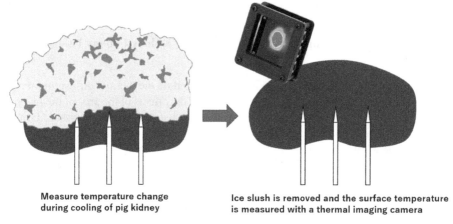

Measure temperature change
during cooling of pig kidney

Ice slush is removed and the surface temperature
is measured with a thermal imaging camera

Fig. 7. Temperature measurement of the whole pig kidney.

6 Discussion

Surgical treatment for renal cell carcinoma used to be radical nephrectomy, in which the entire kidney was removed. Partial nephrectomy emerged as the widely recommended treatment for small renal tumors after better oncologic and functional outcomes than radical nephrectomy was published [6]. In the 1960s, the technique of "cold ischemia," in which the kidney is cooled, greatly advanced the use of partial nephrectomy[7]. In the 1970s, many reports were published on the use of needle thermometers inserted into human kidneys during surgery to measure the optimal deep kidney temperature for cold ischemia [2]. Since it is generally known that the appropriate deep kidney temperature is reached after approximately 10 min of renal cooling, and since minimally invasive surgery has been pursued, few reports of deep kidney temperature measurement using a needle thermometer puncture have been reported. However, if ice slush is placed around the kidney for cooling, the cooling rate varies depending on the thickness of the fat around the kidney and the extent of exposure to the renal surface. It has been reported that the time required to cool the kidney to a sufficient temperature varies greatly from case to case [3]. Given this current situation, a technique to noninvasively measure deep kidney temperature is needed to further improve the outcome of partial nephrectomy.

Although this study aims to improve outcomes in partial nephrectomy, the minimally invasive technology for predicting deep organ temperatures has potential applications in other fields. For example, in renal transplantation, the donor kidney must be maintained at a low temperature until the blood flow is reperfused. However, since temperature measurement by puncture with a needle thermocouple, which can damage the donor's kidney, is not appropriate, only the surface temperature is almost always measured [8]. Therefore, if a predictive model for deep organ temperature is developed, it could be applied in transplant surgery, where organ cooling is required.

The limitation of this study is the difficulty of collecting temperature measurement data using living kidneys. The best way to more accurately predict changes in deep kidney temperature up to 20 °C would be to conduct experiments using live human kidneys. However, this is ethically difficult. Instead, in this study, we used pig kidney sections to estimate the thermal diffusivity. In the future, we plan to conduct experiments using whole pig kidneys. It has been reported that the morphological characteristics of pig kidneys have many similarities and few morphological differences with human kidneys [9], and the experimental data using whole pig kidneys have a high potential for application to actual surgery. In addition, the appropriate deep temperature for the preservation of renal function is not required to be exactly 20 °C. Depending on the report, the appropriate renal deep temperature ranges from 15 °C–20 °C [2, 10]. In light of these considerations, the experimental technique used in this study is considered acceptable.

References

1. Yoo, S., Lee, C., Lee, C., You, D., Jeong, I.G., Kim, C.-S.: Comparison of renal functional outcomes in exactly matched pairs between robot-assisted partial nephrectomy using warm ischemia and open partial nephrectomy using cold ischemia using diethylene triamine penta-acetic acid renal scintigraphy. Int. Urol. Nephrol. **48**(5), 687–693 (2016). https://doi.org/10.1007/s11255-016-1220-4
2. Ward, J.: Determination of the optimum temperature for regional renal hypothermia during temporary renal ischemia. Br. J. Urol. **47**, 17–24 (1975)
3. Thompson, R.H., Lane, B.R., Lohse, C.M., et al.: Every minute counts when the renal hilum is clamped during partial nephrectomy. Eur. Urol. **58**(3), 340–345 (2010)
4. Koeda, M., et al.: Internal thermal damage simulation of body tissue by electrocautery. In: The Institute of Electronics, Information and Communication Engineers, Session number D-16 (2020)
5. Orvieto, M.A., Zorn, K.C., Lyon, M.B., et al.: Laparoscopic ice slurry coolant for renal hypothermia. J. Urol. **177**(1), 382–385 (2007)
6. MacLennan, S., Imamura, M., Lapitan, M.C., et al.: Systematic review of oncological outcomes following surgical management of localized renal cancer. Eur. Urol. **61**(5), 972–993 (2012)
7. O'Connor, E., Timm, B., Lawrentshuk, N., et al.: Open partial nephrectomy: current review. Transl. Androl. Urol. **9**(6), 3149–3159 (2020)
8. Torai, S., Yoshimoto, S., Yoshioka, M., et al.: Reduction of warm ischemia using a thermal barrier bag in kidney transplantation: study in a pig model. Transplant Proc. **51**(5), 1442–1450 (2019)
9. Gómez, F.A, Ballesteros, L.E, Estupiñan, H.Y.: Anatomical study of the renal excretory system in pigs. A review of its characteristics as compared to its human counterpart. Folia Morphol. **76**(2), 262–268 (2017)
10. Wickham, J.E., Hanley, H.G., Joekes, A.M.: Regional renal hypothermia. Br. J. Urol. **39**(6), 727–743 (1967)

Study for Presenting Information on Smartwatch to Assist in Determining Whether to Evacuate by Passing Outside the Road

Akari Mase[1] and Takayoshi Kitamura[2(✉)]

[1] Graduate School of Science for Creative Emergence, Kagawa University, Takamatsu, Japan
[2] Faculty of Engineering and Design, Kagawa University, Takamatsu, Japan
kitamura.takayoshi@kagawa-u.ac.jp

Abstract. In the event of a disaster such as a large-scale tsunami or torrential rain that threatens to inundate a city, evacuation to a safe zone is a matter of time. Even if you have prepared for disasters in your daily life, there is a possibility that you may be damaged in a strange place where you happen to be, such as on a business trip or a vacation. In such a situation, when there are no reliable people or signs around to guide people to an emergency evacuation site, information obtained from a mobile information terminal can be relied upon. In addition, if information on how to get off the road is provided, it will assist in evacuation as soon as possible. However, there are no such efforts, especially in the area of route guidance support on smartwatch. In this study, we investigate whether it is possible to shortcut through off-road areas by presenting the minimum necessary information on a narrow screen such as a smartwatch. For this purpose, we conducted an experiment in which a video shot by a 360-degree camera was projected in a VR space, and the screen of a smartwatch was presented within the video.

Keywords: Mobile · Evacuation · Route selection

1 Introduction

In the event of a disaster such as a large-scale tsunami or a sudden torrential downpour that threatens to inundate the area, evacuation to a safe zone is a matter of time. Even if you have prepared for disasters in your daily life, there is a good chance that you may be damaged in a strange place where you happen to be, such as on a business trip or on vacation. In such a situation, when a person needs to evacuate to an emergency evacuation site but there are no reliable people or signs around, information obtained from a mobile information terminal can be relied upon. Therefore, there is a need to expand research on information provision methods in order to save as many lives as possible by assisting evacuation during disasters. One of the representative information provision methods is evacuation guidance using portable information terminals such as smartphones and smartwatches. In the field of route guidance using mobile information terminals, applications that guide evacuees by combining the camera function of smartphones with location information technology and augmented reality technology, and applications that show directions to routes on smartwatches with GPS functions have been proposed and studied [1, 2]. In addition, as a search aid for route determination, the following methods are being considered: displaying a deformed map based on landmarks instead of a detailed map, using the vibration function of a smartwatch, and using map view and directional view to show the surrounding environment and route [3–5].

All of these route guidance information is considered to be useful for evacuation to emergency evacuation sites. However, these existing route guidance methods select routes based on the locations registered as roads in map information services such as the Geospatial Information Authority of Japan (GSI) and Google Maps. In other words, it does not cover "off-road but passable areas" such as parks, shrine and temple precincts, parking lots, etc., which are not registered as roads but are passable. One of the reasons for this is the lack of a procedure or framework for registering "off-road but passable points" as routes. In addition, there has not been sufficient study of information presentation methods for judging "can pass here or not" from visual information obtained from scenery outside the road and from mobile information terminals.

Therefore, the purpose of this study is to investigate what requirements exist in information provision methods for evacuation guidance that assist in "judging whether it is possible to pass outside the road" in order to realize evacuation in a time-sensitive manner. For this purpose, we will explore the conditions necessary to notice when people do not know that they can pass, and to tell them that they cannot pass where they think they can pass, based on the screen information on their smartwatches. In the experiment, we asked participants to view a 360-degree video of the target location taken beforehand, both with and without the assistance of smartwatch screen information, and to respond to a questionnaire about their impressions of the guided route. From the results obtained from this experiment, we aim to identify requirements to assist users in their route selection decisions.

2 Related Study

For research on route guidance using smartwatch, Wenig et al. [6] noted that the displayable area of a smartwatch is considerably smaller than that of a smartphone, and proposed an easy-to-handle map representation specifically for smartwatch. In addition, the study proposed by Amemiya et al. [7] is well known for presenting route information based on force-feedback vibration information. These studies involve walking a predefined course and target areas that are recognizable as paths to the user.

In addition, there are various proposals and studies on information presentation for evacuation guidance during disasters [8–10]. For example, Yasui et al. [8] have achieved some success in verifying the usefulness of a route guidance experiment employing only a vibration function in a mobile information terminal. However, there have been only a few studies on the use of smartwatch vibration functions and screen information to guide users to routes, and no studies on the provision of information on the availability of off-road information.

Therefore, in this research, we will work on the design of information on smartwatch to assist in "judging whether it is possible to pass through off-road areas" such as parking lots, farmlands, and riverbeds, which have not been the subject of research, assuming that the information will be used in the event of a disaster.

3   Design

This study identifies requirements that facilitate the consideration of adopting non-road routes from the road in a smartwatch-based evacuation guidance application. For this purpose, we propose the following two patterns for the design of information to be presented on a smartwatch.

- Information to assist in judging whether or not passage is possible when visual information indicates that passage is "not possible.
- Information presentation to assist in judging whether or not pas sage is possible when the user feels that passage is "possible" based on visual information

The more information that is presented to assist in the decision of whether or not to allow passage, the better. And it is thought to be possible with a smartphone that has a certain amount of screen area. However, when similar expressions are used on a narrow screen such as a smartwatch, it is difficult for users to grasp and understand the full picture. In addition, presenting detailed map information in times of disaster can lead to "stop-and-go" evacuation, in which people stop to select an evacuation route, or "evacuate while walking" while operating a mobile device [11]. In particular, evacuation may take a long time, or a dangerous situation such as a collision may occur, even though it is a time-critical evacuation. Therefore, in this study, we will consider the minimum necessary screen information, such as that shown in Fig. 1, for example, which is shown after the vibration function by the smartwatch to provide awareness. This limited information provides the user with "awareness in cases where the user does not know that the route is passable" and "awareness that the route is not passable in places where the user thinks it is passable" to assist in route selection decisions.

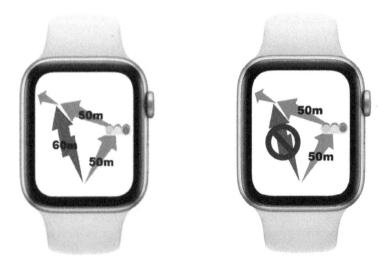

Fig. 1. The image of the system studied in this research. The left image shows that the area outside the road (red arrow) is passable, and the right image shows that the area outside the road is impassable or difficult to pass. The right figure shows that the area outside the road is impassable or difficult to pass. (Color figure online)

4 Experiment

4.1 Outline of the Experiment

In this study, as a prototype for evaluating the design of information presented on smartwatch, we asked our experimental participants to do the following. First, the relevant off-street locations were filmed and collected for one minute in advance with the RICHO THETA Z1 from the evacuee's point of view, and projected into a VR space viewable with the Oculus Quest head-mounted display. Then, the participant was asked to watch this VR video and write on paper all possible routes that they could judge to be passable. The participant was then asked to wear the Oculus Quest head-mounted display again and view a 360-degree video of the same location as before. As shown in Fig. 2, an image with screen information of a smartwatch is attached to the bottom of the screen in the direction of evacuation, and an image of an approaching tsunami is attached to the opposite direction, as shown in Fig. 3. The respondents were asked to answer which route they felt they would choose in reference to these images. Finally, the participant was asked to answer a paper questionnaire about the guided route (the route indicated by the red arrow on the smartwatch in Fig. 2), regarding physical factors such as physical strength and their own equipment, as well as their impression of the route, such as whether the route was safe and whether it was passable without getting lost. The same sequence of steps was followed at all five selected sites shown in Fig. 4.

Fig. 2. Smartwatch image pasted in VR space (shortcut path presented on the right).

Fig. 3. Image showing the direction of the tsunami (blue area) pasted in the VR space. (Color figure online)

4.2 Design of the Experiment

To conduct this study, a preliminary experiment was conducted with five participants (two males and three females) by selecting the spots shown in Fig. 5. At the preliminary experiment target location, all participants recognized the guided evacuation route as a route. In terms of impressions of the route, the respondents tended not to choose a route if their negative impression of the route was high in terms of whether it was safe to pass. On the other hand, in terms of "will it take long?" not much influence on route selection was observed, even if the negative impression tended to be slightly higher. In addition, there was no difference in the impression of "I can get there without getting lost" at the target locations used in this experiment. The high negative impression in terms of "physically demanding" did not affect the choice of route in terms of physical fitness and usual equipment problems by participants. On the other hand, no difference was observed in terms of "seems to be no problem even with ordinary equipment. As a result, among the participants in this experiment, four "chose the guided route" and one "did not choose the guided route.

In the preliminary experiment, all of the participants were aware of the evacuation route to be guided before the guidance, and this result may be due to the size of the entrance to the route and the presence of a structure that allowed them to imagine the presence of a shrine connected by the route, even if they did not know the area near the target evacuation route. In terms of impressions of the route, the choice of route was influenced more by impressions of the safety of the road to pass through than by the time it takes to reach the evacuation site or the clarity of the route. The effect of the route choice was not shown even if the negative impression was high for the problems with physical fitness and usual equipment by the participants. However, in the preliminary experiment, the evacuation behavior was set up for a tsunami. Therefore, it is considered that there are cases where the decision to use a guided route was made based on the idea

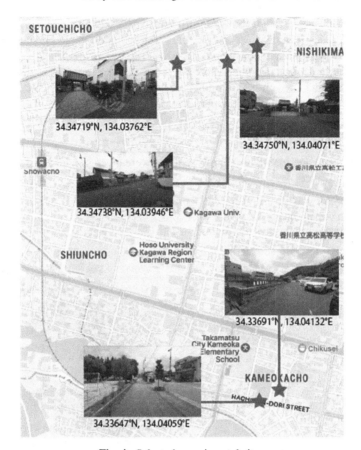

Fig. 4. Selected experimental sites.

of "wanting to go to a point of height" even if the user felt that it would be "physically demanding. Therefore, it was thought that by targeting sites where no slope was observed on any of the paths in this experiment, it might be possible to obtain results different from those in the preliminary experiment.

Based on the above, it was decided that the present experiment would be conducted under the same conditions as the preliminary experiment, but the locations would be considered for five sites with no slope.

4.3 Experimental Video

The experimental video was filmed on a road in the vicinity of Kagawa University that meets the following conditions: "The road is outside the area where people feel it is passable or difficult to pass, and there is no problem with normal traffic. As a method for selecting locations, the characteristics of locations that were considered "passable" or "impassable" at off-road locations were examined. Specifically, we removed the sections that were registered as roads from the existing map information services, and selected sections that were not registered but were still safe to pass through under normal circumstances. Such areas include, for example, parks, shrine and temple precincts, parking lots, and other areas that are considered passable even in an emergency. A 360-degree video was shot for 1 min at the point where all paths could be seen at the selected location using a Ricoh Theta Z1 with the tripod height set at 160 cm, which is considered to be close to the average viewpoint of the participants.

4.4 Selection of Participants

In conducting the experiment, the following items were given special consideration and confirmed in advance.

- Whether or not you have experienced a disaster
- Evacuation experience
- Presence of trauma or difficulty with disasters

Fig. 5. An example of a location examined in this study (created from a screenshot of a Google Maps screen).

The reason for confirming these items is that the experiment in this study assumes that the participants will be affected by a tsunami, and therefore, there is a possibility that participation in the experiment will remind them of their experience of a large-scale disaster, such as the Great East Japan Earthquake, and may cause them distress. We also checked in advance whether the participants had experienced or had difficulty with VR sickness using a head-mounted display, and those who gave the corresponding answers were removed from the list of potential participants.

Furthermore, in this study, it is assumed that the participants knows the actual road connections to the locations selected for the experiment and can select the route to be guided even without the guidance of the smartwatch. Therefore, we decided to exclude from the analysis the cases where we knew the location of the experiment, whether it was accessible or not.

In accordance with the Kagawa University Code of Ethics for Research on Students, we carefully examined whether there were any problems in conducting the experiment, and obtained informed consent from all participants before and after the experiment.

4.5 Survey

Panoramic photographs of the 360-degree scenery used in the video and a questionnaire about their impressions of the guided route were prepared for the participants to answer during the experiment. After watching the first video, the participants were asked to draw arrows with a white pen on a 360-degree panoramic photo of the landscape, as shown in Fig. 6, for all the paths that the experimenter judged to be "passable. Then, after viewing the second video, which was processed as shown in Figs. 2 and 3, the participants were asked to answer a questionnaire about their impressions of the guided path using a 100 mm visual analog scale, as shown in Fig. 7. For example, the respondents were asked to draw a vertical line in the range from "I feel I can get there without getting lost" to "I feel I can get lost without getting lost" to indicate their impression of the route. Thus, for each question, the experimenter responded on a scale from 0 (the most positive impression) to 100 (the most negative impression). Table 1 shows the questionnaire items regarding impressions of the guided route. Items 1, 4, and 5 asked whether the respondents had positive or negative impressions of the route, i.e., "I can use this route to get there safely without getting lost" or "This route is dangerous and I might get lost" in the event of a disaster. Figure 2 and 3 asked about the physical fitness of each participants and whether he or she had problems with his or her usual equipment. In addition, the participants were interviewed about whether they understood the guided route guided by the smartwatch and whether they had experienced taking shortcuts in unfamiliar places.

Fig. 6. Example of a white arrow on a road that is deemed passable.

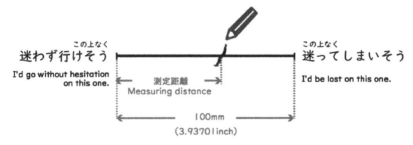

Fig. 7. Example of a visual analog scale entry used in this study.

Table 1. Questionnaire on impressions of guidance routes.

No.	Question Content vs. (All questions are prefaced with the qualifier "above all this.")	
	Positive impression	Negative impression
1	Looks like I can go without hesitation	Looks like you're going to get lost
2	Seems to be physically fit	Looks physically demanding
3	Looks fine in everyday equipment	Looks too difficult with normal equipment
4	Looks safe to pass through	Looks like it will be dangerous
5	Looks like it won't take too long	Looks like it will take a long time

4.6 Experimental Results

The experiment was conducted with 20 participants (10 males and 10 females) who did not know the geography of the surrounding area for the sites selected for the experiment. Five of the participants had experienced a disaster and one had experienced evacuation. The respondents were defined as having experienced an earthquake or tsunami that affected their daily lives, even if only slightly. None of the participants had any trauma or aversion to disasters.

Regarding the impression of the guided route, we checked the results of drawing arrows on the panoramic 360-degree photographs of the landscape for all the routes that the experiment participants judged to be passable, and found that all the experiment participants recognized the guided evacuation route as a route.

Table 2 shows the results of the questionnaire presented in Table 1. In terms of impressions of the route, the respondents tended not to choose a route if they had a high negative impression of the route in terms of "can I get there without getting lost" and "is it safe to pass through?".

In terms of physical fitness and usual equipment problems by participants, the participants tended not to choose a route if they had a high negative impression in the question of whether it would take much time. On the other hand, in terms of "whether or not I would have a problem physically" and "whether or not I would have a problem with my usual equipment," the respondents did not select the guided route if the clothing

Table 2. Results of the questionnaire on impressions of the guidance route (red arrow).

Predictor Variables	$X2$	degree of freedom	p
Can you go without getting lost?	10.469	1	0.001
Are you physically fit?	0.666	1	0.415
Is it safe to use your usual equipment?	0.412	1	0.521
Is it safe to pass through?	11.676	1	<.001
Does it take time to get through?	7.065	1	0.008
Did you recognise it as a road?	0.193	1	0.660

they usually wear is not suitable for overcoming obstacles such as fences, although the negative impression tended to be slightly higher, it did not have much influence on the route selection. As a result, among the participants in this experiment, "those who chose the guided route" were 16 in the park, 18 in the parking lot, 9 in front of the shrine, 3 next to the shrine, and 10 at the temple.

4.7 Considerations

In this experiment, the evacuation behavior was set up for a tsunami. It is possible that the simple information-providing characteristics of smartwatch made it important for the respondents to know whether they could get around without getting lost. It is possible that the large values are due to the fact that many routes were presented as "safe" routes where falling objects were likely to occur. It is thought that the presentation of the information about the tsunami, which "seems to take little time," had a strong psychological impact on the participants. Based on the above, it is quite possible that fluctuations in the rankings of the predictor variables in Table 2 may occur depending on the experimental conditions. The importance of the other items, "seems to be no problem physically" and "seems to be no problem with usual equipment," may vary depending on the quantity and quality of the information presented.

5 Conclusion and Future Prospects

In this study, we proposed the design of an application using a smartwatch as a means of presenting information when there is no one around to guide you or no signposts to guide you in a situation where you have to move quickly to an emergency evacuation site in an unfamiliar or unknown place, or when you can evacuate more quickly by passing outside a road, such as a parking lot or park. Preliminary experiments were conducted to validate the effectiveness of this design, and understanding through these experiments how to reinforce the design of the UI provided insight for full-scale experiments.

As a future prospect, we plan to gather more participants and conduct experiments in a variety of locations. In addition, it is necessary to study the design of the information design that shows that the paths that are judged to take "less time" are actually "less time-consuming," and whether the design can be applied to disasters and regions that were not targeted in this study. In addition, we plan to investigate what requirements are necessary in cases where adaptation is difficult.

Acknowledgement. This work was supported by JSPS KAKENHI Grant Number JP21K14392.

References

1. Izumi, T., Takarai, F., Kitamura, T., Nakatani, Y.: Investigation of information requirements for smartwatch-based evacuation support system (2021)
2. Kitamura, T., Gang, Y., Izumi, T., Nakatani, Y.: Proposal of the onion watch application for enjoying a stroll. In: Meiselwitz, G. (ed.) HCII 2020. LNCS, vol. 12195, pp. 559–568. Springer, Cham (2020). https://doi.org/10.1007/978-3-030-49576-3_41
3. Kono, K., Nitta, T., Ishikawa, K., Yanagisawa, M., Togawa, N.: Comprehensive deformed map generation for wristwatch-type wearable devices based on landmark-based partitioning. In: Proceedings on IEEE 5th Global Conference on Consumer Electronics (2016)
4. Dobbelstein, D., Henzler, P., Rukzio, E.: Unconstrained pedestrian navigation based on vibro-tactile feedback around the wristband of a smartwatch. In: Proceedings of the 2016 CHI Conference Extended Abstracts on Human Factors in Computing Systems, pp. 2439–2445 (2016)
5. Perebner, M., Huang, H., Gartner, G.: Applying user-centered design for smartwatch-based pedestrian navigation system. J. Locat. Based Serv. **13**(3), 213–237 (2019)
6. Wenig, D., Hecht, B., Malaka, R.,: StripeMaps: improving map-based pedestrian navigation for smartwatches. In: MobileHCI 2015, Proceedings of the 17th International Conference on Human-Computer Interaction with Mobile Devices and Services, pp. 52–62 (2015)
7. Amemiya, T., Maeda, T.: Directional force sensation by asymmetric oscillation from a double layer slider-crank mechanism. Trans. ASME J. Comput. Inf. Sci. Eng. **8**(3) (2008)
8. Yasui, T., Kitamura, T., Izumi, T., Nakatani, Y.: Evaluation of a vibration-based route indication for children who are not familiar with maps. In: IEEE 8th Global Conference on Consumer Electronics (GCCE 2019), pp. 40–44. IEEE (2019)
9. Rahman, K.M., Alam, T., Chowdhury, M.: Location based early disaster warning and evacuation system on mobile phones using OpenStreetMap. In: Proceedings of the 2012 IEEE Conference on Open Systems, pp. 1–6 (2012)
10. Inoue, Y., Sashima, A., Ikeda, T., Kurumatani, K.: Indoor emergency evacuation service on autonomous navigation system using mobile phone. In: Proceedings of the Second International Symposium on Universal Communication, pp. 79–85 (2008)
11. Oishi, Y., Furumura, T., Imamura, F., Mihara, Y., et al.: Tsunami evacuaton using real-time hazard information provided by smartphone application. J. Jpn. Soc. Civ. Eng. Ser. B2 (Coast. Eng.) **75**(2), I_1381–I_1386 (2019). (in Japanese)

Comparison of the Accuracy of Pouch Replacement Timing Decisions Using Image Generation Artificial Intelligence and Machine Learning

Michiru Mizoguchi[1]([⊠]), Shun Watanabe[2], Masaya Nakahara[2], and Hiroshi Noborio[2]

[1] Nara Gakuen University, Nakatomigaoka, Nara 631-8524, Japan
`michiru-m@nara-su.ac.jp`
[2] Department of Computer Science, Osaka Electro-Communication University, Kiyotaki 1130-70, Shijo-Nawate, Osaka 575-0063, Japan
`nobori@osakac.ac.jp`

Abstract. This study developed a system that determines when to remove the pouch from the stoma to detect faecal leakage in non-contact stoma holders. Around January 2020, new coronary outbreaks occurred worldwide, making it difficult for hospitals and care homes to collect data from many stoma holders. Collecting data from many stoma holders in hospitals and care centers has generally been challenging. Therefore, sufficient training and correct data were obtained using artificial intelligence (AI) image generation containing more images. These training data were then used to determine the appropriate tame to change the pouch. Finally, the accuracy of the decisions was compared using two learning algorithms, the Microsoft lobe machine learning and the Google teachable machine learning modelling tools. The results showed that the percentage of correct decisions for the two learning algorithms was 100%, from the first day to approximately three days after the faceplate was fitted, but tended to be lower, ranging from 40% to 87.5%, from one to three days before the replacement date. The Google teachable machine learning modelling tool was also less accurate than the Microsoft lobe machine learning modelling tool.

Keywords: stoma · machine learning algorithms · image processing · AI image generation

1 Introduction

In Japan, the projected number of colorectal cancer cases, including rectal cancer, is approximately 156,800, and the estimated annual number of deaths is approximately 53,900 [1]. Colorectal cancer is the leading cause of death in both men and women, but men are more affected than woman. Depending on where the cancer is, the excretory route must be altered, and an artificial anus constructed in the abdomen must be maintained for the rest of one's life.

M. Kurosu and A. Hashizume (Eds.): HCII 2023, LNCS 14014, pp. 107–120, 2023.
https://doi.org/10.1007/978-3-031-35572-1_8

When a stoma is constructed, a pouch that stores excretions must be attached to the abdomen using an adhesive base called a faceplate. The pouch and faceplate need to be replaced periodically. Although there is a certain cycle for the replacement timing, the replacement timing may be earlier or later, depending on the condition of the faceplate, stoma holder, and himself/herself. When the adhesive strength of the faceplate weakens, excretions leak out, resulting in soiled and smelly clothing, which interferes with daily life and social activities [2]. Additionally, the replacement timing is difficult to determine from the body surface, and it must be determined through feeling using the faceplate replacement timing provided by the manufacturer.

However, artificial intelligence (AI) has advanced significantly and can learn in configurations with complex algorithms, such as the human cerebral cortex. Machine learning is influencing technology and science because of its ability to effectively learn and process data and images. It has applications in robotics, automatic driving control, speech processing, and computers [3] and is easing our lives as computers and smartphones have become common. Supervised machine learning algorithms are being researched in disease prediction and several other medical fields [4]. For example, machine learning has been used in the critical care domain to predict the prognosis of cell-level image sections of poor-prognosis malignancies that require early treatment [5] and to identify risk factors for cognitive impairment in post-intensive care syndrome (PICS). The researchers also compared the applicability of decision tree (DT), random forest (RF), XGBoost, neural network (NN), naive bay (NB), and support vector machine (SVM) with seven different machine learning methods, including logistic regression (LR) and generating predictive models [6]. Other studies have used free machine learning and complex combinations of machine learning algorithms to predict the prognosis of diseases and symptoms.

Furthermore, few studies have used AI in the nursing field, such as its impact on health-related quality of life and risk prediction [7], and the development of triage systems for emergency patients [8]. Future nursing education curricula will likey include AI and other machine learning techniques [9].

This study aims to develop a system to evaluate when to remove a pouch from a stoma to detect excretory leakage in non-contact stoma holders. We used the Microsoft lobe machine learning modeling tool (hereafter Microsoft lobe), Google teachable machine learning modeling tool (hereafter Google teachable machine) to determine the appropriate time to change the pouch. We compared the accuracy of the decisions made based on the two machine learning algorithms.

Section 2 describes the two machine learning algorithms used in this study Sect. 3 describes AI image generation. Section 4 describes the use of stoma holder images for machine learning. Section 5 describes the stoma holder image processing process. Section 6 compares the two machine learning algorithms using artificially generated images. Section 7 presents the findings of the init image strength function adjustment validation and comparison of the two machine learning algorithms. Finally, Sects. 8 and 9 provide discussion, conclusions, and future work.

2   Machine Learning Algorithm

The Microsoft loeb and Google teachable machine is used to determine when to release the pouch from the stoma by uploading the images taken by the stoma holder at home using a smartphone or other device via the Internet.

2.1   Microsoft Lobe

This learning algorithm is a free machine-learning tool from Microsoft, which can be used on your computer without a code or uploading data to the cloud. Once an image classification model is created, the label classification can be performed by training the model. To identify labels, the system learns from patterns in image appearance, color, shape, hand movements, and facial reactions. The largest image that can be processed is 178,956,970 pixels; however, the image can be resized and cropped to reduce the image resolution to a 224 × 224 square, to speed up processing. A maximum of five labels can be added, each label requires five images, and 100 to 1,000 images can be trained per label [10, 11] (Figs. 1 and 2).

2.2   Google Teachable Machine

The Google teachable machine is a free machine learning tool from Google that trains models created in a web browser using the TensorFlow.js JavaScript machine learning library. It can be used without a code by accessing the site from a browser. Files and samples can be collected in real-time, and all work can be conducted from a personal computer (PC) on the same device. It is possible to train images, sounds, and poses [12] (Figs. 1 and 2).

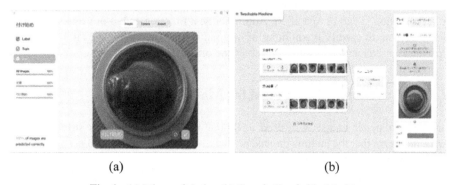

(a)   (b)

Fig. 1.   (a) Microsoft Lobe. (b) Google Teachable Machine.

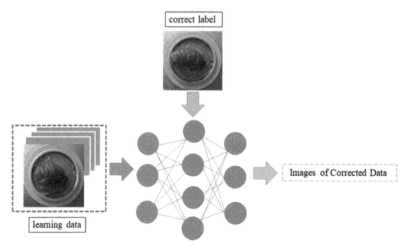

Fig. 2. Supervised learning Algorithm. The training and correct data are given as a set, and the differences between labels are learned.

3   AI Image Generation

The world started experiencing coronavirus disease 2019 (COVID-19) around January 2020, which-made it difficult to collect data from many stoma holders in hospitals and care centers. Therefore, to increase the number of images for training, we used NMKD stable diffusion, which is a Windows GUI tool used for creating AI images and is available in the GUI. Python was used to establish a development environment. The software can be run without command-line arguments. The number of images to be generated at once (Num), the detail of the generated image (Steps), the resolution (Width × Height), and the characteristics of the original image to generate an image that closely resembles the original image can be specified. Additionally, a function called init image strength allows the user to specify the number of original image's characteristics to be retained to produce an image that closely resembles the original image [13].

4   Image of Stoma Pouch Used for Machine Learning

Three types of pouch images were used: an iPhone 12ProMax image of the stoma holder's stoma, an image that the authors created artificially, and an AI-generated propagation of the stoma holder-derived image (Fig. 3).

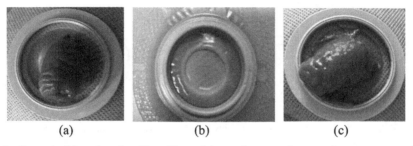

(a)   (b)   (c)

Fig. 3. Supervised learning algorithm. The training and correct data are given as a set, and the differences between labels are learned.

5   The Process of Image Processing of Stoma Holders

The actual dissolution of the faceplate of the stoma holder's actual pouch was filmed using the Apple iPhone 12ProMax's camera function, and the entire faceplate of the stoma or pouch, including the abdomen and other body parts, was filmed. The shooting environment was under indoor fluorescent light, and the same conditions were used each time. The images of the faceplate on the first day of the pouch application, the day of replacement, and at other times during the pouch application were distinguished. However, images after the replacement day had ended were absent because they were taken after the pouch was removed.

Next, because the image of the stoma holder shows a part of the body, such as the abdomen, the image was cropped until the entire faceplate area was captured to reduce the amount of information (Fig. 4). Then, in addition to the normal images, the pattern and number of images for learning were increased by processing the images in the "Photo" application for photo management in Windows 10 to be inverted vertically and horizontally (Fig. 5).

Fig. 4. Cropped image of a stoma holder.

Fig. 5. Stoma holder image cropped and inverted vertically, horizontally, and horizontally.

6   Comparison of the Accuracy of Two Machine Learning Algorithms Using Artificially Created Images

The pouch was attached to a clear file, water was stored in the center of the faceplate, and the faceplate was artificially dissolved over time to about 1 cm, which is the standard time for a replacement. The new part of the image's faceplate is brown, and the dissolved part is white. The images were always taken under the same conditions in an indoor fluorescent lighting environment using the Apple iPhone 12 ProMax's camera function.

The images were classified into four faceplate dissolution size categories. For the training data, 160 images were used: 40 images of 2 mm, 40 images of 5 mm, 40 images of 6 to 10 mm, and 40 images of 10 mm or more. The training data were cropped (Fig. 6), then images in normal and inverted up, down, left, and right were used (Fig. 7). For the evaluation data, we used ten images of each cropped item that was excluded in the training data of 40 images. The data were then validated using the training and evaluation data for each period.

The results showed that the correct images on the Microsoft lobe were six out of ten, five out of seven, five out of five, and four out of four for 2 mm, 5 mm, 6–10 mm, and 10mm, respectively. On the Google teachable machine, the correct images were seven out of ten, five out of five, four out of five, and five out of five for 2 mm, 5 mm, 6–10 mm, and 10mm, respectively.

Fig. 6. Stoma holder image cropped and inverted vertically, horizontally, and horizontally.

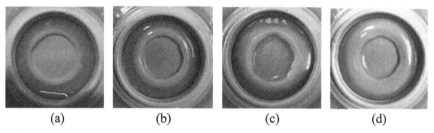

| (a) | (b) | (c) | (d) |

Fig. 7. Four classifications of images created by artificially dissolving 2 mm (a), 5 mm (b), 6–10 mm (c), and more than 10 mm (d) were compared using two different machine learning algorithms.

7 Verification of the Init Image Strength Function Adjustment and Comparison of Two Different Machine Learning Algorithms

Although stoma orthotics are constantly evolving, to prevent leakage, it is still necessary to avoid physical factors such as skin problems, excretory properties, and stoma size incompatibility with the faceplate, and external environmental factors, such as activity and perspiration. Although replacement times vary depending on the type of faceplate, there are products on the market that are used approximately once every four to six days [14, 15].

While it is necessary to prevent excretory leakage and replace the faceplate at the appropriate replacement time, the time around the next replacement date is important to determine the faceplate replacement date. The above experiments classified the first day of wearing the faceplate and the replacement date. We use images from each period from the first day of wearing the faceplate to the replacement date, and compare them with two different learning algorithms, Microsoft lobe and Google teachable machine. With the replacement date functioning as the boundary, the day before the replacement date is specifically defined as one, two, and three days before the replacement date, and the day after the replacement date is defined as six, five, and four days before the replacement date. Particularly, one day before is the oldest state with the longest period of use, while six days before is the newest state of the faceplate (Fig. 8).

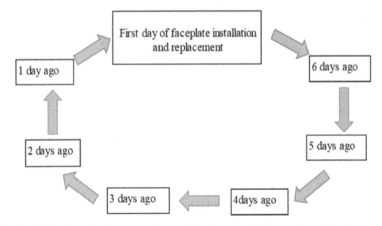

Fig. 8. Cycle from the first day of mounting the faceplate to the day of replacement.

7.1 Verification of Init Image Strength Function Adjustment for AI Image Generation

In addition to using AI image generation to propagate images, the init image strength function was adjusted to increase similarity and bring the images closer to the original images, and the results were verified by varying the similarity.

Images from each period from one to six days before the replacement date were used, except for the first day the faceplate was attached and the day of replacement. However, it was impossible to collect a uniform number of images because the stoma holder had a leak, and the faceplate was removed on the next scheduled faceplate replacement date. Therefore, AI was used to generate images and increase the number of images for learning. The init image strength function was adjusted and derived because it was important to increase the number of images while making the images as close to the original as possible. This function ranges from zero to one. The larger the value, the greater the influence of the original image, and the smaller the value, the more the image is arranged and the farther it is from the original image.

Ten original images of the stoma holder from the day before the faceplate replacement date, eight images from two days before, eight images from three days before, four images from four days before, three images from five days before, and one image from six days before were used. Next to generate AI images, which were used as training data, one image was randomly selected from each of the stoma holder's original images from one to five days before the faceplate replacement date, and the number of images was unified to one image from six days before the faceplate replacement date, which was the minimum number of images.

The training data were cropped images of stoma holders from one to six days before the faceplate replacement date. One hundred images, each from one to six days before the faceplate replacement date were multiplied at 0.05 intervals, from 0.6 to 0.9 init image strength values (Fig. 9). For the evaluation data, we used ten images cropped to the stoma holder's original image faceplate replacement date, ten images from one day before the faceplate replacement date, eight images from two days before, eight images from three days before, four images from four days before, three images from five days before, and one image from six days before, with each init image strength value of 0.6 to 0.9. The training and evaluation data were trained on a Google teachable machine at 0.05 intervals from 0.6 to 0.9 (Fig. 10).

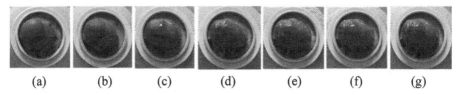

(a)   (b)   (c)   (d)   (e)   (f)   (g)

Fig. 9. The Init Image Strength function of AI image generation was adjusted. The values were 0.6 (a), 0.65 (b), 0.7 (c), 0.75 (d), 0.8 (e), 0.85 (f), and 0.9 (g) at 0.05 intervals.

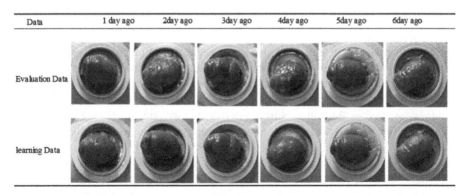

Fig. 10. The evaluation of each period up to the date of faceplate replacement with the init image strength function of AI image generation adjusted. The value and training data are shown.

The results showed that these data were accurate for each 0.05 interval range of the init image strength value, ranging from 0.6 to 0.9. There were nine 0.8 and one 0.9 one day before the faceplate replacement; five 0.7, two 0.75, and one 0.9 two days before; two 0.7, three 0.8, two 0.85, and one 0.9 three days before; one 0.7, two 0.75, and one 0.9 four days before; two 0.7 and two 0.9 five days before; and two 0.7 and one 0.9 four days before. Prior to six days, there was one 0.8 (Fig. 11).

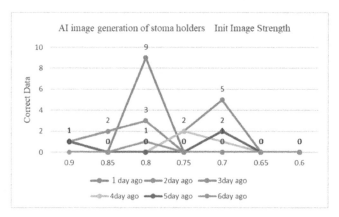

Fig. 11. Training results after adjusting the init image strength function of the AI image generation.

7.2 Comparison of the Two Machine Learning Algorithms Assuming Faceplate Replacement Time

As previously mentioned, it was impossible to collect a uniform number of faceplates for stoma holders because leaks occurred before the next scheduled faceplate replacement date, and each time a faceplate was removed. Therefore, the following method was used to verify the results.

First, 500 images were multiplied by AI image generation from the 34 original images of the stoma holder on the first day of wearing the faceplate. Next, the number of original images from each period, ten images from a day before the faceplate replacement day, eight images from two days before, eight images from three days before, four images from four days before, three images from five days before, and one image from six days before were used. Because the number of original images of stoma holders at each period on the day of faceplate replacement was lower than that of original images on the first day of faceplate attachment, ranging from one to ten, and the number of images was not standardized, the percentage was calculated using ten images one day before the day of replacement, which were more original images on the faceplate replacement day, making the total images to be 500. The evaluation data consisted of 34 original images of stoma holders on the first day of wearing the faceplate: ten original images from each period, ten images one day before the faceplate replacement day, eight images two days before, eight images three days before, four images four days before, three images five days before, and one image six days before.

By cropping images of stoma holders from the first day they wore the faceplate and from one to six days before the date of replacement, AI image generation multiplied the training data. We used 500 images from the first day of wearing the faceplate: 100 from one day before the faceplate replacement date, 100 from two days before, 100 from three days before, 100 from four days before, 70 from five days before, and 30 from six days before.

Next, using the correct data results verified at every 0.05 interval from 0.6 to 0.9 for the init image strength values, the image from one day before the faceplate replacement was set to 0.8, while that from two, three, four, five, and six days before was set to 0.7, 0.8, 0.75, 0.7, and 0.8 respectively. The init image strength values were also set.

For the evaluation data, we used 34 images on the day of the faceplate replacement, ten images one day before the faceplate replacement, eight images two days before, eight images three days before, four images four days before, three images five days before, and one image six days before from the original images of the stoma holder with cropping that was excluded from the training data. The training and correct data for each period were then trained on the Microsoft lobe and a Google teachable machine (Fig. 12).

Therefore, the Microsoft lobe found 32 of 34 images from the day of faceplate replacement, six of ten images from one day before replacement, seven of eight images from two days before replacement, six of eight images from three days before replacement, and six of eight images from four days before a replacement was correct for four of four images, three of three for five days ago, and one of one for six days ago. In the Google teachable machine, 33 of 34 images for faceplate replacement date, one day before the replacement date was correct for four out of ten images, four out of eight for the two-day-old image, four out of eight for the three-day-old image, four out of four for the four-day-old image, three out of three for the five-day-old image, and 1 out of 1 for the six-day-old image (Fig. 13).

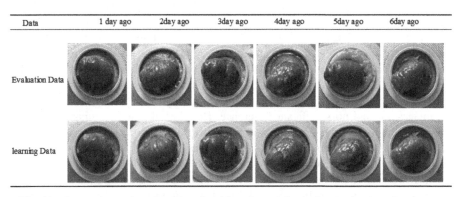

Data	1 day ago	2day ago	3day ago	4day ago	5day ago	6day ago
Evaluation Data						
learning Data						

Fig. 12. Comparison of two learning algorithms from 1 day before to the day of exchange.

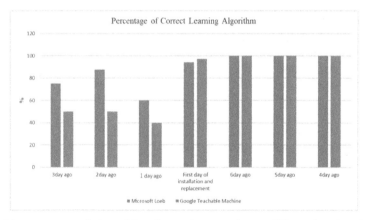

Fig. 13. The correct at each time of faceplate replacement by two different learning algorithms.

8   Consideration

Here, to determine the appropriate time to change the pouch using machine learning, we first increased the number of stoma holder images, artificially created images, and AI-generated images of the stoma holder. Finally, a comparison of the two machine learning algorithms is discussed. Particularly, around January 2020, when COVID-19 was raging around the world, it was difficult to collect data from a large number of stoma holders in hospitals and care centers. Therefore, to proliferate stoma images, we used NMKD stable diffusion, which is available in the GUI. The Microsoft lobe and Google teachable machine, that were used in this study are available for free and are simple to use on the user's computer. Stoma holders can upload photos taken with their smartphones via the Internet and be informed when it is time to exchange their stoma, which is the best part.

Second, a comparison between the two learning algorithms using artificially created images showed no significant difference. However, the two learning algorithms were more accurate for the faceplate with a narrower dissolution range than for the one with a wider dissolution range. Because the percentage of correct answers was 40–50% at approximately 10 mm, which is essentially the guideline for when to replace the faceplate, we believe that the accuracy may be reduced by the dissolution range being significantly too wide or the boundaries of the dissolution being unclear.

After further validation of the init image strength function adjustment, the init image strength function of the AI image generation was adjusted, and the similarity was validated. It was found that the similarity level changed at each period from one to six days before the faceplate replacement date. This may be due to the complex adhesion of excrement to the faceplate [16]. We also considered that the parameters are finely adjustable and may not have reached the point of optimization.

Finally, the init image strength function was adjusted to change the similarity at each period from one to six days before the faceplate replacement date to be closer to the stoma holder's image. The two learning algorithms had differences. For the Google teachable, although the accuracy was lower for the machine algorithm than for the Microsoft lobe algorithm, we believe that the period from one to three days before the replacement date is important because a time when it leaks must be detected.

9   Conclusions and Future Works

Future challenges for determining the appropriate time to replace pouches through machine learning include the following:

1. Although we believe that the accuracy of the two learning algorithms is almost equal, we must continue to evaluate their accuracy to determine the appropriate time for the pouch replacement. This includes determining whether there are differences between pouch types and whether they can detect the faceplate's condition when it is close to the time of replacement.
2. Will the result be the same as this time when the evaluation data are aligned, regardless of the variation in the number of original images of stoma holders used as evaluation data?
3. We will compare the two algorithms with Keras, an open-source neural network library written in Python, which is one of the machine learning options, and can run on TensorFlow and be trained for rapid implementation [17].

Acknowledgment. This study was partly supported by the 2021 Specific Joint Research, Fundamental Mechatronics Research Institute, Osaka Electrocommunication University.

References

1. Foundation for Promotion of Cancer Research. Cancer Statistics in Japan of 2022. https://ganjoho.jp/public/qa_links/report/statistics/pdf/cancer_statistics_2022.pdf. Published 12. Accessed 18 Dec 2022
2. Jeppesen, P.B., Vestergaard, M., Boisen, E.B., Ajslev, T.A.: Impact of stoma leakage in everyday life: data from the Ostomy Life Study 2019. Br. J. Nurs. **31**(6), 48–58 (2022)
3. Jordan, M.I., Mitchell, T.M.: Machine learning: trends, perspectives, and prospects. Science **349**(6245), 255–260 (2015)
4. Shahadat, U., Arif, K., Hossain, Md.E., Mohammad, A. M.: Comparing different supervised machine learning algorithms for disease prediction. BMC Med. Inform. Decis. Mak. **19**(281) (2019)
5. Forchhammer, S., Abu-Ghazaleh, A., Metzler, G., Garbe, C., Eigentler, T.: Development of an image analysis-based prognosis score using Google's teachable machine in melanoma. Cancers **14**(2243), 1–12 (2022)
6. Wu, T., Wei, Y., Wu, J., Yi, B., Li, H.: Logistic regression technique is comparable to complex machine learning algorithms in predicting cognitive impairment related to post intensive care syndrome. Sci. Rep. **13**(2485) (2023)
7. Lee, S.-K., Son, Y.-J., Kim, J., et al.: Prediction model for health-related quality of life of elderly with chronic diseases using machine learning techniques. Healthc. Inform. Res. **20**(2), 125–134 (2014)
8. Yu, J.Y., Jeong, G.Y., Jeong, O.S., Chang, D.K., Cha, W.C.: Machine leaning and initial nursing assessment-based triage system for emergency department. Healthc. Inform. Res. **26**(1), 13–19 (2020)

9. Geum, H.J.: Artificial intelligence, machine learning, and deep learning in women's health nursing. Korean J. Women Health Nurse **26**(1), 5–9 (2020)
10. Microsoft Lobe. https://lobe.ai/. Accessed 9 Jan 2023
11. Microsoft Lobe's Image Classification Overview. https://learn.microsoft.com/ja-jp/ai-builder/lobe-overview. Accessed 9 Jan 2023
12. Google Machine Learning. https://teachablemachine.withgoogle.com/. Accessed 9 Jan2023
13. Github, Stable Diffusion Helper. https://github.com/fladdict/stable_diffusion/blob/main/Stable_Diffusion_Helper.ipynb. Accessed 22 Jan 2023
14. Hollister. https://www.hollister.com/en. Accessed 20 Feb 2023
15. Coloplast. https://www.coloplast.us/. Accessed 20 Feb 2023
16. Malahina, E.A.U., Hadjon, R.P., Bisilisin, F.Y.: Teachable machine. Real-time attendance of students based on open source system. Int. J. Inform. Comput. Sci. **6**(3), 140–146 (2022)
17. Python deep learning library. https://keras.io/ja. Accessed 14 Jan 2023

Message Notification System to Reduce Excessive Smartphone Use by Displaying Smartphone Usage Status as a Character's Condition

Kazuyoshi Murata(✉) and Hiroki Tanaka

Aoyama Gakuin University, Sagamihara, Kanagawa, Japan
kmurata@si.aoyama.ac.jp

Abstract. Many smartphone users frequently check their smartphones daily, and excessive smartphone use can cause various problems. In a previous study, we proposed the CHIAPON message notification system to reduce smartphone use. The CHIAPON system notifies users of messages from anthropomorphic characters that encourage them to reduce excessive smartphone use according to their smartphone usage data. In this paper, we incorporate status factors common to role-playing games into the CHIAPON system to encourage users to become more emotionally involved with the anthropomorphic character. By changing the character's condition based on the values of these status factors and providing feedback to the user regarding how the anthropomorphic character is weakening due to excessive smartphone use, the user can feel more encouraged to reduce smartphone use. We evaluated whether notifying users of changes in their character's condition improved their motivation to refrain from using their smartphones. We also evaluated whether the time spent using a smartphone was reduced. Experimental results demonstrated that the proposed system could change the participants' motivation to reduce smartphone use.

Keywords: Excessive smartphone use · Message notification system · Anthropomorphic character

1 Introduction

Smartphones have become the central information terminal, and the widespread use of smartphones has enabled easy access to various information over the Internet. However, many smartphone users frequently check their smartphones during daily activities, e.g., working, studying, or taking a walk, and excessive use of these smartphones can cause various problems. For example, excessive smartphone use has been reported to cause distraction, and excessive dependence on smartphones leads to stress for users [11]. In addition, nighttime use of smartphones interferes with sleep and can reduce activity daytime levels [10]. Other risks associated with blue light from smartphone screens [18] and health problems, e.g., neck pain [1, 2], depression, and anxiety [5] have been

© The Author(s), under exclusive license to Springer Nature Switzerland AG 2023
M. Kurosu and A. Hashizume (Eds.): HCII 2023, LNCS 14014, pp. 121–134, 2023.
https://doi.org/10.1007/978-3-031-35572-1_9

reported. Regarding the influence of smartphone use on learning, studies of college students have reported a negative relationship between smartphone use and grades [7, 12]. It has also been reported that using smartphones and social media while studying can interfere with daily life [4]. Accidents caused by using a smartphone while walking have been increasing, and it has been reported that smartphone use is distracting to pedestrians [17] and reduces situational awareness [13]. Experiments conducted using virtual environments have demonstrated that talking, texting, listening to smartphone music, and using the Internet on smartphones while crossing the street affect pedestrian safety [3, 22]. Thus, excessive smartphone use is an important social problem, and methods are required to reduce or eliminate the risks associated with excessive use of smartphones.

Digital wellbeing has gained increasing attention as an effort to address excessive use and dependence on digital devices, including smartphones, and various tools have been released to help users control their use of digital device [25]. These tools attempt to help people understand and prevent overuse and addiction to digital devices, and many involve interventions, e.g., app blocking, or self-monitoring, e.g., usage visualization [15]. However, while interventions, e.g., app blocking, can be effective in terms of curbing smartphone use temporarily, frustration has been reported when usage restrictions are overly severe [8]. In addition, it has been reported that pop-up notifications indicating excessive smartphone use do not reduce the frequency of smartphone use [14]. Roffarello et al. analyzed qualitative reviews of current digital wellbeing apps and quantitative experimental data from their tools [20]. They found that although self-monitoring-based modern digital wellbeing apps are helpful for specific use cases, they are insufficient to change user behavior effectively.

Habit formation is considered one of the key element in digital wellbeing. Habits are defined as automatic responses to contextual cues, and when a behavior associated with specific cues is repeated in a stable context, the behavior becomes a habit. Stawarz et al. demonstrated that reminders support repetition and help users remember to complete tasks but do not lead to habit formation. They also showed that reliance on triggering events as cues for task completion increases the automaticity of the behavior; however, the effect is weak [23].

In a previous study, we proposed the CHIAPON message notification system to encourage users to reduce smartphone use [16]. The CHIAPON system notifies users of messages from anthropomorphic characters that encourage them to reduce excessive smartphones use according to their smartphone usage data (Fig. 1). The CHIAPON was designed to encourage users to refrain from excessive smartphone use naturally, and it attempts to make users more receptive to messages encouraging them to change their behaviors than simple warning notifications by having anthropomorphic characters notify them of the messages.

An experiment was conducted to compare the CHIAPON with a system that only notifies users of smartphone usage status. We found that using CHIAPON may improve user motivation not to use smartphones; however, it did not reduce the time spent using smartphones. In addition, interviews with the experimental participants revealed that those who found the CHIAPON effective, especially those who actually decreased their smartphone use, focused on the character of the anthropomorphic character. In contrast, those who did not change their behavior focused on their usage status. This result indicates that users who could establish a close relationship with CHIAPON's anthropomorphic character, rather than viewing it merely as a self-monitoring tool, sensed the intent of the messages, and their behavior was more likely to change. These findings suggest that incorporating a mechanism that allows users to become emotionally involved with the anthropomorphic character of the CHIAPON may strongly encourage users to refrain from using their smartphones excessively.

Fig. 1. The CHIAPON system to encourage users to reduce smartphone use.

In this study, we incorporated status factors used in role-playing games into the CHIAPON system. Specifically, we added fatigue, recovery, and physical strength factors to CHIAPON's anthropomorphic character, and these factors vary according to the user's smartphone usage time. The anthropomorphic character's condition changes based on these changes, and the condition is fed back to the user. By changing the anthropomorphic character's condition and providing feedback to the user about how the anthropomorphic character is weakening due to excessive smartphone use, the user is expected to feel more encouraged to refrain from using their smartphone.

2   Related Work

2.1   Anthropomorphic Character

Anthropomorphism is the attribution of human-like properties, characteristics, or mental states to real or imagined nonhuman agents and objects [6]. There are two possible anthropomorphism methods, i.e., attributing human-like physical characteristics, e.g., face and hands, and attributing human-like emotions, e.g., intention, awareness, shame, and joy [24]. The former method is a representation technique that anthropomorphizes the appearance of an object, which can facilitate understanding the purpose and behavior of the anthropomorphized object or its value and attractiveness. The latter method anthropomorphizes the object's behavior. This technique uses emotional expressions through movements and facial expressions, or words, and actions that provide a sense of social behavior, to convey a sense of intent. Many anthropomorphic systems utilize only one of these two techniques but often integrate both.

The proposed system anthropomorphizes message notifications from smartphones. To anthropomorphize the appearance, the system displays a human-like character that talks to the user, which allows the user to feel familiarity and attraction to the system and better understand the messages. In addition, to personify behavior, the system expresses the fatigue and recovery of the character based on how much time the user has spent using the smartphone. We expect that users who receive these messages will respond favorably to the suggestions made by the anthropomorphic character.

2.2 Behavior Change

Prochaska et al. categorized the process of behavior change into five stages [19], i.e., precontemplation (where people do not intend to change their behavior in the foreseeable future), contemplation (where people recognize the existence of a problem and seriously consider overcoming it but have not yet taken action), preparation (where people intend to take action in the near future), action (where people take action), and maintenance (where people maintain the action). Rothman stated that, to realize long-term behavior changes, different approaches are required for behavior initiation and behavior maintenance [21]. It was suggested that two types of support are required to change the smartphone use habit, i.e., support to make people aware of the problem and initiate the behavior, and support to maintain the change in behavior. In this study, we focus on the support for making people aware of the problem and then initiating the behavior change.

Although warnings about excessive smartphone use make users aware of their problematic smartphone behaviors, this mechanism does not effect change in user awareness. Thus, it is difficult to change user awareness about changing their behavior although it may lead to temporary actions. In this study, we attempted to increase user interest in the messages by anthropomorphizing the entities that issue them, rather than simply notifying users of warning messages, and to direct the user's awareness toward reducing smartphone use.

2.3 Reducing Smartphone Use

Rather than issuing warnings or forcibly prohibiting excessive smartphone use, several methods have been proposed to induce users to reduce smartphone use by incorporating gamification elements, e.g., visualization of usage status or competition. For example, a previously proposed system encourages users to continuously curb their use of smartphones by having them compete with their peers to see how long they spend without using their smartphones [9]. In such systems, the user proactively provides input to the system, and the system presents information to the user to encourage a reduction in smartphone use. In these cases, the user is already in the process of curbing smartphone use; thus, such systems support the maintenance of behavioral change. By combining our system with the advantages of these methods, we expect it would be possible to provide integrated support for both the initiation and maintenance of desired behavior changes.

3 Overview of Proposed System

In the CHIAPON system, which was developed in our previous study [16], an anthropomorphic character notifies smartphone users of messages to encourage a reduction in excessive smartphone use depending on the number of times the smartphone is used or the continuous usage time. In the current study, we modified the CHIAPON system to change the character's condition according to how long the smartphone has been used and to notify messages corresponding to the character's condition. In addition, by sending messages at regular intervals, the system maintains interaction with the user even when anthropomorphic character's state remains unchanged. As in our previous study, we implemented the system as an iPhone application. Figure 2 shows an example of the CHIAPON screen. As can be seen, the CHIAPON application is launched, the main screen shows the CHIAPON's character (an anthropomorphized rice cake). Then, the CHIAPON system notifies the user of messages in response to changes in the character's condition.

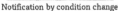

Notification by condition change   Regularly scheduled notification   CHIAPON's appearance

Fig. 2. Examples of CHIAPON screens.

3.1 Condition Changes

In this study, CHIAPON's character has three status values, i.e., fatigue, recovery, and physical strength levels. The value of the fatigue level increases as the time the smartphone is in use increases, and the value of the recovery level decreases when the smartphone is not in use. In addition, the physical strength value is reduced when a certain amount of fatigue value is accumulated. In contrast, the physical strength value increases when a certain amount of recovery value is accumulated. The physical strength level determines the condition of the CHIAPON character. The character's condition goes fluctuations between the five conditions shown in Fig. 3, i.e., the "Fine," "Normal," "Fatigue," "Weakness," and "Dead" conditions, which are described as follows.

– Fine: 75% or greater of the maximum physical strength level
– Normal: 50% or greater but less than 75% of the maximum physical strength level
– Fatigue: 25% or more, but less than 50% of maximum physical strength level
– Weakness: less than 25% of maximum physical strength level
– Dead: 0% of maximum physical strength level

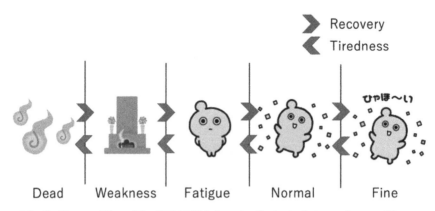

Fig. 3. The condition of the CHIAPON character fluctuates between five conditions.

As the character's physical strength level is reduced, the character becomes increasingly weak, and as the character's physical strength level recovers, the character becomes increasingly energetic. When the physical strength level reaches zero, the character's condition changes to "Dead." As a result, the user is aware that their smartphone usage is linked to the character's condition. Note that the amount of change and the threshold in the status level were determined in preliminary experiments.

As shown in Fig. 3, the character's image on the screen changes according to the character's current condition. For example, a cheerful character appearance is displayed when the character is in the "Fine" condition. As the character gets closer to fatigued state, the displayed character's appearance becomes less energetic. This allows the user to observe and recognize the character's condition visually.

The proposed CHIAPON system notifies the user of messages according to the changes in the character's condition. The message content changes depending on the character's condition. When the character is in the "Fine" state, CHIAPON sends a message indicating that the character is cheerful, and when the character is weak, the system sends a message indicating that the character is tired. By sending messages with content linked to the character's state, users are encouraged to become emotionally involved with the character, which is expected to have a more significant effect on reducing excessive smartphones use.

3.2 Notification Message

The CHIAPON system notifies the user of messages when the character's condition changes and at regular intervals. The title of the notification message is the condition of the CHIAPON character at the time of the notification, and the message contains the character's dialog to inform the user of the character's condition.

Notifications are issued when the CHIAPON character's condition changes from "Normal" to "Fatigue" and from "Fatigue" to "Weakness" to make the character feel tired. For example, when transitioning from "Normal" to "Fatigue," the character says, "I am getting a little tired. You should use your smartphone a little less." In addition, when the character's condition changes from "Fatigue" to "Weakness," the system notifies the user with a message that indicates the character is getting weak, e.g., "I am at the limit of fatigue." Conversely, when the character's condition changes from "Weakness" to "Fatigue" or from "Fatigue" to "Normal," the system indicates the character is recovering. For example, when the condition changes from "Weakness" to "Fatigue," the presented message says, "I am feeling a little better, but I still want to rest." When the condition becomes "Dead," the system repeatedly notifies the user for a short period with a message that indicates the need to recover immediately, e.g., "Oh,... I am dying... I want to come back to life as soon as possible." When the condition changes from "Fatigue" to "Normal," the message states, "I am feeling better now that I have rested." Note that no notifications are given when transitioning from "Fine" to "Normal" and from "Normal" to "Fine" because overly frequent notifications can cause user discomfort. In our previous study, we reported that users found the notifications irritating when the notification frequency was too high [16].

If the character's condition repeatedly changes only between "Fine" and "Normal," this system does not send any notification messages. In addition, the system does not notify the user when the character stays in one condition. Thus, the system provides regularly scheduled notifications to maintain effective interaction even with users whose conditions infrequently. The content of the regularly scheduled notification refers to the usage status based on the character's condition. Here, the user is informed whether their smartphone usage is desirable or undesirable. For example, with the "Fine" condition, the character says, "You are refraining from using your smartphone! Keep it up!" When the condition is "Weak," the character says "I am exhausted... Let's take a break."

As mentioned previously, the system notifies the user when the condition changes and at regular intervals. Depending on the situation, the system may notify the user many times in a short time. For example, assume that the user repeatedly uses the smartphone for a short period when the character's physical strength is close to the boundary of the condition change threshold. In this case, the system will send a notification each time, which may cause user discomfort. Thus, except for the "Dead" condition, when the system notifies the user once, the notification function is turned off for thirty minutes to prevent repeated notifications caused by condition changes.

4 Experiment

We conducted an experiment to evaluate whether notifying users of changes in the CHI-APON character's condition improved their motivation to reduce excessive smartphone use when they observed such changes. In addition, we evaluated whether the time spent using the smartphone was reduced.

4.1 Participants

Thirteen students (six males and seven females) aged 20–24 years participated in this experiment. We first explained the purpose and methods of the experiment both in writing and orally to the participants. Note that each participant received a gift card worth 1,000 yen in compensation, regardless of the time they spent using their smartphone or the extent to which they engaged with the CHIAPON system.

4.2 Experimental Procedure

The experiment was conducted as follows:

1. The participants were asked to report the amount of time they spent using their smartphones each day over the past week. The daily smartphone screen time and pickups were self-reported as a value displayed by the iPhone's Screen Time function.
2. The participants installed the CHIAPON application on their smartphones, activated the system, and spent one week using the system.
3. After the one-week usage period, the participants were asked to report the amount of time they spent using their smartphones with CHIAPON each day over the past week.
4. The participants were asked to uninstall the CHIAPON application.

At the end of the experiment, the participants answered the following questionnaire.

- Q1. Has this system improved your motivation to refrain from using smartphones?

  - ("1. disagree" to "5. agree")

- Q2. How annoying were the notifications?

  - ("1. annoying" to "5. not annoying")

- Q3. Did you read the contents of the notification message?

  - ("1. did not read" to "5. did read")

- Q4. Did you care about the condition of your character?

  - ("1. did not care" to "5. did care")

- Q5. Did you feel attached to the characters?

  – ("1. not attached" to "5. attached")

In addition, the participants were asked to respond in free description format to indicate what was good about the system, what was terrible about the system, and their overall impression of both the characters and messages displayed by the system.

We analyzed the effect of the proposed system by comparing the time and frequency of smartphone use before and during the experimental period. We also analyzed the effect of the proposed system on the motivation to reduce smartphone usage through a post-experiment questionnaire.

5 Results and Discussion

5.1 Smartphone Usage Time and Number of Pickups

One participant did not use the CHIAPON application sufficiently during the experimental period. Therefore, we used the results of the remaining 12 participants (six males and six females) in our analysis. In addition, the screen time function measures the accumulated usage time and the number of device pickups per day. We could not accurately measure the usage time and the number of pickups on the day the questionnaire was administered. As a result, we used data from the previous six days, excluding the questionnaire day.

The smartphone usage time before and after using CHIAPON is shown in Fig. 4. As can be seen, seven of the 12 participants exhibited a reduction in smartphone usage time. In contrast, the smartphone usage time of the remaining five participants increased. We categorized the participants into two groups, i.e., those who reduced their smartphone usage time (A to G in Fig. 4) and those who increased their smartphone usage time (H to L in Fig. 4). In this paper, we refer to the former and latter groups as the "decrease group" and "increase group" respectively.

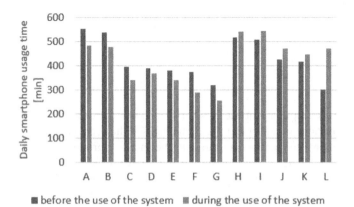

■ before the use of the system   ■ during the use of the system

Fig. 4. Daily smartphone usage time before and during the use of the CHIAPON system.

Figure 5 shows the daily smartphone usage time of both groups, and Fig. 6 shows the number of pickups. We observed no differences between groups in terms of smartphone usage time (Fig. 5). There was also no difference between with and without use of the proposed system. In contrast, the number of pickups in the decrease group was greater than that of the increase group, and the Mann–Whitney test confirmed a significant difference ($p < .05$).

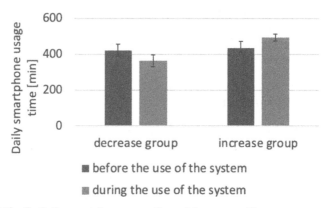

Fig. 5. Daily smartphone usage time of decrease and increase groups.

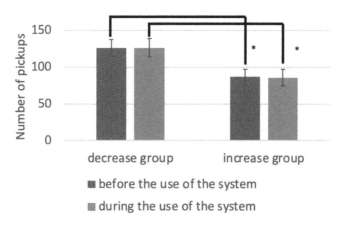

Fig. 6. Number of device pickups of decrease and increase groups.

Under the assumption that the number of pickups corresponds to the number of times the smartphone was checked, the participants in the decrease group checked their smartphones more frequently than those in the increase group but for less time per use. In other words, the proposed system was effective for the participants who check their smartphones frequently but spend a short amount of time per use. However, the proposed system was less effective for the participants who checked their smartphones less frequently and spent more time looking at their devices. There was likely a difference in the smartphone usage patterns between the decrease and increase groups. For example, in the case of tasks that only require a short time, e.g., sending, and receiving text messages, the number of times the smartphone is checked is high; however, it is easy to interrupt the work and control the time. In contrast, for tasks that require a long time per use, e.g., watching videos, or playing games, the number of times the smartphone is checked is low; however, it may be difficult to control the time spent even if a message comes in the middle of the task.

5.2 Questionnaire Results

The results of Q1 are shown in Fig. 7. Rating 1 indicates that the participants did not feel that the system improved their motivation to refrain from using smartphones, and rating 5 indicates that they felt that the system improved their motivation. Based on these results, we categorized the participants into two groups, i.e., the "not-refraining group," who selected a rating of 1 or 2, and the "refraining group," who selected a rating of 4 or 5. Figure 8 shows the results for Q2–Q4 categorized into these two groups.

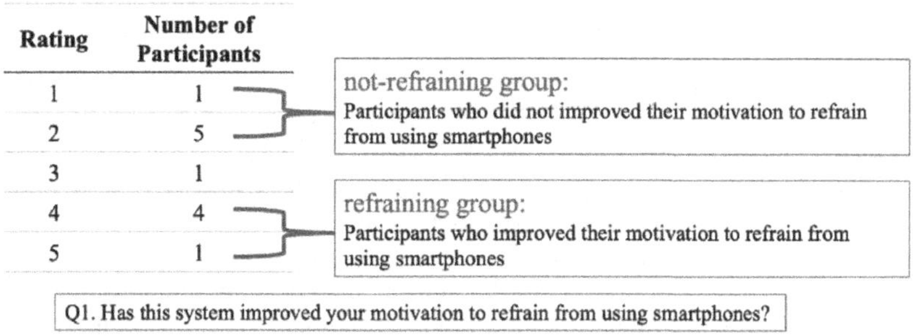

Rating	Number of Participants	
1	1	not-refraining group: Participants who did not improved their motivation to refrain from using smartphones
2	5	
3	1	
4	4	refraining group: Participants who improved their motivation to refrain from using smartphones
5	1	

Q1. Has this system improved your motivation to refrain from using smartphones?

Fig. 7. Results of Q1. The participants were categorized into the not-refraining and refraining groups based on the results.

Mann-Whitney tests were performed for all questionnaire results; however, no significant differences were observed. Nonetheless, we found that the refraining group responded with greater values than the not-refraining group, which indicates that the participants who attempted to refrain from using the smartphone felt attached to the character and were concerned about the character's condition. They also found the notifications from the proposed system annoying. These results demonstrate that the participants cared about the notifications from the proposed system. In contrast, the participants who did not attempt to refrain from using their smartphones did not care much about the character's condition or the notifications.

5.3 Discussion

The experimental results demonstrate that participants who became attached to and paid attention to the character were able to increase their motivation to refrain from using their smartphones. In contrast, the proposed system was ineffective for participants who did not care about the characters or notification messages. The proposed system may be

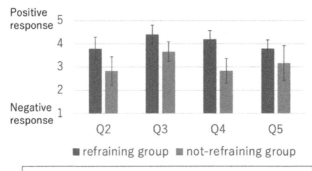

Q2. How annoying were the notifications?
Q3. Did you read the contents of the notification message?
Q4. Did you care about the condition of your character?
Q5. Did you feel attached to the characters?

Fig. 8. Results for Q2–Q5.

more effective if the users' attachment to the character is increased and their empathy for the character is heightened.

Among the participants in the refraining group, we found that three participants reduced their smartphone usage time, and conversely, the other two participants increased their smartphone usage time. Although the two participants were encouraged to refrain from using their smartphones, this motivation did not result in reduced usage of their smartphones.

In addition, the feedback we received regarding the character and notification messages was generally favorable. However, some participants stated that the messages were fixed phrases and there were not enough condition patterns for the character. These issues can be addressed by introducing a message-updating mechanism and an automatic message-generation mechanism.

The duration of the experiment was only one week, which was insufficient to transform smartphone use behaviors. To fully evaluate the usefulness of the proposed system, it is necessary to conduct long-term use experiments and analyze the subsequent usage conditions and habits. In addition, we must analyze the users' attitudes and trust toward the anthropomorphic character and examine the effects of the degree to which users paid attention to or ignored the anthropomorphic character's messages.

6   Conclusions

The effects of excessive smartphone use have become problematic, and a solution to this problem is urgently needed. However, existing methods that warn or inhibit users against their intention to use a smartphone are not likely to improve user behavior. In this paper, we have proposed a system that sends message notifications from an anthropomorphic character and incorporates both character status elements and condition changes. The proposed system attempts to increase the effectiveness of message notifications from the anthropomorphic character and reduce the user's smartphone usage time. The proposed system was evaluated experimentally, and the results demonstrated that the proposed system may change the motivation of the participants to refrain from using their smartphones. In future, we plan to reconsider the pattern of messages and the timing of notifications. In addition, we plan to conduct long-term experiments to confirm the system's effectiveness.

Acknowledgements. This work was supported by JSPS KAKENHI Grant Number JP20K11909.

References

1. AlAbdulwahab, S.S., Kachanathu, S.J., AlMotairi, M.S.: Smartphone use addiction can cause neck disability. Musculoskelet. Care **15**, 10–12 (2017)
2. Berolo, S., Wells, R.P., Amick, B.C.: Musculoskeletal symptoms among mobile hand-held device users and their relationship to device use: a preliminary study in a Canadian university population. Appl. Ergon. **42**, 371–378 (2011)
3. Byington, K.W., Schwebel, D.C.: Effects of mobile internet use on college student pedestrian injury risk. Accid. Anal. Prev. **51**, 78–83 (2013)
4. David, P., Kim, J.H., Brickman, J.S., Ran, W., Curtis, C.M.: Mobile phone distraction while studying. New Media Soc. **17**, 1661–1679 (2015)
5. Elhai, J.D., Levine, J.C., Dvorak, R.D., Hall, B.J.: Fear of missing out, need for touch, anxiety and depression are related to problematic smartphone use. Comput. Hum. Behav. **63**, 509–516 (2016)
6. Epley, N., Waytz, A., Cacioppo, J.T.: On seeing human: a three-factor theory of anthropomorphism. Psychol. Rev. **114**, 864–886 (2007)
7. Felisoni, D.D., Godoi, A.S.: Cell phone usage and academic performance: an experiment. Comput. Educ. **117**, 175–187 (2018)
8. Kim, J., Jung, H., Ko, M., Lee, U.: Goalkeeper: exploring interaction lockout mechanisms for regulating smartphone use. Proc. ACM Interact. Mob. Wearable Ubiquitous Technol. **3**, 1–29 (2019)
9. Ko, M., et al.: NUGU: a group-based intervention app for improving self-regulation of limiting smartphone use. In: CSCW 2015 - Proceedings of the 2015 ACM International Conference on Computer-Supported Cooperative Work and Social Computing, pp. 1235–1245 (2015)
10. Lanaj, K., Johnson, R.E., Barnes, C.M.: Beginning the workday yet already depleted? consequences of late-night smartphone use and sleep. Organ. Behav. Hum. Decis. Process. **124**, 11–23 (2014)
11. Lee, Y.K., Chang, C.T., Lin, Y., Cheng, Z.H.: The dark side of smartphone usage: psychological traits, compulsive behavior and technostress. Comput. Hum. Behav. **31**, 373–383 (2014)
12. Lepp, A., Barkley, J.E., Karpinski, A.C.: The relationship between cell phone use, academic performance, anxiety, and satisfaction with life in college students. Comput. Hum. Behav. **31**, 343–350 (2014)
13. Lin, M.I., Huang, Y.P.: The impact of walking while using a smartphone on pedestrians' awareness of roadside events. Accid. Anal. Prev. **101**, 87–96 (2017)
14. Loid, K., Täht, K., Rozgonjuk, D.: Do pop-up notifications regarding smartphone use decrease screen time, phone checking behavior, and self-reported problematic smartphone use? Evidence from a two-month experimental study. Comput. Hum. Behav. **102**, 22–30 (2020)

15. Lyngs, U., et al.: Self-control in cyberspace: applying dual systems theory to a review of digital self-control tools. In: CHI 2019: Proceedings of the 2019 CHI Conference on Human Factors in Computing Systems, Paper No. 131, pp. 1–18 (2019)
16. Murata, K.: CHIAPON: an anthropomorphic character notification system that discourages their excessive smartphone use. In: Kurosu, M. (eds.) HCII 2021. LNCS, vol. 12763, pp. 432–445. Springer, Cham (2021). https://doi.org/10.1007/978-3-030-78465-2_32
17. Nasar, J., Hecht, P., Wener, R.: Mobile telephones, distracted attention, and pedestrian safety. Accid. Anal. Prev. **40**, 69–75 (2008)
18. Oh, J.H., Yoo, H., Park, H.K., Do, Y.R.: Analysis of circadian properties and healthy levels of blue light from smartphones at night. Sci. Rep. **5**, 11325 (2015)
19. Prochaska, J., Diclemente, C.C., Norcross, J.C.: How people change, prochaska 1992. Am. Psychol. **47**, 1102–1114 (1992)
20. Roffarello, A.M., Russis, L.D.: The race towards digital wellbeing: issues and opportunities. In: CHI 2019: Proceedings of the 2019 CHI Conference on Human Factors in Computing Systems, Paper No. 386, pp. 1–14. Association for Computing Machinery (2019)
21. Rothman, A.J.: Toward a theory-based analysis of behavioral maintenance. Health Psychol. **19**, 64–69 (2000)
22. Schwebel, D.C., Stavrinos, D., Byington, K.W., Davis, T., O'Neal, E.E., Jong, D.D.: Distraction and pedestrian safety: how talking on the phone, texting, and listening to music impact crossing the street. Accid. Anal. Prev. **45**, 266–271 (2012)
23. Stawarz, K., Cox, A.L., Blandford, A.: Beyond self-tracking and reminders: designing smartphone apps that support habit formation. In: CHI 2015: Proceedings of the 33rd Annual ACM Conference on Human Factors in Computing Systems, pp. 2653–2662 (2015)
24. Waytz, A., Cacioppo, J., Epley, N.: Who sees human? The stability and importance of individual differences in anthropomorphism. Perspect. Psychol. Sci. **5**, 219–232 (2010)
25. Widdicks, K.: When the good turns ugly: speculating next steps for digital wellbeing tools. Association for Computing Machinery (2020)

Walking Posture Correction Using Mixed Reality for Self Visualization

Yumiko Muto[1]([⊠]), Jo Kasuya[2], Masaki Oshiba[3], Ryuhei Yamada[3], Yuuna Suzuki[3], Mizuki Hagiwara[3], and Takeshi Muto[3]

[1] Tamagawa University, 6-1-1, Tamagawagakuen, Machida, Tokyo 194-8610, Japan
muto@lab.tamagawa.ac.jp
[2] Tele Business Inc., 2-12-24, Yaei, Chuo-ku, Sagamihara 252-0229, Kanagawa, Japan
[3] Bunkyo University, 1100, Namegaya, Chigasaki 253-8550, Kanagawa, Japan

Abstract. With the aim of proposing a personalized training method for walking to maintain the health of elderly people, we employed mixed reality (MR) technology and recreated a person's gait in real space and time using HoloLens as they walked freely based on the skeletal coordinates identified via IMU motion capture suit. It is made in such a way that users could perform movements, such as walking, while visually confirming their projected postures and allowed for projecting individual posture characteristics of the free movements unique to each person. The results of the experiment showed that by using our proposed system, the swaying of head and lateral difference in shoulder height were reduced while walking.

Keywords: Mixed Reality · Walking Posture · Health Care · Self-projection

1 Introduction

The impact of aging on posture is known to cause falling accidents, fractures, and brain diseases [1]. The authors previously examined the relationship between changes in posture and aging and showed that the impact of aging was more prominent while in motion than at rest (e.g., [2, 3]). Furthermore, by surveying posture, age, sex, bone density, height, weight, body fat, left- and right-arm strengths, leg strength, and the history of falls in 272 people with ages of 65 years or older, the authors showed that there were individual differences in their health, muscle strength, and body fat and that posture parameters can be used to classify their health status [3]. Moreover, the authors showed that the impact of aging on posture is more prominent during motion, such as while walking and standing, than when at rest, with a tendency to tilt forward [3]. Based on these findings, this study focused on individual differences in the health status of elderly people and aimed to propose a technique to improve postures while in motion.

Conventional methods for improving posture usually involve measuring the degree of spinal curvature when at rest and giving advice based on the results; however, it is difficult to improve in-motion posture based on the posture measurements at rest. Moreover, basic posture control consists of postural reflexes that maintain the posture against disturbances

M. Kurosu and A. Hashizume (Eds.): HCII 2023, LNCS 14014, pp. 135–145, 2023.
https://doi.org/10.1007/978-3-031-35572-1_10

and subconscious posture corrections that involve involuntary movement of body parts such as arms. During motion in a real environment, such as while walking, attention must be paid to the surroundings and disturbances for safe movement; consciously responding to disturbances while improving in-motion posture not only puts a burden on the user but also raises safety concerns.

Meanwhile, as computer technology has advanced in recent years, rehabilitations employing virtual reality (VR) and augmented reality (AR) have been proposed [4]; they can be an effective complementary treatment tool for rehabilitation [5]. Moreover, VR/AI makes repetitive exercises easy and reduce the workload for specialists [6]. VR is completely immersive, and using a head-mounted display (HMD) or headset, a user feels completely immersed in a different reality. AR [7] is characterized by the ability to overlay digital information on real elements[8].Research works on VR technology have shown that this technology effectively improves walking and balance after a stroke [9, 10]. Using VR technology, rehabilitations that would be difficult in real- time are being carried out under training conditions and environments. AR technology has been shown to have a positive effect on physical functions in the elderly, lower and upper limb functions in stroke, and phantom pain in combination with conventional therapies [5]. Mixed reality (MR) [11], which includes both AR (inclusion of virtual elements in a real environment) and augmented virtuality (inclusion of real elements in a virtual environment), has been used in new rehabilitation programs [12, 13].

In our study, therefore, we focused on possibilities of new rehabilitation programs using MR technology [8]. We constructed a system that visualizes a user's posture in real space and time via the MR goggles. Three Dimensional Computer Graphics (3DCG) video of a user, which was transmitted to a computer through wireless LAN, was projected based on data acquired by the IMU sensors built into the motion capture suit worn by the user. The skeletal position coordinates and angular data were then transmitted to the MR goggles in real-time. In this manner, it was not only possible for the user to perform movements such as walking while visually confirming their projected posture but also to visualize individual postural characteristics in the free movements that are unique to each person. As conventional assistive technologies for walking that employ CG and MR technology [14, 15], a method that guides the leg movements of users by controlling the movements and distance to the displayed video and a method that is used to evaluate walking abilities have been previously proposed [16, 17]; however, these are different from our proposed system, in which user's movements of the entire body during free walking are measured and recorded in a motion capture suit, allowing the user to visually confirm their body movements.

In the experiment, following three 5-min walking tasks were prepared. In Task 1, 3D CG avatar was not displayed. In Task 2, instead of 3D CG display of self, an animated character was displayed. In Task 3, 3D CG of self was displayed (the proposed method). In all these conditions, the user wore MR goggles and a motion capture suit. Studying these three conditions, we showed the effectiveness of the proposed method from the perspective of gait posture.

2   Self-projection Using MR Technology

2.1   System Overview

Figure 1 shows an overview of the proposed system. Participants can freely walk and move while visually confirming the 3D CG video that recreates their skeletal frame in real space by wearing a wireless motion capture suit (ENETERPRSE BioMed Suits, NANSENSE Inc.) and HoloLens 2 (Microsoft).

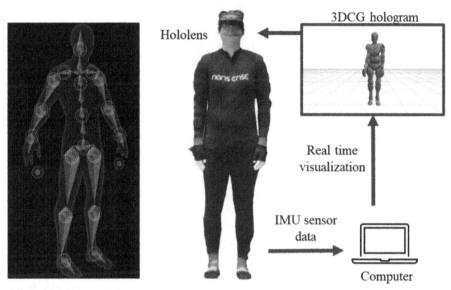

Fig. 1. Self-projection method using MR technology. The self 3D CG video was projected based on the data acquired by the IMU sensors built into the motion capture suit (ENETERPRSE BioMed Suits, NANSENSE Inc.) worn by the user, which in turn is transmitted to a computer through wireless LAN. The skeletal position coordinates and angular data are forwarded to the HoloLens in real-time.

Table 1. IMU 22 sensors

Channel #	
CH1	Spine, Spine1, Left Shoulder, Right Shoulder and Head
CH2	Left Upper Arm and Left Lower Arm (and Left Glove)
CH3	Right Upper Arm and Right Lower Arm and (Right Glove)
CH4	Left Upper Leg, Left Lower Leg, Left Foot and Hips
CH5	Right Upper Leg, Right Lower Leg and Right Foot

The self 3D CG video was created using the 22 IMU sensors of the motion capture suit worn by the user; the wireless motion data was measured at a sampling rate of

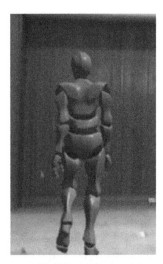

Fig. 2. An example of the projected 3D CG. When a participant wears MR goggles, 3D CG can be viewed as a hologram. It moves in front of the participant while maintaining a certain distance. Based on the previous study [18], the avatar's orientation was back to the participant.

120 Hz (Table 1). This motion data was transmitted to a computer via wireless LAN; taking the starting position of the measurement as the origin, it was then converted into skeletal position coordinates (36 locations) and angular data and recorded in FBX and CSV formats. The FBX format data were also transmitted to the MR goggles worn by the user in real-time using wireless LAN.

Figure 2 shows an example of 3D CG that a user wearing MR goggles could see as a hologram. Within the MR goggles, the user themself was projected as a recreation based on the data acquired by the IMU motion capture suit worn by the user. This hologram was based on the acquired data and recreated based on the humanoid CG character (Y-bot, walking, Adobe) installed in the 3D CG character data Mixamo published by Adobe. It was set to walk at a certain distance from the user, facing away from the user. As the size and position of the CG character could be arbitrarily set by the user, the video could be adjusted so that the character would not block the user as they walked.

2.2 Acquired Data

The data acquired by the IMU motion capture suit were used to recreate a hologram of the user wearing the MR goggles; meanwhile, for analysis, the data were recorded in the computer as a time series of the skeletal positional coordinates for 36 points (x, y, z) and Euler angles (φ, θ, ψ) of each axis. Recording was done at a sampling rate of 120 Hz. Notably, the system was calibrated before the use for each user for eight types of postures (1. I-pose, 2. T-pose, 3. Hands 4. Head, 5. Thumbs, 6. Fingers, 7. Walking, 8. Sitting). The origin of the acquired data was determined from the calibration (Fig. 3).

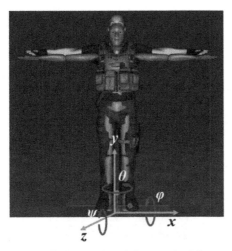

Fig. 3. Three-dimensional coordinate system of the acquired data. With the calibration point as the origin, the data were recorded on the computer as a time series of the 36 skeletal positions coordinates (x, y, z) and the Euler angles (φ, θ, ψ) of each axis at a sampling rate of 120 Hz.

3 Experiment

3.1 Participants

Participants included seven male university students (age: 21.125 ± 1.053). They were given sufficient explanation before their consent was taken to participate in the experiment. This experiment was performed with the approval of the Faculty of Information and Communications Research Ethics Review Committee of Bunkyo University (approval number: 2016-1).

3.2 Experimental Tasks

The experiment participants wore the MR goggles and motion capture suit and were asked to walk counterclockwise around a circular track that was 7 m in diameter for 5 min at their own pace. Three experimental tasks were prepared with different 3D CG display conditions for the MR goggles (Table 2). Before starting the experiment, calibration was performed for each participant. Additionally, participants were informed beforehand that the 3D CG image that they would be seeing would be their own.

In Task 1, no 3D CG video was displayed. Participants wore the MR goggles and motion capture suit and walked at their own pace for 5 min. In Task 2, a 3D CD animated character (Fig. 4), such as those used for video games, was displayed. This character was constructed using the FBX data of a humanoid CG character from Mixamo by Adobe (walking). In Task 3, the proposed system was used; the 3D CG was displayed that recreated the participants' postures (Fig. 5).

Table 2. Three different tasks in our experiment

Task No.	
Task 1	Non-3DCG
Task 2	Anime-3DCG
Task 3	Our proposed system

Fig. 4. An example of an anime–3D CG image in Task 2. For the 3D CG animated character, akin to those used in video games, we used the FBX data of a humanoid CG character from Mixamo by Adobe (walking).

Fig. 5. Walking image using the proposed system for Task 3. A participant wore the MR goggles and motion capture suit. A hologram that recreated his posture was displayed as a 3D video at a certain distance.

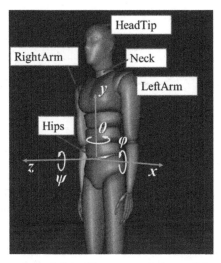

Fig. 6. Overview of the analytical data. The posture during walking was assessed with hip as the origin (in other words, $\left\{ Hips_x, Hips_y, Hips_z \right\} = \{0, 0, 0\}$), with a focus on the degree of spinal curvature. With the participant as the reference, x-axis was along their left and right direction, y-axis was along their vertical direction, and z-axis lied along their front and rear.

4   Results and Discussion

4.1   Movements of the Head

The posture was assessed based on previous studies [3–5]. Among the data acquired by the IMU sensors, we used the $HeadTip, Neck, RightArm, LeftArm$, and $Hips$ coordinates (x, y, z) and Euler angles (φ, θ, ψ) of each axis for analyzing the changes in the degree of spinal curvature while walking (Fig. 6).

The acquired data (Fig. 3) used the calibration point as the origin; therefore, we used the rotation matrix to convert the $Hips$ for the hip into a coordinate system where $HeadTip_x, HeadTip_z, Neck_x, Neck_z, RightArm_z, LeftArm_x$, and $LeftArm_z$ can be obtained (Eqs. (1)–(4)).

$$\begin{pmatrix} HeadTip_x \\ HeadTip_z \end{pmatrix} = \begin{pmatrix} \cos(-\theta) & -\sin(-\theta) \\ \sin(-\theta) & \cos(-\theta) \end{pmatrix} \cdot \begin{pmatrix} HeadTip_{x0} \\ HeadTip_{z0} \end{pmatrix} \tag{1}$$

$$\begin{pmatrix} Neck_x \\ Neck_z \end{pmatrix} = \begin{pmatrix} \cos(-\theta) & -\sin(-\theta) \\ \sin(-\theta) & \cos(-\theta) \end{pmatrix} \cdot \begin{pmatrix} Neck_{x0} \\ Neck_{z0} \end{pmatrix} \tag{2}$$

$$\begin{pmatrix} RightArm_x \\ RightArm_z \end{pmatrix} = \begin{pmatrix} \cos(-\theta) & -\sin(-\theta) \\ \sin(-\theta) & \cos(-\theta) \end{pmatrix} \cdot \begin{pmatrix} RightArm_{x0} \\ RightArm_{z0} \end{pmatrix} \tag{3}$$

$$\begin{pmatrix} LeftArm_x \\ LeftArm_z \end{pmatrix} = \begin{pmatrix} \cos(-\theta) & -\sin(-\theta) \\ \sin(-\theta) & \cos(-\theta) \end{pmatrix} \cdot \begin{pmatrix} LeftArm_{x0} \\ LeftArm_{z0} \end{pmatrix} \tag{4}$$

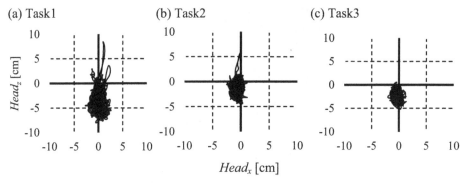

Fig. 7. **An example of the position of the head** $\{Head_x, Head_z\}$ **in Tasks 1–3.** The x-axis is along the left and right direction of the head [cm], while the y-axis lies along the front and rear of the head [cm].

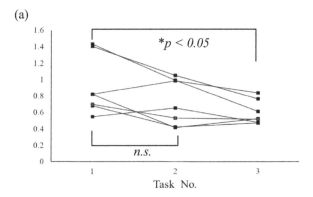

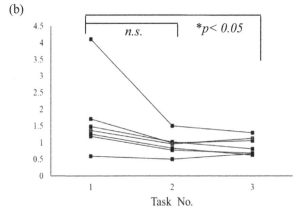

Fig. 8. Comparing results of the standard deviation (SD) of the head position in Tasks 1–3 for (a)$Head_x$ and (b)$Head_z$.

Figure 7 shows the changes in the head position of a participant while walking for Tasks 1–3. The x-axis is along the left and right direction of the head [cm], while the y-axis lies along the front and rear of the head [cm]. $Head_x$ and $Head_z$ were calculated using the Eqs. (5) and (6). To analyze the degree of swaying of the head, we used the neck position $(Neck_x, Neck_z)$ as the reference and calculated the SD of the head movements. If $Head_x$ was positive, it indicated that the head was positioned forward to the neck. Notably, from the start of a walk, the data were excluded for 30 s from the analysis. The results showed that for Task 1, the range of the head movements was wide; however, for Tasks 3, this range became smaller, becoming relatively more stable.

$$Head_x = HeadTip_x - Neck_x \qquad (5)$$

$$Head_z = HeadTip_z - Neck_z \qquad (6)$$

To further examine these results, we calculated the SD of the head movements for all participants and made a comparison among Tasks 1–3 (Fig. 8). The result showed that during the first half of the 5-min walk (2.5 min from the start), there was a significant difference between the results of Tasks 1 and 3 (*Dunnet multiple comparison*, $p = 0.041$); however, when the entire 5-min walk was considered, there was no significant difference ($Head_x : p = 0.0618$, $Head_z : p = 0.060$). The average of the head movements also did not present any significant difference among Tasks 1–3.

In Eqs. (5) and (6), when $Neck_x$ and $Neck_z$ were $Hips_x$ and $Hips_z$, respectively, that is, when the variations in the head position were examined with the hip as the reference, significant difference in its SD was found between Tasks 1 and 3 during the first half (2.5 min from the start) (*Dunnet multiple comparison*, $p = 0.043$).

The above results show that, compared to the non–3D CG condition of Task 1, when self–3D CG was present in Task 3, the SD for the head position was reduced, indicating the reduction in swaying of the head.

4.2 The Lateral Difference in the Shoulder Height

To assess the lateral difference in the shoulder height while walking, we examined the vertical changes in the armpits on both sides; in other words, we examined the difference in the y axial direction $(RightArm_y, LeftArm_y)$. In Eq. (7), $Shoulder(R - L)_y$ represents the lateral difference in the shoulder height, $RightArm_y$ represents the right-armpit height, and $LeftArm_y$ represents the left-armpit height.

$$Shoulder(R - L)_y = RightArm_y - LeftArm_y \qquad (7)$$

For each participant, we calculated $Shoulder(R - L)_y$ for Tasks 1–3 and compared the average values (Fig. 9). The results showed that there was a significant difference in the $Shoulder(R - L)_y$ between Tasks 1 and 3 (*Dunnet multiple comparison*, $p = 0.044$). The lateral difference in the shoulder height while walking was less in Task 3 compared to that in Task 1.

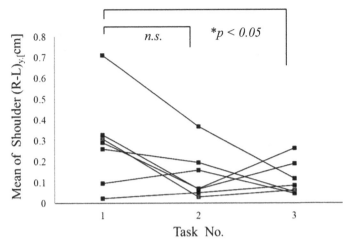

Fig. 9. Comparison of the left- and right-shoulder heights for Tasks 1–3 { $Shoulder(R - L)_y$ }.

5   Conclusion

We employed MR technology to construct a system that visualizes a user's posture in real space and time via the MR goggles. The self 3D CG video was projected based on data acquired by the IMU sensors within the motion capture suit worn by the user; the video was transmitted to a computer via wireless LAN. The skeletal position coordinates and angular data were forwarded to the MR goggles in real-time. In this manner, the user could perform movements such as walking while visually confirming their projected posture. This also allowed for projecting individual posture characteristics of the free movements unique to each person.

The results of the experiment showed that compared to Task 1, Task 3 led to lower standard deviations in the head movements; therefore, it is clear that there was an effect that reduced the swaying of the head. The lateral difference in the shoulder height while walking was lesser in Task 3 compared to that in Task 1. In other words, by using the proposed system, the swaying of the head and lateral difference in shoulder height reduced while walking.

The results of Task 2 (animated character) and Task 3 suggest that not only was there an impact on participants by the addition of visual feedback through the 3D CG walking rhythm, but there was also a psychological motivated impact by seeing themselves in the video projected in front of them. We have planned to study the details of these effects in our future research. Conventional posture correction methods mainly involve providing posture improvement advice; however, in the proposed system, by displaying their own video in front of them, users' gait spontaneously improves. Moreover, our method based on MR technology demonstrated its potential in health care and rehabilitation. In future, we hope to perform an experiment concerning elderly individuals.

Acknowledgments. This study was funded by JSPS Grants-in-Aid for Scientific Research (JP 21H03857).

References

1. Kado, D., Huang, M., Nguyen, C., Barrett-Connor, E., Greendale, G.: Hyperkyphotic posture and risk of injurious falls in older persons: the Rancho Bernardo study. J. Gerontol. Ser. A **62**(6), 652–657 (2007)

2. de Groot, M.H., van der Jagt-Willems, H.C., van Campen, J.P.C.M., Lems, W.F., Beijnen, J.H., Lamoth, C.J.C.: A flexed posture in elderly patients is associated with impairments in postural control during walking. Gait Posture **39**(2), 767–772 (2014)

3. Muto, Y., Sugou, M., Tsumurai, K., Ito, H., Hosono, Y., Muto, T.: Posture analysis and evaluation for modeling in elderly adults. In: Kurosu, M. (ed.) HCI 2017. LNCS, vol. 10271, pp. 506–521. Springer, Cham (2017). https://doi.org/10.1007/978-3-319-58071-5_38

4. Kiani, S., Rezaei, I., Abasi, S., et al.: Technical aspects of virtual augmented reality-based rehabilitation systems for musculoskeletal disorders of the lower limbs: a systematic review. BMC Musculoskelet. Disord. **24**, 4 (2023). https://doi.org/10.1186/s12891-022-06062-6

5. Vinolo Gil, M.J., Gonzalez-Medina, G., Lucena-Anton, D., Perez-Cabezas, V., Ruiz-Molinero, M.D.C., Martín-Valero, R.: Augmented reality in physical therapy: systematic review and meta-analysis. JMIR Serious Games **9**(4), e30985-e (2021). https://doi.org/10.2196/30985. PMID: 34914611;PMCID: PMC8717132

6. Taslimipour, S., Rojhani-Shirazi, Z., Hemmati, L., Rezaei, I.: Effects of a virtual reality dance training program on kyphosis angle and respiratory parameters in young women with postural hyperkyphosis: a randomized controlled clinical trial. J. Sports Med. **30**(2), 293–299 (2020)

7. Makhataeva, Z., Varol, H.A.: Augmented reality for robotics: a review. Robotics **9**, 21 (2020)

8. Palumbo, A.: Microsoft HoloLens 2 in medical and healthcare context: state of the art and future prospects. Sensors **22**(20), 7709 (2022). https://doi.org/10.3390/s22207709. PMID: 36298059, PMCID: PMC9611914

9. Heeren, A., et al.: Step by step: a proof of concept study of C-Mill gait adaptability training in the chronic phase after stroke (2013)

10. de Rooij, I.J., van de Port, I.G., Meijer, J.W.G.: Effect of virtual reality training on balance and gait ability in patients with stroke: systematic review and meta-analysis. Phys. Ther. **96**(12), 1905–1918 (2016)

11. Hu, H.Z., et al.: Application and prospect of mixed reality technology inmedical field. Curr. Med. Sci. **2019**(39), 1–6 (2019)

12. Howard, M.C., Davis, M.M.: A meta-analysis and systematic literature review of mixed reality rehabilitation programs: investigating design characteristics of augmented reality and augmented virtuality. Comput. Hum. Behav. **130** (2022)

13. De Luca, V., et al.: Virtual reality and spatial augmented reality for social inclusion: the "Includiamoci" project. Information **14**(1), 38 (2023). https://doi.org/10.3390/info14010038

14. Held, J.P.O., Yu, K., Pyles, C., Bork, F., Heining, S.M., Navab, N., Luft, A.R.: Augmented reality-based rehabilitation of gaitimpairments: case report. JMIR mHealth uHealth **8**, e17804 (2020)

15. Wolf, J., Wolfer, V., Halbe, M., Maisano, F., Lohmeyer, Q., Meboldt, M.: Comparing the effectiveness of augmented reality-based and conventional instructions during single ECMO cannulation training. Int. J. Comput. Assist. Radiol. Surg. **2021**(16), 1171–1180 (2021)

16. van Duijnhoven, H.J., et al.: Effects of exercise therapy on balance capacity in chronic stroke: systematic review and meta-analysis. Stroke **47**(10), 2603–2610 (2016)

17. Miller, D.A., Ogata, T., Sasabe, G., Shan, L., Tsumura, N., Miyake, Y.: Spatiotemporal gait guidance using audiovisual cues of synchronized walking avatar in augmented reality. IEEE Access **10**, 90498–90506 (2022)

18. Meerhoff, L.A., De Poel, H.J., Jowett, T.W.D., Button, C.: Walking with avatars: gait-related visual information for following a virtual leader. Hum. Mov. Sci. **66**, 173–185 (2019)

VisRef: A Reflection Support System Using a Fixed-Point Camera and a Smartwatch for Childcare Fields

Shigeru Owada[1]([✉])(iD), Sawako Fujita[3], Naho Tomiki[1,2], Masami Ogura[4], Yuki Taoka[3](iD), Momoko Nakatani[3](iD), and Shigeki Saito[3](iD)

[1] Sony Computer Science Laboratories, Inc., Tokyo, Japan
owd@hoikutech.com
[2] The University of Tokyo, Tokyo, Japan
[3] Tokyo Institute of Technology, Tokyo, Japan
[4] Iwasaki Gakuen, Kanagawa, Japan

Abstract. We propose VisRef, a video-based reflective support system incorporating a fixed-point camera and a smartwatch, and investigate its application for improved retrospection in childcare fields. When a childcare worker wearing a smartwatch encounters a situation he or she hopes to reflect upon later, the worker can press a button on the smartwatch to record a video of the immediately preceding few minutes. Depending on the button pressed, a preset text tag or transcribed voice tag is added to the video when they are posted to a chat system, shared with the relevant parties, or stored as a private record. We conducted experiments using the proposed application at a nursery school and at a daycare center for children with disabilities in Japan. The efficacy of this system in improving different field activities was evaluated through questionnaires and interviews. The results indicate that the acceptance of the system varied considerably depending on the differences in the facility environments. We identified several points can be explored in the future.

Keywords: Childcare · Reflection · Recording · Wearable · Voice recognition · Smart Watch · Chat · Communication · Education

1 Background

The declining birth rate and increasing aging population in Japan are expected to continue [3]. Such demographics can adversely affect the social and industrial structure of the country. If these trends continue, competition among childcare facilities will likely intensify, and providing high-quality childcare service will therefore become critical. We focused on the skills of childcare workers [19] and developed tools to support their learning.

To ensure the progress of childcare workers in the field, they should be allowed the opportunity to reflect upon their professional practice, identify any issues,

M. Kurosu and A. Hashizume (Eds.): HCII 2023, LNCS 14014, pp. 146–166, 2023.
https://doi.org/10.1007/978-3-031-35572-1_11

and resolve specific problems. However, the opportunity to make a recording or reflect on one's activities at work (e.g., contact time (CT)) while at a nursery school is limited, and even the time not in contact with children (i.e., noncontact time (NCT)) is mostly spent in performing miscellaneous tasks (Table 1).

To resolve these problems, the development of a system that causes limited stress during field activities, encourages video recording and self-reflection based on reviewing activities at work is critical. Furthermore, because teamwork is required in the field, reflection with other individuals involved, as well as individual reflection are necessary.

With the progress of ICT in the field of childcare, smartphone applications for electronic recording are becoming increasingly popular. However, most of these devices require direct interaction with a smartphone apps [4,24], which could interfere with the on-site activities of childcare workers. We developed VisRef, a system that uses a smartwatch (Apple Watch) as a recording medium during practice, facilitates recording using touch or voice input, and immediately shares the results of the input through a chat system (Slack), thereby allowing immediate feedback from other workers or outside experts. Voice recognition through a smartwatch eliminates the necessity of carrying or retrieving a notepad and writing instruments and allows the user to focus on the child while recording.

2   Related Work

In this chapter, a brief psychological and pedagogical background on self-reflection is provided, and the history of human - computer interface (HCI) in relation to our system is presented. We also briefly review ICT usage under an educational setting.

Psychological and Pedagogical Background. Dewey postulated that the reconstruction or reorganization of experience is the foundation of education [6]. According to Dewey, a continuum of experience exists, and to process an experience, past experiences are used as tools. Based on the results of a behavior analysis, Schön considered experts to be reflective practitioners and argued that teachers should learn through reflection on their own practice [21]. Schön states that excellent practitioners reflect upon their activity when producing unexpected results. The proposed system is intended to trigger a sense of awareness or discomfort during practice and allow practitioners to clip and share videos from a fixed-point camera and subsequently objectively reflect on the situation within the field.

Lifelogging and Sensing. With HCI, the conversion of all experiences into data is called lifelogging [2,8,15]. Activity trackers, particularly those focused on health management, have achieved success as commercial products [23]. Over time, the storage capacity has increased and the recording of an entire lifetime has become possible [9,10]. However, data have become so abundant that the extraction of meaningful parts has become a challenge. To overcome this challenge, VisRef users are allowed to mark meaningful scenes themselves during their professional practice.

Table 1. Usage of CT and NCT (N = 650) [17]

CT (Contact Time)	
Responding to parent inquiries	2.0%
Visual inspection upon arrival and Management of arrival and departure from preschool	6.4%
Leading a park-wide assembly	2.0%
Guidance and assistance in play and activities	24.7%
walk	0.8%
Dietary guidance and assistance	12.0%
Guidance and assistance with siesta	7.7%
Guidance and assistance with toileting	3.3%
Guidance and assistance in bathing	0.0%
Health guidance and first aid	2.6%
Individual guidance and assistance for each child (including care for children with disabilities)	3.1%
Other childcare guidance and assistance	0.5%
Other lifestyle guidance and assistance	0.8%
NCT (Non-Contact Time)	
Rest and Recess	6.1%
Environmental Configuration	1.3%
Staff meeting	1.8%
Contact consultation and meeting (informal)	1.6%
Preparation, cleanup, cleaning and disinfection of germs	3.2%
Filling out and handing in contact sheets	3.6%
Long-term instructional planning	0.6%
Short-term instructional planning	0.5%
Creation of individualized instructional plans	0.3%
Creation of childcare records	2.7%
Evaluation of instructional plans	0.4%
Display of artworks and interior decoration	0.3%
Event preparation, management, and cleanup	4.5%
Photography, organization and sales	0.3%
Communication with Home	0.7%
Consultation and communication with parents	0.6%
Events for Parents	0.5%
induction course	1.2%
Preparation of practical training reports	0.0%
Supervision of trainees	0.1%
tallying up operations	0.1%
general affairs	0.1%
accounting	0.0%
Human resources (shift management for extended day care)	0.0%
Material management and ordering	0.1%
None of the above	3.3%

Sensing in Education. There are many attempts to use sensing to support learning [7]. Examples of sensing include measuring the levels of stress and excitement in students by measuring their heart rate while in the classroom [12]. Other approaches include combining perspiration, blood flow, and brain waves measurements [22]. Furthermore, wearable electrocardiographs and accelerometers are used to review one's behavior in the medical field [18]. Systems using cameras to support an understanding of learning are a critical area of research owing to their low-cost and noncontact nature [11,13,28]. In addition to color information, three-dimensional cameras are used for specific shapes and easy recognition [25] as well as for measuring the state of concentration of students [27]. We focused on developing a low-cost, non-contact, and casual system that can be easily installed using a regular RGB camera, or even a smartphone, as a fixed-point camera.

3   Our System

The proposed video reflection system, VisRef, consists of an **Apple Watch app** operated by the user that accepts voice recognition and a trigger input, an **iPhone App** that continues to record video as a fixed-point camera, and **Slack**, which functions as the information-sharing destination (Fig. 1).

Apple Watch App   **iPhone App**   **slack**

Fig. 1. Overall Architecture

If multiple iPhones install our application and write to the same Slack channel, they can film the same room from different angles. At this stage, the video sharing operation from the Apple Watch is sent to all other iPhones, allowing videos from different angles to be posted to Slack at the same time.

App for Apple Watch. The appearance of an Apple Watch app on a user's arm is shown in Fig. 2. The "Share Memo" and "Share Video" buttons at the top are used for sharing a note or movie clip with other users and staff members. When pressed, both buttons activate the voice recognition mode. Only text is posted to the Slack shared channel when the "Share Memo" button is pressed, and when the "Share Video" button is pressed, the iPhone, which functions as a fixed-point camera, extracts video from the past few minutes (which is configurable with a default of 90 s) and posts it to the Slack shared channel with the text of speech recognition results, if speech recognition is used.

The "Personal Memo" and "Personal Video" buttons at the bottom operate similarly to the two buttons at the top. However, the post destination to Slack becomes a direct message to oneself, instead of a shared channel.

The six buttons at the center are used for posting preset text and video. This button functions similarly to the "Share Video" button in the upper right corner but differs in that it does not activate the voice recognition function and posts the preset text (and previous videos) that the user has set on the iPhone settings screen in advance.

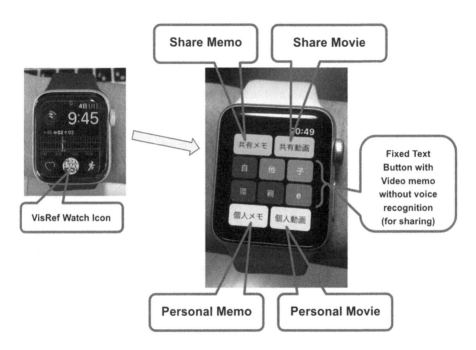

Fig. 2. Smart watch app user interface

Posting to Slack and Logging. Slack was selected as the information-sharing platform because its channel allows detailed settings such as the extent of information-sharing and a mute function. Furthermore, from an implementation perspective, its well-designed API allows the easy development of a corresponding application.

Postings to Slack are conducted through the Slack API. The iPhone applications post messages from the logged-in user, and they can therefore be deleted or modified. To anonymize the users during the experiment, a separate workspace was set up for each experimental field, and the username was simply a number representing the ID of the experiment participant. This ID was affixed to the

Apple Watch with a sticker, and the participants were instructed to use the same Apple Watch each time they started working. We developed a Slack bot to collect logs of recorded direct messages. When this bot is installed in the workspace, direct messages can be cross-posted to the bot. The researcher can then analyze the results.

4   Experimental Study

VisRef is a general-purpose video review system that is intended to support the reflection of various field activities. When applying VisRef to a specific field, it is necessary to consider the constraints specific to that field and emphasize the values. The purpose of the field experiment was to clarify those conditions allowing our video review system to be useful within the context of childcare and to consider future development items. Therefore, the participants were not provided concrete information on how to use the system efficiently and were expected to find a meaningful use of the system on their own.

4.1   Experiment Overview

First, one or several sets of iPhones and Apple Watch pairs that had been set to the Slack workspace were given in the target field, and basic instructions regarding the voice recognition and preset text buttons were then provided. Each preset text button allows the tagging of videos without the user of voice recognition, and these six buttons can be customized to efficiently classify videos on field-specific axes. However, this customization was not enforced.

We requested the participants to operate the system in this state for several days while in the field. They were then requested to answer a questionnaire evaluating the system. The questionnaire consisted of the following three types of questions and a free-text section.

- TSRI :   A set of questions for evaluating HCI systems that allow reflection [1].
- TAM :   An index for evaluating information technology, widely known as the Technology Acceptance Model [5]
- NPS : Net Promoter Score

After the questionnaire, when necessary, individual interviews with the experiment participants were conducted.

4.2   Target Facilities

Because the objective of this study was to clarify those conditions under which the proposed video reflection system is useful, deploying the system in as many different environments as possible could be beneficial. We conducted field experiments at two locations in Japan: a nursery school and an after-school daycare center.

Japanese nursery schools have long working hours, including a long contact time (CT) with children, and it is difficult to have noncontact time (NCT). This limits the amount of time that can be spent on documentation or discussions with other staff members. Furthermore, the number of children per adult is high, making the job difficult. Most staff members are certified nursery teachers, and the percentage of women is extremely high, rendering the workplace relatively homogeneous. The industry is also characterized by a high turnover rate.

Japan's "after-school daycare" centers were established in accord with the 2012 revision of the Child Welfare Law and accept children in need of support. More than 220,000 children between the ages of 6 and 18 years received this service in FY2019.

Because after-school daycare services are designed for children with disabilities, the skills of the workers in this industry differ considerably from those working in nursery schools, which can consist only of childcare workers. After-school daycare service centers are composed of various specialists, including childcare workers, nursery teachers, child development support management supervisors, and functional training staff. In certain cases, commissioned doctors and nurses are also employed.

Because the program targets school-year children, no students are present in the facility when the students are at school (e.g., during the morning). This aspect is very different from nursery schools..

4.3   Field Experiment 1: Nursery School

Methods
The field experiment was conducted in May 2022 at a nursery school in Kanagawa, Japan. This school has approximately 100 infants and toddlers from 0 to 6 year in age. Less than 20 children were present in each grade. Slack has been used for daily communication in the nursery system since FY2020, and by the time the field experiment was conducted, the Slack application had been installed on most of the personal smartphones of the nursery teachers.

From May 16 to May 24 (7 working days), a total of five teachers (four full-time teachers and one part-time teacher) in the 1-year-old class (16 children) were asked to wear an Apple Watch in the morning. Five iPhones paired with the watches were placed at various locations in the room. Because all iPhone apps were set to post to the same Slack channel, when a teacher pushed a button from her watch, videos from all five cameras were posted.

After the experiment, a questionnaire consisting of the TSRI, TAM, NPS, and free-text fields was given out.

Results
Prior to the experiment, the following six preset terms for the watches were determined through a discussion among the participants: **biting, injury, near-miss, good attitude, difficulty, other**.

The results of the questionnaire are presented in Table 2. In the table, the number of posts per person during the entire experiment period is counted. The max score indicates the sum of the highest scores for all questions.

Table 2. Results of the questionnaire given out at the nursery school

	Average	Standard deviation	Max score
TSRI: Insight	10.8	5.50	21
TSRI: Exploration	9	3.39	21
TSRI: Comparison	9.6	2.88	21
TAM: Perceived Usefulness	17.2	11.56	42
TAM: Perceived Ease of Use	14	8.69	42
TAM: Behavioral Intention	8.6	7.37	21
Public posts	21.2	16.78	
Private posts	3.4	2.70	
NPS	−80%		

For the TSRI, TAM, and NPS, the higher the score, the better the system is; however, for the nursery school experiment, the score was less than half of the full score. In particular, the average score for "TAM: Perceived Ease of Use" was extremely low at 14 (out of 42), indicating a difficulty in using the system.

In this field experiment, we chose items from a free-text section that we considered to be issues of our video reflection system. Sc1 to Sc5 indicate the IDs of the experiment participants.

Input Difficulty

> ⎧ Participant statement ⎫
>
> – [Sc5] Although the voice input was convenient, it required taking my eyes off the child to see if the letters were converted correctly. Furthermore, the child's name almost never converted correctly, and often resulted in a different word when redoing the task.

Although the standard method provided by Apple Watch was used for the input, particularly the voice input, many of the experiment participants complained of the difficulty of pressing the completion button or the inaccuracy of the voice input.

However, a preset text was rarely used in the nursery school experiment, and voice recognition was extensively applied. When we asked individually why the use of the speech recognition, which has a low accuracy and is prone to problems, was so predominant, one nursery teacher stated, "I wanted to include the child's name at least because it is difficult to find the video later when looking back based only on preset sentences." However, from an implementation perspective, recognizing proper nouns such as the children's names is particularly difficult, and with current technology, the accuracy of such recognition is quite low.

Difficulty in Viewing

> **Participant statement**
>
> – [Sc1] Although I learned to capture a video, it took time and space to look back on it, and unfortunately I could not find the time to do so. [Sc5] Pressing "Share video" sends all videos from each camera to Slack at once, making it difficult to look back on the huge number of videos recorded each day.

In the field experiment, five iPhones were used and set to post to the same channel. Therefore, if any user conducted a shared video posting operation, the videos captured by all iPhones were posted to Slack simultaneously. Although this concept is based on a prior request from a participant who was concerned that a single camera would create blind spots, the technique may make it difficult to view the videos because many of them flow into a single timeline. The Slack video posted here was viewable on a Chromebook installed in class; however, the Chromebook was typically installed on a wall, and because using a mouse on a vertical wall is difficult, it was unsuitable for viewing each video in detail while moving the slider.

Although not shown here, some of the respondents wanted to see the video not only before but also after the button was pressed.

Operational Issues at the Facility

> **Participant statement**
>
> – [Sc2] I was unable to view the video during the workday. I was also busy after the workday, so it was difficult to view them then, and there was a lack of time for staff to reflect on the situation.

In a 1-year-old class, watching over the children without interruption is necessary.

Furthermore, the CT is affected by the timing of parent pick-up or when the teachers have to spend the entire working time with their children, making it difficult to ensure an available time for a video review during the ordinary workflow. This issue should be discussed with the managers to allow some time to be set aside for viewing the videos.

4.4   Discussion Regarding Nursery School Experiment

Issues emerging from the results of this field experiment are as follows:

- Difficult to search through and view the videos taken
- Inadequate speech recognition precision
- User interface with safety concerns for children
- Lack of time for reflection

To address these issues, the following future improvements are desirable:

- Develop a user interface that allows users to freely move back and forth on the video timeline from start of the recording, and find meaningful parts of the video through an analysis.
- Develop superior speech recognition technology or user interface to facilitate the input of the children's names, such as the use of expanded preset text buttons.
- The use of input devices other than an Apple Watch, as well as physical buttons or gestures that can be operated without interrupting the monitoring of the children.
- Ensuring NCT

In addition to these items, the lack of feedback from other staff members regarding information sharing through Slack is another problem. Although reflection involves reviewing one's own data, reflection from a different perspective has been attempted through the sharing of data with others [14, 16, 20, 26].

As a possible reason why our video review system did not stimulate feedback, although the facility had been using Slack on a daily basis, the message frequency was not high, and daily and casual messaging among staff members was conducted through another service (LINE). Therefore, options other than Slack should be considered. As another possible reason, an online discussion of the shared videos had not been part of the daily on-site activities of childcare workers. Therefore, effort should be made to raise awareness, such as by holding reflection workshop sessions on how to utilize the videos.

4.5   Field Experiment 2: After-School Daycare Service

Methods. The after-school daycare service considered in this field experiment is in Okinawa, Japan and has 5 staff members and 16 children (13 boys and 3 girls) between the ages of 3 and 12. Thus, the number of children per staff member is approximately 3. For this field experiment, only one iPhone and one Apple Watch with VisRef installed were sent to the field, and the participant (classroom leader) was asked to install and operate the system. A tutorial on how to use the system was given on September 20, 2022, and the system was put into operation on the following day. No customization of the preset text buttons was conducted. The experiment did not have a definite end period.

The results of this experiment were reported online by the classroom leader on October 11, 2022, followed by a survey of the classroom leader who directly operated the Apple Watch and a staff member who referred to the video and participated in the review.

An individual online interview was conducted with the classroom leader, who has approximately 8 years of experience in social service facilities, 5 in after-school daycare and 2 as a classroom leader. The individual is a certified caregiver, level 2 helper, social worker, high school teacher, and childcare worker.

The points of the interview were set as follows.

- Work schedule
- Video review before introduction of VisRef
- Usage Forms of VisRef
- Effectiveness of VisRef

As the reason for including the item on the work schedule, we hypothesized that the major difference from the nursery schools could be attributed to the length of the NCT. Questions regarding the video review prior to the introduction of VisRef were included because the initial results reported by the classroom leader stated that this facility was already conducting video reviews prior to the experiment.

Results

Three participants responded to the questionnaire. A comparison with the results of the experiment conducted in the nursery school is presented in Table 3. Here, n = 5 for the nursery school and n = 3 for the after-school daycare service. In the after-school daycare service, the Apple Watch trigger was input by only one participant. In the table, the max score indicates the sum of the highest scores for all questions.

Table 3. Comparison of survey results between nursery school and after-school daycare

		TSRI			TAM			NPS
		TSRI: Insight	TSRI: Exploration	TSRI: Comparison	TAM: Perceived Usefulness	TAM: Perceived Ease of Use	TAM: Behavioral Intention	
Nursery School	Average	10.8	9	9.6	17.2	14	8.6	-80%
	Std. Deviation	5.50	3.39	2.88	11.56	8.69	7.37	3.21
After-school daycare	Average	18.3	18.7	20	30	30	16	33%
	Std. Deviation	3.06	2.08	2.31	8.96	6.43	3.51	4.36
	Max score	21	21	21	42	42	21	11

	Total Posts (private posts)	Number of posts without movie	Days of Experiments	Number of people with watch	Post # per (day*person)
Nursery School	106 (17)	36 (5)	6	5	3.53
After-school daycare	107 (0)	0(0)	21	1	5.10

In the top table, red cells represent the average values. Compared with the nursery school, most of the items achieved scores approximately double those of the after-school daycare service, which revealed a higher level of satisfaction with the system.

The bottom table presents details of the posts. The number of subjects was small (five for the nursery school and only one for the after-school daycare service), and 3.53 and 5.10 posts were added per person per day, respectively. Neither private nor text-only posts were observed for the subject in the after-school daycare service. For the nursery school subjects, notably, the ratio of the total posts to text-only posts was almost the same for both public and private posts (about $\frac{1}{3}$). However, although most users of the public posts applied both with-movie and text-only posts, users of the private posts used only one type of post.

The facility was open five days a week on weekdays, and the work schedule was as follows:

10:00 Conferences among staff members while reviewing the business records, etc.

10:15 Each does the job for which he or she is responsible. Documentation, cleaning and disinfecting equipment, purchasing snacks, preparing for other activities.

12:00 Break. Lunch on one's own

13:00 End of break

14:00 Start of individual child pick-up

16:10 All children gather

16:30 Start of group activity

17:10 End of group activity

17:30 Wrap-up meeting, followed by individual transportation home.

19:00 The official closing time of the facility. Although the hours may be extended when children have unresolved issues, when individual attention must be given to the parents, or when associated record keeping duties occur, the work time ends by 7:30 p.m. at the latest.

As a difference between the nursery school and daycare center, the CT with the children is 5.5 h, from 14:00 to 19:30 at the longest, and the NCT is 4 h, from 10:00 to 14:00. These times differ considerably from those of nursery schools. However, because the program targets children with disabilities, the difficulty of work during NCT differs from that of a nursery school. Therefore, a simple comparison cannot be applied.

Next, we received a few remarks from the results of the question regarding the video review given prior to the introduction of VisRef.

Video Review Prior to Introduction of VisRef

┌─ Participant statement ───

- "The staff members have a habit of taking out their smartphones as soon as they want to record something. We have a lot of videos. Although they move the data to our shared computer hard drive within a week, we're running out of storage space."
- "We take a lot of videos when we're doing exercises. We sometimes assess the way the children move their bodies during the exercise. I consider not only panic and emotional factors, but also the way they move their legs, their posture, and other factors."

└──

As mentioned, the facility had been reflecting on captured videos prior to our experiment. They had also captured so many videos that they were required to organize them by file name, and were running out of hard disk space. The reason for this measure was the necessity for after-school daycare services to record emotional or motor impairments and sharing them with the parents. However, taking photographs with hand-held smartphone cameras changed the children's behavior. When they wanted to capture the facial expressions of the children, they occasionally placed their smartphones in their breast pockets and captured the images without the children noticing.

Next, we asked how they used VisRef, a fixed-point camera. The following statements were made regarding the shooting conditions.

How to Record with VisRef

┌─ Participant statement ───

- I don't really have a concrete reason for pushing the buttons of VisRef. I do this when people gather and something is likely to happen. I often push them with a sense of excitement, hoping to discover something.
- I use a combination of VisRef and a hand-held iPhone... When we want to see a facial expression of children, we place the iPhone in our pockets and look at it. Another staff member is behind me, hiding while approaching, and we are all using the method well together.

└──

Notably, rather than pressing a button after a specific scene to be recorded, the participant recorded the video in advance when she thought something was likely to happen at the time, and then analyzed the video clip to find the occurrence later. If the videos obtained from VisRef are used to search for information that was overlooked during on-site activities, this type of operation can be used.

The size of the facility is small, with only one room. In addition, no major problems were observed when leaving the watch on the desk in the same room and pressing it whenever the user felt the need to do so, rather than wearing it on her wrist. Because it is difficult to read the facial expressions of each individual in the overhead video provided by VisRef, videos were still captured using hand-held cameras or smartphones placed in the users breast pockets.

The next question is regarding information captured by the fixed-point camera. First, many comments were made regarding the individual children, particularly the fact that the camera could capture their natural appearance when not being pointed at them.

Subject of Observation in VisRef: Individual Child

Participant statements

- Some of the children will notice if we are taking a normal video and some will cringe. At these moments, VisRef is useful. It allows the natural behavior of the child to be captured.
- (Taking videos of children having fun) That's a lot of it. ...because we have to assess how the children are involved when the adults are not there. I think it's different when adults are there, and friendships are being formed.
- After all, we know what it's like to talk about things like this in the absence of adults...

In contrast to the previous method using a hand-held smartphone, in which the children are aware that they are being filmed and occasionally change their behavior, the children did not know when they were being filmed using VisRef, which allowed the system to capture more natural scenes. VisRef also rendered it possible to observe children helping each other in the absence of adults, which was desirable.

Some of the participants commented that VisRef had an advantage when a notable event occurred, allowing a specific child as well as his/her relationship with the surroundings to be filmed.

Subject of Observation in VisRef: Relationships Between Children

┌─ Participant statements ──────────────────────────────────────

- Some of the children already have a negative feeling when other children are being scolded, even though they themselves are not. If there is a crying child, another child may bring him or her a tissue. ...I've recently come to realize that it's not only the child who is receiving instruction, and the reactions of those around the child are also quite important. When we use VisRef, we can capture such scenes.
- When we are teaching, we are mostly focused on the child, looking at his or her expression and wondering how much they understand, or whether they are getting the message. Using VisRef, however, I realized that the reactions of those around them are also very important.

└──

During field activities, cognitive resources are utilized in dealing with the child in front of the caregiver. Therefore, the awareness of events taking place in the background is low. However, as an advantage of VisRef, we can recognize signs of a child's nature and development, and we can subsequently reflect upon them.

As another benefit of the proposed method, the caregivers could observe not only the children but also themselves and other staff members.

Behavior of Staff

┌─ Participant statements ──────────────────────────────────────

- I am not very aware of the staff, so I use it to see what they are saying and doing. Until now, we have never photographed the staff.
- (Regarding the staff's resistance to being filmed,) We don't have that. ...We pretty much share our values...We're an easy team to work with now.
- Just as children become tense when they realize they are being photographed, we also become tense. We are human beings, and we tend to say too much at times.

└──

When taking images of an object we want to record at work, we tend to only record the object. However, for the purpose of reflection, it is important to know how the teacher dealt with a certain situation, and the bird's eye camera was beneficial for this purpose.

The participant also described her perspective on information recorded in VisRef.

View VisRef Information

⎡ Participant statements ⎤

- At 10:00 a.m., the staff first looks back over yesterday's work diary. We discuss how we handled the situation yesterday, why it did not go well, and how we will handle it from today onward. At such times, we all look back at the video on our smartwatches and reflect on how we handled the situation.
- To be honest, I still find it difficult to do so every day. When I have meetings (or other commitments), I occasionally end a 15-minute meeting (in the morning) by just standing around and talking.
- I have to evaluate the support plan every day. When I look back, I think, "Oh, wait a minute, this VisRef might have taken the picture."
- Sometimes, we review the images during the morning meetings.
- We also thought it would be inappropriate to spend so much time reviewing the videos and neglecting the work that needs to be done, so we told everyone that they didn't have to do everything.
- When I can afford it, I look at it. I think VisRef is just a support tool for our job, and thus I also think that it is not right to focus too much on it.
- (In terms of the time spent on looking back on a video compared to shooting in a hand-held style with an iPhone,) it's the same.
- I would try watching it at 2x speed for the time being. If it feels strange, you can always try to watch it again.

4.6   Discussion of After-School Daycare Field Experiment

The response at the after-school daycare centers was generally positive. As in the case of the daycare centers, we only explained how to operate the system at the beginning and did not provide any instructions or requests on how to operate the system during their daily activities. However, the videos were filmed on a daily basis, and although not every day, the videos were frequently used in discussions at the beginning of the workday. The main findings are summarized below.

- Even before the field experiment, a 15-min review of the previous day's activities was conducted sporadically starting at 10:00, and a video review without VisRef was conducted during this time.
- Because they were already capturing videos and using them to reflect on the situation to better observe the children's behavior, the meaningfulness of VisRef was explored along with the difference from the existing video reflection approach.
- The differences could be attributed to the fact that VisRef captures videos at all times, rendering less frequent disruptions of the children's natural behavior.

– Meetings with the parents are a milestone for teachers. Videos are expected to be used to gather information for this purpose.
– The button was not pressed when an event that they wanted to look back on occurred but was pressed when they thought a notable event was *about to happen*, and subsequently the users searched for meaningful situations in the video. Even with such uncertain use, notable behaviors were found.
– The shifts indicate that the NCTs are long. However, the NCTs are not comparable to those of the nursery school because the amount of work to be conducted during an NCT is not compared.
– No supporting words were obtained from the interviews regarding the effectiveness of the video reflections achieved by VisRef and whether a change occurred with or without an NCT. This phenomenon could have occurred because it is self-evident to the workers in the daycare center that long periods of NCT will occur.

5   Comprehensive Discussion

The results of the two experiments revealed that video reviews are easily accepted in certain fields while not easily accepted in others. Although these two fields are both childcare institutions, differences exist in many aspects, including institutional, operational, and personnel problems. A comparison of some of the items is as follows:

Element	Nursery School	After School Daycare
Video reflection in advance	Not performed	Performed
Voice transcription	Used	Not used
Difficulties in video viewing	Yes	Not mentioned
Safety concerns	Yes	No
TSRI (possible 63)	29.4	57
TAM (possible 105)	39.8	76
NPS (possible 100%)	33%	–80%
Children types	Mostly able-bodied	Disabled
Proportion between adult and children	1:4	1:3
Age range	1–2	3–12
Staff attributes	Mostly nursery teachers	Diversified
NCT (Non-contact Time)	Short	Long

Because of varying differences, narrowing down the direct factors of success or failure among the TSRI, TAM, and NPS is not possible. However, we list below those factors that we subjectively noted based on the free-text sections of the questionnaires and individual interviews.

- **Need for a detailed observation of the child** An after-school daycare is a rehabilitation and education facility for children with disabilities and requires a professional understanding of the child's situation and detailed explanations provided to the parents. Therefore, a high level of motivation is to include cameras to objectively assess the condition of a child.
- **Familiarization with video review activities** This was the first video retrospective to be conducted at the nursery school where the experiment was performed, and the participants were likely perplexed. By contrast, the after-school daycare services were already routinely filming and discussing situations using videos captured by smartphones and other devices, and the participants were aware of the limitations of existing filming methods (e.g., changes in attitude of the children when a camera is pointed at them).
- **With or without voice recognition** In many cases, the nursery school tried to use voice recognition extensively to distinguish the children and were bound by its performance. By contrast, in the after-school daycare, voice input was rarely used, which reduced the stress while using the system.
- **Time constraints: viewing and reviewing** Several of the nursery school participants commented that they could not find adequate time for viewing the videos. In the after-school daycare, while having longer NCTs, some videos were not viewed.

The system was not intended to be prioritized over more important discussion topics. Because the 15-min review they had been conducting before our system was introduced remained unchanged, this operational knowledge may have also reduced the stress of the video review.

5.1 Areas for Future Improvement

To solve these problems, the items we consider necessary and the requirements for the experimental environment are as follows:

- **Better video viewer** Currently, the length of a video is limited, and videos can only be viewed on Slack. These concerns have caused viewing difficulties. In the future, we hope to record a full-day's video and use the timings when the trigger was pressed as bookmarks. If navigation from a marked time toward the past or future direction, or a fast playback, can be smoothly performed, stress from browsing could be reduced. Furthermore, videos can be analyzed using AI or other means to easily find meaningful moments. Although the system can synchronize multiple cameras and extract videos simultaneously, this feature increases the number of videos posted and renders viewing more difficult. A feature that automatically selects a critical viewpoint can be developed to reduce the stress of viewing.
- **Trigger input device** A non-Apple Watch input system that requires less cognitive resources is desired to reduce the burden during field activities. For example, devices with only physical buttons can be used.

– **An alternative to Slack that facilitates live discussions should be developed for information sharing.** In both fields, staff members used LINE rather than Slack on a daily basis. By selecting a sharing backend that suits the field, online communication can be made more active.

– **The method used to efficiently input a child's name tag** Although nurseries have extensively used voice recognition to include children's names, the precision is not good as expected. Therefore, a voice recognition capable of recognizing children's names, or a device with a user interface that allows an efficient input of their name tags, even with the use of buttons, would make the system more easy to use and the search for data more practical.

Before and during the experiment, the participants should be made aware of the following:

– Provide an explanation of the benefits of video reflection and how it has operated in other experiments.

– Even in fields with significant time constraints, have the users allocate as much as time and equipment (e.g., a computer) as possible to review the records while using VisRef every day.

– The accuracy of the voice recognition is not very high, and preset text buttons can be used.

6   Conclusion and Future Work

In this study, field experiments were conducted using our proposed VisRef video reflection system at two childcare facilities. Considerable differences were observed between the two types of fields, providing considerable insight into the requirements for acceptance of the video review system. This discussion focused only on the limited aspects of the childcare environments. Other factors, such as leadership and staff disposition, were not explored, despite some field personnel indicating such influences.

The number of participants of the experiment was small, and we relied on qualitative interview results. Statistically valuable analysis results were not sufficiently evaluated. In the future, we can expand the scale of the experiment, increase the number of standardized questions provided, and reduce the number of verbal interviews to strengthen quantitative evaluation.

Limited cases of video-based reflection have been recorded under childcare settings. However, an objective understanding and improvement of on-site activities of childcare workers are essential for improving the quality of childcare services. We will continue to improve the system based on the findings of this study.

All childcare service providers should not only provide an application for video reviews, but also hold workshops and plan other activities to help their childcare staff realize the benefits of such a system and reflect on the findings in their future on-site activities. This aspect of the study will be explored in the future.

Acknowledgements. We are sincerely grateful to the staff and children at Kuraki Nagata Nursery School and Shuhoukai Tomishiro Classroom for participating in the experiment. This study was supported by the JST-Mirai Program, Japan, Grant Number JPMJMI22H3.

References

1. Bentvelzen, M., Niess, J., Wozniak, M., Woźniak, P.: The development and validation of the technology-supported reflection inventory. In: CHI 2021: CHI Conference on Human Factors in Computing Systems, pp. 1–8 (May 2021)
2. Bush, V.: As we may think. The Atlantic Monthly **176**(1), 101–108 (1945)
3. Child Care Division, Child and Family Affairs Bureau, Ministry of Health, Labor and Welfare, Government of Japan (日本政府厚生労働省子ども家庭局保育課): The situation surrounding childcare (保育を取り巻く状況について) (May 2021)
4. CoDMON, I.: CODMON. https://www.codmon.com/
5. Davis, F.D., Bagozzi, R.P., Warshaw, P.R.: User acceptance of computer technology: a comparison of two theoretical models. Manage. Sci. **35**(8), 982–1003 (1989)
6. Dewey, J.: Experience and Education. Simon and Schuster, New York (1938)
7. Faisal, M., Bourahma, A., AlShahwan, F.: Towards a reference model for sensor-supported learning systems. J. King Saud Univ. Comput. Inf. Sc. **33**(9), 1145–1157 (2021)
8. Gurrin, C., Smeaton, A.F., Doherty, A.R.: LifeLogging: personal big data. Found. Trends® Inf. Retr. **8**(1), 1–125 (2014)
9. Healey, J., Picard, R.W.: StartleCam: a cybernetic wearable camera. In: Digest of Papers. Second International Symposium on Wearable Computers (Cat. No.98EX215), pp. 42–49 (October 1998)
10. Hodges, S., Williams, L., Berry, E., Wood, K.R.: SenseCam: a retrospective memory aid. In: Proceedings of the 8th International Conference on Ubiquitous Computing 4206, pp. 177–193 (September 2006)
11. Hong, S.B., Broderick, J.T.: Instant video revisiting for reflection: extending the learning of children and teachers. Early Childhood Res. Pract. **5**(1) (March 2003)
12. Hwang, J.P., Wu, T.T., Lai, F.J., Huang, Y.M.: A sensor-assisted model for estimating the accuracy of learning retention in computer classroom. In: 2011 Fifth International Conference on Sensing Technology, pp. 650–654 (November 2011)
13. Isreb, S., Attwood, S., Hesselgreaves, H., McLachlan, J., Illing, J.: Synchronized video-review as a tool to enhance reflection and feedback: a design-based feasibility study. J. Surg. Educ. **78**(1), 1–8 (2021)
14. Kientz, J.A., Arriaga, R.I., Abowd, G.D.: Baby steps: evaluation of a system to support record-keeping for parents of young children. In: Proceedings of the SIGCHI Conference on Human Factors in Computing Systems, pp. 1713–1722. CHI 2009, Association for Computing Machinery, New York, NY, USA (April 2009)
15. Lamming, M., Flynn, M.: "forget-me-not" - intimate computing in support of human memory (September 1997)
16. Lin, J.J.W., Mamykina, L., Lindtner, S., Strub, H.B.: Fish'n'Steps: encouraging physical activity with an interactive computer game. In: UbiComp 2006: Ubiquitous Computing, 8th International Conference, UbiComp 2006, Orange County, CA, USA, 17–21 September 2006. vol. 4206, pp. 261–278. unknown (September 2006)

17. Ministry of Health, Labour and Welfare (厚生労働省): Survey and research on reducing the workload of child care workers in fiscal year 2022 project report (令和元年度保育士の業務の負担軽減に関する調査研究 事業報告書). Tech. rep. (2020)

18. Müller, L.: Pervasive monitoring to support reflective learning. In: Proceedings of the 2013 ACM Conference on Pervasive and Ubiquitous Computing Adjunct Publication, pp. 349–354. UbiComp 2013 Adjunct, Association for Computing Machinery, New York, NY, USA (September 2013)

19. OECD(2006): Starting strong II: Early Childhood Education and Care (2006)

20. Rivera-Pelayo, V., Fessl, A., Müller, L., Pammer, V.: Introducing mood Self-Tracking at work: empirical insights from call centers. ACM Trans. Comput.-Hum. Interact. **24**(1), 1–28 (February 2017)

21. Schön, D.A.: The Reflective Practitioner : How Professionals Think in Action. Basic Books (1984/9/23) (1983)

22. Shen, L., Wang, M., Shen, R.: Affective e-learning: using "emotional" data to improve learning in pervasive learning environment. Educ. Technol. Soc. **12**(2), 176–189 (2009)

23. Shin, G., Jarrahi, M.H., Karami, A., Gafinowitz, N., Lu, X.: Wearable activity trackers, accuracy, adoption, acceptance and health impact: a systematic literature review. J. Biomed. Inform. **93**(September 2018)

24. Storypark: Storypark. https://storypark.com/. Accessed: 22 Oct 2022

25. Walczak, N., Fasching, J., Toczyski, W.D., Papanikolopoulos, N.: Locating occupants in preschool classrooms using a multiple RGB-D sensor system. In: 2013 IEEE/RSJ International Conference on Intelligent Robots and Systems (IROS), pp. 2166–2172. unknown (November 2013)

26. Xue, M., Liang, R.H., Yu, B., Funk, M., Feijs, L.: AffectiveWall: designing collective stress-related physiological data visualization for reflection. IEEE Access (99), 1–1 (2019)

27. Yu, S., Kondo, K., Nakamura, Y., Nakajima, T., Dantsuji, M.: Learning state recognition in Self-Paced E-Learning. IEICE Trans. Inf. Syst. E100.D(2), 340–349 (2017)

28. Zhang, H.: Learning from Experience : The Use of Structured Video-Assisted Debriefing Among Nursing Students. unknown (November 2020)

Body-Centric Vibrotactile Display for Social Support During Public Speaking

Yulia Sion[(✉)] [iD], Sercan Selvi [iD], and David Lamas [iD]

Tallinn University, Tallinn, Estonia
yulia.sion@tlu.ee

Abstract. The expression and impact of social support have been studied over the years in different fields. The purpose of this study is a preliminary exploration of how to mediate social support through touch remotely by using a vibrotactile device during a public presentation. With this study, we aim to explore (1) what are the patterns of expressing social support through touch during public speaking and (2) how can these patterns be mediated through technology. Through the User Enactment method, we identified common ways of providing social support and when to express physical support during the public speaking scenario. We gathered insights on the perceived meaning and overall experience of receiving vibrotactile feedback as a form of social support during public speaking.

Keywords: Vibrotactile · Mediated touch · Wearable

1 Introduction

Public speaking is a common situation where people feel threatened and stressed. A study conducted by Furmark et al. [8] about social phobias identified public speaking as the most common social fear among the participants. A study by Dwyer & Davidson [5] showed that speaking in front of a group was chosen as the top fear, second after the fear of death. Touch coming from close friends and family might help to mitigate the potential influence of stress factors [7].

In today's global world it is not always possible to have our loved ones around, while human interactions are increasingly mediated through different technologies, often through screen-based interfaces. Although there is more proof that mediated touch can afford affective communication and resemble real touch, the sense of touch is still not well supported by the current communication systems [6]. Advancements in technology, especially Virtual Reality (VR), bring more attention to haptic feedback and haptic wearables. As Hamza-Lup et al. [9] mention, a range of commercial haptic wearable products is available today and the field is gaining popularity.

© The Author(s), under exclusive license to Springer Nature Switzerland AG 2023
M. Kurosu and A. Hashizume (Eds.): HCII 2023, LNCS 14014, pp. 167–179, 2023.
https://doi.org/10.1007/978-3-031-35572-1_12

Prior research on mediated touch technology investigated how vibrotactile feedback may enhance remote communication and make it more intimate and engaging [1], elicit various emotions and alleviate stress [11]. Other studies investigated the various vibrotactile actuation technologies and how they were perceived by users in terms of pleasantness and naturalness [4,12]. Nonetheless, more context-specific studies, such as public speaking, would be important to pursue to understand the nuances of perception and usefulness of mediated touch technologies. Our study focuses on providing social support over distance during public speaking and mediating it through body-centric vibrotactile feedback. The research is driven by two guiding questions:

- How do people express social support through touch in the public speaking scenario?
- How to mediate a subset of social support practices, specifically focused touch, through body-centric vibrotactile interfaces?

We conducted two user enactment studies to gather preliminary answers to our guiding questions. The first study was meant to investigate how people prefer to express and receive social support through touch during public speaking. In the second study, we piloted our prototype that simulated a gentle double tap on the left shoulder during the speech and at the end of the speech. The results from the first enactment study revealed preferable ways of providing social support, common parts of the body where the support was provided and when the tactile support is desirable. The prototype piloting showed that the vibrotactile feedback was generally perceived as a positive and useful experience but could have a stronger meaning if it was sent by a close friend or a partner.

These findings further our understanding of how wearable vibrotactile technology may mediate social support during public speaking. We will use these findings to develop a hypothesis for our future study.

2   Related Work

2.1   Touch and Social Support

Cutrona et al. [3] describe social support as the assistance available to a person due to their social bonds. Family members, close friends, co-workers, and the greater community are among the social relationships described in the concept of social support. Social support can be instrumental (e.g., borrowing a car), informational (e.g., giving advice), or emotional. Emotional support is when people show sympathy, care, value, or encourage each other and it can be expressed in various forms (e.g., a hug.) One of the great benefits of emotional support is reducing anxiety and other stress-related symptoms. Emotional support expressed through touch has the strongest effect on reducing stress. According to Morrison, social touch is "well-situated to act as a stress buffer" [15].

The most common meanings of emotional support include encouragement, praise, and emotional reflection [14]. Jones et al. investigated types of supportive touches and their meanings in social interactions [13]. Forty-one percent of supportive touches in close relationships are expressed with spot touches, pats, and squeezes. The support touches usually mean "It is OK", "Let me take care of you", or "I will be there for you". Moreover, in the study by Grewen et al. [17], the researchers demonstrated that the group of people who had partner tactile contact before public speaking exhibited significantly lower systolic and diastolic blood pressure, and heart rate increases than the no contact group. These findings are especially motivating for our study in the context of public speaking.

2.2   Remote Mediated Touch

Since the very beginning of mediated touch technologies history one of the primary goals for mediating real touch was to enable a sense of presence and connectedness in remote relationships, including conveying emotions and providing support [1]. The recent spike in VR research added another angle to mediated touch such as recreating real sensations in virtual environments for immersive experiences [9].

The majority of the studies are dedicated to developing conceptual "mediated touch" prototypes and exploring how these "mediated touches" are interpreted in terms of emotional meaning. Some examples include the Tactile Sleeve for Social Touch (TaSST) [10] and EmoEcho [20] to convey various emotions through vibrotactile feedback. The Force Jacket [4] and Shoulder Tap [19] are examples of prototypes meant to communicate emotions and real touch sensations (e.g., a hug) using force feedback. A recent study by Chan et. al showed a significant reduction in stress indicators (measured via EDA) for emotionally charged conversations between partners accompanied by mediated touch (a hand-held device that allows sending and receiving squeezes) compared to conversations without touch accompaniment [2].

Most of these prototypes are evaluated in controlled environments and lack context-dependent aspects of mediated touch and insights into what people think about being touched in a specific situation. Some researchers identified a great need in researching the mediated touch in ecological environments of a specific context [18]. To the best of our knowledge, there was no study conducted on mediated touch in the context of public speaking in a semi-controlled or fully ecological study.

3   Public Speaking Enactment

The goal of the Public Speaking Enactment was to understand how people provide social support in person and what elements of this interaction could be simulated with the help of technology. We chose User Enactment (UE) as our method. The UE allows to immerse users in the specific context through role play and investigate through observations how people deal with specific problems in context. Odom et al. claim that the approach helps to open up the dialogue about emerging trends and technologies and critically consider what they prefer and why [16].

3.1   Participants

Eight pairs from ten countries took part in the study (11 males, 5 females) with an average age of 26 (range: 20 to 36 years.) While the newest participants' relationship (duration of knowing each other) was six months long, the oldest one was four years. All pairs identified themselves as close friends who know each other well. The gender distribution for pairs was the following: five male-male, two female-female, and one male-female pairing. Participants were recruited by word of mouth at the student dormitory. The consent form was provided and signed before the session.

3.2   Procedure

In each session there were two participants - one would act as a speaker (SP), the other - as a supporter (SU). The vibrotactile feedback was not provided during this enactment. The session scenario foresaw the speaker giving a short speech of fewer than 400 words while watching a video that showed a conference room filled with an audience. The video was played on a big screen while in front of the speaker. The video started with the audience giving a standing ovation for the speaker and ended in the same way. The standing ovation, lasting around 20 s, was provided to give the second participant (a SU) a chance to engage in social support in a way they felt appropriate. Specifically, SUs were instructed to provide support to SP at any moment during the speech, before, or after, and in any way and as often as they see it was needed (Fig. 1).

Fig. 1. Participants during the Public Speaking Enactment session.

3.3   Data Collection and Analysis

A questionnaire was administered before the session to collect demographic information. Semi-structured interviews were used for debriefing, focusing on the feelings of both participants, facts from the role play, and in general the relationship between the participants and how they provide support to one another. The interview was structured around these main questions:

- What was the feeling/gesture that you were expecting? (to SP);
- Why did you decide to do the gesture you did? (to SU);
- Why did you touch that part of the speaker's body?(to SU);
- How did you feel after the touch? (to SP)

The role play was video recorded and the interview was voice recorded. The interviews were transcribed and coded by two researchers. The Thematic Analysis was used to analyze the text and to agree on common themes using the Affinity Diagram tool through several iterations of discussions and sorting.

4   Findings

4.1   When and How to Support

In four cases physical contact happened to provide support where three of them were provided on the upper back and one was provided as a high five. The rest of the support was provided as eye contact and various hand gestures (e.g., thumbs up). People who provided support with a physical touch on the back said that it "seemed natural", "it is a way of communicating to relax", it was "to back up a friend like you can do it".

For instance, SU1 gave a tap on the shoulder to the speaker at the end of the speech and mentioned that it "seemed natural". He also mentioned the following: "I probably wouldn't touch him during the speech. In a normal situation. I would have either, like, say 'Good Luck' at the beginning with like, a pat on the shoulder or something like that. And then I would congratulate at the end. But I wouldn't have interrupted him during the speech". The SP1 agreed that the physical contact during the speech felt disturbing. SU2 also gave a tap on a shoulder during the speech to express his support and mentioned that a pat on the shoulder "is like, bro, kind of a thing. Like... I'm trying to communicate, ask him to relax a little bit". SP2 on the other hand preferred eye contact as a way of support during public speaking. SU4 also gave a tap on the shoulder during the speech to the speaker and said that touching his friend's back was "to back up a friend like "you can do it" in a normal nonverbal way". SP4 mentioned that it made him feel "better". SU5 gave a high-five before the speech and right at the end of the speech. SU5 mentioned the following: "I was thinking hugging or fist bump. But I chose high-five because it is more you know, warm". SP5 said that those moments "felt good" and "...encouraging for me to get going". Even though the rest of the supporters did not provide physical support, they mentioned that they were considering it but were concerned to disturb the speakers from the speech.

We see that half of the participants provided physical support and the speakers appreciated it, especially when it was provided before and after the speech.

The physical contact provided during the speech was disturbing in one case and perceived positively in another case. Overall, all the speakers were looking for continuous support in a form of eye contact, thumbs up, or head nod to receive encouragement and approval. The most common gesture of physical support was a tap on the shoulder, given on the upper part of the back. This finding is consistent with the prior research on the common parts of the body for expressing support in social communication [13].

4.2 Why to Support

The speakers mentioned that receiving support from a friend during public speaking was "encouraging", and "motivating", and even helped them "to focus on the speech". This is consistent with the prior research on the benefits of social support in reducing stress and providing a feeling of connectedness [15]. For instance, the SP5 said, "I felt really good about that (eye contact) because I was looking at her constantly, I think and I like, looking at a familiar face who is supporting me". SP1 mentioned that looking at friends and focusing on them made him feel comfortable. SU2 who provided support with a physical touch on the back said that it was "to back up a friend like 'you can do it'". In one of the instances, the physical support during the speech was perceived as if the speaker did something wrong. In another instance, the mediated touch during the speech was perceived as "you are doing great". The physical support after the speech was perceived as "applause" and "good job" across all speakers.

The findings show that social support is desirable in the context of public speaking. At the same time, when it comes to providing real physical support it generates contradicting experiences when provided during the speech. Most of the speakers appreciate support in a form of a hug or a tap on a shoulder in real-life situations but they were concerned that such support could distract them from focusing on the speech. The real touch support requires a visible presence in the private space of a speaker which makes it more disturbing and less realistic in real-life public speaking scenarios. Since mediated touch can be provided discretely and social support is desired, we believe that it is worth investigating further how mediated touch is perceived before, during, and after public speaking.

5 Experiencing Mediated Touch

The goal was to explore the perceived meaning and overall experience of receiving mediated touch during the public speaking scenario. As in the first study, we used User Enactment as our method. Six participants received the mediated touch at the end of the speech, and the other six participants received it in the middle of the speech. The mediated touch was provided remotely by the researcher.

5.1   Apparatus

The prior work on mediated touch and social support and findings from our first enactment study motivated us to display the vibrotactile feedback on the upper back. The feedback was meant to simulate a gentle tap on a shoulder. The design of the prototype was motivated by prior research on creating a gentle tap on the upper back using vibrotactile feedback [1]. The prototype consists of eight ERM vibration motors that are connected to a NodeMCU (ESP8266) board and controlled over Wi-Fi. All motors vibrated simultaneously (250 Hz) twice for two seconds with a 1-millisecond delay. All of the components were placed on felt fabric (the motors faced the body directly), which was attached to a strap. The strap was made adjustable by using a hook and look tape for participants to feel more comfortable while wearing it. When activated, the prototype would connect to the wireless network and would be controlled via a web interface from a mobile device (Fig. 2).

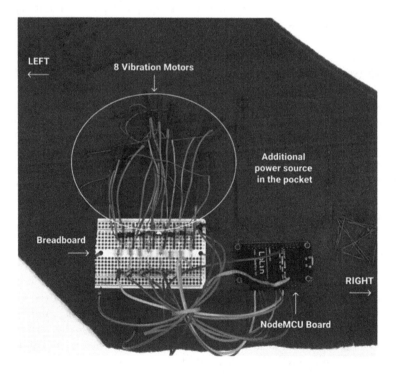

Fig. 2. The inner parts of the prototype.

5.2   Participants

Twelve people took part in this exploratory study (7 males, 5 females) with an average age of 34 (range: 25 to 44 years.) All were professionals with higher education or students in graduate school. Recruitment took place through social networks. Each session began with informing the participants about the task during the study. Before the study, the participants signed a consent form and completed a demographic questionnaire. These participants did not participate in the previous enactment study.

5.3 Procedure

The study procedure used the same setup and environment as the previous study but this time included the prototype and only one participant, the speaker without a supporter. The session began with informing the participants about the process and providing time for addressing any possible questions the participants might have. No information about the purpose of the prototype was given. Afterward, the participants were asked to read and sign a consent form. This was followed by filling out a short demographic questionnaire and having a brief discussion with the researcher about the participant's public speaking experience. Participants were introduced to the prototype before the role-play and received a test vibration to make sure the vibration was felt clearly. Then they experienced a public speaking role-play scenario wearing the prototype on their back (see Fig. 3). The speech was the same for all participants and it was given to the participants after the prototype was placed on their backs. Each participant had 2 min to read the text and prepare.

Six participants received one vibrotactile feedback at the end of the speech, and the other six participants received one vibrotactile feedback in the middle of the speech. The time and duration of the vibrotactile feedback were consistent for all participants. The vibration was sent by the researcher remotely who was present in the same room as the speaker. None of the participants knew when or how many times the stimuli were going to be provided. A semi-structured interview was conducted with all participants at the end of the session.

5.4 Data Collection and Analysis

The participants were asked to fill out a short demographic questionnaire, evaluate their experience with public speaking, rate the pleasantness of the vibration on a scale (one is not pleasant at all and five being very pleasant), and how they felt after receiving it on a scale (one being very tense and five being very relaxed). In a semi-structured post-study interview we asked the participants about their overall experience receiving the mediated touch during (group 1) and after the speech (group 2) and how they would feel if the vibration they received was coming from a close friend or family member. All sessions were video-recorded and the interviews were audio-recorded. The transcribed interviews were analyzed by two researchers using Thematic Analysis. The Affinity Diagram was used to agree on the common themes through several iterations of discussions.

6 Findings

6.1 Perceived Pleasantness and Relaxation

Sixty percent of participants reported that they felt anxious to present publicly in real life. Only two participants identified themselves as confident public speakers. Forty percent identified themselves as intermediate-level speakers, and the other 37 percent rated themselves as beginners. All participants (except for two of them) felt the study resembled a real public speaking experience and they felt nervous. 15 percent of the participants who felt the vibration during the speech rated it as pleasant, and 25 percent rated it as somewhat pleasant. 50 percent of participants rated the vibration as not pleasant during the speech. When the participants were asked how they felt after receiving the mediated touch during the speech, 25 percent said they felt somewhat relaxed, 15 percent felt relaxed, and 50 percent said they did not feel relaxed. One participant did not feel the vibration at all. Contrary, all participants who felt the vibration after the speech found it pleasant. When asked about how relaxed they felt after feeling the vibration, 80 percent said they felt relaxed and 20 percent rated it as neutral.

6.2 Perceived Meaning

Participants described the feeling of getting the vibration after their speech as "applause" and perceived it as if it "poked them back to the real world" and they can "kind of chill, relax". The participants who received the vibration during the speech interpreted it mostly as a corrective signal as if they "did something wrong", talked "too fast", or "too slow", or were "not understood by the audience". Both groups of participants stressed that the meaning of the vibration would differ if it was sent by a close friend or a relative. Then it would "symbolize a feeling" or "some sort of emotion". This is especially the case for those who received vibration during the speech. Most of them mentioned that if the vibration was sent by a close person they would interpret it as an "encouragement", "keep going", or "I am with you" type of meaning. The meaning of vibration would also depend on the nature of the relationship that they had with the sender. For instance, P8 and P10 mentioned that if the vibration was sent by the mother, it would be interpreted as something "positive and supportive". They also mentioned that if the vibration was sent by a friend or a trainer, then it would be interpreted as "a signal to correct".

6.3 Overall Experience

Generally, the participants who received the vibration after the speech did not find it disturbing but rather as positive feedback. On the other hand, the participants who received the vibration during the speech found it slightly disturbing. This was also observed in the videos where several participants paused the speech for a moment after receiving the vibration. None of the speakers, though, found it to negatively affect their quality of speech. The majority of the participants from

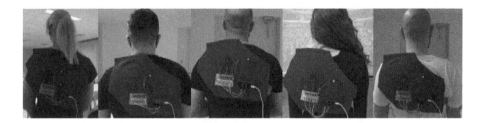

Fig. 3. Participants wearing the prototype

both groups saw the potential value in mediating touch at a distance, especially if it is sent by a close friend or a relative. P1 said that non-verbal interactions, such as touch, had "double, triple value" in helping her stay in touch with her close friends and parents living away. P3 considered it a good idea in the public speech scenario, because the significant other, whose support they would like to receive, "cannot be with them physically". P7 mentioned that such mediated touch support "is a way to bring them [family] closer". P4, on the other hand, said that giving control of your own body to someone else through technology might not be a convenient idea for every other daily use case. P7 and P9 mentioned that they would agree in advance with their close friend or family member on the specific moments to send mediated touch (e.g., speaking too fast or when diverting from the main topic).

7 Discussion and Future Work

The goal of the study was to conduct a preliminary exploration of how people express social support through touch in stressful situations and how to mediate tactile support by means of vibrotactile feedback.

The first study showed that social support is desired during public speaking and that a common body part for expressing tactile support specifically is the upper back (tap on a shoulder). Further, we found that the preferable time for receiving mediated touch (in terms of both relaxation and pleasantness) was after the speech. The mediated touch during the speech was somewhat distracting and perceived as corrective feedback. At the same time, the findings revealed that the nature of the relationship between the sender and the receiver of the vibrotactile feedback may make a great difference in the interpretation of the meaning of the received feedback and potentially the level of pleasantness and relaxation. If participants received the feedback from their close friend or a family member it would have been perceived as an "emotion" and a supportive gesture. This observation confirmed prior research that social touch is highly personal and perceived very differently depending on the degree of a relationship. An opportunity for future research is to explore how participants would react if the prototype was controlled by someone they choose. Based on these findings we can hypothesize that mediated touch sent by a close friend or a partner can be perceived as helpful and encouraging when sent not only at the end of the speech but also during the speech. We can also assume that depending on the nature of the relationship (a close friend vs a colleague) the mediated touch may have a different meaning.

We plan to test this hypothesis in our future study where we will invite pairs of close friends or partners one of whom will give a speech and another send the support. We then want to provide freedom of choice regarding the time of sending support and the ability to terminate this support at any given time. We will continue exploring the same body part (upper back) but will keep in mind that other body parts may be worth exploring. For instance, placing the prototype on the forearm could provide another research opportunity, because touching that part of the body was also seen as pleasant and is commonly chosen for providing a feeling of sympathy through physical touch. Designing other vibrotactile sensations (in addition to the gentle tap) is yet another direction for research. It is important to investigate and design a range of tactile sensations that could reliably communicate various meanings for more nuanced communication using mediated touch. Our hope is that this work will spark interest in the development of novel design, prototyping, and evaluation methods within the scope of body-centric computing.

8 Conclusion

We presented insights from two studies where we investigated the patterns of expressing social support through touch during public speaking and then explored how these patterns were mediated through a vibrotactile display. The results showed that continuous social support is desirable during a stressful situation and that vibrotactile feedback could potentially provide such support if sent by a close friend or a partner. As working, studying, professional and close relationships are increasingly moving to the remote format, the importance of technologies that foster a sense of presence between partners in personal and professional settings that goes beyond screen-based interaction is growing in importance. This research aims to contribute to the growing body of knowledge on mediating the sense of presence in remote interactions by means of haptic technologies.

References

1. Bonanni, L., Vaucelle, C., Lieberman, J., Zuckerman, O.: Taptap: a haptic wearable for asynchronous distributed touch therapy. In: CHI 2006 Extended Abstracts on Human Factors in Computing Systems. Association for Computing Machinery (2006). https://doi.org/10.1145/1125451.1125573
2. Chan, A., Quek, F., Yamauchi, T., Seo, J.H.: Co-verbal touch: enriching video telecommunications with remote touch technology. In: Proceedings of the 2021 International Conference on Multimodal Interaction, ICMI 2021, pp. 186–194. Association for Computing Machinery, New York (2021). https://doi.org/10.1145/3462244.3479924. https://doi-org.ezproxy.tlu.ee/10.1145/3462244.3479924

3. Cutrona, C.E.: Stress and social support-in search of optimal matching. J. Soc. Clin. Psychol. **9**(1), 3–14 (1990). https://doi.org/10.1521/jscp.1990.9.1.3

4. Delazio, A., Nakagaki, K., Klatzky, R.L., Hudson, S.E., Lehman, J.F., Sample, A.P.: Force jacket: pneumatically-actuated jacket for embodied haptic experiences. In: Proceedings of the 2018 CHI Conference on Human Factors in Computing Systems. Association for Computing Machinery (2018). https://doi.org/10.1145/3173574.3173894

5. Dwyer, K.K., Davidson, M.M.: Is public speaking really more feared than death? Commun. Res. Rep. **29**(2), 99–107 (2012). https://doi.org/10.1080/08824096.2012.667772

6. van Erp, J.B.F., Toet, A.: Social touch in human-computer interaction. Front. Digit. Humanit. **2** (2015). https://doi.org/10.3389/fdigh.2015.00002

7. Field, T.: Touch. MIT Press, Cambridge (2001)

8. Furmark, T., Tillfors, M., Everz, P.O., Marteinsdottir, I., Gefvert, O., Fredrikson, M.: Social phobia in the general population: prevalence and sociodemographic profile. Soc. Psychiatry Psychiatric Epidemiol. **34** (1999). https://doi.org/10.1007/s001270050163

9. Hamza-Lup, F.G., Bergeron, K., Newton, D.: Haptic systems in user interfaces: state of the art survey. In: Proceedings of the 2019 ACM Southeast Conference. Association for Computing Machinery (2019). https://doi.org/10.1145/3299815.3314445

10. Huisman, G., Darriba Frederiks, A.: Towards tactile expressions of emotion through mediated touch. In: CHI 2013 Extended Abstracts on Human Factors in Computing Systems, CHI EA 2013, pp. 1575–1580. Association for Computing Machinery, New York (2013). https://doi.org/10.1145/2468356.2468638

11. Huisman, G., Frederiks, A.D., van Dijk, B., Heylen, D., Kröse, B.J.A.: The tasst: tactile sleeve for social touch. In: 2013 World Haptics Conference (WHC), pp. 211–216 (2013)

12. Israr, A., Abnousi, F.: Towards pleasant touch: Vibrotactile grids for social touch interactions. In: Extended Abstracts of the 2018 CHI Conference on Human Factors in Computing Systems, p. LBW131. ACM (2018)

13. Jones, S.E., Yarbrough, A.E.: A naturalistic study of the meanings of touch. Commun. Monogr. **52**(1), 19–56 (1985). https://doi.org/10.1080/03637758509376094

14. Kindness, P., Masthoff, J., Mellish, C.: Designing emotional support messages tailored to stressors. Int. J. Hum.-Comput. Stud. **97**, 1–22 (2017). https://doi.org/10.1016/j.ijhcs.2016.07.010. https://www.sciencedirect.com/science/article/pii/S1071581916300866

15. Morrison, I., Löken, L.S., Olausson, H.: The skin as a social organ. Exp. Brain Res. **204**(3), 305–314 (2010). https://doi.org/10.1007/s00221-009-2007-y

16. Odom, W., Zimmerman, J., Davidoff, S., Forlizzi, J., Dey, A.K., Lee, M.K.: A fieldwork of the future with user enactments. In: Proceedings of the Designing Interactive Systems Conference, DIS 2012, pp. 338–347. Association for Computing Machinery, New York (2012). https://doi.org/10.1145/2317956.2318008

17. PhD, K.M.G., Anderson, B.J., PhD, S.S.G., PhD, K.C.L.: Warm partner contact is related to lower cardiovascular reactivity. Behav. Med. **29**(3), 123–130 (2003). https://doi.org/10.1080/08964280309596065

18. Smith, J., MacLean, K.: Communicating emotion through a haptic link: design space and methodology. Int. J. Hum.-Comput. Stud. **65**(4), 376–387 (2007). https://doi.org/10.1016/j.ijhcs.2006.11.006. https://www.sciencedirect.com/science/article/pii/S1071581906001911. Evaluating affective interactions

19. Stratmann, T.C., Sadeghian Borojeni, S., Heuten, W., Boll, S.C.: Shouldertap - pneumatic on-body cues to encode directions. In: Extended Abstracts of the 2018 CHI Conference on Human Factors in Computing Systems. Association for Computing Machinery (2018). https://doi.org/10.1145/3170427.3188624

20. Woodward, K., Kanjo, E., Burton, S., Oikonomou, A.: Emoecho: a tangible interface to convey and communicate emotions. In: Proceedings of the 2018 ACM International Joint Conference and 2018 International Symposium on Pervasive and Ubiquitous Computing and Wearable Computers, UbiComp 2018, pp. 746–749. Association for Computing Machinery, New York (2018). https://doi.org/10.1145/3267305.3267705, https://doi.org/10.1145/3267305.3267705

Designing an Evidence-based Mental Health Intervention Alongside University Students

Lucretia Williams[1]([envelope]) [iD], Melissa Pinto[1], Heather Abrahim[1] [iD],
Arpita Bhattacharya[3] [iD], Timothy Harrison[2] [iD], Candace Burton[1] [iD],
Jonathan McIntyre[1] [iD], Lobsang Tenzin Negi[2], and Gillian Hayes[1] [iD]

[1] University of California Irvine, Irvine, CA, USA
{lucretiw,habrahim,jrmcinty}@uci.edu, {mdpinto,cwburton}@hs.uci.edu,
gillianrh@ics.uci.edu
[2] Emory University, Atlanta, GA, USA
{timothy.harrison,snegi}@emory.edu
[3] University of Washington, Seattle, WA, USA
arpitab@uw.edu

Abstract. Digital mental health tools can help university students access cost-effective and timely resources for mental health challenges. However, direct involvement by university students during the design of these tools has been limited. Early involvement can help design teams understand how mental health applications can tailor support to student's unique needs alongside evidence-based interventions. We used a participatory design approach to understand how we might translate an in-person, evidence-based intervention into a mobile application for university students. Our findings indicate that students perceived the need for the application to (1) provide healthy reminders, (2) connect with peers and counselors, (3) support personalized experiences and (4) teach informational and instrumental life skills. We discuss implications for designing evidence-based mental health applications for university students to balance their need for customized support for self-help and professional help.

Keywords: Mental Health · Mobile Applications · University Students

1 Introduction

Over the last decade, the number of university students with mental health challenges has risen intensively, with mental health conditions like anxiety and depression being among the most common [83]. University students struggling with mental health are at increased risk for death by suicide—the second leading cause of death among university age students [80]—and a host of, economic, social, emotional [81], and long-term health consequences [82]. Social and economic challenges from the COVID-19 pandemic (e.g., public health mitigation efforts like social distancing, fear of contracting SARS-CoV-2, and loss of stable income) have resulted in higher stress and anxiety among students [66]. Students have reported further worsening of mental health since the start of full-time remote learning during the COVID-19 pandemic in March 2020 [63]. Additionally, students experienced isolation, worried over their academic progress, and were met with substantial financial burdens [66]. Students from communities that have been historically excluded from educational institutions and research, report higher levels of anxiety and depression than their non-underrepresented peers [67,68].

Prior to the pandemic, university counseling centers reported client loads at or near capacity with high demand for student services exceeding the available mental health workforce [87] leading to long wait times, treatment caps, and other measures to portion out limited resources. At the same time, many students do not seek treatment because they find services inappropriate for them [85] or prefer to manage their mental health independently [84]. Thus, poor access to and knowledge of timely and acceptable mental health services have left students without the mental health care they need [64].

Mental health apps are seen as a possible solution to the overwhelmed systems of care [5,13,86]. Counseling services are increasingly relying on digital mental health tools to supplement therapy and provide greater access to mental health resources [45,62,69]. Digital mental health applications are a promising approach for university students who tend to be tech-savvy and have quick access to these applications [5], in part because they are generally inexpensive and scalable [56].

The variety of digital mental health technologies offer a subset of timely, reliable, acceptable, and cost-efficient access to resources for university students [6]. Smartphone apps include resources for skill-development [7], cognitive behavioral therapy [70], mood tracking [9], and learning through gamification [8]. Virtual therapy is similar to in-person treatment in terms of patient satisfaction, number of sessions completed, cost and cost-effectiveness, and other clinically significant outcomes [71]. Using evidence-based strategies in digital interventions can support the mental health of students in engaging and accessible formats.

However, the usability and adoption of these tools lag behind student needs and expectations [57–61]. The reasons for this lack of uptake of tools that otherwise seem to be an excellent fit for the challenges are many and still somewhat unknown. In particular, mobile mental health applications were by and large not designed with the unique needs of university students in mind, and students tend to have poor views of them [47–49]. As just one example, in a study of 100 university students, all with smartphones, students reported that sharing clinical information was a key benefit but expressed concerns about privacy and cost [50]. Designing technologies for this population requires a better understanding of the unique needs of young adults and the social contexts within which they are situated.

In this work, we describe issues that university students consider when engaging with digital mental health applications. We sought to understand the challenges for the translation of an evidence-based in-person intervention named cognitively-based compassion training (CBCT®), to a scalable, digital format, particularly for university students experiencing anxiety and depression. CBCT is an in-person intervention that aims to improve mental health through building the skills of attention, thought examination, and cognitive-behavioral strategies all within the context of strengthening compassion through meditation [78]. We conducted a series of participatory design sessions with 20 university students to understand how they use and perceive existing technical and non-technical resources and envision support for their mental well-being. Our findings demonstrate that students perceived the need for (1) healthy reminders, (2) human connection with peers and counselors, (3) personalized experiences and (4) informational and instrumental life-skill building. We discuss implications for designing evidence-based mental health applications for university students to balance their need for customized support for self-help and professional help. This work contributes to the empirical understanding of design needs for evidence-based mental health tools for university students experiencing anxiety and depression.

2   Background and Related Work

In this section, we describe existing literature from within human-computer interaction (HCI) as well as other fields around the evidence-based mental health support for university students and how these intersect with interactive technologies.

2.1   Designing Digital Evidence-Based Mental Health Tools for University Students

The number of young adults with mental health difficulties attending university has considerably grown in the past decade [81]. Yet, university students report not receiving services at an alarming rate (e.g., as high as 37% to 84% depending on the concern in one study [46]). Administrative personnel at university counseling centers have difficulty with managing students with numerous co-occurring mental health conditions, as well as the usual developmental obstacles of adapting to university life [72]. As concerns of university students' mental health grow and mobile technological solutions become pervasive, HCI researchers [5,10] and health researchers [43,65,73] have been working to bridge the gap between the two.

University students with mental health concerns engage with a wide variety of coping and health management strategies to meet their needs [74]. Like many other people their age, they gravitate towards using applications on mobile devices for self-management and coping with their mental health [75]. These applications tend to be an affordable option [6] and help overcome mental health stigma [44]. Medical literature suggests that most young adults see mobile mental health apps as a viable alternative or adjunct to in-person services [76]. Individuals who self-manage their depression and other mental health conditions have also repurposed a variety of digital tools that were not specifically created for mental health, such as utilizing digital calendars and to-do lists [77]. In a focus group study, students identified personalization, tracking and feedback, live support, community, and providing motivational content and relaxation exercises as key features [43].

While some studies have examined the effectiveness of digital mental health tools, there are very few that focus on evidence-based mental health tools with the university student demographic. Despite their potential, the limited involvement of university students in the early design of these applications may have resulted in relatively low utilization by university students, an issue we sought to remedy with this work.

2.2 Participatory Design and Mental Health

In recent years, design researchers have increasingly used participatory design to create digital mental health tools and interventions. While it is not uncommon to design and evaluate early concepts or prototypes of mental health applications with clinicians (e.g., [20,21]), research studies that engage people with mental health challenges in the design process are few. A few researchers have discussed the difficulty with conducting participatory design activities with people experiencing mental health challenges [21] but by not doing so, we are missing out on documenting and understanding their lived experiences and challenges interacting with various digital mental health applications.

Participatory design has been commonly used for designing technical solutions with marginalized groups because it gives them a space and opportunity to communicate their opinions, and a sense of empowerment and responsibility to work collaboratively with professional researchers on a project that has the potential to significantly impact their community [18]. One study example aimed to provide technological solutions to foster peer support amongst young adults with mental health challenges were identified through the facilitation sketching and storytelling activities, and later asking participants to elaborate on it during interviews [1]. In another study, university students and counseling center staff participated together in co-design workshops, brainstorming features and access to a stress management tool [5]. They found the role in which peers and non-peers influence student interaction with digital mental health apps and they ways in which they would like to be educated about such tools.

The use of participatory design allows for knowledge exchange between the researcher and the participant's expertise. Findings from previous research investigating the use of technology to support university students' mental health strongly suggest that designing alongside them can provide better solutions that include their current practices and future goals to improving their mental well-being [2,5]. Therefore, we chose to use a participatory design approach to allow university students to act as subject matter experts in providing an evidence-based technological solution that can be a supplemental solution for their mental well-being improvement efforts.

3   Methods

This study was conducted as a part of a broader study focusing on the development and implementation of an evidence-based mobile application for university students experiencing anxiety and depression. In this study, we conducted a series of three participatory design workshop sessions that each centered on a specific design activity: (1) card sorting (2) storyboarding and user personas, and (3) designing mockups (low-fidelity prototypes). All the activities were conducted via Zoom video-conferencing platform and lasted for approximately 90 min.

Table 1. Participant Demographic Data

ID	Age	Gender	Race	Card Sorting (N=18)	Storyboarding (N=18)	Design Mockups (N=19)
P1	19	Female	Asian	X	X	X
P2	20	Female	Asian	X	X	X
P3	20	Male	White	X	X	X
P4	21	Female	Asian	X	X	X
P5	22	Male	Asian	X	X	X
P6	20	Female	Mixed	X	X	X
P7	21	Male	Mixed		X	
P8	25	Female	Asian	X	X	X
P9	25	Female	Mixed	X		X
P10	21	Female	Asian	X	X	X
P11	24	Female	Asian	X	X	X
P12	22	Female	Asian	X	X	X
P13	22	Female	Unknown	X	X	X
P14	21	Female	Asian	X	X	X
P15	21	Female	Unknown	X	X	X
P16	24	Female	Asian	X	X	X
P17	21	Female	Asian	X	X	X
P18	20	Nonbinary	Asian	X	X	X
P19	18	Female	Asian		X	X
P20	20	Female	Asian	X		X

Participants were recruited from the University of California Irvine through emails to university student listservs and student Facebook groups. This study was approved by the university's institutional review board prior to recruitment. There were a total of (N = 20) participants in this study who were between the ages of 18–25, majority female, and majority Asian (Table 1). For all three workshop sessions, we split the consented participants into four groups. Participating in all three design workshops was not required. All 20 participants were invited to all sessions, however, 16 of them attended all three sessions. The groups were reshuffled each session to prioritize participant scheduling and flexibility. Thus, each workshop activity included 4–6 participants but never the exact same 4–6 students, with some participants missing out on workshops due to scheduling conflicts. A total of 12 workshops (4 groups per workshop) which resulted in 18 h, 340.5 h of participant engagement in our data corpus. In the following sections we will describe each workshop activity in detail.

3.1   Card Sorting

The card sorting activity [51] enabled understanding of the hierarchy of students wants and needs in a mental health app specifically catered to their demographic. A total of 18 students participated in the card-sorting activities. Participants organized pre-made "cards" of potential features for a hypothetical mental health app. The potential mental health app features chosen for the pre-made cards were drawn from prior literature and research conducted surrounding mental health applications [43,55,77]. During the workshop, we used Whimsical[1], an online collaborative space. To protect their privacy, participants did not access the Whimsical board themselves as they remained anonymous during the study. The lead facilitator shared their screen with participants and moved cards on Whimsical to columns based on instructions from the participants. We asked participants to collaboratively discuss and vote together on whether a card, that had a potential app feature, should be placed in the following columns: (a) absolutely want to have, (b) potentially want to have, and (c) would not want to have. The students worked together as a group to place 20 cards across these categories. The card with majority votes was placed in its respective column. After completion of the card sorting activity, facilitators asked participants a series of questions surrounding their thoughts on certain potential app features.

3.2   Storyboarding and User Personas

The storyboarding activity [52] and creation of user personas [54] helped participants to visualize how they or a peer may want to ideally experience a mental health app. A total of 18 students participated in the storyboarding and user-persona activities. Each of these workshops began with participants collectively creating two user personas. We asked participants to think about the types of students that will "most likely use or be in great need of a mental health app geared towards students". Participants listed pain points, wants or needs, and goals for the persona [79]. After creating the two personas, participants collaboratively created a story on what an ideal experience would look like for a student to use a mental health app geared towards them. For this storyboarding activity, participants chose an app feature that a student would use based on the problem they have.

3.3   Design Mockups

Based on the two participatory design activities described in 3.1 and 3.2, the students designed a simple mockup [53] in response to the two most discussed

---

[1] Whimsical: https://whimsical.com/.

scenarios. A total of 19 students participated in the sessions to create design mockups. Participants were asked to choose between two scenarios to design a mockup for a mental health application: (1) finding a therapist in the app and (2) personalization features in the app. Each participant was given access to a design software called Canva[2], with a template to create their app prototypes. Participants also had the option to use their own design software or at-home materials to create their app prototype. Participants were given 45 min to design their prototypes following a series of questions asking participants their opinions and preferences on popular health apps on the market. Examples of these apps included Calm and the Nike app, mentioned by students during previous focus groups that were conducted as a part of the broader study mentioned at the beginning of Sect. 3.

3.4   Data Analysis

All twelve participatory design workshops were audio and video recorded and transcribed through Zoom video conferencing software and then manually corrected for transcription errors by the first and last authors. The lead workshop facilitator, also the first author, de-identified participant information from the transcripts and replaced participant names with their respective participant identification numbers. The workshop transcripts, storyboards, and designs prepared by participants were then analyzed by the first and last authors.

Each of the two coders read all of the transcripts independently to immerse themselves in the findings. They then met to discuss overall themes, identifying key aspects of the students' feedback and brainstorming: in-app reminders, virtual connection to others (e.g., peers, counselors), personalization (e.g., aesthetic, content), and knowledge of evidence-based resources. The researchers then analyzed the transcripts again with specific attention to these categories, coding them, and identifying evidence, in the form of both quotes and artifact exemplars, in each of these categories. Throughout this iterative process, the two coders met regularly to discuss their findings and analysis of specific exemplars. Finally, they each wrote memos detailing their findings both independently and collaboratively. These memos and the exemplars identified in this process, alongside those identified through the deductive coding, then became the basis of our results.

Our goal for this study was to understand the challenges for the translation of an evidence-based in-person intervention to a digital application format, by leveraging the CBCT evidence-based intervention throughout this study. We conducted a thematic analysis [19] of transcripts of the group conversation and artifacts they created. We used the elements of CBCT [78] as one lens for examining participant responses given its strong evidence-based in the area of mental health for university students. These elements included reflection on emotions, mindfulness, and attention and focus. However, emergent themes were also uncovered during this process as described in the results section.

---

[2] Canva: https://www.canva.com/.

4   Results

The results of our analysis indicate that students value a variety of social, informational, and active intervention support offered in a tiered and personalized fashion. Additionally, this support was seen to be most useful when delivered by using modalities of interaction most appropriate to their needs and contexts. In this section, we highlight key themes from these results: (1) healthy reminders, (2) human connection, (3) personalized experiences and (4) informational and instrumental life skills.

4.1   Providing Healthy Reminders

Building on existing mental health research, our participatory design activities were initially scoped to include some discussion around reminders and prompting of reflection and awareness activities [4,40–42]. We were particularly interested in using participatory design to address the mismatch between efficacy in research studies and reports from students in past participatory design work that mentions goal-setting or personal assistance to provide suggestions around goal-setting were not appealing nor necessary [43].

Reminders, in particular, emerged early in our design sessions as problematic for students. The stories they described while sorting their priorities in the card sorting exercises or developing their own designs, match the image of over-scheduled students we have seen increasingly represented in research about them. As students become more digitally connected [37], and as universities attempt to automate and move student services online [39], students will be increasingly interrupted by such reminders, which can be distracting and problematic [38]. Students in our workshops by and large viewed reminders as generally helpful, but the type of reminders being received matters. Notification prompts in the form of affirmations or reminders to relax or breathe would set a relaxing and encouraging tone in contrast to a notification prompting them to complete or start a task which can be seen as more daunting and intrusive. For example, one undergraduate student described their interest in being reminded of positive approaches:

> P20: You will be reminded to take the day in a very positive manner [...] Like, 'oh don't forget that', 'don't forget [to] take a breath', and things like that. And this one [reminder feature] kind of ties in a little bit with affirmations but I think the affirmations one is my personal favorite.

Instead of high volumes of generic reminders, the majority of students emphasized the need for tailoring the content of the reminder to their mental state (e.g., stressed and need to relax) and to indicate the time needed for attending to that content. This way, the reminders would be sensitive to the situational ability, increasing the chances that students can actually attend to it and the intervention is helpful (Fig. 1).

Fig. 1. A student design mockup displaying how they envision an affirmation being displayed in a mobile app.

4.2 Human Connection

As in prior work [36], human connection—in the form of both peer and professional support—was considered to be essential by workshop participants. Such support, traditionally offered through a mix of in-person counseling and support groups as well as online engagements, was particularly tenuous at the time of this study during the COVID-19 pandemic. Thus, it is perhaps unsurprising that students viewed technological supports as particularly advantageous to providing such human connection. In this section, we detail both their interests in and potential instantiations of such connectivity through mobile mental health tools.

Seeking Peer Support. During the COVID-19 pandemic in 2020–2021, when this research was conducted, students had little to no in-person social interaction with their peers. This put an even bigger strain on students who are starting their first year of undergraduate [34], graduate school or new transfers [35]. Students expressed wanting in-app capabilities to connect with peers anonymously in a forum-based setting. Students want such a peer-connected space for purposes of venting anonymously, listening to others' experiences, feeling heard, and connecting with mentors.

Students already naturally seek out information and experiences from their peers through searching various blogs and unofficial online closed student groups. A student described wanting to browse the online contributions of students who may have "issues similar to theirs".

> P7: To look for someone who had issues similar to theirs, and they can kind of read through their experiences and relate to their experiences and see how they ended up solving their problems or mitigating them.

However students recognized that the challenge of keeping such space for students to vent and share their experiences has to have a high level of anonymity and regulation to keep the environment safe. Having a space of this sort may expose a students' identity, depending on the information they choose to share.

University students have some advantages over other communities in that they typically spend time together, often live on or near campus, and have at least a minimal shared identity. Capitalizing on these connections should make provision of peer support possible in a way that appropriately engages notions of privacy and synchronicity. However, peer support alone is insufficient. Thus, technological platforms that engage this population must have a tiered-services approach that also engages mental health professionals.

Seeking Support from Therapists or Counselors. The students brainstormed self-help solutions but also acknowledged the need for professional support from a therapist or a counselor on an "as needed" basis depending on the context of their difficulty. Participants mostly expressed that having virtual access to counselors is necessary for students who really need to speak to a mental health professional rather than a peer. Friends and other peers may not be well equipped to handle certain situations and responses so they would want to receive guidance from a counselor. Professional support, particularly through on-demand digital services, was described as "an absolute must" (P11), particularly when provided by "reputable people" (P20).

Knowing when and how to access professional services can be difficult for students [46]. Students in our workshops spoke at length about the need for technological support to guide them through the "progression" of what they would need to schedule a virtual counseling appointment. More detailed instructions on how to access services, including but not limited to concerns around what information would be needed to book an appointment and what health insurance options are available (this study was conducted in the United States, which has limited financial support for mental health services). Students expressed that they are often caught off guard with the amount of personal information they needed to provide for virtual counseling services. For example, P16 described needing a checklist of sorts before starting to find professional services (Fig. 2):

Similarly, P13 described the need for technologies to help people to be in the right mindset for seeking and navigating support from a therapist to find a therapist-client fit.

> P13: This little blurb kind of talks about how finding a therapist takes time and to kind of have patience with that because I feel like that is something that is kind of difficult for folks to grasp sometimes like the first therapist isn't always the right therapist.

Thus, to reduce barriers to seeking therapy, students suggested that the app should reduce apprehensions by automatically flagging issues to encourage seeking professional help, provide scaffolds for steps to acquire information about what is needed to find therapists and book appointments, and set appropriate expectations.

Fig. 2. Example of student showing the steps they would like to see before choosing professional services (left) and the outcomes of therapists displayed after someone has gone through the process (right).

4.3   Support a Personalized Experience

Students were enthusiastic for a personalized app experience. Students described wanting self-help resources that focused on resources that are available to them locally and based on their needs. For example, during the storyboarding activity, participants predominantly presented features to personalize self-help resources and individualized activities such as a journaling space and an online community forum in response to a student dealing with high stress and anxiety. They explained such personalization would incline students to use and have continued engagement with the app. For example, one student described daily engagement in app as a goal of such a system (Fig. 3).

Additionally, students in our workshops described personalizing the aesthetics, information architecture, services offered, and other elements of interaction with the app. Students described wanting a calming and simplified aesthetic that they could customize such as picking out their own background colors, customizing dark and light modes.

Technological solutions that are translated from evidence-based practices, such as cognitive behavorial therapy or dialectical behaviorial therapy, often include guided interactions wherein the participants learn and "unlock" certain skills, step by step, to progress to the next module (e.g., [11]). This kind of gamification is a type of personalization in that the leveling is associated with past engagement. However, the effectiveness of this approach and the associated skill development may differ based on individual characteristics and preferences

Fig. 3. A student design that shows various goal setting topics to choose from in mobile app.

[3]. P8 suggested allowing participants to select options in the beginning, to let the user select their own pathways through the different activities in the mental health app.

The sheer volume of information produced by university counseling centers [12] can be overwhelming. Filtering, and other personalization solutions, can reduce the number of options within intervention modules and simplify the experience for each individual user. The feedback that too many options in a menu system might feel overwhelming is not in itself particularly surprising. What is notable here, is the tendency of both clinical design partners and the students themselves in our workshops tend to generate such long lists. As university counseling centers and other stakeholders race to make as much information and support available as possible, this tendency to pack menus and apps with information must be monitored carefully and addressed when possible.

4.4   Informational and Instrumental Life-Skill Development

The connection between satisfaction of basic needs and mental well-being has previously been considered but needs additional research [31,33]. Preliminary studies indicate that such a connection may have been exacerbated by the pandemic [32]. In our results, this connection was incredibly salient in the minds of participants. In every workshop, at some point the students turned the discussion to the importance of navigating the challenges of adult life, which were very new for some of them. Students described needing a variety of support, including both informational and tangible resources.

Informational support described in our workshops included the teaching of financial literacy skills, such as managing a budget, loan policies and practices, and tax filing. Time management, given the busy schedules of students, was a frequently discussed feature, particularly if such management could be tailored to their needs as described in the personalization Sect. 5.3:

Financial management concerns were just as popular as those related to time management, perhaps in part due to the challenges of transitioning from childhood to adulthood for this population as well as in response to the growing cost of university undergraduate and postgraduate education in the United States [15].

Beyond learning to manage resources, many students described needing more financial resources to even begin to need to manage them. In these cases, students may need instrumental and tangible support, such as acquiring emergency funds, in addition to the informational support that would help them to follow procedures or manage those funds once procured.

In this age of misinformation, students need ways to understand if the informational and instrumental support they find online is trustworthy [29,30], a particular challenge for low-income and first-generation students, many of whom are otherwise very high performing [16,28]. While students described these concerns to some degree regarding financial, time management, and other somewhat transactional needs, this concern about what information is trustworthy appeared to be even more salient for information and concerns around mental health in particular. When accessing information about mental health online, students spoke about wanting to verify whether the source of information was trustworthy such as from scientific sources.

P20: [...] but links, where you can scroll and see and see supported and well-cited sources, there were articles talking about it [mental health] in a very gentle manner, and I think being very compassionate about these topics are very important.

Students want to educate themselves about mental health and gain the skills needed to actively meditate and relieve stress. Consuming content activity in small, easily digestible portions are ideal for current university students. Thus, designing to support transitional needs of university students calls for combining emotional support with informational and instrumental support. These findings indicate that any intervention will have to be multi-layered, including both technological engagement as well as human and financial resource deployment.

5   Discussion

The tangibility of the design workshops provided participants the opportunity to not only comment on their general needs and perceptions of technological support for mental health but also to develop designs themselves. In this section, we build on participants' design needs and solutions to synthesize recommendations for the HCI community in adapting evidence-based mental health interventions.

5.1   Customizing Support for Self-help and Professional Help

Students requested therapy on an "as-needed" basis instead of seeking therapy at regular intervals (e.g., weekly). Such support is ideal when human support is augmented with machine intelligence. Automated mental health tools can guide them through evidence-based self-support skills, help them reflect on the context of their problems, suggest when they might need help from a professional counselor, and assist them with informational support to find one.

This approach can guide the user in moving back and forth between self-help and professional support. However, there are real-world constraints to implementing and integrating such a solution with existing mental health systems on campuses [87]. Ad-hoc therapy from professionals is accessible through telehealth options (e.g., [90,91]). However, students may experience financial barriers in accessing these online resources, particularly in the United States where this work was conducted and access depends on insurance. Understanding the feasibility of integrating university mental health and counseling services with mobile tools requires a broader understanding of the human and digital ecosystem into which such tools might be introduced.

Between truly automated digital support and on-demand professional engagement, there may be an important middle ground: technologically supported and mediated peer support. Peers who know how to successfully navigate the mental health system or have some training as peer counselors can act as a bridge between self-help and professional support. For example, some universities have peer educator programs for well-being [89], but even peer programs struggle to scale to the level of need present on campuses. Our findings suggest that machine-enabled personalization and prompting, may enable improved, sustainable, and scalable peer support, such as that seen in other domains (e.g., [26,27].

Algorithmic approaches can tackle many customization challenges, but they require a huge amount of personal data collection, such as tracking usage patterns within the app or on the phone more broadly, geo-location, and even personal content of messages, phone calls, and voice recordings (e.g., MoodRhythm [17]). Researchers and designers should engage in discussions and practices around the protection and use of such sensitive personal data, only some of which is protected in the US by rules governing health data [88] or educational data in the case of university students [92]. For European students [95] or those living in states in the US with their own privacy laws (e.g., California [94] and Massachusetts [93]), these trade-offs may become even more complex for designers to understand and meaningfully engage. Privacy and ethics around such data use becomes even more consequential when these systems are scaled beyond research studies.

Providing options for anonymity and regulations on online peer support groups can help, but institutions need to be mindful about staffing human moderators, either peer leaders or professionals, to maintain a safe online space [14]. Beyond the opportunities and challenges associated with data collection for personalization, students may inherently struggle with the need for support from other people and the commensurate need to share personal and private information with those people. Based on the empirical understanding from this study, we list recommendations for designers to consider when creating digital evidence-based mental health interventions for students (Table 2).

Table 2. Design takeaways for student mental health.

Self Help
1. Provide students with app notification reminders that reflect their current mental health journey and/or mental state. Try to minimize generic reminders as much as possible.
2. Design for engagement by using AI capabilities to allow for greater personalization of information and goal completion (e.g. recommender system).
3. Address concerns of privacy and personal data use of students for such personalization.
Peer Support
1. Match students who have the same goals, similar experiences, and or shared identity in an anonymous online peer forum.
2. Address privacy concerns of students when making connections outside the app.
Professional Support
1. Display journey road map of what information is needed to obtain professional counseling service (e.g. insurance information, location).
2. Design for supportive practices when desired professional support is not available.
3. Provide students with agency in transitioning back and forth between self-help and professional support

6 Limitations and Future Work

Although participants were from diverse backgrounds and included both undergraduate and graduate students, the majority of workshop participants were Asian-American undergraduate students, matching the demographics of the majority at the university at which this study was conducted. In the next phase of our research we will strive for more diversity in recruitment. This work was conducted remotely during the COVID-19 pandemic which ultimately put a strain in reaching more students. A pandemic, particularly one that has stretched on for multiple years, tends to result in general feelings of insecurity, uncertainty, and anxiety in the global population [63]. Thus, students may avoid the added burden of participating in research studies.

This work contributes to the growing trend of using co-design to support the design and development of mental health interventions and support services [22–25]. The engagement of the students and the connection to their daily life challenges, enabled us to question assumptions and approaches and to bring in additional insights beyond those that stem from the evidence-based intervention. Future work will focus on expanding recruitment to a diverse set of student participants as well as translating their insights into design and usability testing.

7 Conclusion

In this study, we conducted a series of online participatory design workshops with 20 university students to understand their design needs for translating an evidence-based in-person mental health intervention to a digital application. Analysis of both student statements and artifacts from these design sessions indicate that any technological support for this population should provide healthy reminders, connect them with peers and counselors, personalize content and aesthetics on the app, and support informational and instrumental life skills. This analysis contributes empirical evidence of the needs of university students and their unique contexts. By designing with students, we translate these concerns into design implications and broader considerations for the trade-offs one might encounter in different design solutions to support this group.

In particular, we find that technological solutions must work alongside existing resources to integrate self and automated help with help from peers and professionals. These interventions should support a variety of transitional life skills not traditionally thought of as "mental health" concerns, and navigate the tension between disclosures and privacy or confidentiality in a highly stigmatized context. University students represent a uniquely vulnerable population for mental health challenges who are also particularly well-suited to make use of technological interventions, making this an integral challenge for additional HCI research in the future.

Acknowledgments. This research was supported by the National Institute of Health under the Small Business and Innovation Research program grant 1R44MH121219-01. We thank Benten Technologies for their support and assistance throughout this research.

References

1. O'Leary, K., Bhattacharya, A., Munson, S. A., Wobbrock, J. O., Pratt, W. Design opportunities for mental health peer support technologies. In: Proceedings of the 2017 ACM Conference on Computer Supported Cooperative Work and Social Computing, pp. 1470–1484 (2017). https://doi.org/10.1145/2998181.2998349
2. Kelley, C., Lee, B., Wilcox, L. Self-tracking for mental wellness: understanding expert perspectives and student experiences. In: Proceedings of the 2017 CHI Conference on Human Factors in Computing Systems, pp. 629–641 (2017). https://doi.org/10.1145/3025453.3025750

3. Schroeder, J., et al.: Data-driven implications for translating evidence-based psychotherapies into technology-delivered interventions. In: Proceedings of the 14th EAI International Conference on Pervasive Computing Technologies for Healthcare, pp. 274–287 (2020). https://doi.org/10.1145/3421937.3421975

4. Moraveji, N., Adiseshan, A., Hagiwara, T. Breathtray: augmenting respiration self-regulation without cognitive deficit. In: CHI 2012 Extended Abstracts on Human Factors in Computing Systems, pp. 2405–2410 (2012). https://doi.org/10.1145/2212776.2223810

5. Lattie, E.G., Kornfield, R., Ringland, K.E., Zhang, R., Winquist, N., Reddy, M.: Designing mental health technologies that support the social ecosystem of college students. In: Proceedings of the 2020 CHI Conference on Human Factors in Computing Systems, pp. 1–15 (2020). https://doi.org/10.1145/3313831.3376362

6. Park, S.Y.: Social support mosaic: understanding mental health management practice on college campus. In: Proceedings of the 2018 Designing Interactive Systems Conference, pp. 121–133. (2018). https://doi.org/10.1145/3196709.3196787

7. Rohani, D.A., et al.: Personalizing mental health: a feasibility study of a mobile behavioral activation tool for depressed patients. In: Proceedings of the 13th EAI International Conference on Pervasive Computing Technologies for Healthcare, pp. 282–291 (2019). https://doi.org/10.1145/3329189.3329214

8. Chan, L.T., Wallace, J.R.: Changing peer support attitudes with avatar-based gamification. In: Extended Abstracts of the 2018 CHI Conference on Human Factors in Computing Systems, pp. 1–5 (2018). https://doi.org/10.1145/3170427.3188497

9. Canzian, L., Musolesi, M.: Trajectories of depression: unobtrusive monitoring of depressive states by means of smartphone mobility traces analysis. In: Proceedings of the 2015 ACM International Joint Conference on Pervasive and Ubiquitous Computing, pp. 1293–1304). (2015). https://doi.org/10.1145/2750858.2805845

10. Wang, R., et al.: StudentLife: assessing mental health, academic performance and behavioral trends of college students using smartphones. In: Proceedings of the 2014 ACM International Joint Conference on Pervasive and Ubiquitous Computing, pp. 3–14 (2014). https://doi.org/10.1145/2632048.2632054

11. Schroeder, J., et al.: Pocket skills: a conversational mobile web app to support dialectical behavioral therapy. In: Proceedings of the 2018 CHI Conference on Human Factors in Computing Systems, pp. 1–15 (2018). https://doi.org/10.1145/3173574.3173972

12. Williams, L., et al.: Analysis of distance-based mental health support for underrepresented university students. In: Extended Abstracts of the 2021 CHI Conference on Human Factors in Computing Systems, pp. 1–6 (2021). https://doi.org/10.1145/3411763.3451708

13. Eisenberg, D., Golberstein, E., Hunt, J. B. Mental health and academic success in college. BE J. Econ. Anal. Policy. 9(1) (2009). https://doi.org/10.2202/1935-1682.2191

14. Seering, J., Wang, T., Yoon, J., Kaufman, G.: Moderator engagement and community development in the age of algorithms. New Med. Soc. 21(7), 1417–1443 (2019). https://doi.org/10.1177/1461444818821316

15. Looney, A., Yannelis, C.: A crisis in student loans?: How changes in the characteristics of borrowers and in the institutions they attended contributed to rising loan defaults. Brook. Pap. Econ. Act. 2015(2), 1–89 (2015). https://doi.org/10.1353/eca.2015.0003

16. Hoxby, C.M., Turner, S.: What high-achieving low-income students know about college. Am. Econ. Rev. 105(5), 514–517 (2015). https://doi.org/10.1257/aer.p20151027

17. Matthews, M., et al.: Development and evaluation of a smartphone-based measure of social rhythms for bipolar disorder. Assessment **23**(4), 472–483 (2016). https://doi.org/10.1177/107319111665679

18. DiSalvo, C., Clement, A., Pipek, V. Participatory design for, with, and by communities. In: International Handbook of Participatory Design, pp. 182–209 (2012)

19. Hashimov, E. Qualitative data analysis: a methods sourcebook and the coding manual for qualitative researchers. In: Miles, M.B., Michael Huberman, A., Saldaña, J., (eds.), pp. 308–381. SAGE, Thousand Oaks, CA, 2014 (2015)

20. Hoefer, M.J.D., Van Kleunen, L., Goodby, C., Blackburn, L.B., Panati, P., Voida, S. The multiplicative patient and the clinical workflow: clinician perspectives on social interfaces for self-tracking and managing bipolar disorder. In: Designing Interactive Systems Conference 2021, pp. 907–925 (2021). https://doi.org/10.1145/3461778.3461995

21. Wadley, G., Lederman, R., Gleeson, J., Alvarez-Jimenez, M.: Participatory design of an online therapy for youth mental health. In: Proceedings of the 25th Australian Computer-Human Interaction Conference: Augmentation, Application, Innovation, Collaboration, pp. 517–526 (2013). https://doi.org/10.1145/2541016.2541030

22. Ospina-Pinillos, L., Davenport, T., Mendoza Diaz, A., Navarro-Mancilla, A., Scott, E.M., Hickie, I.B.: Using participatory design methodologies to co-design and culturally adapt the Spanish version of the mental health eClinic: qualitative study. J. Med. Internet Res. **21**(8), e14127 (2019). https://doi.org/10.2196/14127

23. Hodson, E., Dadashi, N., Delgado, R., Chisholm, C., Sgrignoli, R., Swaine, R.: Co-design in mental health; mellow: a self-help holistic crisis planning mobile application by youth, for youth. Des. J. **22**(sup1), 1529–1542 (2019). https://doi.org/10.1080/14606925.2019.1594975

24. Tee, S., Özçetin, Y.S.Ü.: Promoting positive perceptions and person centred care toward people with mental health problems using co-design with nursing students. Nurse Educ. Today **44**, 116–120 (2016). https://doi.org/10.1016/j.nedt.2016.05.024

25. Larkin, M., Boden, Z. V., Newton, E. On the brink of genuinely collaborative care: experience-based co-design in mental health. Qual. Health Res. **25**(11), 1463–1476 (2015).https://doi.org/10.1177/1049732315576494

26. Bonar, E.E., Chapman, L., Goldstick, J.E., Young, S.D., Bauermeister, J.A., Walton, M.A.: Feasibility and acceptability of a social media intervention for cannabis use in emerging adults. In: SPR Virtual 29th Annual Meeting. SPR (2021)

27. Jaganath, D., Gill, H.K., Cohen, A.C., Young, S.D.: Harnessing Online Peer Education (HOPE): integrating C-POL and social media to train peer leaders in HIV prevention. AIDS Care **24**(5), 593–600 (2012). https://doi.org/10.1080/09540121.2011.630355

28. Carlana, M., La Ferrara, E., Pinotti, P.: Goals and gaps: educational careers of immigrant children. Econometrica **90**(1), 1–29 (2022). https://doi.org/10.3982/ECTA17458

29. Horwedel, D.M.: The misinformation about financial aid. Divers. Issues High. Educ. **23**(14), 34 (2006)

30. Phippen, A., Bond, E., Buck, E. Effective strategies for information literacy education: combatting 'fake news' and empowering critical thinking. In: Future Directions in Digital Information, pp. 39–53. Chandos Publishing. (2021). https://doi.org/10.1016/B978-0-12-822144-0.00003-3

31. Martinez, S.M., Frongillo, E.A., Leung, C., Ritchie, L.: No food for thought: food insecurity is related to poor mental health and lower academic performance among students in California's public university system. J. Health Psychol. **25**(12), 1930–1939 (2020). https://doi.org/10.1177/1359105318783028
32. Cénat, J.M., Dalexis, R.D., Kokou-Kpolou, C.K., Mukunzi, J.N., Rousseau, C.: Social inequalities and collateral damages of the COVID-19 pandemic: when basic needs challenge mental health care. Int. J. Public Health **65**(6), 717–718 (2020). https://doi.org/10.1007/s00038-020-01426-y
33. Weaver, L.J., Hadley, C.: Moving beyond hunger and nutrition: a systematic review of the evidence linking food insecurity and mental health in developing countries. Ecol. Food Nutr. **48**(4), 263–284 (2009). https://doi.org/10.1080/03670240903001167
34. Goodwin, J., Behan, L., Kelly, P., McCarthy, K., Horgan, A.: Help-seeking behaviors and mental well-being of first year undergraduate university students. Psychiatry Res. **246**, 129–135 (2016). https://doi.org/10.1016/j.psychres.2016.09.015
35. Mehr, K.E., Daltry, R.: Examining mental health differences between transfer and nontransfer university students seeking counseling services. J. Coll. Stud. Psychother. **30**(2), 146–155 (2016). https://doi.org/10.1080/87568225.2016.1140996
36. Bhattacharya, A., Nagar, R., Jenness, J., Munson, S.A., Kientz, J.A.: Designing asynchronous remote support for behavioral activation in teenagers with depression: formative study. JMIR Form. Res. **5**(7), e20969 (2021). https://doi.org/10.2196/20969
37. Arthur-Nyarko, E., Agyei, D.D., Armah, J.K.: Digitizing distance learning materials: measuring students' readiness and intended challenges. Educ. Inf. Technol. **25**(4), 2987–3002 (2020). https://doi.org/10.1007/s10639-019-10060-y
38. Rozgonjuk, D., Elhai, J.D., Ryan, T., Scott, G.G.: Fear of missing out is associated with disrupted activities from receiving smartphone notifications and surface learning in college students. Comput. Educ. **140**, 103590 (2019). https://doi.org/10.1016/j.compedu.2019.05.016
39. Griffin, R. A. Socially distant but digitally connected: how one online literacy teacher educator responded to the COVID-19 pandemic. Teaching/Writing: J. Writing Teach. Educ. **9**(1), 13 (2020). https://scholarworks.wmich.edu/wte/vol9/iss1/13
40. Sullivan, M.: Development of a Scalable Self-Regulation Intervention in Support of Lifelong Learning for First-year Engineering Students (Master's thesis, Schulich School of Engineering) (2019). http://dx.doi.org/10.11575/PRISM/37080
41. Woodward, J., Chen, Y.P., Jurczyk, K., Ross, K.M., Anthony, L., Ruiz, J.: A survey of notification designs in commercial mHealth apps. In: Extended Abstracts of the 2021 CHI Conference on Human Factors in Computing Systems, pp. 1–7 (2021). https://doi.org/10.1145/3411763.3451639
42. Lee, R.A., Jung, M.E.: Evaluation of an mhealth app (destressify) on university students' mental health: pilot trial. JMIR Mental Health **5**(1), e8324 (2018). https://doi.org/10.2196/mental.8324
43. Alqahtani, F., Winn, A., Orji, R.: Co-designing a mobile app to improve mental health and well-being: focus group study. JMIR Form. Res. **5**(2), e18172 (2021). https://doi.org/10.2196/18172
44. Bakker, D., Kazantzis, N., Rickwood, D., Rickard, N.: Mental health smartphone apps: review and evidence-based recommendations for future developments. JMIR Mental Health **3**(1), e4984 (2016). https://doi.org/10.2196/mental.4984

45. Reetz, D. R., Krylowicz, B., Mistler, B. The association for university and college counseling center directors annual survey. Retrieved from Association for University and College Counseling Center Directors (2016). https://www.aucccd.org/director-surveys-public

46. Eisenberg, D., Golberstein, E., Gollust, S. E. Help-seeking and access to mental health care in a university student population. Medical Care, pp. 594–601 (2007)

47. Palmer, K.M., Henderson, S.G.: College students' attitudes about mental health-related content in mobile apps. J. Technol. Behav. Sci. **4**(4), 381–389 (2019). https://doi.org/10.1007/s41347-019-00102-0

48. Kern, A., Hong, V., Song, J., Lipson, S. K., Eisenberg, D.: Mental health apps in a college setting: openness, usage, and attitudes. Mhealth **4** (2018). https://doi.org/10.21037/mhealth.2018.06.01

49. Levin, M.E., Hicks, E.T., Krafft, J.: Pilot evaluation of the stop, breathe & think mindfulness app for student clients on a college counseling center waitlist. J. Am. Coll. Health **70**(1), 165–173 (2022). https://doi.org/10.1080/07448481.2020.1728281

50. Melcher, J., Camacho, E., Lagan, S., Torous, J.: College student engagement with mental health apps: analysis of barriers to sustained use. J. Am. Coll. Health **70**(6), 1819–1825 (2022). https://doi.org/10.1080/07448481.2020.1825225

51. Wood, J.R., Wood, L.E.: Card sorting: current practices and beyond. J. Usability Stud. **4**(1), 1–6 (2008)

52. Truong, K N., Hayes, G.R., Abowd, G.D. Storyboarding: an empirical determination of best practices and effective guidelines. In: Proceedings of the 6th conference on Designing Interactive systems, pp. 12–21 (2006). https://doi.org/10.1145/1142405.1142410

53. Peavey, E. K., Zoss, J., Watkins, N.: Simulation and mock-up research methods to enhance design decision making. HERD: Health Environ. Res. Des. J. **5**(3), 133–144. (2012). https://doi.org/10.1177/193758671200500313

54. LeRouge, C., Ma, J., Sneha, S., Tolle, K.: User profiles and personas in the design and development of consumer health technologies. Int. J. Med. Inform. **82**(11), e251–e268 (2013). https://doi.org/10.1016/j.ijmedinf.2011.03.006

55. Zhang, R.E., Ringland, K., Paan, M.C., Mohr, D., Reddy, M.: Designing for Emotional Well-being: integrating persuasion and customization into mental health technologies. In: Proceedings of the 2021 CHI Conference on Human Factors in Computing Systems, pp. 1–13 (2021). https://doi.org/10.1145/3411764.3445771

56. Donker, T., Blankers, M., Hedman, E., Ljotsson, B., Petrie, K., Christensen, H.: Economic evaluations of Internet interventions for mental health: a systematic review. Psychol. Med. **45**(16), 3357–3376 (2015). https://doi.org/10.1017/S0033291715001427

57. Torous, J., Nicholas, J., Larsen, M.E., Firth, J., Christensen, H.: Clinical review of user engagement with mental health smartphone apps: evidence, theory and improvements. BMJ Ment Health **21**(3), 116–119 (2018). https://doi.org/10.1136/eb-2018-102891

58. Baumel, A., Muench, F., Edan, S., Kane, J.M.: Objective user engagement with mental health apps: systematic search and panel-based usage analysis. J. Med. Internet Res. **21**(9), e14567 (2019). https://doi.org/10.2196/14567

59. Pratap, A., et al.: Indicators of retention in remote digital health studies: a cross-study evaluation of 100,000 participants. NPJ Digit. Med. **3**(1), 21 (2020). https://doi.org/10.1038/s41746-020-0224-8

60. Torous, J., et al.: Characterizing smartphone engagement for schizophrenia: results of a naturalist mobile health study. Clin. Schizophrenia Relat. Psychoses. (2017). https://doi.org/10.3371/csrp.jtps.071317

61. Flett, J.A.M., Hayne, H., Riordan, B.C., Thompson, L.M., Conner, T.S.: Mobile mindfulness meditation: a randomised controlled trial of the effect of two popular apps on mental health. Mindfulness 10(5), 863–876 (2018). https://doi.org/10.1007/s12671-018-1050-9

62. Johnson, K.F., Kalkbrenner, M.T.: The utilization of technological innovations to support college student mental health: Mobile health communication. J. Technol. Hum. Serv. 35(4), 314–339 (2017). https://doi.org/10.1080/15228835.2017.1368428

63. Xiong, J., et al.: Impact of COVID-19 pandemic on mental health in the general population: a systematic review. J. Affect. Disorders. 277, 55–64 (2020). https://doi.org/10.1016/j.jad.2020.08.001

64. Mowbray, C.T., et al.: Campus mental health services: Recommendations for change. Am. J. Orthopsych. 76(2), 226–237. (2006). https://doi.org/10.1037/0002-9432.76.2.226

65. Morey, B.N.: Mechanisms by which anti-immigrant stigma exacerbates racial/ethnic health disparities. Am. J. Public Health 108(4), 460–463 (2018). https://doi.org/10.2105/AJPH.2017.304266

66. Browning, M.H., et al.: Psychological impacts from COVID-19 among university students: Risk factors across seven states in the United States. PloS one. 16(1), e0245327 (2021). https://doi.org/10.1371/journal.pone.0245327

67. Eisenberg, D., Hunt, J., Speer, N.: Mental health in American colleges and universities: variation across student subgroups and across campuses. J. Nerv. Ment. Dis. 201(1), 60–67 (2013). https://doi.org/10.1097/NMD.0b013e31827ab077

68. Herman, S., Archambeau, O.G., Deliramich, A.N., Kim, B.S., Chiu, P.H., Frueh, B.C.: Depressive symptoms and mental health treatment in an ethnoracially diverse college student sample. J. Am. Coll. Health 59(8), 715–720 (2011). https://doi.org/10.1080/07448481.2010.529625

69. Dosaj, A., et al.: Rapid implementation of telehealth services during the COVID-19 pandemic. Telemed. e-Health 27(2), 116–120 (2021). https://doi.org/10.1089/tmj.2020.0219

70. Aguilera, A., Muench, F.: There's an app for that: information technology applications for cognitive behavioral practitioners. Behav. Ther. AABT. 35(4), 65 (2012). PMID: 25530659; PMCID: PMC4270287

71. Veazie, S., Bourne, D., Peterson, K., Anderson, J. Evidence brief: video telehealth for primary care and mental health services (2019)

72. Pedrelli, P., Nyer, M., Yeung, A., Zulauf, C., Wilens, T.: College students: mental health problems and treatment considerations. Acad. Psychiatry 39(5), 503–511 (2014). https://doi.org/10.1007/s40596-014-0205-9

73. Fripp, J.A., Carlson, R.G.: Exploring the influence of attitude and stigma on participation of African American and Latino populations in mental health services. J. Multicult. Couns. Dev. 45(2), 80–94 (2017). https://doi.org/10.1002/jmcd.12066

74. Kumar, S., Bhukar, J.P.: Stress level and coping strategies of college students. J. Phys. Educ. Sports Manage. 4(1), 5–11 (2013). https://doi.org/10.5897/JPESM12.001

75. Huberty, J., Green, J., Glissmann, C., Larkey, L., Puzia, M., Lee, C.: Efficacy of the mindfulness meditation mobile app "calm" to reduce stress among college students: Randomized controlled trial. JMIR Mhealth Uhealth 7(6), e14273 (2019). https://doi.org/10.2196/14273

76. Horgan, A., Sweeney, J.: Young students' use of the Internet for mental health information and support. J. Psychiatr. Ment. Health Nurs. **17**(2), 117–123 (2010). https://doi.org/10.1111/j.1365-2850.2009.01497.x

77. Mohr, D.C., et al.: IntelliCare: an eclectic, skills-based app suite for the treatment of depression and anxiety. J. Med. Internet Res. **19**(1), e10 (2017). https://doi.org/10.2196/jmir.6645

78. Ash, M., Harrison, T., Pinto, M., DiClemente, R., Negi, L.T.: A model for cognitively-based compassion training: theoretical underpinnings and proposed mechanisms. Soc. Theory Health **19**, 43–67 (2021). https://doi.org/10.1057/s41285-019-00124-x

79. Martin, B., Hanington, B., Hanington, B.M.: Universal methods of design: 100 ways to research complex problems, develop innovative ideas, and design effective solutions. Rockport Pub

80. Turner, J.C., Leno, E.V., Keller, A.: Causes of mortality among American college students: a pilot study. J. Coll. Stud. Psychother. **27**(1), 31–42 (2013). https://doi.org/10.1080/87568225.2013.739022

81. Duffy, M.E., Twenge, J.M., Joiner, T.E.: Trends in mood and anxiety symptoms and suicide-related outcomes among US undergraduates, 2007–2018: Evidence from two national surveys. J. Adolesc. Health **65**(5), 590–598 (2019). https://doi.org/10.1016/j.jadohealth.2019.04.033

82. Scott, K.M., et al.: Association of mental disorders with subsequent chronic physical conditions: world mental health surveys from 17 countries. JAMA Psychiatry. **73**(2), 150–158 (2016). https://doi.org/10.1001/jamapsychiatry.2015.2688

83. Blanco, C., Okuda, M., Wright, C., Hasin, D.S., Grant, B.F., Liu, S.M., Olfson, M.: Mental health of college students and their non-college-attending peers: results from the national epidemiologic study on alcohol and related conditions. Arch. Gen. Psychiatry **65**(12), 1429–1437 (2008). https://doi.org/10.1001/archpsyc.65.12.1429

84. Xiao, H., Carney, D.M., Youn, S.J., Janis, R.A., Castonguay, L.G., Hayes, J.A., Locke, B.D.: Are we in crisis? National mental health and treatment trends in college counseling centers. Psychol. Serv. **14**(4), 407 (2017). https://doi.org/10.1037/ser0000130

85. Zauszniewski, J.A.: Intervention development: assessing critical parameters from the intervention recipient's perspective. Appl. Nurs. Res. **25**(1), 31–39 (2012). https://doi.org/10.1016/j.apnr.2010.06.002

86. Lattie, E.G., Lipson, S.K., Eisenberg, D.: Technology and college student mental health: challenges and opportunities. Front. Psych. **10**, 246 (2019). https://doi.org/10.3389/fpsyt.2019.00246

87. Thielking, M.: A dangerous wait: colleges can't meet soaring student needs for mental health care STAT (2017). https://www.statnews.com/2017/02/06/mental-health-collegestudents

88. Secretary, HHS Office of the, and Office for Civil Rights (OCR). Summary of the HIPAA Privacy Rule. Retrieved from HHS.gov: www.hhs.gov/hipaa/for-professionals/privacy/laws-regulations/index.html. (2013)

89. University of Washington. LiveWell Peer Health EDUCATORS: Husky Health & Well-being (2021). https://www.wellbeing.uw.edu/get-involved/peer-health-educators

90. Free Care & Therapy. Retrieved from 7 cups: www.7cups.com. (2021)

91. Online Therapy. Talkspace: (2021). https://www.talkspace.com

92. US Department of Education. Family Educational Rights and Privacy Act (Ferpa) (2021). https://www2.ed.gov/policy/gen/guid/fpco/ferpa/index.html ¡error l="305" c="Invalid
command: paragraph not started." /¿
93. Tufts Technology Services. Guide to Massachusetts Data Privacy Laws. https://it.tufts.edu/about/policies-and-guidelines/guide-massachusetts-data-privacy-laws
94. State of California Department of Justice - Office of the Attorney General. Privacy Laws (2018). https://oag.ca.gov/privacy/privacy-laws
95. European Union. General Data Protection Regulation (2018). https://gdpr.eu/tag/gdpr/

HCI for Learning, Culture, Creativity
and Societal Impact

The Context of War and Cognitive Bias: An Interactive Approach in Accessing Relations of Attitude, Behavior and Events in Ancient Texts and Online News

Christina Alexandris[1,3(✉)], Jiali Du[2], and Vasilios Floros[1,3]

[1] National and Kapodistrian University of Athens, Athens, Greece
calexandris@gs.uoa.gr, florosbas2002@yahoo.gr
[2] Guangdong University of Foreign Studies, Guangzhou, China
dujiali68@126.com, 201310039@oamail.gdufs.edu.cn
[3] European Communication Institute (ECI), Danube University Krems, Austria and National Technical University of Athens, Athens, Greece

Abstract. Access to knowledge from ancient classical texts for a comparison and understanding of current events and situations poses challenges, especially to non-experts, especially if information searched concerns behaviors, attitude and mentality linked to war and not facts, events and names. Geopolitical and diplomatic information concerning behavior and intentions is also connected to the challenge of precision, correction and capturing subtle details. These resources may be a valuable -yet often obscure- source of information to a broader User group, requiring expertise, language skills and a remarkable period of time to access and to evaluate these resources in order to combine and compare information with the current state-of-affairs. Easy access to the Classical Texts and the display of detailed and/or specific information in a user-friendly interaction is the main target of the designed user-interface and partially implemented applications. The approach integrates expert-knowledge and user requirements and also manages Cognitive Bias. The designed user-interface and partially implemented applications by-pass Cognitive Bias but also take advantage of specific types of Cognitive Bias.

Keywords: Cognitive Bias · Interface Design · Seed Ontology

1 Comparing Online News and Ancient Texts

1.1 Challenges in Accessing Information for the Understanding, Comparison and Evaluation of Attitude, Behavior and Events

The analysis and study of classical ancient historical texts concerning political-geopolitical and military information is a common practice for non-academic professionals of the field of Geopolitics and Diplomacy, such as military personnel, diplomats and journalists. In the present approach and applications, expert knowledge is targeted to be integrated in an attempt to utilize resources from World History in evaluating the current state of affairs and in decision-making. In particular, the targets involve knowledge extracted from ancient texts in respect to politics, diplomacy, human nature and attitudes linked to government, war, conflicts, internal politics and relations with other countries and powers.

Classical ancient historical texts provide (1) information as reference work, which is compared to the current state-of-affairs and (2) text structure allowing a better analysis and organization of the text content for the creation of possible models.

Non-experts and many categories of professionals alike may wish to access knowledge from ancient classical texts for a comparison and understanding of currents events and situations. Information from spoken political and journalistic texts and online written political and journalistic texts may be compared and evaluated in respect to knowledge and information to classical texts. However, unlike most types of language resources, both the linguistic features of the ancient texts concerned and the related knowledge and expertise do not facilitate access to a broader, international public and non-experts. Recent research and accomplishments in the field of Digital Humanities [18, 22] may provide a large variety of resources. However, accessing in-depth dimensions of their information content to a broader and international public remains a challenge.

Geopolitical and diplomatic information constitutes a type of information that is not easily processed with standard Information Extraction practices, since it does not concern mere facts, but behavior and intentions. In this case, the type of information content concerned does not allow a direct training and implementation of "off-the-shelf ontologies" [6] without the requirement of hand-labeled training data, as in the case of medical data [6]. Geopolitical and diplomatic information concerning behavior and intentions is also connected with the challenge of precision, correction and capturing subtle details. Furthermore, experts and professionals in the field of geopolitical and diplomatic information benefit from sources containing experience from the Past, describing geopolitical states-of-affairs, rhetoric and diplomacy. These resources may be a valuable yet often obscure source of information to a broader User group, requiring (a) expertise, (b) a remarkable period of time to access and to evaluate these resources in order to combine and compare information with the current state-of-affairs and (c) language skills, in many cases.

We note that these types of texts often are characterized by a particular structure of text and information and use of vocabulary. This means that the employment of expert knowledge in the analysis of the text structure and content is necessary. This is of essential importance since the text content is not in a (dated) modern language such as English or German as is the case of other classical references in the domain of War (for example, Carl Philipp Gottfried (or Gottlieb) von Clausewitz: "Vom Kriege" (About War), Alfred Thayer Mahan "The Influence of Sea Power upon History": 1660–1783).

The main challenge concerned is the process of guiding non-expert users and expert users alike in searching the respective information in the ancient classical texts. The content, language and structures of these text types requires a specialized customization of search techniques in addition to standard Information Extraction practices. This is especially necessary in the case of accessing information in regard to behaviors, attitude and mentality linked to war and not only facts, events and names.

Precision and expert knowledge are factors contributing to an interactive approach versus a fully automatic approach in accessing and extracting complex information such as behavior and intentions resulting to decisions and events in History and Geopolitics. Employing an interactive approach in this case is similar to the practice of employing interactive approaches in interactive versus fully automatic approaches in Machine Translation – especially in cases where precision and completeness in the transfer of information content are of crucial importance.

As an example of ancient texts of World History, the "Peloponnesian War" of Thucydides (Ancient Greek) is taught in military academies, such as West Point. The present application concerns Ancient Greek historic texts, specifically, the "Peloponnesian War" of Thucydides, however, the general modelling approach used can be a starting point for possible adaptations to the specifications of other (ancient) texts, also in other languages.

Sun Tzu's "The Art of War" (Ancient Chinese) was written about 515 BC to 512 BC during the Spring and Autumn Period. Sun Tzu summarized the theories and principles of war and discussed the nature of war, the planning of war, danger in war, the preparations for war, strategic means in war, material supply in war, the general deployment in war, the analysis on situations in war, military virtue of an army in war, the use of the special battle in war (fire attack and espionage warfare) - among others.

1.2 Design Specifications and Cognitive Bias

For the proposed interface, first of all, the user's search strategy should address the question whether information from classical references is relevant and useful in respect to understanding and/or analyzing current events and state-of-affairs. This information should be directly accessed in the respective texts and passages. Furthermore, specialized and/or detailed information should be made available, according to the type of classical text accessed. These specifications are summarized by the following questions: "If?", "Where?" and "How?".

The general approach for the modeling and implementations presented here are compatible with practices in spoken dialog systems allowing the options of both fast and slower-paced interaction [14]. The "If?" question corresponds to quick interaction whereas the "Where?" and "How?" questions correspond to intermediate and slower-paced levels of interaction speed [14] respectively.

For the modelling of the interface the way the information is presented to the user (Presentation) as well as the quality of information presented (Content) are of equal significance.

The present designed interface and partially implemented applications are based on modelling the knowledge provided by the (1) combination of existing language resources and expert knowledge contained in them, with (2) a strategy similar to practices employed in editors for Controlled Languages. This strategy is applied because the historic texts and translations concerned are resources with sublanguage-specific sub-domains and text-specific features presenting expert knowledge, formulated in the writer's or translator's style. Furthermore, the sub-domain of War and Geopolitics - Diplomacy in these resources allows the creation of ontologies and the formalization of entity relationships from text content and text structure such as Source-Outcome/Cause-Result relationships.

2 User Requirements and Cognitive Bias

2.1 Cognitive Bias

The designed user-interface and partially implemented applications for accessing knowledge from ancient classical texts targets to by-pass Cognitive Bias - but also to take advantage of specific types of Cognitive Bias. In particular, types of Cognitive Bias such as "Anchoring Bias", "Confirmation Bias" and "Bandwagon Effects" [4] are avoided whereas types of Cognitive Bias such as "Availability Bias", and "Framing Effects" [4] are used to the advantage of the interface creation and application implementation. The main target is to allow easy access to the Classical Texts and display detailed and/or specific information in a user-friendly interaction. The Cognitive Biases in the user's search are listed as following, according to Azzopardi, 2021:

"Availability Bias leads people to overestimate the likelihood of an answer or stance based on how easily it can be retrieved and recalled." [4] "Framing Effects occur when people make different decisions given the same information because of how the information has been presented" [4] "Anchoring Bias stems from people's tendencies to focus too much on the first piece of information learnt, or observed (even if that information is not relevant or correct)". [4] "Confirmation Bias stems from people's tendency to prefer confirmatory information, where they will discount information that does not conform to their existing beliefs." [4] "Bandwagon Effects occur when people take on a similar opinion or point of view because other people voice that opinion or point of view. Researchers have been concerned that search engines may be influencing people's opinions, either by presenting confirmatory information reinforcing people's existing beliefs […], or by presenting information to sway their decisions through exposure effects (dubbed the Search Engine Manipulation Effect (SEME)." [4] Searchers rated articles as more useful if they were easier to read and understand" [4].

2.2 Expert Users and Cognitive Bias

For professionals, precision and correctness are of crucial importance in information searched in ancient and historical texts (Requirement A), constituting a resource of expert knowledge from lessons learnt from the Past. If the information from these resources is to be compared with the current spoken journalistic and political texts, especially for decision-making, quick access to the requested content is a desired feature (Requirement B). Additionally, User requirements regarding the content of the information to be extracted were formulated with the aid of a questionnaire made available to prospective Users, especially journalists and military personnel.

Questionnaire –based User Requirements confirm that information from the Past can be relevant to the understanding of the current-state-of affairs, with the following topics consisting typical examples: In particular, Users strongly agreed with the following factors playing a crucial role in understanding Cause-Result relations in current affairs, directly related to geopolitical and diplomatic information from the "Peloponnesian War" of Thucydides: "Expert"-Users believed that the following applied in most cases: "Pressure from Allies is always a major factor", "Citizens' emotions are an unpredictable factor in decision-making", "Personality of leader is crucial in success of strategy",

"Even today, war may be lost due to bad advisors". Users believed that the following applied in some cases: "Events may be explained by seemly irrelevant incidents" and "Unpredictable behavior of Allies may be due to factors related to domestic politics".

We note that the a-priori knowledge of expert-users is linked to word-entities and expressions such as "unpredictable", "emotions" and "domestic politics". However, a-priori knowledge, on the other hand, may also result to Confirmation Bias, where confirmatory information may be preferred, according to one's knowledge and experience. In other words, expert-users are not exempt from Cognitive Bias.

In order for the practices of professionals to be simulated by the implemented application, the nature and complexity of the information to be extracted requires the integration and formalization of expert knowledge as a starting point of analysis and investigation (Requirement C).

2.3 Non-expert Users and Cognitive Bias

In contrast to expert-users, non-expert users may not be aware of the types of information content in the ancient texts. Therefore, types of Cognitive Bias such as Availability Bias and Anchoring Bias related to the accessibility and completeness of information are characteristic examples of Cognitive Bias that may be related to non-expert-users. Non-expert users may not always be able to evaluate the quality of precision and correctness of information searched in ancient and historical texts (Requirement A), however, as in all applications, precision is a essential requirement - for all users.

Quick access to the requested content is a desired feature (Requirement B) and may be a requirement of particular importance to non-expert users. Specifically, expert-users have, by default, due to their interests and expertise, a higher level of interest and engagement in the use of the application accessing information content of the ancient texts. Non-expert users have, by default, a lower level of interest and engagement in the use of the application and any errors and delays may discourage the users from any further interaction.

For non-expert users, the integration of expert knowledge (Requirement C) for accessing information in the ancient texts concerned involves the creation of a user-friendly interface, allowing easy interaction and formulation of queries.

Since the nature of the information to be extracted is not always easy to formulate as a query, because - in contrast to most applications - behavior, attitude and politics in general are concerned, the User's query is designed to be assisted by the sublanguage of the application. The sublanguage specifications and resulting ontologies function both for the search and extraction of information and for assisting User queries.

The interface targets to adapt the user's queries to the "world" of the ancient text. Specialized modules targeting to process distinctive linguistic features of the ancient texts are a necessary function. The same query word(s) can be related to different contexts and types of information in the Classical texts. The User cannot know or foresee the possible contexts and variations in information content of the query word.

In the case of ancient Classical Texts, information is often presented in a different way than in most (international) online texts. This results to non-expert and/or international users facing difficulties in accessing the information. In addition, non-expert and/or international users may not have a complete overview of the type of information available in the texts. Therefore, the targeted basic functions of the application interface are:

- to allow direct access to information not easily extracted
- to connect spoken texts from the live stream of current event to their "echoes" of related information in the resources concerned, in the present case, the resources from the ancient Past and
- to provide the necessary resources for understanding and providing possible clusters and associations of complex information concerning behavior and diplomacy.

2.4 Interaction and Specialized Functions

As described above, the design and creation of the interface focuses both on (a) the way the information is presented to the user (Presentation) and (b) the quality of information presented (Content)- in accordance with Requirements A, B and C.

In respect to the presentation of the information, the interaction concerns the following basic steps: (1) the selection of the ancient text to be processed (TEXT-SELECT), (2) the insertion of the query word(s) (QUERY-WORD), (3) the refinement of the search (SPECIFY-TERM) and (4) the viewing of the specialized query word(s) options/choices displayed in the interface (SPECIFY-TERM results). Additional, optional steps are (5) the display of specialized and/or detailed information upon request (ENBL.CONTEXT) and (6) the extension and upgrading of the ontology used in the search process extension and upgrading of the search ontology - recommended for expert users (UPGRADE-ONTOLOGY).

The insertion of the query word(s) (2) and the refinement of the search (3) address the questions of "If?" and "Where?" and the specialized and/or detailed information (5) additionally addresses the question of "How?". The "Availability Bias" and "Framing Effects" Cognitive Biases [4] are used to the advantage for the modelling of the interface design and interaction.

Regarding the content of the information, the following three features are targeted to ensure the quality of the information presented: Choice of translation(s), text-specific and language-specific parameters of content and linguistic features, sublanguage-specific seed domain ontologies [8, 17]. These features are integrated in the design and implemented modules of the application for the avoidance of Cognitive Bias such as "Anchoring Bias", "Confirmation Bias" and "Bandwagon Effects" [4].

The presentation (Presentation) and (Content) of information are linked to the activation of the "Specify Term" and "Enable Content" processes in the interface. The activation of the "Specify Term" process with the respective button in the interface assists the user's query by guiding the search and providing possible options in respect to the information content of the word. In other words, if the word(s) inserted from the online journalistic text (QUERY-WORD) cannot be directly linked to corresponding passages in the Ancient Text, the activation of the "Specify Term" process refines the search.

After the words and expressions from user queries are matched to the content of the ancient Classical Text and the respective passages are displayed on the interface, the user may choose to activate the "Enable Context" button for the optional display of specialized and/or detailed information, according to the Classical Text selected. The optional fifth

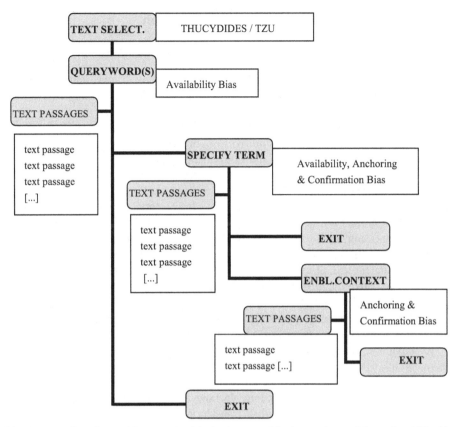

Fig. 1. Overall outline and framework of the basic steps of the interaction and the optional "Enable Context" (ENBL.CONTEXT) function.

step of the interaction activated by the "Enable Context" process displays the word(s) selected within their possible contexts of specialized and detailed information.

For example, in the case of the Thucydides' Peloponnesian War, with the activation of the "Enable Context" button, a connection of the query word(s) with a sequence of "Cause-Result" and other types of relations related to the behavior of politicians and citizens is displayed in the respective passages. In the case of the "Art-of-War", the activation of the "Enable Context" button displays passages with characteristic forms of structure and content expressing significant information such as repetitions or other types of content characteristic of the ancient text, such as the skills and qualities of military leaders.

The "Update Ontology" button (optional step 6) allows the extension and upgrading of the ontology used in the "Specify Term" search process.

3   Content and the "Enable Context" Function

3.1   The "Enable Context" Function: Corpora and Translations

The integration of expert knowledge and the choice of multiple corpora and translations are the necessary condition and requirement for the development and implementation of the "Specify Term" and "Enable Content" functions.

The choice of multiple corpora and translations allowing a broader range of options and information minimizes the possibility of Cognitive Bias, in particular, Availability Bias and especially Anchoring Bias and Confirmation Bias [4].

Translations, often bound by language-specific factors, often may not reflect the style of author and the "patterns" of the original text – an important feature in the text structure and content – and sometimes may not convey subtle but essential types of information [7]. The latter is important for the full transfer of the original information, while the feature of text structure contributes to detecting and extracting information. Ideally, translations of the classical texts (such as the Peloponnesian War of Thucydides) can be paired with the original ancient text, along with additional "assistive" translations by scholars and experts whose native tongue is closely related to the language of the original text. This allows a larger set of structural and other linguistic similarities closer to the original text: Essential/subtle information may also be contained in the morpho-syntactic structure of words (or characters, in languages such as Chinese).

To maximize the coverage and precision of the information extracted, in previous research [16] multiple resources are used both in widely spoken languages such as English and with the above-stated "assistive" translations that can be processed with easily accessible and non-specialized online Machine Translation systems such as Google Translate. The resource for the English translation employed here is the MIT Classics Archive - Internet Classics Archive of the Massachusetts Institute of Technology (http://classics.mit.edu/Thucydides/pelopwar.mb.txt - Thucydides' Peloponnesian War, translated by Richard Crawley. J.M. Dent and Co., London 1903) [5].

The assistive "Katharevousa" translation here is the translation of the "Peloponnesian War" (in Katharevousa Greek - a "compromise" between Ancient Greek and Modern Greek mainly in formal texts and official documents, especially before the 1980's) by the prominent Greek statesman and political leader Eleftherios Venizelos (1864–1936). It was published in 1940 in the University of Oxford, after his death, also provided online (Centre for the Greek language: Portal for the Greek Language: www.greeklanguage.gr, E.Venizelos Translation [1940] 1960 [21]). The translation is very close to the original Ancient Greek text, however, it explicitly presents most of the information implied by pronouns and other forms of anaphora and context-dependent expressions in the original Ancient Greek text, facilitating the direct access to the text content with the use of the sublanguage-specific keywords. Furthermore, in this translation, an increasing number of causal relations is visible with pointers such as "because", which might not be available in an original English translation [2]. In order to be processed by Google Translate in English, the translation in "Katharevousa" Greek can be submitted to partial editing [2]. As observed from the evaluation of the translations from previous research [2], Google Translate could successfully handle the partially processed Katharevousa Greek text (Assistive Translation). The following example illustrates the additional information (in brackets) from the Assistive Translation, as well as its similarity to the original ancient text (We note that the Athenians and Lacedaemonians (Spartans) were the superpowers of the time):

English translation (for Queries) (MIT Classics Archive): The Mantineans and their allies were the first to come over [become allies with] through fear of the Lacedaemonians. [Because] Having taken advantage of the war against Athens to reduce a large part of Arcadia into subjection, they thought that Lacedaemon would not leave them undisturbed in their conquests, now that she had leisure to interfere, and consequently gladly turned to a powerful city like Argos, the historical enemy of the Lacedaemonians, and a sister democracy.

Assistive Translation (for Search and Extraction): [5.29.1] Πρῶτοι οι Μαντινείς και οι σύμμαχοί των προσεχώρησαν εις την συμμαχίαν ταύτην, εκ φόβου των Λακεδαιμονίων. Διότι, διαρκούντος ακόμη του προς τους Αθηναίους πολέμου, οι Μαντινείς είχαν υποτάξει μέρος της Αρκαδίας, και ενόμιζαν, ότι οι Λακεδαιμόνιοι δεν θα τους επέτρεπαν να διατηρήσουν την επ' αυτού κυριαρχίαν, ήδη οπότε αι χείρες των ήσαν ελεύθεραι. Ώστε προθύμως εστράφησαν προς το Άργος θεωρούντες αυτό πόλιν ισχυράν, και ανέκαθεν αντίπαλον των Λακεδαιμονίων, και επί πλέον δημοκρατουμένην, όπως και αυτοί.

Original Ancient Text: [5.29.1] Μαντινῆς δ' αὐτοῖς καὶ οἱ ξύμμαχοι αὐτῶν πρῶτοι προσεχώρησαν, δεδιότες τοὺς Λακεδαιμονίους. τοῖς γὰρ Μαντινεῦσι μέρος τι τῆς Ἀρκαδίας κατέστραπτο ὑπήκοον ἔτι τοῦ πρὸς Ἀθηναίους πολέμου ὄντος, καὶ ἐνόμιζον οὐ περιόψεσθαι σφᾶς τοὺς Λακεδαιμονίους ἄρχειν, ἐπειδὴ καὶ σχολὴν ἦγον· ὥστε ἄσμενοι πρὸς τοὺς Ἀργείους ἐτράποντο, πόλιν τε μεγάλην νομίζοντες καὶ Λακεδαιμονίοις αἰεὶ διάφορον, δημοκρατουμένην τε ὥσπερ καὶ αὐτοί.

We note that respective texts related to events from current spoken journalistic or political texts from which queries may be formulated were not presented here for reasons of political correctness.

A similar observation - in respect to the translation proximity to the ancient text- is also observed in "The Art of War" by Sun Tzu. As quoted from Zheng (2019): "Lin Wusun is a Chinese scholar who is 19 years older than Roger T. Ames, so he has the advantage of understanding the original text". These differences are illustrated in the following example:

[24]: 静以幽, 正以治. This term is from chapter eleven, in which the whole sentence is: "将军之事, 静以幽, 正以治". Ames's translation: As for the urgent business of the commander: He is calm and remote, correct and disciplined. Lin's translation: It is the responsibility of the commander to be calm and inscrutable, to be impartial and strict in enforcing discipline [24].

3.2   The "Enable Context" Function: Implemented Modules and Parameters

Parameters for the "Peloponnesian War" by Thucydides. In previous research [1, 2], for the extraction of Source-Outcome/Cause-Result relations from the "Peloponnesian War" of Thucydides, a sublanguage-based approach was employed, based on the structure and linguistic features of the source text (Ancient Greek) and the linguistically related "Assistive" ("buffer") translation (Katharevousa Greek).

Standard Information Extraction techniques are based on the universal or text-dependent (syntax) [15, 22, 23] logical relations between entities - facts, names, objects, actions as concepts, whether text-dependent or text-independent [3, 10, 11]. However, information related to mentality, intentions, beliefs and emotions as well as socio-cultural factors for the presentation and presentation of Source-Outcome/Cause-Result relations is not easily processed with standard Information Extraction techniques. This is due to the fact that the above described type of information is not easily analyzed and categorized in sublanguage-independent detectable and extractable entity groups and patterns of sequences of words and entities. Although typical practices in Digital Humanities provide a necessary basis for any forms of Information Extraction, here, the employment of a customized approach is necessary.

Additionally, precision and correctness are here a basic requirement, as in the case of technical texts, where practices of a traditional in-depth analysis are used to create Controlled Languages. The strategy employed is a sublanguage-based formalization of ontologies in the vocabulary and sentence structure, typical in Controlled Languages [12, 13] which were originally based on features of technical texts and extended to other task-oriented domains and applications. To conform to the requirements of precision and correctness but also to achieve speed for an easy access to the requested information, a strategy with features and practices of Controlled Languages is employed, such as controlling input in relation to a restricted set of words and processing predefined types of sentence structure related to respective types of content.

The implemented application is based on three types of ontologies. These ontologies are used for the extraction of the requested information in the text passages presented: The Topic-Keyword Ontology (the actual word-entries from the online political and journalistic texts as user-input -extendable by the User); The assistive Query Ontology (visible to the User); The Search Ontology (extracting the passages from multiple [other] corpora- primarily the "Assistive" Translation).

We note that these ontologies used in previous research presented here [1, 2, 16] correspond to the proposed Seed-Domain ontologies depicted in Sect. 4, namely: The Topic-Keyword Ontology corresponds to the proposed general search ontology ("Start-Up" ontology, Sect. 4) and the Query Ontology and Search Ontology both correspond to the proposed singular "Search Term" ontology presented here in Sect. 4. These modifications target to simplify the search process. However, for analysis purposes, we present the original ontology types used in the implemented specialized application.

The Topic-Keyword Ontology and the sublanguage-specific Query Ontology are combined (TQ) and used to assist the User's query as a singular search list and to refine the User' search. The Search Ontology operates in resources consisting translations from ancient texts (MIT Classics Archive -Crawley Translation [5]) in combination with the "Assistive" translation in languages closer to the original ancient texts (Portal for the Greek Language – Venizelos Translation [21]). The Search Ontology functioning as a search and extraction tool is based on the Source-Outcome/Cause-Result relationships explaining politics, diplomacy and geopolitical relations from the "Peloponnesian War" of Thucydides.

The sublanguage-specific Query Ontology [1, 2] is in English and in the language of the "Assistive" Translation (Katharevousa Greek). It is used to assist the User's query and to refine the User's search and is based on keywords clustered around three basic concepts. These concepts extend the formalization of the sublanguage of "Diplomacy" from previous studies [2]: State (for example: neutrality" or "disadvantage"); Action (for example: "response"- "reaction"- "answer" or "accept" and "rejection"); Result (for example: "gain"- "benefit"- "profit" or "loss"). Furthermore, the Query Ontology contains an additional small set of words with sublanguage-specific tags such as "Athenians-[Superpower]", to assist Users queries (currently approximately 280 words).

The specialized Search Ontology performs the actual search in the translation close to the ancient text. The strategy employed for extracting the requested information from passages in the "Assistive" translation is based on: (1) the recognition of a defined set of conjunctions (CONJ) and (2) the recognition of a set of words concerning intention and behavior, annotated as "Intention-Behavior"- IB words (verbs and participles). Multiple IB words contained in passages extracted can be related to a singular query containing keywords from the Topic-Keyword Ontology and the Query Ontology (TQ-Keyword):

Query: [TQ-Keyword(s)] IB < CONJ > IB [TQ-Keyword(s)] [2, 16].

The IB words occur "before" and "after" the conjunction (CONJ). The text containing the IB word(s) before the conjunction CONJ expresses the "Result (Outcome)" relation and the text containing the IB word(s) after the conjunction CONJ expresses the "Cause (Source)" relation. However, for some types of conjunctions, the reverse order applies [2, 16]. The order and type of "Cause (Source)" and "Result (Outcome)" is dependent on the type of conjunction concerned. This type of order is defined according to the information structure in the Assistive Translation, which allows a strict formalization of information content based on syntactic structure similar to formalizations for creating Controlled Languages. This is the basis on which the Cause-Result relations are extracted.

The group of specified conjunctions describing causal relations contains expressions such as "because" and "due to" ("διότι", "επειδή", "άλλωστε", "δια το", "δηλαδή", "ένεκα", "ένεκεν", "ώστε").

Relations between topics may concern "IB verbs" of the following types:

"Feeling-Intention-Attitude" type (what was believed, what was felt, what was intended, what attitude prevailed -Int-Intention) (for example: "were intended to" ("διατεθειμένοι"), "ignored", "were ignorant about" ("ηγνόουν"), "expected", "calculated", "took into account" -"υπελόγιζαν");

"Speech-Behavior" type - Sp-Speech (what was said - for example: "asked", "demanded" ("εζήτουν"), "convinced" ("πείσουν"), "supported", "backed" -"υπεστήριζε");

"Benign-Malignant Behavior" type (actual behavior -Bh-Behavior) (for example: "secured" (in context of negotiation) ("εξασφαλίσας"). [2, 16].

In the following example (implementation in JAVA [16]), the passages contain Cause-Result relations related to the keywords "subjects (of superpowers)" from the Topic-Keyword Ontology paired with "revolt" and "carried away" from the Query Ontology (TQ). A query concerning the possibility of a revolution by people controlled by a superpower ("subjects (of superpowers)" "revolt") is refined and assisted with the aid of keywords from the Topic-Keyword Ontology and the Query Ontology. The search and extraction is performed by the Search Ontology (IB verbs and CONJ), extracting one or multiple passages containing the keywords from the Topic-Keyword Ontology:

Query Content: [subjects (of superpowers), revolt (TQ)]
Search Ontology match: (IB-Int: showed desire) <CONJ:because> (IB-Sp: admit)

The extracted passages of the matches in the text are presented to the User (The Eighth Book, Chapter XXIV, Nineteenth and Twentieth Years of the War - Revolt of Ionia - Intervention of Persia - The War in Ionia). The additional information from the Assistive Translation (Katharevousa Greek text) is depicted in square brackets, as demonstrated in the following example:

English Translation: But above all, the subjects of the Athenians showed a readiness to revolt [against rule] even beyond their ability, [because] judging the circumstances with [carried away by] [revolutionary] passion, and refusing even to hear of the Athenians being able to last out the coming summer.
Assistive Translation: Before: CONJ ("διότι")-IB: "εκτιμώμεναι":[Αλλ' οι, υπήκοοι προ πάντων των Αθηναίων εδείκνυαν μεγάλην επιθυμίαν όπως αποτινάξουν την κυριαρχίαν των και αν ακόμη αι δυνάμεις των ορθώς εκτιμώμεναι δεν ήσαν επαρκείς εις τούτο]
After: IB: "παραδεχθούν": [διότι εις τας κρίσεις των παρεσύροντο από τον επαναστατικόν οργασμόν, και δεν ήθελαν να παραδεχθούν καν ότι οι Αθηναίοι ήτο ενδεχόμενον να ανθέξουν κατά το προσεχές θέρος].

We note that keywords in the Topic-Keyword Ontology and the Query Ontology (TQ) may also be subjected to Machine Translation. In the previous approaches concerned [1, 2], this included Universal Words, with the use of the Universal Networking Language (UNL - www.undl.org) originally created for processing UN documents in languages as diverse as English, Hindi and Chinese [20].

Parameters for "The Art of War" by Sun Tzu. In the case of "The Art of War" by Sun Tzu, we note the characteristic use (and repetition) of verbal anaphora in the text content and structure [19] and particular types of military terms [24].

For the detection of repetitions, indicating content of emphasized significance, the respective process for the detection of this specialized and detailed information can be activated by the "Enable Context" button.
Example [24]: "十六字诀" This term refers to "上兵伐谋, 其次伐交, 其次伐兵, 其下攻城", which is from chapter three of Sun Tzu.
Ames's translation: The best military policy is to attack strategies; the next to attack alliances; the next to attack soldiers; and the worst to assault walled cities.
Lin's translation: The best policy in war is to thwart the enemy's strategy. The second best is to disrupt his alliances through diplomatic means. The third best is to attack his army in the field. The worst policy of all is to attack walled cities.
Example [19]: 是故军无辎重则亡, 无粮食则亡, 无委积则亡. (军争 第七)
Pinyin: Shigu jun wu zizhong ze wang, wu liangshi ze wang, wu weiji ze wang. (Chapter 7 Manoeuvring)
Version (1). An army without its baggage train is lost; without provisions it is lost; without bases of supply it is lost. (L. Giles)

Version (2). For this reason, if an army is without its equipment and stores, it will perish; if it is without provisions, it will perish; if it is without material support it will perish. (Roger Ames)

Diverse meanings of a seemingly singular term are another characteristic feature of "The Art of War" by Sun Tzu. For example, according to the description in "The Art of War", there are five types of spies in war, and 反间(fǎn jiàn) is the third one. The discussion about the military terminologies of spies in "The Art of War" is as follows:

Example of diverse terms from "The Art of War" by Sun Tzu:

(1) The first kind of spy is called 因间 (yīn jiàn). Sun Tzu said"因间者 (yīn jiàn zhě), 因其乡人而用之 (yīn qí xiāngrén ér yòng zhī)".That means 因间 is a special spy whom you can make work for you because he is your fellow countryman. Therefore, the military term of 因间 (yīn jiàn) can be translated into "a fellow countryman spy".

(2) The second kind of spy is called 内间 (nèijiàn). "内间者 (nèijiàn zhě), 因其官人而用之 (yīn qí guānrén ér yòng zhī)".That means 内间 is a special spy whom you can make work for you because he is an enemy government official. Therefore, the military term of 内间 (nèijiàn) can be translated into "an enemy government official spy".

(3) The third kind of spy is called 反间 (fǎnjiàn). "反间者 (fǎnjiàn zhě), 因其敌间而用之 (yīn qí díjiān ér yòng zhī)". That means 反间 is a special defecting spy whom you can make work for you because he is an enemy spy. Therefore, the military term of 反间 (fǎnjiàn) can be translated into "an enemy's converted spy".

(4) The forth kind of spy is called 死间 (sǐjiàn). "死间者 (sǐjiàn zhě), 为诳事于外 (wèi kuáng shì yú wài), 令吾间知之 (lìng wújiān zhīzhī), 而传于敌间也 (ér chuán yú díjiān yě)".That means 死间 is a betraying spy who is doomed to die. To deceive the outside world, we intentionally make certain information collected and disseminated to the enemy by the spy who betrayed us. The military term of 死间 (sǐjiàn) can be translated into "a doomed spy".

(5) The fifth kind of spy is called 生间 (shēngjiàn). "生间者 (shēngjiàn zhě), 反报也 (fǎn bào yě)".That means 生间 is a surviving spy who can come back alive to report. The military term of 生间 (shēngjiàn) can be translated into "a surviving spy".

The implementation of modules concerning the processing and evaluation of the content of political and journalistic texts from international English-speaking news networks can be adapted to the content type and linguistic features selected English translations of the "The Art of War" by Sun Tzu. These modules implemented in previous research [2, 16] involve the signalization of occurrences of word repetitions in sentences and paragraphs of political and journalistic texts from international news networks [16]. The implemented modules also involve the signalization of particular word classes and their percentages with the aid of the Stanford Log-Linear Part-of-Speech Tagger [2, 16, 25]. Unlike the content of political and journalistic texts from international news networks, where mostly nouns, proper nouns, adjectives and adverbs were selected and processed [2, 16], in the case of "The Art of War by Sun Tzu, verbs and verbal anaphora play a significant role. In contrast to proper names and nouns, verbs and verbal anaphora constitute word types that are less commonly selected by application users in Information Extraction strategies and other forms of search mechanisms. In other words, there is a lexical category bias in respect to verbs and verbal anaphora [9]. However, in the case of "The Art of War by Sun Tzu, these less commonly sought word types are observed to be links to essential information.

The different word types are detectable with a POS Tagger. The respective words and word categories may constitute a small set of entries in a specially created lexicon or may be retrieved from existing databases or WordNets. In this case, sublanguage-specific Seed Domain ontologies.

4 Presentation: Modelling the "Specify Term" Function

4.1 Modelling Domain-Specific Seed Ontologies

As described above, the Interface is designed to provide possible options to the User in order to assist the query. These options are both in respect to the information content of the word ("Specify Term") and its possible contexts ("Enable Context" button).

In the previously mentioned "Specify Term" function, the User chooses a word from an online written or spoken text and enters it into the interface. The User selects the type of Classical Text concerned and then activates the "Specify Term" button. The function of query assistance minimizes the possibility of Cognitive Bias, in particular, Availability Bias [4].

In the first step of the interaction of the "Specify Term" function, namely the "Select query word(s)" sub-task, individual keywords of User queries in form of free input are recognized by the application. Words and expressions from the free input of User queries can be directly matched to the content of the ancient Classical Text. The user can directly proceed with search and extraction in the respective passages displayed in the interface. If there is no match, the user proceeds to the next step of the interaction of the "Specify Term" function, namely to "Refine search words" sub-task (sublanguage-specific) ("Specify Term" function - Message: No matches found. Proceed with Search anyway? OR Refine Search). In this case, keywords from sublanguage-specific ontologies appear as an option (selected from the menu or as a pop-up window) to assist the User's query. In particular, the User's query is assisted by ontologies presented as a singular search list in the interface of the application ("Specify Term" function - Menu: Assist Search), with a similar function as an interactive Controlled Language editor for the management of input for texts to be processed (for example, max. 20 English words of average size).

These ontologies constitute a sublanguage-specific domain ontology [22] functioning as a prior knowledge [8, 17], which can be extended and adapted, if necessary, for example, for term clustering with seed knowledge-based LDA models [8]. These ontologies constitute hand-labeled training data for further training and implementation [17]. As described above, we note that the nature of the information content concerned does not allow a direct training and implementation of ontologies without the requirement of hand-labeled training data, as in other types of information and related applications [6].

There is a general search ontology (Start-Up ontology) for both types of Ancient Texts. To facilitate User's queries, the extendable Start-Up ontology contains a "start-up" set of predefined general sublanguage expressions such as "war", "allies" and "rebellion" of currently approximately 100 words (Start-Up).

There is a specialized ontology for each type of text, namely the Thucydides Search Term Ontology and the Sun Tzu Search Term Ontology, which are connected to the respective "Enable Content" modules specializing in the information content of the type of Ancient Text. One ontology is based on terms from Thucydides' Peloponnesian War and the other ontology is designed to be based on the terms of "The Art of War" by Sun Tzu. Both ontologies are extendable.

With the "Update Ontology" function, the (expert) user may choose to update and/or extend the general search ontology (Start-Up ontology) or one of the specialized Search Term Ontologies, the Thucydides Search Term Ontology or the Sun Tzu Search Term Ontology. The sublanguage-based formalization of ontologies in the vocabulary and sentence structure allows the use of keywords, a feature typical of Spoken Dialog Systems, where speed is of crucial importance [14]. The Topic-Keyword Ontology is extendable. There is the option for its extension by expert users ("Update Ontology" function Menu: Save Query) (not presented in Fig. 1).

Typical examples from the Seed-Domain ontology of Thucydides' Peloponnesian War are general search ontology (Start-Up ontology) terms "war", "allies" and "rebellion" and text and sublanguage-specific terms connected to the respective nodes in the Search Term Ontology, namely "State", "Action" and "Result". Examples of sublanguage-specific terms connected to the "State" node are "neutrality" and "disadvantage". Examples of sublanguage-specific terms connected to the "Action" node are "response", "reaction", "answer"," accept" and "rejection". Examples of sublanguage-specific terms connected to the "Result" node are "gain", "benefit", "profit" and "loss" (Fig 2).

Typical examples from the Seed-Domain ontology of "The Art of War" by Sun Tzu include the above-described general search ontology (Start-Up ontology) terms "war" "allies" and "rebellion" and text and sublanguage-specific terms concerning "Military policy". They are connected to the Search Term Ontology subset of the "The Art of War" Seed-Domain ontology. The Search Term Ontology contains sublanguage-specific verbs and the respective nodes namely "Strategy", "Battlefield-Tactical" and "Objects". Examples of sublanguage-specific terms connected to the "Strategy" node are "military policy", "strategies", "alliances", "enemy", "diplomatic means", "soldiers". Examples of sublanguage-specific terms connected to the "Battlefield-Tactical" node are " enemy field", "(walled) cities", "bases of supply", also "soldiers". Examples of sublanguage-specific terms connected to the "Objects" node are "baggage train", "provisions", "equipment", "stores", "material support" (Fig. 3).

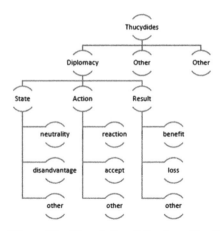

Fig. 2. Overview of Thucydides "Search Term" Ontology (Seed Domain Ontology).

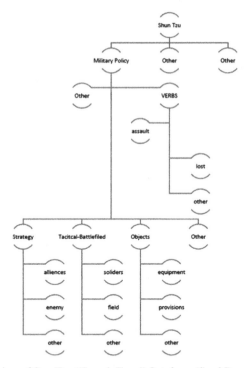

Fig. 3. Overview of Sun Tzu "Search Term" Ontology (Seed Domain Ontology).

5   Conclusions and Further Research

Information from spoken political and journalistic texts and online written political and journalistic texts is targeted to be linked to knowledge and information to classical texts for its comparison and evaluation. However, access to knowledge from ancient classical texts for a comparison and understanding of currents events and situations poses challenges, especially to non-experts. This process can become of increased complexity especially if information is searched regarding behaviors, attitude and mentality linked to war and not facts, events and names. Easy access to the Classical Texts and the display of detailed and/or specific information in a user-friendly interaction is the main target of the designed user-interface and partially implemented applications. The approach integrates expert-knowledge and user requirements and also manages Cognitive Bias. The designed user-interface and partially implemented applications by-passes Cognitive Bias but also takes advantage of specific types of Cognitive Bias.

The upgrading and updating of the existing ontologies by expert-users is expected to play a key-role in the full implementation and overall improvement and upgrading of the application and interface. The target of the application and interface is its function as a "two-ended" collaborative search interface, with the user on the one end and the expert/expert-user on the other end, updating /upgrading the ontology.

A possible future step in the implementation of the application is the generation of models created from the relations between the words processed in the "Enable Context" functions. The strategy used in the present application can also function as a corpus builder, as a training platform and as starting point for further adaptations and additional goals. However, for any further developments full implementation of all the interface functions and extensive evaluations are necessary.

Acknowledgements. In loving memory of our co-author Vasilios Floros who passed away before the completion of the present research paper.

References

1. Alexandris, C., Mylonakis, K., Tassis, S., Nottas, M., Cambourakis, G.: Implementing a platform for complex information processing from written and spoken journalistic data. In: Kurosu, M. (eds.) HCI 2017. LNCS, vol. 10271, pp. 549–558. Springer, Cham (2017). https://doi.org/10.1007/978-3-319-58071-5_41
2. Alexandris, C.: Accessing cause-result relation and diplomatic information in ancient "journalistic" texts with universal words. In: Kurosu, M. (eds.) HCI 2014. LNCS, vol. 8511, pp. 351–361. Springer, Cham (2014). https://doi.org/10.1007/978-3-319-07230-2_34
3. Angeli, G., Premkumar, M.J., Manning, C.: Leveraging linguistic structure for open domain information extraction. In: Proceedings of the 53rd Annual Meeting of the Association for Computational Linguistics and the 7th International Joint Conference on Natural Language Processing, Stroudsbourg, PA, USA, pp. 344–354. Association for Computational Linguistics ACL (2015)
4. Azzopardi, L.: Cognitive Biases in search: a review and reflection of cognitive biases in information retrieval. In: Proceedings of the 2021 ACM SIGIR Conference on Human Information Interaction and Retrieval (CHIIR 2021), New York, NY, USA. ACM (2021). https://doi.org/10.1145/3406522.344602
5. Crawley, R.: Thucydides' Peloponnesian War, translated by Richard Crawley. J.M. Dent and Co., London (1903)
6. Fries, J.A., et al.: Ontology-driven weak supervision for clinical entity classification in electronic health records. Nat. Commun. **12** (2021). https://doi.org/10.1038/s41467-021-223 28-4

7. Hatim, B.: Communication Across Cultures: Translation Theory and Contrastive Text Linguistics. University of Exeter Press, Exeter (1997)

8. Huang, H., Harzallah, M., Guillet, F., Xu, Z.: Core-concept-seeded LDA for ontology learning. Procedia Comput. Sci. **192**, 222–231 (2021). https://doi.org/10.1016/j.procs.2021.08.023

9. Jia, H., Liang, J.: Lexical category bias across interpreting types: implications for synergy between cognitive constraints and language representations. Lingua **239** (2020)

10. Jurafsky, D., Martin, J.H.: Speech and Language Processing, an Introduction to Natural Language Processing, Computational Linguistics and Speech Recognition, 2nd edn. Prentice Hall series in Artificial Intelligence, Pearson Education, Upper Saddle River (2008)

11. Jurafsky, D., Martin, J.H.: Speech and Language Processing, an Introduction to Natural Language Processing, Computational Linguistics and Speech Recognition, 3rd edn. (2022). Draft: https://web.stanford.edu/~jurafsky/slp3/ed3book_jan122022.pdf

12. Kuhn, T.: A survey and classification of controlled natural languages. Comput. Linguist. **40**(1), 121–170 (2014)

13. Lehrndorfer A.: Kontrolliertes Deutsch: Linguistische und Sprachpsychologische Leitlinien für eine (maschniell) kontrollierte Sprache in der technischen Dokumentation. Tübingen, Narr (1996)

14. Lewis, J.R.: Introduction to Practical Speech User Interface Design for Interactive Voice Response Applications. IBM Software Group, USA, Tutorial T09 presented at HCI 2009 San Diego, CA, USA (2009)

15. Mausam, N.V., Schmitz, M., Bart, R., Soderland, S., Etzioni, O.: Open language learning for information extraction. In: Proceedings of EMNLP-CoNLL 2012 -Joint Conference on Empirical Methods in Natural Language Processing and Computational Natural Language Learning, Stroudsburg, PA, USA, pp. 523–534. Association for Computational Linguistics ACL (2012)

16. Mylonakis, C.: Processing and extracting complex information in written and spoken journalistic data and historic (ancient) texts. Masters thesis, Department of Informatics and Telecommunications, National University of Athens, Greece (2016)

17. Rawsthorne, H.M., Abadie, N., Kergosien, E., Duchêne, C., Saux, E.: ATONTE: towards a new methodology for seed ontology development from texts and experts. In: Corcho, O., Hollink, L., Kutz, O., Troquard, N., Ekaputra F.J. (eds.) EKAW 2022, Proceedings of the 23rd International Conference on Knowledge Engineering and Knowledge Management, Bolzano, Italy (2022). hal-03794323

18. Suissa, O., Elmalech, A., Zhitomirsky-Geffet, M.: Text analysis using deep neural networks in digital humanities and information science. J. Assoc. Inf. Sci. Technol. (JASIST) **73**, 268–287 (2022). https://doi.org/10.1002/asi.24544

19. Tao, Y.: Translation of verbal anaphora in "the art of war." Theory Pract. Lang. Stud. **3**(6), 1040–1044 (2013). https://doi.org/10.4304/tpls.3.6.1040-1044

20. Uchida, H., Zhu, M., Della Senta, T.: Universal Networking Language. The UNDL Foundation, Tokyo, Japan (2005)

21. Venizelos, E.: Thoukudidou Istoriai: Kata Metaphrasin Eleutheriou Benizelou. [Thucydides' History: translated by Eleftherios Venizelos]. In: Caclamanos, D. (ed.) Two Vols. Oxford University Press, Oxford (1940)

22. Zhang, B., Kumpulainen, S., Keskustalo, H.: A review on information retrieval in the historical digital humanities domain. In: Proceedings of the Asian Conference on Arts & Humanities 2021 ACAH2021, Tokyo, Japan (2021). https://doi.org/10.22492/issn.2186-229X.2021.1

23. Zhao, G., Zhang, X.: Domain-specific ontology concept extraction and hierarchy extension. In: Proceedings of the 2nd International Conference on Natural Language Processing and Information Retrieval (NLPIR 2018), Bangkok, Thailand, pp. 60–64. ACM, New York (2018). https://doi.org/10.1145/3278293.3278302

24. Zheng, J.: A comparative study on English translations of military terms in Sun Tzu: "the art of war". Theory Pract. Lang. Stud. **9**(5), 537–544 (2019). https://doi.org/10.17507/tpls.090 5.07
25. The Stanford Log-linear Part-Of-Speech Tagger. https://nlp.stanford.edu/software/tagger. shtml. Accessed 6 Nov 2022

Development of MLOps Platform Based on Power Source Analysis for Considering Manufacturing Environment Changes in Real-Time Processes

Ji-hyun Cha[1]([✉]) [iD], Heung-gyun Jeong[1] [iD], Seung-woo Han[1] [iD],
Dong-chul Kim[1] [iD], Jung-hun Oh[1] [iD], Seok-hee Hwang[2] [iD],
and Byeong-ju Park[2] [iD]

[1] Cloudnetworks Co., Ltd, 20, Yeongdong-daero 96-gil, Gangnam-gu, Seoul, Korea
{jh.cha,harris.jeong,sw.han,dc.kim,jh.oh}@cloudnetworks.co.kr
[2] Ijoon Co., Ltd, 410, 75, Techno 1-ro, Yuseong-gu, Daejeon, Korea
{seokhee,bjpark}@Ijoon.net

Abstract. Smart factories have led to the introduction of automated facilities in manufacturing lines and the increase in productivity using semi-automatic equipment or work auxiliary tools that use power sources in parallel with the existing pure manual manufacturing method. The productivity and quality of manual manufacturing work heavily depend on the skill level of the operators. Therefore, changes in manufacturing input factors can be determined by analyzing the pattern change of power sources such as electricity and pneumatic energy consumed in work-aid tools or semi-automatic facilities used by skilled operators. The manual workflow can be optimized by modeling this pattern and the image information of the operator and analyzing it in real time. Machine learning operations (MLOps) technology is required to respond to rapid changes in production systems and facilities and work patterns that frequently occur in small-batch production methods. MLOps can selectively configure Kubeflow, the MLOps solution, and the data lake based on Kubernetes for the entire process, from collecting and analyzing data to learning and deploying ML models, enabling the provision of fast and differentiated services from model development to distribution by the scale and construction stage of the manufacturing site. In this study, the manual work patterns of operators, which are unstructured data, were formulated into power source consumption patterns and analyzed along with image information to develop a manufacturing management platform applicable to manual-based, multi-variety, small-volume production methods and eventually for operator training in connection with three-dimensional visualization technology.

Keywords: Pneumatic pattern analysis · Manual work standardization · Image information analysis · Machine learning

© The Author(s), under exclusive license to Springer Nature Switzerland AG 2023
M. Kurosu and A. Hashizume (Eds.): HCII 2023, LNCS 14014, pp. 224–236, 2023.
https://doi.org/10.1007/978-3-031-35572-1_15

1   Introduction

In manual manufacturing sites, managers oversee tracking and managing the quality of manual work performed by operators through standard operating procedures such as work instructions. Recently, manual tasks have been standardized using the deep learning technology of artificial intelligence (AI) smart cameras, and analysis models with evaluation accuracy of 99% have been introduced in some electrical and electronic parts industries that value work quality. Although AI cameras may generate an abnormal signal when the work pattern of an operator deviates from a trained model, there is a limit to detecting actions that can occur within the same work pattern, such as the action of slightly changing the button-pressing strength of an electric or pneumatic driver, which is a work-aid tool. In the event of changes in the manufacturing environment, such as materials, equipment, and manpower, which may lead to quality defects upon proceeding with the existing work method, skilled operators can avoid defects by temporarily changing their working manner based on their experience. However, non-skilled operators frequently generate defects due to a lack of information on the change points and countermeasures.

In manual manufacturing, productivity and quality are also different depending on the skill of the operator in handling jigs and semi-automatic equipment. However, product inspection mainly relies on the initial product and sampling method, and defects are often monitored late in the subsequent process. Therefore, to minimize the defects caused by manual work, a system enabling real-time management and tracking by linking the energy consumption pattern and the status information of semi-finished products in the manufacturing of each unit process must be developed.

As the pneumatic actuator has non-linear characteristics owing to the compressibility and friction of air and its working fluid, implementing accurate modeling is very difficult, reducing control performance. Many studies on pneumatic actuators have been conducted to compensate for these nonlinearities and limitations to improve driving precision. As the compressed air generated by the compressor and delivered to the pneumatic actuator is affected by the load design of the entire system, piping valves, dryer filters, etc., pneumatic consumption patterns need to be studied from a comprehensive perspective. In particular, the original technology for virtual sensing and energy saving can be secured by reinterpreting the pneumatic pattern on the secondary side of the pneumatic regulator used to reduce the pressure on the primary side, while the leak pressure and excessive use of the manufacturing line can be improved by detecting abnormal signs and optimizing the pneumatic consumption pattern for the operation units of automatic and semi-automatic facilities. Furthermore, the developed technology can predict abnormalities in the process, quality, and manufacturing facilities by analyzing the electricity, pneumatics, and image information (vibration, particle, and equipment operation information) acquired from manufacturing facilities. This proposed technology can be applied to most small and medium-sized enterprises operating various types of semi-automated and automated facilities without being limited to manual manufacturing sites. To analyze the final consumption of pneumatic pressure, this study aimed to develop a manufacturing management platform technology that can be applied to the manual work-based, multi-variety, small-volume production method by formalizing the manual work patterns of operators, which are unstructured data, into power source consumption patterns and analyzing them in conjunction with image information.

2   Manufacturing Power Source

The main power sources used in manual-based manufacturing sites are electricity and pneumatic energy. For electricity, energy management systems, such as a factory energy management system, monitor and control the power supply feeders (distribution and distribution boxes). For pneumatic pressure, only a pressure regulator is installed at the inlet end of the facility, with the operator managing only the upper and lower limit specs.

2.1   Pneumatic System

Driving Principle. The main components of a pneumatic system include a compressor, a pneumatic regulator, and an air cylinder. When the air pressure is consumed at the outlet due to the operation of the air cylinder, the main valve, diaphragm, and pressure control spring of the pressure-reducing regulator operate to restore the set air pressure, where the load-side pneumatic pressure shows various instantaneous patterns depending on the set time of the solenoid valve (Table 1 and Fig. 1).

Table 1. Pneumatic working principle.

No	Unit	Motion
1	Air cylinder primary inlet	Compressed air input when the air cylinder moves forward
2	Pressure reducing regulator	Pneumatic filling
3	Solenoid valve switching	Pneumatic holding
4	Air cylinder secondary side outlet	Compressed air input when the air cylinder moves backward
5	Pressure reducing regulator	Pneumatic filling

Fine Pattern Analysis. Collecting the data generated when the air pressure is consumed in tens of ms units and converting them into big data enables analyzing patterns that cannot be analyzed in seconds; moreover, the difference in workability can be verified by standardizing manual movement, know-how, and skill.

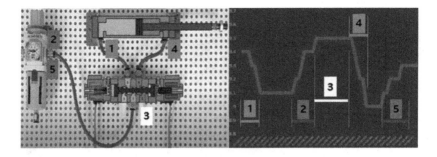

Fig. 1. Pneumatic system diagram.

For example, in an ultrasonic welding machine that fuses manually assembled upper and lower panels of an enclosure with a horn mounted on an air cylinder, if a defect such as a crack occurs due to a work mistake at the lowest point of the air cylinder piston, the piston speed decreases and the stroke distance is shortened, affecting the load-side pneumatic pattern. To verify the factors affecting the pneumatic pattern at the lowest point of the air cylinder, after supplying 90 to 150 kPa of pneumatic pressure to two types of double-acting cylinders with bore diameters of 10 and 16 pi, a 6–12 N force is applied with a push-pull gauge to generate artificial resistance pressure at the stroke end point, confirming "a significant difference in the fine pattern" compared to the normal operation.

The mechanism of occurrence can be explained through adaptive control modeling (Table 2 and Fig. 2, 3).

Table 2. Pneumatic pattern test.

Item	Specification	
	Manufacturer	Model
1. Sensor	Autonics	PSAN-D1CV(2.5~1,000ms)
2. Data collector	Autonics	PSM4-VR(Modbus RTU)
3. Converter	Autonics	SCM-US481(RS-485)
4. SMPS	Phoenix Contact	2910586
5. Software	Autonics	DAQ Master
6. Push pull gauge	HANDPI	NK-20 (Max 20N)
7. Air Cylinder	KCC	B10-S100
	FTEC	KM16-125

Cylinder bore (Pi)	Water pressure (Kpa)	Stroke (mm)	Resistance value (N)	Operation time (s)			
				Forward	Standby	Backward	Wait
1.10	140	100	6	2	2.5	0.7	2.5
	90	100	6	2	2.5	0.7	2.5
2.16	140	125	12	1.4	0.5	0.7	1.2
	90	125	12	1.4	0.5	0.7	1.2

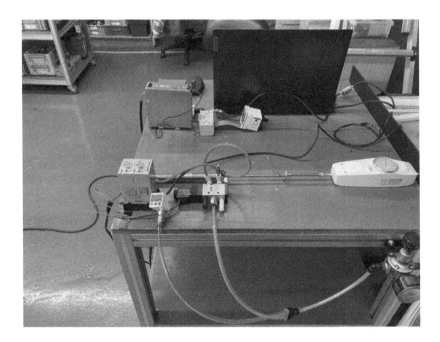

Fig. 2. Installation of pneumatic test bed.

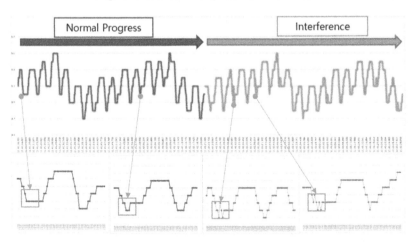

Fig. 3. Pneumatic pattern comparison.

Example of Manufacturing Facility Application. As the consumption patterns of all the pneumatic actuators are reflected in the secondary side pneumatic pattern in the T.C.A (Trip Coil Assembly) assembly process, where the operator sequentially stacks eight types of parts, the frictional force of the piston can be monitored, which is difficult to detect even with a displacement sensor and PLC time-out interlock and provides negligible progress due to air leakage (Fig. 4).

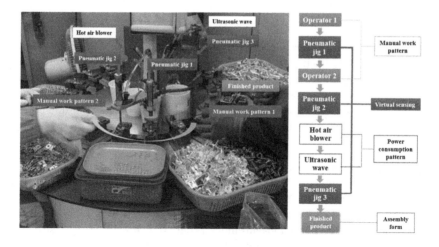

Fig. 4. Example of T.C.A assembly.

Energy Saving Effect. The pneumatic pressure of the facility should be selected by calculating the appropriate air consumption and load factor considering the productivity and quality requirements for the object to be processed, such as the collaborative robot pneumatic system. In most sites, the pneumatic pressure must be optimized considering the work characteristics, as it is usually standardized at a level of 4–6 kg/cm^2 without analysis of the pneumatic margin, and determined according to the required pressure of the compressed air equipment. The formula for calculating the power savings rate that can be obtained when the discharge pressure is reduced is as follows, where the reduction obtained when the discharge pressure of 7 kg/cm^2 is lowered to 6 kg/cm^2 is approximately 8.3%:

$$L_{ad} \propto \left\{ \left(\frac{P_2}{P_1} \right)^{\frac{(k-1)}{(a+1)k}} - 1 \right\} \right\} ; \varepsilon = \frac{L_{ad1} - L_{ad2}}{L_{ad1}} \times 100,$$

where Lad is the theoretical adiabatic air power (kW), ε is the power savings rate (%), P1 is the atmospheric pressure (suction pressure), and P2 is the absolute discharge pressure before and after improvement.

The main components of a pneumatic system include a compressor, a pneumatic regulator, and an air cylinder. When the air pressure is consumed at the outlet due to the operation of the air cylinder, the main valve, diaphragm, and pressure control spring of the pressure-reducing regulator operate to restore the set air pressure, where the load-side pneumatic pressure shows various instantaneous patterns depending on the set time of the solenoid valve.

2.2 Power System

Supply System. Each electric feeder can be supplied to the facility by referring to the water substation unit disconnection diagram, power trunk line diagram, and distribution panel wiring diagram among the electrical drawings. If a facility using a motor is connected to a transformer dedicated to power facilities, it can be checked through the distribution panel (MCC) feeder in the single-line diagram of the water substation facility.

Monitoring System. By analyzing the energy consumption pattern of a facility, optimal operation, detection of abnormal symptoms, and maintenance plans can be secured for electricity, which is the main power source of manufacturing facilities; thus, a place where the operating state can be measured must be selected and monitored as a measurement point. In a manufacturing site where an energy management system is installed, a module for collecting power quality data in the main distribution box or a smart type circuit breaker is installed, enabling the collection of data on manufacturing facilities, freight elevators, electric heat, and lights; the collected data are transmitted to the central control system through the gateway. In a manufacturing site where an energy management system is not installed, it is necessary to check whether it is possible to install a meter, such as a watt-hour meter, for checking the real-time load and consumption at each feeder of the facility.

Power Quality Control. The Electricity Supply Terms and Conditions of Korea Electric Power Corporation (KEPCO) and the international standard IEEE C57.12.00 - 1987 set harmonic limits, and the upper limit should not exceed 5% of the rated current. Measurements are conducted on the secondary side of the load, which is the low voltage part of the distribution panel, and measures to reduce harmonics include the installation of passive or active filters, installation of reactors (ACL, DCL), increase in the transducer multipulse output constant (rectifier polyphase), adoption of pulse width modulation converters, installation of phase shift transformers, system separation, increase in harmonic immunity, and increase in short-circuit capacity (Tables 3 and 4).

3 Analysis Platform

The predictive model, one of the components of the analysis platform, is a machine learning operations (MLOps) technology that collects data in the form of a data lake and enables rapid re-learning and distribution. The developed model enables efficient management from development to distribution while minimizing the involvement of specialists, even when it is necessary to quickly switch to a multi-variety, small-volume production system (common in manual work sites) or to modify the model due to changes in equipment and operators. The components and functions required by the platform are as follows.

Table 3. Electricity supply terms and conditions of KEPCO.

Voltage Classification	Supplied from S/S with underground lines		Supplied from S/S with overhead lines	
	Voltage distortion factor (%)	Equivalent disturbing current (%)	Voltage distortion factor (%)	Equivalent disturbing current (%)
66 [kV] or lower	3.0	-	3.0	-
154 [kV] or lower	1.5	3.8	1.5	-

Table 4. IEEE C57.12.00 - 1987 regulation.

Circuit voltage	Each harmonic maximum	Maximum total harmonic distortion
69 [kV] or lower	3.0	5.0
115 to 161 [kV]	1.5	2.5
161 [kV] or higher	1.0	1.5

3.1 Platform Components

Data Collection Unit. Through red-green-blue (RGB) and time-of-flight (ToF) cameras, images of operators performing manual work and product images are collected, and the pose estimation algorithm for manual pattern analysis is applied. By applying the upper body joint data and hand joint detection algorithm and extracting detailed joint data from the hand, three-dimensional (3D) joint data for visualization analysis is collected [1].

Data Analysis Unit. After defining the range of the work motion data and process elements, the classification system of two types of data is expressed in a hierarchical structure and analyzed by dividing it into task, motion, and posture. A convolutional neural network binary classification model is used to classify products as normal or defective based on image data. The final result is collected through Dense operation and SoftMax function application after extracting the DenseBlock optimization structure and feature from the backend model DenseNet.

3.2 Platform Features

Anomaly Detection Function. Process abnormality detection and feedback based on manually collected data require the analysis of influence and correlation between data, management chart, identification of data relationships through various visualization analyses, definition of key standard information for manual anomaly detection, development of standard information pre-processing technology for manual anomaly detection data analysis, outlier detection and removal, missing value treatment, normalization, principal component analysis, and development of a facility anomaly detection data analysis algorithm using correlation analysis and ML techniques.

Manual Operation Support Function. An input/output support service system between the execution services of work standards-based analysis model and the automatic update function of the data analysis model generated as a result of data analysis algorithm execution is required to share and improve the data analysis model for manual manufacturing operation support, standard-based analysis model modification and supplementation and schema implementation for manual anomaly detection analysis.

Interfacing Function. The development of a technology for generating patterns using image device interlocking power sources requires the extraction of interlocking patterns of data and image information generated during work-aid tool operation to compare and verify the operation sequence pattern of the work-aid tool and the power source consumption (Fig. 5).

3.3   Machine Learning Operations

MLOps can selectively configure Kubeflow, the MLOps solution, and the data lake based on Kubernetes for the entire process-from collecting and analyzing data to learning and deploying ML models-thereby enabling the provision of differentiated services from model development to distribution by the scale and construction stage of the manufacturing site [3].

Network Configuration. Powered by the cloud-native computing foundation, KubeEdge is built on Kubernetes to extend cloud-native containerized application orchestration capabilities to the edge. EdgeMesh can be configured by implementing a communication tunnel between subnets using Auto Relay, multicast DNS, and Hole Punching based on the implementation of LibP2P with Proxier, which is responsible for configuring the iptables rules of the kernel for communication between multiple middle-edge nodes and intercepting requests to the EdgeMesh process, and LoadBalancer and LibP2P to forward requests between nodes. EdgeMesh allows users to access edge-to-edge, edge-to-cloud, and cloud-to-edge applications from different local area networks [4] (Fig. 6).

Protocol Integration Support. The integration support between devices is secured by developing Driver Mapper and implementing the MQTT protocol to interface with OPC UA, MODBUS, and BLE, an industrial protocol based on IEC 62541, between the data collection device, pneumatic sensor and camera, and middle edge. After data preprocessing through Logstash in the ELK stack, data are distributed and stored in multiple nodes of ElasticSearch, with log data visualization and monitoring possible through Kibana [2].

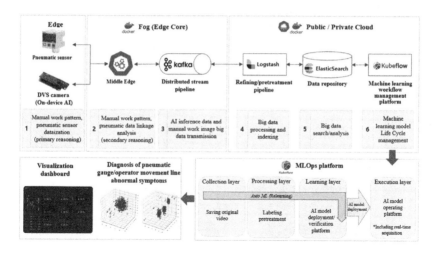

Fig. 5. Platform diagram.

Distribution Setting Management. Rapid deployment and rollback by recording and tracking changes is possible by developing a GitOps-based CI/CD pipeline for source distribution management and managing application sources and distribution settings through Git. When a push or pull request event occurs in Github, a deployment progress command is issued to Jenkins, which compresses the source code of the repository where the event occurred using the AWS Certification set in advance in the AWS Cloud in a zip format and uploads it to S3, the AWS Storage service. In sequence, it calls the AWS CodeDeploy service to start the deployment task, receives the source code from S3, and completes the deployment on the AWS EC2 server.

Machine Learning Workflow Configuration. Through Kubeflow Pipelines, a tool for building and deploying Kubernetes ML workflows, the code that is performed in all stages of the workflow, such as data preprocessing, data transformation, hyperparameter tuning, and model learning, is made in advance as a pipeline component and connected in the form of a directed acyclic graph. With Katib, a hyperparameter tuning system, the prediction accuracy and performance of the model can be improved through the automatic tuning of several ML frameworks such as Tensorflow, Pytorch, and XGBoost. Components are easily accessible through the configured Kubeflow UI dashboard, and a list of components running in the cluster, such as pipelines and katibs, can be consulted.

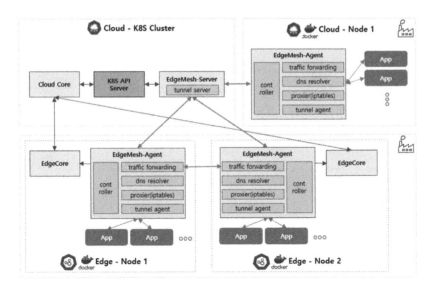

Fig. 6. EdgeMesh schematic diagram.

4   Education Platform

Summary. Working patterns can be standardized by converting the data collected from the image acquisition device into 3D skeleton coordinate values after primary inference. By comparing and analyzing them with the golden samples obtained by combining manual patterns and process elements, it can be used as a knowledge management platform to devise an optimized work method for each worker.

Schematic Diagram. The platform consists of a user interface layer, a process layer, and a data layer. Visualizations realized by 3D modeling can be used to manage, disseminate, and train optimized manual methods (Fig. 7).

Work Standardization. Standardizing the work guide and QC process chart by reflecting the golden sample and performing a comparative analysis of step practice and work patterns between workers by skill level using the work pattern image are expected to improve productivity and work quality.

Standard Operating Procedure. New and inexperienced operators can remove the factors that reduce productivity and quality due to workability in advance by performing comparative practice and correction through work pattern images for each step.

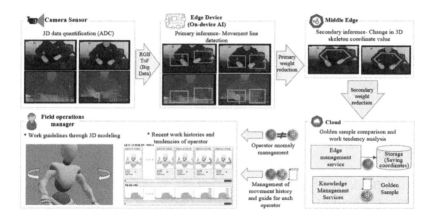

Fig. 7. Education platform.

Maximizing Yield. Real-time monitoring of work patterns of skilled operators in response to unexpected changes in 4M1E occurring at the manufacturing site and reflecting them in the production site can ensure a stable yield. A stable yield can be secured by monitoring the work patterns of the corresponding skilled workers in real time and reflecting them on the production site. In addition, by continuously reflecting, comparing, and analyzing data between experts in the golden samples for each period, points for improvement in work patterns can be continuously discovered.

Work Environment Improvement. Repetitive motions that can occur in the manual process at the manufacturing site, continuous motion in a fixed position, and inappropriate working posture can cause symptoms of pain, numbness, and aching in the neck, shoulder, elbow, and wrist. Standardizing the manual work patterns for each operator prevents excessive actions that cause these musculoskeletal disorders in advance, thereby improving the working environment.

5   Conclusion

As a measure to improve productivity and quality at manual-based manufacturing sites, this study aimed to propose a method to collect patterns of power sources, such as pneumatic energy and electricity, used by operators in ms units and analyze them in conjunction with image and product status information. Efficient management from development to distribution is required to quickly respond to model modifications due to the rapid conversion of small-batch production systems of various types and changes in facilities and workers, which frequently occur in manual work sites. These issues can be solved by the developed platform incorporating MLOps technology. Finally, improvement points can be derived and corrected by establishing an education platform and comparing and analyzing the work patterns of skilled workers through step-by-step work, a QC process chart, and work pattern videos for new personnel. These processes are expected to improve productivity and work quality.

Acknowledgements. This work was supported by project for Smart Manufacturing Innovation R&D funded Korea Ministry of SMEs and Startups in 2022 (RS-2022-00141143).

References

1. Van den Bergh, M., Van Gool, L.: Combining RGB and ToF cameras for real-time 3D hand gesture interaction. In: 2011 IEEE Workshop on Applications of Computer Vision (WACV), pp. 66–72. IEEE (2011)
2. Le, V.C., Yoo, M.: Lightweight kubeedge tool for edge computing environments. **46**(9), 1507–1514 (2021)
3. Raj, E., Buffoni, D., Westerlund, M., Ahola, K.: Edge MLOps: an automation framework for AIoT applications. In: 2021 IEEE International Conference on Cloud Engineering (IC2E), pp. 191–200. IEEE (2021)
4. Santos, J., Wauters, T., Volckaert, B., De Turck, F.: Towards network-aware resource provisioning in kubernetes for fog computing applications. In: 2019 IEEE Conference on Network Softwarization (NetSoft), pp. 351–359. IEEE (2019)

Application of Polymer Composite Material Reaction Vessel with IoT Monitoring System

Bai-Chau Chen and Jui-Hung Cheng(✉)

Department of Mold and Die Engineering, National Kaohsiung University of Science and Technology, Kaohsiung, Taiwan
`rick.cheng@nkust.edu.tw`

Abstract. In most cases, precise polymer composite reaction vessels require a lot of human resources. In addition to monitoring whether the reaction process is abnormal, it requires frequent manual adjustments of chemical raw materials and reaction parameters. In addition to being expensive, industrial-grade automated production equipment needs an excellent modular design, and there needs to be a standardized method to choose the most suitable method for the evaluation goal. Therefore, this study will use open-source software to implement products into the Internet of Things (IoT) to set standards and classify the scores of these methods in this regard. Moreover, set a complete user interface (UI) that, According to different usage environments, users can meet the requirements that meet the conditions, such as: "physical quantity inventory," "parameter control rate," and "data availability," and finally verify it through feasibility analysis., which includes: production cycle assessment, multiple feeding and discharging systems, and real-time monitoring of pressure and temperature in the reaction process to achieve quality control, provide a good user experience (UX), and realize automated production.

Keywords: Modular design · IoT · UI/UX · Real-Time Monitoring

1 Introduction

In an ever-advancing industrial environment, improving equipment intelligence leads to higher reliability of process results. Research in this field should utilize the Internet of Things (IoT) and cloud services provided by new technologies such as the Internet and various sensors. They are particularly suitable for chemical sensors and related equipment for continuous online monitoring of parameters. Therefore, obtaining these parameters is very important for the reaction process. The reaction vessels for polymer composite material apply with the Internet of Things as automatic reaction vessels for temperature, pressure control, and stirring with data. Industry 4.0 and the Internet of Things have become a trend in the current industry. In addition to precisely controlling each Item, parameters can also be controlled in and out of raw materials, using an intelligent monitoring system to reduce personnel costs and operational errors and significantly improve production stability. This study found that real-time monitoring and automatic production are essential in the overall reaction vessel, so there must be a way to build this system. When necessary, the modular expansion and combination of sensors can use for various Choose from different environments.

M. Kurosu and A. Hashizume (Eds.): HCII 2023, LNCS 14014, pp. 237–244, 2023.
https://doi.org/10.1007/978-3-031-35572-1_16

2   Materials and Methods

2.1   Pre-assessment

We extensively evaluate previous research and practice to define benchmarks for comparison, including benchmarks for experimental methods. These studies provide several ways to classify and compare existing processes, adding to the feasibility analysis. The traditional reaction vessels rely on empirical decisions, as shown in Fig. 1. They need relevant standards, such as feasibility assessment, method maturity, and process stability.

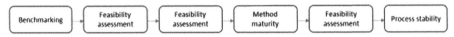

Fig. 1. Pre-Assessment Flow Chart

2.2   Pressure Reactor Vessels for IoT Applications

An overview of the application of a reaction vessel of polymer composite material with an IoT monitoring system showed as in Fig. 2. The proposed device design has sensors, MCU, and a reaction vessel used to monitor the process of raw chemical materials. In addition to controllable parameters such as pressure and temperature, the system allows further evaluation of process parameters to gain insight into current conditions. Establish data collection between the program and the cloud for data integration and historical investigation. Implement IoT in the system to improve overall process efficiency.

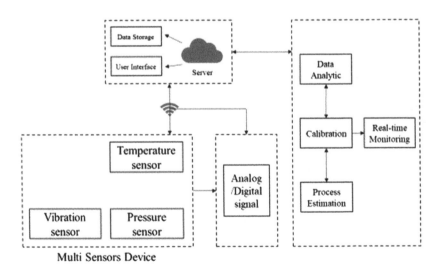

Fig. 2. Overview of IoT Sensors Applied to Polymer Reaction vessels

2.3 Node-Red for Real-Time Monitoring Screen

In order to define an exemplary user interface, the control element uses a development board based on open-source software so that users can make modular modifications to the device according to different usage scenarios in the future. At the same time, the monitoring system is developed with Node-Red for signal collection and processing, as shown in Fig. 3. Sensors collect the original parameters in the pressure vessel monitoring system connected to the Internet of Things. Then the information is sent to Raspberry Pi for data collection. At the same time, the information will import into the database. It is convenient to have a complete historical record verifying in the future. As shown in Fig. 4, it is no longer necessary to follow the traditional experience but to replace it with more convincing data.

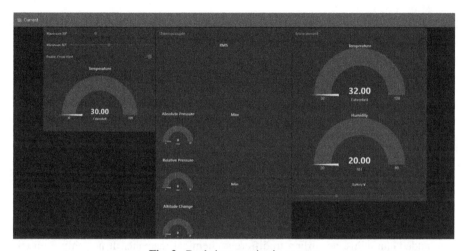

Fig. 3. Real-time monitoring screen

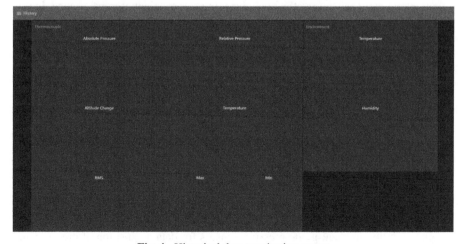

Fig. 4. Historical data monitoring screen

2.4   Components Used in Implementation

Today, there is an increasing focus on preventing emergencies. Furthermore, new-generation mobile technologies and their services discuss for wireless networks. Different sensors for temperature, humidity, pressure, and agitation for a few seconds use to collect reaction parameter information for diagnosis. Raspberry Pi and IoT are used satisfactorily for health monitoring, and this article gives the concept of these two platforms. The popular Raspberry Pi platform offers a complete Linux server in a small platform with IoT at a meager price. Raspberry allows for the provision of interface services and mechanisms through a generic I/O interface. By using this combination, the proposed structure is more efficient. At the same time, it ensures the possibility of its modularization and provides a better user experience.

A. Raspberry Pi

The Raspberry Pi is a small single-board computer. Connecting peripherals such as a keyboard, mouse, and monitor to Raspberry Pi will act as a mini-PC and reach a wide range of real-time image/video processing, IoT-based applications, and robotics applications. The connection between the Raspberry Pi and the Internet may be through a LAN (LAN) cable/Ethernet or a USB modem. The main advantage of Raspberry Pi is that it has a large number of applications. It also has a 4-pole stereo output and composite video port. Raspberry Pi runs an operating system based on Linux, an open-source operating system. We use Raspbian OS, a Linux-based operating system in this system. The programming language implementation of this Raspberry-Pi system in Python. Use raspberry Pi to integrate information into a database through the Modbus communication protocol so that users can receive and monitor the process status anytime, anywhere.

B. Modular Sensors

Modular sensors are the most flexible piece of equipment in this research. The sensors to be added can adjust according to different chemical reactants. It not only dramatically improves the extensibility of this research equipment but also reduces the cost of equipment maintenance, more effectively bringing a convenient user experience. In this study, the temperature and pressure sensors of NCD-io use as the default configuration, which is a node independently developed by Node-Red. So that this device can not only provide accurate parameter feedback but also can use according to different needs. The parameters can monitor and adjust on the development page and exported to the dashboard to realize an unmanned factory.

1. **IoT Long Range Wireless Temperature Humidity Sensor:** This sensor measures body temperature through voltage. It has advantages in Kelvin to Celsius conversion, is also suitable for wireless applications, outperforms thermostats, and does humidity sensing simultaneously.
2. **IoT Long Range Wireless Pressure Sensor Bidirectional Differential:** This IoT pressure sensor offers an effective wireless range of 2 miles and uses a 900 MHz wireless mesh architecture to transmit data across large networks when a more excellent range is required. This IoT pressure sensor uses the AMS5812 series of high-resolution medical-grade pressure sensors for data acquisition of pressure and temperature data. Then it transmits this data to a user-defined receiver.

3. **Heating Element:** In order to provide a good temperature performance for the pressure vessel, use a heating coil to replace the traditional silicone heating belt. Moreover, add a thermocouple to ensure that the specified temperature can maintain under long-term high-temperature operation. The information is sent back promptly for use and account monitoring adjustments in cooperation with the monitoring system.
4. **Vibration Sensor:** Use a vibration sensor to ensure that the materials in the pressure vessel are stirred accurately and uniformly during the chemical reaction process. Ensuring that the agitator is generally operating under the ideal process reduces the instrument replacement cost and improves production capacity.

C. Communication Network

A health monitoring system uses a wireless network to forward measurements to the cloud through a gateway. The leading network used here is IoT. IoT is the Internet of Things, referred to as the Internet of Everything. Communication technology can use to (i) connect IoT devices as local networks and (ii) connect these local networks (or individual IoT devices) to the Internet. In this article, we use the Modbus RTU communication protocol for the Ethernet/IP protocol gateway, which can improve the efficiency of equipment management and support equipment with different protocols, forming a large data relay station.

3 Data System Design

The system divides into two parts, including hardware & software; the hardware unit consists of sensors and receivers, while the software unit includes software languages such as Node.js and C++ and their interfaces. Here, we discuss the IoT application monitoring valuable process for the following aspects. The general operational phases of an IoT application, as shown in Fig. 5, include (1) Data acquisition, (2) Data processing, (3) Data calibration, (4) Data storage, and (5) Data transmission. The first and last stages exist in every application, while processing and storage may or may not be present in some applications. Here data collection is taken as real-time raw data transmission, raw data transmission, and real-time process. Many IoT applications already have data sparsity and can utilize the compressive sensing paradigm. Ultra-low power near-threshold processors, as well as high-performance processors, bring energy efficiency to IoT applications in addition to task scheduling frameworks.

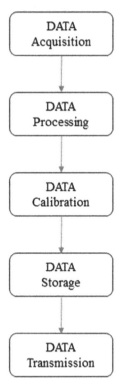

Fig. 5. Data application stages

4 The Proposed Method

As mentioned in Sect. 3, the system divides into hardware and software parts. Software is responsible for the work of a better system and also for interfaces. Work in parallel processes. The hardware further divides into a sensor part and a receiver part. Implementing the sensor is an essential part since the sensor is mounted directly on the pressure vessel. Raspberry Pi is the primary device in the proposed system; other devices, like different sensors, are connected to it. An IoT server connects to the system, allowing data exchange connections with other devices. IoT allows connected objects to identify and control remote access networks. After the data send to the receiver or client, all data is first acquired, processed, and stored in the internal memory of the Raspberry Pi. The stored information is then transmitted to the receiver employing an IoT server. The receiver part is on the user side. In the receiver section, it received all messages. It is collected and sent to the cloud via Raspberry Pi to provide monitoring, as shown in Fig. 6.

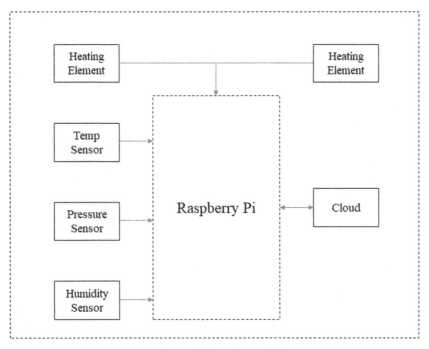

Fig. 6. Data Transmitter Section

5   Conclusion

A Raspberry Pi-based health monitoring system analyzes through IoT. There are two ways to connect and operate the Raspberry Pi device; one is to connect to the peripherals using LAN directly, and the other is to install the putty software and connect to the computer, enter the IP address, subnet mask, and gateway to that system. It will pre-establish MQTT to report directly to the user or authorized person if any abnormality finds in the experimental parameters. The proposed method aims at being easy to use and convenient to record, and it is more effective to establish a database under such a premise. The system is a good communication tool between the user and the equipment. This paper analyzes a Raspberry Pi-based polymer composite material reaction vessel with an IoT monitoring system. The conditions of any process can be more intuitive, and the data that can be made transparent through the Internet is more credible. Using this system enables users to not rely on previous manufacturing experience. Through the modular design, the correct experimental direction provides in a data-based manner, and the complete database not only provides complete historical information but also presents the real Industry 4.0. The appearance that it should have makes its industry perfect.

References

1. Capella, J.V., Bonastre, A., Campelo, J.C., Ors, R., Peris, M.: IoT & environmental analytical chemistry: Towards a profitable symbiosis. Trends Environ. Anal. Chem. **27**, e00095 (2020)
2. Phan, D.T., Phan, T.T.V., Huynh, T.C., Park, S., Choi, J., Oh, J.: Noninvasive, wearable multi biosensors for continuous, long-term monitoring of blood pressure via internet of things applications. Comput. Electr. Eng. **102**, 108187 (2022)
3. Mayer, M., Baeumner, A.J.: A megatrend challenging analytical chemistry: biosensor and chemosensor concepts ready for the Internet of Things. Chem. Rev. **119**(13), 7996–8027 (2019)
4. Naik, S., Sudarshan, E.: Smart healthcare monitoring system using raspberry Pi on IoT platform. ARPN J. Eng. Appl. Sci. **14**(4), 872–876 (2019)
5. Salih, S.Q., Alsewari, A.A., Yaseen, Z.M.: Pressure vessel design simulation: implementing of multi-swarm particle swarm optimization. In: Proceedings of the 2019 8th International Conference on Software and Computer Applications, pp. 120–124, February 2019
6. Christos, S.C., Christos, G.: Data-centric operations in oil & gas industry by the use of 5G mobile networks and industrial Internet of Things (IIoT). In: Proceedings of the 13th International Conference on Digital Telecommunications, p. 16 (2018)
7. Odette, G.R., Lucas, G.E.: Recent progress in understanding reactor pressure vessel steel embrittlement. Radiat. Eff. Defects Solids **144**(1–4), 189–231 (1998)
8. Dong, P., Brust, F.W.: Welding residual stresses and effects on fracture in pressure vessel and piping components: a millennium review and beyond. J. Press. Vessel Technol. **122**(3), 329–338 (2000)
9. Meng, Y., Zhao, H., Yin, Z., Qi, X.: IOT medical device-assisted foam dressing in the prevention of pressure sore during operation. In: Mathematical Problems in Engineering, 2021 (2021)
10. Mansfield, S., Vin, E., Obraczka, K.: An IoT system for autonomous, continuous, real-time patient monitoring and its application to pressure injury management. In: 2021 IEEE International Conference on Digital Health (ICDH), pp. 91–102. IEEE, September 2021
11. Lin, W.F.: Analysis of thick-wall hollow functionally graded material under temperature and pressure loads. In: 2020 IEEE Eurasia Conference on IOT, Communication and Engineering (ECICE), pp. 279–281. IEEE, October 2020
12. El Zouka, H.A., Hosni, M.M.: Secure IoT communications for smart healthcare monitoring system. Internet Things **13**, 100036 (2021)
13. Reddy, K.U.K., Shabbiha, S., Kumar, M.R.: Design of high security smart health care monitoring system using IoT. Int. J. **8** (2020)
14. Pardeshi, V., Sagar, S., Murmurwar, S., Hage, P.: Health monitoring systems using IoT and Raspberry Pi—a review. In: 2017 International Conference on Innovative Mechanisms for Industry Applications (ICIMIA), pp. 134–137. IEEE, February 2017

Research on the Representations of Information in Koto Music Scores

Sachiko Deguchi[✉]

Kindai University, Higashi-Hiroshima Hiroshima 739-2116, Japan
deguchi@hiro.kindai.ac.jp

Abstract. This research analyzes the information in traditional koto scores, and proposes the representations of the information. Playing techniques and shoga are analyzed in koto part. The illustrations and icons of several playing techniques of left hand are proposed and evaluated by an experiment. The result indicates that these icons can be used in koto scores. Shoga (verbal description of melody or playing technique) is analyzed based on the most fundamental koto scores of Ikuta school and Yamada school. The result indicates that shoga has important information in koto scores. Then, score data format of koto part is proposed, and score display system of koto part has been implemented. On the other hand, melismas and rhythms are analyzed in voice part. Melismas (melody in syllable) are analyzed on the scale of koto music and the representation of melisma is proposed. The difference of rhythms between koto part and voice part is also indicated. Then, score data format of voice part is proposed. The score display system of voice part is under development.

Keywords: Koto Music Score · Tablature · Playing Technique · Shoga · Melisma

1 Introduction

Staff notation is widely used today, however, many kinds of tablatures are used in the world and methods of encoding and notations have been researched from many points [1–3]. Tablatures are also used in Japanese traditional music. An editing system is provided [4] for several genres of Japanese traditional music and an editing system for undeciphered musical notation is also proposed [5], however, it is difficult to use these systems for complicated traditional pieces.

The author's previous research [6] proposed a universal design of musical performance system and score display system in HCII 2021. It was shown that the design of UI and score format can be extended for non-Western music. However, precise research is needed for the musical scores of non-Western music based on a specific example. In this research, the information in koto scores is analyzed.

The aim of this research is to clarify the information in musical scores of koto music in order to develop display software of koto scores. There is information about playing techniques of right hand and left hand, shoga (verbal description of melody or playing technique), and melisma (melody in syllable) of voice part in koto scores along with the melodies and rhythms of koto part and voice part.

M. Kurosu and A. Hashizume (Eds.): HCII 2023, LNCS 14014, pp. 245–257, 2023.
https://doi.org/10.1007/978-3-031-35572-1_17

2 Analysis of the Koto Part: Playing Techniques and Shoga

Koto is a music instrument with thirteen strings [7]. Each string has a string name: 1, 2,... 10, and to, i, kin. In this research, each string is represented as a string number 1, 2,... 12, 13. Thirteenth string is the nearest string to a player. There are several tunings, e.g. in Hira-joshi (most fundamental tuning), strings are tuned in [D4, G3, A3, A#3, D4, D#4, G4, A4, A#4, D5, D#5, G5, A5].

Since a koto is a stringed instrument, there are many playing techniques about plucking strings for both right hand and left hand [8, 9]. It is sometimes confusing to use technique based on the instruction described on the original scores [10, 11]. Also, some descriptions use Japanese characters and it would be difficult for people abroad to understand the meanings.

2.1 Right-Hand Techniques

There are many playing techniques including fingerings for right hand as follows.

(1) kaki dume: pluck two strings (one string and the next string) at almost the same time using index finger.
(2) wari dume: pluck two strings at almost the same time as kaki dume twice sequentially using index finger and middle finger.
(3) awase dume: pluck two strings (the interval between two strings is one octave) at the same time using thumb and middle finger.
(4) ura ren: strike strings from the thirteenth string using the back sides of plectrums of index finger and middle finger, and then pluck two strings indicated on a koto score using thumb.
(5) hiki ren: pluck the first and the second strings at almost the same time using middle finger, and stroke other strings, and then pluck the last two strings (the twelfth and the thirteenth strings).
(6) other 12 techniques: hiki sute, nagashi dume, nami gaeshi, otoshi, wa ren, sukui dume, furi dume, suri dume, chirashi dume, hajiki, ko dume, uchi dume.

This research provides some icons of playing techniques for right hand based on the traditional descriptions of Yamada school [11]. Figure 1 shows icons used for the playing techniques (1)-(5) described above. Kaki dume and wari dume use the same icon of vertical wiggly line. Awase dume uses the icon of parenthesis, ura ren uses the icon of horizontal wiggly line, and hiki ren uses the icon of horizontal line. Each icon is usually put over a string number on a koto score. Sometimes same icons are put over two or three string numbers. Ura ren and hiki ren use icons over string numbers. Hiki sute and nagashi dume use similar icon of hiki ren. Namigaeshi uses similar icon of ura ren. Otoshi uses icons of dot line over string numbers.

Other playing techniques are described by using symbols or characters.

– Wa ren is described as "wa" at the row of string number on a score.
– Sukui dume is described as "V" over the string number or at the row of string number on a score.
– Furi dume is similar to sukui dume.

Fig. 1. Icons of (a) kaki dume and wari dume, (b) awase dume, (c) ura ren and (d) hiki ren.

- Suri dume is described as " < --" or "-- >" (arrow symbol) at the row of string number on a score.
- Chirashi dume, hajiki, ko dume, and uchi dume are described as "chi, ha, ko, u" respectively over the string number on a score.

2.2 Left-Hand Techniques

Since Yamada school explains playing techniques in each koto score explicitly and uses some icons of playing techniques [11], we analyze left-hand techniques based on Yamada school's description. There are several playing techniques for left hand as follows.

(1) oshi hanashi, (2) oshi tome, (3) oshi tome hanashi, (4) oshi hibiki, (5) tsuki iro, (6) yuri atooshi, (7) yuri sakioshi, (8) hiki iro, (9) oshi awase, (10) soe dume, (11) keshi, (12) kake oshi, (13) oshi iro.

A playing technique oshi iro listed above (13) means sharp, double sharp, or triple sharp. Since the pitch is increased by pushing a string by left hand in koto music, sharp is described as a playing technique in traditional scores. However, in this research, sharp, double sharp and triple sharp are described using #, * and & symbols respectively.

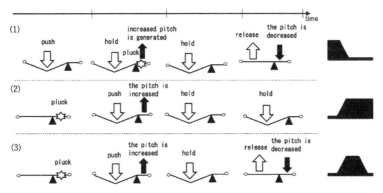

Fig. 2. The top illustration and icon are used for oshi hanashi, the center illustration and icon are used for oshi tome, and the bottom illustration and icon are used for oshi tome hanashi.

On the other hand, this research proposes eight illustrations and icons of left-hand playing techniques listed above (1)-(8). Figure 2 shows illustrations and icons used for (1) oshi hanashi, (2) oshi tome and (3) oshi tome hanashi. The illustration of (1) means "push the left side of string, and pluck the right side of string, and then release the string". The icon of (1) means "increased pitch is generated, and then the pitch is decreased". The illustrations and icons of (2) and (3) show the different ways to modify pitches.

Figure 3 shows illustrations and icons used for (4) oshi hibiki and (5) tsuki iro. Figure 4 shows illustrations and icons used for (6) yuri atooshi and (7) yuri sakioshi. Figure 5 shows illustration and icon used for (8) hiki iro. Other left-hand techniques (oshi awase, soe dume, keshi, kake oshi) use icon, character or symbol.

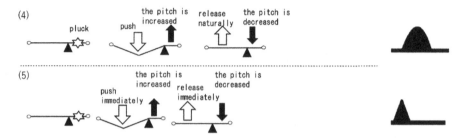

Fig. 3. The top illustration and icon are used for oshi hibiki, and the bottom illustration and icon are used for tsuki iro.

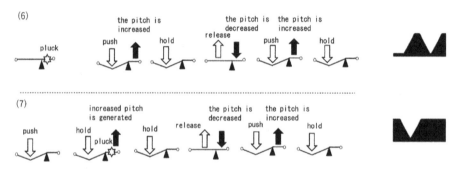

Fig. 4. The top illustration and icon are used for yuri atooshi, and the bottom illustration and icon are used for yuri sakioshi.

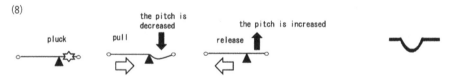

Fig. 5. These illustration and icon are used for hiki iro.

Figure 6 shows the comparison of the icons of this research with original notations of Yamada school and Ikuta school. Top row shows the notation of Ikuta school [10], where vertical scores are used and playing technique is written by using katakana character (one kind of Japanese characters) near string number. In Fig. 6, a circle symbol means the place where string number is to be written. Center row shows the notation of Yamada school [11], where horizontal scores are used and playing technique is written by using icon and/or katakana character over string number. Bottom row shows icons of this research which are written over string numbers. The left three notations (top, center, bottom) represent oshi hanashi described above, the next three notations represent oshi tome, and so on.

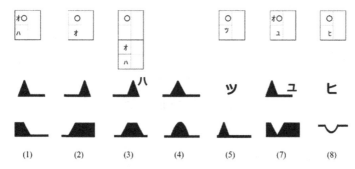

Fig. 6. Comparison of notations of Ikuta school, Yamada school and this research.

2.3 Experiment of Left-Hand Techniques

Pre-experiment. The pre-experiments were done to determine the method of evaluation experiment as follows.

Pre-experiment 1. Three examinees were given a list of eight illustrations (1)-(8) (Japanese version of Fig. 2–5) and a list of eight icons lined up randomly, and they were told to find suitable icon for each illustration. The average time to finish the experiment was 6′ 02″ and average percentage of correct answers (total) was 62.5%.

Pre-experiment 2. Other three examinees were given a list of eight illustrations (1)-(8) and a list of eight icons lined up randomly, where the illustration (2) (in Fig. 2) had the answer (corresponding icon). Then, they were told to find suitable icon for each illustration except (2). The average time to finish the experiment was 3′ 39″ and average percentage of correct answers (total) was 85.7%.

Since the aim of this research is to provide icons which are distinguishable and understandable, the method of pre-experiment 2 was chosen to be used for evaluation experiment.

Experiment. The evaluation experiment was carried out in November 2022.

Methods. Examinees were 34 students (age: 18–22). They were given a list of eight illustrations (1)–(8) and a list of eight icons lined up randomly, where the illustration (2) had the answer. Then, they were told to find suitable icon for each illustration except (2).

Result and Discussion. The average percentage of correct answers of each illustration and total average are shown in Table 1. The percentages of correct answers of (6) (7) (8) are higher than those of (1)-(5). Two examinees mistook (1) for (3), and two examinees mistook (1) for (4), and four examinees mistook (1) for others. It would be difficult to understand that a string is pushed before plucking. On the other hand, the percentage of correct answers of (7) is higher than that of (1). Examinees might understand the meaning by comparing (7) with (6). Since the total average is 87.4%, these icons can be learned easily when people play the koto. Therefore, these icons of playing techniques are added to the score display system.

Table 1. The average percentage of correct answers for each illustration and total average.

illustration	(1)	(3)	(4)	(5)	(6)	(7)	(8)	total
average percentage of correct answers	76.5%	82.4%	79.4%	88.2%	94.1%	91.2%	100%	87.4%

2.4 Shoga

Shoga is used to memorize melody or playing technique verbally in shamisen music. Koto music is closely related to shamisen music, and shoga is also used in koto music. Since koto music had been transmitted orally for more than 200 years in Edo period, shoga had been used as an aid to memorize melody or playing technique. Shoga has been analyzed by several researchers in Japan [12, 13], however, it has not been analyzed statistically. Also, shogas of two schools (Ikuta and Yamada) have not been compared.

In this research, shoga in Rokudan which is the most fundamental piece of koto music is analyzed using koto scores of two schools [10, 11].

"Ton", "ten", "tsun", "chin" and their variations are used to describe pitches but they are not assigned to absolute pitches, however, these words could be the aid for the memory.

- Duration: Usually "to-n", "ton" and "to" (te-n, ten and te, etc.) are corresponding to half note, quarter note and eighth note respectively.
- Relative pitches: Usually, "ton" is lower than "ten", "tsun" or "chin". "Chin" is usually higher than "ton", "ten" or "tsun" (but "chin" is sometimes lower than "ten" in Ikuta school). "Ten" is sometimes lower than "tsun", and sometimes higher "tsun".
- Fingering: If a note (string number) has a description of fingering "3" (using middle finger), "ton" is described as shoga.
- Playing technique of left hand: When a string number is described with left-hand technique "oshitome", shoga is usually "chi/chin" (sometimes "tsu/tsun" in Ikuta school).
- Sharp and double sharp: When a string is pushed by left hand to increase pitch by whole tone, shoga is usually "tsu/tsun" for most strings. To increase pitch by half tone for some strings, shoga is usually "chi/chin".
- Sequence: "Ten" follows "shan" or "sha sha" if the interval is 1 octave or 1 degree, e.g., 5 shan, and 10 ten. "Ten" follows "ton" if the interval is 1 octave and fingering of "ton" is 3, e.g., 2 ton, and 7 ten.

"Shan", "sha sha", "chan", "sa- ra rin" etc. are used to describe playing techniques of right hand. "shan" is used for kaki dume, "sha sha" is used for wari dume, "chan" is used for awase dume in Yamada school, "sa- ra rin" is used for ura ren. "Ko- ro rin" is used to describe rhythm (sequence of dotted eighth note, sixteenth note and quarter note) and melody (sequential three string numbers, e.g. 8 7 6). "Shu" and "Zoo" are onomatopoeia, e.g., "shu" represents the sound of wind.

There are differences between two schools: Yamada and Ikuta. Table 2 shows the difference of shoga in Rokudan. E.g., the number of times that chi/chin in Yamada score corresponds to tsu/tsun in Ikuta score is 10, and so on. These differences are relatively low, because there are around 800 notes in Rokudan and this piece had been transmitted orally for 200 years.

Today, shoga is not usually used for practicing the koto, however, the result of the analysis indicates that shoga has important information. Therefore, shoga is added to the score display system using Roman characters.

Table 2. The difference of shoga between two schools.

Yamada	chi/chin	tsu/tsun	chi/chin	te/ten	tsu/tsun	te/ten	chi te tsun	ko- ro rin	tsu to
Ikuta	tsu/tsun	chi/chin	te/ten	chi/chin	te/ten	tsu/tsun	ko ro rin	ten ton	ton ka ra
number of times	10	7	11	6	2	1	6	8	3

3 Representation of the Koto Part

3.1 Score Data Format of the Koto Part

Koto music uses tablature scores (numbered notation scores) and the numbers in a score correspond to the string numbers of koto instrument (11th, 12th and 13th strings are notated as "to, i and kin" in original scores and they are notated as "11, 12 and 13" in this research). The strings are tuned, e.g. the pitches of strings (1–13) in hira-joshi are [D4, G3, A3, A#3, D4, D#4, G4, A4, A#4, D5, D#5, G5, A5]. Therefore, in koto score of hira-joshi, 1 means D4, 2 means G3, and so on. '0' means rest. This research provides score data format of text file, where pitches are notated by using string numbers.

In this format, there are nine columns as follows.

string # dur right finger left shoga string2 #

- "string" means string number, which is described above.
- "#" means if the pitch is increased or not. If the value of this column is 1/2/3, the pitch is increased by half tone/whole tone/minor third.
- "dur" means duration, which is notated using number and '.' symbol. 4 means quarter note, 8 means eighth note, 4. means dotted quarter note, and so on.
- "right" means right-hand technique including tie. The value of this column is notated using katakana (Japanese characters) because it is recognizable for a Japanese

encoder. Kaki dume and wari dume are notated as "sha" in katakana, awase dume is notated as "awase" in katakana, ura ren is notated as "sara" in katakana, and so on.

- "finger" means fingering. The value of this column is 2 (for index finger) or 3 (for middle finger). 1 (for thumb) is default value and it is not described.
- "left" means left-hand technique. The value of this column is also notated using katakana. Oshi hanashi is notated as "oshiha" in katakana, oshi tome is notated as "oshitome" in katakana, hiki iro is notated as "hiki" in katakana, and so on.
- "shoga" means shoga as described above. The value of this column is notated using Roman characters, which is same as the notation appeared on the displayed score.
- "string2" means the second string (pitch) of chord.
- "#" after string2 means if the second string is increased or not as described above.

An example of score data file of Rokudan is shown in Fig. 7.

string	#	dur	right	finger	left	shoga	string2	#
=	=1	1dan						
5	0	2			ヒキ	te-n		
3	0	4				ton		
1	0	4	シャ			shan	2	
=	=2							
0	0	4						
3	0	8	シャ	2		sha	2	
3	0	8	シャ	3		sha	2	
8	0	8.				ko-		
7	0	16				ro		
6	0	8				rin		
7	0	8			オシトメ	chin		

Fig. 7. Score data file of Rokudan.

3.2 Score Display System for the Koto Part

The author developed a score display system in 2018 and improved the system in 2019 [14] and 2021 [6]. This score display system can generate four kinds of notations about pitches (numbers, note names, note names in Japanese, and colors), and can generate two types of notations about duration (space length and symbol). This system can be used to display koto scores for novice players, however, playing techniques and other information are described in traditional koto scores, therefore, the system has to be enhanced.

Traditional koto music is classified into instrumental music and vocal music. This research has rebuilt score display software to describe koto part and voice part. Based on the previous system where a pitch was described by number and duration was described by space length, rows are added to the score display format of koto part in order to describe chord, fingering, playing technique and shoga.

Figure 8 shows an example of Rokudan score displayed by the system, which is instrumental piece. The format of koto part has five rows which are defined as follows.

- The first row (bottom) is used for string number (which represent pitch).
- The second row is used for chord.

– The third row is used for fingering.
– The fourth row is used for icon of playing technique.
– The fifth row is used for shoga.

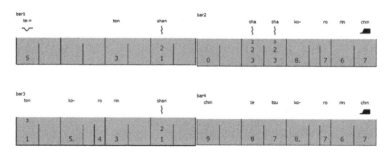

Fig. 8. Displayed score of Rokudan.

4 Analysis of the Voice Part: Melisma and Rhythm

4.1 Melisma

A melisma is a melody in a syllable. In European religious music, melismas have been analyzed and their notations have been researched [15, 16]. In Japanese religious music, melismas have been analyzed [17], however, research of melismas is not so common in Japanese traditional music.

In koto music, melismas are clearly described with precise pitches and durations on koto scores. This research analyzes melismas in Sakuragari [18] which is a representative song of Yamada school. For example, the first word of Sakuragari: "nodoka" is pronounced as "no o o do o o ka a a a a", and vowels in the syllables are sung in different pitches using string numbers as follows.

[String numbers] no: 9## 10 9##, do: 10 9## 10, ka: 10 9 10 9## 8.

These melodies are described by using MIDI note numbers as follows, where the middle C is 60, half tone is 1 and whole tone is 2.

[MIDI note numbers] no: 72 74 72, do: 74 72 74, ka: 74 70 74 72 69.

Also, these melodies are described using intervals as follows.

[Intervals] no: $(2 -2)$, do: $(-2\ 2)$, ka: $(-4\ 4\ -2\ -3)$.

The author analyzed several songs of koto music by using n-gram [19], and found that limited melodic patterns $(2 -2)$, $(-2\ 2)$, $(-1\ -2)$, $(-2\ -4)$, etc. occurred in melismas. The author also analyzed melodic patterns on koto mode (koto musical scale), and explained that the scale is the basis of the patterns. The scale of koto music [20, 21] is described using tones on the scale and intervals between two tones as Fig. 9, where d1 is the first tone of the scale, and the interval between d1 and d2 is 1 (half tone), the interval between d2 and d3 is 2 (whole tone), and so on.

Since the melody does not jump in koto songs, the author analyzed transitions whose interval is equal to or smaller than a major third (4 in the MIDI notation). E.g., from the first scale degree d1, transitions to d2(+1), d3(+3), d7(-2) and d6(-4) are possible. Since four transitions are possible from each scale degree, sixteen transitions are possible as 3-note patterns, e.g., from d1, (−2 −2), (−2 −3), (−2 2), (−2 3), (−4 −1), (−4 −3), (−4 2), (−4 4), (1 −1), (1 −3), (1 2), (1 4), (3 −2), (3 −3), (3 2) and (3 4) are possible. However, mainly four 3-note patterns (−2 −3), (−4 −1), (−2 2), and (−4 4) actually occur.

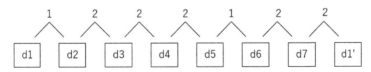

Fig. 9. Scale of Koto Music.

Based on the previous result, this research proposes a notation of melisma. The result showed that melismas were composed of typical melodic patterns and that the pitches of each pattern were on the scale. Therefore, important information is whether the melody is up or down and whether the interval is 2nd degree (e.g. 2nd degree of d1 is d2) or 3rd degree (e.g. 3rd degree of d1 is d3).

This research proposes notation / for up by 2nd degree, // for up by 3rd degree, \ for down by 2nd degree, and \\ for down by 3rd degree, e.g., (2 −2) is represented as (/ \), (−4 4 −2 −3) is represented as (\\ // \ \\). To represent the interval of 4th degree, /// or \\\ is used. These symbols are added to the score display system of voice part.

4.2   Rhythm: Voice Part and Koto Part

The relationship between koto part and voice part is complicated. In general, the rhythm of Japanese traditional music is complicated and several genres are analyzed qualitatively [22]. In koto music, the author reported that the melodies of both parts are slightly different especially in rhythms [14]. It is difficult for a novice player to sing a koto song and play the koto at the same time.

Figure 10 shows an example of simplified score data files of Sakuragari [18]. In the 4th bar of voice part of Fig. 10, the vowel "o" in syllable "no" is pronounced in pitch of 10th string. At the beginning of the 5th bar of koto part of Fig. 10, string 10 is plucked. In the 5th bar of voice part of Fig. 10, syllable "do" is pronounced in pitch of 10th string after dotted quarter note from the beginning. The voice part sometimes precedes the koto part, and the voice part often follows the koto part. It is difficult to represent the difference between koto part and voice part, and it is also hard to know how a performer recognize the correspondence between koto part and voice part.

5   Representation of the Voice Part

5.1   Score Data Format of the Voice Part

This research provides score data format of text file for voice part separately from koto part. There are six columns in this format as follows.

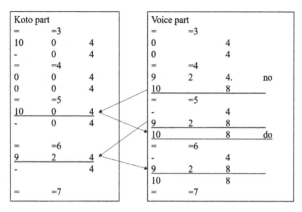

Fig. 10. Koto part and Voice part of Sakuragari.

string # dur right lyric melisma.

- "string" means string number as the koto part.
- "#" means if the pitch is increased or not as the koto part.
- "dur" means duration as the koto part.
- "right" means tie in voice part.
- "lyric" means syllable.
- "melisma" means the symbol of melisma: /, //, \, \\, ///, \\\.

An example of score data file of the voice part of Sakuragari is shown in Fig. 11.

string	#	dur	right	lyric	melisma
=	=3				
0		4			
0		4			
=	=4				
9	2	4.		no	
10		8			/
=	=5				
-		4			
9	2	8			\
10		8		do	
=	=6				
-		4			
9	2	8			\
10		8			/

Fig. 11. Score data file of the voice part of Sakuragari.

5.2 Score Display System for the Voice Part

The score display system of voice part with koto part is under development. The voice part is described below the koto part. In the voice part, syllables and melismas are described with string numbers which represent pitches. The format of voice part has two rows which are defined as follows.

- The first row (bottom) is used for string number (which represent pitch).

– The second row is used for syllable and melisma.

It is difficult to sing a koto song while playing the koto. We are developing a prototype support system where the timings of koto part (plucking koto string) and voice part (pronouncing syllable or vowel) are displayed on the koto score. This prototype system is under development and the effect of the system should be evaluated.

6   Conclusion and Future Work

This research analyzed the information in traditional koto scores, and proposed the representations of the information. Playing techniques and shoga were analyzed in koto part. The illustrations and icons of several playing techniques of left hand were proposed and evaluated by an experiment. The result indicates that these icons can be used in koto scores. Shoga was analyzed based on the most fundamental koto scores of Ikuta school and Yamada school. The result indicates that shoga has important information in koto scores. Then, score data format of koto part was provided, and score display system has been implemented. On the other hand, melismas and rhythms were analyzed in voice part. Melismas were analyzed on the scale of koto music and the representation of melisma was proposed. The difference of rhythms between koto part and voice part was also indicated. Then, score data format of voice part was provided. The score display system is under development.

Future work includes the completion of score display system of voice part, and the development of a support system which can indicates the timings of the koto part and voice part.

Acknowledgments. The authors would like to thank Atsunori Sasaki and Koki Kanbara for their contribution to the development of score display system.

References

1. de Valk, R.: Crafting TabMEI, a module for encoding instrumental tablatures. Music Encod. Conf. Proc. **2020**, 75–82 (2020)
2. Shaw, R.A.: The Kassel-Wolfenbüttel tablature system: a convergence of lute tablature and mensural notation. In: Music Encoding Conference Proceedings 2015, 2016 and 2017, pp. 63–72 (2016)
3. Wiggins, A., Kim, Y.: Guitar tablature estimation with a convolutional neural network. In: Proceedings of the 20th ISMIR Conference, pp. 284–291 (2019)
4. Wagaku Hitosuji: https://jonkara.com/soft/wagaku/. Accessed 18 Jan 2023
5. Arasaki, T., Yako, M.: Specification of software for building database of out-of-date and/or undeciphered musical notation. The Special Interest Group Technical reports of IPSJ, 2012-MUS-97(12), pp. 1–6 (2012)
6. Deguchi, S.: A study on universal design of musical performance system. In: Kurosu, M. (ed.) Human-Computer Interaction. Design and User Experience Case Studies. LNCS, vol. 12764, pp. 18–33. Springer, Cham (2021). https://doi.org/10.1007/978-3-030-78468-3_2
7. Hirano, K., et al. (Ed.): Nihon Ongaku Daijiten (in Japanese), Heibonsha, Tokyo (1989)

8. Sakamoto, M. et al.: Koto no tame no Handbook (in Japanese), Katei-ongakukai, Fukuoka (1993)
9. Ando, M.: Ikuta-ryu no Sokyoku (in Japanese), Kodansha, Tokyo (2005)
10. Miyagi, M.: Rokudan no Shirabe, Koto Score of Ikuta School, Hogakusha, Tokyo (2005)
11. Nakanoshima, K.: Rokudan no Shirabe, Koto Score of Yamada School, Hogakusha, Tokyo (2008)
12. Kikkawa, E.: Shoga no Rekishi to Genri (In Japanese). Bull. Musashino Acad. Musicae **7**, 1–23 (1974)
13. Noto, K.: Sound Symbolism of KOTO. Osaka Univ. J. Lang. Cult. **17**, 83–96 (2008)
14. Deguchi, S.: Multiple representations of the UI, score and scale for musical performance system and score DB. In: Kurosu, M. (ed.) Human-Computer Interaction. Design Practice in Contemporary Societies. LNCS, vol. 11568, pp. 177–191. Springer, Cham (2019). https://doi.org/10.1007/978-3-030-22636-7_12
15. Apel, W.: Gregorian Chant. Indiana University Press, Bloomington (1958)
16. Holman, H.J.: Melismatic tropes in the responsories for matins. J. Am. Musicol. Soc. **16**(1), 36–46 (1963)
17. Sasagima, M.: Japanese song and ornamental Melody. Bull. Chiba Keiai Junior College **15**, 1–17 (1993)
18. Nakanoshima, K.: Sakuragari, Koto Score of Yamada School, Hogakusha, Tokyo (1996)
19. Deguchi, S., Shirai, K.: An analysis of melismatic patterns in Koto songs. Comput. Musicol. **14**, 159–170 (2006)
20. Deguchi, S., Selfridge-Field, E., Shirai, K.: The temperament, scale and mode of Koto music, In: Proceedings of International Congress of Musicological Society of Japan 2002, 434–438 (2002)
21. Toyo Ongaku Gakkai (Ed.): Nihon no Onkai (In Japanese), Ongaku-no-tomo-sha, Tokyo (1982)
22. Koizumi, F.: Nihon Dento Ongaku no Kenkyu –Rhythm (in Japanese). Ongaku-no-tomo-sha, Tokyo (1998)

Supporting and Motivating Re-integration of Justice-Involved Individuals Through Dynamic Gamification

Nicholas Diliberti[1] , Haeyong Chung[1(✉)], Yansi Keim[2], Marc Rogers[2],
Umit Karabiyik[2], Sudhir Aggarwal[3], Tathagata Mukherjee[1],
and Carrie Pettus[4]

[1] Department of Computer Science, The University of Alabama in Huntsville,
Huntsville, AL 35899, USA
{nd0006,hc0021,tm0130}@uah.edu
[2] Department of Computer and Information Technology, Purdue University,
West Lafayette, IN 47905, USA
{ykeim,rogersmk,ukarabiy}@purdue.edu
[3] Department of Computer Science, Florida State University, Tallahassee,
FL 32304, USA
sudhir@cs.fsu.edu
[4] Justice System Partners, P.O. Box 970, South Easton, MA 02375, USA
carrie@justicesystempartners.org

Abstract. The United States prison system faces staggering levels of
recidivism – the observed phenomenon wherein justice-involved individuals (JII) on parole are re-convicted and entered back into correctional
facilities. Combined with the large existing prison population, this leads
to an overtaxing of the human resources available for JII management
and a worsened quality of life for previously-incarcerated individuals.
A framework for successful reintegration – the Five Keys of Reentry –
has been formulated, but the process risks user un-investment due to the
heavily differing perceived difficulties between seemingly-equal tasks. We
solve both problems at once by creating a JII-facing smartphone app and
case-manager facing web app which collectively guide JII through the
Five Keys using a gamified task system with dynamic point reallocation
to account for signs of mismatch between effort and reward. We show the
usefulness of our system using the use case of possible user interaction
with the resulting application. We also discuss the hurdles of its practical
implementation, system evaluation methodology and additional points of
academic intrigue.

Keywords: Justice-involved individuals · Gamification · Criminal
Justice · HCI

This work was supported by the National Institute of Justice Award No. 2019-75-CX-
K001. We would like to thank Jessica Le for her comments and suggestions.

M. Kurosu and A. Hashizume (Eds.): HCII 2023, LNCS 14014, pp. 258–275, 2023.
https://doi.org/10.1007/978-3-031-35572-1_18

1   Introduction

Recidivism, the observed tendency for an individual in the penal system to offend again after judiciary action, is a core concern in criminal justice. Both the psychological repercussions of incarceration and the material concerns of reintegrating into society place individuals in circumstances which inflate chances of relapse. Were these factors to be addressed, those affected would be afforded the maximal chance of being able to return to nominal psychological health, re-enter society, and lead stable, fulfilling lives.

The criminal justice system in the United States currently faces a problematic overabundance of justice-involved individuals (JII); such as those convicted of crimes, those who have been arrested, and those who have served time in the penal system; who need to be monitored compared to the human resources the system commands. This is caused through various contributing factors, such as mass incarceration, recidivism, and the unavailability of JII management solutions. At the same time, the management of JII on parole has become an understaffed field in the United States. Current tools do not avail themselves of our Information Age capabilities, and instead rely on the rote, human evaluation of JII compliance. Although methods for automatically capturing data exist, they neither sufficiently serve the privacy concerns of JII nor present themselves to case managers in a form which enables efficient, parallelized mass JII administration.

To address the problems by both JII and case managers, we have created a full-stack application with two interfaces-the GOALS (Gaining Occupational and Life Skills) smartphone app and the dashboard web app. This system uses the Five Keys of Reentry [30], a psycho-social prescriptive model of behavior for JII reintegration, and applies it to the target population through a novel dynamic gamification system.

In doing so, we tackle a problem which appears during the gamification of life-altering actions of such magnitude: when points are the quantification of importance and progress, a static gamification scheme, which applies the same points to tasks regardless of the user's circumstances, risks losing user engagement due to disagreements in the difficulty and importance of prescribed actions. In order to dynamically re-balance the system's point allocation without need for constant manual oversight, we developed a "rubber-band" type system which translates automatically-gathered performance metrics into a point-shuffling procedure which better aligns the reward a user receives with the difficulty they have in fulfilling each task.

The novelty of our contribution lies in the dynamic re-organization of points in our gamification scheme, the application of information-age techniques to JII management, and the use of gamification as a motivational tool to promote JII self-betterment. In total, we seek to make the following contributions to the fields of criminal justice, human-computer interaction, and computer science:

1. The analysis, design, and implementation of the gamified system, including use cases for an example system implementation

2. The adaption of the Five-Key Model for Reentry into a gamified context
3. A framework for dynamic gamification that attempts to optimally incentivize the pursuit of parallel objectives
4. An increase in the ability of gamified self-help applications to motivate parallel vectors of user self-betterment.

2 Related Work

Our gamified system builds on existing research at the intersection of gamification and criminal justice. We will first review prior work in the relevant areas, including mobile apps used in Criminal Justice, gamification apps for different demographics, mechanics used in gamification techniques, and apps used in criminal justice.

2.1 Gamified Applications

Generally, gamification is referred to as the method of applying game systems in non-game contexts to engage users in solving problems [3]. It has been proposed as a preferred solution for engaging individuals in self-improvement behaviors such as exercising [4], education [5,6], mental health [7], and stress management [8] among others [9]. Over the years, researchers have studied and used various attractive mechanisms in gamification [10] such as entertainment [11], loyalty programs, point scoring, and competition with others for enhanced engagement with specific tasks within these apps.

The gamification aspect has the ability to advance specific goals of specific groups of people [9]. To further understand the perceived benefits of gamification, researchers study specific gamer demographics and gamification goals [12–14]. These studies show an increase in attempts to understand the relationship between user demographics and user behavior.

Broadly, prior work above suggests that any new gamification system should support different demographics and focus their tasks to each demographic's needs. It is hypothesized that by engaging with customized activities within the app, any individual under said population might improve their strengths and psychological well-being. As a result, they remain crime-free and contribute positively to society [19,20].

2.2 Mobile Apps in Criminal Justice

In recent years, community supervision has started exploring reentry programs focusing on smartphone app technology to curb recidivism.

The use of JII-focused re-entry apps is expected to lower incarceration rates and possibly replace GPS ankle bracelets. Several parole apps also have enabled a new kind of observation to track parolees without having to report or meet with a probation officer. For example, voice-recognition in the Shadowtrack app [1] allows users to speak answers to a series of questions that a probation officer would normally ask. Another app, SmartLink [1], can integrate a variety of software products from Business Intelligence (BI) tools, such as Total Access. This tool uses predictive analytics to predict a person's likelihood of fleeing and identify their potential risk locations.

Three other apps for those on parole or probation are The Guardian, Tracktech, and Uptrust. These programs are designed to help probation and parole officers keep track of their massive caseloads, but each program has its own unique approach [2]. For instance, The Guardian collects information about users' locations and activities, and is very invasive. It forces users to check in with the app several times a day, which can lead to issues, such as losing sleep and even losing their jobs. Over a dozen cities have already invested in The Guardian technology, which is very problematic because it could lead to the wrongful return of people who were previously incarcerated. This could also make it harder for probation and parole officers to help their clients reintegrate into society.

2.3   Points, Badges, and Level Mechanics

There are frequently-recurring game mechanics that are commonly observed in gamified systems. Particularly, game mechanics of points, badges, and levels (PBL) can be leveraged to drive behavior in a variety of application domains. It is cited as an important combination of status or performance communication of an individual. Moreover, Muangsrinoon and Boonbrahm emphasize on game mechanics from advanced gamified systems such as feedback, levels, leaderboards, challenges, badges, avatars, competition, and cooperation [21].

Points. Our gamification system primarily employs points for the purposes of guiding user behavior and driving motivation like many other prior gamification systems [21–24]. Muangsrinoon and Boonbrahm (2019) define points as virtual rewards against the player effort [21]. To that end, we aim to use the point system and extend its support to individuals on house arrest and day reporting to improve their overall psychological well-being [19,20].

In the Lai et al. study [25], the participants earned points for completing high-value activities, such as accessing the app on a regular basis, responding to push notifications, earning badges, advancing to a higher level, and completing trigger surveys. Participants could also advance to a different level based on the points awarded for high-value activities. The use of game mechanics in survey research can engage respondents and reduce burden, but there are challenges to effectively implementing these techniques.

Badges and Levels. Both badges and levels can be incorporated into different applications to drive engagement. According to Lai et al. [25], gamification of survey tasks gives a positive survey experience leading to making web surveys more engaging, interesting, and enjoyable. Using virtual badges and other intangible social rewards can increase response rates among participants with the drawback of introducing response bias.

Key	Definition
Healthy thinking patterns	Adaptive mental actions or processes, the presence of empathy, and the acceptance of internalization of values and norms that promote prosocial behavior
Meaningful work trajectories	Sustainable compatibility of an individual's goals and abilities and the demands of that individual's occupation (obligations/job paid or unpaid) is sustainable
Effective coping strategies	Adaptive behavioral and psychological efforts taken to manage and reduce internal/external stressors in ways that are not harmful in the short or long term
Positive social engagement	Social experiences organized for beneficial social purposes that directly or indirectly involve others, engaged in during discretionary time, and experienced as enjoyable
Positive relationships	Reliable, mutually beneficial relationships between two people that range from brief to enduring in duration within formal or informal social contexts

Fig. 1. The Five Keys of Reentry, with specific breakdowns for each key.

Akpolat and Slany considered the potential of employing gamified techniques to education [27]. In their study, which focused on educating software development processes, they found gamification may be successful, but it could lose its benefits if the students lost interest in "playing the game". They argued that a suitable reward system with sufficiently, but not overly, difficult badges is critical to students' continued engagement.

2.4   The Five Key Model

The Five Keys of Reentry are an academic model that will serve as the foundational theory for the tasks to be gamified in our dynamic gamification's implementation. The model is a rehabilitation initiative uniquely well-suited to gamification, as it prescribes a set of recommended actions for the JII to take, which in totality provide the foundation for a successful rehabilitation.

This active component to the model makes it uniquely suited for gamification. Similarly to how exercises make up the foundational tasks of an exercise game, and lessons and quizzes form the core of an educational game [3], these Five Key activities form the foundation of a rehabilitative game. The five keys are explained in Fig. 1.

3   Gamification

In this section, we will detail the ways in which tasks are gamified, the expected user experience, and the novel way in which we dynamically re-allocate gamified rewards in order to maximize user engagement with the application.

3.1 Gamification Setup

The process of fulfilling the Five Keys of Reentry [30] is gamified into a set of tasks with both cosmetic and non-cosmetic rewards for reaching task-completion milestones. Mechanically speaking, the game is lightweight and optimized towards ease of teaching. To set up the gamification, we must decide how users will generate points upon task completion, set up overarching goals that those points will count towards, and display the users' overall progress in a way that reinforces their motivation to continue participating in the app.

Points are the primary motivating system that guides user behavior, and the system dispenses both material and immaterial rewards as points are accumulated. Given that each user's experience with the application is isolated, and as such is not compared with other users' experiences, the point values are tweaked on a per-user basis to best fit multiple criteria. These criteria include the user's expected length of engagement with the application (which drives the point value of individual interactions) and the user's assessed areas of strength and weakness (which are adjusted using the Rubber-Band System).

Gaining points triggers two different reward mechanisms. The first is the automated dispensation of the rewards currently used to reward good behavior. For example, a correctional facility might have a system by which participants can earn or purchase "vacation passes" which allow for the temporary suspension of parole limitations during specific holidays. This first mechanism could dispense anything from free vouchers for these vacation passes to an accumulating set of rewards that increase the length of time over which the pass is in effect.

The second reward mechanism is the vista, a purely cosmetic reward mechanism that acts as a virtual trophy case of the users long-term achievement in the game. Each of the Five Keys is represented by an element within the vista. The five elements; the house, the car, the boat, the greenery, and the crowd; can be viewed as independent tracks of advancement, with continued investment in each Key resulting in larger and more impressive assets representing that track within the vista.

The automated behavior rewards are awarded for total user progress within the app, for tasks which both do and do not involve the Five Keys. Vista progress is rewarded for normalized progress on the path towards the total number of points that can be gained in each key, which is finite. This places the restriction on the gamification that the total number of points available to earn must remain constant, regardless of changes made by the Rubber-Band System.

3.2 The Rubber-Band Process

Tuning of gamified rewards is handled by the Rubber-Band System, a gamification subroutine that allows the system to automatically incentivize activity in the areas where the user shows the least aptitude. The motivating idea behind the system is reflected in the name: similar to elastic force exerted by a rubber band, we wish for the motivating force to grow the farther away the user feels from their goal.

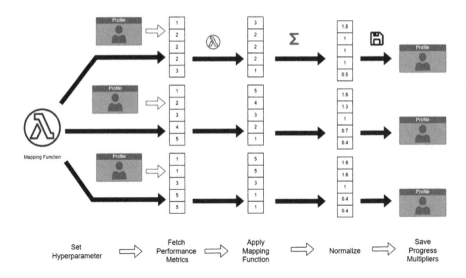

Fig. 2. Progress adjustment under the Rubber-Band model.

During system intake, each user undergoes an assessment that gauges their lifestyle situation and their relative aptitude towards creating and maintaining positive change through each of the Five Keys. Using this assessment of relative aptitudes, the system distributes the points gained from the Five-Key assignments among the various keys in amounts that are inversely proportional to the user's aptitude in each key. The goal of this system is that when users seek points in the gamification system, they will receive additional rewards when making strides in areas in which they show a lack of aptitude or progress, subsidizing their motivation in those areas.

In general, the process for Rubber-Band adjustment is as follows. First, a mapping function is set as a system hyper-parameter. Next, user performance on a per-goal basis is transformed into a numeric representation. Then, the mapping function is applied and the results are normalized. Finally, the normalized results are used as point-gain multipliers for the user's gamified tasks until the next Rubber-Band invocation. This process is visualized in Fig. 2.

Let us use an example of a hypothetical user experiencing dynamic gamification of the Five Key model. Suppose that the user performs their entry examination to have their aptitudes in each key evaluated. Further suppose that the user shows weak prospects in Positive Relationships, strong prospects in Meaningful Work Trajectories, and medium prospects in the other three keys. Given their weak prospects in Positive Relationships, the gamification system wishes to boost their motivation in that key using points as an external incentive. Additionally, given that the user already shows aptitude in Meaningful Work Trajectories, the gamification system "borrows" these bonus points from that, seeing as the user already excels in that key without any behavioral incentives.

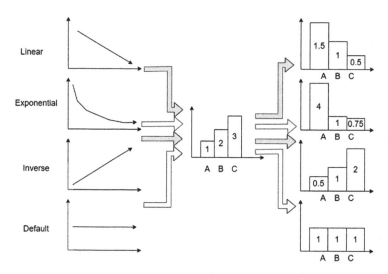

Fig. 3. The evaluation function acts as the system hyper-parameter, resulting in different behaviors being incentivized in different amounts. Different evaluation functions result in different relative incentivizations of unequal categories. Linear decreasing functions create a smooth reallocation of points, exponential functions heavily reward initial progress in a category, increasing functions reward focused investment in a singular area, and constant functions result in no change to point allocation.

3.3   System Parameters

The Rubber-Band System's behavior is controlled by a function on scalars that acts as a system hyper-parameter. The function maps relative progress in the different areas of advancement (the Five Keys, in this case) to relative value scalars. These relative value scalars are normalized to an average of 1, and then the normalized values are used as multipliers for the points gained in that particular area.

The net result of this operation is that the user is incentivized more in areas where they are struggling and less in areas where they excel. We assume that because a user is already excellent in an area in which the function will deem them lacking in need for aid, excellent performance will continue without relatively-outstanding reward. Thus, in effect we "borrow" points from areas in which they are not needed and place them in areas which need additional incentivization. As the gamified system uses points as its sole motivator for action, this changing of points changes the allocation of the gamified system's motivating power.

This shuffling of points does not affect the total points gained, only the relative point gain from different areas. Thus, we are able to invoke the psychological benefit of anchoring to increase motivation without changing the rate at which the user progresses along the first, point-total reward track.

Examples of how different evaluation functions incentivize different spreads of behavior are shown in Fig. 3. Each has specific scenarios where it might be useful in real-world applications. For example, in a gamified environment where beginning each objective feels daunting to the user, such as becoming proficient in different mediums of art, an exponentially decaying evaluation function would compensate users for the large initial investment it takes to begin a category. On the other hand, an increasing function rewards continued investment in a single area. Suppose, for example, tasks were built around beating more and more difficult challenges, or repeatedly overcoming one's own performance record; in this case, the increasing function would compensate the user for the increasing challenge posed by each successive task.

3.4   Implementation

In implementation, this simultaneous pursuit of multiple independent objectives maps neatly onto the Five Key model for reentry. By using each key as a category, we can tune the degree to which progress at different points in the process is incentivized. All the while, the total number of points is preserved due to normalization, and so total gamification progress remains a viable metric for the dispensation of behavior-based rewards. Since each of the Five Keys has a set number of tasks to complete, we can determine percentage completion for each category, and use that percentage as a simple metric for performance in each key. From there, applying a linear evaluation function results in a dynamically-rebalancing allocation of point incentives.

However, the gamification of reentry does not map perfectly to the real-world implementation. Certain categories ancillary to the Five Keys, such as the incentivization of health and the point rewards for avoiding off-limit areas, are recurrent tasks which do not have a set number of total points. This disparity prevents clean integration between these recurrent, uncapped categories and the finite points available under the Five Key tasks. In practice, we resolved this discrepancy by only treating non-recurrent sources of points with the Rubber-Band System.

4   The SMS4CS System

The SMS4CS (Support and Monitoring System for Community Supervision) system is a software package built to serve the needs of the JII population, empower case specialists to mass-manage them, and employ dynamic gamification to provide appropriate, tune-able incentivization of Five Key tasks. It serves as both an example of Five Key gamification and an implementation of the rubber-band system.

4.1   System Overview

The SMS4CS system serves as a real-world implementation of the gamification of parallelized advancement. The system refers to the totality of the GOALS phone app, the dashboard web app, and their shared backend.

The user-base of the SMS4CS system is split by interface endpoint. The GOALS phone application is used by JII in order to interact with the SMS4CS systems like location tracking and task gamification. The dashboard web application is used by case specialists in order to review and interact with the cases under their supervision. The primary method by which these two interfaces overlap is the issuance of tasks, which are elements of the gamification system which are issued by specialists, fulfilled by JIIs, and monitored for completion by the SMS4CS subsystems.

The gamification aspect of the SMS4CS system issues tasks to the participants, checks for task completion using a persistence layer as an intermediary, and issues both cosmetic rewards and prize progress upon point gain. Additionally, the gamification system reads input from case specialists, who can shape the gamified experience through issuing tasks, decide the prize track, and query snapshots of the users' overall gamification progress.

One of the key components to the SMS4CS JII experience is the inclusion of the **vista** (Fig. 4, center). The vista is a portion of the task-handling interface which represents the user's progress as a collection of cosmetic rewards. Each element of the Five Key model is mapped to an element of the vista, and reaching progress milestones in a key will result in the respective vista element ranking up, becoming more opulent or impressive. In doing so, the vista view acts like a digital trophy case of the user's long-term progress.

4.2   The GOALS App

The GOALS app allows participants to interact with the SMS4CS system using their smart phone, giving them access to the required tasks, assessments, sessions, and meetings that are assigned by their case specialist.

Since participants are expected to engage with the system during a long period of time (at least 3 months), we thought it prudent to cultivate features and designs that would foster longer-term, voluntary engagement with the gamified aspects of the app. Thus, the GOALS app is incorporated with the game mechanics, such as points, rewards, levels, and supportive visual feedback. The Five Key Model for Reentry is central to the game's design, encouraging participants in completing tasks and assessments related to each key. The GOALS app as a whole also helps them comply with court orders without direct interaction with case specialists.

When the GOALS app starts, the participant is asked to log in. Afterwards, he or she may access several views. They may switch between these views at any time using tabs at the bottom of the app screen. The GOALS app's functionality is divided into the following five views:

1. The **Home** view: Giving a general overview into the participants current progress levels, upcoming tasks, a chart detailing their points, and access to a map with their current location and exclusion information
2. The **Tasks** view: Listing the currently assigned tasks, reward information, and an interactive game vista using their progress

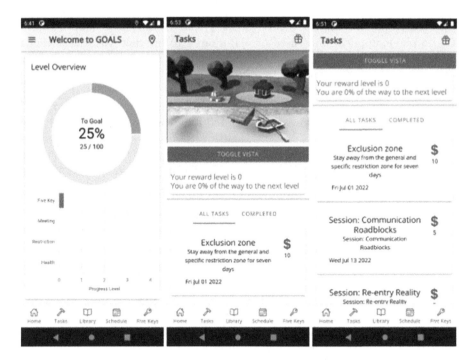

Fig. 4. Examples screens of the GOALS app. From left to right: The home screen, the topmost view of the task screen, and a body view of the task screen.

3. The **Library** view: Supporting important resources and documents
4. The **Schedule** View: showing a calendar with all scheduled meetings, allowing the participants to request meetings themselves
5. The **Five Keys** View: giving the participants the ability to complete assessments and sessions through forms and chat bot sessions

   Select screens of the GOALS app are shown in Fig. 4.

4.3   The Dashboard

The Dashboard system is designed to empower caseworkers to monitor and analyze a large amount of data produced by participants through their interactions with the SMS4CS system. In terms of gamification, this interface allows case specialists to issue new tasks; set rewards, their ordering, and their point thresholds; adjust the rubber-band system by tuning the function hyper-parameter; and view user vistas as snapshots of their overall progress.

For this goal, the dashboard system enables case specialists to access a large amount of data produced by participants and identified by the SMS4CS via multiple user interfaces. Additionally, the dashboard is designed to give the specialist clear insight into critical patterns and impactful factors related to participants' activity data collected by the GOALS app. The interconnected visualizations

Fig. 5. The Five Key view of the dashboard web app. From here, the case specialist will be able to monitor the user's progress through the Keys of Reentry, as well as manually dispatch evaluations and follow-ups at their discretion.

also aid in pattern-recognition in spatial and temporal data concerning participants' daily activities.

The intended use of the dashboard is to make monitoring participants easier for specialists, who typically manage about 50–60 participants at any given time. Select screens of the dashboard web app are given in Figs. 5 and 6.

5   Use Case Scenario

Within the following use case scenario, we use the gamification system as part of a support and management tool for community supervision. The support system consists of two main components: the term "dashboard" refers to the web-accessible dashboard used by case specialists and the term "GOALS (Gaining Occupational and Life Skills) app" refers to the phone app used by JII.

The following actors are used to illustrate the operation of the GOALS app and how it relates to the operations of JII and case specialists who use the system. **James** is a JII on parole. He was arrested for public intoxication, and so his terms of parole require him to avoid any locations within 100 yd of a store that sells alcohol. He has elected to receive a smartphone pre-loaded with the GOALS app to help him through this process. **Sarah** is a 35-year-old case specialist who works for the corrections agency of the facility in which James was incarcerated. It is her responsibility to manage James' parole by meeting with him, evaluating his progress, and helping him understand the terms of his parole. Her department has elected to use the SMS4CS system through the dashboard interface in order to let each case specialist effectively handle more JII.

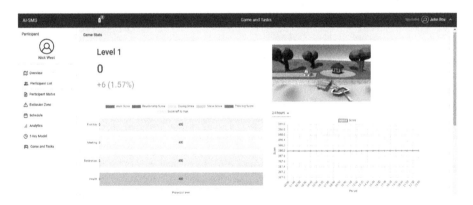

Fig. 6. The Game Progress view of the dashboard app. For each user, this screen will show their case manager their progress in the Five Key gamification, the vista they are using to represent their progress, and their completion rate for time-limited tasks.

5.1   Intake

As James is released from incarceration to begin his parole, he has a face-to-face meeting with Sarah to clarify and explain the terms of his sentence. Sarah uses the dashboard web app to set up James as a new user of the GOALS app. James is handed his smartphone and is told how to launch the app.

To start, James and Sarah are co-located at the site of the hand-off of the smartphone. James enters the username and password given to him by Sarah, his case specialist. James is sent to the Home screen, which has no data to show on his dashboard yet. He begins to ask Sarah about all the different windows he can navigate to. James taps onto the Tasks screen and sees both the vista and the task list. Sarah explains the cosmetic rewards present in the vista, and the difference between the "Today's Tasks" and the "All Tasks" tabs of the task list.

James taps onto the Prize screen and sees both the unclaimed and claimed prize list. Neither is populated because James has not earned any prizes yet. Sarah's office has opted in to prize distribution, so she explains both tabs' functionality. Next, James taps onto the Library screen. Sarah explains that it stores documents related both to his specific case and to the general parameters of parole. From there, James taps onto the Schedule screen. Sarah explains that it will list meetings when the two of them agree on a date and time to host one. To finish, James asks for clarification on anything he doesn't understand, which Sarah provides. Additionally, James opts in to Health and Location tracking.

James is given a smart-watch by Sarah, which syncs with the smartphone. At the end of the interaction, James is released from the facility and begins his parole. His new smartphone is in his pocket, and is collecting location data. His new smart-watch is on his wrist, and is measuring his vitals.

5.2   JII Fulfills Five-Key Task

As part of the Meaningful Work Trajectories key of the Five Keys, James is issued the task of learning about when and how applying for a job requires him to disclose his parolee status. He decides to complete this task at home.

To start, James checks the Tasks screen of his GOALS app. He sees that "Learn about applying to jobs as a parolee" has been added as a new task. James taps on the task. It opens a window which explains that he needs to read a specific document from the Library screen that contains this information. James closes the window and goes to the Library screen. Then, he searches for the document by name and selects it. James reads the document. When he gets to the bottom, he answers a short series of quiz questions that ensure he has comprehended the material. James returns to the Task screen. The task is marked completed, and James immediately receives 5 points in the Meaningful Work Trajectories key, moving him some percentage of the way towards his next cosmetic reward in the vista.

5.3   JII Earns and Claims Prize

While browsing the app, James notices that Sarah has added a free movie ticket as a reward, set at a point value of 60 points. Over the next few weeks, James ensures that he does not fail any tasks, since he wants that movie ticket. After obtaining enough points, he gains and claims the prize.

To start, James opens the Task list and verifies that he has finished the 12th task worth points, bringing his total to 60 points more than when the tickets were added. From there, James opens the Prize screen and sees that the tickets are in his Unclaimed Prizes tab. James taps on the tickets to claim them. Sarah is alerted to this. In response, Sarah mails James one of the tickets, then sends James a message informing him she's done so.

5.4   JII Levels Up Vista

During his interaction with the GOALS app, James crosses over the 100-point threshold in the Meaningful Work Trajectories key. This gives him a cosmetic reward in the vista.

To start, James opens the Task list and taps on the house. The house is the vista element that is related to the Meaningful Work Trajectories key. He notes that he has 95 points in the key. From there, James completes one more five-key task in the Meaningful Work Trajectories key. James then taps on the house again. His point bar is full, and a yellow arrow indicates he is allowed to update the house to the next level. James taps on the arrow. The house he had been seeing disappears, replaced with a more extravagant three-story house. This element upgrade acts as a virtual trophy for his overall progress in the Meaningful Work Trajectories key. James taps away from the Tasks screen, then returns to it later. The vista remembers his choice of element levels, and more visually represents the house he chose by default.

5.5 JII is Motivated by Dynamic Gamification

Over several weeks, James avoids the kinds of tasks he finds most difficult: those in the Meaningful Work Trajectory key. The dynamic gamification will step in here to increase the rewards after detecting his lower-than-average performance in this key.

To start, the Rubber-Band System is invoked by Sarah through the dashboard web app. She chooses a simple decreasing linear function, provided to her as a template by the application. The system goes into effect, scanning through James' progress, and finds that his Meaningful Work Trajectory progress is far behind his progress in the other keys. It borrows points from the other keys' tasks and adds them onto those in the Meaningful Work Trajectories key, and James finds that the new tasks he's issued in that key become more rewarding. This process repeats itself until the motivation provided by the points exceeds James' hesitancy to perform his tasks in his most difficult key, helping him make initial progress and starting him down the path to well-balanced Five-Key reentry journey.

6   Discussion

The dynamic gamification of the rubber-band system has been successfully deployed to the SMS4CS system, but real-world considerations present the implementation of the system with several significant problems.

Unlike most gamified systems, which layer a helpful set of motivational psychology over something that the user wishes to do, our system gamifies a process in which users must, legally, participate. This limits the extent of what we can implement in the gamification system in terms of tasks, progress tracking, and responding to user successes and failures. The second limitation of the gamification system is that it cannot be too complex. Preliminary surveys of the target demographic and interviews with case specialists have indicated to us that technical literacy in the prospective user base is low. A nontrivial number will have never used a smartphone before, and an even greater number will never have interacted with a gamification system. Thus, anything we wish to add must be clear, concise, and understandable to a layperson.

Regardless of these problems, we believe that the gamification of life-improvement habits and rehabilitation will lead to a humanitarian benefit in the SMS4CS target population, regardless of the degree to which alteration of the gamified system improves user engagement.

In the future, we hope to carry out a pilot study that analyzes the difference in motivation between traditional gamification and dynamic gamification across the same set of issued tasks. From this, we ought to be able to judge whether dynamic gamification creates an instant, significant change in the metrics which measure player engagement, such as task completion rate and screen time. This study ought to compare users who receive traditional, statically-valued gamified tasks against users who receive experimental, dynamically-valued gamified tasks.

A control group who receives a task list without gamification might prove useful, but are not strictly necessary in a comparison between static and dynamic gamification methods.

Over a longer period of time, we hope to use the data generated by the users of the SMS4CS system to longitudinally observe how the system affects motivation over a long period of time. This second analysis will allow us to view the gamification in a situation in which the novelty of shifting points and exposure to the rewards mechanisms no longer influences participant behavior. Additionally, it will allow us to gather subjective evaluations from both the JII population and the case-specialist populations who engage with the system, after they have engaged with the system over a long period of time. Feedback from these groups will, respectively, give valuable information on long-term motivational impact and the system's ability to facilitate time-efficient JII mass management.

Finally, we wish to investigate the different short- and long-term impacts of different evaluation functions hyper-parameters on user behavior. The difference between, say, a linear and exponential decreasing evaluation function might reveal that a linear function provides less initial motivation and a larger total gain in engagement, while the exponential function highly motivates initial progress but anchors point-gain expectations too high to be sustainable.

7 Conclusion

We believe strongly in the capability of the core system idea: the allocation of rewards so that under-performing areas are reinforced with extra gamified incentive. This could be applied in any area in which simultaneous pursuit of performance metrics among independent paths is needed. For one example, the system could be used to gamify an elementary school student's pursuit of high test scores in math, language, science, and other mutually-independent classes. in another example, a tennis player could set themselves goals in independent areas that leads to in-game success, such as stamina, reflexes, reaction speed, serves, receives, and net-play.

The benefit of this dynamic point reallocation over traditional, static gamification remains to be seen. We believe that either that the alignment between effort and reward will improve total engagement with the gamification, or that users will become aware of the point-rebalancing mechanism and become resentful that their rewards are being manipulated.

In either case, we hope that deploying this system will add another tool to the belt of gamification design, and that it will be used to craft more effective tools of motivating self-improvement.

References

1. Feathers, T.: They track every move': how US parole apps created digital prisoners. In: The Guardian, March 4 2021

2. Harness, J.: The benefits and drawbacks to using probation and parole apps (2020). https://vistacriminallaw.com/probation-apps/

3. de Sousa Borges, S., Durelli, V.H., Reis, H.M., Isotani, S.: A systematic mapping on gamification applied to education. In: Proceedings of the 29th Annual ACM Symposium on Applied Computing, pp. 216–222 (2014)

4. Kari, T., Piippo, J., Frank, L., Makkonen, M., Moilanen, P.: To gamify or not to gamify? Gamification in exercise applications and its role in impacting exercise motivation (2016)

5. Nicholson, S.: A RECIPE for meaningful gamification. In: Reiners, T., Wood, L.C. (eds.) Gamification in Education and Business, pp. 1–20. Springer, Cham (2015). https://doi.org/10.1007/978-3-319-10208-5_1

6. Barata, G., Gama, S., Jorge, J., Gonçalves, D.: Improving participation and learning with gamification. In: Proceedings of the First International Conference on Gameful Design, Research, and Applications, pp. 10–17 (2013)

7. Fleming, T.M., et al.: Serious games and gamification for mental health: current status and promising directions. Front. Psychiatry 7, 215 (2017)

8. Hoffmann, A., Christmann, C.A., Bleser, G.: Gamification in stress management apps: a critical app review. JMIR Ser. games 5(2), e7216 (2017)

9. Koivisto, J., Hamari, J.: Demographic differences in perceived benefits from gamification. Comput. Hum. Behav. 35, 179–188 (2014)

10. Zatwarnicka-Madura, B.: Gamification as a tool for influencing customers' behaviour. Int. J. Econ. Manag. Eng. 9(5), 1461–1464 (2015)

11. Porcino, T., Oliveira, W., Trevisan, D., Clua, E.: Gamification for better experience in queues during entertainment events. In: SBC Proceedings of SBGames, pp. 162–168 (2018)

12. Hanus, M.D., Fox, J.: Assessing the effects of gamification in the classroom: a longitudinal study on intrinsic motivation, social comparison, satisfaction, effort, and academic performance. Comput. Educ. 80, 152–161 (2015)

13. Hamari, J.: Do badges increase user activity? A field experiment on the effects of gamification. Comput. Hum. Behav. 71, 469–478 (2017)

14. Xi, N., Hamari, J.: Does gamification affect brand engagement and equity? A study in online brand communities. J. Bus. Res. 109, 449–460 (2020)

15. Rodrigues, L.F., Costa, C.J., Oliveira, A.: How does the web game design influence the behavior of e-banking users? Comput. Hum. Behav. 74, 163–174 (2017)

16. Nasirzadeh, E., Fathian, M.: Investigating the effect of gamification elements on bank customers to personalize gamified systems. Int. J. Hum.-Comput. Stud. 143, 102469 (2020)

17. Huang, L., Lau, N.: Enhancing the smart tourism experience for people with visual impairments by gamified application approach through needs analysis in Hong Kong. Sustainability 12(15), 6213 (2020)

18. Caton, H., Greenhill, D.: The effects of gamification on student attendance and team performance in a third-year undergraduate game production module. In: European Conference on Games-Based Learning, Academic Conferences International Limited, p. 88 (2013)

19. Pettus-Davis, C., Kennedy, S.C.: Building on reentry research: a new conceptual framework and approach to reentry services and research. In: Handbook on Moving Corrections and Sentencing Forward, Routledge, pp. 367–378 (2020)

20. Pettus-Davis, C., Renn, T., Veeh, C.A., Eikenberry, J.: Intervention development study of the five-key model for reentry: an evidence-driven prisoner reentry intervention. J. Offender Rehabil. 58(7), 614–643 (2019)

21. Muangsrinoon, S., Boonbrahm, P.: Game elements from literature review of gamification in healthcare context. JOTSE: J. Technol. Sci. Educ. **9**(1), 20–31 (2019)
22. Çubukçu, Ç., Wang, B., Goodman, L., Mangina, E.: Gamification for teaching Java. In: Proceedings of the 10th EAI International Conference on Simulation Tools and Techniques, pp. 120–130 (2017)
23. Bartel, A., Hagel, G.: Engaging students with a mobile game-based learning system in university education. In: 2014 IEEE global engineering education conference (EDUCON), pp. 957–960. IEEE (2014)
24. Urh, M., Vukovic, G., Jereb, E.: The model for introduction of gamification into e-learning in higher education. Procedia-Soc. Behav. Sci. **197**, 388–397 (2015)
25. Lai, J.W., Link, M.W., Vanno, L.: Emerging techniques of respondent engagement: leveraging game and social mechanics for mobile application research. In: 67th Conference of the American Association for Public Opinion Research (2012)
26. Abramovich, S., Schunn, C., Higashi, R.M.: Are badges useful in education?: It depends upon the type of badge and expertise of learner. Educ. Technol. Res. Dev. **61**(2), 217–232 (2013)
27. Akpolat, B.S., Slany, W.: Enhancing software engineering student team engagement in a high-intensity extreme programming course using gamification. In: 2014 IEEE 27th Conference on Software Engineering Education and Training, pp. 149–153. IEEE (2014)
28. Landers, R.N., Sanchez, D.R.: Game-based, gamified, and gamefully designed assessments for employee selection: definitions, distinctions, design, and validation. Int. J. Sel. Assess. **30**(1), 1–13 (2022)
29. Denny, P.: The effect of virtual achievements on student engagement. In: Proceedings of the SIGCHI Conference on Human Factors in Computing Systems, pp. 763–772 (2013)
30. Pettus-Davis, C., Renn, T., Veeh, C.A., Eikenberry, J.: Intervention development study of the five-key model for reentry: an evidence-driven prisoner reentry intervention. J. Offender Rehabil. **58**, 1–30 (2019). https://doi.org/10.1080/10509674.2019.1635242

How Can We Encourage Ownership to Social Challenges?: Comparison of Three Types of Workshop Themes

Nana Hamaguchi[1]([envelope]), Momoko Nakatani[2], Yuki Taoka[2], Mika Yasuoka[3], Tomomi Miyata[2], Shigeki Saito[2], Erika Ashikaga[1], Kakagu Komazaki[1], Ushio Shibusawa[1], and Yoshiki Nishikawa[1]

[1] NTT Social Informatics Laboratories, 1-1 Hikarinooka, Yokosuka-shi, Kanagawa, Japan
nana.hamaguchi@ntt.com
[2] Tokyo Institute of Technology, 2-12-1 Ookayama, Meguro-Ku, Tokyo, Japan
[3] Roskilde University, Universitetsvej 1, 4000 Roskilde, Denmark

Abstract. We designed a data-driven workshop program to encourage ownership to social challenges. Three different social challenges were the themes of the workshops; "future food," "future community child-rearing," and "future work style". In each workshop, both statistical and video data were provided. Participants were asked to answer questionnaires before and after the workshops to measure how much ownership was encouraged. The results confirmed that the proposed workshops encourage ownership regardless of the theme, indicating that the effectiveness of the workshops is versatile. The workshop also provided several findings to increase the effectiveness of the workshop. For example, even small numerical changes should include statistical data to show that changes are taking place. We have found that using such data to engage in dialogue about the future with a diverse group of people can better facilitate ownership of social challenges.

Keywords: future design · workshop · psychological ownership

1 Introduction

The society we live today is faced with various social issues. Global warming, in particular, is an urgent situation, and action is needed not only at the national level, but also at the corporate and individual levels to solve it. In the past few years, the United Nations has set forth the Sustainable Development Goals (SDGs), and corporate activities are now evaluated on the basis of environmental, social, and corporate governance (ESG) criteria, and the movement to encourage collaboration to solve social issues is accelerating.

However, many people may find it difficult to see social issues as their own business on an individual level, even if they are suddenly told that "we should all collaborate to solve social issues." Because social issues are large in scale, it is difficult to find a

M. Kurosu and A. Hashizume (Eds.): HCII 2023, LNCS 14014, pp. 276–293, 2023.
https://doi.org/10.1007/978-3-031-35572-1_19

connection to one's own daily life, and at first glance, it may seem like a problem far away from oneself, or one may feel that taking some action on an individual level will have no impact. However, it is difficult to solve social issues only at the organizational level, such as at the national or corporate level, and it is ultimately important that each individual perceives social issues as his or her own, feels the significance of addressing them, and accumulates actions to solve them.

We believe that to solve social issues, it is essential for each individual to feel the significance and take action. The first step in this process is for each individual to see social issues as his or her own personal matter. We have developed a workshop program that encourages participants to make social issues their own. This paper introduces the workshop program we developed and describes how the workshop brought about changes in the participants' awareness, on the basis of questionnaires before and after participation in the workshop and their post-participation impressions.

2 Previous Study

2.1 What Ownership is

To see things as his or her own personal matter is called a "sense of ownership" or "psychological ownership," and research has long been conducted in fields such as social psychology, educational psychology, and business administration to clarify the determinants of this sense of ownership (e.g. [1, 2]). For example, in a study aimed at fostering a sense of ownership of disaster countermeasures among municipal employees [2], two factors were found to affect the sense of ownership: "I know this job well" (i.e., sense of knowledge) and "I am capable of performing this job" (i.e., sense of control). They hypothesized that by fostering a sense of ownership, an attitude that "we should actively implement this job from now on" (i.e., positive attitude toward the job) would be formed. The results of the experiment indicated that a "positive attitude toward the job" was formed by improving the "sense of control," which in turn needs to be improved to foster an "awareness of the parties concerned".

With regard to environment-conscious behavior, there are models created in reference to four representative Western models [3]. The models state that there are two stages before people take environmentally conscious actions: "general goal intention," in which they have an attitude of wanting to contribute to the problem, and "specific behavior intention," in which they take actions that match their goal intention. The three factors that define a goal intention are "perceived seriousness of environmental problems," "ascription of responsibility for environmental problems," and "belief in the effectiveness of a pro-environmental lifestyle," while the three factors that define a behavioral intention are "feasibility evaluation," "cost-benefit evaluation," and "social norm evaluation". However, the author states that there is no relationship between goal intentions and behavioral intentions, and that they are solely independent.

Some literature advocates a process in which individuals and organizations make the SDGs their own [4]. First, we need to know and understand what the SDGs are, and then to relate oneself to the goals in a bidirectional way, by seeing how the goals expressed in the SDGs relate to the individuals and the organizations they belong to, and what contribution they could make to the goals. This contention addresses the phase of determining the relevance between oneself and the goals is very important in sensing an ownership.

These studies imply that to deepen one's understanding of the subject with some new information, including risk, and to find relevance with oneself, such as feeling a sense of responsibility or self-efficacy in resolving the issue, leads to behavioral intentions (until one has the will to act). Furthermore, whether one actually takes action is not rationally defined, as it is affected by various factors such as cost-effectiveness and feasibility. We believe that "ownership" is only a matter of awareness, and that actual action is the result of an advanced awareness of "ownership". Therefore, the goal of "ownership" in this study is to have the will to act.

2.2 How to Encourage Ownership to Social Challenges

In light of the previous section, encouraging ownership to social challenges means deepening one's understanding of the target issue and determining a connection between oneself and the issue. We believe that temporal and psychological distance make it difficult to sense ownership to social challenges (Fig. 1) [5]. Temporal distance refers to the sense of how much one perceives the event to be a story in the far future. Since it is difficult to imagine one's own or society's situation in the distant future, it is difficult to take action to prepare for the future. Psychological distance refers to the feeling of how much one feel irrelevant to the issue or the feeling that a problem that involves others different from oneself and one does not know what to do. We believe that reducing these distances will encourage ownership to social challenges.

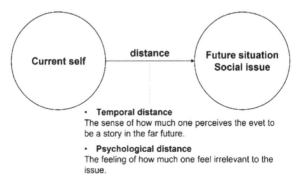

Fig. 1. Distance between social issue and current self.

A number of systems, such as chatbots, are used as a means to promote ownership [6], but as previously mentioned, temporal and psychological distance have a strong effect on ownership to social challenges. Therefore, we believe it is necessary to intervene with stronger means. Therefore, we would like to focus on a dialogue with a diverse group of people as a strong means to bring about a transformation in people's consciousness. In the context of living labs and workshops (WSs), many previous studies have stated that learning and interaction occur through dialogue with a diverse group of people, resulting in positive feelings toward things and behavioral changes [7, 8]. We will also focus on the use of data as it has been reported that presenting data that explains the subject matter under discussion during dialogue accelerates learning [9].

2.3 Approach to Ownership Focused on in this Study

On the basis of the aforementioned previous study, we designed a WS in which statistical data on the target social issue and video interviews with people from overseas were presented, and a diverse group of members engaged in a dialogue about the issue and their ideal vision of the future. In our previous study [5], we conducted a WS on the theme of "future food in 2030" among the social issues and confirmed that the WS encouraged participants' ownership. With regard to statistical data, surprising information for participants aroused their interest in the theme. In addition, data that could be connected to their own daily lives and relevant to themselves were more suitable for a sense of ownership than overly large-scale data. Video data contributed to a more realistic understanding of future situations and issues. Empathy, a sense of detailed discomfort, and a sense of surprise provided an opportunity to deepen their awareness of the crisis and their thinking.

However, the aforementioned results were limited to one theme. To confirm our designed WSs universal effectiveness in addressing other social issues, we conducted similar WSs on "future community child-rearing" and "future work style in 2030". In this paper, we compare the results of the three themes and discuss the effect versatility of our designed WSs. We also derive findings to enhance the effectiveness of the WSs.

3   Verification Through Workshops

3.1   Themes Implemented

The WS programs were conducted on the following three themes, which are detailed in the next section. The themes and dates of implementation are listed in Table 1.

Table 1. The themes and dates of implementation

theme	dates
Future food in 2030	March 23, 2022
Future community child-rearing	September 29, 2022
Future work style in 2030	October 31, 2022

The theme of "future food in 2030" (hereafter, "future food") was selected because it is familiar to everyone, but it also causes relatively familiar social problems such as food loss, and is actually connected to larger-scale social issues such as its impact on carbon dioxide emissions. We considered it appropriate because it is a theme that can easily feel both temporal and psychological distances.

The theme of "future community child-rearing" (hereafter, "future child-rearing") was co-sponsored by a non-profit organization (NPO) involved in child-rearing support. The NPO aims to eliminate solitary child-rearing, and has so far provided support to relatively small families raising children. Isolation of the child-rearing population is a major social issue in today's world, where interaction with local people is becoming increasingly sparse, and considering how local people who are not involved in child-rearing can help solve this problem is an appropriate theme because it means reducing psychological distance.

The theme of "future work style in 2030" (hereafter, "future work style") is familiar with working people, as it occupies the majority of their daily lives. However, both the present and future are changing at a dizzying pace, with new ways of working, such as remote work, emerging due to the COVID-19 pandemic, and the declining trend of the productive population in the future. As the future is uncertain and uncontrollable, it is easy to feel temporal distance. In addition, since work styles need to be considered in the context of relationships with people who have different values, this theme was considered appropriate because it is easy to feel psychological distance as well.

3.2 Workshop Program

Each WS was 3 h long and consisted of the following.

1. Explanation of the purpose of the WS
2. Self-introduction
3. Presentation of statistical data
4. Presentation of video interviews with people living abroad
5. Dialogue about the ideal image of the future
6. Presentation

First, the purpose of the WS was explained, introducing the theme and explaining that the activity was a place for everyone to think about a better future society. After introducing the facilitators including authors, and participating organizations, the participants were divided into groups of 4–6. In Programs 3, 4, and 5, participants worked in groups, and at the end, each group presented their results to the whole group. The following is a detailed description of Programs 3, 4, and 5, which were unique to this WS.

Presentation of Statistical Data

Statistical data related to the theme were collected, and made into cards before the WS. They were distributed to each participant and explained verbally to the entire group. The statistical data were collected from the Internet by the national government and private companies. The data were collected from various perspectives to deepen the understanding of the theme and to enable the participants to realize the relationship between the theme and themselves. For "future food," we collected data that showed the relationship between social trends and daily life to find as many connections as possible with daily life in relation to large-scale social issues. For "future child-rearing," we included data from the perspectives of those involved and not involved in child-rearing since the people of the local community are the stakeholders in this issue. For "future work style," we collected data showing signs of diversification in work styles, environments, and values, as well as changes in how people perceive their time outside of work so that we can expand our thinking beyond the current work styles and environments.

The following are examples of the statistical data presented in each theme (Table 2).

Table 2. Example of the statistical data presented in each theme

theme	example of the statistical data
future food	• Vegetable consumption per person per year in Japan and the USA • Annual amount of food loss in Japan • Climate change and its impact on familiar foods • Sources of methane in the world • Percentage of the world's land area used for food production
future child-rearing	• Population by age group in the community • Importance of community support for those raising children • Actual support actions taken for parents with children • Relationship between the number of community members interacting with children after school and their enjoyment • Connection to community members and babies for those without children
future work style	• Changes in the working-age population • Changes in the employment rate of the elderly • International comparison of working well-being related to working • Relationship between telework and work motivation • Percentage of workers with a second job • Changes in leisure time activities

Regarding the "future child-rearing" and "future work style," the group shared their impressions and questions about the data just after checking the statistical data to deepen their understanding. For "future food," on the other hand, their impressions and questions were collectively shared after viewing the video data described later, due to time constraints.

Presentation of Video Interviews with People Living Abroad

All participants viewed the interview videos, which were approximately one minute each. The interviewees in the videos were people living in Denmark, which ranks high in terms of happiness and SDGs, so that the participants could learn about the thinking of people who are highly aware of the themes, are actually taking action, and are, in a sense, advanced for Japanese people. One of the author members, who lives in Denmark, asked each of the interviewees about the theme and their own situation in 2030, and they answered the questions. However, for "future child-rearing," we asked them about the good things about Denmark in the present, rather than its situation in the future, in accordance with the theme.

Six videos were prepared for "future food," three for "future child-rearing," and four for "future work style." All interviewees for each theme were men and women in their teens to 60 s living in Denmark, and their nationalities and languages were different. This was done to investigate whether having something in common with the WS participants would affect their sense of ownership. All videos were subtitled in Japanese. Table 3 shows a summary of a number of interviewee's statements in the video prepared for each theme.

Table 3. Summary of a number of interviewee's statements in the video

theme	Summary of a number of interviewee's statement
future food	• I think we will start to eat less meat. I also We think will be in a situation where we only have automatic cars, and climate change has become a serious issue, and we are have started to take action • I think we will have diverse food choices such as insect- and vegan-based foods and vegan, etc. I will be in my 50 s, so I think I will eat less and spend more money on what is good for my body
future child-rearing	• There are three good things I felt while raising children in Denmark: first, people around me are kind; second, many people can handle children; and third, parents are accepted as one imperfect human being • Unlike Japan, I feel that people have more financial and psychological leeway. For the national character, people does not interfere too much with others, so they do not care what others think. People around me don't mind if my children make a lot of noise
future work style	• High school teacher. I work from before 8 a.m. until about 4 p.m. I don't think my work style will change much in 2030, because I am satisfied with the way things are now • I work 39 h a week in a food processing company developing production machinery. In 2030, I will be 62 years old, so I would like to work a little less and have more leisure time. However, I would like to continue working as well, and at that time, I would like something that enables me to work flexibly like I do now

After viewing the videos, participants shared their impressions and questions about the videos within their groups to deepen their understanding.

Dialogue About the Ideal Image of the Future

After deepening their understanding of the theme through statistical data and videos, the participants engaged in a dialogue about the theme within the same group. First, individuals filled out worksheets on "The situation in the future in 2030" and "My situation in the future in 2030," and shared them with the group. Next, the entire group drew an ideal scenario of the future.

3.3 Participant

To attract as many diverse people as possible, both working professionals and students were brought together using the snowball sampling method. Working people were acquaintances of the authors engaged in work or activities related to the theme, and were contacted directly by the authors and their acquaintances. For students, recruitment flyers were prepared and distributed to laboratories and clubs with which the authors were connected. Table 4 shows the demographics and number of participants for each theme. The future child-rearing WS was hosted by an organization that provides childcare support, so people from the organization participated and was held at a café operated by the organization. The other WSs were held on the university's campus.

Table 4. Demographics and number of participants for each theme

theme	working people/adults	students	total
future food	8 (5 men, 3 women)	13 (10 men, 3 women)	21 (15 men, 6 women)
future child-rearing	11 (3 men, 8 women)	3 (1 man, 2 women)	14 (4 men, 10 women)
future work style	12 (5 men, 7 women)	12 (7 men, 5 women)	24 (12 men, 12 women)

3.4 Evaluation

To determine how much the participants' ownership to the theme had progressed as a result of their participation in the WS, a questionnaire was prepared to ask about the degree of ownership to the theme, and was distributed both before and after the WS. The questionnaire consisted of 8 questions (Table 5 left), and all responses were on a 7-point Likert scale ("1 not at all agree" to "7 very much agree").

Questions 1–4 of this questionnaire refer to the process of sensing ownership in [4], with questions 1 and 2 measuring the phase of knowing and understanding the subject, and questions 3 and 4 measuring the phase of finding its relevance to oneself. Questions 5–7 refer to the attribution of responsibility, as described in Sect. 2.1, from the aspect of whether it is something that one should work on. Finally, question 8 refers to action intention. Questions 2, 6, and 8 were adapted from questions in [2] to measure a sense of knowledge, sense of ownership, and positive attitude toward countermeasures, respectively, while questions 3, 5, and 7 were adapted from questions in [10] to measure crisis awareness and sense of ownership, respectively. Questions 1 and 4 were newly added by the authors.

Qualitative data were also collected by conducting 20 or 60 min semi-structured interviews with consenting participants after the WS. They were asked about their impressions of and reasons for the statistical data and videos, as well as the impact or changes they experienced as a result of participating in the WS.

3.5 Analysis

Questionnaire responses were tested for two-way analysis of variance (ANOVA) (mixed design) for the theme ("future food," "future child-rearing," "future work style") and timing of response (before and after the WS). All analyses were conducted using the statistical software SPSS 29.0.

4 Workshop Results

Table 5 shows the mean values of each questionnaire item by theme before and after the WS. Note that invert scales (questions 3, 5) are treated by inverting the values.

Table 5. Result of each questionnaire item before and after WS

No.	question	future food		future child-rearing		future work style	
		before	after	before	after	before	after
1	I have a concrete image about the "theme"	3.33 (1.71)	5.00 (0.84)	4.20 (1.01)	4.93 (1.28)	3.50 (1.38)	4.38 (1.16)
2	I can generally imagine what kind of "theme"-related issues will arise in the future	3.50 (1.54)	4.88 (0.78)	4.53 (1.19)	5.13 (0.99)	3.84 (1.26)	4.62 (0.97)
3	I don't think the various issues related to the "theme" will become more serious during my lifetime. (invert scale)	5.39 (1.24)	5.50 (1.20)	5.60 (0.99)	5.60 (1.12)	5.11 (1.45)	5.33 (1.28)
4	The "theme" feels relevant to me	5.61 (1.46)	6.39 (0.78)	6.40 (0.83)	6.73 (0.46)	5.84 (1.30)	5.57 (1.29)
5	Various issues related to the "theme" are difficult for me to consider as my own problem. (invert scale)	4.61 (1.75)	5.17 (0.86)	5.00 (1.11)	6.21 (0.89)	4.22 (1.87)	5.00 (1.52)

(*continued*)

Table 5. (*continued*)

No.	question	future food		future child-rearing		future work style	
		before	after	before	after	before	after
6	It is our job to be prepared to achieve the "theme" ideal	5.33 (1.09)	5.89 (1.08)	6.07 (0.88)	6.33 (0.90)	5.32 (1.46)	5.48 (1.25)
7	We should strive to achieve our "theme" ideal for the sake of future generations	5.50 (1.15)	5.89 (0.83)	6.07 (0.80)	6.33 (0.82)	5.16 (1.34)	5.57 (1.08)
8	I intend to actively work toward achieving the ideals of the "theme" in the future	4.50 (1.58)	5.17 (1.15)	5.87 (0.92)	6.33 (0.82)	4.74 (1.63)	5.05 (1.47)
		Values are means (standard deviation)					

The results of the two-way ANOVA were as follows.

- Question 1: I have a concrete image about the "theme."

The main effect was found only before and after the WS ($F(1,47) = 31.40$, $p < .001$). In other words, regardless of the theme, participants had a concrete image about the theme after participating in the WS.

- Question 2: I can generally imagine what kind of "theme"-related issues will arise in the future.

The main effect was found only before and after the WS ($F(1,48) = 28.43$, $p < .001$). In other words, regardless of the theme, participants were able to imagine what issues might arise in the future as a result of participating in the WS.

- Question 3: I don't think the various issues related to the "theme" will become more serious during my lifetime.

No significant differences were found among the theme or between before and after the WS.

- Question 4: The "theme" feels relevant to me.

The interaction was significant ($F(2,48) = 5.96$, $p < .01$) and the main effect of the theme was significant ($F(2,48) = 3.41$, $p < .05$). When the simple main effects of each factor were checked, significant differences were found between "future food" and "future work style," and between "future child-rearing" and "future work style" after the WS ("future food" and "future work style": $F(2,48) = 7.98$, p < .05; child-rearing and future workstyle: $F(2,48) = 7.98$, p < .01). In "future food," there was a significant difference between before and after the WS ($F(1,48) = 9.39$, p < .01). In other words, in "future work style," participants were less aware that it was relevant to them after the WS than in the other two themes. In "future food," the participants' awareness of "it is relevant to me" increased after participating in the WS.

- Question 5: Various issues related to the "theme" are difficult for me to consider as my own problem.

  The main effect was found only before and after the WS ($F(1,47) = 9.08$, p < .005). In other words, regardless of the theme, participation in the WS led participants to consider the issue as their own.

- Question 6: It is our job to be prepared to achieve the "theme" ideal.

  The main effect was found only before and after the WS ($F(1,50) = 4.23$, p < .05). In other words, regardless of the theme, participation in the WS increased the participants' awareness that it is our job to prepare to achieve the ideal.

- Question 7: We should strive to achieve our "theme" ideal for the sake of future generations.

  The main effects of before and after the WS and theme were both significant (before and after the WS: $F(1,50) = 6.70$, p < .05; theme: $F(2,50) = 3.66$, p < .05). For theme, there was a significant difference between "future child-rearing" and "future work style" ($F(2,50) = 3.66$, p < .05). In other words, regardless of the theme, participation in the WS increased awareness for "we should strive to achieve our ideals for the sake of the next generation." In addition, regardless of whether it was before or after the WS, the awareness was higher for "future child-rearing" than for "future work style."

- Question 8: I intend to actively work toward achieving the ideals of the "theme" in the future.

  The main effects of before and after the WS and the theme were both significant (before and after the WS: $F(1,47) = 4.29$, p < .05; theme: $F(2,47) = 6.30$, p < .01). For the themes, significant differences were found between "future food" and "future child-rearing," and between "future child-rearing" and "future work style" ("future food" and "future child-rearing": $F(2,47) = 6.30$, p < .01; "future child-rearing" and "future work style": $F(2,47) = 6.30$, p < .01). In other words, regardless of the theme, participation in the WS increased the participants' awareness in that they "intend to actively work toward the realization of the ideal." In addition, regardless of whether before or after the WS, the participants' awareness was higher for "future child-rearing" than for the other two themes.

5   Discussion

5.1   Versatility of WS Effects

The results of the questionnaire showed that participation in the WS improved their sense of knowledge by having a concrete image of the theme and being able to imagine problems that may arise in the future, regardless of the theme (questions 1 and 2). They also began to think of the issue as "my own problem" and to have a sense of responsibility that "it is our job to prepare and strive to achieve the ideal" (questions 5, 6, and 7). These changes eventually led to the behavioral intention to "actively work toward achieving the ideal" (question 8), indicating that the proposed WS program, regardless of the theme, is effective in encouraging ownership to social challenges.

However, for questions 3 and 4, which measure the relevance of the theme to oneself, only a significant difference was found for question 4, "future food," indicating that the effect of finding a relevance to oneself is low. These results show that after the understanding of the theme has deepened, a sense of responsibility and behavioral intention arises, even if a relevance to oneself is not necessarily found.

We then focused on the following three points where we observed differences by theme.

1. Only "future food" showed a difference in awareness of "it is relevant to me" after participating in the WS.
2. "Future work style" had a lower awareness of "it is relevant to me" after the WS than the other two themes.
3. Regardless of before or after the WS, participants in "future child-rearing" had high awareness in that they "intend to work actively toward achieving the ideal" and "should work toward achieving the ideal" than the other two themes.

Regarding 1, we believe that the theme of "future food" is affected by the fact that it is so commonplace compared with the other two themes that we rarely have the opportunity to think about it on a daily basis. For child-rearing and work style, people have opportunities to feel dissatisfied and to envision their ideal image on a daily basis. However, many people, especially in Japan, have few opportunities to feel dissatisfied with food, and do not consider it as a subject worth considering. They probably do not do much research on the future of food. We believe that the participants felt the most change before and after the WS because they participated in such a situation, gained new knowledge from statistical data and videos, and had a dialogue with people who are thinking deeply about food in the future.

Regarding 2, we believe that the theme of "future work style" is affected by the fact that, compared with the other two themes, the scope of change at one's discretion is very narrow or almost non-existent. As seen in the following statements, the way one works depends more on the policies of the organization to which one belongs and the capitalistic philosophy that is the basis of economic activities than on the individual. The Japanese national characteristic of not objecting to decisions made by superiors may have had an effect, but we do not think it was insufficiently effective to change the mindset of individuals to change the major trends in the world and the decisions made by superiors at the individual level.

- *I can't change the current world. (Why?) It depends on the solution, but to take an extreme example, unless I leave my child at daycare during the week and have a daycare provider take care of her from morning to night throughout the day, my sleep deprivation will not be solved. ["future work style," Working people/Adult 7]*
- *Japanese private companies, or maybe it is our company, do not consider it acceptable to be satisfied with the present or with the way we work, including whether or not we enjoy the way we work. They are saying, "We have to grow more." They are saying that the present status is not good enough. I felt that this is also connected to the level of individual happiness. Should we all be dissatisfied with the present status? Being happy and being satisfied with the current job is equal. Not being happy and being unsatisfied with the current environment and feeling the need to grow is equal. That is where the link is. ["future work style," Working people/Adult 5]*

Regarding 3, we believe that this was affected by the fact that many of those who participated in the theme of "future child-rearing" had strong feelings about the theme on a regular basis. The WS on this theme was co-sponsored by a local NPO involved in childcare support, and many of the participants were NPO staff members or people who were involved with the NPO. Since the vision of "raising children in the community" was proposed by this NPO, the participants were more motivated to achieve the ideal regardless of the WS than those who participated in the other two themes. A participant who is one of the staff members of this NPO said the following, indicating that she was highly motivated to solve the problem from the beginning for personal reasons and that she could easily imagine taking some action to achieve the ideal because she belonged to the NPO.

- *My child stopped going to school and became recluse.... I would say people who are the majority look at things a little differently, even if only a little. I would like to help people expand their perspective a little bit, or perhaps to make a new move in their own way. ["future child-rearing," Working people/Adult 11]*
- *We are trying to build a cafe (the NPO is planning to open a new one). I would like to explore what we can do there, and I think we can do it. (Why so positive?) Because I believe in everyone in the NPO. I have been involved with the current store since it was established, and although I am a person who originally thought negatively and did not participate in social activities, seeing how many things have happened in the past seven years and how many people are involved, I believe that they will happen again in the future and that we can make them happen. ["future child-rearing," Working people/Adult 11]*

While 1 and 3 are not a problem because they are positive differences with respect to the objective of encouraging ownership, it is 2 that needs to be considered. It is suggested that themes that are beyond an individual's discretion in actually trying to take action will hinder ownership. It is necessary to set themes within the range of what can be done at individuals' discretions, determine what can be done at the individual level, and incorporate elements into the WS that make people feel that there is something they can do.

5.2   Elements that Enhance the Effectiveness of WS

Next, on the basis of the participants' comments, we will discuss the factors that contributed to the effectiveness of this WS in encouraging ownership, and extract the factors that enhance the effectiveness of the WS.

Statistical Data

The clear visualization of signs of change in the current situation and in the future, both numerically and graphically, had an impact on the way of thinking about the theme and on future actions. In particular, data showing that change is definitely occurring, even if it is only a slight numerical change, is thought to have the effect of raising expectations that the future may change and prompting people to change their thinking and behavior.

- *The working-age population is changing rapidly, the number of young people is decreasing, and the elderly are making up a larger proportion of the overall population. I thought it was necessary to change the working style in accordance with the changes in the working-age population, or to clarify tasks so that the elderly can also work. ["future work style," Student 12]*
- *This data made me reflect on the fact that vegetable consumption in Japan is decreasing… And that when we eat out, we don't eat vegetables as much as we should. I felt that I should eat more vegetables so that consumption will not lead to a decrease, but rather to an increase. ["future work style," Working people/Adult 8]*
- *Statistics were useful in terms of thinking about the future. (Which data?) The data on the percentage of people who have a second job…. Right now, we can only think about the immediate future. I think it was easier to enter the WS after seeing the data that the working style will change in the future. ["future work style," Student 4]*

In particular, the group that was able to utilize the same statistical data in a way that focused on positive aspects rather than negative ones to find solutions had a positive attitude toward working to achieve their ideals. Conversely, in a number of cases, focusing on negative aspects led to thoughts of being stuck in the present status. On the basis of this, we believe that statistical data with additional information that encourages an awareness of positive aspects will positively affect thinking and behavior, and develop thinking toward solutions that go beyond that.

- *I was very impressed by the positive attitude of the participants, and the way they talked about how they could do this, that, and other things…. I thought that when Japanese people hear overseas people talk, they tend to think that Japan is not good enough, but I was surprised to hear that this was not the case…. We didn't see the statistics of Japan in a negative light. ["future child-rearing," Working people/Adult 11]*
- *The part about wages (data showing that the average wage in Japan has not increased) bothered me. I knew it was true…. I thought we have to design our life within this level of income. From now on, I will have more opportunities for free labor, but few ones for paid labor due to my age…. If we don't resist, it will be free labor, and if we can't*

resist, we will live while saving money? ["future work style," Working people/Adult 5]

Although previous studies show that facts such as statistical data are unsuitable for changing people's opinions [11], it can be said that in this WS, statistical data were effective in changing participants' awareness. One reason is that in this WS, statistical data were not used to lead to a specific conclusion, but rather as material to deepen participants' understanding of the theme and to help them think for themselves. In addition, the fact that the data were open to interpretation and that participants had the opportunity to discuss how to interpret the data with each other may have had an impact. The fact that the group that focused on the positive aspects of the data in this WS showed a positive attitude toward achieving ideals is consistent with the findings of [11] that "people listen more to messages delivered from a positive perspective and are more likely to be affected as a result." This suggests that statistical data should be collected from a variety of perspectives with the goal of deepening one's understanding of the theme, and that while leaving interpretation of the data to the participants, it would be best to make them aware of the positive aspects as much as possible.

Video Interviews with People Living Abroad
By comparing the information obtained from the video with the situation in Japan, where they live, the participants conversely became aware of the characteristics of Japan, and this led them to have an image of how things will change in the future. When living in the same environment for a long time, it is difficult to notice things that are characteristic of Japan because they are taken for granted. Information about advanced foreign countries that are different from one's own country provides an opportunity to think about the future without being bound by the present status.

- *I thought that the work-life balance required differs depending on age, position, and job title, so working styles are broader than I had thought. I thought that remote work had spread because of COVID-19, but after watching the video of the Danish people, I realized that this was not the case at all. I wondered if more flexible work styles will increase in the future. ["future work style," Student 12]*
- *By listening to the messages from Scandinavia,... I was able to expand my image and talk about them.... The interviewee was Japanese, so she talked about the differences between Japan and the other side of the world. Her comments naturally made it easy for me to compare Japan with the other country. It was easy to bring it to the situation we live in. It might have been different if it had been a completely foreign interview by a foreigner. The foreigner might not notice the goodness of his own country. Maybe it was easier to draw her in because she was talking about the good points of the foreign country as seen from the Japanese perspective. ["future child-rearing," Working people/Adult 11]*

It also confirmed the impact of obtaining information from a real person as opposed to statistical data. For the participants who had never thought much about the theme before the WS, after they saw real people speaking their own opinions on video, they began to feel that they should have their own opinions as well. This change in awareness is thought to have been a factor in making the theme one step more personal.

– *Until now, I have always felt as if it were someone else's problem, but through the WS, I have begun to develop a sense of ownership to the theme.... I thought I should at least have an opinion about what I think should happen.... I think it was important for me to see people actually speaking, and to hear them speak, not to read something written down.... I could feel that this person was really thinking. ["future food," Student 3]*

There were also examples where the attributes of the speakers of the videos affected their ownership. For example, as for the aforementioned comment ["future child-rearing," Working people/Adult 11], a Japanese person, rather than a foreigner, was closer to the speaker, and thus the video was perceived as more personal to him or her. Another example was when a small child clearly expressed his own opinion, which made a participant feel that he should also face the theme, as in the following statement. Although it was not possible to analyze whether there was some kind of correlation between the speakers' attributes and their effect on ownership only in this experiment, it is thought to be one of the factors.

– *A number of them were still in elementary and junior high school, and I was surprised to see that even they had their own ideas about food, the environment, and the future more clearly than we had imagined. ["future food," Working people/Adult 3]*

Dialogue with a Diverse Group of People
Having the opportunity to talk about the theme with someone else is in itself a trigger for thinking, and that alone has the effect of bringing it closer. In particular, when the members include experts who know or think about the theme well, they tend to gain new knowledge and stimulation, and their awareness of the theme tends to increase.

– *I thought I'm blessed because I'm raising my kids now in an environment where cafés are nearby that hold such a WS. When I speak at such places, I have the opportunity to reflect on myself and notice new things. I am grateful to have some kind of connection and place around me because I think it is hard to raise a child without being able to see what is going on around me.... Opportunities to notice new things are not usually found in the places where we usually go to play. ["future child-rearing," Working people/Adult 6]*
– *I knew there are people close to me who are aware of this issue (food loss), and the importance of the food loss issue has been raised in my mind. ["future food," Working people/Adult 8]*

In addition, having positive dialogues about the theme with people from different positions and backgrounds made them think about what they could do and the possibility of changing the world for the better. A number of examples were seen that changed their usual way of thinking. Positive dialogue depends in part on the personality and compatibility of the participants, but as mentioned earlier, they are encouraged by focusing on the positive aspects of the data. In other words, it is believed that dialogues with a diverse group of people about the positive aspects of the data will encourage ownership.

- *I thought it was a group of people from various positions, each with their own opinions and what they could do in their respective capacities. This made me think more strongly about what I can do. ["future child-rearing," Working people/Adult 6]*
- *Even if intuitively it seems a little unthinkable,… Perhaps, at some stage, it will exceed the limit in some way and will happen…. I came to think so while watching videos and talking with people…. When I talked with people in reference to the videos, one of the members who initially had a cautious attitude like myself, saying that "Food might not change so easily," said after watching the videos that "Maybe it's not true." So, I think other participants also realized this like me. ["future food," Student 9]*
- *I started to think about work-life balance. The main thing that has changed was that before attending the WS, I was thinking about what skills I could acquire by working rather than achieving a work-life balance, but after meeting various people at the WS, I felt that having a fulfilling personal life and having enough time to live like that would help me maintain motivation for my work. ["future work style," Student 12]*

6   Conclusion

We confirmed that the proposed WS program encourages ownership in three different social challenges, and showed that it is effective and versatile. We also found a new hypothesis that it would be better to include additional information to enable participants to focus on the positive aspects of statistical data. In addition, video data in which real people talk about advanced foreign information could be more persuasive and raise expectations that the future might change without being limited by the present status. Using such data to engage in dialogue about the future with a diverse group of people is expected to further promote the ownership to social challenges.

In the future, we would like to improve the WS program on the basis of this knowledge and systematize it so that it can be implemented in a variety of situations. In addition, each of the three WSs mentioned in this paper was followed by two or three more sessions (Ideation WSs) to discuss solution ideas. We plan to gain further knowledge to encourage ownership by analyzing those Ideation WSs in the same way.

Acknowledgments. This research is based on a joint research project between Nippon Telegraph and Telephone Corporation and Tokyo Institute of Technology. Tokyo Institute of Technology is also promoting this research with a grant from the Tokyo Institute of Technology's DESIGN Organization for Future Society (dLab).

References

1. Pierce, J.L., et al.: Work environment structure and psychological ownership: the mediating effects of control. J. Soc. Psychol. **144**(5), 507–534 (2004)
2. Ryo, T., et al.: Effectiveness of workshop training method on development of intentions and attitudes towards disaster waste management preparedness action. J. Jpn. Soc. Nat. Disaster Sci. **34**, 99–110 (2015)

3. Yukio, H.: Determinants of environment-conscious behavior. Res. Soc. Psychol. **10**(1), 44–55 (1994)
4. Masaaki, I.: PBL to cultivate the sensitivity to inclusiveness and sustainability. J. Kyosei Stud. **11**(11), 66–79 (2020)
5. Momoko, N., et al.: How can we achieve ownership to societal challenges?: through a workshop on food for the future. Hum. Interface Soc. (2022)
6. Sora, M., et al.: Prototyping dialogue agent for encouraging sense of ownership on social problems. In: The 36th Annual Conference of the Japanese Society for Artificial Intelligence (2022)
7. Mika, Y.: Keys for CoDesign: living lab and participatory design. Serviceology **5**(3), 36–44 (2018)
8. Fumiya, A., Atsunobu, K.: Living Labs as a methodology for service design: analysis based on cases and discussion from the viewpoint of systems approach. J. Jpn. Soc. Kansei Eng. **15**(2), 87–92 (2017)
9. Fumiya, A., et al.: Research on living lab methodology with data. A case of living lab practices using disaster data archive. Bull. Jpn. Soc. Sci. Des. **66**(0), 76 (2019)
10. Rie, I., et al.: The study of awareness about global warming issues and environmentally concerned behaviors from a survey of elementary and junior high school teachers. J. Home Econ. Jpn. **52**(9), 827–837 (2001)
11. Tali, S.: The Influential Mind: What the Brain Reveals About Our Power to Change Others. Little, Brown Book Group (2017)

CallMap: A Multi-dialogue Participative Chatting Environment Based on Participation Structure

Masanari Ichikawa[✉] and Yugo Takeuchi

Shizuoka University, 3-5-1, Johoku, Naka-ku, Hamamatsu, Shizuoka 4328011, Japan
ichikawa.masanari.18@shizuoka.ac.jp, takeuchi@inf.shizuoka.ac.jp

Abstract. Voice communication is the most familiar interaction mode for people in face-to-face scenarios. People can participate in multiple dialogues by controlling their gaze, body orientation, and physical distance from the speaker. Participation in multiple dialogues results in sharing of opinions and information transfer among groups and can be useful for learning and generating ideas in classes and meetings. However, many telecommunication systems do not allow for such multi-dialogue participation. In addition, there are no clear technical guidelines for achieving multi-dialogue participation online. The purpose of this study is to propose a design guideline to realize multi-dialogue participation online. Based on the participation structure, this study defined symbols for describing the participation structure non-verbally and described statutes of multi-dialogue participation using graphs. This study also implemented CallMap, a telecommunication system, based on the graph. A method to realize multi-dialogue participation online was discussed, as were the advantages of representing the participation structure as a graph, issues in implementing the system, and the possibility of online communication independent of the physical interface.

Keywords: Participation Structure · Graph Theory · Multi-Dialogue Participation · Telecommunication System

1 Introduction

Voice communication in face-to-face situations is the most familiar form of interaction for people. In recent years, telecommunication systems such as Zoom [24] and Microsoft Teams [15] have become popular as a means of voice communication as the COVID-19 pandemic spreads. These systems allow people to talk with a group of people online and to see the faces and gestures of participants. They enable people to conduct some classes and meetings in a manner similar to face-to-face scenarios. However, some people find communication in these systems inconvenient and unsatisfactory, and they may still prefer face-to-face as a means of communication. Some classes, meetings, and conferences are still conducted face-to-face, even with the widespread use of telecommunication systems. Existing telecommunication systems are effective as a means of

M. Kurosu and A. Hashizume (Eds.): HCII 2023, LNCS 14014, pp. 294–313, 2023.
https://doi.org/10.1007/978-3-031-35572-1_20

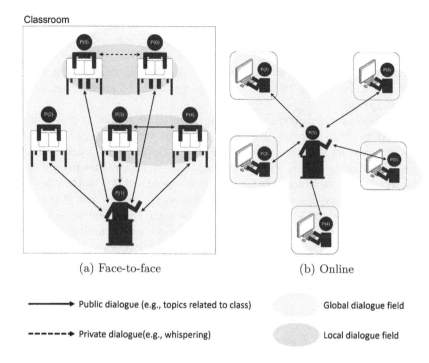

(a) Face-to-face   (b) Online

———▶ Public dialogue (e.g., topics related to class)   Global dialogue field

------▶ Private dialogue(e.g., whispering)   Local dialogue field

Fig. 1. Examples of dialogue fields generated by face-to-face and online classes

voice communication based on verbal information but have many limitations as a means of communication from the perspective of nonverbal information. For example, one limitation is that people cannot simultaneously participate across multiple dialogues online.

People routinely participate simultaneously in multiple dialogues in face-to-face situations. For example, in face-to-face lectures, students listening to the lecturer often talk with each other (Fig. 1a). Sometimes the conversation is just chatting, but sometimes students are discussing the content of the class or clarifying doubts. The conversation may contain useful content that should be shared with all students to help them better understand the lesson. Similarly, incidental chat occurs during a meeting and can turn into a general discussion. Unlike a public speech in classes and meetings, an environment where participants can engage in private conversations is a meaningful opportunity for stimulating discussion and generating learning and ideas. However, it is structurally difficult for participants to engage in private conversations with each other in contemporary telecommunication systems, and opportunities to realize the afore-described dialogue are lost (Fig. 1b). Therefore, this study discusses how to realize multi-dialogue participation online.

In this study, multi-dialogue participation is defined as a situation in which a person participates in multiple dialogues at the same time. For example, the captain of an airplane participates in multiple dialogues with the copilot, attendants, the captains of other airplanes, and the ATC tower on the ground concurrently. However, the captain may not always be the speaker, may not always be the addressee, and may not always be listening to all of the dialogue. It is important to emphasize that multi-dialogue participation refers to participating in multiple dialogues, not to being able to hear and understand all of the dialogues in which one is participating.

As some telecommunication systems have breakout rooms, it would not be technically difficult to have separate dialogue fields within a single application. However, no existing telecommunication systems claim to be capable of multi-dialogue participation. There may be an implicit perception that people cannot participate in multiple voice communications concurrently. On the one hand, when a person is approached by several people at the same time, it is difficult for the person to respond to each of them at the same time. On the other hand, as in the previous example, there are situations in which multiple dialogues can be handled simultaneously, such as talking during classes or meetings. People have the capacity for multi-dialogue participation [1,2,5]. However, certain conditions must be met for it to function properly. Based on the theory of a participation structure, it has been reported that people can participate in multiple dialogues under certain conditions [3,8]. The theory posits the existence of a hierarchy of participation levels among participants in a dialogue field, and it is widely understood in peripheral research fields that people engage in dialogue according to the structure. It also has been reported that nonverbal information such as participants' gaze [4,9,12,18], body distance [10], and body placement [13,20] in face-to-face interaction contributes to the formation and visualization of the participation structure, and participants determine their own behavior by recognizing this nonverbal information. However, it is difficult to properly form and recognize participation structures online because much of the nonverbal information is restricted. As a result, there is a peculiar awkwardness that permeates online communication. Some telecommunication systems, such as Gather [6] and oVice [17], partially resolve this restriction by adding a virtual body to the interface. Many studies attempt to solve the constraints in online communication using similar approaches (e.g., [11,14,16,23]). However, the aforementioned restrictions have not yet been fully resolved. There is also scope for consideration of whether it is appropriate to develop telecommunication systems based on the idea of imitating a face-to-face situation. Therefore, this study proposes a method to realize multi-dialogue participation online based on academic findings such as the theory of the participation structure.

The purpose of this study is to propose a design guideline to realize multi-dialogue participation online. To achieve this goal, this study defines a symbolic system for describing the participation structure non-verbally based on the theory of the participation structure and surrounding academic knowledge and describes statutes of multi-dialogue participation using graphs. While there is considerable academic and qualitative discussion of the participation structure in dialogue research, there is no sufficient set of technical and quantitative indicators. Therefore, this study adopted graphs as a symbolic system for quantita-

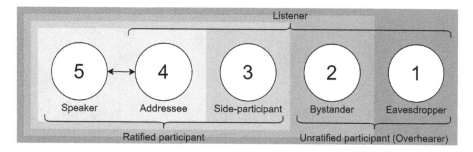

Fig. 2. Model in the theory of participation structure [based on Clark et al. 1996] Note: The number of loads is assigned by the participating states (cf. Sect. 3.1).

tively describing the structure of dialogues and defined its own symbolic system. Graphs are a typical means of representing discrete structures. For example, servers and the Internet have a discrete structure, and their network diagrams are often represented by graphs. As the structure of dialogue also has a data type that is discrete and similar to a network in terms of information transfer, this study adopted graphs as the symbolic system. This study also implemented a telecommunication system based on the described graphs. Based on these processes, this study discusses a method to realize multi-dialogue participation online, the advantages of representing the participation structure as a graph, issues in implementing the system, and the possibility of online communication independent of a physical interface.

2   The Participation Structure and Human Cognition

2.1   Concept of the Participation Structure

In a dialogue field composed of many people, the participation status of listeners is not uniform. For example, when a teacher poses a question to one of the students in class, that student may speak to the teacher or the entire classroom. However, other students are not allowed to speak without a show of hands or nomination. In this case, it can be said that the position in the dialogue differs between the nominated student who has the right to speak, and the other students. The participation structure distinguishes the following five levels for a listener's participation positions within a hierarchy: speaker, addressee, side-participant, bystander, and eavesdropper (Fig. 2). All participants are also classified into two categories: ratified participants and unratified participants [3, 8].

Ratified participants are those who have been assigned the right to be the speaker. The speaker is the most central person in the dialogue. The addressee is the person to whom the dialogue is addressed. In most cases, the addressee is the person who speaks immediately before the speaker or is prompted to speak immediately after the speaker, but it is not always possible to determine the

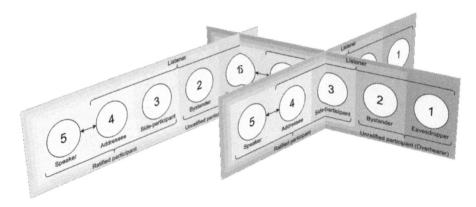

Fig. 3. Example of multi-dialogue participation in the participation structure model

receiver in actual dialogue without some ambiguity. Side-participant is a ratified participant other than the speaker and the addressee. Unratified participants are often described as overhearers, and they are those who have not been given the right to be a speaker (e.g., parents visiting class on parents' day and a person who happens to be passing by). In the participation structure, overhearers are treated as participants in a broad sense. The distinction between a bystander and an eavesdropper is whether or not their presence is recognized by others. The participation status changes according to the progress of the dialogue and the change of speakers.

The participation structure can uniquely assign the positions of participants in a single dialogue field, which marks an improvement. However, it is difficult to describe multiple participant states using this diagram because this model is not scalable (Fig. 3). Furthermore, this diagram is not suitable for designing telecommunication systems. Therefore, the concept of the participation structure should be used as a reference when designing a telecommunication system. It is also necessary to develop an original symbolic system for the description method.

2.2   Role of the Body in Multi-dialogue Participation

It is widely understood that participants' body positioning (e.g., interpersonal distance, F-formation, body torque) and gaze (e.g., eye contact, addressing, gaze awareness) play a role in face-to-face interaction. By using the interface of the body, people can adjust their participation status in the participation structure appropriately and realize multi-dialogue participation. This section organizes the physical interactions observed in face-to-face situations, focusing on their relationship with the participation structure.

The F-formation is a concept related to the dialogue field formed by the physical arrangement of the participants [13]. The space constructed by the F-formation is concentric, with participants located in the center having a higher degree of participation than those located on the outer edge. Concerning the participation structure, both of them explain a hierarchy in the degree of participation within a single dialogue field. There are also similar studies that discuss the correlation between physical distance and the degree of participation [10].

When three or more people interact in a face-to-face situation, the speaker needs to quickly determine the next speaker to keep the dialogue going smoothly [18]. Many studies have pointed out the importance of gaze information such as eye movements and facial orientation when changing speakers [4,9,12]. In the case of a three-way dialogue, eye gaze plays the role of determining the addressee or the next speaker, i.e., it plays the role of an address [21]. In the model shown in Fig. 2, the address is indicated by an arrow.

In face-to-face situations, body placement and eye contact make the concept of participation structure visible and contribute as cues for people to behave appropriately. However, in online situations, these bodily interactions are not represented, resulting in unnatural silences and difficult speaker changes [19,22]. Some telecommunication systems, such as Gather [6] and oVice [17], partially overcome this restriction by adding a virtual body to the interface. However, the aforementioned restrictions have not yet been fully resolved. Body position and eye contact are means used within the constraints of a face-to-face situation. The constraints of face-to-face situations include, for example, limitations in vision, hearing, and the number of people in the room. In face-to-face situations, participants often have difficulty looking into the dialogue room at a distance or are forced to move from one seat or room to another. Therefore, the question of whether it is appropriate to develop telecommunication systems based on the idea of imitating a face-to-face situation needs to be considered.

It has been reported that people experience unforced interaction, a state in which they perceive that they are perceived by each other, in the process of verbal interaction [7]. It is also reported that messages exchanged through body movements in an unforced interaction are perceived through visual reification [7]. In other words, this suggests that the important thing in interaction is not eye contact or body positioning, but rather nonverbal information such as participation status and address perceived through certain actions. Therefore, it is necessary to provide an appropriate interface for online communication to send and receive participation status and addresses, such as eye gaze and body positioning in face-to-face situations.

2.3   Multiple–Participation Design for Telecommunication Systems Based on Participation Structure

We have focused on the participation structure and interfaces in face-to-face situations and described their academic importance and technical applications. While academic findings are often well organized, they are not yet ready to be used for technological application. Consequently, multi-dialogue participation in telecommunication systems has not yet been achieved. This study proposes a method to realize multi-dialogue participation online based on academic findings such as the theory of the participation structure. In Sect. 3, we define a symbolic system for implementing the participation structure as a system and prepare the foundation for creating a telecommunication system based on the participation structure. In Sect. 4, we examine appropriate means of expressing nonverbal information such as participation status and addresses online. We then design CallMap, a multiple participative chatting environment.

3   Graphing the Participation Structure Applying Graph Theory

A graph is a mathematical structure composed of vertices (nodes) and edges. A graph can represent how elements are related in some context in a set with a discrete structure. Considering the aspect of information transfer in dialogue and the fact that dialogue has a discrete structure involving participants and dialogue fields, we thought it appropriate to use a graph.

3.1   Definition of Symbols

Nodes. A node is an abstraction that represents an element in a set. The elements that make up the participation structure are the participants and the dialogue field.

We define "participant node" as a symbol of a participant and "dialogue node" as a symbol of a dialogue field. To distinguish between them, a participant node is labeled $P(m)$ and denoted by a white circle. A dialogue node is labeled with the label $D(n)$ and denoted by a black circle. m and n are serial numbers and integers greater than or equal to 1.

The Edges. Edges are abstractions that represent relationships between elements. The relations between elements in the participation structure include the participation status relation between the participant and the dialogue field as well as the address relation between the speaker and the addressee.

We define "status edge" as a symbol of the participation statute. The status edges are classified into five based on the number of loads shown in Fig. 2. Each edge is defined as one of the following: speaker edge, addressee edge, side-participant edge, bystander edge, and eavesdropper edge. Each statute edge is assigned a weight according to the number of loads. Weight is a concept in graph theory that expresses the magnitude of the relationship between nodes. Status edges are undirected edges because there is no direction in the relationship between a participant and a dialogue field.

We define "address edge" as a symbol of the address that a speaker is sending to an addressee. An address edge is a directed edge because an address has a direction. To improve readability, the address edge is indicated by a dashed line.

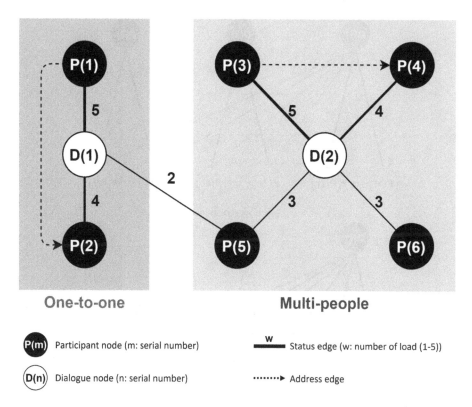

Fig. 4. Example of a participation graph in a restaurant (Color figure online)

3.2 Tutorial on Participation Graphs

We refer to a participation graph as a graph described based on the symbols defined in Sect. 3.1. This section describes three basic forms of a participation structure graph: one-to-one, multi-people, and multi-dialogue participation.

The participation graph shown in the red background of Fig. 4 represents a one-to-one dialogue. $D(1)$ is a dialogue field containing two ratified participants. At this moment, $P(1)$ is the speaker and $P(2)$ is the addressee, and the participation status changes over time. For example, let $P(1)$ and $P(2)$ be a customer and a waiter, respectively, and a scenario involving placing an order in a restaurant is represented by the graph including $P(1)$, $P(2)$, and $D(1)$.

The participation graph shown in the blue background of Fig. 4 represents a multi-people dialogue. $D(2)$ is a dialogue field containing four ratified participants. At this moment, $P(3)$ is the speaker, $P(4)$ is the addressee, $P(5)$ and $P(6)$ are side-participants, and the participation status changes over time. For example, assuming $P(3)$ to $P(6)$ are customers, so a situation of four people chatting is represented by the graph including $P(3)$ to $P(6)$ and $D(2)$.

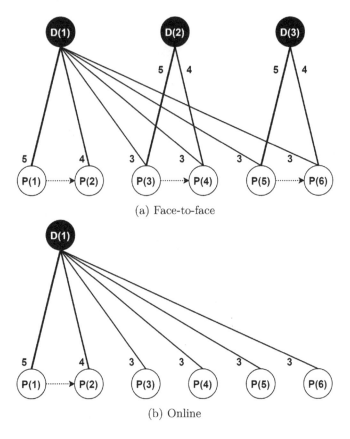

(a) Face-to-face

(b) Online

Fig. 5. Example of a participation graph in a classroom

The participation graph can represent multi-dialogue participation states. Connecting a participant node and dialogue nodes with status edges represents multi-dialogue participation. In Fig. 4, $P(5)$ is connected to both $D(1)$ and $D(2)$. $P(5)$ participates in $D(1)$ as an observer and in $D(2)$ as an observer. For example, people sometimes listen to conversations of nearby customers in a restaurant. A situation that belongs to one dialogue field while listening to another is represented by $P(5)$, $D(1)$, and $D(2)$. This multi-dialogue participation, which was difficult to describe in Fig. 2, could be described by the participation graph.

3.3   Participation Graphs of Classroom

Section 1 mentioned some limitations of online communication, such as the inability to chat. It suggests that there are differences in the structure of dialogue between face-to-face and online scenarios. In this section, we use participation graphs to quantitatively clarify these differences.

Figure 5a and 5b show the situations in Fig. 1a and 1b represented by the participation graphs. The participants consist of $P(1)$ as a teacher and $P(2)$ to

$P(6)$ as students. From Sect. 3.2, $D(1)$ in Fig. 5a and 5b is a dialogue between multiple participants. Given that $D(1)$ in both figures is a public dialogue field to which all participants are connected, it can be assumed to be a dialogue field where a class is being held. For example, let a teacher, $P(1)$, be the speaker, a student, $P(2)$, be the addressee, and the other students, $P(3)$ to $P(6)$, are the side-participants. A situation wherein the teacher asks the student some questions is represented by Fig. 5a.

From Sect. 3.2, $D(2)$ and $D(3)$ in Fig. 5a, which shows a face-to-face situation, are both one-to-one interactions. $P(3)$ to $P(6)$, which are connected to $D(2)$ and $D(3)$, are all connected to $D(1)$ as well, and are thus involved in multi-dialogue participation. As $D(2)$ and $D(3)$ are private dialogue fields to which only some participants are connected, they can be assumed to be dialogue fields where chats are being held. Incidentally, in Sect. 1, it was pointed out that chats in the classroom include not only idle talk but also useful information. However, the participation graph cannot describe what participants are talking about. In Fig. 5b, which shows an online situation, $D(2)$, $D(3)$, and the edges connected to them in Fig. 5a do not appear because current telecommunication systems cannot generate multiple dialogue fields in a single space. Figure 5a and 5b reveal the difference between face-to-face and online dialogue structures in a classroom situation.

4 CallMap: A Multiple Participative Chatting Environment

Section 2.2 mentioned the limitations of representing interactions used in face-to-face situations, such as eye gaze and body placement, directly online. This chapter describes the design of CallMap, which has an interface adapted to telecommunication systems. CallMap is a telecommunication system designed based on the graph set up in Sect. 3. This chapter presents the specification of CallMap and its relationship to the participation structure. Section 4.1 descrives the development environment and network configuration of CallMap, Sect. 4.2 describes the components of CallMap, and Sect. 4.3 describes its functions. Sections 4.4 and 4.5 describe how participation status and addresses are abstracted and designed.

4.1 Application Development

CallMap is software designed for use on a personal computer (PC). Its output mechanism uses a PC display and headset while input mechanism uses a cursor, keyboard, and headset microphone (Fig. 6).

Table 1 shows the development environment. CallMap was produced with Unity, a game engine. CallMap uses Photon, a multi-player engine, for its communication. Photon is often used as a communication platform for multi-player games. In CallMap, Photon plays the role of a relay server that passes variables

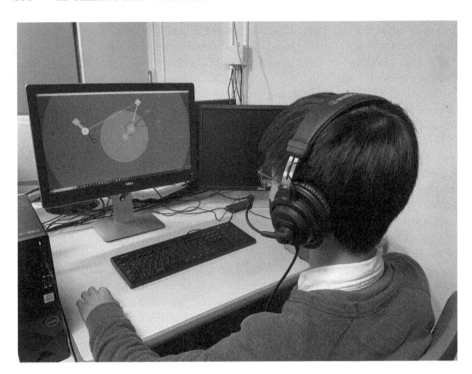

Fig. 6. Backshot for CallMap usage

and voice information between terminals (Fig. 7). Among user operations, network connection updates are processed by Photon Unity Networking2 (PUN2), and voice communications are processed by Photon Voice2 and reflected in the room on the photon cloud. Unlike the channels described below, the room here refers to the server that controls CallMap communication.

4.2 Elements

The CallMap screen is shown in Fig. 8. The CallMap screen consists of four elements: user nodes, channel nodes, participating edges, and speech ripples. All nodes can be moved via drag-and-drop, except for the user's self-user node.

User Node. In Fig. 8, the square object marked with a letter is called a user node. A user node is an abstraction of a participant (i.e., a participant node in Sect. 3). User nodes are colored with a unique color, hereafter referred to as "symbol color". When CallMap is started, the user's node is placed in the center of the screen and cannot be moved. Other users' nodes can be moved to any position by drag-and-drop.

Table 1. Development Environment

Classification	Name(Remarks)
Operating System	Windows 10
Processor	Intel Core i5 10th gen
Development Platform	Unity (ver. 2020.3.32f1)
Communication Platforms	Photon Unity Networking (for network connection) Photon Voice2 (for voice communication)

Channel Node. In Fig. 8, the numbered circular objects are called channel nodes. Channel nodes are abstractions of the dialogue field (i.e., dialogue nodes in Sect. 3). Channel nodes can be created freely by performing specific operations described below. By connecting a participating edge to an arbitrary channel node, the user can participate in the dialogue field. All channel nodes can be moved to any position by drag-and-drop. The size of a channel node increases with the number of connected edges.

Participating Edge. The line connecting the user node and the channel node in Fig. 8 is called the participating edge. A participating edge is an abstraction of the degree of participation (i.e., a status edge in Sect. 3). A user connected to any channel by a participation edge can listen to the spoken dialogue on that channel. The width of a participating edge is negatively correlated with the distance between the user node and the channel node. That is, the shorter the distance between them, the thicker the width of the corresponding participating edge.

Speech Ripple. The annular object in Fig. 8 that extends around the channel node is called the speech ripple. A speech ripple is an abstraction that represents the presence of a speaker. The speech ripple indicates that the user with that symbol color has his/her microphone turned on. The speech ripple is synchronized between all user screens. This allows all users to know in real-time on which channel each of the users is speaking.

4.3 Functions

Table 2 lists the functions of CallMap. This section describes in detail the three central functions of CallMap: participation, speech, and status adjustment.

Participation. A left double-click on a channel node that is not participating allows the user to participate in the dialogue field on the CallMap. The participating user can listen to the spoken dialogue on that channel. A symbol-colored participation edge is drawn between the user's node and the corresponding channel node (from Fig. 9a to Fig. 9b). The participating edges are synchronized with

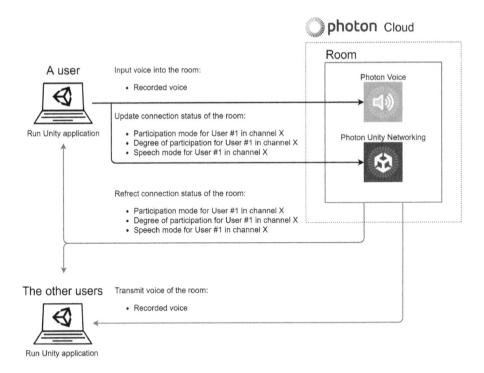

Fig. 7. Network configuration diagram

the screens of all users. This allows all users to know which channels all users are participating in. It is also possible to participate in multiple channels in parallel.

By left double-clicking on participating channel node, the user can leave the channel. In this case, the participation edge and the audio output from the channel are disconnected.

Speech. A right double-click on a participating channel node allows the user to speak on CallMap. The user in the speaking state can speak on that channel. At this time, the corresponding channel node is colored using the symbol color. Symbol-colored speech ripples are generated from the channel node (from Fig. 9b to Fig. 9c). The speech ripples are generated every three seconds while the user is speaking and spread out like rings on the water. The ripples are synchronized with the screens of all users. This allows all users to know which channels each user is speaking on. The speech state is exclusively controlled and a user cannot be a speaker on more than one channel at the same time.

A right double-click on a channel node in the speech state, i.e., a channel node colored with a symbol color, will release the speech state. In this case, the participation state is maintained while the audio input to the corresponding channel is disabled (i.e., muted).

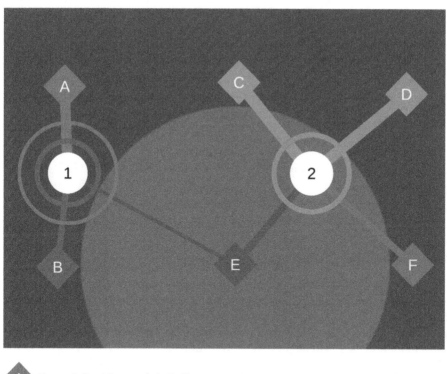

Fig. 8. CallMap screen. Figure 8 depicts the participation structure graph in Fig. 4 on CallMap.

Status Adjustment. The degree of participation can be adjusted by moving the participating channel node closer to or further away from the user node (from Fig. 9b to Fig. 9d). The distance between a channel node and the user's node is negatively and exponentially correlated with the volume output from the channel: the shorter the distance, the exponentially louder the volume of the channel. The distance between a channel node and the user's node has a negative linear correlation with the width of the participating edge: the shorter the distance, the thicker the width of the corresponding participating edge. The widths of the participating edges are synchronized with the screens of all users. This allows all users to know the degree of participation of all users in each channel.

Table 2. Functions of CallMap

Functions	Input
Create a channel node	Ctrl + N
Delete a channel node	Middle double-click on a channel node
Participate in/Leave from a channel	Left double-click on a channel node
Turn on/off the mic	Right double-click on a channel node
Status Adjustment	Move channel nodes closer/further away
Move nodes	Drag-and-drop
Zoom in/out on a viewpoint	Mouse wheel scroll
Shift of viewpoint	Arrow keys
Reset viewpoint	Space key

4.4   Abstraction of Participation Status

This section describes how the participation status is designed in CallMap. Based on the theory of the participation structure, there are five levels of participation (cf. Fig. 2). From an ethical standpoint, CallMap does not implement a mechanism that corresponds to an eavesdropper. Therefore, we consider four participant statuses, leaving out the eavesdropper.

Side-Participant and Bystanders in CallMap. A participation position in the participation structure corresponds to the participation status in CallMap. A user in the participating mode can listen to the dialogue on the channel. They can also switch to speech mode at any time. This aspect corresponds to that of a participant in the participation structure.

No mode in CallMap corresponds to the bystander mode of the participation structure; however, this is intentional. For example, based on the example given in Sect. 2.1, there is no environmental factor that distinguishes between students who are side-participants and parents who are bystanders in the classroom. The distinction between side-participants and bystanders is a distinction implicitly generated based on the members of the dialogue field and the content of the dialogue and is not an environmentally controlled concept. Therefore, CallMap does not have a factor that distinguishes between the side-participants and the bystanders.

Speaker and Addressee in CallMap. A speaker in the participation structure corresponds to the speech mode in CallMap. A user in speech mode can speak in a channel. This aspect corresponds to the speaker of the participation structure.

No mode in CallMap corresponds to the addressee of the participation structure. The reason for this is the same as the reason there is no explicit notion of address in CallMap, and will be explained in detail in the next section.

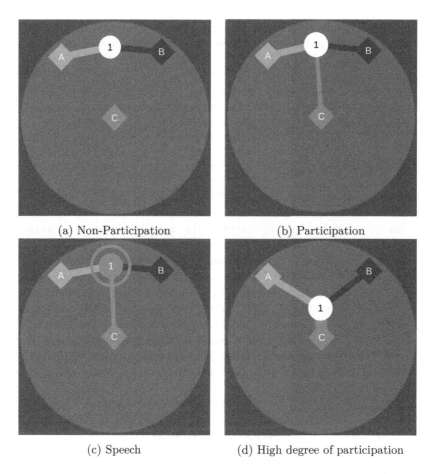

(a) Non-Participation   (b) Participation

(c) Speech   (d) High degree of participation

Fig. 9. Output screens for each function in CallMap

4.5 Abstraction of the Address

This section describes how addresses are designed in CallMap. Addressing by eye gaze or nonverbal signals in face-to-face situations is important for determining the next speaker and thus facilitating smooth dialogue. However, there are also linguistic means of address, such as invocation, context, and the use of specific vocabulary, e.g., personal pronouns and the distinction between polite and non-polite forms of speech. People already use linguistic signals in spoken dialogues via telecommunication systems, telephones, and other information media. Therefore, CallMap does not have a mechanism that corresponds to addresses. Instead, CallMap uses speech ripples as a clue to identify the addressee. As mentioned in Sect. 4.2, CallMap generates symbol-colored speech ripples for the user whose microphone is turned on. This is not synonymous with the user being the speaker. This is the same as the fact that the user with the microphone on is not always the speaker in a typical interactive situation in a current telecommunication system. In such situations, it is often the case that the user turns to the listener with the microphone still on, and then turns to the speaker as soon as another finishes speaking. This behavior of turning to the listener with the microphone still on and then immediately turning to the speaker is consistent with the behavior of the addressee in the participation structure. Therefore, it can be understood that users who are not speaking are likely to be addressees in CallMap, even though speech ripples appear.

5   Discussion

This study focused on the fact that multi-dialogue participation cannot be realized in the current telecommunication systems and aimed to provide a solution. First, this study focused on the structure of dialogues and interactions at the cognitive level and attempted to describe them symbolically. This study proposed a participation graph as a means of quantitatively describing the structure of dialogues. Second, this study focused on the interface in communication and implemented CallMap, a telecommunication system with an interface suitable for information media, based on the participation graph. CallMap abstracts and expresses the degree of participation that people express using body and eye contact in face-to-face interaction by using participating edges, speech ripples, and so on. The above approaches differ from conventional remote dialogue systems that mimic aspects of face-to-face communication and can be considered a novel aspect of this research.

The next step of this research is to conduct experiments to verify whether CallMap can realize multi-dialogue participation. If CallMap, a remote dialogue system that appropriately follows and abstracts the participation structure, can realize multi-dialogue participation, it means that people can communicate with each other through non-verbal information even in situations where they do not have physical and spatial resources such as body distance and eye-gaze. This mode of interaction is completely different from online communication using VR or the metaverse. Traditionally, spoken dialogue has been interpreted as an interaction centered on the body. However, depending on the results of this study, this research may be part of a pioneering effort to establish a new communication system that eliminates the body as well.

In Sect. 3, we developed the necessary symbols and described the participation structure in terms of the graph. It has been pointed out that there is a gap in terms of dialogue structure between face-to-face and online communication scenarios. However, the differences between the two became apparent when their structure was described graphically, as shown in Fig. 5a and 5b. Participation graphs were used to depict these differences. The graphs could be used for reference and comparison of dialogue structures in another situation. For example, if a teacher knows another teacher's dialogue structures in their classes, it may improve the quality of his/her classes. Knowing dialogue structures that produce good results in a workplace environment may contribute to improving the work environment.

Participation graphs may also be useful in the design of telecommunication systems. The fact that dialogues can be described by graphs means that it is possible to freely design the intended dialogue field by connecting and composing graphs as needed. For example, in a face-to-face situation, moving from one dialogue field to another requires moving seats or rooms. In existing telecommunication systems, it is necessary to leave the breakout room you are in and re-enter another room. In contrast, switching the dialogue field on the graph is as simple as switching the destination of the connected node. In addition, even in the case of multi-dialogue participation, a new edge needs to be created and connected to an arbitrary dialogue field. It is important to emphasize that public beliefs about voice communication are still strongly dependent on face-to-face situations, even though telecommunication systems are becoming increasingly popular. A variety of online interactions have been realized, and there has been a lot of interest in how to mimic a face-to-face situation, e.g., by setting up breakout rooms, attempting to virtualize the body using avatars, and visualizing eye contact. However, as described in Sect. 2.2, these approaches may lose the advantages unique to telecommunication and may inadvertently introduce constraints unique to face-to-face situations. Therefore, when considering minimalistic and appropriate design for online communication, the structure and logic of the spoken dialogue interaction itself should be focused on.

CallMap has specific implementation issues. When there are simultaneous utterances in multiple channel nodes, it is more complicated than in face-to-face situations to identify them simultaneously. In a face-to-face communication scenario, the physical characteristics of the environment, such as the distance between the speakers, the direction of the sound source, and the device used to produce the sound, can be used to identify the speaker and understand the content of their speech, even in situations where multiple speakers are speaking simultaneously. However, CallMap does not have real dialogue space. Therefore, it can distinguish who is speaking, while it is difficult to distinguish what each person is talking about. It is desired that this problem can be solved by a design that does not rely on imitation of face-to-face situations (e.g., using stereophonic sound). In addition, CallMap is intended to be used with a PC so that the interaction involves the heavy use of hands and fingers. In CallMap, all actions of participating, speaking, and changing the participating states are performed through cursor operations and mouse clicks. Compared to making eye contact quickly or torquing one's body naturally, these operations require more delicate manipulations. While CallMap's design takes advantage of being unique to the information media, it may place an enormous cognitive burden on the user. We believe this burden can be eliminated if eye gaze and facial orientation can be used as input methods.

6   Conclusion

This study focused on the limitations of existing telecommunication systems in online situations due to the impossibility of multi-dialogue participation. Existing systems have not been designed based on academic knowledge of human cognition, such as the participation structure. This study proposed a design guideline for realizing multi-dialogue participation in telecommunication systems based on the participation structure. First, a symbol system for describing dialogues was defined. Second, dialogues and their multi-dialogue participation states were described based on the defined symbols, and a design guideline was proposed for telecommunication systems. The design guidelines of the telecommunication system are quantitatively described by the symbols and the graphs. Third, CallMap was implemented based on the graph described. CallMap abstracted nonverbal interactions in face-to-face situations such as participation status and addresses to fit the telecommunication system and designed an interface. The participation structure graph proposed in this study is considered useful for quantitative analysis of dialogue structure in face-to-face situations and for designing a telecommunication system to realize multi-dialogue participation. CallMap, a telecommunication system based on the participation structure graph, is expected to realize online communication with multi-dialogue participation. To realize multi-dialogue participation with CallMap, designed to abstract the body and gaze, suggests that the body and gaze are not necessary for human interaction and will be a precursor to the design of next-generation communication systems with an approach different from virtual reality. Further experiments will be conducted to demonstrate the effectiveness of the design proposed in this study.

Acknowledgement. This work was supported by JSPS KAKENHI Grant Number 22H04862.

References

1. Bee, M.A., Micheyl, C.: The cocktail party problem: what is it? how can it be solved? and why should animal behaviorists study it? J. Comp. Psychol. **122**(3), 235 (2008)
2. Bregman, A.S.: Auditory Scene Analysis: The Perceptual Organization of Sound. MIT Press, Cambridge (1994)
3. Clark, A.E., Oswald, A.J.: Satisfaction and comparison income. J. Public Econ. **61**(3), 359–381 (1996)
4. Duncan, R.B.: Characteristics of organizational environments and perceived environmental uncertainty. Adm. Sci. Q. 313–327 (1972)
5. ul Fazal, M.A., Ferguson, S., Saeed, Z.: Investigating cognitive workload in concurrent speech-based information communication. Int. J. Hum.-Comput. Stud. **157**, 102728 (2022)
6. Gather. https://www.gather.town/. Accessed 26 Dec 2022
7. Goffman, E.: Embarrassment and social organization. In: Personality and Social Systems, pp. 541–548 (1963)
8. Goffman, E.: Forms of Talk. University of Pennsylvania Press, Philadelphia (1981)
9. Goodwin, C.: Conversational organization. Interaction between speakers and hearers (1981)
10. Hall, E.T., Hall, E.T.: The hidden dimension, vol. 609. Anchor (1966)

11. He, Z., Wang, K., Feng, B.Y., Du, R., Perlin, K.: Gazechat: enhancing virtual conferences with gaze-aware 3D photos. In: The 34th Annual ACM Symposium on User Interface Software and Technology (UIST), pp. 769–782. Association for Computing Machinery, Virtual Event, USA (2021)

12. Kendon, A.: Some functions of gaze-direction in social interaction. Acta Physiol. **26**, 22–63 (1967)

13. Kendon, A.: Conducting interaction: patterns of behavior in focused encounters, vol. 7. CUP Archive (1990)

14. Li, J.V., Kreminski, M., Fernandes, S.M., Osborne, A., McVeigh-Schultz, J., Isbister, K.: Conversation balance: a shared VR visualization to support turn-taking in meetings. In: CHI Conference on Human Factors in Computing Systems Extended Abstracts, pp. 1–4 (2022)

15. Microsoft teams. https://www.microsoft.com/microsoft-teams/group-chat-software. Accessed 26 Dec 2022

16. Morikawa, D., Ishii, Y., Watanabe, T.: Speech support system using a noise environment including multiple non-participants in VR space. Trans. Hum. Interface Soc. **22**(4), 403–410 (2020). (in Japanese)

17. ovice. https://ovice.in/. Accessed 26 Dec 2022

18. Sacks, H., Schegloff, E.A., Jefferson, G.: A simplest systematics for the organization of turn taking for conversation. In: Studies in the Organization of Conversational Interaction, pp. 7–55. Elsevier (1978)

19. Sato, R., et al.: Eye contactable multi-party video conferencing system. In: The 28th Annual Meeting of the Japanese Cognitive Science Society, pp. 205–212 (2011). (in Japanese)

20. Schegloff, E.A.: Body torque. Soc. Res. 535–596 (1998)

21. Takanashi, K.: Units of analysis for understanding conversational structure - participation structure. Jpn. Soc. Artif. Intell. **23**(4), 538–544 (2008). (in Japanese)

22. Yamamoto, S., Teraya, N., Nakamura, Y., Watanabe, N., Lin, Y., Takeuchi, Y.: Implement of simple multi-party video chatting system focused on direction of participants' gaze: operation and effectiveness of ptolemaeus. Technical report of IEICE. HCS **112**(176), 31–36 (2012). (in Japanese)

23. Zhu, Y., Yerkovich, B.C., Zhang, X., Park, J.I.: Realtime facial expression representation method for virtual online meetings system. In: Proceedings of the Korean Society of Broadcast Engineers Conference, pp. 212–214 (2021)

24. zoom. https://explore.zoom.us/products/meetings/. Accessed 26 Dec 2022

Interoperable Findability: Investigating an Information Ecology of Graded Feedback in Higher Education

Michael Lahey[✉] [iD]

Kennesaw State University, Kennesaw, GA 30144, USA
mlahey@kennesaw.edu

Abstract. This paper investigates a specific information ecology related to how students make sense of and organize graded feedback at a higher education institution in the United States. Based on qualitative research findings that suggest students are struggling to make sense of where and when to find information in an information ecology defined by a proliferation of tools and platforms, I argue for the importance of academic administrators and instructors dealing with the problem of interoperable findability—the ability for different software to speak to one another and make information findable across multiple channels. To do this, I first describe how the online survey and interviews were administered. Second, I explain the interoperable findability present in this information ecology. Third, I mention other findings relevant to graded feedback to get a fuller sense of this information ecology. Finally, I speculate on what this discussion of grading feedback says about how institutions and students relate through software-enabled tools and platforms.

Keywords: Findability · Information Architecture · Information Ecology · Interoperability

1 Introduction

The Covid-19 pandemic accelerated trends that impact academic structures of knowledge and communication. One such trend is how the necessity for distance learning during the pandemic increased the use of tools and platforms through which instructors and students communicate [1, 2]. The proliferation of tools and platforms is increasingly mundane, an accepted part of everyday life in higher education in the United States.

I wanted to understand if and how an increase in tools and platforms might be affecting student behavior since this increase changes the information ecologies of higher education. How are students adapting? What role do all these tools and platforms play? What changes should instructors and/or administrators make regarding how they interact with students? In the Spring of 2023, an online survey of 83 students and interviews with 18 students in a user experience (UX) design program in the United States was administered to better understand a specific information ecology through which students make sense of communications with their instructors and schools.

M. Kurosu and A. Hashizume (Eds.): HCII 2023, LNCS 14014, pp. 314–324, 2023.
https://doi.org/10.1007/978-3-031-35572-1_21

While participants spoke on a range of issues regarding how they communicate with their institution and instructors, a significant pattern arose related to graded feedback. Feedback on graded assignments is an important part of the dynamic between instructors and students in higher education [3, 4]. Effective feedback provides "the foundations for learner autonomy," helps students assess their capabilities, and potentially prepares them for post-collegiate environments in which they will apply skills learned in school [5, pg. 153].

The most consistent concern students had was struggling to keep track of feedback as tools and platforms used to deliver feedback proliferate. Where do they look for that feedback? How do they remember where it is? Will they always have access to that feedback?

In this paper, I highlight the importance of findability across increasingly complex, cross-channel academic information ecologies that often include software that is not interoperable—the ability of software to exchange information [6, 7]. I argue that, if an information ecology existing between institutions, instructors, and students does not include some form of interoperable findability, then things like graded feedback—a crucial aspect of students' academic experience—risk getting lost in the shuffle. As Peter Morville notes, information that is hard to find is information that is hardly found [8].

To make the case for how poor interoperable findability shapes student engagement with graded feedback, I first describe how the online survey and interviews were administered. Second, I focus on the theme of confusion around where to find and what to do with feedback and how information ecologies that lack interoperable findability intensify this problem. Third, I mention other findings relevant to graded feedback, including the importance of mobile platforms to students, a preference for richer forms of feedback, and how articulating in-class assignments to the job market might enhance the utilization of instructor feedback. Finally, I speculate on what this discussion of grading feedback can hint at regarding the implications for how institutions and students relate through software-enabled tools and platforms.

2 Student Access to Institutional and Classroom Information

What follows is a description of an online survey regarding student perceptions of access to institutional and classroom information and a description of follow-up interviews with a subset of students to more fully understand patterns discussed in the online survey.

2.1 Online Survey Description

During the month of January in 2023, an online survey titled "Understanding Student Access to Institution and Classroom Information in College" (IRB-FY22-199) was published that targeted UX design-related students at Kennesaw State University. 83 students completed the survey. 38 (46%) of students had more than 8 classes in the degree signifying their closeness to graduation. 40 (48%) had between 4 and 8 classes in the degree while 6 participants (6%) had fewer than 4 classes in the degree.

There was no special emphasis in the survey placed on the proliferation of tools and platforms. The survey asked opened-ended questions regarding student experiences with communication from either their academic institutions or instructors. Since the questions were posed as short answers rather than logging an answer on a scale, the answers were coded using qualitative research techniques. Codes were employed by the researcher to search for patterns amongst the participants. A code is a "researcher-generated construct that symbolizes and thus attributes interpreted meaning to each individual datum for later purposes of pattern detection, categorization, theory building, and other analytic processes" [9, pg. 4].

The goal of the survey was to understand how students make sense of communications coming from their academic institution and classrooms. From this data, I extrapolated findings regarding information architecture (how students store and access information from their teachers and/or schools), preferences (which types of communications students prefer), and speculation (what students hope could be done differently regarding the software used).

As stated above, a significant pattern seen in the online survey regarded graded feedback. Many participants made voluntary disclosures regarding the importance of graded feedback when answering questions about how they relate to communications from their instructors. To better understand student perceptions of feedback, I completed interviews with students from this study.

2.2 Interview Description

At the end of the online survey all participants were asked if they would be willing to complete an in-depth interview. 18 students were chosen to better understand patterns seen in the survey with a specific focus on graded feedback. 10 (55%) of students had more than 8 classes in the degree signifying their closeness to graduation. 7 (39%) had between 4 and 8 classes in the degree while 1 participant (6%) had fewer than 4 classes in the degree. Interviews were an hour long with a focus on better understanding of responses to the survey. As with the survey results, the interviews were coded using qualitative research techniques.

A confusion over where to find and how to store graded feedback in this information ecology is discussed in Sect. 3 and other insights from interviews regarding graded feedback is discussed in Sect. 4.

3 Interoperable Findability

It is often reported that instructors are "frustrated by a perceived lack of student engagement and responsiveness to feedback" [3, pg. 400]. While it certainly is true that students do not always engage in feedback in the ways instructors would like, can we ask questions about the information ecology itself? What if it is organized in ways that are not conducive to student engagement?

Following Bonnie Nardi and Vicki L. O'Day, I define an information ecology as a "system of people, practices, values, and technologies in a particular local environment" with a focus on how information circulates [10, pg. 49]. An ecology metaphor highlights relationships and how different elements within an ecology adapt to change over time. This approach also emphasizes the agency of different elements within an ecology to adapt to change.

This specific ecology is made up of information, instructors, students, learning platforms, third-party software tools, institutional rules, and personalized strategies for organizing information. It is experienced locally but includes information held on a range of servers far away.

Tools and platforms for communication at this specific academic institution include D2L Brightspace (D2L), an online learning platform that is used in almost all classes (there is no rule that an instructor must use it). On D2L, instructors can post a syllabus, run a discussion board, create online quizzes and tests, post content like lectures or articles to read, create a calendar, add announcements, create "intelligent agents" that automate some instructor-student communication, and incorporate a range of other "widgets" that are not well understood by students and haphazardly used by instructors. Some instructors craft their syllabi on websites outside D2L and use Dropbox, an online file hosting service, to collect assignments. There is an official school email in addition to an email embedded within D2L courses that instructors can use to communicate with students. Since the pandemic, this institution implemented a version of Zoom, a video conferencing tool, embedded inside D2L course shells but also appears to have prioritized Microsoft Teams as the preferred option for video and audio conferencing. Teams is also utilized by some instructors to organize files for their classes outside D2L as well as a messaging service for communication with students. Some instructors eschew Teams and use Discord, an online messaging application many students use outside of class for video game-related activities. Instructors sometimes create videos for students to watch outside of class on YouTube, Loom (an asynchronous video messaging service targeted at workspaces), or Kaltura Mediaspace (a video service that embeds media inside D2L course shells). Some instructors utilize digital whiteboarding tools like Miro and FigJam, although the use of these tools is most likely more germane to instructors and students in a UX design-related degree and may have limited applicability outside this degree.

The dissemination of graded feedback exists within this larger information ecology. Some of the tools and platforms above can be utilized for feedback with certain stipulations. For instance, actual grades (i.e., education records) can only be posted in spaces allowed under the Family Educational Rights and Privacy Act (FERPA) [11]. This does not preclude instructors from sending feedback through a variety of channels provided it does not include a grade. At this institution, an instructor can include the grade on D2L or the official email, which are FERPA protected.

Interviewed students reported receiving feedback on D2L embedded inside the assignment they turned in, on D2L in a field next to their grade, via official email, on Discord, on Teams, on YouTube, on Loom, on FigJam, on Miro, and written on paper. Further, students expressed frustrations regarding the different feedback practices of instructors. One student remarked that "feedback in all these different places means I might miss something." Another student said they disliked that "different teachers keep it in different places" while another said they "just don't know where to look."

The lack of clarity over where feedback may be housed is amplified by time constraints. Many students simply cannot get to feedback "right at that moment." If students are allowed to improve their grade, they look at the feedback "relatively quickly." If the feedback is future-facing, they might not look at it for quite some time. One student said they often "guess where the feedback was sent" when seeking it out later. Another student said they "go fishing" through their student email or D2L or Discord or Teams to find where the feedback is located.

This information ecology has many tools and platforms that do not speak to one another and the locus of responsibility for dealing with this ecology falls on the students and instructors. Students need to create organizational strategies to deal with the complexity of when and where to find feedback and instructors need to spend time in class better explaining and reinforcing when and where to look for communications like feedback.

In short, this information ecology lacks interoperable findability. When essential tools and platforms within a system are not interoperable, i.e., they do not share information with one another, disconnected pools of data are created. Furthermore, with no search system, there is no other way for people to find information. This creates confusion and friction for tasks that should be, in a healthy information ecology, relatively easy. In this specific information ecology, information is "inconsistent, incomplete, redundant, [and] uncoordinated" [12, pg. 7]. This is often a problematic feature of digital environments where information exists differently across "devices and situations" [7, pg. 25].

While issues with interoperable findability largely define this information ecology, what strategies do students employ to collect and organize feedback? Eight of the students interviewed "mentally noted" feedback or "filed it away in [their] brain." Yet, ten of the students found different strategies for how to organize that feedback so they could access it later. From a media studies perspective, John Collins has shown that the increased information brought on by digital technologies gave rise to management strategies at the "local" level [13, pg. 16]. Students use "practical classifying" strategies to make local sense of administrative structures [14]. In short, people find ways to deal with complex information ecologies.

In a fascinating example of how humans often use tools to their own ends [15], two students took screen captures of written feedback from fields on D2L where teachers wrote comments related to a graded assignment. This allowed these students to "unlock" feedback from D2L and place it in folders specifically organized for feedback, either on their desktop screen or within a file folder dedicated to a specific class.

Students employed a range of other strategies as well. If an instructor gave video-based feedback, and the tool allowed it, students downloaded the file and kept it with all their other feedback. Another student took feedback, whether written or video-based, and wrote "room for improvement" comments on a list stored in a personal FigJam file. Another student copied "important" feedback into a Google Document while another transcribed feedback notes in Apple Notes in a checklist format so they could check off items when they "find time." Another kept all career-related feedback in a handwritten journal while another transcribed feedback notes in Notion, a productivity and note-taking application.

These strategies are important because many students were concerned about losing access to feedback if it was posted in place for which they might lose access. These fears are not without warrant; students lose access to D2L 30 days after their final grade is posted. As one student told me, "I didn't realize that feedback [from a class] would be important until later when I started setting up my portfolio." A few students complained that videos on Teams—recorded lectures and feedback videos—have access windows that close. If a student wants to look at the video after they lose access, they must email the instructor who then needs to go into Teams and change the access window dates. Two students thoroughly collected every single asset related to class. One of these students said they did it "because all these assets on academic-run software can be cut off."

Three students talked about how they created Discord servers to house all their notes and documents regarding class. Discord allows its users to create servers (i.e., a space) dedicated to topics. On a server, users can create channels for specific topics in addition to being able to add, pin, and tag content. These three students all used Discord to their own ends as a repository to store information regarding classes. One student showed me how they set up the channels by their current classes. They would upload assignments in one channel, leave notes in another, and copy and paste feedback notes into a third channel.

All three mentioned that the powerful search function incentivized them to use Discord. One student loved that the search function can easily find information and noted that "if more teachers put their feedback there, it would be easy to find when the student needed it." Although, one student admitted that they learned to use Discord from another student, which is an interesting example of how practical classifying strategies circulate in an information ecology.

It's clear that students are finding ways to make sense of graded feedback and organize it in ways that work for them. Yet, these strategies are cognitively taxing and most likely lead to more students mentally noting feedback rather than engaging with it more deeply. This specific information ecology has organized information in seemingly slapdash ways that create constraints that discourage engagement more so than affordances that demand or encourage engagement [16]. Perhaps, with a better ecology, students who "file away feedback mentally" would be encouraged to search it out.

4 Additional Insights

In addition to a focus on better interoperable findability in this information ecology, there were other interesting patterns of thought regarding graded feedback. These patterns are helpful to note for instructors and administrators trying to make their information ecologies more usable.

4.1 Designing for Mobile Interactions

Almost all the students interviewed could be classified as "mobile first," i.e., using their mobile phone to engage with communications and content sent from instructors. Getting feedback on the phone, whether written or video-based, needs to deal with the problem of experiencing content on mobile platforms. As Peter Morville notes, "size will remain an inherent problem of mobile computing" [8, pg. 68]. Students were frustrated that Pulse, a third-party application that opens certain content from D2L on mobile phones, would cut off messages, including feedback. At that point, the student would have to move to a web browser to see more information. As one participant put it, "my computer is slower than my phone" and this has implications for what devices students will gravitate toward.

4.2 Video-Based Feedback

There is no one size fits all form of feedback that works for all students in all instances [5]. That said, many students in interviews professed a desire for video feedback. They liked that they could connect feedback comments directly to something visual. Many students complained that written feedback could be too ambiguous [17]. As one student said, "I read it and still don't know what it really means."

They also liked that that video affords them the chance to pause and rewind, something you cannot do with face-to-face feedback. It is noted that video feedback may be better for specific types of assignments, like the visual-based assignments found in UX design-related programs [18]. That said, research has shown that personalized video feedback helped students feel supported, valued, and encouraged [19, 20].

Considerable pressures exist on instructors to deliver feedback in higher education environments in the United States identified by increasingly large class sizes. As a student said in the survey, their "100 plus student" General Education classes were largely "Scantron-based" with no additional feedback. Although, Borup et al. note that text feedback can be equally as effective, video feedback has become increasingly easier for instructors and students to utilize [21].

While many students responded positively to video feedback, there were limitations. Video feedback is difficult to skim and, for students seeking to do that, video poses issues. In short, if a video is too long, they are less likely to watch it.

4.3 Connecting Feedback to the Job Market

While this paper has focused on the challenges of interoperable findability in a specific information ecology, I should note that the feedback from instructors does not always live up to the mental models students have for what good feedback should be. Many students responding to the survey and during interviews wished instructors gave "detailed feedback." One student argued that the feedback they did receive was "too nice" and did not "prepare them for the future." Other students wanted feedback that included visual components and "not just words." Research shows that "comments such as 'good', 'shows insight' or 'well referenced' do little to develop increased understanding" [3, pg. 400].

While students do seem to appreciate the "corrective function" of feedback [22], the results of this research show that feedback framed for future growth and/or the job market to be the most important to these students. One participant said that it is important they "perceive it to be helpful for the [job] market." Others echoed this sentiment when suggesting feedback was most important if it was on a project that might go in their portfolio. One student summed it up by saying, "prepare me for my future, prepare me for a job."

5 Conclusion

This paper, using feedback from students, shows how the proliferation of tools and platforms has created interoperable findability problems for a specific information ecology. The qualitative research carried out here can only speak to this specific instance and these specific students and, thus, more research would need to be done to understand how information ecologies differ across public and private institutions (both large and small) and across different boundaries (i.e., states, regions, countries). Even so, there can still be some tentative conclusions drawn from this research on what we might do to make graded feedback better for students.

First, from an administrative perspective, more work needs to be put into architecting total experiences that considers the wide range of tools and platforms used in the classroom for graded feedback. A systems approach to this ecology imagines where siloed data might exist and how to deal with the complexity of multi-channel environments [7, pg. 27]. Additionally, this approach acknowledges the need for a better understanding of real student and instructor behavior and how that shapes the design possibilities. Doing more usability testing and broad user research with both instructors and students when deciding what tools or platforms administrators are going to allow within an information ecology would be a good start [23].

One thing to consider is the role application programming interfaces (API) might place in creating a more interoperable ecology. APIs allow communication between different, defined data sets with the proper access key. This has created an environment where one entity, like Google, can share some its data, like their Google Maps, with other platforms. Perhaps APIs could be used to create an experience for students that minimizes the need to hunt and peck for feedback when they are ready to address it. This could be some type of software that acts as a checklist or notification board that tells students when information is available and where to link to it.

Another way this could be addressed is through the overlay of a robust, cross-channel search system that students could use to effectively find relevant information across a range of software that have contracts with an academic institution. This would be particularly helpful to current students, as "Gen Z" students are far more likely to preemptively use the search functionality on their computers to find files [24].

Search systems have historically been an important part of information architecture, with increased emphasis as information architecture became more pervasive in our everyday lives as it moved "beyond the confines of the Web" [25, pg. 42]. There needs to be an information architecture that makes sense of all this complexity. In this specific information ecology, students are consuming and producing information across multiple contexts and through multiple devices, tools, and platforms. As Jon Fisher et al. say, a successful cross-channel experience can be judged by how it creates "an architecture of meaning or understanding within the minds of its users, irrespective of which channel they engage with" [26, pg. 6].

Designing information architecture for an ecology full of tools and platforms that might include better interoperability and has cross-channel searching is a daunting task. As noted above, many academic ecologies have a diverse third-party software mix. The rate at which some institutions cycle through software might create challenges for even the best IT departments at academic institutions. Furthermore, the Edtech market seems to focus more on cost-efficiency as a driver of innovation than teaching or learning [27]. This means that a lot of that software does not afford the opportunity to easily connect with other software. Finally, many private companies treat data as proprietary, which makes the likelihood of data pools that do not communicate higher.

If nothing can meaningfully be changed on an administrative level, instructors need to imagine what interventions they can make. First, instructors need to take pains to explain to students what to do with feedback, and esp. First year students [3, pg. 401]. This includes carving out time in their syllabus schedules to explain the information architecture of that class clearly.

This means setting aside more time than the first session of the class to fully explain procedures. While it is good to go over the syllabus and classroom expectations, a healthy amount of time should be focused on the information architecture of that class, including which tools and platforms will be used. Since it is highly unlikely that all students are very familiar with all these tools, instructors need to carve out time to teach students best practices with these tools and platforms. This may be seen as "off topic" relative to the content in the classroom, but it is important for the health of that classroom ecology.

Since most feedback on meaningful assignments is not delivered near the start of a term, instructors need to remind students of the information architecture of the class. As one student told me, "I kind of just forget about where everything is [located]." This includes what to do with feedback now (i.e., can it be implemented now for a revised grade?) and later (i.e., how might students address feedback after the class is over?).

A more effective information architecture strategy might also include prioritizing messaging apps over the use of email. Students showed a considerable preference for messaging apps because it allowed them to message instructors quickly and in a way that was more comfortable to students. These apps allow instructors to send more updates and reminders to places students are more likely to check, an important aspect to note in a complex information ecology. These updates and reminders allow instructors to steer students back to best practices in that classroom.

Finally, what does this discussion of an information ecology of graded feedback teach us about designing better interactions and future experiences in the educational realm? It shouldn't be shocking that student issues regarding graded feedback mirror their larger confusion with keeping track of information coming from their schools and/or instructors. Higher education institutions are trying, in their own ways, to keep pace with the complexity of digital information environments to create meaningful connections with students. Yet, as evidenced by the results of the online survey and interviews, much of the information coming from institutions and classrooms is easily lost. One piece of software may not interact with another piece of software, creating easily siloed information. Some instructors use unique software in their classes that students never experience in other classes. A lot of Edtech software is modular and can be set up however the instructor chooses. This creates potential confusion, as one student said, "I cannot find the announcements in this class." While confused, students do have their own idiosyncratic organizational strategies to "make do" with these cognitively overwhelming academic information ecologies. By focusing efforts to reduce interoperability and make information more easily findable across a range of channels, administrators and instructors can create better experiences for students. Yet, if we keep rapidly adding and/or cycling through software—with each new software adding new interaction patterns—then this problem will remain. Interactions will still be caught up in ecologies of information that shape their possibilities.

References

1. Turnbull, D., Chugh, R., Luck, J.: Transitioning to e-learning during the COVID-19 pandemic: how have higher education institutions responded to the challenge? Educ. Inf. Technol. **26**(5), 6401–6419 (2021). https://doi.org/10.1007/s10639-021-10633-w
2. Pokrhel, S., Chhetri, R.: A literature review on impact of COVID-19 pandemic on teaching and learning. High. Educ. Future **8**(1), 133–141 (2021)
3. West, J., Turner, W.: Enhancing the assessment experience: improving student perceptions, engagement and understanding using online video feedback. Innov. Educ. Teach. Int. **53**(4), 400–410 (2016)
4. Yang, M., Carless, D.: The feedback triangle and the enhancement of dialogic feedback processes. Teach. High. Educ. **18**, 285–297 (2013)
5. McCarthy, J.: Evaluating written, audio and video feedback in higher education summative assessment tasks. Issues Educ. Res. **25**(2), 153–169 (2015)
6. Resmini, A., Rosati, L.: Pervasive Information Architecture: Designing Cross-Channel User Experiences. Morgan Kaufmann Publishers, Burlington (2011)
7. Haverty, M.: An ecological framework for information architecture. J. Inf. Architect. **6**(2), 25–46 (2021)
8. Morville, P.: Ambient Findability. O'Reilly Press, Sebastopol (2005)
9. Saldaña, J.: The Coding Manual for Qualitative Researchers, 2nd edn. Sage Publications, London (2013)
10. Nardi, B., O'Day, V.L.: Information Ecologies. MIT Press, Cambridge (1999)
11. Family Educational Rights and Privacy Act (FERPA), U.S. Department of Education Website, https://www2.ed.gov/policy/gen/guid/fpco/ferpa/index.html. last accessed 2023/01/28
12. Martin, A., Dmitriev, D., Akeroyd, J.: A resurgence of interest in information architecture. Int. J. Inf. Manage. **30**(1), 6–12 (2010)
13. Collins, J.: Architectures of Excess: Cultural Life in the Information Age. Routledge, New York (1995)
14. Bowker, G.C., Star, S.L.: Sorting Things Out: Classification and Its Consequences. MIT Press, Cambridge (2000)
15. Akrich, M.: The description of technical objects. In: Bijker, W., Law, J. (eds.) Shaping Technology/Building Society. MIT Press, Cambridge (1994)
16. Davis, J.L.: How Artifacts Afford: The Power and Politics of Everyday Things. MIT Press, Cambridge (2020)
17. Ryan, T., Phillips, M., Henderson, M.: Written feedback doesn't make sense': enhancing assessment feedback using technologies. In: AARE Conference 2016 (2016)
18. Lowenthal, P.R.: Video feedback: is it worth the effort? A response to Borup et al. Educational Tech. Research Dev. **69**(1), 127–131 (2021). https://doi.org/10.1007/s11423-020-09872-4
19. Ryan, T.: Designing video feedback to support the socioemotional aspects of online learning. Education Tech. Research Dev. **69**(1), 137–140 (2021). https://doi.org/10.1007/s11423-020-09918-7
20. Henderson, M., Phillips, M.: Video-based feedback on student assessment: scarily personal. Australas. J. Educ. Technol. **31**(1), 51–66 (2015)
21. Borup, J., West, R.E., Thomas, R.: The impact of text versus video communication on instructor feedback in blended courses. Education Tech. Research Dev. **63**(2), 161–184 (2015). https://doi.org/10.1007/s11423-015-9367-8

22. Mahoney, P., Macfarlane, S., Ajjawi, R.: A qualitative synthesis of video feedback in higher education. Teach. High. Educ. **24**(2), 157–179 (2019)
23. Shell, A., Tare, M., Blemahdoo, E.: Incorporating research and educator voice in edtech design. In: Gresalfi, M., Horn, I.S. (eds.) The Interdisciplinarity of the Learning Sciences, 14th International Conference of the Learning Sciences (ICLS) 2020, vol. 3, pp. 1573–1576 (2020)
24. May, E.: Gen Z doesn't understand file structures (Ep. 415). Stack Overflow blog, https://stackoverflow.blog/2022/02/15/gen-z-doesnt-understand-file-structures-ep-415. last accessed 2023/01/24
25. Resmini, A., Rosati, L.: A brief history of information architecture. J. Inf. Architect. **3**(2), 33–46 (2011)
26. Fisher, J., Norris, S., Buie, E.: Sense-making in cross-channel design. J. Inf. Architect. **4**(2), 5–30 (2012)
27. Mintz, S.: Why Most Ed Tech fails. Inside Higher Education website, https://www.insidehighered.com/blogs/higher-ed-gamma/why-most-ed-tech-fails. last accessed 2023/01/7

Proposal of Seoul's UAM Routes and Vertiports with Spatial Data Analysis

Juho Lee[1] , Donghyun Yoon[2] , Jinyong Lee[3] , and Jahwan Koo[2(✉)]

[1] Graduate School of Computer and Information Technology, Korea University, 145 Anam-ro, Seongbuk-gu, Seoul, Republic of Korea
wngh577@korea.ac.kr
[2] Graduate School of Information and Communications, Sungkyunkwan University, 25-2 Sungkyunkwan-ro, Jongno-gu, Seoul, Republic of Korea
jhkoo@skku.edu
[3] Pilot Training Group, Republic of Korea Airforce Academy, 635 Danjae-ro, Sangdang-gu, Cheongju, Republic of Korea

Abstract. Since UAM is a new mobility that does not exist before, all domains such as operating concept, demand, and safety are uncertain, and this uncertainty can reduce the acceptance of all related parties to the UAM industry. Therefore, for stable commercialization of UAM, it is necessary to consider all possible situations and remove uncertainties by analyzing them from various perspectives. Especially, it is necessary to 'reassure' people by presenting an objective basis for the utility and safety of the UAM industry through data-based analysis. At that point, UAM route and vertiport location are key elements to verify their utility and safety.

Thus, we presented a spatial data analysis methodology through the Grid-based analysis method for UAM route design and Vertiport location selection and proposed practical and immediate UAM route and Vertiport location using spatial data in Seoul. In this process, comprehensive and reliable research results were derived by reflecting various factors such as the aviation operation aspect of the existing air traffic system, properties of UAM, urban transport demand aspect and topographical properties from the perspective of aviation experts.

Keywords: UAM · Flight route · Vertiport · Spatial Data · QGIS · Seoul

1 Introduction

Urban Air Mobility (UAM), a new concept that can quickly move places in the city, has been rapidly realized by more than 200 companies around the world with the goal of commercial operations before 2030 due to technological advances in materials, battery, software, telecommunication, and Carbon-neutral policies of each country. In particular, the development of electric Vertical Take-Off and Landing (eVTOL) aircraft technology has the advantages of low noise, vertical takeoff and landing, and rapid movement, it is emerging as a new means of transportation that can compensate for the limitations of crowded public transportation. In addition, the concept of Regional Air Mobility (RAM) for wide-area movement of short-range cities is also emerging.

© The Author(s), under exclusive license to Springer Nature Switzerland AG 2023
M. Kurosu and A. Hashizume (Eds.): HCII 2023, LNCS 14014, pp. 325–340, 2023.
https://doi.org/10.1007/978-3-031-35572-1_22

According to the Korea UAM (K-UAM) roadmap, the manned aircraft is initially operated, but in the final stage, it aims to operate unmanned. According to the roadmap above, to grow the UAM industry and form popularity step by step, it is necessary to design a safe UAM route in the city and locations of the UAM vertiport for takeoff, landing, and maintenance. In particular, in order to lower the public's uneasy perception of UAM stability, UAM routes and UAM vertiport will have to be determined through aeronautical and geographical aspects. Also, for the continuous business of the UAM operation company, it is necessary to grasp whether urban planning is reflected, population liquidity, and payment ability in terms of economy in advance. Based on this, it is important to set the optimal UAM route and vertiport.

Therefore, this study aims to derive UAM route setting and location selection for UAM vertiports, which are essential elements for UAM commercialization, through QGIS based on spatial data and be used for future UAM network construction.

2 Related Work

2.1 UAM

There are various definitions of UAM for each institution and industry. In this study, we intend to use representative definitions officially announced by state institutions.

The Ministry of Land, Infrastructure and Transport (Government) of Korea defined UAM (Urban Air Mobility) as a new air transport system operated in connection with other means of transportation for passengers or cargo using eco-friendly electric power vertical takeoff and landing (eVTOL) that can be used in the city center [1].

The Federal Aviation Administration FAA [2] defined UAM as follows. "UAM is a subset of the Advanced Air Mobility (AAM), a National Aeronautics and Space Administration (NASA), FAA, and industry initiative to develop an air transportation system that moves people and cargo between local, regional, intraregional, and urban places previously not served or underserved by aviation using revolutionary new aircraft."

2.2 UAM Route Design

Most of the studies presented standards for the route of operation and the location of vertiport based on Con-Ops (Concept of Operation) published by state institution. For example, the Ministry of Land, Infrastructure and Transport (Government) of Korea published operational concept book to build the UAM ecosystem. Also, in the United States and Europe, there is Con-Ops published mainly by the Federal Aviation Administration, NASA [3], and EASA [4]. These studies suggested ways to minimize the impact on the existing air traffic system and utilize the existing helicopter infrastructure [1]. And based on the essential items of the UAM operating system, study presented operating routes in terms of airspace, control, air traffic, and environmental factors [1]. But the existing studies of UAM routes presented limitations in part.

First, the routes proposed by the Ministry of Land, Infrastructure and Transport (Government) of Korea connected departure and arrival points straightly and simply [2]. These routes were insufficient such as altitude and direction for the operation of UAM, which operates in performance-based navigation (maintaining altitude and direction through self-navigation performance).

Second, the UAM route presented in [6] was designed to consider abnormal operating scenarios, but also presented insufficient components such as specific design standards and reasonable data to cope with abnormal scenarios.

Finally, the route designed based on the helicopter VFR route in the Seoul metropolitan area, focusing on the fact that UAM will utilize the existing helicopter infrastructure, was designed without considering the characteristics of UAM operating with different flight rules from helicopters [6].

2.3 UAM Vertiport Location Analysis

In the previous studies on Vertiport location, a model was built by aspect of personal ownership type, MaaS(Mobility as a Services) type, demand response [7]. Also, a model for the costs required for location selection was built [8]. And the importance of the factors needed for location selection was calculated through a survey by experts. [9]. In addition, clustering analysis of locations was conducted based on commuting demand through the K-means algorithm [10] and a study was conducted to comprehensively analyze location, route, and travel time based on population density, commuting statistics, and eVTOL type specifications [11].

Our study referred to various methods of these studies and established our own standards for selecting vertiport locations. In addition, spatial data which is not considered in previous studies were added and visualized to evaluate the safety and efficiency of the location.

3   Method

To select the UAM routes and vertiports, it is necessary to select locations that meet various criteria based on the spatial data. Setting up a Vertiport location by simply connecting the departure point and arrival point [1, 6] or considering only the decision-making or real estate location of government/business policymakers suggested [8] may be groundless and threaten stability of UAM flights or failed to create initial demand that can lead risk that the industry may not be activated.

So, we developed a methodology for creating a spatial location map by five procedures and selected the most valid areas as route and vertiport locations according to the spatial location map created. The five procedures are as follows.

1. Setting criteria for selecting UAM route based on current policy.
2. Setting criteria for selecting UAM vertiport in aspects of geography, economics, and aeronautics
3. Collecting spatial data that meets the set criteria into Positive factor and Negative factor.
4. Expressing the collected data on a 100 M grid using geographic information SW (QGIS).
5. Scoring each data in layer of grid and making final layer of grid by summing layers.
6. Creating and visualizing a spatial location map with the sum of the layers.

3.1 Setting Criteria for Selecting UAM Route Based on Current Policy

We checked the results of UAM operation policy studies in the United States (FAA) [3], Europe (EASA) [5], and Korea (Ministry of Land) [1] to establish the criteria for setting the UAM route and selected four criteria for setting the route. The criteria are as follows.

7. The UAM route should minimize the impact on existing air mobility. According to the report, the UAM requires vertical separation to minimize the impact from the existing air mobility, but horizontal separation is also required to prevent the existing air mobility from being paralyzed due to violations of take-off and landing sections and no-fly zones at airports [1].
8. The UAM shares the helicopter's route. It was noted that UAM is similar to the current characteristics of helicopters, and the official and customary routes frequently used by helicopters were investigated and related data were collected, reflecting the policy that future helicopters would share their routes [3, 4].
9. The UAM route criterion is that an immediate response should be possible in the event of an abnormal situation. Since an UAM is a mobility operated in a three-dimensional space, unlike a car operated in a two-dimensional space, it is restricted from stopping and responding to the situation in an emergency. Therefore, the UAM route should be designed to respond immediately to possible emergency situations such as aircraft defects, occurring emergency patient, holding, and off course.
10. It must be designed in compliance with UAM's own flight rules called Managed Flight Rules (MFR). Currently, aircraft fly using two flight rules, Visual Flight Rules (VFR) and Instrument Flight Rules (IFR), each defining control and operational responsibilities. In a VFR environment, the pilot takes full responsibility for the visual flight, and in an IFR environment, the controller is given operational responsibility, and the pilot is subject to the control of the controller. However, Airbus Corp. Proposed a new flight rule called Managed Flight Rules (MFR). MFR is a flight rule operated through the control of a traffic management service that manages a large numbers of flight traffic based on two-way data communication, flying along a route connected to a certain corridor or waypoint [13]. Because the two existing flight rules (VFR, IFR) are limited only when pilots are on board and controlled, it is difficult to apply to the operation of low-altitude aircraft that implement autonomous flight technology [13].

3.2 Setting Criteria for Selecting UAM Vertiport in Aspects of Geography, Economics, and Aeronautics

UAM vertiport is a terminal actually used by users, their departure and arrival. Therefore, in order to select a vertiport location, it is necessary to consider it in various aspects such as transportation, economics, and urban design as well as aviation engineering and aeronautics for UAM. However, since our study presents a methodology, we selected three criteria for economic, geographical, and aeronautics by referring existing studies.

First, for stable operation and business feasibility when commercializing UAM, vertiport must be established in an area that can generate sufficient profits and generate stable demand. Economic criterion has been established for this, and detailed standards are as follows.

1. If the number of UAMs used per month is 50 times, the affordability per household is upper 20% or more based on a daily fee of 40,000 won [14].
2. The moving population is over 25,444, which means median number of people who moves in administrative districts to another districts in Seoul.
3. The daily estimated traffic volume is over 4,800 vehicles, which means median number of vehicles in administrative districts in Seoul.

The second is geographical criterion from a transportation and urban design approach, the location of the transportation terminal must satisfy accessibility and convenience. Considering the connection with the currently operating transportation system, the distance from the area where initial demanders are concentrated is important. In addition, topographical stability must be secured in geographical standards. There should be no obstacles that violate flight safety, such as high mountains or buildings, and there should be fewer risk factors such as birds and should be a geographically stable location. Detailed criterions are as follows.

1. Within 300 m of existing transportation systems such as subways and buses.
2. Within 500 m with 1000 major companies.
3. Geographically unusable areas are excluded due to the establishment of restricted altitude and green areas.
4. Under 500 m or less above sea level.
5. Under 20 species of bird species.

Finally, the previously established criteria of the UAM route must be considered to minimize the impact of the existing air mobility, consider suitability in terms of air operations, and be an accessible area for the UAM. Therefore, we applied all criteria of UAM route for selecting UAM vertiport location due to meet aeronautics aspect.

3.3 Collecting Spatial Data and Scoring Each Data

We collected the spatial data that meets each of the established criteria as shown in Tables 1 and 2. The list of data that meets each criterion and score were selected through Focus Group Interview (FGI) methods to participate experts.

A focus group is, according to Lederman (see Thomas et al. 1995), 'a technique involving the use of in-depth group interviews in which participants are selected because they are a purposive, although not necessarily representative, sampling of a specific population, this group being 'focused' on a given topic' [15]. The selection of participants in this group is important for FGI. Therefore, this method mainly selects experts on topics and interviews them in depth. Since this method is conducted through social interaction and coordination of opinions among participants, deeper and more meaningful data can be collected than the one-to-one interviews method of collecting individual thoughts. On the other hand, in FGI, selecting participant is one of the most important factors. If it is wrong, the wrong opinion may be selected as the right opinion, and there is a possibility that an opinion that is completely different from the direction of the study may be selected as the final opinion. In addition, the role of the interviewer is important

Table 1. Data List for Creating Route Spatial Location Map

Category	Data	Score
Criterion 1	Flight forbidden area	−200
	Aircraft flight route	−100
	Airport	−10
Criterion 2	River	+100
	Road	+100
	Helicopter VFR flight route	+100
Criterion 3	Heliport	+50
	Highway rest area	+30
	Interchange	+30
	Highway Sleeping area	+20
	Hospital	+20
Criterion 4	Buildings	−2 (per building)
	Mountains	−50
	Waypoints	+100

Table 2. Data List for Creating Vertiport Location Map

Category	Data	Score
Criterion 1	Estimate Traffic	Y/N
	Population	Y/N
	Income per house	Y/N
	House account	Y/N
Criterion 2	Subway	Y/N
	Bus	Y/N
	DEM	Y/N
	Birds	Y/N
	Land Usage	Y/N
	Company location data	Y/N
Criterion 3	[Table 1]	

because it is necessary to put the opinions of all participants together by mediating so that the opinions of one participant are not emphasized or alienated during the interaction process.

Fig. 1. Interview for processing FGI

We proceeded FGI to select a list of data for UAM route and vertiport and score the weights of each data (Fig. 1). A total of 14 aviation experts, fighter pilots, helicopter pilots, mechanics, and controllers working in the Air Force, were participated to specify a list of data for the selection of UAM routes and Vertiports. For example, data such as flight forbidden Area, Aircraft flight route, and airport location of existing air traffic were selected to satisfy < criterion 1 > that interference with the existing air traffic system should be minimized. After that, FGI participants scored the selected data of each Criterion with weight. In this process, scoring was conducted by dividing the route spatial location map and the Vertiport spatial location map because the scoring system applied to each map was different.

Each data composed the route spatial location map were relative attributes. Therefore, we score weight of each data and aggregate each data layer and used a method of selecting regions that are relatively likely to be selected as routes compared to other regions according to the distribution of the data. In detail, the list of data was divided into positive data and negative data, and the score was defined through FGI according to the importance of each data on UAM route selection. For example, in < Criterion 1 > of the Flight route Spatial Location Map, UAM aircraft should never enter a flight forbidden area, so the flight forbidden area score was given −200 points, making it impossible to offset with any score (Most data scores were scored between −100 and +100) and in < Criterion 2 >, roads and rivers area score was given +70 points due to sharing with helicopter's route.

On the other hands, each data composed the vertiport spatial location map were absolute attributes. For example, if the traffic and population number are not met in the economic standard < Criterion 1 >, it cannot be selected as a Vertiport location. And the connection with other public transportation in the geographical standard < Criterion 2 > is an absolute criterion to be satisfied by the government policy of establishing a UAM Vertiport. Therefore, the score for the vertiport spatial location map was defined as Pass or Fail rather than numerically assigned, and if all the conditions are satisfied, it marked positive on the map.

Most of the collected data were public data provided by the Seoul Metropolitan Government and the Ministry of Land, Infrastructure and Transport of Korea with CSV or SHP file format [16–18]. The data with CSV format consisted of the location and details of the components, and the data with SHP format contained information on the spatial shape as well as the location and details of each component. Public data is one of the public services made by government to use research and application development for free.

3.4   Creating Map with Each Standard

Table 3. Method of Making Grid by Data Type

Spatial Relationship	Geometry Type of Statistical Data		
	Point	Line	Polygon
Contain	•		
Count			
	Counts = 4	Counts = 2	Counts = 2

To create a special location map, all the selected scored data was visualized on the map. In this process, it was necessary to quantitatively synthesize and compare various data. However, data may have various depending on the institution, purpose, character, and the regional scope of data were different. For example, highway data is in the form of a line, and buildings are in the form of polygon. In addition, Heliport locations are provided with data based on coordinates, but the number of people is provided by administrative district. Therefore, a pre-processing process is needed to facilitate data aggregation and comparison.

We used the Grid based analysis method [19] for Spatial Data. The Grid based analysis method reflects pre-processed data on the grid to determine which grid's cells contain data or to compare cells including data with each other. The Grid based analysis method allows data to be visualized on the map in the same format regardless of the collection unit (administrative movement, coordinate), and data type (point, line, and poly-gon), and has the advantage of objectively understanding statistical information.

At this time, there were two main ways to reflect data in the cell: contain and count. As expressed in Table 3, the container determined whether the cell contains data. The formats of the data were meaningless and reflected the score if some or all of the data overlaps with the cell. On the other hand, count is a procedure for checking the number of data contained on the cell. For example, if there are two road data on the cell, and Cell is a method of reflecting the score '2'.

In our study, the entire map of Seoul was divided into 100 M × 100 M grid for the generation of a special location map through the grid-based analysis method. At this time, the reason for setting grid in units of 100 M was the most conservative criterion (0.1 NM) among the Final Approach GPS TSE (0.1 to 0.3 NM) in RNPAR, which is currently considered the most utilizable of UAM's navigation procedures. In other words, 0.1 NM, the lowest value of the GPS system tolerance when approaching, was applied to land in the RNPAR method. Through this, it may be assumed that the UAM aircraft applying RNPAR is regarded as the same position in any region in the cell of gird.

After that, the grid in the form of a Rectangle generated in Seoul was set to default grid map (G_n).

$$
G_n = \begin{bmatrix} C_{0,0} & C_{0,1} & \cdots & C_{0,j} \\ C_{1,0} & C_{1,1} & \cdots & C_{1,j} \\ \vdots & \vdots & \ddots & \vdots \\ C_{i,0} & C_{i,1} & \cdots & C_{i,j} \end{bmatrix}
$$

If data ($d_{i,j}$) in Data Layer (L_n) was not zero and overlapped with the grid cell ($C_{i,j}$), data ($d_{i,j}$) is added to the corresponding cell ($C_{i,j}$).

$$
L_n = \begin{bmatrix} d_{0,0} & d_{0,1} & \cdots & d_{0,j} \\ d_{1,0} & d_{1,1} & \cdots & d_{1,j} \\ \vdots & \vdots & \ddots & \vdots \\ d_{i,0} & d_{i,1} & \cdots & d_{i,j} \end{bmatrix} \text{where } d_{i,j} = 0 \, or \, data \, score
$$

$$
\text{If } d_{i,j}! = 0 \tag{1}
$$

$$
\text{Then } C_{i,j} = d_{i,j} + C_{i,j} \tag{2}
$$

By repeating this method, we created each Grid map (G_n) for all Data Layer and added all Grid map (G_n) to create a final Spatial location Map (G_T).

$$
G_T = \sum_{i=i}^{n} G_i
$$

The entire process of dividing the Seoul city map into grid in the form of a rectangle, reflecting data, and generating a special location map used QGIS [20] S/W. QGIS is a GIS application based on Free and Open-Source Software (FOSS) that provides the ability to visualize, manage, edit, analyze data, and implement it on a map [20]. Also, it is highly compatible with Python, so it is easy to link data analysis with AI programming.

4 Proposal of Seoul's UAM Route and Vertiport

4.1 UAM Route Spatial Location Map

Figure 2 shows the data visualization for the creation of the UAM route spatial location map. As shown in the first figure in Fig. 2, 100 M grid was drawn on the map of Seoul, and data selected through FGI was visualized to create a Data Layer (L_n). After that, a Grid map (G_n) for each data layer was generated according to the above formula, and the final UAM route spatial location map (G_T) generated as shown in the last figure of Fig. 2.

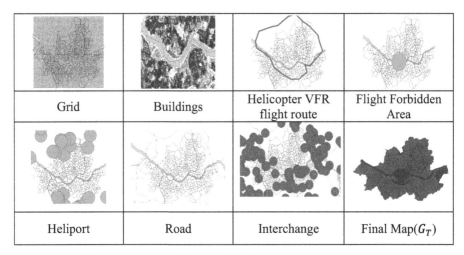

Grid	Buildings	Helicopter VFR flight route	Flight Forbidden Area
Heliport	Road	Interchange	Final Map(G_T)

Fig. 2. Procedure of Creating UAM Route Spatial Location Map

Table 4. Score categorization & Visualization

Score Range	Grid Color	Fly Zone
X<-100		X
-100$\leq$ X $\leq$1		X
1$\leq$ X $\leq$100		O
100$\leq$ X		O

In the generated UAM route spatial location map, the score for each grid is the sum of the scores of each Data Layer. Among them, a grid with a score of 1 or more is an area where flight is possible, and a grid with a score of 1 or less is an area where flight is impossible. We visualized the grid of fly zone as blue and the impossible grid as red for more appropriate analysis and perfect map generation (Table 4). The fly zones from Map were mainly centered on the Han River, roads, and rivers, and some areas outside of Seoul. Meanwhile, major downtown areas, including the presidential office, were expressed in red, indicating that flying is impossible. Therefore, to operate UAM inside Seoul, road and river-oriented routes must be established.

In addition, in terms of aviation operations, Vertiport must be built in an area where UAM can fly, so when selecting Vertiport, it must also be selected in a blue area where flight is possible by considering the map. This is why the UAM route spatial location map was set to < Criterion 3 > for creating a Vertiport spatial location map.

To design a detailed route thereafter, the most suitable route among the fly zone should be selected by considering Vertiport, Waypoint, emergency landing, etc. Among the lines connecting the Vertiport of the origin and destination with a fly zone grid, the line containing Waypoint may be selected as route. At this time, the following criteria were applied to the topography or structure being used as a waypoint can be easily seen from the sky, such as high mountains and buildings.

6. If the scale is more than 100% larger than the surrounding structures and geographical features.
7. If the color contrast ratio is 50% or more with the surrounding structure.
8. Terrain features above a certain height (with two-way communication) that can be easily used for performance-based navigation.

4.2 Vertiport Spatial Location Map

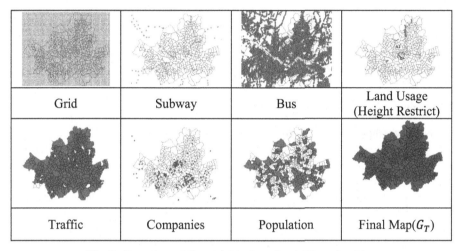

Grid	Subway	Bus	Land Usage (Height Restrict)
Traffic	Companies	Population	Final Map(G_T)

Fig. 3. Procedure of Creating Vertiport Spatial Location Map

Figure 3 shows the data visualization for generating the Vertiport spatial location map. As shown in the first figure in Fig. 3, 100 M grid was drawn on the map of Seoul, and data selected through FGI was visualized to create a data layer (L_n). After that, a grid map (G_n) for each data layer was generated according to the above formula, and the final Vertiport partial location map (G_T) was generated as shown in the last figure of Fig. 3.

Table 5. Score categorization & Visualization

Score Range	Grid Color	Vertiport Availability
$X<1$		X
$1 \leqq X$		O

The score by grid is the sum of the scores of each Data Layer. Among them, a grid with a score of 1 or more is an area where Vertiport can be constructed, and a grid with a score of 1 or less is an area where Vertiport cannot be constructed. We visualized the vertiport construction-capable grid in blue and the impossible grid in red for more appropriate analysis and perfect map generation (Table 5). The areas where vertiport can be constructed were mainly Gangnam-gu, Songpa-gu, Guro-gu, and Jung-gu. The characteristics of these areas were mainly business areas, areas with large population or traffic, or areas with high income levels. This was same with the prediction [5] that UAM demand will initially be centered on entrepreneurs or people with high income levels. The initial consumer of UAM is expected to be rich people who want a private trip, or people who want to save time while paying high fees (e.g., C.E.O). The fact that the local characteristics of vertiport candidates produced by our study were same with the predictions in [5] also proved that the list of data selected to generate the map is appropriate.

The vertiport spatial location map, which was established through the study, considered not only the demand aspect but also the aviation operation aspect through the UAM route spatial location map. As a result, it suggested that vertiport should be built in an area where it is possible to take off and land.

4.3   Proposal UAM Route and Vertiport Location

To check whether the methodology suggested so far works normally, we would like to suggest a Vertiport candidate site in Seoul and a route connecting Vertiport through the generated spatial location map. We arbitrarily selected candidate sites that can be built Vertiport according to various criteria, verify the validity of our suggested Vertiport location selection methodology for those sites, and propose a route between valid candidates. For example, the second stage of the K-UAM Grand Challenge [23] promoted by the Ministry of Land, Infrastructure and Transport (Government) of Korea is planning to commercialize the Gimpo-Jamsil section, to explore appropriate Vertiport locations in Gimpo and Jamsil and design[1] routes between them.

At this time, the appropriate Vertiport location suggested in our study was able to take future policy research and commercialization by presenting accurate locations and coordinates considering surrounding topography and obstacles, unlike the previous study proposed by location.

Creating Candidates of Vertiport Location. Vertiport candidates were selected in two ways. First, in accordance with the Seoul Metropolitan Government's policy of constructing Vertiport at a regional base transfer center [21, 22], 19 areas of the regional base transfer centers were selected as the first green point in (Fig. 4).

According to [21], the Seoul Metropolitan Government plans to build a UAM Vertiport at its regional transfer center to provide various urban complex functions such as public services, logistics, business, and commerce. So, we included a transit center as a candidate to verify the validity of Vertiport locations based on these plans.

Second, pilots (especially helicopter pilots) and controllers were asked to select an area in Seoul that has easy access to roads or rivers and can enter the air without obstacles

---

[1] Currently, Vertiport of the second stage of the K-UAM Grand Challenge was decided as Gimpo Airport and Jamsil Station [23] as a policy. As a result, we excluded those sites from the Vertiport candidate site of this study.

Fig. 4. Candidates of Vertiport

during takeoff and landing through FGI. As a result, 25 areas were selected as shown in the second picture (Fig. 4). These were candidate sites that considers where UAM operation is possible in terms of air operation rather than customer demand.

Selecting Candidates of Vertiport Location. 41 candidate sites selected in two ways were created on the Vertiport Special location map as shown in the first figure in (Fig. 5). Among them, candidate sites in the Vertiport construction area were included, while other candidate sites were excluded. As a result, the finally selected 10 vertiport locations are as follow (the second figure in Fig. 5).

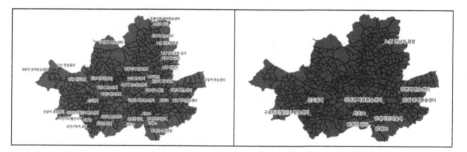

Fig. 5. Vertiport Candidates on the Vertiport Spatial Location Map

1. Nowon Meeting Plaza
2. Sindorim Station
3. Seocho IC
4. Yangjae IC
5. Yangjae Citizens' Forest Station
6. Yangjaecheon vacant lot
7. Gangbyeon Station Transfer Center
8. Jamsil Metropolitan Transfer Center
9. Gangnam Station Complex Transfer Center
10. Guro Digital Complex Transfer Center

Design Routes Between Candidates of Vertiport. The UAM route spatial location map was used to design the route between the finally selected Vertiport locations. After visualizing the Vertiport location selected on the map, the route through the most appropriate grid was designed considering the way-point and emergency landing areas among the blue areas, and the following criteria were additionally applied considering the results of the existing research and the government's policy direction.

1. If possible, it must travel via the Han River [1].
2. If there is a Waypoint or an emergency landing place nearby, it must be via [6].
3. Prioritize the higher-scoring grid among the same blue grid [12].

By applying these criteria, the path was finally designed as red line (Fig. 6).

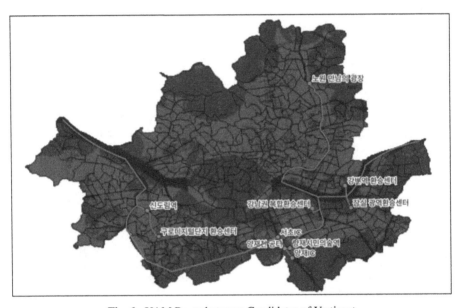

Fig. 6. UAM Route between Candidates of Vertiport

5   Conclusion

As a result of designing Seoul's UAM route and Vertiport location through our methodology based on the spatial information data of Seoul, we were able to meet the government's proposal of concept of operation and suggest a specific plan that can be operated in practice. Based on the criteria, we suggested the safest and most efficient UAM route, and selected a Vertiport location that meets the initial demand and allows UAM aircraft to be accessed via flight.

Since the methodology was based on spatial data, it is possible to provide specific design criteria and an objective and reasonable basis for selecting the route and vertiport location. In addition, it is meaningful that it is a developable methodology that can further reflect various types of data in the future to enhance the validity and effectiveness of the methodology. Through this, it is expected to increase acceptability in the government or the private sector by reducing the rejection that may occur and to secure the credibility of UAM.

For future research and development, it is necessary to verify the demand of vertiport selected in terms of business administration and urban engineering, and to design an entry and departure procedure considering holding pattern in preparation for operating many UAM aircrafts. In addition, it is necessary to create UAM procedure at the UAM route through the flight simulator and procedures how to cope with various emergency situations.

Acknowledgment. We participated and won the "2022 Land, Infrastructure and Transport Data Utilization Contest" hosted by the Ministry of Land, Infrastructure and Transport (Government) of Korea, and participated and won the "2022 Seoul Digital Spatial Information Utilization Contest" hosted by Seoul Metropolitan Government.

References

1. UAM Team Korea: K-UAM Conops 1.0, 1st. Ministry of Land, Infrastructure and Transport, Sejong (2021)
2. KAIA(Korea Agency for Infrastructure Technology Advancement): K-UAM Technology Roadmap, 1st. KAIA, Anyang (2021)
3. FAA(Federal Aviation Administration): Urban Air Mobility(UAM) Concept of Operations v1.0, 1st. FAA, Washington D.C. (2020)
4. NUAIR, NASA: High Density Automated Vertiport Concept of Operation, 1st. NUAIR and NASA, Washington D.C. (2021)
5. EASA(European Union Aviation Safety Agency): Urban Air Mobility Survey Evaluation Report, 1st. EASA, Cologne (2020)
6. Lee, Y., Kwag, T.H., Jeong, G.M., Ahn, JH., Chung, B.C., Lee, J.W.: Flight routes establishment through the operational concept analysis of urban air mobility system. J. Korean Soc. Aeronaut. Space Sci. **48**(12), 1021–1031 (2020)
7. Lee, J.-H., Hong, S.: Classification of operation model and ground infrastructure for Urban Air Mobility (UAM). J. Urban Policies **12**(1), 89–111 (2021)
8. Kim, S., Lee, J.: The initial concept of a generalized cost model to verify the economic feasibility of city-level UAM operation. In: Proceedings of the 85th KOR-KST Conference, pp. 587–588. KOR-KST, Jeju (2021)
9. Kim, W.-J., Park, J.-H.: A study on the factors affecting UAM vertiport location selection. J. Urban Stud. Real Estate **13**(2), 119–137 (2021)
10. Jeong, J.Y., Hwang, H.Y.: Selection and evaluation of vertiports of Urban Air Mobility (UAM) in the Seoul metropolitan area using the K-means algorithm. J. Adv. Navig. Technol. **25**(1), 8–16 (2021)
11. Oh, J.S., Hwang, H.Y.: Selection of vertiport location, route setting and operating time analysis of urban air mobility in metropolitan area. J. Adv. Navig. Technol. **24**(5), 358–367 (2021)
12. Lee, J., Lee, J.Y., Yoon, D.H.: Development of UAM route design methodology using transportation bigdata. In: Proceedings of The Korean Society for Aeronautical and Space Sciences 2022 Autumn Conference, pp. 630–631. KSAS, Jeju (2022)
13. Balakrishnan, K., Polastre, J., Mooberry, J., Golding, R., Sachs, P.: Blueprint for the sky: The Roadmap for the Safe Integration of Autonomous Aircraft, 1st. Airbus Acubed, California (2018)

14. Bae, Y.: A study on the improvement of regional equality of public transit services based on indicators from a public transit-user perspective. KRIHS **545**, 1–8 (2015)
15. Rabiee, F.: Focus-group interview and data analysis. Proc. Nutr. Soc. **63**(4), 655–660. University of Cambridge, London (2004)
16. National Spatial Data Infrastructure Portal, http://www.nsdi.go.kr. last accessed 2023/1/7
17. Seoul Open Data Flatform, https://data.seoul.go.kr/. last accessed 2023/1/7
18. National Open Data Portal, https://www.data.go.kr/. last accessed 2023/1/7
19. Kim, M., Lee, J.: A data transformation method for visualizing the statistical information based on the grid. J. Korea Spat. Inf. Soc. **23**(5), 31–40 (2015)
20. QGIS, https://qgis.org/. last accessed 2023/1/8
21. Seoul Metropolitan Government: 2040 Seoul Urban Basic Plan. 1st. Seoul Metropolitan Government, Seoul (2022)
22. Ministry of Land, Infrastructure and Transport: Metropolitan Transportation Implementation Plan. 1st. Ministry of Land, Infrastructure and Transport, Sejong (2021)
23. K-UAM Grand Challenge, http://kuam-gc.kr/. last accessed 2023/1/18

Why are Some Makerspaces not so Male-Dominated

Mizan Rahman[1]([⊠]) and Michael L. Best[1,2]

[1] College of Computing, Georgia Institute of Technology, Atlanta, GA 30332, USA
{mizan,mikeb}@gatech.edu
[2] Sam Nunn School of International Affairs, Georgia Institute of Technology, GA 30332
Atlanta, USA

Abstract. Makerspaces have been shown to play a significant role in promoting innovation and entrepreneurship by providing users with the tools and resources to produce and create products. Nonetheless, the makerspace movement has been scrutinized for exhibiting severe gender disparity, often causing women to feel excluded from participation. As a result, many women are deprived of the tools and educational opportunities commonly available in a typical makerspace. This study utilizes a qualitative research method to investigate makerspaces located across the United States. The results of our research indicate that some makerspaces do not exhibit the gender bias that is often associated with the movement, and we explore the factors that may be contributing to these makerspaces' success at gender balance. Our findings reveal that women in leadership, inclusive policies and regulations, women-focused activities, and safe and accessible facilities are instrumental in attracting a more diverse demographic. This study holds the potential to inform the design of innovation spaces that prioritize inclusivity and foster a greater sense of community among makers of all genders.

Keywords: makerspaces · Fablabs · women empowerment · gender · feminist HCI · digital fabrication · DF4D · open innovation · gender inclusion

1 Introduction

Innovation spaces such as makerspaces are a complex socio-technical system (O'Donovan and Smith, 2020) that has been shown to be fertile ground for innovation and entrepreneurship development (Browder et al., 2019; Greenberg et al., 2020; Dammicco, 2022). The positive impact of innovation and entrepreneurship on numerous sectors, such as healthcare, information technology, transportation, and agriculture, is well-documented and underscores their vital role in driving economic growth (Andrews et al., 2022). The role of gender diversity in innovation spaces cannot be overstated, as gender has been shown to influence technology utilization in unique ways (Bardzell, 2010). Nevertheless, socio-technical systems are not immune to biases and often fail to effectively represent marginalized groups (Ogbonnaya-Ogburu et al., 2020), and innovation spaces are no exception. However, the gender disparity in innovation spaces is not

© The Author(s), under exclusive license to Springer Nature Switzerland AG 2023
M. Kurosu and A. Hashizume (Eds.): HCII 2023, LNCS 14014, pp. 341–354, 2023.
https://doi.org/10.1007/978-3-031-35572-1_23

consistent across all makerspaces. Some makerspaces invite gender diversity among its members more willingly than others. This intriguing situation motivated our investigation into understanding the reasons behind the reduced gender disparity in some makerspaces compared to most innovation spaces. The goal of this inquiry is to establish a foundation for developing strategies to address gender disparities in other innovation spaces.

Makerspaces provide a communal workspace for individuals with similar technical interests to collaborate on projects while sharing resources, ideas, equipment, and knowledge (Diaz et al., 2021). According to Dammicco (2022), makerspaces offer access to a range of manufacturing technologies, including both digital and traditional tools such as laser cutters, 3D printers, lathes, wood and metal working machines, sewing stations, and drills. These collaborative innovation environments are growing in popularity among the general public (Corsini et al., 2021). The communities that form within makerspaces can be viewed as communities of practice (Khanapour et al., 2017), where a group of individuals unite based on shared interests.

The impact of gender disparity in technology and product development cannot be underestimated. Perez (2019), in her book Invisible Women, exposes these biases present in everyday artifacts. She describes how voice recognition software in cars exhibits a male voice bias, resulting in better performance for men than women. Instead of redesigning the software, manufacturing companies offer training for women to use it. In addition, she asserts that popular tech products marketed as gender-neutral often exhibit male bias and fail to meet the needs of women, such as oversized smartwatches and VR headsets that are too big for the average woman's head. Women continue to be underrepresented in the tech industry, holding only 26% of jobs in the US professional computing profession and 14% in the UK STEM workforce (Perez, 2019). While designers may believe they are creating gender-neutral products, these products are often geared toward men, highlighting the need for pluralistic representation of gender in product design to avoid designing products that cannot be used by everyone (Bardzell, 2010). This argument shows how innovation spaces need gender balance if they are to avoid perpetuating these biases.

Makerspaces provide a collaborative ecosystem for individuals with similar technical inclinations to participate in project development, and exchange thoughts, resources, and technical expertise. These spaces exhibit unique characteristics, as reflected in the type and availability of equipment and methods employed. The communities that inhabit these makerspaces can be considered as communities of practice (Khanapour et al., 2017), as they are established based on shared interests and goals. Individuals with non-technical backgrounds tend to focus more on the product they desire to create, rather than the tools they utilize. Consequently, they adopt technology to produce art, crafts, jewelry, or streamline processes in their daily lives, with the utilization of technology being a consequence of seeking the most efficient means to achieve their objectives (Faulkner & Mcclard, 2014).

Despite the widespread recognition of the benefits and contributions of makerspaces, they are not immune to significant issues of gender inequality. Research has indicated that women often view the makerspace environment as hostile and unwelcoming (Menold et al., 2019). Menold et al. (2019) found that women make up only 19% of people in makerspaces and tend to avoid these spaces due to their male-dominated nature. As the makerspace movement continues to gain traction in pedagogical contexts, it is imperative to consider and address the gender-related issues present in these environments.

Gender equality in work, including in makerspaces, benefits all people in society, not only women. Investing in women's economic empowerment can contribute directly to gender equality, poverty eradication, and inclusive economic growth (UN Women, 2022). According to the World Bank (2022), 2.4 billion working-age women do not have equal economic opportunities. With increasing numbers of makerspaces and FabLabs globally, many women will gain access to resources and could enjoy empowerment. Considering such a change can help to achieve the UN's Sustainable Development Goals (SDGs) of gender equality and women's empowerment by 2030. As UN Women is committed to developing tools and methodologies to facilitate gender-responsive innovation in collaboration with industry partners (UN Women, 2022), makerspace and FabLabs could play a vital role in achieving this.

2   Implications

Contemporary HCI theory focuses on flourishing of human values (Dourish, 2019), and human values are influenced by entrepreneurship (McCabe, 2012). Makerspaces play a significant role in learning and entrepreneurship building. In accordance with the analytical lens of Feminist HCI (Bardzell, 2010), the factors underlying higher female participation in a makerspace could be helpful to all makerspaces and other related innovation spaces in opening opportunities for more women in makerspaces and other related innovation spaces.

3   Related Work

Makerspaces provide noticeable opportunities for digital empowerment (Smolarczyk & Kröner, 2021; Diaz et al., 2021), making the maker movement into a user-led innovation platform that offers a supportive environment for aspiring entrepreneurs (Neumeyer & Santos, 2019). Consequently, makerspaces have increased significantly in recent years, which coincides with an increased need for manufacturing space and access to expensive digital manufacturing technologies (Browder et al., 2019; Farritor, 2017). Despite the growing demand for access to digital manufacturing technologies, makerspaces are becoming widespread, but gender inequalities persist in these spaces (Fox, 2015; Maric, 2018; Melo, 2020; Menold et al., 2019; Whelan, 2018; Sherrill, 2017).

Though makerspaces could contribute to more equity in education (Smolarczyk & Kröner, 2021), a significant gender disparity exists among makerspace members, with studies indicating that 81% are male (Faulkner & Mcclard, 2014). This gender imbalance has led to women being deterred from utilizing makerspaces, thereby limiting their access to tools and learning opportunities (Capel et al., 2020). According to Lauren (2015), many making activities have been highly gendered. For example, woodwork is one of the most common activities in a makerspace, and men dominate this space, while 41% of women makers in the US come from an arts-and-crafts background (Axup et al., 2014). Thus, most makerspaces are geared toward men and are equipped with tools and services less sought after by many women, making it challenging for them to participate actively (Menold et al., 2019).

The male-dominated and sometimes hostile environment of certain makerspaces has led to the establishment of women-only hackerspaces, also referred to as "feminist hackerspaces" (Fox, 2015; Fuchsberger et al., 2022; Henry, 2014). The use of the term "feminist hackerspace" reflects the intention of these spaces to maintain a community based on shared values. These spaces provide a safe and supportive environment for their women members to express themselves, develop resistance strategies, and build a community centered around these shared values. The goal of these spaces is to address the limitations of hacktivism and foster a stronger feminist hacker culture (Toupin, 2013; Guthrie, 2014).

Capel et al., (2021) found that women-only makerspaces can provide a safe environment for female learners and help them overcome their inhibitions to join co-ed makerspaces, thus increasing the level of gender inclusion in makerspace communities. However, according to Smit and Fuchsberger (2020), the isolation of women-only hackerspaces can result in a "maker-bubble." In this situation, members may feel excluded from other makerspaces and miss out on opportunities for knowledge-sharing, professional networking, and building social connections. Although the above intervention was introduced in response to gender imbalance in makerspaces, some female members disagree and believe that women and men have equal access to makerspace (Bean et al., 2015). Clearly, such a position raises the possibility that some makerspaces may operate differently than others and offer more gender equality and inclusivity.

The gender gap in makerspaces is not limited to a particular region. According to Geser et al. (2019), the European research and innovation project DOIT which aims to help young people develop an entrepreneurial mindset and skills through practice-based learning in makerspaces. The project has revealed that makerspaces can be useful environments for promoting social innovation and entrepreneurial learning, but there are challenges regarding the underrepresentation of girls in these activities. To address this issue, recommendations arising out of the DOIT project include implementing gender-sensitive measures in communication, organization, and conduct of maker education (Geser et al., 2019). Researchers also find that socio-cultural barriers, including gender stereotypes, male dominance, and a lack of female role models, may explain women's underrepresentation in the Maker community in southern France (Maric, 2018) and similar work in Australia (Hedditch & Vyas, 2021).

According to the theory of "framing," the failure to confront gender inequity at the micro-level, specifically within makerspaces, may have persistent implications at the macro level. Maalsen et al. (2022) bring to the fore the predicament of gender myopia in decision-making, which could result in the neglect of salient variables. For example, criticism has been levied at the City of Sydney's initiative to alleviate gender asymmetry in the innovation domain due to its narrow focus. Rather than addressing the male conduct and culture prevalent in entrepreneurial ecosystems, the initiative primarily emphasizes training women to navigate competently in male-dominated milieus. This approach has been perceived as problematic since networking constitutes a critical facet of the industry, as underscored by Feldman et al. (2017).

4 Methods

This study exclusively focuses on independent makerspaces that operate outside the purview of libraries, museums, or educational institutions. To investigate our research question, "why are some makerspaces not so male-dominated", we adopt a qualitative research design. Our research process involved employing a one-on-one interview instrument in order to shape our semi-structured interviews to elicit qualitative information. Data obtained from the interviews were manually transcribed and analyzed using AtlasTi, a computer-assisted qualitative data analysis software, using a thematic analysis procedure.

4.1 Recruitment Protocol

The recruitment of participants for this study was accomplished through a trifold approach. Firstly, individuals were curated from Facebook groups that catered to makerspace management, thereby tapping into a pre-existing network of makerspace enthusiasts. Secondly, contact information for makerspaces across the United States was gathered from the website of Maker Magazine (https://makerspaces.make.co/), and outreach efforts were initiated through a multiplicity of channels including electronic mail, social media platforms such as Facebook and LinkedIn, and telephone communication. Lastly, the technique of snowballing recruitment was utilized, where interested participants were encouraged to recommend additional individuals with similar characteristics for inclusion.

4.2 Interview Instrument

This project was part of a larger mixed-methods study that included a survey sent to makerspaces. The survey data helped to provide a basic understanding of the makerspace, which guided the interview instrument development process. As an example, if a makerspace reported a non-male membership surpassing the average female representation in makerspaces, which is 19% according to Faulkner & Mcclard (2014), the inquiry was designed to determine what measures the makerspace took to achieve such a proportion of female participation. Alternatively, when the non-male membership rate was below 20%, the investigation concentrated on elucidating the reasons for the low women's participation rate. The questioning focused on aspects such as the makerspace's management structure, leadership composition, and strategies for fostering inclusivity. Participants were forthcoming in describing the underlying problems, and various questions were asked. We paid special attention to carefully framing the interview questions to elicit candid responses and gain a comprehensive understanding of the research question. It is important to note that as semi-structured interviews, the conversations were different with each individual based on their responses to the quantitative survey.

4.3 Interview Participants

We conducted interviews with 27 participants, consisting of 6 females and 21 males. The interview respondents' job titles reflect a diverse range of positions within the makerspaces, with 42.50% identifying as Founder/Co-founder, 3.75% as managers, 11.25%

as executive management, 16.25% as directors, 23.75% as the board of directors, and 2.5% as officers (Table 1).

Table 1. List of participants.

Participant	Position	Gender	Year Est.	% of members not male	Location (State)
P01	Director	F	2016	50	NY
P02	Board of Director	M	2009	35	WI
P03	Founder/Co-founder	M	2014	33	WA
P04	Founder/Co-founder	M	2012	8	IL
P05	Executive Management	M	2006	35	AZ
P06	Director	M	2010	20	PA
P07	Founder/Co-founder	M	2008	30	OH
P08	Founder/Co-founder	M	2015	48	OR
P09	Founder/Co-founder	M	2014	50	KY
P10	Board of Director	F	2009	45	PA
P11	Director	M	2015	0	SC
P12	Founder/Co-founder	M	2016	30	SC
P13	Founder/Co-founder	M	2019	50	KY
P14	Board of Director	M	2015	10	IA
P15	Director	M	2013	10	MA
P16	Board of Director	F	2015	40	TN
P17	Director	M	2009	15	NM
P18	Founder/Co-founder	M	2010	10	WI
P19	Board of Director	M	2013	12	NC
P20	Executive Management	F	2013	35	GA
P21	Founder/Co-founder	M	2014	20	MA
P22	Executive Management	M	2018	10	GA
P23	Founder/Co-founder	M	2021	15	TX
P24	Founder/Co-founder	F	2017	41	MN
P25	Board of Director	M	2017	40	CA
P26	Founder/Co-founder	M	2015	20	PA
P27	Founder/Co-founder	F	2019	50	MN

4.4 Coding

We utilized Atlas.ti for coding and thematic analysis of interview data, using open coding and inductive coding methods for interview transcripts. Subsequently, we performed the first cycle of coding using descriptive and in-vivo methods to categorize the data at a basic level and capture participants' direct stories, ideas, and meanings. We then compared codes to identify differences and similarities, which were organized into categories and subcategories before performing a second coding cycle. For a better understanding of the perspectives and experiences of the participants, in vivo coding was particularly useful. We performed a total of 3 coding cycles, and eventually, 43 codes were transformed into four final themes. Those themes were: women in leadership, inclusive policies and regulations, women-focused activities, and safe and accessible facilities.

5   Findings

The study results underscore the importance of creating a welcoming environment to increase women's participation, which can be achieved through various interrelated attributes. These attributes include having women in leadership, inclusive policies and regulations, women-focused activities, and safe and accessible facilities. The makerspaces that prioritized these attributes fostered female participation, gender diversity, and an atmosphere of inclusivity.

5.1   Women in Leadership

The presence of women who are actively working and involved in a particular community can create a sense of belonging and support for other women. This can break down stereotypes and provide role models and mentors for women who are starting out in a field. This community can also support women facing discrimination or other challenges, empowering them to speak up and push back against obstacles. For example, [P26] said, *"what I saw was the facilities that had higher female participation because when the female comes, they see other women are working and involved. It really helps."*

According to participants of both genders, having women in management, staff, or even in the founding team is a way to create a women-supportive environment. This suggests that having women in leadership roles can be important in promoting gender diversity and creating an environment where women feel welcome and valued. For example, when asked about their recruitment of an impressive female population, participant [P24] stated that one of the factors contributing to a more inclusive environment is the significant representation of women in the company's leadership. Specifically, [P24] noted, *"60% of our board members are women."* By having women in positions of power, it can help to break down gender stereotypes and provide women with role models and mentors to guide them in their careers. Overall, this highlights the importance of promoting gender diversity in all aspects of an organization in order to create an environment that is inclusive and supportive of women. [P03] highlighted the importance of having women in leadership and founder positions and said, *"what helped a lot is having a co-founder who's female."* Having women in volunteer positions was also seen as engendering a friendly atmosphere for women. [P08] said, *"if I was to go out there right now and show you our volunteers, you'd see that we encourage volunteers of both sexes, we make everyone feel comfortable. So, when a new female comes, they do not feel like they're a fish out of water."*

Some makerspaces have taken creative measures to address male dominance and promote more inclusivity. One such approach was initiated by a female member who suggested hosting a special night where men leave the space and women, trans, and femme members can socialize and establish stronger bonds with each other. According to this participant, this approach empowers and supports women, trans, and femme members by providing a safe and supportive environment for building community and solidarity. He said,

"I would say our fourth year, there was this awesome woman that came in, and she started our WTF (women, trans, and femme) night every Tuesday, where men just kind of exit the space. When we started doing that, suddenly, we started getting really, really creative people out of the diverse gender orientation." [P05]

The persistent gender stereotype that makerspaces are dominated by men has made it challenging to attract individuals of other genders. Consequently, some participants have implemented alternative marketing strategies to promote gender inclusivity. [P24] said, *"A lot of our marketing pictures show women working that I think that making them comfortable when they get to the space is really, really important."*

5.2 Inclusive Policies and Regulations

Our findings suggest that makerspaces that have well-defined rules and policies are more likely to exhibit a greater balance of gender representation than organizations without established policies. The impact of rules and enforcement of them is particularly notable, as some participants reported that a few male members had caused discomfort for female members. However, when a makerspace adopts rules and procedures that enforce tolerance, respect, and inclusivity, it can help to mediate these harms. The results highlight the importance of implementing clear policies and guidelines in makerspaces to promote a safe and inclusive environment that supports all members. For example, participant [P10] reported *"there's always that one [...] and like, he is just the most recent one, just self-selected himself out of there. He was a very mediocre [...] dude. But, you know, we don't have huge problems that often when they do, they tend to self-select themselves out."*

Similarly, participant [P05] reported that the code of conduct of their makerspace removes members who exhibit toxic behavior that can make women and other gender members uncomfortable. A code of conduct that prioritizes tolerance and respect can promote diversity and inclusivity and ensure the removal of individuals whose behavior violates these values.

"we have a code of conduct that's very, very strict, that has to do with harassment has to do with, you know, asserting yourself onto someone else, or asserting your ideas on somebody else without unsolicited advice. Like, there's a lot of those

things that we have in our code of conduct. For those reasons, we found that those were causing problems that do not come back."

In addition, participants emphasized that a strong organizational commitment to diversity significantly influences the gender balance in makerspaces. In this regard, participant [P20] stated:

"we've heard that from lots of people and being inclusive and diverse is definitely something that was grounded in our founding, so we wanted to be a place for all people, regardless of sex, income, skill level, or I guess the gender, you know, religious backgrounds political back or whatever, we just, we just want to be a place where people can come in feel welcome and make things awesome."

Similarly, in agreement with participant [P20], participant [P07] indicated the following:

"we have emphasized gender diversity. The COO I had hired to be a CEO replacement for me is a woman. She's very empowering. We to do things like all women's welding classes, and all women's blacksmithing classes, bring the Girl Scouts in, and they would get their product design merit badge. We were grateful to be connected to many female startups and businesses and the culture in general."

5.3 Women-Focused Activities

According to participants, men and women may prefer different activities within makerspaces. In general, men are more likely to participate in activities that involve tools or machinery, such as woodworking and metalworking. Conversely, women expressed a greater interest in activities that involved textiles or crafts, such as knitting and sewing. As a result, organizations that offer women-focused activities draw more women. As stated by participant [P22]:

"Woodworking is our big draw, and it's stereotypically a guy thing. That's why we tend to attract more men than women. You know, most people who come to our shop for the first time are interested in woodworking, and that's why they're usually dudes. I get a lot more women interested in laser cutting because they see the potential for how they can cover a lot of different domains with one tool, which is very interesting because men don't think that way."

Further, other participants expressed similar opinions, with [P25] saying: *"I believe ceramics is a significant draw for women to our space",* as well as [P16] stating,

"ceramics is the reason behind our impressive women population. We probably only got about four women in the woodshop, and maybe not even one in welding. But we have a lot of women in ceramics, and they are go-getters. I mean, these are people who have immense talents. A lot of them are interior designers, kitchen designers, a lot of them are coders. They're people who run all kinds of very technical programs for their companies. They're not, you know, I mean, you think of pottery just being sort of a craft thing. For them, it's a way of carrying relief

from their jobs, but these people, in a pinch will help you out with anything. We have one of them drawing architectural plans to put in a large studio to try and get a grant. Things like that, are really just an incredible bunch of talent there."

Similarly, participant [P08] confirmed that higher female participation in makerspaces is the result of the following factors *"our jewelry studio, for example, all these equipments are specifically for making jewelry; really nice professional-level jewelry. And so, this has attracted an entirely huge demographic of women."*

Participants further disclosed that many men within the maker community have a limited understanding of women makers and overlook services designed for women. One manager, for instance, struggled to explain why so few women were attending his makerspace, suggesting that making was not an activity in which women typically engage. However, the study findings indicate that making is a popular pursuit among women. For example, our interviews with a women-only makerspace revealed that they had a waiting list of potential members and were limited by their capacity to accommodate more people. As participant [P12] noted, overcoming bias is essential for promoting inclusivity:

"I think women need to know that they can do it, and you don't have to do it for them; you just have to set them up and say, there's the target, here's what you need to do, go for it, and let them do it. I think that's one of the reasons why we have such a diverse group. We do have significant numbers of females... I think that's the culture that we set and the openness and, inclusive, as inclusive part none of those diverse parts."

5.4 Safe and Accessible Facility

Our participants highlighted the critical role of a makerspace's location in promoting gender diversity. Given the tight budgets of many makerspaces, rent often represents a significant expense, and decision-makers may opt to rent cheaper spaces in industrial areas. However, this location choice may deter women from participating in makerspaces, as some areas may be perceived as unsafe. For instance, one participant [P11] explained that their makerspace had no female members due to its location in a terrible part of town while participant [P26] attributed their low female participation to the spooky location within an old hospital. These findings emphasize the importance of considering location when establishing makerspaces and suggest that makerspaces in areas perceived as unsafe may struggle to attract and retain women. For example, according to the participant [P09]:

"it's inviting, well, that easy to get to downtown in a safe space. Female members are the winners, the ones that want to build more, they're looking to leapfrog and do more. So they've got a lot more of all the ones that are working in there. Now. There are the go-getters."

Moreover, participant [P24] expressed a similar sentiment regarding the relationship between location and the ability to attract female members. They said, *"you try to get yourself location is important. You know, to be too far on the outskirts of town is going to limit the people who can get to you. So, find a place inside the city in the communities you're trying to reach."*

6 Discussion

Based on our participant interviews, we have gathered evidence as to why some makerspaces have better gender diversity than others. This research highlights that makerspaces that establish a "safe and welcoming" environment for women and other gender-orientation groups tend to attract a more gender-diverse membership than traditional male-dominated makerspaces. According to our research, the act of making itself is not gendered - women are as prolific makers as men but each group favors different activities; most makerspaces do not understand their potential audience, causing gender disparity in innovation and creative spaces.

This study identified four strategies that some makerspaces employed that create a more gender-inclusive environment and reduce male dominance. Firstly, the presence of women in leadership roles - both in management and volunteer capacities - was found to create a more welcoming environment for potential new women members. Secondly, makerspaces that adopted inclusive policies and regulations were able to eliminate disruptive behavior that caused discomfort for some female members. Thirdly, makerspaces that offered women-focused activities - such as ceramics, which tends to be more appealing to women, were successful in attracting more female members. Finally, makerspaces that were in safe and accessible facilities were found to be more effective in drawing a diverse membership. Although some makerspaces may prioritize low rental costs when selecting a location, this decision may contribute to diversity issues.

Studies have illuminated the immense potential of makerspaces in promoting innovation and entrepreneurship, thereby enabling individuals to access the necessary tools and resources for the creation and production of goods (Browder et al, 2019; Greenberg et al., 2020; Dammicco, 2022). Nevertheless, the makerspace movement has been subject to noteworthy criticism due to the profound gender disparity that persists, where women are frequently precluded from participating in such spaces (Menold et al., 2019). Unfortunately, the under-representation of women in the technology industry has resulted in asymmetric product innovation and design, as women's ingenuity and unique perspectives are not being effectively harnessed (Maalsen et al. 2022). Eckhardt et al., (2021) claim that the absence of female role models in makerspace leadership is one of the causes of this gender disparity. It is worth noting that since most makerspaces are male-dominated, certain women have taken refuge in establishing feminist makerspaces (Fox, 2015), which has created a distinct maker-bubble (Smit and Fuchsberger, 2020), hindering cooperation and collaborative innovation.

We found that several makerspaces have been founded by many creative and well-intentioned individuals with limited business and organizational expertise. Operating a makerspace poses significant challenges, including recruiting and retaining members, as well as making sure bills are paid consistently. This perpetual demand for operational stability prevents the organization from addressing crucial concerns such as promoting diversity, fostering community awareness through mass marketing, and establishing organizational rules and policies. Despite these challenges, the leaders and founders of these spaces make considerable sacrifices to sustain their operations and facilitate creative expression, thus warranting recognition and admiration. Nonetheless, with access to financial and organizational resources, in addition to comprehensive training and exposure, such makerspaces have the potential to become exceptional spaces that welcome all individuals.

7   Conclusion

Makerspaces play a vital role in promoting innovation and entrepreneurship. However, gender disparity has been observed in many of these spaces, with women being significantly underrepresented. The prevalence of a male-dominated environment in these spaces can create feelings of discomfort and exclusion for women. Nonetheless, our study has identified makerspaces that have successfully fostered an inclusive ecosystem. The research suggests that makerspaces with a "safe and welcoming" environment for women and other gender-orientated groups tend to attract a more gender-diverse membership than those dominated by males. We found that achieving gender diversity requires a sustained and dedicated effort. Organizations must adopt a systematic approach and pay attention to several critical factors such as women in leadership, inclusive policies and regulations, women-focused activities, and safe and accessible facilities are instrumental in attracting a more diverse demographic of makers.

References

Andrews, M., Chatterji, A., Lerner, J., Stern, S.: The Role of Innovation and Entrepreneurship in Economic Growth. University of Chicago Press (2022). https://www.hbs.edu/faculty/Pages/item.aspx?num=58240

Axup, J., et al.: The world of making. Computer **47**(12), 24–40 (2014). https://doi.org/10.1109/MC.2014.373

Bardzell, S.: Feminist HCI: taking stock and outlining an agenda for design. In: Proceedings of the SIGCHI Conference on Human Factors in Computing Systems, pp. 1301–1310 (2010). https://doi.org/10.1145/1753326.1753521

Bean, V., Farmer, N.M., Kerr, B.A.: An exploration of women's engagement in makerspaces. Gifted and Talented Int. **30**(1–2), 61–67 (2015). https://doi.org/10.1080/15332276.2015.1137456

Browder, R.E., Aldrich, H.E., Bradley, S.W.: The emergence of the maker movement: implications for entrepreneurship research. J. Bus. Ventur. **34**(3), 459–476 (2019). https://doi.org/10.1016/j.jbusvent.2019.01.005

Capel, T., Ploderer, B., Brereton, M.: The wooden quilt: carving out personal narratives in a women-only makerspace. In: Proceedings of the 2020 ACM Designing Interactive Systems Conference, pp. 1059–1071 (2020). https://doi.org/10.1145/3357236.3395562

Capel, T., Ploderer, B., Brereton, M., O'Connor Solly, M.: The making of women: creating trajectories for women's participation in makerspaces. In: Proceedings of the ACM on Human-Computer Interaction, 5(CSCW1), pp. 35:1–35:38 (2021). https://doi.org/10.1145/3449109

Corsini, L., Dammicco, V., Moultrie, J.: Frugal innovation in a crisis: the digital fabrication maker response to COVID-19. R&D Management **51**(2), 195–210 (2021). https://doi.org/10.1111/radm.12446

Dammicco, V.: The emergent process of entrepreneurial innovation: Evidence from Fabrication Spaces, Thesis, University of Cambridge (2022). https://doi.org/10.17863/CAM.87836

Diaz, J., Tomàs, M., Lefebvre, S.: Are public makerspaces a means to empowering citizens? The case of Ateneus de Fabricació in Barcelona. Telematics Inform. **59**, 101551 (2021). https://doi.org/10.1016/j.tele.2020.101551

Dourish, P.: User experience as legitimacy trap. Interactions **26**(6), 46–49 (2019). https://doi.org/10.1145/3358908

Eckhardt, J., Kaletka, C., Pelka, B., Unterfrauner, E., Voigt, C., Zirngiebl, M.: Gender in the making: an empirical approach to understand gender relations in the maker movement. Int. J. Hum Comput Stud. **145**, 102548 (2021). https://doi.org/10.1016/j.ijhcs.2020.102548

Farritor, S.: University-based makerspaces: a source of innovation. Technol. Innov. **19**(1), 389–395 (2017). https://doi.org/10.21300/19.1.2017.389

Faulkner, S., Mcclard, A.: Making change: can ethnographic research about women makers change the future of computing? Ethnographic Praxis in Industry Conference Proceedings **2014**(1), 187–198 (2014). https://doi.org/10.1111/1559-8918.01026

Feldman, R., Armitage, A., Wang, C.: The Gender Gap in Startup Catalyst Organizations: Bridging the Divide Between Narrative and Reality (2017). https://scholarsbank.uoregon.edu/xmlui/handle/1794/22323

Fox, S.: Feminist hackerspaces as sites for feminist design. In: Proceedings of the 2015 ACM SIGCHI Conference on Creativity and Cognition, pp. 341–342 (2015). https://doi.org/10.1145/2757226.2764771

Fuchsberger, V., et al.: Making access: increasing inclusiveness in making. In: Extended Abstracts of the 2022 CHI Conference on Human Factors in Computing Systems, pp. 1–5 (2022). https://doi.org/10.1145/3491101.3503696

Geser, G., Hollauf, E.-M., Hornung-Prahauser, V., Schon, S.: Makerspaces as Social Innovation and Entrepreneurship Learning Environments: The DOIT Learning Program - ProQuest. Discourse and Communication for Sustainable Education (2019). https://www.proquest.com/openview/3defa8ee89e6015141144879cbeee52a/1?pq-origsite=gscholar&cbl=2026372

Greenberg, D., Calabrese Barton, A., Tan, E., Archer, L.: Redefining entrepreneurialism in the maker movement: a critical youth approach. J. Learn. Sci. **29**(4–5), 471–510 (2020). https://doi.org/10.1080/10508406.2020.1749633

Guthrie, G.: Where Are the Women in Makerspaces? Make: DIY Projects and Ideas for Makers (2014). https://makezine.com/article/maker-news/where-are-the-women/

Hedditch, S., Vyas, D.: A gendered perspective on making from an autoethnography in makerspaces. Designing Interactive Systems Conference **2021**, 1887–1901 (2021). https://doi.org/10.1145/3461778.3462015

Henry, L.: The Rise of Feminist Hackerspaces and How to Make Your Own. Model View Culture (2014). https://modelviewculture.com/pieces/the-rise-of-feminist-hackerspaces-and-how-to-make-your-own

Khanapour, P.R., DesPortes, K., Cochran, Z., DiSalvo, B.: Framing makerspace communities. In: Proceedings of the 7th Annual Conference on Creativity and Fabrication in Education, pp. 1–4 (2017). https://doi.org/10.1145/3141798.3141814

Lauren, B.: Power, Access, Status: The Discourse of Race, Gender, and Class in the Maker Movement | Technology & Social Change Group (2015). https://tascha.uw.edu/2015/03/power-access-status-the-discourse-of-race-gender-and-class-in-the-maker-movement/

Maalsen, S., Wolifson, P., Dowling, R.: Gender in the Australian innovation ecosystem: planning smart cities for men. Gend. Place Cult. **30**, 1–22 (2022). https://doi.org/10.1080/0966369X.2022.2053068

Maric, J.: The gender-based digital divide in maker culture: features, challenges and possible solutions. J. Innov. Econ. Manage. **27**(3), 147–168 (2018). https://doi.org/10.3917/jie.027.0147

McCabe, L.: Human Values of Entrepreneurship: An Empirical Analysis of the Human Values of Social and Traditional Entrepreneurs. Regent University (2012)

Melo, M.: How Do Makerspaces Communicate Who Belongs? Examining Gender Inclusion through the Analysis of User Journey Maps in a Makerspace. Undefined (2020). https://www.semanticscholar.org/paper/How-Do-Makerspaces-Communicate-Who-Belongs-Gender-a-Melo/291054affde97ce6125674f5a931bb911915fb90

Menold, J., et al.: BUILDing a community of female makers through hands-on experiences in a university MakerSpace. IEEE Frontiers in Education Conference (FIE) **2019**, 1–8 (2019). https://doi.org/10.1109/FIE43999.2019.9028553

Neumeyer, X., Santos, S.C.: Makerspaces and entrepreneurship: the effect of team dynamics and prototyping efficacy on entrepreneurial performance. In: 2019 IEEE Technology & Engineering Management Conference (TEMSCON), pp. 1–6 (2019).https://doi.org/10.1109/TEMSCON.2019.8813727

O'Donovan, C., Smith, A.: Technology and human capabilities in UK makerspaces. J. Hum. Dev. Capabilities **21**(1), 63–83 (2020). https://doi.org/10.1080/19452829.2019.1704706

Ogbonnaya-Ogburu, I.F., Smith, A.D.R., To, A., Toyama, K.: Critical race theory for HCI. In: Proceedings of the 2020 CHI Conference on Human Factors in Computing Systems, pp. 1–16 (2020). https://doi.org/10.1145/3313831.3376392

Perez, C.C.: Invisible Women: Data Bias in a World Designed for Men (First Printing edition). Abrams Press (2019)

Sherrill, J.T.: Gender, technology, and narratives in DIY instructions. In: Proceedings of the 35th ACM International Conference on the Design of Communication, pp. 1–8 (2017). https://doi.org/10.1145/3121113.3121214

Smit, D., Fuchsberger, V.: Sprinkling diversity: hurdles on the way to inclusiveness in makerspaces. In: Proceedings of the 11th Nordic Conference on Human-Computer Interaction: Shaping Experiences, Shaping Society, pp. 1–8. Association for Computing Machinery (2020). https://doi.org/10.1145/3419249.3420070

Smolarczyk, K., Kröner, S.: Two decades in the making: a scoping review on research on digital making and its potential for digital empowerment in non-formal settings. J. Res. Technol. Educ. **55**, 1–18 (2021). https://doi.org/10.1080/15391523.2021.1974987

Toupin, S.: Feminist Hackerspaces as Safer Spaces? Feminist Journal of Art and Digital Culture, 27 Hacktivism (2013)

UN Women: UN Women - Economic Empowerment (2022). https://www.unwomen.org/en/what-we-do/economic-empowerment

Whelan, T.: We are not all makers: the paradox of plurality in the maker movement. In: Proceedings of the 2018 ACM Conference Companion Publication on Designing Interactive Systems, pp. 75–80 (2018). https://doi.org/10.1145/3197391.3205415

World Bank: Nearly 2.4 Billion Women Globally Don't Have Same Economic Rights as Men (2022). https://www.worldbank.org/en/news/press-release/2022/03/01/nearly-2-4-billion-women-globally-don-t-have-same-economic-rights-as-men

Prototype of a Facilitation System for Active Learning Using Deep Learning in Body Movement Classification

Sotaro Suzuki[(✉)] and Tomohito Yamamoto

Department of Information and Computer Science, College of Engineering, Kanazawa Institute of Technology, 7-1 Oogigaoka, Nonoichi, Ishikawa 921-8501, Japan
c6101651@planet.kanazawa-it.ac.jp,
tyama@neptune.kanazawa-it.ac.jp

Abstract. Active learning has gained attention in recent years and has been implemented across various education fields, as it is considered more effective than the conventional lecture style of learning. In active learning, it is necessary for teachers to provide appropriate facilitation to improve the quality of learning. However, it becomes more difficult to keep track of the activities of each group as the number of groups increases. Therefore, in this study, we analyzed body movements based on the values obtained from the accelerometer and gyroscope of a smartphone worn around the neck or placed in pant pockets to evaluate the learning state of students. Furthermore, we proposed appropriate facilitation based on the evaluated students' learning states according to the analyzed body movements and constructed a prototype system enabling a robot to perform facilitation.

Keywords: Group work · Deep learning · Facilitation · Body movement · and Active learning

1 Introduction

Recently, various educational institutions, particularly universities, have introduced "active learning." This learning style, which includes presentations and group work, can achieve higher learning outcomes than the conventional lecture style [1–3]. In this style, it is necessary to provide appropriate facilitation according to the learning capabilities of students to improve the quality of learning. In higher education institutions, some of the teachers are very good at facilitation, but this is not always true. In addition, it becomes more difficult to monitor the participants' learning status as the number of groups increases [4]. If it is possible to monitor student activities during active learning, such as group work, and suggest appropriate facilitation for teachers, these problems can be solved.

From this point of view, several studies have analyzed students' body movements with accelerometers to understand their activities during learning [5, 6]. Our research group has also recorded the body movements of learners during group work using sensors installed in smartphones and analyzed the relationship between learning outcomes

M. Kurosu and A. Hashizume (Eds.): HCII 2023, LNCS 14014, pp. 355–365, 2023.
https://doi.org/10.1007/978-3-031-35572-1_24

and subjective communication quality [7, 8]. In addition, the data obtained from the experiment are classified by deep learning to analyze the body movements during group work in detail [9]. The results suggest that a group of data consisting of body movements can be detected with high accuracy. The final goal of these studies [7–9] is to support teachers in understanding the state of group work and facilitating appropriately. However, such a system has not yet been developed. In addition, body movements are typically recorded using a smartphone worn around the neck during the experiment; however, in this case, students may feel the physical burden of the analysis instrument. Hence, it is necessary to consider methods to reduce the burden on the participants.

In this study, we develop a prototype system that evaluates the body movements during group work using smartphone sensors and suggests facilitation to teachers according to students' situations. Furthermore, we develop a system prototype in which a robot performs facilitation instead of teachers. To develop these systems, as in the previous studies, we record body movements both using a smartphone worn around the neck and placed in the pocket of the pants to clarify the accuracy of the classification of the body movements in each measurement.

2 Overview of Facilitation System

Figure 1 shows the configuration of the facilitation support system. The system consists of a measurement, monitoring, and robot facilitation system. The measurement system uses a three-axis accelerometer and gyro sensor mounted on a smartphone to measure body movements during group work. In this system, the smartphone sends the terminal number to the server to identify each terminal's subsequent communication first. Then, the smartphone starts measurements at a sampling frequency of 60 Hz and sends the data to the server using UDP. The system displays the measured data, results of the classification of the body movements, and contents of facilitation generated based on the results. In addition, the facilitation robot makes speeches for facilitation based on the results.

The latest measured data are input into the trained classification model when the system is executed to evaluate the body movements in real time. Simultaneously, the sensor data received from the smartphone and classified body movements are displayed on the screen in real time for presenting information regarding the group work to the teacher. Moreover, the system generates facilitation content based on the classified body movements and presents it as text on the monitoring screen. The robot receives the generated text data and facilitation actions from the server and performs speech and actions.

3 Classification of Body Movements Using Deep Learning

3.1 Dataset and Training Model

In this study, a classification model was constructed to evaluate the body movements during group work. We used the 10 movements listed in Table 1 as detection targets, which were previously studied: M01–05 represent the data of body movements related to communication, and M06–10 denote the data of relatively small body movements [9].

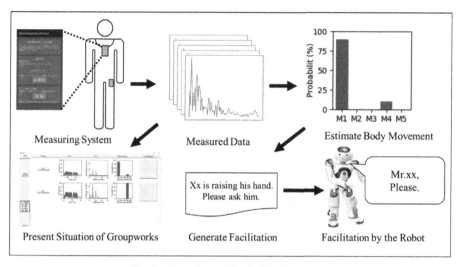

Fig. 1. Overview of the facilitation system

These movements were performed with the smartphone hanging from the neck and with the smartphone in the right front pocket of the pants. In this measurement, the values of the accelerometer and gyro sensor were acquired. Each motion was performed 50 times by four participants, and a total of 2,000 data points were obtained. Before training the body movement classification model, the following preprocessing was performed on the measured data.

1. Split the measured data into three-second segments.
2. Calculate the L2 norm of the three-axis acceleration data and subtract 9.8.
3. Add 0.0 values before and after to make the data length as 256.
4. Apply a Hann window to the data and perform fast Fourier transform.
5. Normalize the data such that the data value is approximately 0.0–1.0.

In this study, we prepared the following six types of training data to clarify how the results change depending on the input data.

1. Five types of chest data (M01–M05)
2. Five types of pocket data (M01–M05)
3. Five types of chest data (M06–M10)
4. Five types of pocket data (M06–M10)
5. Ten types of chest data (M01–M10)
6. Ten types of pocket data (M01–M10)

After the preprocessing, the data were labeled and grouped according to the specific body movement they correspond to. Grouped data were randomly divided into four groups, one of which was used for the test, and the rest were employed for the training data. A convolution neural network, with the structure shown in Fig. 2, was used for training. The acceleration data had a data length of 1 channel × 128, and the gyro data had a data length of 3 channels × 180 in this model.

Table 1. Body movements for classification

ID	Movement Name	Pictures
M01	Remaining stationary	
M02	Clapping	
M03	Raising hands	
M04	Nodding	
M05	Turning around	
M06	Stretching	

(continued)

Table 1. (*continued*)

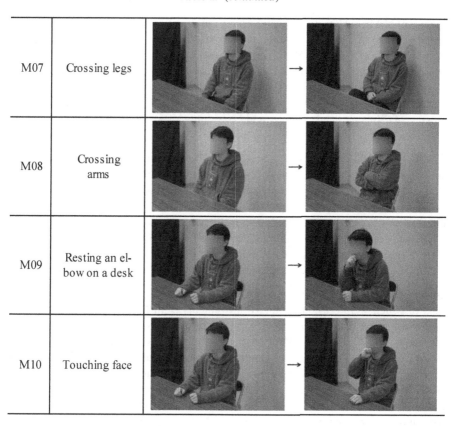

M07	Crossing legs	
M08	Crossing arms	
M09	Resting an elbow on a desk	
M10	Touching face	

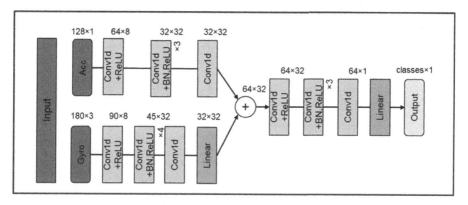

Fig. 2. Classification model of body movements

3.2 Results of Body Movement Classification

Movement of M01–M05. Tables 2 and 3 show the classification results for Datasets 1 and 2, which consist of five types of body movements: "Remaining stationary," "Clapping," "Raising hands," "Nodding," and "Turning around." From the results, the chest data is classified with a high accuracy of 99.6%. The pocket data show a lower accuracy rate of 92.4% compared to the chest data. However, the pocket data still achieved a high accuracy level, similar to that of the chest data. Among the results of pocket data, the accuracy of "Raising hands (M02)" and "Nodding (M04)" are lower than those of the chest data.

Movement of M06–M10. Tables 4 and 5 show the results of classification for Datasets 3 and 4, which consist of five types of body movements: "Stretching," "Crossing legs," "Crossing arms," "Resting an elbow on a desk," and "Touching face." The accuracy rate for the chest data is 72.0%, while that for the pocket data is 75.2%. The results indicate that the pocket data is more accurate than the chest data for the body movements of "Crossing arms (M08)," "Resting an elbow on a desk (M09)," and "Touching face (M10)." These actions are upper body-driven actions, but the lower body actions that appeared in the pocket data may have been more effective in discriminating these actions.

Movement of M01–M10. Tables 6 and 7 show the results of classification for Datasets 5 and 6, which were created for all 10 movements from M01 to M10. The accuracy rate for the chest data was 80.6% for the 10 movements, 91.2% for the M01–M05 movements, and 70.0% for the M06–M10 movements. For the pocket data, the accuracy was 74.2% for the 10 movements. Compared to the chest data, the pocket data showed a significant decrease in the accuracy rate for the "Raising hands (M02)" and "Stretching (M06)" movements. These are upper body-driven body movements, similar to the motion detection results in Datasets 1 and 2. However, the detection accuracy for the upper body-driven motions, "Clapping (M02)," "Nodding (M04)," and "Resting an elbow on a desk (M09)," were almost the same as those of the chest data. The movements of M02 and M04 are continuous. In addition, even if the movements of the lower body are small, the specific frequency spectrum becomes large, and the characteristics of the movements are observed. In the "Resting elbow on a desk (M09)," a forward-leaning motion was included, and this movement is captured by gyro sensors in the experiment.

Table 2. Accuracy of classification of body movements classification in Dataset 1

| | | Prediction | | | | |
		M01	M02	M03	M04	M05
	M01	**1.00**	0.00	0.00	0.00	0.00
	M02	0.02	**0.96**	0.02	0.00	0.00
Input Data	M03	0.00	0.00	**1.00**	0.00	0.00
	M04	0.00	0.00	0.00	**1.00**	0.00
	M05	0.00	0.00	0.00	0.00	**1.00**

Table 3. Accuracy of classification of body movements classification in Dataset 2

		Prediction				
		M01	M02	M03	M04	M05
Input Data	M01	**0.98**	0.00	0.02	0.00	0.00
	M02	0.00	**0.84**	0.06	0.10	0.00
	M03	0.06	0.02	**0.90**	0.02	0.00
	M04	0.04	0.00	0.02	**0.94**	0.00
	M05	0.00	0.00	0.00	0.04	**0.96**

Table 4. Accuracy of classification of body movements in Dataset 3

		Prediction				
		M06	M07	M08	M09	M10
Input Data	M06	**0.74**	0.02	0.06	0.08	0.10
	M07	0.06	**0.86**	0.02	0.06	0.00
	M08	0.12	0.00	**0.62**	0.02	0.24
	M09	0.10	0.16	0.04	**0.68**	0.02
	M10	0.06	0.00	0.20	0.04	**0.70**

Table 5. Accuracy of body movements' classification in Dataset 4

		Prediction				
		M06	M07	M08	M09	M10
Input Data	M06	**0.52**	0.00	0.28	0.18	0.02
	M07	0.16	**0.72**	0.06	0.06	0.00
	M08	0.10	0.06	**0.76**	0.08	0.00
	M09	0.14	0.02	0.02	**0.80**	0.02
	M10	0.00	0.00	0.02	0.02	**0.96**

4 Facilitation System for Active Learning

4.1 Monitoring System

In this study, we developed a monitoring system that displays the measurement data of the smartphone sensors of the students, types of classified body movements from the measurement data, and facilitation contents based on the results. Figure 3 shows the

Table 6. Accuracy of body movements' classification in Dataset 5

		Prediction									
		M01	M02	M03	M04	M05	M06	M07	M08	M09	M10
Input Data	M01	**0.94**	0.00	0.00	0.00	0.00	0.00	0.00	0.00	0.00	0.06
	M02	0.02	**0.92**	0.00	0.00	0.00	0.00	0.00	0.04	0.00	0.02
	M03	0.00	0.00	**0.78**	0.00	0.02	0.10	0.00	0.00	0.04	0.06
	M04	0.00	0.00	0.00	**0.92**	0.00	0.02	0.02	0.02	0.02	0.00
	M05	0.00	0.00	0.00	0.00	**1.00**	0.00	0.00	0.00	0.00	0.00
	M06	0.00	0.00	0.02	0.00	0.04	**0.84**	0.00	0.04	0.06	0.00
	M07	0.00	0.00	0.02	0.02	0.00	0.10	**0.78**	0.04	0.00	0.04
	M08	0.00	0.02	0.02	0.04	0.00	0.18	0.08	**0.58**	0.00	0.08
	M09	0.00	0.00	0.02	0.00	0.02	0.16	0.02	0.08	**0.70**	0.00
	M10	0.02	0.00	0.20	0.00	0.00	0.04	0.08	0.04	0.02	**0.60**

Table 7. Accuracy of body movements' classification in Dataset 6

		Prediction									
		M01	M02	M03	M04	M05	M06	M07	M08	M09	M10
Input Data	M01	**0.94**	0.00	0.00	0.00	0.00	0.00	0.00	0.00	0.00	0.06
	M02	0.02	**0.88**	0.02	0.00	0.00	0.02	0.00	0.04	0.00	0.02
	M03	0.06	0.02	**0.58**	0.10	0.00	0.04	0.00	0.10	0.00	0.10
	M04	0.02	0.02	0.00	**0.86**	0.00	0.00	0.00	0.04	0.06	0.00
	M05	0.02	0.00	0.00	0.00	**0.92**	0.02	0.00	0.00	0.04	0.00
	M06	0.00	0.02	0.08	0.00	0.02	**0.50**	0.02	0.16	0.08	0.12
	M07	0.00	0.00	0.00	0.00	0.04	0.02	**0.92**	0.02	0.00	0.00
	M08	0.00	0.02	0.08	0.00	0.00	0.16	0.04	**0.54**	0.04	0.12
	M09	0.04	0.00	0.04	0.02	0.00	0.10	0.00	0.00	**0.78**	0.02
	M10	0.02	0.00	0.20	0.04	0.00	0.12	0.00	0.08	0.00	**0.54**

screen of the system. The IP address of the host computer is displayed at the upper left corner of the screen. The measured values are automatically displayed on the screen by entering this IP address in the measurement application on the smartphone and pressing the start button.

The ID of the terminal, measured data and analysis results, type of body movement classified, and content of the facilitation based on the results are displayed on the screen. The values displayed on the system screen represent the L2 norm of the acceleration sensor values for the three axes, which have been obtained through the Fourier transform of the values. Moreover, the system shows the results of the classification of body movements using the model developed in Sect. 3, and results of the facilitation based on these results.

In the accelerometer window, the latest 5 s of data are displayed, and these are updated every 0.5 s. Then, in the frequency analysis window, the frequency analysis of the acceleration data for the latest 3 s is displayed in the range of 0–30 Hz. The body movement window displays the results of the body movement classification with a confidence level of 0.0 to 1.0. Currently, the classification model of body movements is selected from several options based on the position and number of body movements (worn around the neck or in the pocket and 5 or 10 movements, respectively). In the final facilitation window, the specific facilitation content generated based on the results are displayed as texts.

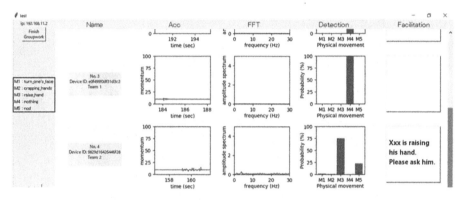

Fig. 3. Monitoring system

4.2 Prototype of Robot Facilitation System

The monitoring system can present facilitation contents to the teacher based on the body movements of the student. In this study, we also developed a facilitation robot (Softbank Robotics Nao) to present these facilitation contents.

The purpose of this system is to assist teachers in providing effective facilitation. The role of the robot and teacher facilitation in a class should be determined based on factors, such as the skill level of the teachers the strengths of both human and robot facilitation. However, at present, the following operation is suggested.

The teacher will either look around the classroom or observe each group from the podium during group work. At the time when facilitation is needed, such as when only one student is speaking, there are cases where facilitation is not provided in a timely manner. In that case, if the robot is be placed at each desk, it can provide immediately the necessary facilitation based on the estimated body movements. If a robot can perform facilitation as well as a teacher, more cases will be handled by the robot because of its time advantage.

However, it is difficult for robots to support discussions to create new ideas or interpret and summarize a series of conversations. In the future, it may be possible to achieve these tasks using a language model based on deep learning, but it is difficult to achieve this at present from the perspective of the processing speed. Therefore, teacher facilitation will be provided for such content.

Currently, two types of facilitation are implemented in this system: (1) facilitation that encourages those who raise their hands to speak and (2) facilitation that encourages those who do not participate in the discussion to join in. We assume that effective group work involves ensuring that all members participate in the discussion and implement these facilitations at first.

In the system, if the body movements of students are "Remaining stationary" for more than 30 s, the robot will say "Mr. XXX, how about you?" or when "Raise your hand" is detected, the robot will say "Mr. XXX, please". In addition to these facilitations, it is also possible to explain the contents of the group work or present cues for the start and end of the group work (Fig. 4).

Fig. 4. Facilitation by the communication robot

5   Conclusion

In this study, we developed a system that classifies the students' body movements using smartphone sensors and suggested facilitation to the teacher. We also developed a prototype of a robot facilitation system.

In future works, we will use not only the data obtained in the experimental environment but also the data obtained in the actual group work to investigate the necessary accuracy for practical classes. For the variation of facilitation, currently, several facilitations based on a single detected body movement have been implemented. To provide more facilitations in suitable situations, we will estimate the progress of the discussion based on the total movements of all group members and generate sequential facilitation for students. Moreover, we will improve the robot facilitation system to enable more natural facilitation, such as pausing for a moment to facilitate at the appropriate time.

Furthermore, we will introduce this system in the group work of the actual class and evaluate whether the facilitation content is effective or not for the teacher and students.

References

1. Springer, L., Stanne, M., Donovan, S.: Effects of small-group learning on undergraduates in science, mathematics, engineering, and technology: a meta-analysis. Rev. Educ. Res. **69**, 21–51 (1999)
2. Tanner, K., Chatman, L., Allen, D.: Approaches to cell biology teaching: cooperative learning in the science classroom—beyond students working in groups. Cell Biol. Educ. **2**, 1–5 (2003)
3. Freeman, S., et al.: Active learning increases student performance in science, engineering, and mathematics. Proc. Natl. Acad. Sci. U. S. A. **111**, 8410–8415 (2014)
4. Forsell, J., Forslund, F.K., Hammar, C.E., Hui, S.K.F.: Teachers' perceived challenges in group work assessment. Cogent Educ. **8**(1) (2021)
5. Yamamori, K., Ito, T., Nakamoto, K., Hagiwara, Y., Tokuoka, M., Oouchi, Y.: Recording elementary school students' academic engagement or on-task behavior using accelerometers. J. Sci. Educ. Technol. **41**(2), 501–510 (2018). (in Japanese)
6. Mathie, M., Celler, B., Lovell, N.: Classification of basic daily movements using a triaxial accelerometer. Med. Biol. Eng. Comput. **42**(5), 679–687 (2004)
7. Harada, N., Yamamoto, T., Miyake, Y.: Relationship between learning outcomes and communication behavior in active learning. Corresp. Hum. Interface **20**(9), 1–6 (2018). (in Japanese)
8. Watanabe, I., Yamamoto, T.: Relation between body movements and outcomes or communication quality of group work. Trans. Hum. Interface Soc. **23**(2), 201–208 (2021). (in Japanese)
9. Sakon, H., Yamamoto, T.: Body movements for communication in group work classified by deep learning. In: Kurosu, M. (ed.) HCII 2019. LNCS, vol. 11567, pp. 388–396. Springer, Cham (2019). https://doi.org/10.1007/978-3-030-22643-5_30
10. Hofmann, R., Mercer, N.: Teacher interventions in small group work in secondary mathematics and science lessons. Lang. Educ. **30**(5), 400–416 (2016)

A Multilevel Perspective for Social Innovation: Three Exemplary Case Studies in Collaborative Communities Toward Sustainability

Jing Wang[1]([✉]), Yunyun Weng[2], Mohammad Shidujaman[3], and Salah Uddin Ahmed[4]

[1] College of Design and Innovation, Tongji University, Shanghai, China
wangjing7733@tongji.edu.cn
[2] Hangzhou College of Childhood Teachers' Education Zhejiang Normal University, Zhejia, China
wengyunyun77@zjnu.edu.cn
[3] Department of Computer Science and Engineering, Independent University, Dhaka, Bangladesh
[4] School of Business, University of South-Eastern Norway, Kongsberg, Norway

Abstract. Social innovation research involves new ways of doing, organizing and seeking relationship-based collaboration in community so that it enhances the community resilience to adapt to environmental changes, and generate social and economic synergies dealing with unsustainable crises. In this paper, the authors draw on the MLP (Miltilevel Perspective) framework and focus on 3 cases to illustrate the characteristics of a sustainable society, and summarize the value advocacy of social innovation from the perspective of values in usage level, infrastructure level and governance level.

Through the case studies, the authors put forward the conceptual design supports social innovation. Understanding the social innovation from a cultural perspective is a human spirit and a culture of survival for the vulnerable. More importantly, a deep cultural structure needs to be found to support these marginalized networks (Design for social Innovation and Sustainability networks), to practice the solidarity economy. In Chinese Zen culture, such a kind of value proposition is advocated, and those who live in inferior positions can have the state of mind of living in heaven. Design is not just a practice of making things, it is a practice of changing the way designers and others think about a subject. Imagining, planning, and producing both material and immaterial things are expressions of these views. This paper revisits the definition of 'design' beyond a question of form and function and place the role of 'citizen-designer' in the front and center of society, where they drive the aestheticization of infrastructures and generate scenario-based designs following bottom-up needs of a community.

Keywords: Social innovation · Infrastructuring · Collaborative design · Aesthetics

M. Kurosu and A. Hashizume (Eds.): HCII 2023, LNCS 14014, pp. 366–391, 2023.
https://doi.org/10.1007/978-3-031-35572-1_25

1   Introduction

The environmental and economic problems we face today involve a society that is more humane, fairer, and most importantly less destructive to humans and nature. In designing a sustainable society, design can guide sustainability in practice can be evaluated by its attempt to respond to inclusivity, justice, care, resilience and community building.

From the perspective of China's Marxist economic theory, China's initial design policy reflects the government's design awareness: for example, sustainable product design, looking for green, environmentally friendly, and non-polluting materials. Design is not the mainstream of the economy, but a visual propaganda tool. However, such a design is only superficially sustainable. To some extent, just changing in form, doesn't really inspire a change in people's behavior. The design of sustainable products cannot be achieved through isolated and single products, it requires a kind of cultural operation. Gavin Melles proposed a list of practical criteria and believes that socially responsible design can be judged from the following criteria: 1) Does it meet the needs of the community? 2) does it create jobs for the community? 3) is the design result affordable locally and regionally? 4) Is the solution understood, controlled and maintained locally?

The current change is that the role of design has changed from endowing product styles to business innovation, industrial strategy, and even national competitiveness. In the study of designing for innovation, the concept of human-centered design breaks the traditional design framework and extends to technical, economic and social background. From a technological point of view, it means fundamental changes in materials, resources, processes and innovation methods. From a social perspective, the characteristics of network and intelligence, openness and integration, co-creation and sharing gradually form an inclusive, diverse and effective social environment; from an economic point of view, designers are strategic planners, committed to serving and creating social value in the era of knowledge.

To cite a typical case, for example, the MacArthur Foundation, as a non-profit public welfare organization, links enterprises, governments, and related institutions to form a systematic solution under a common vision and pushes the circular economy to an important agenda in the business, political, and academic circles. The emerging design culture has developed from a new product development process led by experts and professional brands to a leader in innovation activities. The practice of design has also been described as 'managing as design'. New relationships between design, innovation, and users, also described as promoting fundamental innovation through meaningful language, and technological application.

How to Understand the Concept of Citizen Designer? The author thinks that the market model can be used for reverse derivation. A market-based society characterized by individualism, materialism, privatization, short-termism, and a dogmatic focus on economic growth. It is focused on excessive consumption of natural resources and raw materials without regard to social and ecological values. This decades-long economic model has resulted in reduced biodiversity, environmental degradation, and the depletion of natural resources and raw materials. Civic relations or public relations replaces the dominant economic model by 1) questioning the current economic system, 2) demonstrating an appreciation for the values of public relations, including trust, collaboration, and (mutual) empowerment based on holistic view of human development.

The development of human being depends on sharing weal and woe with others, working and helping each other. Only in this way can we create a bright future belonging to society. The author believes that citizen designers need to consciously cultivate the following three important capabilities: firstly, aesthetic ability, which refers to having an appreciation for people, society, and all things; secondly, imagination, creativity, cognitive ability, which is the heart of human wisdom; and thirdly, empathy, which refers to understanding the feelings and behavior tendencies of others. At this level, it means that citizen designers have transcended some worldly troubles and be good at thinking about problems from the standpoint of the other people.

Our team member used to work as a health care program design manager in the Chinese Medicine hall in Shanghai. For many sub-health diseases, Chinese medicine provides a traditional and special treatment plan for example, Chinese Acupuncture therapy which carrying and delivering the thinking of Humanistic Care which is beneficial to the physical and mental development of people. There are many commonalities between Chinese medicine physiotherapy and Human-Centered Design. For example, the Five Elements theory of Chinese Medicine, regards the five substances: metal, wood, water, fire, and soil as the basic substances that constitute the universe. These five substances not only promote each other but also restrain each other (相生相克), forming a unity of opposites. Ancient Chinese philosophers used the theory of five elements to explain the formation of everything in the world, and describe the movement forms of things and their transformation relationships. The Five Elements Theory is the original system theory in ancient China. In this article, we propose a Human-Centered collaborative community approach, in which designers act as cultural intermediaries to integrate participatory design processes, such as social communication, discourse engagement, meaning construction and peer-to-peer connection, as emancipatory ethos, into the institutional practice.

The human-centered design is mainly reflected in the fact that we need to examine the value, the meaning from a systematic and holistic perspective. Value is generated through the creative recombination of resources. For example, coordinating the two major problems of excess waste and insufficient resources is an effective way to alleviate environmental pressure and expand resource stocks. People-oriented also refers to the concept of emphasizing individual freedom, human dignity, and personal value. At the same time, it is also emphasized that the system as an organic whole with certain functions formed by the connection of several elements in a certain structural whole. The objective of systemic design is to affirmatively integrate systems thinking and systems methods to guide human-centered design for complex, multi-system, and multi-stakeholder services and programs across society.

A valid question is, what is the ontological underpinnings of 'design'? The first and second author come from Design for social innovation and sustainability Network (Sustain X Laboratory, Shanghai). The Head of the Laboratory, advocated that creative problem-solving needs iterative experiment [1], and it (creative problem-solving) creates a social context for open and participatory innovation flow of social relations [2]. In this environment, Design practice is set as a social collaboration process of meaning, ideas and continuous negotiation to nurturing new socio-economic activities. Based on such research background, the author proposes a hypothesis that 'design', as a co-evolution socio-technical system, interacts with various factors in the process of social collaboration to achieve convergence of economic interests of multiple subjects.

In this article, we attempt to discuss the role of designers as cultural mediators, strategically approaching institutional actors, and addressing sensitive topics related to social exclusion. The position of participatory design is that participation is expected to happen anywhere, including public institutions in cities, private companies, grassroots advocacy groups. More recent understandings of design as 'infrastructuring' see design as a dynamic process through which publics coalesce and are maintained [3]. Furthermore, in its best guises, design creatively reframes complex problem spaces [4], offers ideas and possibilities in response to situations and develops infrastructures that enable collective action [5]. This is visible in movements such as social design [6], participatory design [7] and adversarial design [8]—each of which are developments with roots in Deweyan pragmatist and/or social democratic ideals [9].

Focus: This Research focuses on the intersection of SDG9 industry, innovation and infrastructure and SDG11 sustainable cities and communities among the 17 SDG goals proposed by the European Union in 2015 [10], and reports an community-based approach [11], enhance the community resilience to adapt to environmental changes, and generate social and economic mixed synergies.

1.1 The Aim of This Research

The aim of the research is to improve social value within the community and enhance community resilience. **Resilience (governance)** first appeared in the literature on climate change and ecosystem adaptation, originally known as the ability of a system to retain its properties after ecological disturbance [12], it is the ability of man-made and natural systems to respond to external shocks.

Although community resilience is a relatively new topic in design research, there has been research that contributes to social and ecological resilience, particularly in the area of design for sustainability, related issues including the cultures of resilience [13], design for relations and relational qualities [14], design and social-ecological diversity [15] , user empowerment [15].

Besides, resilience research is a topic that spans multiple interdisciplinary fields including ecology, psychology, public policy, and complex systems research. There are many analytical models for assessing resilience across disciplines, with some frameworks directed towards ecosystems and others applicable to social systems. This framework developed in this paper is applicable to human communities and surrounding ecosystems and aimed to observe how interventions can be designed to enhance social connections within communities, and foster collaborative engagement, enhance social capital.

The Research Purposes are as Follows

1. Exploring how to enhance ecosystem services to achieve sustainable goals [16], especially using new forms of organization and creating social networks, developing public interests [17];
2. In exploratory research activities, provide insights into a hybrid governance model for adaptive co-management, foster inclusive community dialogue, thus build consensus;
3. Placing the citizen-designer front and centre where they drive the aestheticisation of Infrastructures

1.2 Research Question

Before design was used as a tool to reveal social complexity, people have always viewed it as a tool for problem solving. However, in the last decade, people has tended to explore the modest role of design(er) in addressing social issues. For example, as revealing the relationship between complex social issues and advocated that design practice needs to open up new understandings of the relationship between people, communities, institutions and common practice as new research directions.

This Paper Focused on the Following Questions

1) What is social innovation? How to understand designing for Social Innovation ? (2.2 Social innovation and collaborative communities)
2) What are the characteristics of a sustainable society? (3.1 MLP Perspective Collaborative Community)
3) How does Design Thinking experiment with novel organizational forms to effectively connect people, places and resources? (5.1, 5.2, 5.3, Relational Assets and Social Capital)

2 Theoretical Background

2.1 Design for Sustainability

The famous Brundtland Report coined one of the most frequently cited definitions of sustainable development in 1987 as 'development that meets the needs of the present without compromising the ability of future generations to meet their own needs' [18]. Studies have shown that our theoretical understanding of the concept has evolved from a view that perceived sustainability as a static goal to a dynamic and moving target responding to our ever increasing understanding of interdependencies between social and ecological systems [19].

Ulm school of design pointed out that efficient use of natural resources and pass on the caring for the environment and residents convey a value of sustainability [20]. Victor

Papanek, points out the designers' responsibility in terms of social and environmental challenges [21]. Design attitude, is committed to collaboration with the most pressing challenges facing human society and the natural environment. Designing for Transformation is breaking down the big vision into small, achievable, autonomous actions. In Manzini's words, it is to actively initiate action to solve the problems of daily life [22] .

In china, design for sustainability is an environmentally friendly approach, and the formation of concepts is a long-term process that goes through three stages: The first stage is green design and ecological design. The deteriorating ecological environment and scarcity of natural resources force designers to respond to environmental issues; In the second stage, people's attitudes towards the natural environment have changed, not just as a source of resources, but as a habitat for survival. People as an organic element in the environment, actively participate in the construction of an ecologically harmonious environment; In the third stage, the issues in sustainable design are no longer just the harmony between human society and nature, but issues such as racial discrimination, marginalized groups, and imbalance between economic and environmental development are also included in the discussion.

In summary, achieving sustainability requires a process-based, multi-scale and systemic approach to planning for sustainability guided by a target/vision instead of traditional goal-based optimization approaches [12].

What is the Ontological Underpinnings of 'Design'?

In a broad sense, what is design? Buchanan proposes Design Four Orders, from the perspective of interaction, from symbols, object, actions and system which correspond to all stakeholders in the design process [23]. Symbols, as things that talk with people; Objects, as things a person interacts with; Actions, as groups of people and things in interaction; and Systems and environments, as groups of people and things in interaction with other groups of people and things [23]. Seen in isolation, these four parts are associated with fragmented design practices, but from a broader and interdependent perspective, a larger and organic whole can be seen. Therefore, the Design Four Orders is often used to reconstruct values of aesthetics in design. Dorst proposed the problem framework that plays a role in guiding and structuring design tasks throughout the design process [24], the co-evolution process of problem framing, solution, synthesis and evaluation is an iterative process, and recognizes the problem and solutions are in a state of dynamic changing and continuous improving states.

In China, Zou Qichang, systematically put forward design governance which outline the basic issues of social design, clarify the connotation of design governance that is related to norms, standards, interests, aesthetics, and quality [25]. Design governance as a good, reasonable and high-quality design, is the spiritual realm pursued by contemporary designers [25]. Domestic scholars believe that emphasizing the theory of meta-governance is more in line with China's national conditions. Based on a deliberation of complex society, it is difficult to achieve the optimal governance effect only by relying on the power of the state. At practical level, taking society as the orientation, gathering various social forces, participating in the management of public affairs which more effectively promote political civilization. In general, the definition of governance emphasizes that it is a process based on the coordination and interaction of multiple subjects, and special emphasis is placed on the important role of social negotiation in the design process. Brereton attributes good design to the success of the collaborative design process [26].

From the perspective of organization and culture, Kimbell proposed that design thinking is a general theory of design, organizational resources, and a framework for social and cultural transformation [27], Design Thinking as a Mindset and Attitude [28], the transformation is a broad and complex social learning process in which all mainstream old world ways of thinking and behaving are re-examined - from everyday life styles to wellbeing concepts [22].

2.2 Social Innovation and Collaborative Communities

What is social innovation? The author tries to support people in designing useful, usable, enjoyable, and meaningful products or services through the process of community design, program setting, and people-centered principles.

In the process, we further saw the difference between traditional design and emerging design. Traditional design usually focuses on the 'product', while emerging design focuses on a specific goal. In particular, it focuses on knowledge about humans and their interactions with the environment in order to produce products or services that meet their needs. A community-based innovation process that can be used to create and deliver a wide variety of solutions or proposals. Design outputs range from products to services, processes, organizational approaches, and even strategy and common governance process. A design output that satisfies the following requirements is considered as innovation:

1) The solution or suggestion is novel. The degree of novelty is considered as a continuum ranging from incremental to radical, and from discontinuous to continuous;
2) Provide value for potential stakeholders. Value includes two aspects, one is commercial value which is usually seen as the result of innovation in the public or social sector; the other is related to social and public value, such as improving service quality, enhancing trust, legitimacy and confidence in government;
3) Innovation is more than products and services. There must be a corresponding organization and system to put ideas into practice which involves designing an organization or system that can implement and disseminate solutions, including designing business models, agendas, strategies;

The purpose of social innovation is to improve economic or financial performance. But the economy here is not exactly synonymous with business. The essence of the economy is goods + service, in which 'good' implies a value orientation. In Chinese characters, Good (好) can be disassembled as '女' + '子'. In the context of Chinese, it implies a relationship of affiliation between parents and children. At the family or community level, that is, parents as guardians, or protectors, of their children. From the micro level to the macro level, that is, the national level, the children here refer to the people (citizens).

In traditional Chinese Confucianism, the ideology of governing the country holds that the people are the most important, the country is second, and the monarch is the least important. Confucianism advocates that human beings are inherently good at the beginning, and advocates benevolent government, and believes that the king should love his own people (citizen). In other words, it is to put the fundamental interests of the common people first. In such a situation, we can extend the understanding of 'good' into a kind of love, which is a kind of paternal love, maternal love, and friendly love at the micro level. On the macro level, it is the benevolence (仁爱) of the country to its people.

In popular language, social innovation refers to using the power of the social system to enhance the influence of the current technical system. In other words, let technological innovation better serve the society and improve the well-being of people's lives.

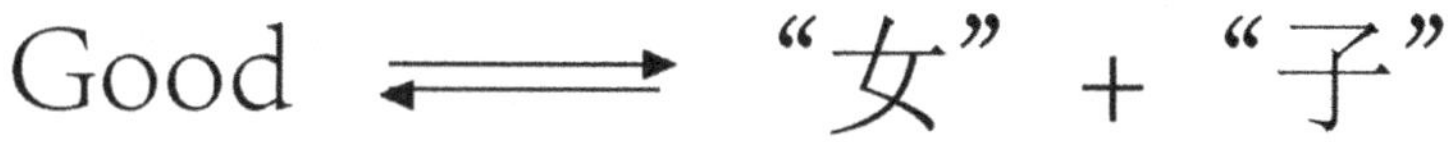

$$\text{Good} \rightleftharpoons \text{“女”} + \text{“子”}$$

Fig. 1. Good and Benevolence

Giddens proposes that traditional forms of society have disintegrated, a society in which modernity and individualized social processes have fully unfolded and society is represented as a fluid set of individuals [29]. Mulgan even used the term 'contemporary community 'to describe the emerging social form formed due to the wave of social innovation [30]. The social innovation group refers to the pioneering of new and relational practices and ways of doing things within existing social structures, heralding popular social forms. In social innovation design, a collaborative community is defined as a group of people who actively and voluntarily participate in social collaboration to provide solutions to current problems, such as social exclusion, business failure, depression, which are also called collaborative services [31].

Community resilience transforms adversity into personal, relational and collective growth by strengthening existing social engagement and developing new relationships through creative collective action. Community-based collaboration occurs when people meet, exchange resources, and create shared value. Community-based problem solving has several characteristics:

1) Transforming values into dynamic actions which achieve common expectations [22];
2) Prototype iteration as an innovative representation which link the expectations of different stakeholders [32], create dynamic collaborative network;

Community formation is a strategic design action that develop shared values and construct collective identity through open dialogue. Design-driven innovation create environment to form key interpreter network [33], which intertwined with relationship assets and foster people, ideas, information and resources to flow through network. Creative communities and collaborative networks that bring social capital and increase awareness of sustainability which help dispersed people gain power from the network, Manzini calls it a multi-local society [34]. In the process of multi-stakeholder dialogue, people's recognition of meaning does not stop at material design process, but to obtain some kind of spiritual well-being. Quality social connection refers to the community consciousness which create a sense of belonging and kinship between people [35].

2.3 Designer as the Culture Mediator: Commoning and Institutioning

Citizen designers refer to ordinary people who are in the position of bottom-up and actively participate in design decisions. The status quo of China's grassroots public sector affairs management faces the following challenges: low public participation; unsmooth channels for public participation; lack of participation mechanisms for social citizens; insufficient public participation capabilities and high participation costs. How to strengthen citizens' sense of responsibility and mobilize citizens' enthusiasm for active participation is an urgent problem to be solved.

Figure 1 shows the role of mediator capable of transferring the concepts from the bottom-down, integrating the resource to carry the new concepts from the bottom-up, and facilitate the practice of innovation [36]. In china, IDAC, the designer innovation design alliance, which plays the role of the new mediator (Fig. 2).

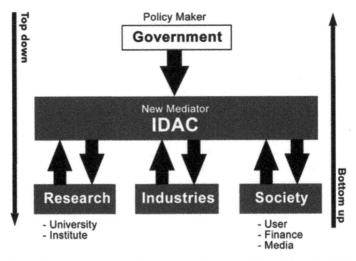

Fig. 2. Designer as the mediator (image Resource: Sylvia Xihui Liu [36])

In the context of this article, the role of designer focuses on action interventions as cultural mediators. The designer integrates the participatory design process into the institutional practice to promote the agenda of community cooperation, and transform the nature of the institution from the private to public form. Moore argues that the creation of public value depends on the expression of collective decisions and preferences mediated by politics [37]. The service ecosystem theory proposes that the participants and actors of public services do not passively consume public services, that is, the value cannot be pre-defined by service providers. Therefore, in collaborative design, how to make users active and equal contributors is a problem that needs to be considered. Social and cultural resources exist in visible and implicit ways, and novel art and cultural expressions play a role in infiltrating people's hearts in the management of public values. The paper put the citizen designer in prime positions to influence the aforementioned making of values from bottom-up.

3   Research Framework

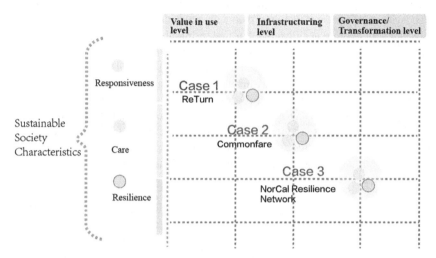

Fig. 3. Case Study Framework (Image Source: Adapted from Nicola Morelli Multilevel approach for social Transformations [38])

Value in Use Level. The purpose of social innovation is to promote more groups to reach consensus on public Common. As a meaning-driven strategy, designers usually bring stakeholders together through event-driven processes, such as workshops, co-analysis seminars to facilitate the process of open collaborative activities among different stakeholders. Design activities focus on the interaction between stakeholders involved in the service (Fig. 3).

Infrastructuring Level. Social transformation is a systemic innovation, and as a long-term process, it requires the cooperation of socio-technical infrastructure and social culture [39] changing the habits of practice [40]. Discussions related to infrastructure include the citizens' ability to participate [41], and the formation of the public [42]. Some authors believe that the purpose of infrastructure is to help ordinary citizens build communication skills in the complex design process [41], and develop tools for stakeholders in a community-based environment [43]. The concept of capabilities in infrastructure, based on Sen and Nussbaum, refers to individuals, groups, organizations or institutions that explore a set of predetermined issues, relationships, options and goals, thus the process of building capabilities.

Morgan [44] defines the concept of competence from the individual level, and subdivided the ability into soft skills and hard skills. Soft skills refer to relationship building, trust, and legitimacy; while hard skills are problem-solving techniques, logistical and project management skills. Friedman, from the perspective of designer, believes that competence generally refers to the designer's ability to be an analyst, synthesizer, generalist, leader, and critic [45].

Governance and Transformation Level. Design at this level focuses on an identity ecosystem of service elements that will make the solution replicable and scalable. Designers operate at this level that may bring about incremental or fundamental changes to the socio-technical environment surrounding services. Transformative Socio-Ecological Innovation (TSEI) requires collective action and effective multi-sector, and multi-level collaboration, as well as institutional change and new governance models that recognize the complexity of social-ecological systems. Focusing on social learning is broad and diverse governance research Part of the field. In addition, the community mentioned in this paper is not the same as the spatial location of the community, but the natural form of the community, and the healthy beliefs and behaviors of the residents who live in the community. This article focuses on investigating communities from cultural and social dimensions.

3.1 Case Selection

The three cases selected by the authors are ReTuren, Commonfare and NorCal resilience network. These three cases have similarities and differences. The commonality is mainly reflected in the social economy of solidarity, and the differences are mainly reflected in the development scale. For example, ReTuren in Malmö, Sweden is a local project to develop a public value management in Malmö, Sweden; Commonfare is developing pilot projects in three countries, connecting people facing difficulties through digital platforms to develop a solidarity economy; The Norcal resilience network is a cross-regional alliance, interacting with organizations, groups, and institutions, and responding to challenges with collective wisdom;

The authors chose these three cases for the following reasons: first, the case has a clear value proposition, embody the human-centered design, and have significance for the theory of sustainable design; second, the cases embodied the characteristics of innovative design, namely green and low-carbon, networking, intelligence, openness and integration, and co-creation and sharing [46].

The purpose of the case analysis is to answer the following questions: If the community is regarded as an ecosystem composed of many project pilots, then in such an ecosystem, what are the social values advocated in the community? Which groups is this community responsible for? What are the positive impacts of current actions on design policy? (Fig. 4)

3.2 Analysis Framework

Designer as the Culture Mediator: Commoning and Institutioning. This paper uses two analytical coding techniques: (1) an formal systematic approach; (2) an informal systematic approach; In a formal systematic approach, the author draws on a scaf-fold that fourth order design which was proposed by Richard Buchanan focused on the way in which designers work and how they take accountability for the success(or failure)of their actions. Culture and community are the subject matter of fourth order design.

Case Name	Brief Description	Reason for choice
ReTuren (waste prevention[47])	In the public sector, organizing social material and cultural practices, managing public values;	This case breaks through traditional waste management and develops public services for waste upgrading through collaboration with multiple stakeholders;
Commonfare Digital Platform https://commonfare.net /en	Focus on heterogeneous groups of people in daily life, and organize people around the problems through the network;	This case is a shift from identifying the needs of users to recognizing the values of the participants, not only focusing on people's participation, but also to their knowledge, abilities, values and relationships
NorCal Resilience Network https://norcalresilience. org/	The Resilience Center allocates resources, coordinates mutual aid networks, and exchanges information during a disaster;	The case is an action-oriented way of doing things, developing real community-to-community synergy

Fig. 4. Reasons for Case Selection

When applying design methods to environmental issues include: 1) why are we doing this task? 2) What does it tell us about our identity and value? The authors gather empirical material from several sources reviewing the entire case, and gain an insight into the infrastructuring process and community based approach which create a contextual understanding of the ongoing case [48]. The informal sys-tematic approach, is an immersive and deeply reflective approach which is a more creative technique [49], related to the researcher's interest in the study. Furthermore, when processing the base material, the authors borrowed a software application (www.wordle.net) to extract the words that occur frequently in the text data and gen-erate a word cloud (Fig. 5).

4 Case Analyzing

4.1 Case1: ReTuren

4th Order of Design (Environments): The Public sector innovation—ReTuren Project, originated in the 1990s, when the public sector in Europe (Sweden), inspired by the market model, reflected on the inflexibility and economically inefficient of the existing system. In response, a new approach and ideas for managing as public values emerged. This new approach to public value management emphasizes the importance of maintaining ongoing dialogue and interaction between public institutions, citizens and other social actors. In this process, the new institution complements, rather than replaces, the old institution [50]. (For more details see Anna Seravalli [47, 51]).

3th Order of Design (Activities & Services): ReTuren is an upcycling station in the neighbourhood of Lindängen in Malmö, Sweden, a place where citizens can dispose

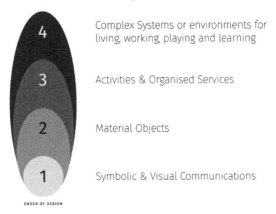

Fig. 5. Four orders of design drew by Sam Rye (Image Source: Buchanan, R. (1992) Wicked Problems in Design Thinking [23], https://kanopi.gitbook.io/mdes-exegesis/appendices/fourth-order-design)

hazardous and cumbersome waste, exchange things in good condition. As a public service for waste production conceived by the municipal government and jointly developed by local citizens, makerspaces, community, and the new service including local trading systems, such as social enterprises, voluntary social welfare services. Co-production is part of a wider discussion, including user practices, markets, policies, regulations, culture, infrastructure, lifestyles and corporate governance. This type of new public service demonstrates structure and openness, where people embrace uncertainty and possibility. Human diversity is the basic condition of action and language, and has the dual characteristics of equality and distinction. Because of the diversity, there is a debate about what is 'good'. The key is to recognize and acknowledge these controversies, which is also a kind of progress. In addition, in the process of interaction, people become very sensitive to issues of identity, origin, belonging and even ethnicity. Due to the limited space of the article, it is not included in the scope of discussion.

2th Order of design (Material Objects): ReTurn organizing public events for prototyping includes fixing bikes, upcycling furniture, remaking old textiles, fixing broken electronics, and more. The role of the design researcher, participate in the running of the scheduling service, and facilitate the shared learning process which also developed the ability to interact with citizens and collaborate with different social actors. Material and activity design methods have also been identified as important for building trust among the businesses, the public sector and communities [52], which makes these relationship of interdependencies visible and create a common understanding among groups of people. Various materials and activities serve as a culture medium to building empathy and foster positive relationships among all participants in the network [53].

1th Order of Design (Visual Communications): Open seminars are held regularly every month to evaluate ongoing public activities and gradually perfect the rules and regulations of waste disposal. Graphic designers create expressions of low-carbon living

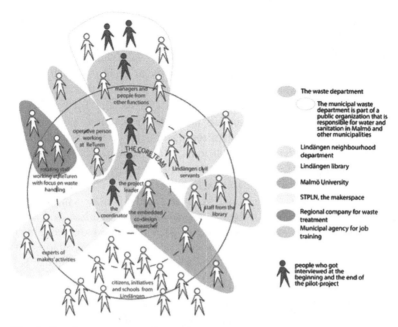

Fig. 6. Sweden waste prevention project (Image Source: Design in public [47])

art, such as food and green space, local economy and welfare and mapping the organizational structure diagram, such as PR and communication, Resource and Finance. The project report also noted that current technological, organizational, and metacultural frameworks often limit the development of public capacity [47]. However, According to huybrecht [54],participatory design cannot dilute the institutional framework, such as government agencies, legal agencies, regulatory agencies. The core idea of this theory advocates an adaptive co-management and governance model aimed at social learning and collective change as a response to complexity and uncertainty [55].

4.2 Case 2: Commonfare Solidarity Network Platform

4th Order of Design (Environments): The European welfare state model cannot cover a wide range of social groups. Nearly 25% of the European population is not covered by state social benefits. In the Netherlands, up to 50% of people are flexible workers, such as temporary contractors or the self-employed. This is a huge group, and they cannot obtain a stable economic income. In order to close the gap in social welfare, people are rebuilding distributed solidarity mechanisms. Commonfare, a digital economy platform, regards social cooperation as a common good. The 'commons' is a form of participatory welfare provision based on cooperation between people. Common Welfare, as a participatory form of welfare delivery, is a civic platform for people living in Europe to develop new ways to collectively deal with the dilemmas and challenges they face and improve their own lives.

3th Order of Design (Activities & Services): The digital collaboration platform serves for the people at risk of material deprivation or social exclusion, such as the young unemployed, precarious workers, welfare recipients [56]. 'Affordance' as an important design tool that creates meaningful and active roles for socially disadvantaged groups, fostering connections in personal support networks. In addition, the designer is also considering how to design a Trust **(Institutioning)** to connect small and micro enterprise in the dominion. In this process, digital tools, as a medium, are exploring a path to address the challenges of fragmented global landscapes. The specific characteristics of sustainable lifestyles are: low growth, exchange networks, eco-communities, sharing resources, and social engagement. At the same time, it also considers the reuse of spaces that have not been reused within the city (such as urban, suburban, and rural areas), emphasizing the preservation of local identities, and cultivating and celebrating regional characteristics. The goal of the service is to build a global innovative platform based on participation, self-management, solidarity and respect for nature and human beings.

2th Order of Design (Material Objects): In order to facilitate the flow of public goods and wealth such as information, emotions and resources, the project structure includes a trust promotion system (Commonshare) and a digital supplementary currency (Commoncoin), which assists communities and groups to create their own digital currencies (As shown in Fig. 6).

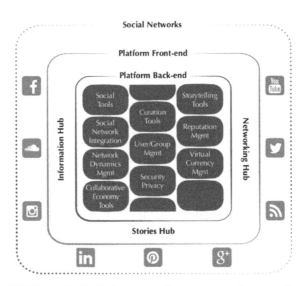

Fig. 7. PIE New technological approach (Image source: Francesco Botto [57])

1th Order of Design (Visual Communications): Commonfare story Hub has created various toolkits (Fig. 6) , such as storytelling tools, reputation mgmt, virtual currency mgnt etc, facilitating a Narrative Based on the Sharing Economy. On the one hand, it focuses on social innovation, that is, to create more sustainable economic and environmental models; on the other hand, Commonfare's website design reflects people's desire to connect with each other to achieve solidarity among peers, which achieved through the following modules:

1) Create and share stories of personal and collective experiences;
2) Create groups around interests;
3) Communicating directly between Commonfare participants via private messages, stories are created and shared to foster mechanisms of mutual solidarity;

Commonfare network platform represent a complex combination of digital, material, social, and informational entities. In most cases, learning environments are highly heterogeneous, with networks of multiple institutions and individual actors. The platform empower actors participating in the network. The concept of empowerment has some pre-set prerequisites, which vary according to different cultural backgrounds, regions, social classes, and group concepts. According to Avelino [58], empowerment is defined as the process by which actors mobilize the capacity and willingness acquire resources to achieve goals; Dispower refers to the process by which an actor loses the ability and willingness; The social resources condensed by the platform include persons, assets, materials or capital, including human, spirit, currency, artifacts and natural resources [58]. The process of networked learning involves the co-configuration of heterogeneous tasks, activities, roles, relations, artifacts and spaces. Its advantage is that it is not limited by time and geographical location, and connects people and resources to facilitate the process of knowledge sharing. The rise of the platform economy has impacted many policy areas, and its novel features make it particularly well-suited for deploying collaborative decision-making and creating new ways of experimenting with policy co-creation.

4.3   Case 3: NorCal Resilience Network

4th Order of Design (Environments): In a world of constant disasters, The NorCal Resilience Network is a grassroots coalition to activate and support community-based, nature-inspired solutions to climate change, economic instability and social inequality in Northern California.

3th Order of Design (Activities & Services): The mission of this Network is to catalyze a Just Transition to an equitable and regenerative region by supporting and activating community-based and ecological solutions. The five Components of resilience hubs are as follows:

1) Resilience Services and Programming. Services and relationships that promote community well-being and resident health. Examples include community garden days, disaster preparedness discussion sessions, water harvesting skills sharing.
2) Resilient Communication; Examples include door-to-door strategies for building relationships inside and outside the service area and connecting community members during times of disaster.
3) Resilient Buildings and Landscape; Refers to examples of solutions that meet operational objectives under seismic conditions, such as seismic retrofits, energy efficiency, greywater and stormwater harvesting systems.

4) Resilient Power; Ensure facilities are provided with electricity, such as solar power, backup batteries and generators, during a disaster.
5) Resilient Operations; Distributing food and other emergency supplies during disasters, coordinating mutual aid networks, and disaster preparedness supplies, etc.

2th Order of Design (Material Objects): The resilience hubs model (See Fig 7) shifts power to neighborhoods and residents while prioritizing their development in Black, Indigenous, and people of color communities that affected by marginalization. Resilience Hubs and spaces providing regular culturally appropriate programming for community members, from workshops to gatherings and promote resource sharing; Regenerative Ecological Features, such as no or low-VOC paints, green cleaning products, rainwater catchment, drip irrigation, solar panels, electric cars and so on; Disaster preparedness and response, for example, A robust supply of water, food and supplies on hand for earthquakes and other disasters (Fig. 8).

Fig. 8. Resilient Hubs Model (Image source: https://norcalresilience.org/)

1th Order of Design (Visual Communications): The vision of the Resilience Hubs Initiative is to create a network of community centers, neighborhoods, schools, parks, churches, and other trusted community sites that are models for resilience. The practice of resilience as a form of common-based peer production, based on collaboration among large numbers of individuals, open access to information and resources, and open innovation tools. More importantly, it is necessary to create virtual visual experiments, so that these ideas can be seen by more people. The concept of resilience is a process of learning and adapting to more positively address current challenges in a resourceful way.

5   Findings

5.1   Designing at the Value in Use Level: Social Relations as Object for Design

Social designer has a double meaning, the first meaning includes care-oriented design activities aimed at improving the well-being of disadvantaged groups, such as the poor, the elderly, and the disabled; The second meaning refers to a social formation that the way society is constructed to facilitate the interaction between individuals and groups.

The designer's social and environmental awareness lies in the fact that the designer first realizes the awakening of the sense of responsibility to apply his ability to social services, and develops the corresponding ability to solve current problems. Design ability is mainly reflected in three aspects: 1) Understanding 2) Transforming 3) Communication (Fig. 9).

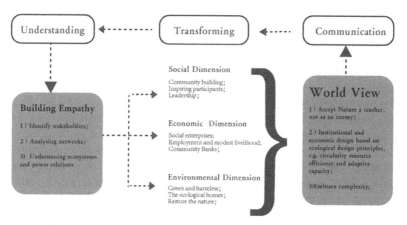

Fig. 9. Design competences at three Dimension for sustainability

Understanding: Issues related to understanding involve Identify stakeholders; understanding power relations; and analyzing the motivations of stakeholders. In particular, designer need to use a more holistic perspective to embrace cultural diversity participants in the social network. Participatory design engages multiple stakeholders and acts as a design material that is drawn into cultural attributes, aligning participants around a common problematic situation. Constructed through an iterative process and design approach, which served as a co-design framework, facilitating discussions of collective governance, experimentalism, and technological justice. Although in this open process, the stakeholders contribute to innovation in the public sector which can also be contentious or cause conflict as stakeholders may have different (and possibly conflicting) needs and interests. Coordinated action is a rather delicate process that can be fraught with conflict and ambiguity. In some cases, it is difficult to reach a consistent agreement among stakeholders.

Transforming: The ability to transform can be discussed from three dimensions. The social dimension mainly refers to the ability to build a community, such as building a healthy community resource center; The environmental dimension refers to creating an environment for social innovation (social change), which can be learned from some experiences in Africa, such as informal burial associations. In rural areas of Africa, there exist a self-organizing association giving a decent funeral to loved ones and practicing humanitarian care; Finally, it is the economic dimension, training social entrepreneurs, building community equity loans, and creating community-based jobs through business model innovations. The main difference between traditional design thinking and systemic design thinking is that stakeholders are the designers of social innovation systems. The outcomes proposed in the case study aimed to benefit both the environment and people engaged in the system, improving the current waste system to recover organic waste in general waste streams.

Communication: Design is a way of communicating that thinks about the connection between the individual and the world of design. It starts with a clear attitude, seeing nature as a teacher, not an enemy. The purpose of the communication is to achieve a shared vision, e.g., an innovative institution that brings together research, business, and the community to create a post-carbon economy and develop low-carbon products and services. What are the techniques of design in the communication phase? Adopt a vision-driven design method to generate visual solutions and formulate a vision for a low-carbon community. The vision lies in recognizing the value of time, transcending objective and subjective paradigms, and seeing time as a mechanism for social synergy.

In the initial stage of communication, irreconcilable contradictions are prone to appear due to the difference in cultural background and metacultural framework. The author borrows the metaphor of water, water is originally a natural resource, only through the interaction with people, it gradually becomes a cultural resource. In the process of transforming from natural resources to cultural resources, a tradition of maintaining common resources is gradually formed, and this transformation is usually completed in the dimension of time.

Designing for sustainability has an implication that we must push people to reflect on their daily lives [59]. We should design for the perception of meaning, design aesthetic sensitivity, and sustainable lifestyle changes. Parsons sees thorny issue as an advantage, explaining why a certain degree of redundancy is important for public organizations to be able to cope with complex contexts and innovate [60]. He uses the spare tire as an analogy, if organizations operate without any spare tires, those organizations inherently lack any robustness and fail to adapt to changing conditions or unexpected events. Spare capacity raises important issues related to innovation which providing basis for the space for people to try, play, experiment, explore new ideas and question existing ways of thinking [60]. The principle of community engagement creates a space away from the existing hierarchy. Participants are encouraged to co-create or repair objects, express individual and collective ideas through material method in the public space.

5.2   Designing at the Infrastructure Level: Digital Platforms as Civic Care Facilities

1) Civic Care Infrastructure: Inequality, social exclusion and social exploitation are a long-standing phenomenon in our society. The union of the Internet and infrastructure opens up new possibilities for a more just and equitable future. Digital platform is the basis for a product, technology or service developed by a company. Jegou and Manzini define digital platforms that Membership within a platform that prioritizes mutual accountability and commitment is a caring facility [61]. For example, in the case of Commonfare, volunteers are recruited to monitor the flow of creeks and rivers, and provide water collection services for families, businesses, and schools; The technical means recorded the steps involved in making community rain garden prototype, annotate the geographic location of specific practices in different communities, and share them with communities in other watersheds; As the organizer, the designer uses the sustainable living camp as the carrier to teach people to perceive and create positive changes through Appreciative Inquiry (AI) and open dialogue.

2) Unique ways of design meet special or basic needs of people: Herbert Simon proposed that designers have a unique way of solving problems [64], and believed that designers can contribute to organizational competitiveness. Care-driven design activities aim to increase the wellbeing of those who are underprivileged. The basic idea is not to design for the (more or less) wealthy consumer, but to see design as a specific way to meet the special or basic needs of people who somehow are disadvantaged, vulnerable, or marginalized.

3) Network: As a civic care facility, digital platforms connect people, resources and needs of different groups through technological means. The role of design in it includes: providing citizens with non-commercial caring space, which is mainly caring for the natural environment. **Technology-based solution** has become indispensable to the functioning of a society and the quality of life of its citizens. Commonfare is a process of commons, communing, as processes of collective experimentation, learning and organizing that emphasis on informal cooperation between citizens [62, 63].

4) Place Making: In addition, design at the infrastructure level emphasizes the importance of local culture. Designers cooperate with local government departments to jointly develop cooperation models and produce Public Good. Places are regarded as important places for shaping social identity and cohesion.

What are the main functions of the infrastructure? For example, organizing entrepreneurship training work; making innovation support scales; enhance the use of design management and technical practices to improve innovation process; support diversified cultural norms; develop organizational innovation climate assessment scales (Fig. 10).

5) Social Capital: Social design is related to the way people construct social forms which brings about sustainable social changes, or solutions for new social forms and economic models, reducing the impact on the environment. In the case of ReTuren which is based on a social process of collaborative learning, involving organizational staff, project managers, civil servants and regional companies. Social capital as the quality/number of relationships and networks that can be mobilized for personal benefit or better cooperation in society [64]; Social capital, in a sense, is a movement, or a form of organization. Through community debate, designers strategically initiate dialogue, designing perceptions and experiences, and form coalitions.

6) Community Norms: Generally speaking, social design usually injects design thinking into organizations to improve the quality of public services. Social design in the

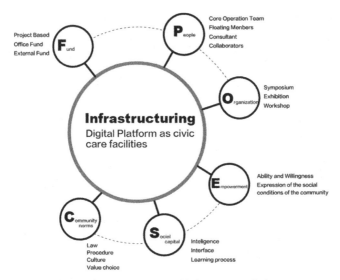

Fig. 10. Concept map of infrastructure design

public sector, as a new approach to public value management embodied in institutional aspects, including law, procedure, organization, culture, social challenges, and interactions between actors [50]. The responsibility of designers is not only to connect the industry and the market, but even influence the value choice (Community Norms) in community. Supported by design methodologies, tools, and techniques, design thinking can significantly improve public/nonprofit organization problem-solving processes and innovation strategies.

7) Empowerment: In the process of managing common resources, empowerment is usually based on the expression of the social conditions of the community [65]. The author believes that empowerment is not only a sociopolitical concept, but also a psychological concept. It is important to create an environment in the community, cultivate the ability and willingness to mobilize resources, and strengthen the belief that people can overcome current challenges. In addition, The focus on the long-term, sustainability of the platform is critical. Sustainability should not be taken for granted. Rather, it should be a long-term process of hard work, especially through the coalition of institutions to promote the formalization of a common resource model.

5.3 Designing at Governance and Transformation Level: Inclusive Learning Process

The purpose of thinking about ontology of design is to think about whether the world can be governed in some way. Ontological commitments to resilience, emphasizing the neolibreal form of governmentality that emphasizes individual adaptability to survive in the uncertainty of complex systems.

The author introduces the definition of resilience from the Resilience Alliance, which refers to the ability of a system to absorb disturbances, undergo changes, and maintain the same basic functions, structures, identities, and feedbacks [66]. Psychological resilience refers to the ability of individuals to stimulate their potential and become stronger to successfully cope with environmental pressure when they encounter adversity, trauma, grief, threats or major life stress events. Resilience is also an effective psychological resource for individuals to cope with setbacks and stress. A healthy and complete ecosystem is composed of a social system and an ecological system, and the impact of the human system on the natural system is completed through the interaction between them. In terms of improving the efficiency of the ecosystem, if the intervention is top-down, there will be some short-term benefits, but in the long-term, it will weaken the resilience.

The radical inclusive design is consistent with the plural ontology theory proposed by Arturo Escobar [67], which studies the interaction of ecological resilience and human adaptation in complex large-scale systems. The design approach is aimed to enable the ecological, social, human and non-human in a mutually reinforcing manner to produce mutually nourishing condition. The ability to bounce back of an individual/community is a process of continuous learning and adaptation. Each Actor has its own intrinsic (Nature) pursuit and driving force, and adapts to the ever-changing environment through learning, planning, and reorganization. An inclusive practice creates a world that respects and welcomes differences. Allowing for diverse viewpoints, heterogeneous voices and spaces for dissent and even conflict [68]. This approach views design as an inter-constitutive process where the relationships between things (including the designer) are as important as the things themselves. In actual practice process, it is important to keep the openness of the ontology that is based on recognizing the existence of the different worlds we inhabit, but which can be bridged by design experiences that constitute one another—a kind of Thoroughly inclusive design.

6 Discussion and Conclusion

Manzini defines social design as design that deals with problematic situations, such as extreme poverty, disease, or social exclusion, as well as design after catastrophic events. Margolin extended the scope of social design to the design of a good society, including the design of social institutions. Although there are various emerging interpretations of social design, it is generally accepted that its main driving value is the public good or common good, sometimes expressed as the concept of social good or good society. Therefore, promoting the common good is the ultimate goal of social design [69].

The Research Leads to Four Key Principles of Designing for Social Innovation and Sustainability

Principle 1: As a situated process, local is an important place for knowledge production through experiential practice. Collaboratively produced through participatory design methods, co-define local context of resilience with potential users, and explore the needs of the local environment for tools and create opportunities to share locally developed knowledge;

Principle 2: As a mediated process, understand local needs for resilience, and build connections with local communities over time, and intervene in local contexts. This is a knowledge space developed through local experimentation. These communities of practice provide the opportunity to investigate practice and process as subject and object of co-design [70], and keeping the process open to allow new communities and practices to join;

Principle3: As a network-related process [71], Through participatory design, facilitating connections between different groups. Networks serve as means of knowledge production to managing connectivity for maintaining resilience within systems.

Principle 4: As an open source process, all knowledge and means of production are recognized as collective ownership. The knowledge produced is passed back to the community in which they emerged and made accessible to other users, maintaining ongoing knowledge production. This process builds on the New Commons movement [72] and is seen as a pathway to new production, use and governance of shared urban resources.

Design thinking has always called for human-centered design. This problem can be broken down into the understanding of people and the cognition of human nature. Human beings are not so much a static attribute as a kind of men, nature and technology emerging from the interaction. The behavior of humans to predict, transform and adapt to the environment, in turn, shapes humans.

6.1 Barriers and Opportunities

The principles of design for sustainability are very simple, such as people-oriented, strengthening interpersonal relationships, embrace diversity, etc. The principles are universal, but specific to different cultural context, the applicability is questionable. Especially when the designer does not live in the community, there are many mistakes in understanding the local customs and community rules.

In daily life, although everyone has a kind heart, the process of building empathy is specific design actions and practices. This article draws some preliminary conceptual designs, detail proposals, and function lists through case study. For more detailed functional simulation and prototype design, it is necessary to take root in a specific community, carry out concrete actions, and acquire local knowledge.

The authors of the paper speculate that the obstacles in advancing the research plan mainly include the following aspects:

1. Difficulty in understanding power relationship in communities/organizations. Whether the cultural atmosphere in an organization is a bottom-up grassroots innovation culture or a top-down hierarchical bureaucracy? The root of this problem is that different organizations have different attitudes towards power, that is, does the organization conquer people with spirit or power? What is the overall cultural ethos?
2. The preconditions of any communities/organizations are different. How do designers find the leverage characters that serve as cultural mediators reconciling diversity and difference?
3. In specific practice, mistakes are tolerated. But there is an overlooked premise here, that is, what is already assumed to be correct. The authors believe that such assumptions need to be examined. In Chinese Zen culture (禅宗文化), such a kind of value

proposition is advocated, and those who live in inferior positions can have the state of mind of living in heaven (当下就是天堂).

The authors believe that human nature has the ability to love, to connect, to have a sense of worth, to be independent, and to have a sense of security. In the discourse system of Chinese Buddhism, it is called pure and good quality.

References

1. Lou, Y., Ma, J.: Growing a community-supported ecosystem of future living: the case of NICE2035 living line. In: Rau, PL. (eds.) CCD 2018. LNCS, vol. 10912, pp. 320–333. Springer, Cham (2018). https://doi.org/10.1007/978-3-319-92252-2_26
2. Lou, Y.: Designing interactions to counter threats to human survival. She Ji J. Des. Econ. Innov. 4(4), 342–354 (2018)
3. Hansson, K., Forlano, L., Choi, J.H.: Provocation, conflict, and appropriation: the role of the designer in making publics. Des. Issues 34(4), 3–7 (2018)
4. Dorst, K.: The core of 'design thinking' and its application. Des. Stud. 32(6), 521–532 (2011)
5. Le Dantec, C.A.: Designing Publics. MIT Press, Cambridge (2016)
6. Margolin, V., Margolin, S.: A social model of design: issues of practice and research. Des. Issues 18, 24–30 (2002)
7. Björgvinsson, E., Ehn, P., Hillgren, P.-A.: Agonistic participatory design: working with marginalised social movements. CoDesign 8(2–3), 127–144 (2012)
8. Disalvo, C.: Adversarial design (2012)
9. Disalvo, C.: Design and the construction of publics. Des. Issues JSTOR 25(1), 48–63 (2009)
10. Transforming our world Agenda Sustainable Development 2030 EngFreSpa AEL 151004
11. Andrade, Á., Córdoba, R., Dave, R.: Draft principles and guidelines for integrating ecosystem-based approaches to adaptation in project and policy design: a discussion document. Turrialba Costa Rica (2011)
12. Holling, C.S.: Resilience and stability of ecological systems. Annu. Rev. Ecol. Syst. 4(1), 1–23 (1973)
13. Manzini, E.: Cultures of resilience: a cosmopolitan localism (2014)
14. Cipolla, C., Manzini, E.: Relational services. Knowl. Technol. Policy 22(1), 45–50 (2009)
15. Cantù, D.: "Ideas sharing LAB". Co-designing multifunctional services with local food communities (2012)
16. Costanza, R.: Valuing natural capital and ecosystem services toward the goals of efficiency, fairness, and sustainability. Ecosyst. Serv. 43, 101096 (2020)
17. Collier, S.J., Mizes, J.C., Von Schnitzler, A.: Preface: public infrastructures/infrastructural publics. Limn 7 (2016)
18. Bruntland, G.: World commission on environment and development. Our Common Future (1987)
19. Ceschin, F., Gaziulusoy, I.: Evolution of design for sustainability: from product design to design for system innovations and transitions. Des. Stud. 47, 118–163 (2016)
20. Martin, A.: Diseño sustentable (2009). Recuperado de. http://foroalfa.org/articulos/diseno-grafico-sustentable
21. Papanek, V., Fuller, R.B.: Design for the Real World. Thames and Hudson, London (1972)
22. Manzini, E.: Design, when everybody designs: an introduction to design for social innovation (2015)
23. Buchanan, R.: Wicked problems in design thinking. Des. Issues JSTOR 8(2), 5–21 (1992)
24. Dorst, K., Cross, N.: Creativity in the design process: co-evolution of problem–solution. Des. Stud. 22(5), 425–437 (2001)

25. Sampsa, H., Marttila, T., Perikangas, S.: Codesign for transitions governance: a mid-range pathway creation toolset for accelerating sociotechnical change. Des. Stud. **63**, 181–203 (2019)
26. Brereton, M.F., Cannon, D.M., Mabogunje, A.: Analysing Design Activity. John Wiley, Chichester (1996)
27. Kimbell, L.: Rethinking design thinking: Part I. Des. Cult. **3**(3), 285–306 (2011)
28. Michlewski, K.: Design Attitude. Gower Publishing, Ltd. (2015)
29. Giddens, A.: The consequences of modernity 1990 (2007)
30. Mulgan, G., Tucker, S., Ali, R.: Social innovation: what it is, why it matters and how it can be accelerated. Skoll Centre Social Entrepreneurship (2007)
31. Meroni, A., Sangiorgi, D.: A New Discipline. Gower Publishing Limited (2011)
32. Sanders, L., Stappers, P.J.: From designing to co-designing to collective dreaming: three slices in time. Interactions **XXI** (2014)
33. Verganti, R.: Design Driven Innovation: Changing the Rules of Competition by Radically Innovating What Things Mean. Harvard Business Press (2009)
34. Manzini, E.: Design research for sustainable social innovation. Des. Res. Now, 233–245 (2007)
35. Huijnen, C.A.G.J., Ijsselsteijn, W.A., Markopoulos, P.: Social presence and group attraction: exploring the effects of awareness systems in the home. Cognit. Technol. Work **6**(1), 41–44 (2004)
36. Liu, S.X., Liu, H., Zhang, Y.: The new role of design in innovation: a policy perspective from China. Des. J. **21**(1), 37–58 (2018)
37. Moore, M.H.: Creating Public Value: Strategic Management in Government. Harvard University Press (1995)
38. Morelli, N., De Götzen, A.: A multilevel approach for social transformations and its implications on service design education. Des. J. **20**(sup1), S803–S813 (2017)
39. Geels, F.: Co-evolution of technology and society: the transition in water supply and personal hygiene in the Netherlands (1850–1930)—a case study in multi-level perspective. Technol. Soc. **27**(3), 363–397 (2005)
40. van de Kerkhof, M., Wieczorek, A.: Learning and stakeholder participation in transition processes towards sustainability: methodological considerations. Technol. Forecast. Soc. Change **72**(6), 733–747 (2005)
41. Huybrechts, L., Dreessen, K., Hagenaars, B.: Building capabilities through democratic dialogues. Des. Issues **34**(4), 80–95 (2018)
42. Dantec, C., Disalvo, C.: Infrastructuring and the formation of publics in participatory design. Soc. Stud. Sci. **43**, 241–264 (2013)
43. Pipek, V., Wulf, V.: Infrastructuring: toward an integrated perspective on the design and use of information technology. J. AIS **10** (2009)
44. Baser, H., Morgan, P.: Capacity, change and performance: study report (2008)
45. Friedman, K.: Theory construction in design research: criteria: approaches, and methods. Des. Stud. **24**(6), 507–522 (2003)
46. Den Ouden, E.: Innovation Design: Creating Value for People, Organizations and Society. Springer, London (2012). https://doi.org/10.1007/978-1-4471-2268-5
47. Seravalli, A., Upadhyaya, S., Ernits, H.: Design in the public sector: nurturing reflexivity and learning. Des. J. **25**(2), 225–242 (2022)
48. Flyvbjerg, B.: Five misunderstandings about case-study research. Qual. Inq. **12**(2), 219–245 (2006)
49. Robson, C.: Real World Research: A Resource for Social Scientists and Practitioner-Researchers. Wiley, Hoboken (2002)
50. Olsen, J.P.: Change and continuity: an institutional approach to institutions of democratic government. Eur. Polit. Sci. Rev. **1**(1), 3–32 (2009)

51. Seravalli, A., Agger Eriksen, M., Hillgren, P.-A.: Co-design in co-production processes: jointly articulating and appropriating infrastructuring and commoning with civil servants. CoDesign **13**(3), 187–201 (2017)
52. Pirinen, A.: The barriers and enablers of co-design for services. Int. J. Des. **10**(3), 27–42 (2016)
53. Gaudion, K., Hall, A., Myerson, J.: A designer's approach: how can autistic adults with learning disabilities be involved in the design process? CoDesign **11**(1), 49–69 (2015)
54. Huybrechts, L., Benesch, H., Geib, J.: Institutioning: participatory design, co-design and the public realm. CoDesign **13**(3), 148–159 (2017)
55. Huntjens, P.: Towards a Natural Social Contract. Transformative Social-Ecological Innovation for a Sustainable, Healthy and Just Society. Springer Cham (2021). https://doi.org/10.1007/978-3-030-67130-3
56. Bassetti, C., Sciannamblo, M., Lyle, P.: Co-designing for common values: creating hybrid spaces to nurture autonomous cooperation. CoDesign **15**(3), 256–271 (2019)
57. Botto, F., Teli, M.: PIE news. A public design project toward commonfare, 2–4 (2016)
58. Avelino, F., Dumitru, A., Cipolla, C.: Translocal empowerment in transformative social innovation networks. Eur. Plan. Stud. **28**(5), 955–977 (2020)
59. Kemp, R., Loorbach, D.: Transition management: a reflexive governance approach. Reflexive Gov. Sustain. Dev., 103–130 (2006)
60. Parsons, W.: Innovation in the public sector: Spare tyres and fourths plinths. Innov. J. **11**(2), 1–10 (2006)
61. Jégou, F., Manzini, E.: Collaborative Services – Social Innovation and dEsign for Sustainability (2008)
62. Federici, S., Linebaugh, P.: Re-enchanting the World: Feminism and the Politics of the Commons. Pm Press (2018)
63. Gibson-Graham, J.K.: A Postcapitalist Politics. U of Minnesota Press (2006)
64. Bourdieu, P.: The forms of capital. In: The Sociology of Economic Life, pp. 78–92. Routledge (2018)
65. Sadan, E.: Empowerment and Community Planning (2004)
66. Alliance, R.: Assessing resilience in social-ecological systems: workbook for practitioners (2010)
67. Escobar, A.: Transiciones: a space for research and design for transitions to the pluriverse. Des. Philos. Pap. **13**(1), 13–23 (2015)
68. Mouffe, C.: Deliberative democracy or agonistic pluralism?. Soc. Res. JSTOR, 745–758 (1999)
69. Tromp, N., Vial, S.: Five components of social design: a unified framework to support research and practice five components of social design: a unified framework to support research and practice. Des. J. **0**(0), 1–19 (2022)
70. Wenger, E.: Communities of Practice: Learning, Meaning, and Identity. Cambridge University Press (1999)
71. Latour, B.: From multiculturalism to multinaturalism: what rules of method for the new socio-scientific experiments? Nat. Cult. **6**(1), 1–17 (2011). Berghahn Journals
72. Benkler, Y.: The Wealth of Networks: How Social Production Transforms Markets and Freedom. Yale University Press (2006)

Research on Transition Design of Site-Specific Art Based on Aesthetic Empathy

Pei Wang[✉] and Xinqun Feng

Donghua University, Shanghai 200051, China
wangpei0911@yeah.net

Abstract. Since Site-Specific Art have different presentation effects in terms of psychological laws, individual differences, periodical ethnicity and local differences, depending on the authors, audiences and venues, etc. The differences in experience are presented through different perspectives of philosophy, aesthetics and literature, and the discursive nature of artistic creation and the intuitive nature of the work experience have analyzed from the perspective of empathy in psychology in order to enhance the presentation results and the degree of participation in the work. Through the identification and definition of the concept of local art, foreign literature is collected and sorted through the Web of Science database, while domestic research is sorted through the literature in the CNKI (China National Knowledge Infrastructure) database, and Citespace is used to analysis the literature for citation clustering. It is hope to help the presentation of local art works and improve audience participation through the perspective of aesthetic empathy.

Keywords: Site-Specific Art · Psychology Empathy · Aesthetic Empathy

1 Introduction

The process of creating artworks requires the synthesis of multiple fields such as visual culture, philosophy, psychology and sociology, and also requires the artist have the knowledge storage base on multiple fields. From the current results, there have been many studies on the issue of the aesthetic function of art in philosophy, literature and aesthetics, but it has also been found that: there are fewer results from the perspectives of psychology, sociology and philosophy to study the aesthetic function of art, while the psychological laws of aesthetics and the individual differences of art aesthetics also lack systematic classification and research; There are more studies on the aesthetic function of art in the fields of philosophy, aesthetics and literature, because of the difficulty are synchronizing their philosophical-based discursive nature with the intuitive experience of the creators of art practice, this has resulted in differences in aesthetics and experience between creators and audience groups, thus weakening the effect of the presentation of art in the field [1].

M. Kurosu and A. Hashizume (Eds.): HCII 2023, LNCS 14014, pp. 392–403, 2023.
https://doi.org/10.1007/978-3-031-35572-1_26

2 Concept Identification and Scoping

2.1 The Concept and Categories

Through the identification of basic concepts and the definition of research background to analyse the research object and keywords, Shunfeng Guan [2] in The *Methods of Artistic Science Research* proposed as shown in Fig. 1: "Four paradigm types of scientific research" to sort through the literature and lock the problem keywords, after elaborating and interpreting the objective problem, through consensus and known knowledge to deduce the theoretical hypothesis, and from the objective problem to cases which verify the authenticity of the theoretical hypothesis, to remove the falsity the truth, and to get a real and effective solution to the problem.

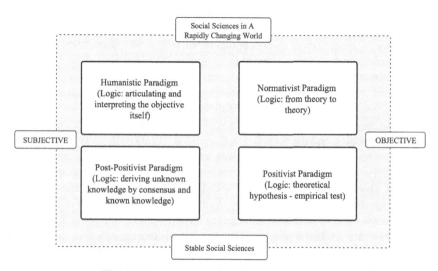

Fig. 1. Four paradigm types of scientific research

The word "Site-Specific Art" was first refined and extended by the American mini-malist artist Robert Irwin (1928-) [3], and became popular among some young American artists in the mid-1970s. In its original sense, the term can be translated as "Site-Specific Art" or "place-restricted art", which refers to work created by artists for the specific place [4]. Tracing its conceptual beginnings back to minimalism, it continues to rein-force the purity of the medium of painting and sculpture, ultimately reducing the work to the material of the medium itself and the need to fill the work with its surroundings. It is as if the viewer is placed in an environment with the work, allowing the ambience to stimulate the viewer's artistic experience, and the artistic perception is transferred from the work itself to the environment, as in the case of Installation Art and Land Art. At the same time the spatial environment in which the work is situated increasingly takes over the judgement of the work of art from its own material medium. It is in this transfer of aesthetic appreciation and participation that the concept of art in place, as shown in Fig. 2.

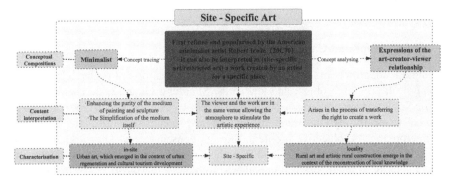

Fig. 2. Concept Analysis of Site-Specific Art

In the course of its development, Site-Specific Art has taken on different characteristic effects, along with changes in its conceptual terminology. Site-Specificity which is the basis of the concept sometimes reduced to 'in-site' and sometimes extended to locality. In Chinese, both 'in-site observation and contemplation' and 'Site-Specific Art' have become terms with a wide range of meanings, and a variety of 'Site-Specific Art' has emerged in contemporary Chinese art at different times.

The shift from 'Site-Specific' to 'Community' and 'Regional' is a contemporary process in public arts, and the booming in Chinese art rural construction in recent years has taken the form of township art festivals, the art in the countryside and intangible cultural heritage protection. Which exist in China's countryside. While complementing the multiple objectives of rural poverty alleviation, new rural construction and tourism promotion, art rural construction activities mostly use the reconstruction of local knowledge as an entry point to show that the activists have reached a conceptual identification with contemporary art. In the process of urban renewal community public art has gradually been promoted as a fictional unity, a community with specific location and cultural attributes, a temporary community formed by the intervention of artistic activities, and a continuous community developed from a temporary community, and these types have been transformed by the intervention of public art and the participation of community residents. The result is that public art has given the clear locating orientation, expressing the idea of the democratization of arts and the integration between arts and life, and accentuating its local character [5].

2.2 The Boundaries of Aesthetic Empathy

The aesthetic function of artistic activity comes with artistic activity. However, as art links all aspects of human thought, emotion and behaviour to particular forms of activity, its multiple functions are gradually recognized and valued [6].

The core essence of art is its aesthetic nature, and in the creation and experience of art, which encompasses a multitude of disciplines and complex processes, not only is the aesthetic art elevated and accompanied by rational activity, but the entire cultural content of the aesthetic process is also experienced. This is the natural regularity and immutability of aesthetic activity, and the cognitive and educational functions of art unfold within the context of the aesthetic. As shown in Fig. 3 constructs builds a framework for the process of moving from aesthetic experience to aesthetic empathy from the encounter [7] (meeting the problem) to the final reflection (recounting the problem).

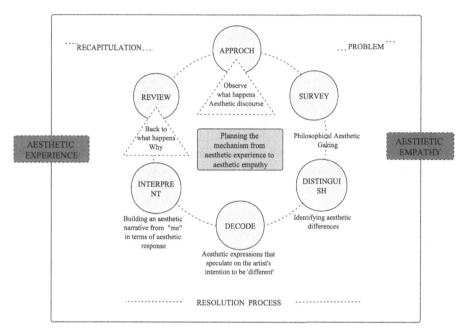

Fig. 3. Framework From Aesthetic Experience to Aesthetic Empathy

3   Relevant Studies Abroad

By precise search of web of science for 'Site-Specific Art' revealed that because the concept of it is an imported thing, it is well documented in foreign literature, particularly in the United States which is the birthplace of Site-Specific Art, Now has become more frequent in recent years especially in Korea and Japan. The content search also revealed that research on Site-Specific Art has focused on its site-specific and local characteristics.

According to Miwon Kwon, the shift from 'local' to 'community' has been the biggest change in public art in the last decade or two, resulting in the growing popularity of community public art as the third form of urban public art [8]. Community public art, the democratization of art is the goal, intervening in community public spaces with the help of project activities in order to mobilize community residents to participate and construct public art together, thereby reshaping and enhancing community culture and feeding back into community life. Miwon Kwon says the Culture in action launched in Chicago in 1993, as a groundbreaking example of community public art, and the annual Sensational City Arts Festival in Cape Town South Africa, as an example of how community public art can be used in a more transform way. It uses the term 'local' as a definitive term in the titles of its various sections, including performance art, visual art and participatory art, which is an attempt to integrate local concepts into community public art.

3.1 General Analysis of the Literature Relating to Site-Specific Art

The fuzzy search for "Site-Specific & art" contains the total of 5,596 articles, of which 494 were published in 2020, mainly in the field of applied research highlighting "Site-Specific" and concentrated in the fields of fine arts, literary theory and education, and less in the field of design and artistic creation. The main focus is on art, literary theory and education, and less on design and artistic creation. Which has thirty-five National Social Science Foundations. A total of 1,824 articles were precise searched for "Site-Specific & art", of which 297 were published in 2020, mainly in the applied category of "Site-Specific" locality, and concentrated on the fields of public art, art and calligraphy, architectural science, and less in the fields of design and artistic creation. Which covers thirty-one National Social Science Foundation projects. The fuzzy search for "Site-Specific Art" contains the total of 4875 articles, of which 1534 belong to the field of computer science and 1421 to the field of engineering, mainly highlighting applied research on "locality", and concentrating on public art, fine art, and architectural science. The search focused on public art, art and calligraphy, architectural science and less on design and creative arts.

3.2 A Categorical Study of Site-Specific Art

One Place after Another; Site-Specific Art and Location Identity by American curator and critic Miwon Kwon [9]. The author firstly compares the genealogy of the development of "Site-Specific Art", arguing that since its birth in the early 1960s, it has undergone three paradigms of evolution: empiricism, institutional criticism and disciplinary construction: in the first phase (early 1960s), "Site-Specific Art" was theoretically based on empiricism and phenomenology, emphasized the physical-spatial properties of place, the sensory-body experience of the viewer and the ephemeral and unrepeatable nature of the work. In the second phase (mid 1960s), "Site-Specific Art" became associated with institutional critique and began to turn towards the political sphere. The rationale was that place had not only physical but also cultural and social properties; galleries, museums, art fairs, etc., which were always spatial and economic complexes that constructed a system of ideologies to regulate the development of art. What art did has to question and criticize this situation. In the third phase (since the end of the 1960s), echoing the frequent practice of "Site-Specific Art" and the variations it produced during its development, attempts were made to explore the boundaries of "Site-Specific Art" in terms of sociological, psychological and other disciplinary directions and around spatial constructions, leading to its disciplinary construction. The research object is not only the space of the art institution, but also the public space outside the institution, the commercial space and even the regional culture.

Since the 1960s and 1970s, when "Site-Specific Art" emerged and continued to flourish, driven by market interventions and the increasingly popular global model of Biennial and Triennial, artists have begun to reproduce 'Site-Specific' works originally created for a specific location elsewhere to suit the needs of different cities and institutional settings. Artists changed from being creators to being promoters of aesthetic culture. At the same time, institutions and markets began to establish rules for the production, display, sale and placement of "Site-Specific Art". This process has undoubtedly fatally destroyed local art in its original sense, as the 'territoriality' that was the basis of its existence no longer exists. Facing this onslaught, Miwon Kwon [10] attempts to return to the phenomenological model of "Site-Specific Art" in order to reclaim its defensive boundaries, she says "rethinking the definition of Site-Specific is that the work is no longer permanent or immovable (as in the sculpture and earth art projects of early practice), but rather that it is impermanent and ephemeral." This is not a simple return to the logic of a negative dialectic, which appears to place particular emphasis on the symbiotic relationship between the works and its location, but in fact shifts its focus to a value position, that of anti-commercialization, manifested in the artist's resistance to the rapid commercialization of artworks by presenting works with fickle forms and short lifespans and controlling the timing and frequency of market transactions.

3.3 A Categorical Study of Aesthetic Empathy

The precise search for "aesthetic empathy" yielded 42 articles, 13 of which were published in 2020, mainly applied research based on "aesthetic experience" and concentrated in the fields of communication, aesthetics, music and dance, and less in the fields of design and artistic creation. Among them, there are three National Social Science Foundation (one in 2017 and two in 2021). The fuzzy search for "aesthetics & empathy" includes 166 articles, of which 32 will be published in 2020, mainly in the field of applied research based on "local" and concentrated in the fields of public art, literary theory and cultural economy, and less in the fields of design and artistic creation. Among them, six National Social Science Foundation (one in 2017, one in 2018, one in 2019, two in 2020 and two in 2021).

The search results shown in Fig. 4, said that the field of aesthetic empathy is widely used in foreign research, including qualitative research in psychology, interdisciplinary character education, early childhood development and care. In the area of language and literature, research is done on creative intent and expressiveness, specifically in fiction and drama; in the area of performing arts, research is done on expressiveness and effectiveness, specifically in singing and opera, aesthetic creativity in film, and hormonal changes in tragedy concerts; in the area of serving the health care system, research is done on empathy psychology, specifically on the themes of sleep quality concern care, science in the field of architecture, we do research on the validity of aesthetic consistency, specifically on sustainable architecture composed of advanced building materials.

4 Relevant Domestic Studies

Some of the exhibitions share the conceptual resources of 'Site-Specific' since 2000 the number of art events in China has been increased which have taken on the name of 'Site-Specific'. First is the rise of urban public art or works in public space, which benefits from the amplification, reproduction and displacement of museum, and the so-called

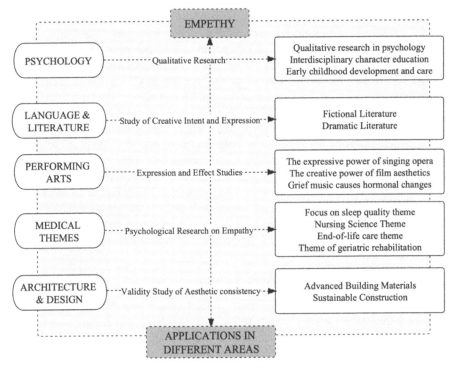

Fig. 4. Research and Application of Empathy in Foreign Countries

public space of art, which refers to the configuration of sculpture and installation works as 'urban furniture'. These two forms have been commonplace in mainland Chinese cities already.

When we talk about 'Site-Specific', the visual of urban public spaces are inevitably superficial, and all the types of arts is inevitably concerned with a deeper sense of questioning [11]. To date, the deeper practice and academic discussion of Chinese local art has been concerned with two main issues: the first is the reconstruction of local knowledge (which in conjunction with the practice of artistic vernacular construction); then the methodology of creation in relation is to specific sites. In terms of the notion of 'Site-Specific' to which they are linked, although the former focuses on 'locality' and the latter is on 'limitation', both are in any case consistent in their emphasis on the relationship between their work and They attempt to bridge the local practices of local knowledge reconstruction and rural construction, and are particularly indicative of the socialization trend of Chinese contemporary art in recent years.

In an era of global spatial production and visual culture increasingly homogeneous period, how to find a sense of belonging and identity among the fragments, the countryside is a physical spatial solution for collecting foot marks of culture and aesthetic values. In this context, the 'artistic countryside construction' has developed into a symptomatic trend in the reconstruction of local knowledge as the concern for local art in mainland China recent years. The influence of outstanding local art achievements from abroad and the lively agricultural art festivals in Taiwan, the import of various fresh ideas, and the promotion of the rural revitalization strategy (translated into the local government's awareness of political performance and the development of regional cultural tourism) are some of the factors. In terms of creation, they generally introduce the popular creative methods of contemporary art, through the deconstruction and imaginative restructuring of local culture.

4.1 Comparative Studies of Site-Specific Art

In mainland China, there is still a lack of systematic theoretical construction of in Site-Specific Art, and the introduction of foreign words is sporadic and scattered, thus leaving more spaces for people to play around. The first is the case of Boyi Feng's practice of "creating in site, showing in site"; the second is Hong Wu's "special location"; The third is "cultural and geopolitical expansion" as elaborated by Hanru Hou. In fact, all the three can be linked to different concepts of 'Site-Specific'. Boyi Feng, as the creator curated the '798 Chinese Contemporary Art Internal Observation Exhibition' in 1998 and subsequently published 'Traces of Survival', which in terms of semantics, clearly favour in-site and ephemeral, with the aim of emphasize a marginal creative position outside the mainstream of urban culture. Hong Wu's 'Site-Specific Art' automatically connects 'in-site art' to 'site-specific art'. It refers specifically to the 'opposition monuments' or 'anti-monuments' that are executed in urban demolition sites and sites of historical monumental, which with a focus on historical reflection and social critique. Han Hou translates his English essay into Chinese as 'Towards a New Locality'. The essay is intended to look at the future of the meaning of global biennials, which begin with: "Every local biennial of contemporary art inevitably carries with it some attempt to expand culturally and attempts at geopolitical expansion [12]. So the local artwork is one that brings together the concept of locality and local culture in an innovative way, while maintaining an openness to international culture.

4.2 Studies on Aesthetic Empathy and Social Engagement

The issue of aesthetic empathy and social participation involves the study of aesthetics and the psychology of empathy in aesthetic research [13], through participation in the completion of aesthetic empathy and the realization of the value and meaning of artworks, as shown in Fig. 5. By combing through the literature, we have identified the original proponents of the concept of 'aesthetic empathy' and the young designers and design educators who have applied it to specific areas of design, as well as the experts in the field of education and research in west who have conducted research on 'aesthetic empathy'. This theory has been used in the construction of behaviour science models and has achieved some results in this field. In the process of combing through the literature, we have reviewed the development of sociology during post-war period in the United States, the most famous of which are the "Chicago School" and the "Los Angeles School", who used the knowledge systems of sociology and urban geography respectively to study the problems encountered in the process of urban development. They used the knowledge systems of sociology and urban geography to study the problems of urban development, from changes in the city to changes in participatory behaviour, and eventually to develop sociological theories that addressed changes in urban-rural relations, which are illustrated by a statistical classification of the key figures identified above.

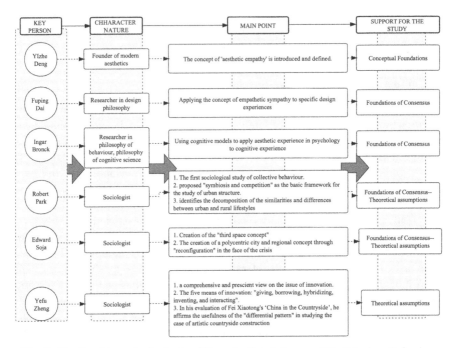

Fig. 5. The Key Figure in the Study of Empathy Psychology and Participatory Behaviour

5 Music of Tiling - A Conversation with Nature

The warm and humid climate of Sichuan produces bamboo which is a kind of natural shallow rooted plant. Bamboo can be used as a tool or a form for potential. Nature is infinitely generous and uncompromising to us, so what kind of posture should we maintain towards nature? As Master Hui Neng said in the Sixth Patriarch's Sutra, "The wind has not yet moved, the streamers have not yet moved, but the heart of the benevolent has moved". In the whole process of design and construction, how to feel nature with heart and how to use the power of nature are the answers we want to find through this project. We hope to alleviate the anxiety and fear caused by the epidemic with a dynamic installation, and to interpret this work through an understanding of nature and traditional culture. The installation does not have to be static, but it can take on different forms depending on the climate and natural conditions in order to redefine the relationship between human and nature. At the beginning of the exploration, we targeted two traditional elements, Tiling and Fou. Tiling refers to the tile gutter formed by the tiles on the house, and combined with the percussion instrument Fou, which represents the sound. The two traditional objects are similar to the shape of a bamboo tube, but also bring the crisp sound after the wind moves. The units extend upward in layers, making the main structure reflect the trend of "flying eaves". The carving of the eaves tiles on the top and the rise of the eaves are our understanding of the unique architectural aesthetics of the Eastern culture. We try to use parametric calculation to make its shape and unit have more flexibility and possibility. The installation has some kind of connection with the environment. Hoping to achieve the best condition to withstand wind resistance and rain pressure, we processed for each modular unit. With the bamboo section as the center, the whole is cut in a 3:2 ratio to obtain a bamboo tube with open ends and an arc cut at the longer end (Fig. 6).

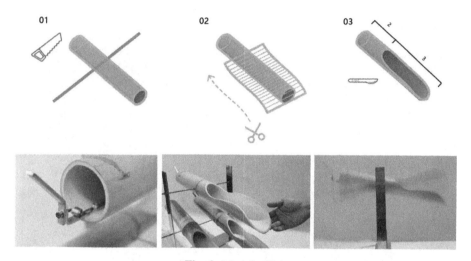

Fig. 6. Modular Unit

This is a complex force structure. The constraints of various reasons forced us to consider the feasibility of the design in a more site-specific manner. We carried out several rounds of optimization and upgrading of the main form and explored the reasonable relationship between the size and number of units. At the same time, we had conducted 1:20 modeling and experiments for each node treatment. It took us four days to complete this first attempt at nature. The first day was spent on material sorting and weight testing of unit parts. The second day was for the main structure construction, skin node placement and positioning. On the third day, we reinforced the main structure and assembled the skin of the unit parts. On the last day, we adjusted the skin of the unit parts and created the environment of flower. In the process of building, we reworked the design for the remaining material cutted (Fig. 7).

The prefabricated stainless steel metal balance bar connects the remaining bamboo pieces at the end like "tiles" to complete the counterweight of the unit. The screws and nuts at the end serve both the function of connection and the function of "weight" leveling by increasing or decreasing the number of nuts and the position of the balancing bar to adjust the angle needed for each unit. The breeze always keeps the unit in a dynamic balance, creating layers of bamboo waves (Fig. 8).

Fig. 7. Structural details

Fig. 8. The General View of Music of Tiling

6 Conclusion

In the context of psychology empathy, the process from aesthetic autonomy to social participation in "Site-Specific Art" is a process from psychological identification to behaviour participation. In the course of a literature search, it was found that Swedish scholar Ingar Brinck through psychoanalysis to behaviour metrics, and through a comprehensive analysis of several disciplines in philosophy of language and philosophy of action. At the same time, the famous young Chinese academic Fuping Dai has applied the concepts of empathy and sympathy to experience design through a combination of these concepts. The main ideas of the two above are detailed through diagrams. A comprehensive analysis of the literature reveals that aesthetic autonomy and social engagement is a process of change from psychological change to behaviour trends, and is currently used in specific fields of design, but there is less relevant research in the field of artistic creation.

Based on the above, the theoretical hypothesis is deduced from consensus and knowledge by establishing the object of study, after elaborating and interpreting the key words of the objective problem, and the truth of the theoretical hypothesis is verified by the landing point of the objective problem (the design case). The specific forms of category of Site-Specific Art need to be organization precisely on the basis of different disciplines. The study of 'aesthetic empathy' is based on psychological research, establishing a complete mechanism from empathy psychology to experiential participation, and category and effectively guiding it according to its local nature, which is in order to get the present act of participation in local art much more better.

Acknowledgments. This project won the first prize in the 2022 Chengdu Park City International Garden Season and the 5th Beijing Forestry University International Garden Construction Week competition under the guidance of Professor Geng Huang, and thanks to the landscape architecture faculty of the School of Landscape Architecture at Beijing Forestry University for their comments and guidance. This project is the result of the collective strength of the "urban link" team, with special thanks to Shuyu Qiu and Jie Lin for their hard work in the design and construction process. This work has been collected by the Chengdu Park City International Garden Season Organizing Committee and is permanently stored in the Chengdu Botanical Garden.

References

1. Gu, Z., Wang, S.: The Theory of Art to the Realm, no. 01. Baihua Literary and Art Press (1999)
2. Guan, S.: Art Science Research Methods, no. 11. Wuhan University of Technology Press (2019)
3. Wang, H.: Public art - in situ. Shanghai Art Rev. (10) (2018)
4. Yi, Y.: Rethinking space-site specific art and in situ art. Shanghai Art Rev. (05) (2018)
5. Zhang, Y.: Historical changes and contemporary practices of site-specific art. Public Art (02) (2018)
6. Peng, F.: The contemporary game of aesthetics and art. Lit. Art Stud. (06) (2017)
7. Zhang, L.: Design ideals and ethics in the Anthropocene. Non Anthropocentrism Object Oriented Des. (01), pp. 27–31 (2021)
8. Li, Y., Mao, Y.: The concept of "locality" and the practice of locality in Chinese contemporary art". Obs. Reflect. (06) (2020)
9. Zhang, Y.: The historical changes and contemporary practices of site-specific art. Public Art (02) (2018)
10. Wang, H.: Public art - in situ sex. Shanghai Art Rev. (10) (2018)
11. Hou, H.: Towards a new in-placeness. Hou Hanru, Translated by Zhou Xuesong, Oriental Art (23) (2010)
12. Zhang, L.: Returning to place - writing art history in the wave of localization. Ethn. Art Stud. (06) (2021)
13. Dai, F.: Building the "I-Thou" relationship: on empathy in experience design. Creat. Des. (04) (2018)
14. Gou, M., Zhang, Y.: Whose art countryside is built. Art Obs. (01) (2019)
15. Zhang, Z.: Intuitive art and aestheticism: Heidegger's thoughts on being and freedom. J. Yuxi Norm. Coll. (01) (2015)

Light-Note: A New Interface for Touchless Laser Digital Instruments

Yu Wang[1,2(✉)], Jie Wu[2], and Hanfu He[2]

[1] School of Pop Music and Dance, Shanghai Institute of Visual Arts, Shanghai, China
asterwangyu@126.com
[2] College of Design and Innovation of Tongji University, Shanghai, China

Abstract. In recent years, the integration of human-computer interaction technology with digital musical instruments has become increasingly common. In this study, we designed a touchless laser digital instrument interface, 'Light-Note', and invited musicians to play the instrument. In the context of human-computer interaction, we explored the interaction patterns between the players and the touchless digital instrument interface and summarised the impact of de-touching on the players' playing experience through their performance interactions. We found that players' playing styles, playing techniques and perceptions of performance were all influenced by the touchless interface, shedding new light on how human-computer interaction can be designed. In addition, we have developed an interaction model of the touchless interface, which provides a reference and guide for the innovative design of human-computer interfaces for digital musical instruments.

Keywords: Tactile-free · interface design · digital musical instrument · interaction · laser sensor

1 Introduction

In recent years, the integration of human-computer interaction technology with digital musical instruments has become more and more common. Firstly, in the field of musical performance, this fusion has been mutually stimulating with innovative forms of performance. The concept of "the instrument as an extension of the musician's body" [1] has been given a new interpretation. At the same time, in the consumer market, relevant applications running on new media devices such as tablets and smartphones not only make up for the shortcomings of traditional electronic musical instruments in terms of human-computer interaction and music education, but can also replace some traditional electronic musical instruments and devices to a certain extent, forcing traditional electronic musical instrument manufacturers to accelerate their innovation and transformation. Today, more and more digital musical instrument interfaces are being designed in conjunction with new media technologies, not only drawing on the experience of human-computer interaction design of existing musical instrument interfaces, but also making appropriate use of the various features of new media technologies. Essl

[2] proposed a framework and methodology for designing new physical musical instruments in 2006, and this study initially explored the working mechanisms of multiple sensory channels such as haptics in the design of digital musical instruments. Based on this, different researchers have attempted to explore and design new interaction modes for digital musical instruments and digital instrument interfaces. For example Lauren [3] investigated and developed an enhanced instrument (hybrid piano) by exploring the concept of multimodal playing information and haptic feedback, treating playing as a perceptually guided act to enhance the player experience. He et al. [4] explored interaction patterns for the Guqin using a physical gesture capture system to classify left-handed playing techniques for the Guqin. Brazi [5] explored approaches to sound interaction design from a human-computer interaction perspective. These works have inspired more scholars to carry out design and development of human-computer interaction interfaces for digital musical instruments, such as the laser harp, a new media instrument [6]. The design of human-computer interaction interfaces for digital musical instruments consists of two main parts: designing the control and feedback process between the player and the instrument and designing the effects presented on components such as audio and display devices.

Considering entanglement HCI in a musical context, the instrument does not become an instrument until it is played by a performer [7], whereas for plucked digital instruments, the way the performer plays relies heavily on the human sense of touch. The tactile perception system of plucked digital instruments determines how they are played and how they are performed. Therefore, the design of the tactile perception interface is often very important in the design of plucked digital instruments. However, with the advent of technology, the design of 'de-tactile' non-tactile instruments is emerging, such as the Tremens and light-sensitive instruments, which extend the interface of digital instruments and innovate performance techniques. In the context of human-computer interaction, we can't help but wonder whether, although tactile perception systems have led to the creation of traditional plucked digital instruments, are the tactile-based techniques themselves a limitation for performers? Would there be more scope for performers to play plucked digital instruments if we did not rely on the sense of touch? Does the use of a tactile-free interface facilitate the playing of digital instruments? These are the research questions of this paper. In addition, we develop an interaction model of a touchless digital instrument interface, which provides a reference and guide for the innovative design of human-computer interaction interfaces for digital instruments.

2   Interaction Model

In the field of human-computer interaction research, a general definition of a tactile-free interface is one that removes the sense of touch and uses other multimodal sensory interaction techniques to replace the tactile senses. Tactile information channels have many unique advantages of their own, but there are also many limitations to using them alone for interaction interface design. The use of de-tactile interfaces in digital musical instruments can break the bonds of traditional performance techniques for players at some level, especially for users with no experience of playing the instrument.

2.1 Explanation of Interaction Models for Touchless Digital Instrument Interfaces

Since the invention of the computer, there have been various discussions about the relationship between the digital world and the real world. In the study of human-computer interaction, the relationship between digital space and physical space has become a key issue that has led to changes in interface design. Professor Yu Ishii of the MIT Media Lab proposed the idea of "Tangible bits" at the end of the last century [8], pointing out that, compared to GUI where the main information is presented in a virtual way, TUI are characterised by the integration of digital technology into physical entities, giving them the ability to process and express information [9] (MIT Media Lab, 2004). The interaction model of the two is shown in Fig. 1.

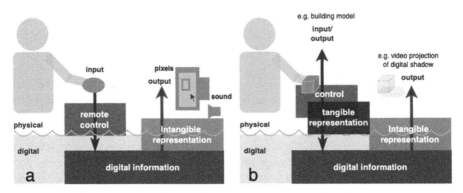

Fig. 1. a: GUI interaction model b: TUI interaction model

The special physical nature of a touchless interface: in contrast to the pixels of a graphical interface and the bits of a digital space, a touchless interface is 'untouchable' and can only replace the information conveyed by touch with information from other sensory channels; in contrast to physical entities in general, the information input to a touchless interface is usually invisible. In a way, therefore, a touchless interface can be considered as an extension or a subclass of TUI, while also having some characteristics of its own. In this paper, an interaction model for a touchless interface is given from this perspective (Fig. 2). For a TUI user, the interface can be controlled directly by controlling the movement of a physical object, but for a non-tactile interface, the user can only control the interface through other sensory channels instead of tactile information, such as light, images, sound, etc. In the case of plucked digital instruments, lasers are often used as a bridge between the player and the instrument when using a tactile-free interface for these instruments. This is because lasers are visible in a given environment, are non-tactile and morphologically simulate the strings of a plucked digital instrument.

As we have already mentioned in the definition of a touchless interface, many touchless interface applications are actually formed by a combination of modalities, and multi-sensory association is one of the key features of a touchless interface. Thus a significant part of the virtual representation of digital information is dominated by audiovisual elements. In the process of introducing the laser as a tactile digital instrument design, the digitised laser-sensitive information can also be converted into other sensory elements for representation, for example in the form of images, sounds and other forms of clearer and more detailed feedback to the performer, although other applications and technologies are not excluded.

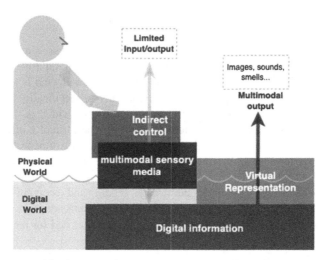

Fig. 2. Interaction models for tactile-free interfaces

2.2 Summary of Interface Components

A user interface for a touchless channel can be broken down into a complete system consisting of several parts. We have tried to generalise and summarise the components associated with a touchless interface from the point of view of the design of plucked digital instruments. Based on the potential order of interface components from input to output, they are divided into an acquisition layer, a processing layer and a presentation layer. The reason for the hierarchical induction is that acquisition-processing-application simultaneously embodies an interdependent relationship between the layers, with the acquisition layer representing the input method for various forms of touchless information, and the processing of touchless information being an embedded layer of a touchless interface that, while does not provide a direct user experience, but plays a very important supporting role, receiving input information on the one hand and processing and modulating the information to be presented on the other; while the presentation layer is the output and presentation of the information.

Collection Layer. The acquisition layer is the input layer to the touchless interface, i.e. the layer where the touchless multimodal information is incorporated into the machine. Based on the special characteristics of plucked digital instruments, this paper proposes that the input of touchless information needs to be carried out in both physical and digital dimensions, i.e. both the player's performance information should be captured through digital acquisition techniques such as laser sensors and the information should be able to be digitally recognised and processed.

At the physical level, the user expects the collected performance information to be recognised and used in multimedia art creation related to the sound of the digital instrument; at the digital level, the user expects the light-sensitive digital capture to be applied to the collection of touchless data, pattern recognition, etc.and thus to provide some data-based services such as music recognition, AI composition, etc.

Processing Level. The processing layer is also divided into two dimensions, digital and physical, which are considered in different senses. The digital dimension refers to the algorithmic processing of the multimodal sensory data collected in addition to the tactile sensation, in the case of plucked digital instruments, specifically the algorithmic processing of the photoreceptor data, the main purpose of which is to identify and correspond to the notes from the collected photoreceptor performance information.

The physical dimension, in the case of the plucked digital instrument interface, refers specifically to the laser sensor beam settings, including the distance between beams and the laser array settings.

The processing layer also includes the storage, sending and receiving of multimodal sensory information, such as note recording and note transmission, which requires the local multimodal sensory information to be sent to the other end for recognition data, results, etc.

Presentation Layer. Currently, the tactile-free channel is presented in plucked digital instruments in a physical form, where the player transmits playing information through a physical form of laser beam, which can replace the strings of a traditional digital instrument on some level. We can use the cross-channel coherence of psychology for some visual and auditory design to replace the tactile experience.

For the presentation of non-tactile laser performance data or the recognition of laser control data, it is often necessary to rely on virtual forms of digital representation, with images and sound being the most common forms of representation, for example visualising laser data in various forms to show the performance effect.

3   Prototype Implementation of a Touchless Digital Instrument Interface

The design of the Light-Note interactive interface for the touchless laser digital instrument consists of two main components: 1) the design of the control-feedback process between the player and the instrument; and 2) the design of the effects presented on the multi-channel sensory (auditory, visual, tactile, etc.) experience components such as audio and display devices.

The Light-Note design model is based on plucked digital instruments, but our design research does not aim to recreate the performance methods and characteristics of traditional plucked digital instruments using new media interaction technologies, but rather to explore a new mode of human-computer interaction for digital instruments that is de-tactile, to innovate and expand new forms of expression and multi-sensory performance experiences for digital instruments, and to establish a framework for the design and implementation of touchless laser digital instruments. The aim is to explore a new mode of human-computer interaction for digital musical instruments, to innovate new forms of expression and multi-sensory performance experiences, and to establish a framework for the design and implementation of touchless laser digital instruments.

The human-computer interaction mode of the Light-Note can be understood as the transformation of manual movements into sound through optical sensors. Therefore, the main research point in designing the Light-Note human-computer interaction model is how to capture human actions and how to translate them into sound. At present, with the spread and advancement of science and technology, there are a variety of ways to achieve the final conversion from triggering an optical sensor to a sound signal, but the actual results are very different. Figure 3 illustrates the flow of the Light-Note human-computer interaction mode for a touchless laser digital instrument.

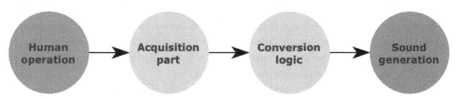

Fig. 3. Human-computer interaction process of the Light-Note, a touchless laser digital instrument

3.1 Overall Design Model

The Light-Note is a touchless laser digital instrument that uses 21 pairs of optical sensors as sensory touch devices to simulate "strings". The human-computer interaction between the player and the Light-Note is as follows: the player triggers the laser strings with gestures of different playing techniques, and the laser strings translate the player's touch into playing information and transmit it. Due to the nature of the laser, the player can play in a way that is not limited to traditional plucked digital instruments, and can even use smoke to trigger and control the laser strings. Special techniques such as glissandos and ornamental notes are achieved with the Pitch Bend, and the transposition of the Light-Note is achieved by means of a dip switch with an integrated transposition program. The Light-Note's feedback process for the player's touch includes translating the player's actions into sound information or visual linkage information.

The design model for the Light-Note touchless interface focuses on exploring the process of converting laser touch signals into acoustic signals. In this regard, the information that can be generated by the laser string simulated by the optical sensor and its transformation information correspond as shown in Fig. 4.

Original information	Corresponding information	Transform information
Trigger laser string	Note information	Note name
Trigger / not trigger laser string	Laser string blocked / not blocked	Note on / off
Laser string occlusion time	Opening speed	Note velocity

Fig. 4. Correspondence table for laser string information conversion

There are 2 main methods of converting and realising the sound signal.

(1) The corresponding information from the acquisition section is collated and transformed in a common way and then passed on to the computer sequencing software, which uses a library of sampled timbres to select and produce the sound that is eventually produced by the sound component. In this approach, the sound generation module is separate from the instrument module.

(2) The sound module is placed in the instrument, i.e. the digital instrument comes with its own sound generator.

We design the corresponding program to realise the conversion of the performance information through the MIDI protocol, the Musical Instrument Digital Interface protocol, a standardised technology whose underlying port is the RS232 communication protocol, which allows communication between devices, between computers or between computers and devices to be accomplished over three wires. At a specific Baud rate, the system can transmit note information to the upper end according to a standard format. The standard MIDI protocol enables the transmission of one note message in less than 1ms, and the sequencing software of the host can implement polyphony algorithms. Thus, we can communicate directly with the computer via a Microcontroller Unit (MCU) that supports the MIDI protocol and eventually connects to the sound system to produce sound (Fig. 5).

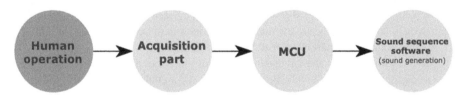

Fig. 5. Information flow for the Light-Note, a touchless laser digital instrument

3.2 Implementation of the Light Note Information Collection Side of the Touchless Interface

Plucked digital instruments form the process of human-instrument interaction primarily through the playing of strings by human fingers. Therefore, we chose a string-like sensing device. By comparing relevant and established devices, we have chosen a pair of laser sensors instead of conventional strings. The playing information is collected by forming a laser array of 21 pairs of laser sensors to simulate 21 strings. The laser sensors are arranged next to each other, with the distance between two adjacent laser strings set at 15mm and the distance between the ends of each pair of laser sensors (laser string length) set at 20cm, as shown in Fig. 6.

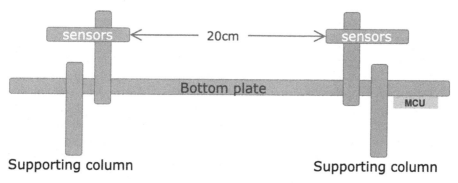

Fig. 6. Design of the collection side of the touchless interface

We have selected the M5 compact laser-to-sensor (Fig. 7) as the laser string with an NPN normally open output.

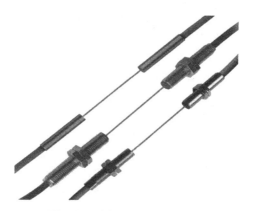

Fig. 7. M5 laser sensor diagram

The NPN normally open output is an inherent property of this laser sensor. NPN is a type of transistor, where the switch in the component breaks when the laser is fired and the load is detected as high. The load in this case is two resistors, as the closed signal of the switch cannot be read directly, but needs to be converted into a voltage change by a 'load' consisting of two resistors (Fig. 8).

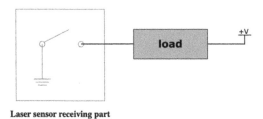

Laser sensor receiving part

Fig. 8. Diagram of how the laser sensor works

When a laser is emitted to the sensor receiving end, the switch inside the sensor is disconnected and the photoelectric effect is used to convert the light signal into an electrical signal, realising the conversion of the human interactive performance information into an electrical signal. The specific human-computer interaction process is as follows: when the finger does not pluck the light string, the light string is unobstructed, the laser of the laser sensor is directed at the sensor, and the switch inside the sensor receiver is disconnected. When the finger toggles the light string, the light string is blocked and the laser from the laser sensor is blocked by the finger, and the switch inside the sensor receiver is closed. The closing and breaking of the switch corresponds to the interaction between the finger and the light string.

As the Input and Output of the Microcontroller Unit can only receive information on the change of analogue quantities in a specific range or the level of the level, the switching signals cannot be captured directly by the Microcontroller Unit system and additional circuitry (Fig. 9) is required to divide the voltage through two resistors so that the internal component switches detect a high level signal when the laser is fired in and a low level signal when the laser is blocked.

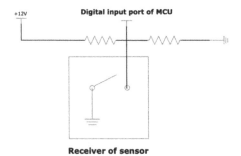

Receiver of sensor

Fig. 9. Additional circuit diagram for laser sensor

3.3 Implementation of the Light Note Information Transformation for Touchless Laser Digital Instruments

We designed the corresponding program to implement the message conversion based on the MIDI protocol. The underlying MIDI communication is RS-232 communication, and we used a USB MIDI adapter to connect the body of the Light Note to the computer. On analysis, the relevant MIDI protocol messages for the Light Note are shown in section (Fig. 10).

Frame type	ID information	Number of data frames	Data Frame 1	Data Frame 2
Note on	0X9X	2	Note name	Opening speed (Velocity)
Note off	0X8X	2	Note name	Closing speed (Velocity)
Pitch Bend data	0XEX	2	Data-low	Data-high

Fig. 10. Related MIDI protocol information

When playing the touch operation, the collector sends the corresponding frame data shown in Fig. 10 to the host computer, which receives, reads and generates the corresponding sound information.

For fast tuning, the Light Note has a 12-digit Dial switch module, where each digit corresponds to a dial switch, and the key settings can be programmed and adjusted according to requirements. The tones can be pre-programmed and adjusted according to the requirements. The tones can be switched to the preset tones in real time by toggling a certain dial switch. In this mode, the Microcontroller Unit of the acquisition system reads the status information of the 12 digits in real time to determine the current key.

In the Light-Note, a touchless laser digital instrument, we have designed the Pitch Bend module to be integrated directly into the light-sensitive acquisition side. The Pitch Bend module operates on the principle that the change in voltage output from the sliding resistor corresponds to the bend data. In the case of the Pitch Bend module, we only need to read the voltage change information through the analogue-to-digital conversion port of the Microcontroller Unit (MCU) and convert the corresponding bend data to play the bend with the Light Note. The corresponding circuit can be designed as shown in (Fig. 11).

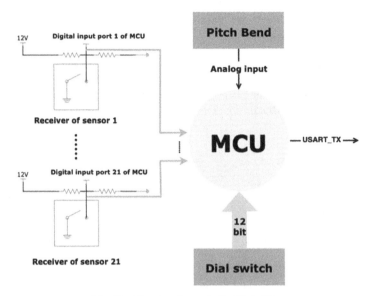

Fig. 11. Circuit schematic for Light Note

The program we have designed according to the MIDI protocol implements the transformation of information on the capture side of the Light Note's touchless laser sensor. A function was designed to correlate the note strength data with the plucking velocity (the time the laser strings were obscured). Based on the actual playing experience and the feedback characteristics of the laser strings, we have initially designed a correspondence between the two (Fig. 12), which can be further refined as the human-computer interaction on the acquisition side is tested and iterated.

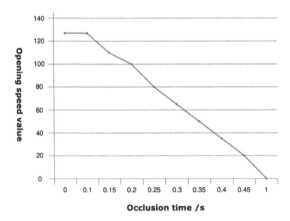

Fig. 12. Correspondence between force and plucking speed

The programming idea for Light Note is shown in (Fig. 13).

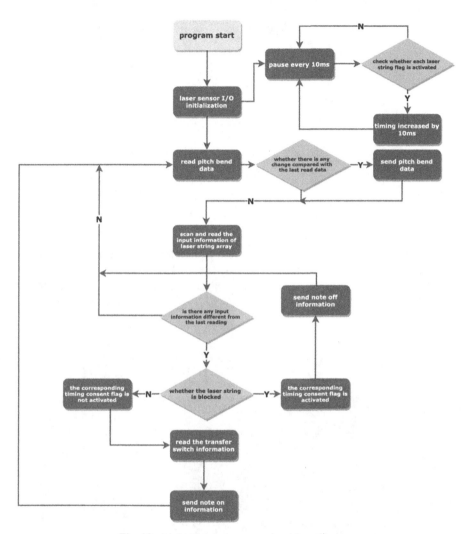

Fig. 13. Light Note's programming ideas diagram

3.4 Achieving Results

After testing, we found that the Light Note can transmit information from the player's touch laser string array to the host computer, that the Pitch Bend works properly and changes the sound bend in real time, and that the 12-position transpose switch allows for real time transposition. The Microcontroller Unit can be integrated and fixed directly into the Light Note's panel, so that the player is not limited in their performance. The finished design is shown in Fig. 14.

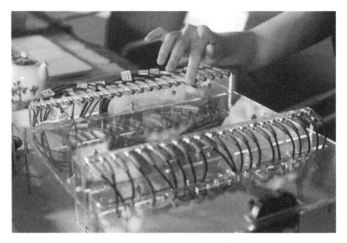

Fig. 14. Finished Light Note

Fig. 15. Visual feedback group diagram for the Light Note system

Since the Light Note can transform laser signals directly into MIDI messages, it is possible to use MIDI messages as a bridge to various sound libraries for sound feedback during human-computer interaction, but also to transmit MIDI messages from the performance to the visual hardware and software system to design different visual effects for the melody played by the player and the different playing techniques of the instrument. Visual effects for the melody the player is playing and for the different playing techniques of the instrument. The Light Note can be used to visualise the sound in real time as it is played (Fig. 15) and the visual effects in Fig. 15 are all visualisations of the sound generated by the Light Note's real time performance information. It is even possible to design MIDI messages from the laser performance signal to the AI music generation system and the AI visual image generation system for real-time musical and visual feedback, with a variety of results.

4 Performer Experience Test

4.1 Research Design Overview

We designed an exploratory study using a de-tactile interface as a probe to explore the effects of a touchless digital instrument interface on the way players play and their performance techniques. The study invited musicians to play music using the Light Note, a tactile, laser-based digital instrument interface. Participants are asked to use their imagination to play the Light Note, a touchless laser digital instrument, without any restrictions, and their performance will be observed and recorded. After playing, the participants will participate in a semi-structured interview. To maintain consistency, one investigator (the first author) manages all sessions.

4.2 Participants

Eight participants (P1–P8) took part in the study, all of whom had received training on a variety of instruments, but not just plucked instruments. The participants' ages ranged from 18 to 30 years old. The participants did not have self-identified conditions that may impact musical performance.

4.3 The Methodology

Before each participant plays the Light Note, a touchless digital instrument, the researcher introduces the participant to the basic use of the Light Note, the digital instrument interface, which is safe to use. After seeing the Light Note, participants confirmed that they would be participating in the study and filled out a consent form. The players were then given the opportunity to practice playing the instrument on their own and finally they were asked to play any melody using the Light Note. Each session ended with a semi-structured interview. The study was reviewed and approved by the ethics committee of the authors' school prior to the start of the study. Each time the participants played the instrument, their interviews were recorded. The interview data were analysed according to thematic analysis methods [10].

Before starting the experiment, the researchers explained how to use the instrument Light Note's touchless laser interface, the transpose switch module and the Pitch Bend module, and demonstrated how to play the instrument. The researchers demonstrated the following gestures: finger plucking of the laser beam, slow sliding of the fingers between several laser beams, fast sweeping of the laser beam by several fingers, finger plucking of a single laser beam while rotating the bending wheel to create a glissando effect, finger plucking of several laser beams while rotating the bending wheel to create a polyphonic glissando effect, and the use of smoke to submerge the laser beam to produce the sound. Each participant was given 5 min to explore the instrument, after which they were given 5 min to play a melody. Upon completion, participants answered questions about their experience of playing the Light Note, a touchless digital instrument interface, during this experiment.

Figure 16 shows one participant (P1) playing the Light Note and Fig. 17 shows another participant (P4) learning and thinking about how to play the Light Note.

Fig. 16. Participant (P1) playing Light Note

4.4 The Results

All eight participants completed the task of playing the melody using the Light Note. As the participants became familiar with the instrument during practice, they added new gestures and playing techniques in addition to those demonstrated by the researcher. The gestures used to manipulate the Light Note included those shown to the participants by the researcher, such as plucking the laser beam, sliding the fingers between several laser beams in slow motion, sweeping the laser beam with several fingers in rapid succession, plucking a single laser beam while rotating the Pitch Bend wheel to create a glissando effect, as well as original playing styles created by the participants.

Four participants (P1, P2, P5, P7) performed new performance gestures. Some creative playing gestures can well control the non-touch instrument interface. P1 and P5 beat the laser beam with the palm of their hands, which produced a wonderful effect when the light note system timbre was adjusted to the percussion timbre. P2 and P7 gently tap the laser beam with both hands and fingers at the same time, which can form a grain-like dispersion of timbre effect. P5 commented that "the non-touch performance

Fig. 17. Participant (P4) playing Light Note

interface has increased her enthusiasm for the exploration of the digital instrument. If more practice time is provided, she will explore more ways to play." P7 commented that "each time I play Light Note, I use different performance gestures. The instrument seems to become a part of my body, and the performance techniques will not become the constraint of this instrument for me to play music." P3 said "The experience of playing musical instruments with smoke is very wonderful. I have never experienced this kind of experience before. I like the sound effect produced by smoke playing very much."

During the study, we noticed that participants also had different perceptions of their bodies when playing the instrument, with P4 commenting positively that the instrument made him feel that his fingers were flexible and strong, an experience he did not have when playing a traditional digital instrument. Some participants such as P8 felt that when playing the instrument, she wanted more fingers because she wanted to produce a more complex effect of playing gestures.

All participants commented on the novelty of the Light Note playing experience and how the non-tactile interface inspired them to play the instrument and stimulated them to innovate their playing techniques.

5 Discussion

We have designed a touchless interface for digital instruments and developed a new touchless interface for laser digital instruments, Light Note, which enables the direct conversion of laser signals into MIDI messages and their output via a MIDI interface, with a microcontroller circuit system at its heart to process the collected light-sensitive signals and convert them.

The performer uses his fingers to block the laser induction string to achieve touchless plucking performance. In terms of plucking velocity control, Light Note controls the velocity at the speed of plucking. Its sound generation system is based on the pre-modulated sample voice library and the connected sound system. In terms of playing experience, the Light Note allows for plucking, sweeping and scraping techniques, as well as slide control via the Pitch Bend. In terms of playing expression, the Light Note allows for innovative playing techniques such as polyphonic glissandos. In addition, due to the malleability of the laser, it is also possible to play with smoke triggered laser-sensitive strings. The capture and transformation of playing information without a tactile interface is proving to be possible.

After playing tests with eight participants, we found that the 'de-tactile' human-computer interface was to some extent conducive to innovation in the players' approach to technique and playing style, breaking with the traditional digital instrument interaction interface that uses mainly the sense of touch for human-computer interaction. The specific interaction between the player and the touchless digital instrument interface leads to a deeper reflection on the fact that interface design also involves the embodied design of the user's body. The use of a touchless interface allows the player's attention to be diverted from the 'strings' of the interactive instrument interface to the performance itself, with the instrument becoming an extension of the performer's body.

While Light Note leaves much to be desired in terms of the correspondence and translation of multimodal information, the playing method of the digital instrument and the musical elements produced by the performance, the touchless interface interaction model we have built provides a clear approach to the design of interactive interfaces for digital instruments, presenting them in a way that is based on HCI design. Our prototype is simple, but lowers the threshold of the player's experience in terms of mastering complex playing techniques: an interactive interface based on 'de-touching' will give musicians a new way of communicating, experiencing and even thinking about playing techniques.

On the technical side, we need to conduct more in-depth research, including more sophisticated information gathering on playing techniques, broader integration of playing music elements and the application of laser matrices to simulate touch depth. In terms of experience design, we need to conduct more in-depth user research (in collaboration with musicians and psychologists) to determine the potential impact of individual playing habits on the design of touchless digital instrument interfaces.

6   Conclusion

Designing a de-tactile digital musical instrument interface is challenging, and we need to break away from the traditional concept of digital musical instrument playing interfaces that mainly use tactile perception for interaction. Based on the existing human-computer interaction design theory and practice of plucked digital instruments, this research fully considers the particularity of musical instrument playing experience according to the principles of physiology, psychology and other disciplines, and explores the human-computer interaction design mode of the non-touch digital instrument interface that comprehensively uses optical touch sensing devices, physical feedback components, intelligent hardware devices and supporting development of interactive programs. The design model of the touchless digital musical instrument interface was established, and a new touchless digital musical instrument Light Note was developed.

In the context of HCI, we explored the interaction model between the player and the touchless digital instrument interface, and summarised the impact of the de-tactile interface on the player's performance experience through the player's performance and interaction experience. We found that players' playing styles and techniques, as well as their perceptions of performance, were influenced by the touchless interface, and that the use of the touchless interface provided an impetus for innovation in players' performance styles.

Funding Information. Chenguang Project of Shanghai Municipal Education Commission and Shanghai Education Development Foundation. Grant/Award Number:19CGB06.

Key Laboratory of Intelligent Processing Technology for Digital Music(Zhejiang Conservatory of Music), Ministry of Culture and Tourism. Grant/Award Number:2022DMKLC 011.

References

1. Nijs, L., Lesaffre, M., Leman, M.: The musical instrument as a natural extension of the musician. In: The 5th Conference of Interdisciplinary Musicology, pp. 132–133 (2009)
2. Essl, G., O'Modhrain, S.: An enactive approach to the design of new tangible musical instruments. Organ. Sound **11**(3), 285–296 (2006)
3. Lauren, H.: Haptic augmentation of the hybrid piano. Contemp. Music. Rev. **32**(5), 499–509 (2013)
4. He, J.Y., Jim, M., Dale, A.C., et al.: Investigating Guqin left hand modulation techniques. In: International Computer Music Conference, pp. 81–86. ICMC, Shanghai, China (2017)
5. Brazil, E.: A review of methods and frameworks for sonic interaction design: exploring existing approaches. In: Ystad, S., Aramaki, M., Kronland-Martinet, R., Jensen, K. (eds.) Auditory Display. CMMR ICAD 2009 2009. LNCS, vol. 5954. Springer, Berlin, Heidelberg (2010). https://doi.org/10.1007/978-3-642-12439-6_3
6. Michae, M.: Electronic harp. USA: US 2012/-272813 A1. (2012)
7. Hardjowirogo, S.-I.: Instrumentality. On the construction of instrumental identity. In: Bovermann, T., de Campo, A., Egermann, H., Hardjowirogo, S.-I., Weinzierl, S. (eds.) Musical Instruments in the 21st Century, pp. 9–24. Springer, Singapore (2017). https://doi.org/10.1007/978-981-10-2951-6_2
8. ISII H.: Towards seamless interfaces between people, bits and atoms. In: Proceedings of ACM CHI 97, vol. 1, Issue 1, pp. 1–11 (1997)
9. Mi, H.P., Wang, M., Lu, Q.Y., et al.: Tangible user interface: origins, development, and future trends. Special Issue on Human-Computer Interaction in the Age of Intelligence, p. 405 (2019)
10. DeCuir-Gunby, J.T., Marshall, P.L., McCulloch, A.W.: Developing and using a codebook for the analysis of interview data: an example from a professional development research project. Field Meth. **23**(2), 1–33 (2011)

A Framework on Digital Communication of Chinese Traditional Handicraft

Jingjing Wang, Yi Ji[(✉)], Minliang Bai, and Yihui Cai

School of Art and Design, Guangdong University of Technology, District of Dongfeng East
Road No. 729, Yuexiu 510000, Guangzhou, China
jiyi001@hotmail.com

Abstract. Increasingly more communication are being digitized, and the mode to spread traditional handicraft culture is important for protecting its profound humanistic heritage and cultural connotation. However, digital communication enabled by new technology is mostly instantaneous, fragmented and absent. This kind of communication mode with compressed time and space dimensions has affected the integrity of traditional handicraft content to a certain extent, which will result a shallow and one-sided cognition of the audience. Cultural exchange, recording and inheritance all depend on the field. This paper examines the current dilemma of digital communication of Chinese traditional handicrafts from the perspective of "Field", and proposes a new framework for the spread of traditional handicrafts, so as to give full play to the role of its profound humanistic heritage and cultural connotation.

Keywords: Traditional handicraft · Digital communication · Field theory

1 Introduction

Chinese traditional handicraft are formed in historical production practice. It represented the essence of production technology that time. Since the extremely high aesthetic value and emotional value nowadays, it is the core of the current productive protection and inheritance of ICH (intangible cultural heritage) [1]. However, traditional handicraft's own complex cultural attributes and forms make it difficult for ordinary people to effectively understand, recognize and learn them. This has resulted in the protection and inheritance of Chinese traditional handicraft limitations. With the rapid development of new media and digital technology, the original communication mode has been replaced, and the traditional handicraft culture has been impacted by the digital communication and promotion directly. Its artistic form and spiritual connotation have taken on a new state. It is an issue worthy of deep consideration to make better use of digital interaction and other technologies to spread traditional handicraft cultdure [2].

Pierre Bouerdieu's [3] field theory provides a new analytical framework for the digital communication of traditional handicraft. Field is a social space with its own unique operation rules, not a physical entity that can be touched or defined. Countless independent social spaces constitute the whole social world. In the space of the field, there

M. Kurosu and A. Hashizume (Eds.): HCII 2023, LNCS 14014, pp. 422–437, 2023.
https://doi.org/10.1007/978-3-031-35572-1_28

are various intertwine and changing objective relationships, and any object can interact with each other. Field is the framework and carrier of cultural communication, and cultural exchange, recording, inheritance, etc. are all dependent on it [4]. In the field, actors receive some conventions and norms, internalize them into self-consciousness or emotional tendencies, and produce a corresponding habitual habit, namely "Habitus". Bourdieu defined "Habitus" as a persistent and convertible tendency system [5], and each field corresponds to a habitus. Field and habitus interact. As far as cultural communication is concerned, when the shaping mechanism and generation strategy of "Habitus" enable culture to produce sustainable effects once it is accepted, and this persistence is relatively stable. Thus the "Field-Habitus" framework can provide a practical basis for cultural communication [6].

From the perspective of the thinking framework of field theory, Chinese traditional handicraft culture, as a dynamic cultural space, is an independent field. Traditional handicrafts are formed in a specific historical and cultural background, and are also closely related to the production and life style of the generation era. For instance, when the export porcelain industry rosed in the Qing Dynasty, merchants in Guangzhou brought plain porcelain from Jingdezhen, and invited Jingdezhen's masters to Guangzhou to paint and teach art, which gave birth to the art of Cantonese Porcelain. Traditional handicraft culture can be roughly divided into two forms: tangible form and intangible form. From the tangible layer, it mainly includes tools, handicrafts, physical objects and cultural sites; From the intangible layer, it mainly includes social practice, concept expression, forms of expression, knowledge, skills and other contents [7]. Before the advent of digital images, traditional handicraft was mainly spread through ethnic activities or apprenticeship [8]. Masters taught apprentices directly through words and actions. This form of face-to-face communication has formed a unique field for the spread of traditional handicraft culture. The apprentice devotes himself to craft learning with concentration and efficiency, forming a habitus of self cognition of traditional handcraft. It has promoted the spread and inheritance of Chinese traditional handicraft. At present, the development of digital technology has broken the boundaries of time and space, and the original "Field-Habitus" system structure has changed, limiting the spread of the spiritual core and charm of traditional handicraft as the intangible cultural heritage [9].

2 Problem Statement

Regis Debray and Manuel Castells et al. believed that every leap in media technology often brought a temporary and big step back to culture [10]. The powerful enabling of technology, on the one hand, has brought new communication space to traditional handicraft culture, on the other hand, it has triggered changes in art forms and communication methods, which make the original presentation form no longer applicable, thus leading to a series of difficulties in the current traditional handicraft communication (Table 1).

Table 1. Status of digital communication of traditional handicrafts

Form	Example	Communication content	Problem
Graphics and texts	WeChat public platform	– News: Notifications of events, lectures and research, etc – Knowledge: Basic introduction, display of handicrafts, presentation of skills and other contents of science, etc – Stories: Stories of traditional handicraft inheritors, etc – Relevant current events related content – Academic related content	– Time of dissemination is unstable. It is difficult to cultivate the stable reading habits of the audience – Less efficient dissemination
Video	Tiktok	– Skill demonstration – Handicrafts demonstration: Multi angle display of handicrafts – Knowledge: Explanation of the history, culture, steps and difficulties of traditional handicraft – Step-by-Step Instruction: Inheritors conducts step-by-step explanation and teaching, and eventually a simple handicraft can be completed	– Quality difference of video content is too large – Display form of handicrafts is simple – Length of the short video limits the display of content
	MOOC	– History: Origin, historical culture, cultural background, etc – Skill demonstration – Artistic appreciation of handicrafts: Introduction to the artistic value and aesthetic value of handicrafts	– Lack of interaction with the audience – Insufficient display of innovative content of traditional handicraft culture

2.1 From the Field Perspective

First of all, the diversified media and immediacy of digital communication have built an equal communication system: anyone can freely participate in the communication and even construction of culture on behalf of himself. This strengthens the role of unidentified individuals in cultural construction [11]. Traditional or modern, elegant or vulgar, serious or entertaining, jumbled cultures coexist and spread wantonly in this huge network "Field". The complicated skills and artistic aesthetics of the traditional handicraft culture have even been simplified and distorted [12]. Secondly, the traditional handicraft field is ultimately a field centered on the communication and inheritance of traditional handicraft culture. The field carries out exchanges with "Ji" and "Tao" as the core, so as to continuously inherit and enrich the cultural connotation. While digital communication attaches importance to dissemination and pursues extensive or enthusiastic effects. Some cultural contents with strong entertainment and high sensory stimulation are more likely to become high attention in the commercial media environment. For example, a traditional handicraft short video blogger with more than one million fans on the Chinese Tiktok platform (Fig. 1) released videos showing the art of Oil Paper Umbrella[1]. More than 10W likes were received in combination with "Love&Green"[2] (a) or "Qianji Umbrella"[3] (b). The ratings of videos that only showed the process of making oil paper umbrellas were within 1K (c). The communicators consciously sacrifice depth and choose to publish simple content to compete for more audience resources. These contents replace the cultural connotation and elegant pursuit carried by traditional handicraft, which may cover the attraction and dissemination value of traditional handicraft.

Fig. 1. Video screenshot released by a short video blogger

---

[1] A kind of umbrella was used in ancient China and is now a Chinese intangible cultural heritage.

[2] Green is often used in Chinese culture to describe infidelity in love.

[3] A prop for a popular game IP character.

2.2   From the Habitus Perspective

When the field changes, it needs to shape the corresponding habit to adapt to this change [3]. In the previous handicraft field, the master, with the help of books, materials, handicrafts and other items, taught the connotation of skills, deep artistic aesthetics and spiritual culture. The communicators (masters) integrate these into practice and unconsciously internalize the temperament system of the audience (apprentices), which affects their value cognition of traditional handicraft. The field plays a role in the self consciousness or emotional tendency of the audiences, which makes it easier for the hearers to form personal cognition and understanding of traditional handicraft culture, and play a role in their subconscious level, so as to promote them to internalize and even explore traditional handicraft independently. In the current digital field, based on the audience's psychology, the form of communication is usually suitable for mobile reading scenarios. For example, images and texts are the main form of WeChat public account, and short videos are the main form of Tiktok platform. The audience forms a fast-food reading habit and tends to use various intervals to receive relaxed, short and highly concentrated communication content in this situation. On the one hand, the emergence of digital media has promoted the integration of traditional handicraft field and digital communication field. However, the habitus changes brought about by the new field: the fragmentation of the audience's attention. It makes the audience form a fragmented and confused traditional handicraft cognition [13]. On the other hand, in order to attract the attention of the audience, the communicator tried to cater to the audience's habitus by adjusting the content of traditional handicraft communication, thus changing the value orientation of traditional handicraft communication.

In general, the impact of field transformation and the incommensurability of habitus are not conducive to the audience's acceptance and cognition of traditional handicraft. According to Bourdieu [3], when the new field encountered by habitus is different from the original field, habitus needs to be adjusted accordingly in order to adapt to the new field [14]. The digital communication trend of traditional handicrafts in the media era has become a reality, which cannot be easily reversed and changed. Therefore, the fundamental strategy to solve the problem is to promote the transformation of the original "Field-Habitus" into a new one, optimize the transmission path of traditional handicraft, and finally achieve the shaping of habitus in the new field, so as to give full play to the role of its humanistic heritage and cultural connotation.

The traditional handicraft digital communication strategy needs to solve the following two main problems from the field perspective:

- Explore how online media can focus on the knowledge system of traditional handicraft culture, and show the intangible and systematic characteristics of traditional handicrafts. It aims to promote the public's cognition and understanding of the cultural symbols associated with it, and enhance the cultural connotation dissemination and value influence.

- From the perspective of the audience's cognitive psychology, create a new "Field-Habitus". Promote the audience to form deep thinking inertia and consciously spread traditional handicraft culture.

The following will propose the transmission path of traditional handicraft and the design strategy of shaping habitus in the digital context.

3   The Communication Layer of Traditional Handicraft Culture

From a philosophical perspective, as a cultural form, the core of ICH must be concepts and spirits, because the essence of culture can only be conceptual existence [15]. Traditional handicraft culture is an important part of ICH, and its essence is also difficult to be clearly defined. There are certain difficulties in its dissemination. Traditional handicraft culture consists of two aspects: tangible and intangible. The tangible content of traditional handicrafts is easier to be accepted and understood. There is no barrier between objects and eyes, which is a bright and direct impression and gives people a more intuitive visual communication [16]. The intangible content is an untouchable form of physical existence, which can only be conveyed to the audience through the materialization process of symbol encoding, transmission and decoding. It usually uses context or tools as the display or realization carrier. For example, the process of paper-cut are intangible and need to be displayed to the audience through traditional handicrafts (paper cutting crafts), tools(clippers, etc.) and scenes. As a culture formed in production and life, the primary feature of traditional handicraft is its immateriality, and more emphasis is on its spiritual and cultural transmission and inheritance. In a word, the concept and spiritual culture at the invisible level are the core elements of the protection and dissemination of traditional handicraft.

According to the view put forward by Luo Feng et al. [17] the content of traditional handicraft culture communication can be deconstructed into three layers based on memetics theory: external, intermediate and core levels, as shown in Fig. 2. The specific contents are as follows:

- The external layer, include the intuitive knowledge of history, colors, shapes, patterns, etc.;
- The intermediate layer (transition layer) is dominated by tools, processes, techniques and other carriers that allow the expression of intangible content;
- The core layer is dominated by intangible spiritual products such as core concepts, cultural traits and value demands.

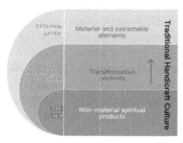

Fig. 2. Deconstruction of traditional handicraft based on memetics theory

The communication of traditional handicraft can be considered as a process of "encoding-transmission-decoding" of cultural contents. The communicator translates and encodes the core concepts and values of the core layer, decodes and transforms them through the carrier of the intermediate layer, and finally presents them to the audience in a tangible form. After the audience intuitively perceives the knowledge elements of the external layer, they can master the transformation of the encoding and decoding process of traditional handicraft through further understanding and cognition, and finally recognize the intangible spiritual products of the core layer. In short, the communicator deconstructs traditional handicraft culture from the inside out, and the content is conveyed to the audience from the outside in, layer by layer (Fig. 3). Establishing a clearer communication hierarchy can, on the one hand, improve the audience's knowledge accumulation of traditional handicraft and, on the other hand, enhance the efficiency of communication.

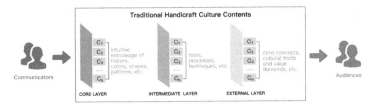

Fig. 3. Dissemination process of traditional handicrafts

4   Proposed Framework

Based on the dissemination hierarchy, a digital communication model of traditional handicraft is further proposed. The ultimate purpose of spreading traditional handicraft is to protect and promote their profound cultural heritage and connotation. Gaining momentary attention and popularity in the media communication environment cannot achieve this purpose. Its real key lies in the audience's continuous recognition of traditional handicraft. Merlin Wittrock, an American educational psychologist, believes that the human brain does not passively learn and record the input information, but selectively focuses on information and connects it with the original cognition to actively construct the meaning of information [18]. This view is consistent with the transformability of habitus, that is, under the influence of habitus, people can summarize past experience and make analogies to each field, so as to complete tasks different from those of previous habitus. The shaping of habitus in the field needs to realize a system with dual structural functions: a structure that simultaneously connects the objective structure of the field with the physical and mental structure of the individual [19]. Therefore, it is feasible and reasonable to construct a digital communication model of traditional handicraft based on "Field-Habitus". We proposes three stages of shaping audience habits for traditional handicraft in the digital context: enhancing the overall cognition, stimulating cultural identity, and promoting active learning. Each stage focuses on different cognitive layers of traditional handicraft as shown in Fig. 4.

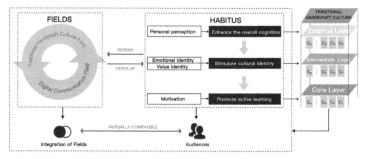

Fig. 4. A framework for digital communication of traditional handicrafts based on "Field-Habitus"

4.1 Enhancing the Overall Cognition

It is important to help audiences build a knowledge system of the content of the external layer (Fig. 2), while guiding them to pay attention to the historical, cultural and aesthetic values behind traditional handicraft, for the purpose of improving their overall knowledge of traditional handicraft. Traditional handicraft culture is a complex knowledge system, so the communicator needs to design the communicated content and form to impact the audience's attention and selection of information. The main approaches include: increasing the structure of traditional handicraft content, increasing the sharing and use value of content, etc. The dual presentation path of dynamic images and static graphics and texts is used to build a narrative path with stability, continuity and integrity, so that audiences can have a more comprehensive understanding of traditional handicraft.

4.2 Stimulating Cultural Identity

Establish a deep emotional link between the traditional handicraft culture and the audience, and promote the audience to form a cultural identity for the traditional handicraft. The cultural identity includes both emotional and value identity. First, pay attention to the emotional attitude of the audience, and pay attention to expressions that respond to the interests and needs of the audience, such as visualize content, situational learning, etc. The content of the transition layer (Fig. 3) is mainly used to activate their cultural memory to strengthen emotional identity. Secondly, teaching is the best way to reach value consensus and gain value recognition. Use high-quality cultural and creative resources to interpret and explain the contemporary value of traditional handicraft in a multi-dimensional way, further enabling the audience to form a cultural identity for the value of traditional handicraft.

4.3 Promoting Active Learning

Guiding the audience to form the habitus of independent cognition and then shaping the corresponding practice of independent cognition can effectively improve the cognitive depth of traditional handicrafts. In order for the audience to recognize the content of the core layer, the communicator should adopt a variety of appropriate strategies to promote the self-learning of the hearer, such as setting up personalized creative practices for traditional handicraft culture and other tasks. The audience will have a sense of achievement and mission in the process of creative practice. When the cultural connotation infiltrates into their hearts, they will realize the profound cultural heritage and cultural connotation among. The practice also renews the audience's memory of traditional handicrafts. Audiences accumulate knowledge in the practice of traditional handicraft culture dissemination and eventually internalizes it into their habitus. It is not only a motive for action, which presupposes the possibility of action, but also impacts the behavior of the actor.

5 Case Study: Validating Framework

For verify the feasibility of the framework, we conducted a practical exercise at the university. We developed a digital course on digital media innovation design with the theme of Cantonese Porcelain. Participants in the program span all grade levels and multiple design disciplines. Cantonese Porcelain, also known as "Guangcai", was included in the second batch of China's national intangible cultural heritage list in 2008. As one of the valuable intangible cultural heritages in the Lingnan area, it has its unique cultural connotation and historical research value. The digital course combines Guangzhou's local traditional handicraft with digital media technology, and is a great opportunity to provide practical validation of digital communication strategies for traditional handicraft.

5.1 Methodology

According to the strategic model, we set the online digital course into three main stages, each stage of which the communicator focuses on the communication of different cognitive layers of the Guangcai culture.

Phase I. The materialized knowledge of Cantonese Porcelain is the main teaching resource for this stage, include the following:

- Tools: pillow cases, ink boxes, raw material boxes, ring color bowls, order ring pens, brushes, etc.
- Porcelains: porcelain plates, bowls, vases, basins, cups, jars, pots, boxes and other porcelain artifacts that have survived from history to the present.
- Modern Guangcai handicrafts made by inheritors.
- Workshops of Guangcai where hand work is performed, scenes and places where crafts are made, etc.

We organized the above resources into seven categories and coded them as history, craft, tool, Subject-Matter, Pattern, color, and model to build a more complete knowledge system (see Table 2). When the communicator talks about the knowledge of Guangcai in the center of the screen, some knowledge cards (Fig. 5) will appear online at the same time. These cards contain brief descriptions and pictures of that seven categories, as well as a QR code. Audiences can scan the QR code to see the detailed content. In the digital classroom field, the teacher, as the presenter, cannot interact with the students and cannot keep an eye on how they are receiving the knowledge. The integrity of the Guangcai culture is likely to be destroyed in this communication process. But those cards can support the communicator's narration and build the audiences' overall knowledge.

Table 2. The seven categories of the knowledge of Guangcai[4]

Category	Contents	Number
History	The origin of Guangcai Porcelain	H-O
	The rise of Guangcai Porcelain	H-R
	The prosperous of Guangcai Porcelain	H-P
	The development of Guangcai Porcelain in the Republic of China era	H-M
	The development of Guangcai Porcelain now	H-N
Tool	"Leise Wan": A bowl for crushing paint	T-Lsw
	"Leise Chui": A rod for crushing paint	T-Lsc
	"Zhenxiang": A wooden box for storing tools	T-Z
	"Mohe": A dish for holding paint	T-M
	"Shuizhong": A bowl for holding water	T-S
	"Maobi": a writing brush for painting	T-Wb
	"Lingquan Bi": A special pen for drawing circles	T-L
Finish	The eight main steps in the process of painting Guangcai porcelain	F-1(8)
Model	Bowl	M-B
	Case	M-Ca
	Cup	M-Cu
	Kettel	M-K
	Plate	M-P
	Tank	M-Ta
	Tub	M-Tu
	Vase	M-V
	Other	M-O

(continued)

---

[4] The coding rule is mainly based on the first letter of the English word of the knowledge element of Guangcai porcelain. For example, the Guangcai modeling code "M" corresponds to the model, the bowl code "MB" corresponds to the Model Bowl and the box code "MC" corresponds to the Model Case. To ensure the uniqueness and correspondence of each code, try to select words with different initials and avoid words with the same initials.

Table 2. (*continued*)

Category	Contents	Number
Subject-Matter	Animal-related motifs	S-A
	Badge-related motifs	S-B
	Character-related motifs	S-C
	Flower-related motifs	S-F
	Landscape-related motifs	S-L
	Now-related motifs	S-N
	Ship-related motifs	S-S
Pattern	"Bianjiao": Patterns used to decorate borders	P-B
	"Doufang": Pattern used to separate the content of a painting	P-D
	"Jindi": Used to fill in blank patterns	P-J
	"Zuzhi": A group of motifs decorated with a combination of content	P-O
Color	Blue series	C-B
	Cyan series	C-C
	Gold series	C-G
	Black series	C-K
	Purpul series	C-P
	Red series	C-R
	White series	C-W
	Yellow series	C-Y

Fig. 5. Knowledge cards with the QR code

Phase II. We have developed an AR mobile application specifically to assist in the digital communication of Guangcai. The application was designed to help audiences understand the intermediate layer of Guangcai culture. Audiences could use it to scan the images of Guangcai porcelain. Some realistic and three-dimensional models will appear on their phones that are demonstrating the process of making the porcelain. This fun and interactive experience can enhance audiences' emotional identification with Guangcai culture. At the same time, we use Guangcai's cultural and creative design including game interaction category (Fig. 6) and physical product category (Fig. 7) which are the results of Intangible Cultural Heritage Workshop [20] as the main teaching resources for Phase II. The former uses elements of Guangcai culture as the main interface and sets up different levels of difficulty according to the cultural background, so that players can experience the contemporary value of the culture in the game interaction. The latter, on the other hand, is the result of a deeper transformation of Guangcai culture. Its visual layer can convey the cultural connotation to the audiences, and its practical performance can enhance the audiences' value identification with Guangcai.

Fig. 6. Games related to Guangcai culture

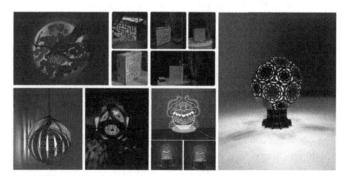

Fig. 7. Practical products related to Guangcai culture

Phase III. When it comes to Phase III, we set the task of creative motifs on the theme of Guangcai culture to motivate students to create. Audiences in this stage are mainly engaged in creative practice using Scratch, an easy-to-use creative programming software that is easy to use for most audiences. The audiences' creative graphic works on the theme of Guangcai created using Scratch are shown in Fig. 8. They are design with the original patterns of Guangcai, such as the Wan Zi Jin pattern and the Bo Gu Dou Fang pattern, as the source of creativity, while their colors are extracted from the main colors of Guangcai porcelain, such as blue, yellow and red. In order to complete the task, students needed to conduct preliminary research, select appropriate elements and applications, and create innovative designs on their own. In this process, they deepen their understanding of Guangcai culture and shape the habit of learning traditional crafts on their own. Phase III is the main part of the entire program of the digital course, which tests the audiences' mastery of what they have learned in the first two stages and allows them to truly understand what they have learned about Guangcai from a level of self-reflection and self-digestion. Eventually, audiences can further practice and continue to study in depth to complete deeper creative design tasks, such as game creative design, product creative design, etc.

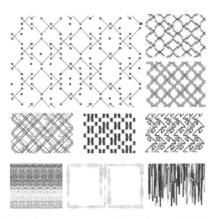

Fig. 8. Creative patterns about Guangcai culture

5.2 Results

We evaluate the results of the digital communication framework in practice by semi-structured interview. The interview is divided into two parts, the first part focuses on the participants' knowledge of the content of Guangcai culture (the knowledge of external later, intermediate layer and core layer) based on the reconstruction of the knowledge system, and the second part focuses on the completion of the milestones of the digital communication strategy. Ten participants were randomly selected for online telephone interviews at the end of each of the three course phases. The participants' professional backgrounds covered information interaction design, perceptual engineering, digital media, industrial design, etc. The final conclusions of the interviews were compiled (see Table 3). Based on the qualitative research analysis, it can be seen that the participants' knowledge of Guangcai varied significantly at different stages, and there was a tendency to gradually form a habitual path that fit the model, which to a certain extent supports the effectiveness of the traditional handicraft knowledge dissemination hierarchy combined with the online digital course field communication model.

Table 3. Results of the interviews in each phase

Phase	Themes	Conclusion
Phase I	Knowledge of Guangcai Porcelain	Participants were generally able to answer questions about Guangcai porcelain culture accurately, indicating a good reception of their knowledge at the external level
	Habitus forming trends	The participants focused on the cultural and aesthetic values of Guangcai, among others, and basically formed a holistic perception
Phase II	Knowledge of Guangcai Porcelain	Participants mostly enjoyed the AR experience format and had a good knowledge of the transitional layer (the process of Guangcai, the content of the skills)
	Habitus forming trends	The addition of cultural and creative content allowed participants to recognise the vibrancy of Guangcai and to shake off the stereotype of a declining and outdated traditional craft culture
Phase III	Knowledge of Guangcai Porcelain	The participants need to refine, transform and express the Guangcai elements in the process of completing the innovation task, where the core layer of knowledge (cultural values, core ideas, etc.) is more easily received and understood
	Habitus forming trends	The completion of the participants' creative works inspires a sense of achievement and the expectation of being better known by their own work; at the same time, a sense of mission to preserve traditional handicraft culture arises and the act of spontaneous dissemination begins

6 Discussion

In analyzing the dilemma of digital communication of traditional handicraft, we found that online digital classes are more suitable than other communication media for presenting traditional handicraft culture to the public. From the perspective of field transformation, the online digital class field and the traditional communication field are more homogeneous, showing a similar knowledge transmission structure, which lays a solid foundation for the in-depth exploration and nurturing of high-quality content to reflect the core spiritual value of traditional handicrafts. From the perspective of habitual cooperation, the audience in the online digital class field has the role of "learner" rather than "spectator", which is conducive to shaping habitus in the fragmented communication context. However, the formation of the dual structure of field and habitus is a long-term and systematic process, which places higher demands on communicators. On the basis of insisting on the field construction of digital communication, we have to continuously reflect and improve, so that the participants can internalize their habits in the increasingly accumulated communication practices. The number of participants in the online digital class practice of the Guangcai theme is limited, and in fact we need more test data to support further research to come up with a long-term effective framework. However, it was surprising that the participants produced many creative works that were recognized by professional Guangcai inheritors, which may trigger a communication circle effect centered on the individual participants and facilitate the further spread of Guangcai culture.

7 Conclusion and Future Work

Based on the field theory, this paper proposes the habit shaping path of cognition, identity and active learning, which provides a theoretical basis and decision reference for the digital inheritance and protection of traditional handicraft. The dissemination of traditional handicraft culture should be based on the present, build the integration mechanism between traditional handicraft culture field and digital communication field, standardize the hierarchical structure of communication content, enhance the public's emotional and value recognition of traditional handicraft, cultivate cultural confidence and spontaneous communication habits, and realize the effective dissemination of traditional handicraft in the context of new technology. In our subsequent research, we will focus on improving the connotation and structure of the "Field-Habitus", and at the same time digging deeper into the study mode that matches the laws of traditional handicraft inheritance, building a deep interaction between the inheritors and the audience, and improving the audience's participation, satisfaction and effect of learning traditional handicraft. The study model is also designed to build a deep interactive relationship between the inheritors and the audience, and to improve the audience's participation, satisfaction and learning effect of traditional handcraft culture.

Acknowledgments. This research was supported by The Ministry of Education's Industry-University Cooperative Education Project (220705242072650), Guangzhou University Innovation and Entrepreneurship Education Project (2020kc007) and Guangdong Provincial Science and Technology Innovation Strategy Special Fund Project (pdjh2023 b0170).

References

1. Zhu, Y.Q.: Production protection and living heritage of traditional skills. Folklore Res. **01**, 81–87 (2015). https://doi.org/10.13370/j.cnki.fs.2015.01.009
2. Yao, L.: Modern choices of ethnic traditional culture inheritance practices–a perspective based on field theory. Guangxi Ethnic Stud. (01), 89–98 (2018)
3. Bourdieu, P., Wacquant, L.D.: Practice and reflection - an introduction to reflective sociology. In: Li, M., Li, K. (eds.), p. 138. Central Compilation and Publishing House, Beijing (2004)

4. Zhao, X.: A study on the cultural memory and transmission field of Huizhou folk songs. J. Jiujiang College (Soc. Sci. Edn.) **40**(04), 109–114 (2021). https://doi.org/10.19717/j.cnki.jjus.2021.04.022

5. Li, Q.S.: A brief analysis of Bourdieu's field theory. J. Yantai Univ. (Phil. Soc. Sci. Edn.) (02), 146–150 (2002). https://doi.org/10.13951/j.cnki.issn1002-3194.2002.02.005

6. Yu, X.F.: Revolutionary culture in the "field" perspective - the cross-field communication of the spirit of Yimeng as an example. Shandong Soci. Sci. (04), 175–181 (2018). https://doi.org/10.14112/j.cnki.37-1053/c.2018.04.026

7. Yao, Z.W., Di, J.: The innovation of traditional handicraft in the context of intangible cultural heritage protection: the case of messy needle embroidery. J. Hubei Univ. National. (Phil. Soc. Sci. Edn.) (02), 101–106 (2020). https://doi.org/10.13501/j.cnki.42-1328/c.2020.02.011

8. Zhang, L., Lei, Y.C.: Communication and transmission of non-traditional heritage in the context of digital survival. China TV (10), 72–76 (2021)

9. Zhou, B.: Dialogue and listening: the inheritance and development of traditional handicrafts in contemporary context. J. Nanjing Art Inst. (Art Design) **06**, 61–65 (2010)

10. Jiang, S.R., Xu, Y.: Communication and inheritance of traditional handicrafts in the era of fusion media. J. Soc. Sci. Hunan Normal Univ. (05), 134–140 (2021). https://doi.org/10.19503/j.cnki.1000-2529.2021.05.016

11. Gong, C.B.: An examination of the survival paradox of new media culture. Shandong Soc. Sci. **10**, 31–34 (2010). https://doi.org/10.14112/j.cnki.37-1053/c.2010.10.026

12. Peng, X.: The realistic dilemma and innovative strategy of traditional culture inheritance in the new media era. Jiangxi Soc. Sci. (12), 233–238 (2014)

13. Chen, Y.: Fragmentation and reconstruction: traditional chinese culture in the context of microcommunication. Contemp. Commun. **04**, 65–68 (2017)

14. Sun, S.Q.: Cultivating socialist core values among ethnic minority college students based on "field-habit" theory. Educ. Rev. **03**, 88–92 (2019)

15. Cai, H.: "Culture" can only be conceptual existence - A discussion on the core concept of the Convention for the Safeguarding of Intangible Cultural Heritage. Ethnic Literat. Stud. **03**, 47–50 (2015)

16. Dong, Y.: On the "art" and "theory" of intangible cultural heritage of traditional handicrafts. Shanghai Arts Crafts **04**, 56–59 (2019)

17. Luo, F., Zhang, Y.J.: Research on the mechanism of video communication of "non-foreign heritage" from the perspective of living heritage. Sight Sound (10), 9–11 (2021). https://doi.org/10.19395/j.cnki.1674-246x.2021.10.003

18. Osborne, R., Wittrock, M.: The generative learning model and its implications for science education. Stud. Sci. Educ. **12**(1), 59–87 (1985). https://doi.org/10.1080/03057268508559923

19. Jing, L.N.: Field integration and shaping habitual habits: the ways and values of red culture communication in the new media perspective. J. Tonghua Normal College **11**, 54–58 (2021). https://doi.org/10.13877/j.cnki.cn22-1284.2021.11.009

20. Ji, Y., Fu, T.M., Tan, P., Sun, X.H.: Research on learning experience of intangible cultural heritage workshop from the perspective of innovation. In: Proceedings of the Seventh International Symposium of Chinese CHI (Chinese CHI 2019), pp. 109–112. Association for Computing Machinery, New York, NY, USA (2019). https://doi.org/10.1145/3332169.3332260

The Art of Artificial Intelligent Generated Content for Mobile Photography

Zhuohao Wu[1]([✉]), Min Fan[1], Ritong Tang[1], Danwen Ji[2], and Mohammad Shidujaman[3]

[1] School of Animation and Digital Arts, Communication University of China, Beijing, China
HiMrHOW@gmail.com
[2] College of Design and Innovation, Tongji University, Shanghai, China
[3] Department of Computer Science and Engineering, Independent University, Dhaka, Bangladesh

Abstract. Mobile photography is the most commonly used way for people to record images of their lives and work. As AI technology advances, specifically in neural style transfer and large-scale multi-modal models, AIGC (Artificial Intelligent Generated Content) provides a new possibility for the evolution of mobile photography. Through analyzing the habits of ordinary people and professional photographers in taking and editing mobile photos, we investigated how AI can help to turn professionals' best practice into standard assistance for ordinary people, effectively improving the quality and efficiency. Through analyzing the visual elements and structure of AIGC, we found how to decompose and reconstruct a style in the aspects of form, color and detail such as line and texture. We found how to fuse AIGC and a photo by blending stylized images and the original photo in different ways for different themes. These specific methods can be summarized into corresponding replicable models and processes, rather than artistically inspired creations, making the automatic implementation possible.

Keywords: AIGC · AI Art · Style Transfer · Artificial Intelligence · Photography · Creativity · Art · Design

1 Introduction

1.1 Mobile Photography

The history of mobile photography dates back to the late 1970s and early 1980s, when portable digital cameras were first developed. However, it was not until the introduction of the first camera phones in the late 1990s that mobile photography truly began to take off [1]. Here are the major milestones since then:

The first camera phone, Kyocera Visual Phone VP-210, was introduced in 1999; The first color camera phone, Sharp J-SH04, in 2000; The first smartphone with a built-in camera, Nokia 7650, in 2001; iPhone was released in 2007, marking a significant turning point in the history of mobile photography, as it popularizes the use of smartphones as a primary means of capturing and sharing photographs;

M. Kurosu and A. Hashizume (Eds.): HCII 2023, LNCS 14014, pp. 438–453, 2023.
https://doi.org/10.1007/978-3-031-35572-1_29

Samsung Galaxy S and iPhone 4, the first modern smartphones with a front-facing cam-era, were released in 2010. This allows for the popularization of self-portraits, or "selfies," taken with a smartphone. The first smartphone with a high-resolution camera, Nokia Lumia 1020, was released in 2013; The first smartphone with dual rear cameras, Huawei P9, was released in 2016, allowing for the creation of depth-of-field effects and improved low-light photography, launching a new round of mobile photography arms race.

As more and more people were using smartphones to take photos and upload to the internet, Instagram, world's most popular photo sharing social network started in 2010, and Twitter added photo-sharing feature in 2011. Today, mobile photography has become a dominant way for people to record their lives and work.

1.2 Digital and AI Photo Filters

Photo filters have been a feature of mobile photography since the early days of smart-phone cameras. Some of the earliest smartphones with camera capabilities, such as Nokia N95, released in 2006, already had a selection of photo filters that users could apply to their images. In the years since, the range and variety of photo filters available on smartphone cameras has continued to expand, with many phones now offering a wide selection of filters that can be applied to images in real-time as they are being taken or after the fact through editing apps.

As AI technology advances, photo filters that use artificial intelligence to apply various effects to images are introduced into photo editing apps to enhance images, change the look and feel of a photo, or create a specific artistic effect [2]. Typical examples include: Prisma, an app that applies artistic effect to images; FaceApp, an app that applies aging, gender swapping, and smiling effects to portrait images.

AI photo filters have had a significant impact on mobile photography. By providing users with an easy and convenient way to apply stylized filters to their photographs, it has made it easier for users to achieve a particular aesthetic with their photos [3]. In addition, AI photo filters have also made it possible for users to achieve more advanced edits and retouching without needing to have a deep understanding of photo editing software. These have contributed to the rise of mobile photography as a mainstream hobby.

AI photo filters also allow professional photographers to work more efficiently and produce a larger volume of work, and has also made it easier for photographers to experiment with different styles and techniques without needing to spend a lot of time on manual editing.

1.3 AIGC

The advance of computer vision, multi-modal machine learning, large-scale models, and diffusion models has led to a boom in AIGC in 2022. The products based on these technologies allows users to generate stunning stylized images with text and/or image prompts [4]. Within the year of 2022, from DALL·E 2 to Disco Diffusion, the door began to open to the all people instead of a small group of researchers; from Disco Diffusion to Stable Diffusion, the time it takes to generate images has decreased from several (tens of) minutes to several (tens of) seconds; from closed Midjourney to open-sourced Stable Diffusion, open source has inspired the developers around the world, and more and more AIGC products are being developed.

Released in November 2022, the Magic Avatars feature of the Lensa app became quickly viral on the internet. It allows users to generate a variety of images based on their portrait photos, transforming themselves into characters from ancient or future times, in different costumes, and in various visual styles. This perfectly demonstrates the potential of AI-generated content for mobile photography.

In our previous papers, AI Creativity and the Human-AI Co-creation Model [5] and Human-AI Co-creation of Art Based on the Personalization of Collective Memory [13], we explained that as AI technologies advance and are used proactively by people [6], more and more potential for human-AI co-creation will be released [7].

2 AI-Assisted Photo Taking and Editing

2.1 Themes of Mobile Photography

There is a wide range of themes that are popular in mobile photography. The specific themes that are most preferred can vary depending on cultural and personal factors [8]. We studied the photos published by ordinary people on Instagram, the world's most popular mobile photo social network, as well as the winning entries in global renowned mobile photography competitions. The most commonly seen themes can be summarized as: Portraits, Landscapes, Nature and Animals, Street and Fashion, Architecture, Travel, Food, Abstract and Experimental, etc.

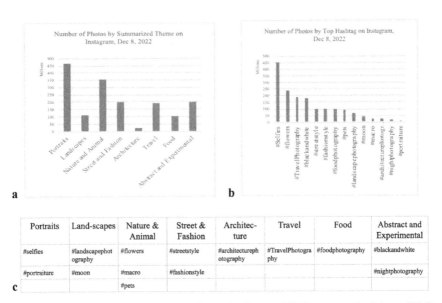

	Portraits	Land-scapes	Nature & Animal	Street & Fashion	Architec-ture	Travel	Food	Abstract and Experimental
	#selfies	#landscapephotography	#flowers	#streetstyle	#architecturephotography	#TravelPhotography	#foodphotography	#blackandwhite
	#portraiture	#moon	#macro	#fashionstyle				#nightphotography
c			#pets					

Fig. 1. Number of photos on Instagram (**a**) by top hashtag and (**b**) by summarized theme [9], Dec 8, 2022. (**c**) The classification between the summarized themes and top hashtag themes.

As we can tell from the numbers based on the top hashtags on Instagram (see Fig. 1), the most popular photo themes by ordinary people include: Portraits, Nature and Animal, Abstract and Experimental, Street and Fashion, Travel, Landscapes, Food, and Architecture. Considering the longtail hashtags unincluded, the real distribution of all photos should be different, but the listed themes here can still reflect the most popular mobile photo categories among ordinary people.

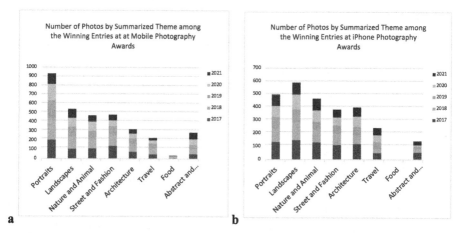

Fig. 2. Number of photos by summarized theme among the winning entries (**a**) at Mobile Photography Awards [10] and (**b**) at iPhone Photography Awards [11], 2017–2021

The study on the winning entries at Mobile Photography Awards and iPhone Photography Awards in the past five years shows professionals' preferences across photography themes (see Fig. 2).

By comparing the categorization data of ordinary people and professionals in mobile photography, we can see that Portraits is the most prominent common preference for both, although ordinary people mainly take selfies. Ordinary people's second preference is for Nature and Animal, especially Flowers, but their interest in Landscape is much less, which is different from the preferences of professionals. The third level of interest for ordinary people falls on Street and Fashion, Travel, Abstract and Experimental, and professionals also have a lot of interest in these three themes. However, ordinary people have little interest in taking photos of Architecture and are quite interested in taking photos of Food, which is different from the preferences of professionals, too.

2.2 AI Assistance in Photos Taking

Although the preferences of ordinary people and professionals in mobile photography are different, the common practices of professionals are the best tips for ordinary people. It is not easy for ordinary people to learn these skills, especially to consciously and actively use them flexibly, but AI can help ordinary people do these things well. As described below, most of the features can be done with the current AI technologies. AI recognizes the scene(s) first, either through image recognition or through getting voice command from the user, and then provides corresponding shooting assistance for each specific theme [12] (Table 1).

Table 1. Proposed AI-assisted features for different photo themes.

Themes		Shooting Tips & AI-Assisted Features
Portraits	#selfies	• Find or add some decent lighting • Lower the exposure, so to capture more details and leave some room for future editing • Make sure the faces are in focus
	#portraiture	• Artistic styles • Blend the real and the virtual
Landscapes	#landscapephotography	• Connect the foreground and background • Panoramic mode • Capture the light and shadow of sunlight • Small aperture
	#moon	• Capture the blue moment • Golden ratio composition • Focus on the moon and lower the exposure • Five times or more telephoto
Nature & Animal	#flowers	• Focus on one main single subject
	#macro	• Capture images: • with backlighting, such as silhouettes; • from a bird's eye view or low angle; • depict humanistic scenes or situations • Use a macro lens to capture close-up, detailed images. Sufficient lighting
	#pets	• Capture the moment • Focus on the nose and eyes • Blur the background
Street & Fashion	#streetstyle	• Find a proper foreground • Make an interesting composition: • Framing composition • Low angle • Mirror reflection
	#fashionstyle	• Focus on the model. Natural pose • Let clothes speak • Decent lighting

(continued)

Table 1. (*continued*)

Themes		Shooting Tips & AI-Assisted Features
Architecture	#architecturephotography	• Composition: • Contrast • Lines and geometry • Reflection • Utilize lens distortion
Travel	#TravelPhotography	• Ensure the composition is skillfully arranged to tell a story through the image • Use a wide-angle lens to capture images with a wide field of view • Use a macro lens to capture close-up, detailed images
Food	#foodphotography	• Capture an overall shot from a high angle • Capture images: • with side backlighting • close-up details • Large aperture
Abstract and Experimental	#blackandwhite	• Capture images: • with high shadow ratios • that show texture and detail • Create balance in the image using positive and negative space
	#nightphotography	• Capture the blue moment • Small aperture creates starburst • Increase exposure compensation to prevent over-exposure of bright areas • Telephoto lens creates a sense of compressed space

2.3 AI Assistance in Photo Editing

As AI technology advances, it can do more and more in photo editing.

Automatic adjustments: For quite a while, photo editing software could only automatically adjust the color, contrast, and other basic image settings based on the overall content of the photo. This can be useful for simple themes such as landscape or architectural photography; however, when it goes to the themes with complex content, such as daily life, such an overall adjustment often can't generate a satisfying result.

Object recognition: With the ability to automatically detect and identify objects within a photo, AI can apply proper effects to different areas; It would be even better if AI could help maintain a cohesive overall image while a specific area is changed. Some users might also want to manually modify the targeted object/area. This can be very useful for themes such as daily life and portrait photography.

Style transfer: With the help of AI, users can apply a specific style, either of a photo/image, or of an artist/art style, to the targeted photo. This can be very useful for themes such as portrait or fashion photography, where users may want to experiment with different looks and styles.

3   The Art of AIGC for Mobile Photography

3.1   Visual Elements in the Eyes of AI

Mobile photography is the most commonly used way for people to record their lives, and AIGC provides new possibilities for the evolution of photos. Users can transform a photo into a specified visual style through text prompts and image references, add or remove something in a photo, and blend reality and fiction in a photo... All of these are based on AI's understanding and manipulation of visual elements of the collective memory among all images it has learned [13].

AI can understand the visual elements of an image through a process called "feature extraction." This involves using algorithms to identify and analyze the various components of an image, such as lines, shapes, colors, and textures. These features are then used to classify the image, identify objects or scenes depicted in the image, or perform other tasks such as image recognition or image generation. There are various ways that AI systems can extract features from images. One common approach is to use machine learning algorithms, which are trained on large datasets of labeled images. These algorithms learn to recognize patterns and features in images and then can be used to identify similar patterns and features in new images. Another approach is to use deep learning algorithms, which are designed to mimic the way the human brain processes visual information. These algorithms can analyze images at a much deeper level and can identify more complex patterns and features in images.

AI does not really understand the visual elements in an image like a human, but only judges the probability of the pixel combination that constitutes the image based on its similarity to known objects which the AI was trained with. Therefore, it is easy to make mistakes in the process of AI generating images, such as generating a human face or body parts with misaligned organs, or generating some human body parts in a landscape painting simply because the referenced artist did many figure paintings. And, naturally, different AIs use different models and different training data, so the generation effect is also different [14].

At least for now, when generating and editing images through AI, it is necessary to communicate and interact with it in a way that is suitable for this specific AI program in order to achieve the desired effect. We're looking forward that AI can be more powerful to cover more knowledge and generate visual content in a smarter way in the future.

3.2   The Structure of Visual Styles in AIGC

Applying a specific visual style to an image is one of the most important foundations of the fusion of mobile photography and AIGC. However, as previously discussed, there is still a lot of room for current AI to improve. We need to find ways for AI to effectively generate high-quality images and make the settings as the best presets for users, otherwise users' aimless attempts and the results below expectation will lead to a poor user experience. We conducted the following research, taking Disco Diffusion as an example, which is a pioneer in this wave of AIGC and the foundation of many followers. Disco Diffusion remains the initial features and reflects the initial training data, which makes it easier to discover the root causes of questions.

Name of Style	Effect Rating	Perspective	Note (Forms, Texture...	Style Samples	Generated Results
Divisionism	Invalid				
Abstract Art	Invalid				
Neo-baroque	Invalid				
Japonism	Invalid				
Purism	Invalid				
Verism	Invalid				
Art Deco	Mediocre				
Precisionism	Poor	Details	会把笔刷的印记附着在画...		
Cloisonnism	Poor	Color			
Regionalism	Invalid				
Socialist Realism	Mediocre	Form	不符合原有画风，但是影...		
Synthetism	Excellent	Texture			
Intimism	Mediocre	Texture	影响了画面的质感，但一...		
New Medievialism	Invalid				
Fauvism	Excellent	Color Texture			
Muralism	Excellent	Color Texture			
Art Nouveau (Modern)	Excellent	Color Texture	不太能分辨飞船和森林的...		
Cartographic Art	Mediocre	Color			
Existential Art	Poor	Color	改变了图片的颜色，但是...		
Pictorialism	Invalid		可能适配人像，不适配风景		
Expressionism	Invalid		可能适配人像，不适配风景		
Lettrism	Invalid		内容和风格不匹配		
Kitsch	Poor		可能适配人像，不适配风景		
Mechanistic Cubism	Mediocre	Color Details	风格不适配		
Miserablism	Mediocre	Texture Color	对色彩的影响不太稳定，...		
Neo-Romanticism	Excellent	Texture Color Details			
Abstract Expressionism	Excellent	Form Color			
Cubism	Mediocre	Color			

Fig. 3. Tests of AIGC on styles, by Zhuohao Wu and his team, 2022

We have tested over 900 artists, 250 art styles, and 220 art media on Disco Diffusion (see Fig. 3) and obtained the following initial insights:

1. By specifying a certain visual style in the form of a text prompt, as long as the style is contained in the AI's training dataset and the name of the style can be uniquely identified without confusion, the effect can be produced. Different AIs have different compositions in their training datasets, text semantic understanding and image generation algorithm models, so the effects of generating images are also different.
2. A specific visual style mainly affects the visual elements of the target image in three aspects: Form, Color, and Detail such as line and texture. Some visual styles have strong effects in all three aspects, while others only perform well in one or two aspects. In order for an image to be successfully stylized by AI, the applied visual style(s) must perform well on all three aspects, so it is necessary to choose a visual style that performs well in all three aspects or use a combination of several visual styles.

3. In the above three aspects, the ability of the Form influence mainly depends on the content of the training data of the visual style, such as figure, landscape, architecture, machine and etc. Some artists' works are more about figure art, so the AI visual style trained with these works is good at presenting figures; and as previously discussed, because AI lacks real semantic understanding of things, but is based on probability judgment, if such a figure-art-based AI visual style is applied to a landscape image, the result could have some strange human body parts in the landscape. Therefore, when applying the AI visual style, it is necessary to pay attention to the matching between the content of the target image and the content that the visual style is good at; even if it cannot be completely matched, it has to find some matching parts in the content that the visual style is good at, so to obtain a better generation effect.

As in the example (see Fig. 4), the AI generated images are affected by the training data significantly not only for the style, but also for the form: When; When Alphonse Mucha's artworks are used as training data, the generated result tends to have human figures unexpectedly.

Fig. 4. AI generated images with the text prompt "A shining sea of mint leaves, clear sky and beautiful clouds" and (**a**) "by Claude Monet" V.S. (**b**) "by Alphonse Mucha", by Zhuohao Wu with Disco Diffusion, 2022

4. Unlike the way humans think and draw, AI has its own unique way of working, such as parameterization. Users can quantitatively mix several different AI visual styles by giving weights, just as they use different amounts of ingredients and seasonings according to different recipes when cooking. As demostrated in Fig. 5, it was not 6 images merged into one, but 6 styles fused to build up a pipeline for generating images in such a specific "new" style. What's more, users can regenerate the target image according to the image composition pattern of a "seed", which is a set of parameters for the representation of a particular image. Users can also quantitatively set various parameters to control how close the generated result to the target image and to the text prompts, the finesse and color details of the image and etc.

5. Before this wave of AIGC, neural style transfer was the main AI stylization method, and it is still effective today. In this method, AI looks for similarities in visual elements between the target image and the style image, and applies the specific styles of the style image to the corresponding similar visual elements in the target image. Because it is purely visual element correspondence, any image can be used as a style to apply, and it is more flexible than using text prompts to specify a style (see Fig. 6). Neural style transfer still has its value and wide application scenarios.

Fig. 5. 6 styles fused to form a new one: 50% as Edmund Dulac's, 18.75% as Martin Deschambault's, 12.5% as Junc Wenjun Lin's, 6.25% as Victo Ngai's, 6.25% as Sylvain Sarrailh's and 6.25% as a randomly picked style trending on Artstation. By Zhuohao Wu with Disco Diffusion, 2022.

3.3 The Fusion of AIGC and a Photo

Today, AI often has defects in the results of style transfer for photos, which makes it difficult to use directly. For example, when using style transfer on landscapes and buildings, the result is often good, but when applying it to people in the photograph, the result becomes aesthetically unpleasing to humans. Another issue is that it can be difficult to balance between overall effect and detailed depiction, either lacking overall effect with too much focus on details or vice versa. Additionally, some styles are better at portraying overall color structure, while others excel at capturing texture and brushstrokes, and using just one style for style transfer does not produce the best results. In these cases, an effective solution is to divide and rearrange the visual elements of the image into layers and merge them to create a fused style effect. Let's discuss a few examples.

Example 1. Blending stylized image and original photo in the targeted area
In this example, a little girl is sitting in front of a window full of flowers (Fig. 7-1) and AI turns the photo into a colorful, brush stroke style oil painting (Fig. 7-2). The overall

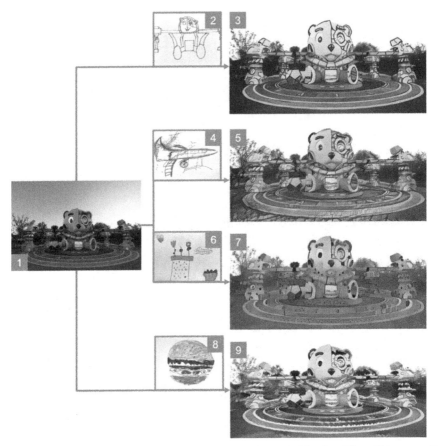

Fig. 6. Using kids' drawings as styles and applied to a photo. By Zhuohao Wu and his team with Deep Dream Generator, 2022.

artistic feel of the image is very good, but the face may appear strange after applying such an artistic style, and needs to be adjusted specifically to match both the overall artistic style and human aesthetics. The following steps are demonstrated manually, but can be fully implemented using current AI technology.

Step 1: Recognize and select the area of the face in the photo, and expand and feather the edge appropriately (Fig. 7-3).

Step 2: Overlay the original photo at 40% transparency on top of the AI-generated stylized image, so that the strange feel of the artistic style is balanced by the realism of the photo in the area of the face (Fig. 7-4).

Step 3: Overlay another layer of the original photo, blend mode Linear Light, transparency 30%, to brighten the skin tone and increase contrast, making it more consistent with the overall visual style (Fig. 7-5).

Step 4: Overlay another layer of the original photo, blend mode Screen, transparency 70%, to further brighten the skin tone and make it more consistent with the overall color of the image (Fig. 7-6).

Step 5: Fine-tune some small details. And the final result is achieved, with a strong overall artistic style and a face that meets the aesthetics of ordinary people (Fig. 7-7).

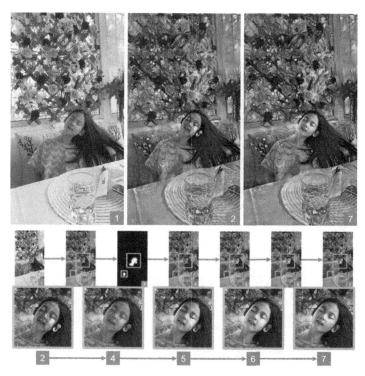

Fig. 7. A Little Girl Sitting in front of a Window Full of Flowers, by Zhuohao Wu with Deep Dream Generator, 2020

Example 2. Blending stylized images and original photo to form the expected color distribution and texture details

In this example, a group of Chinese-style buildings were located next to a rice field, with mountains shrouded in clouds and fog behind them, and several crested ibises flew out of the rice field. I tried to stylize the photo using images of various styles as references. After some trial and error, the best result is obtained by fusing the two stylized results with the original photo.

Step 1: Use style transfer to generate two images, one in watercolor style with preferred texture (Fig. 8-2), and the other in digital art style with preferred colors (Fig. 8-4).

Step 2: Overlay the watercolor stylized image (Fig. 8-2) on the original photo, blend mode Lighten, transparency 0%, to give the photo the texture of a watercolor painting, while weakening unnecessary intricate details (Fig. 8-3).

Step 3: Overlay the digital art stylized image (Fig. 8-4), blend mode Hard Light, transparency 40%, to adjust the color feeling of the image (Fig. 8-5).

Step 4: Fine-tune some details and colors. And the final result is achieved, with a clear watercolor texture and an overall digital art color feeling (Fig. 8-6).

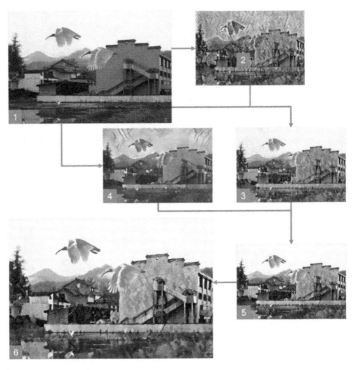

Fig. 8. A Winery on the Mountainside and Crested Ibis in the Rice Fields, by Zhuohao Wu with Deep Dream Generator, 2021

Example 3. Stylized images through style transfer VS through diffusion model
There is no doubt that AIGC based on multi-modal machine learning and diffusion model is the most popular application recently, generating a large number of stunning images. What does this bring to mobile photography? Let's also use the photo of the little girl in front of the flower window as the base image, and let such an AI generate some images (see Fig. 9). High-quality images are constantly produced, but at the same time, a major problem arises: if we want the AI to play freely, it can do a great job at creating various different results; however, there's no direct way to keep a part of the image unchanged in terms of content, while having the overall style changed, because the generation process itself has a certain degree of randomness. Of course, we can use a mask to make a part of the image unchanged. If it is a portrait, we can also train a model specifically for a certain face just what Lensa does, to ensure that the face remains consistent and correct. In other words, to serve mobile photography, this new type of AIGC also needs to establish a matching workflow. After all, the main purpose of ordinary people is to optimize their own photos. When users really want to use their photos to create some new

artworks, just as what the professionals do in the Visual FX & Digital Art competition [15], AI generation can be a great helping hand to enhance efficient initial explorations and high-quality final presentations.

Fig. 9. A Little Girl Sitting in front of a Window Full of Flowers, by Zhuohao Wu with Stable Diffusion optimized by Deep Dream Generator, 2022. Figure 9-0. is the original photo; Fig. 9-s. is the style transferred image as in the example 1; Fig. 9-1., 2., 3., 4., 5., 6. Are generated by diffusion model.

Example 4. Applying a style to a series of photos

When users do mobile photography, they often take a series of photos, either taking different angles of a person/object, or taking different objects/scenes in an environment. These photos form a series, and when they are stylized, a consistent style is often expected. If the photos are processed one by one through manual adjustment, it will be very cumbersome, but AI can easily apply the adjusted artistic style to all selected photos, and can even make automatic fine-tuning based on the specific situation of each photo. It will significantly improve the efficiency and quality of photo processing.

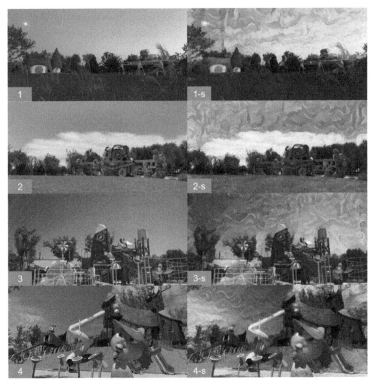

Fig. 10. Views of a kids land in the style of Wheat by Vincent van Gogh, by Zhuohao Wu with Deep Dream Generator, 2022. Figure 10-1., 2., 3., 4. are the original photos and Fig. 10-1-s., 2-s., 3-s., 4-s. are the stylized images.

4   Conclusion and Future Work

In 2022, AIGC, represented by image generation, has made significant breakthroughs in practical applications, turning AIGC from a toy that was only for a small group of researchers and not easy to use into a productivity tool that is almost within reach for everyone. This is the best example of AI Creativity: helping everyone transcend themselves, enabling ordinary people to do things they couldn't even imagine before, and enhancing the abilities and efficiency of professionals; human and AI co-create by playing to each other's strengths to achieve more.

In this paper, we have discussed how AI can be used to improve the aesthetic quality and efficiency of mobile photos. We demonstrated how to artistically process the photos with AI and suggested the corresponding methods and workflows. However, we haven't done enough test yet to validate the methods in a wider range and with a considerate number of users. This is what we need to cover in the coming months. On the other hand, AI can also match an image with beautiful words, music, dynamic effects or generate some videos, based on simple requests from people. More workflows are being or about to be reshaped soon.

Acknowledgements. The authors like to thank Wenrui Liao, Yuan Zhang, Gongkai Luo, Yongkang Lin, Zhiting He, Shenglin Xu, Gen Mai, Dan Wu, Congyu Jiang, Tianpei Zang, Xiangtan Zhao and all the volunteers for their contribution in this paper, as well as Liwen Feng for the technical support on deploying and optimizing AI applications. This work was also supported by the Beijing Nova Program (Z211100002121160).

References

1. Ling, R., Fortunati, L., Goggin, G., Lim, S.S., Li, Y.: The Oxford Handbook of Mobile Communication and Society, p. 392 (2020)
2. Fatima, N.: AI in photography: scrutinizing implementation of super-resolution techniques in photo-editors. In: 35th International Conference on Image and Vision Computing New Zealand, pp. 1–6. Wellington, New Zealand (2020)
3. Mazzone, M., Elgammal, A.: Art, creativity, and the potential of artificial intelligence. Arts **8**(1), 26 (2019)
4. Cetinic, E., She, J.: Understanding and creating art with ai: review and outlook. ACM Trans. Multimedia Comput. Commun. Appl. **18**(2), 1–22 (2022)
5. Wu, Z., Ji, D., Yu, K., Zeng, X., Wu, D., Shidujaman, M.: AI creativity and the human-AI co-creation model. In: Kurosu, M. (ed.) HCII 2021. LNCS, vol. 12762, pp. 171–190. Springer, Cham (2021). https://doi.org/10.1007/978-3-030-78462-1_13
6. Daniele A., Song, Y.: AI + Art = Human. In: AAAI/ACM Conference on AI, Ethics, and Society (AIES 2019) on Proceedings, pp. 155–161. New York, USA (2019)
7. Mikalonytė, E., Kneer, M.: Can artificial intelligence make art?: folk intuitions as to whether ai-driven robots can be viewed as artists and produce art. ACM Trans. Hum. Robot Interact. **11**(4), 1–19 (2022)
8. Manovich, L.: Designing and Living Instagram Photography: Themes, Feeds, Sequences, Branding, Faces, Bodies. Instagram and Contem-porary Image, Chapter 4 (2016)
9. Top themes of photos by hashtag on Instagram. https://instagram.com/. Accessed 8 Dec 2022
10. The annual winners at Mobile Photography Awards 2017–2021. https://mobilephotoawards. com/11th-annual-mpa-winners-honorable-mentions/. Accessed 8 Dec 2022
11. The annual winners at iPhone Photography Awards 2017–2021. https://www.ippawards.com/ gallery/?v=1c2903397d88Online. Accessed 8 Dec 2022
12. Farhat, F., Kamani, M. M., Wang, J. Z.: CAPTAIN: comprehensive composition assistance for photo taking. ACM Trans. Multimedia Comput. Commun. Appl. **18**(1), 1–24 (2022)
13. Wu, Z., et al.: Human-AI co-creation of art based on the personalization of collective memory. In: ACAIT 2022 on Proceedings. Changzhou, China (2022)
14. Das, P., Varshney, L.R.: Explaining artificial intelligence generation and creativity. IEEE Sign. Process. Magaz. **39**(4), 85–95 (2022)
15. VISUAL FX & DIGITAL ART WINNERS | 11TH ANNUAL MPA, https://mobilephotoa wards.com/visual-fx-digital-art-winners-11th-annual-mpa/. Accessed 8 Dec 2022

Building the Regional Identity of Sustainable Architecture
A Participatory Tool Under Systematic Thinking

Lingrui Zhang[1] and Yuan Liu[2(✉)]

[1] Accademia di belle arti di Roma, Roman, Italy
[2] Beijing Institute of Fashion Technology, Beijing 100029, China
yuan.liu@polimi.it

Abstract. One of the keys to understand sustainable architecture is to construct the cultural identity of urban. The losing of urban characteristics is reflected both in the convergence of geography and the passage of cultural identity. This study follows the exploration of two research (Jones & VanPatter 2009; Pereno & Barbero 2020) in complex systems, aims to develop a participatory tool to help facilitate the process co-creation. We analyze the famous regional buildings in China to summarize the corresponding architectural characteristics, also take the reconstruction of Hougou ancient village in Shanxi Province for a pilot research. Urban elements are organized and proposed in a modular way, we aim to explore new methods to engage stakeholders in the activity, in response to sustainable urban needs in the future.

Keywords: Sustainable Architecture · Urban Characteristics · Participatory Tool

1 Introduction: System Design in Cultural Sustainability

Understanding environmental problems with complex systems is not new, communities, governments, and industries work through the corresponding means to enabling resilient territories and social resources, both from the design and non-design side (Jones 2009). Jones defines the four domains of design processes within systemic design, his relevant methodology is used to address the system problems in design, linking generative design guidelines to systematic theoretical principles, for example, activity analysis, hermeneutics, participatory design and visualize problems, graphically shape complexity (Pereno & Barbero 2020). Battistoni and the team (2019) proposed a method named Holistic Diagnosis (HD) to systematically frame state-of-the-art and complex scenarios. Interdisciplinary thinking and synergy are also mentioned, to link the synergies between design, technology, economics, and sociology (Ruttonsha 2018). In subdivided disciplines, the idea of complex social systems has been explored by designing products and services, policy making, territorial systems and urban contexts (Jones 2014; Barbero & Bicocca 2017; Ruttonsha 2018).

Compared with other disciplines, the involvement of design views and methods is relatively young, but it has shown an increasingly vigorous development trend, and its feasibility has been verified in many fields. The purpose of this paper is to discuss how to construct architectural territorial identity through participatory tools, under the framework of systemic thinking, to expand the aspects and ideas of sustainable territorial design.

2 Sustainability Under Systematic Design Thinking

The design of architecture has a strong connection with nature, economic and technical conditions, the impact of a particular social situation on a person usually varies individually (Mallgrave 2013; Ploder & Stadlbauer 2016; Anderson 2006). However, the global cultural convergence caused by integration is widely reflected, where the regional culture of architecture is gradually submerged by the global one, and the national nature of architecture is replaced by the "international nature". Commonality and individuality, architectural convergence and cultural diversity of various nationalities manifest themselves. They are a contradictory unity based on each other and promoting each other.

It is necessary to develop a new understanding between architecture and region, region has two meanings here: one is as a place, a specific location, and a single entity closely related to the geographical environment. The second is to understand it as a record of history and memory, which includes culture components except the objective material facts. We define regional characteristics from the second aspect, where the "region" is the symbolic representative of the nation and history, which is preserved through modern design techniques, and has the potential of cultural sustainability.

Sustainable architecture and its surroundings are a dynamically evolving system that is an assemblage of distinct elements (Ryan 2014), there is a certain hierarchical structure among the components of this system (Lee 2020). Therefore, system design in sustainable buildings is multifaceted. On the one hand, the construction and development of sustainable buildings is a systematic engineering; on the other hand, system design provides new ideas for sustainable architecture.

Thus, we discuss this problem in both resource-based and cultural level. The direction within system design presents two characteristics: the strong nature of time, and the increasing cultural communication.

From the literature, sustainability in architecture is reflected in the following levels:

- **Temporal spirit.** Sustainable design was initially reflected in the focus of climate, forming a design theory called bioclimatic localism. At that time, the sustainable architecture focuses on the overall design thinking in the environmental system. Then it gradually turned to seek the harmonious between man, architecture and nature, and the idea of system design was gradually improved (Ryan 2014; Bennetts, Radford & Williamson 2003; Sevaldson 2011). Nowadays, the route of understanding sustainability is to treat various living systems as entities with organic life and self-sustainable characteristics. The expression of innovative has led the trends and fashion (Sassi 2006; Gauzin-Müller 2002; Opoku 2015).
- **Transmissibility.** Architectural has the role of proceeding social information and apply their language theme in shaping the urban characters (Sondhi 2015). Business occupies social information attached to the building, and the prosperity of the market

economy makes the manufacturers of goods compete for the consumers. Architectural also has the function of spreading non-verbal symbols (Remizova 2015). It is necessary to further understand the characteristics of non-verbal symbols in propagation systems, to form a certain way to transmit communication (Jackson 2006; Stojiljković & Ristić Trajković 2018).

3   Understand Architecture with Regional Characteristics

How to define the self-identity of architecture is essential, what remains corny but important are the natural conditions of the region, social, cultural, economic background, and other factors. Guy and Farmer (2012) emphasize the importance of local culture, and new approaches is necessary to collaborate more closely, energy-efficient buildings that fail to meet cultural needs and services may be prematurely obsolete (Foster & Kreinin 2020).

The regional nature of architecture is reflected in the "local spirit". The geography of building is first influenced by the environment, and then affected by the specific terrain, geomorphic conditions, and the construction environment around the city. It is also important to consider history and cultural environment, architects should always seek their roots in the traditional culture of the region (Liang 2014).

To sum up, the cultural sustainable identity of architecture may have the following two qualities: to reflect the "times", and to connect with the regional nature. The "times" means that new industrial, material, and cultural needs such as the impact on the meaning and language of architecture, and the birth of new technologies like metaverse which brings new design needs. Regional component is not exaggerated paste cultural symbols on architecture, but to let the "audience" feel it, to grasp the climate, natural environment, humanities, history, and consider it as an important factor of design. The richness in intimacy, sense of belonging, all have regional characteristics of living space expressed with it.

3.1   Architectural Identity for Cultural Sustainability

Sustainable construction comes with complexity. Architects around the world take unique construction methods that echo specific lifestyles. But local culture evolves as societies develop, especially as they collide with other countries and cultures, introducing new knowledge as well as new building materials and techniques in the process (Hillier 2012). The sustainability of culture and architecture is reflected in three aspects: the biophilic of architecture; sensory sustainability; regional, national, or political sustainability.

Biophilic Nature of Architecture. The representatives of cultural ecology of architecture includes biophilic. The design of biophilic is naturally embedded into the environment. It requires applying architectural forms and materials to urban space through the consideration of sunshine, natural wind, internal and external landscape (Zhong, Schröder & Bekkering 2021). Biological architecture application has many layers: the overall form and layout of the building; green plants in public areas; urban microclimate caused by ventilation and lighting; and urban biodiversity (Grierson 2009; Opoku 2015;

Ignatieva 2010). These ideas are known as the multi-level greening of high-rise buildings, which also include the "urban geometry" and the resulting complex wind direction and sunlight elements (Aydogan & Cerone 2021).

Sensory Sustainability. Individual sensory preference also response to space and place. By controlling the posture of the building space, different functions can be realized to influence mental conditions (Li 2019). Under the varied aesthetic tastes and values, people have different needs that produce architectural results. Architect Diebedo Francis Kere turned his childhood into the design "a tree", to explore the sustainable impact of group senses on architecture. The British serpentine pavilion uses a circular architectural structure and a rich blue color to evoke natural feelings. This is exactly the influence of the individual senses on the overall architectural structure.

Regional, Ethnic, or Political Sustainability. Due to the different historical traditions, living customs, cultural conditions and aesthetic concepts of ethnic groups, the architecture components vary, such as the plane layout, structural methods and shapes. Details of the buildings in different ethnic areas are also different, presenting a simple and natural style and characteristics (Kistova & Tamarovskaya 2015).

Designed by Marcel Ferencz and opened in 2022, the new building of the Ethnology Museum[1] in Budapest City Park, its spectacular logo is the glass curtain wall around the landscape roof garden, which is made from the ethnological patterns with distinctive ethnic features. The related design method focuses on organically organizing characteristic elements form historical to new and creating buildings that can assimilate into the surrounding. That's the value of design tools in building regional characteristics, as they summarize, organize, and participate in decision-making.

3.2   Measurement of Regional Buildings

To better understand the concept of regional building, this paper considers both the sustainable development and the regional strategies of architectural design under the influence of different factors. We summarize five relevant characteristics to explain sustainable elements under the support of architectural case studies.

Climate Adaptability. As a unique resource of nature, climate directly affects human production, life and social activities, and form adaptation to climate conditions is also a common method in architectural design. Follow people's adaptive responses to environmental climate change will effectively support design methods in existing living spaces (Ryan 2013; Pereno & Barbero 2020). Sustainable buildings can achieve the purpose of reducing emissions and energy conservation to produce better comprehensive benefits. The Dameisha Resort of Shenzhen, China, has designed automatically regulated external shading system according to the height of the sun and the indoor illumination, to achieve the architectural need of "breathing".

Local Material. Regional materials convey strong local information, and their identification inevitably becomes the key content of architecture. Regional materials usually

---

[1] See: https://napur.hu/en/.

have unique color or texture, and it can be easily associated with traditions (Thomas 2006). Sustainable development needs to be coordinated with economy, environment, resources, population, and society. It is necessary to maximize the use of natural resources and energy, also to maximize productivity and reduce energy consumption (Muazu & Alibaba 2017).

Traditional brick, stone, wood, and other natural materials have adaption to the local climate. Modern architects pay attention to the traditional culture and respond to them in the spatial form and formal characteristics. The wall façade design of "Ningbo Museum" is made of bamboo formwork concrete and old bricks and tiles collected from civilians. The fusion of classical materials and modern design is popular, this route can integrate the humanistic color while meeting the functional needs. The example goes in the main media center building of Wuhan Military Games[2], it considers the pattern of Jingchu culture[3] to embody the native living.

Native Terrain. The discussion of social ecologic cannot ignore the utilization and discussion of terrain origin. Under the concept of sustainable development, cities start to divide different regions into natural ecological areas according to regional characteristics. Designers conform to the aesthetic characteristics of regional buildings, and form more "rational" regional design characteristics (Stokols, Lejano & Hipp 2013). For example, the Lotus Hotel in Xiangsha Bay[4], Ordos city, is a green building designed according to the shape of the terrain contour. It fixes the building in the floating sand by using the origin of the terrain.

Energy Saving and Environmental Protection. Sustainability requires the protection of the ecological environment and attention to environmental issues (Olabi 2011). Modern buildings pay great attention to improving the utilization rate of natural resources. Architects use technology to process and recycle the renewable resources in nature with the original materials to proceed energy saving. Guangzhou Pearl River Tower[5] organically integrates climate technology, solar and wind energy, and generates its own electricity to realize the concept of "zero energy consumption".

Cultural Symbolism. Architecture is an expression of regional culture, due to the differences in historical inheritance, lifestyle and local customs vary their regional cultural characteristics. "Bird's Nest"[6] in Beijing perfectly integrates the openwork techniques in traditional culture, that also represents in the ceramic grain and the most advanced modern steel structure design. The shape is like the "nest" of life, which keeps auspicious wishes.

---

[2] See: http://en.hubei.gov.cn/special/7thcism_mwg/.

[3] Jingchu culture is a regional culture that emerged today in the Hubei area of China.

[4] See: https://www.archdaily.com/296725/xiangshawan-desert-lotus-hotel-plat-architects.

[5] See: https://www.som.com/projects/pearl-river-tower/.

[6] See: https://www.chinahighlights.com/beijing/attraction/birds-nest.htm.

4 Project: Participatory Methods Under Systematic Design

As mentioned earlier, design role in complex system contributes to innovative tools such as activity analysis, hermeneutics and participatory design (Pereno & Barbero 2020). Participatory design has been conducted in policy making under the systemic dialogue (Blomkamp 2022), also to improve the sustainability of E-waste management under stakeholders' conversation (Méndez-Fajardo, Böni, Vanegas & Sucozhañay 2020).

For sustainable architecture, we believe that participatory design is particularly advantageous. It includes all aspects of regional architecture composition in a decentralized way, such as ecological materials that reflect natural properties, the standards that reflect regional or political possibilities, along with criteria of narratives and visualization of cultural symbols. It is possible to understand sustainable architecture from several perspectives, including building occupants (residents), architects (designers) and urban planners (government, community, group).

Participatory design, this "democratic" approach is often presenting people's actual feelings. For example, in the Manheim Spinelli Community Center, to improve the lives of the refugees, 18 students from the TU Kaiserslautern School of Architecture worked together with 25 refugees to establish a community center, forming an environment with gardens and public green space (Nettelbladt & Boano 2019). Hybrid Space Lab shows three cases (CITY KIT, DIY Pavilion, SIMPLE CITY)[7], turning residents into "manufacturers" of cities through network-based platforms. These cases build channels for communication among residents' needs, users of the urban environment and construction experts. Applying participatory design in architecture, designers are no longer a small team trying to do their best, but a community of designers, architects, and urban planners from around the world who will collaborate in the specific design of future architecture, landscape, and urban planning.

In this paper, we create a participatory tool including the co-work with several stakeholders, to help them establish sustainable regional identity and characteristics. This approach is seen as a tool visualization of Sanders, the "3-D mock-ups using e.g., foam, clay, Legos or Velcro-modeling" summarized by Brandt and Binder (2010), to help participants without architectural background to present regional feature modules.

4.1 The Participatory Tool Called "Small Squares"

The so-called "Small square" is a participatory analysis tool that co-create the geographical reconstruction by sustainably presenting the identity modules of one target area. This project creates a small data wall with many squares (see Fig. 1), it is used as database specially created by designers for the target groups to participate in information collection, problem analysis and countermeasure research. It aims to establish a user-centered construction mode, giving the right of the living environment to the real individual, to identify the identity of local architecture under sustainable needs.

This project took a pilot study (2020) in author's hometown, Hougou Ancient Village, Shanxi Province, since it retains ancient folk customs and culture. Yet this part of the culture has not been well combined with modern architecture. We understood all aspects of the regional characteristics of Hougou, and split and reorganize the five levels of its regional characteristics according to the previous study (Table 1).

---

[7] Https://hybridspacelab.net/.

Table 1. Analysis of regional characteristics

Place of Measurement	Climate Adaptation	Materials Locality	Territory Originality	Energy Conservation and Environmental Protection	Culture Symbolization
Village	The east, west and north sides of villages are surrounded by soil slopes, and the mountain can effectively break the icy wind from northwest in winter	Residents use local materials, such as loess, gray bricks, timbers, stones, grasses, wheat straws and so on, and take advantage of the properties of those materials	Site selections, layouts and architectural forms reflect the philosophy of "harmony of nature and human". The whole structure of the villages represents the bionics artistic conception of "two dragons playing with a pearl"	The villagers live a self-sufficient life and retain the original production workshops such as vinegar workshops, oil workshops, wine workshops, rice workshops and bean curd workshops	Folk crafts such as paper-cutting, wall painting, cloth tigers and embroidered insoles convey the desires for warding off evil, praying for blessings and longevity and so on
Cave	Rotundas and domes with high windows, penetrate sunlight into the inner of caves deeply in winter	The loess and stone are used for laying heated beds, cutting earth, demoulding and baking bricks to build earth cave dwellings, stone cave dwellings and brick cave dwellings	Dig the earth caves deeply, forming the cave in the cave; And divided caves into sections to form a longitudinal inner and outer kiln	Places where the earth is hard are chosen for cave dwellings to insulate the "walls"	The curved exteriors and arched windows reflect the people's love of life

(continued)

Table 1. (*continued*)

Place of Measurement	Climate Adaptation	Materials Locality	Territory Originality	Energy Conservation and Environmental Protection	Culture Symbolization
Courtyard	The principal room located in the north courtyard faces south, and the front door is set on the south or southeast side, to avoid the monsoon wind. This design takes advantage of the warm and humid summer south-westerly winds to freshen the courtyard air	The streets were built on a slope and paved with rubble. Rainwater can flow down along the slope to prevent erosion to the loess. The wall shelters are set on the gable that are the opposite of the door, to flow the air around the wall and gather qi together	The courtyards are irregularly shaped and built according to the terrain. The yard is lower in front and higher behind, and the ground is paved with gray bricks, which ensure that the ground is dry and conducive to drainage	The courtyard drains were made of stone and covered with iron wires to filter debris and prevent clogs of the waterways. The public drainage system is buried deep underground	Quadrangle courtyards are constituted with the primary room, east and west wing rooms and reversely-set room, surrounding a courtyard in the middle. The trilateral courtyards are distributed in a concave shape
Temple	Temples stress" facing onto the sunny side, backing onto the shadowy side, and fronting water and with hills on the back". They are tend to be built on the slopes of the south due to the warm sunshine	The whole of the shrines are made up of bricks and brick carvings	The 13 temples are built according to "Feng Shui" and are located refer to the eight diagrams, integrating Buddhism, Taoism and Confucianism	The application of brick carving, wood carving and stone carving techniques returns the architectures back to its original nature	There are shrines in the temple, which are moderate in size and exquisite in shape. Because of the disparate beliefs in Confucianism, Buddhism and Taoism, the village temple architectures have different styles

Through the analysis, the author collected a large number of regional building materials with the characteristics of out-field investigation, and placed them in several 10x10cm display boxes. The real objects, pictures and words are arranged neatly according to the five measurement levels and form a beautiful and intuitive regional data wall.

Five levels of sustainable material properties include:

Climate adaptability: pictures including temperature, precipitation change data chart, extreme weather events, geographical distribution.

Local material: materials including loess, broken tiles, blue brick, straw, log and other main materials needed by the building.

Native terrain: schematic diagrams of landform and gully village section, banded architectural distribution along the village contour line, quadrangle courtyard triad courtyard, irregular buildings, etc.

Energy saving and environmental protection: methods (in the form of written words and pictures) of treatment among waste metals, recyclable blue bricks, stone materials, consumer goods waste, and environmental protection methods.

Cultural symbolism: handicrafts, decorative patterns, carving and other physical objects, architectural model drawings, wine, vinegar, tofu and other local characteristics.

Fig. 1. The process of collecting materials and the site of display

The author invited the local craftsmen, folk craftsmen, ordinary residents (the elderly, women, children), and volunteers to form a team of 20 people, which have none background of design. Facing the "little square" wall, the author introduced the significance of the reconstruction of ancient villages and the display content, along with how to use the data wall to the team members. The participants are open to independently discuss and vote on the local characteristic architectural elements and put forward ideas and suggestions on the reconstruction of ancient villages.

The author collected the results, also followed a simple discussion with everyone, then initially established the regional architectural identity suitable for the sustainable development and transformation of the ancient village. The participants formulated the direction, goal, and concept of the transformation, and laid a foundation for the formulation of the transformation plan.

The ideas collected so far include but are not limited to:

– There are various buildings in the village that have been in disrepair, problems such as cracked walls and unstable structures need to be repaired, and private houses and shops are in a mess.
– The awareness of rural cultural characteristics is relatively low, and ancient buildings have been damaged to a certain extent. There is a need to popularize cultural education and improve the quality of housing and the living environment while preserving historical values.
– Increase the cultural identity of the new generation of residents, thereby increasing the attractiveness of the local area.

5   Discussion

In this paper, we discuss the value of participatory tools based on system design which redefine the measurement level of regional architecture, also intervening a polit study in the definition of regional architecture by taking Hougugu village of Jinzhong as an example. The next step is to expand the visual features of the participating design tool, deepen the participating discussion, along with the version of subsequent iterations through a larger experimental sample.

References

Anderson, L.: Analytic autoethnography. J. Contemp. Ethnograp. **35**(4), 373–395 (2006)
Aydogan, A., Cerone, R.: Review of the effects of plants on indoor environments. Indoor Built Environ. **30**(4), 442–460 (2021)
Barbero, S., Bicocca, M.: Systemic design approach in policy-making for sustainable territorial development. Des. J. **20**(sup1), S3496–S3506 (2017)
Battistoni, C., Giraldo Nohra, C., Barbero, S.: A systemic design method to approach future complex scenarios and research towards sustainability: a holistic diagnosis tool. Sustainability **11**(16), 4458 (2019)
Bennetts, H., Radford, A., Williamson, T.: Understanding Sustainable Architecture. Taylor & Francis (2003)
Blomkamp, E.: Systemic design practice for participatory policymaking. Policy Design Pract. **5**(1), 12–31 (2022)

Foster, G., Kreinin, H.: A review of environmental impact indicators of cultural heritage buildings: a circular economy perspective. Environ. Res. Lett. **15**(4), 043003 (2020)

Gauzin-Müller, D.: Sustainable architecture and urbanism: concepts, technologies, examples. Springer Science & Business Media (2002)

Grierson, D.: Towards a sustainable built environment. CIC Start Online Innov. Rev. **1**(1), 70–77 (2009)

Guy, S., Farmer, G.: Contested constructions: the competing logics of green buildings and ethics. In: Ethics and the Built Environment, pp. 89–104. Routledge (2012)

Hillier, B.: The city as a socio-technical system: a spatial reformulation in the light of the levels problem and the parallel problem. In: Arisona, S.M., Aschwanden, G., Halatsch, J., Wonka, P. (eds.) Digital urban modeling and simulation. CCIS, vol. 242, pp. 24–48. Springer, Heidelberg (2012). https://doi.org/10.1007/978-3-642-29758-8_3

Ignatieva, M.: Design and future of urban biodiversity. Urban biodiversity and design, vol. 1 (2010)

Jackson, N.: The architectural view: perspectives on communication. Vis. Commun. Q. **13**(1), 32–45 (2006)

Jones, P.H.: Systemic design principles for complex social systems. In: Metcalf, G.S. (ed.) Social systems and design. TSS, vol. 1, pp. 91–128. Springer, Tokyo (2014). https://doi.org/10.1007/978-4-431-54478-4_4

Jones, P.H., VanPatter, G.K.: Design 1.0, 2.0, 3.0, 4.0: The rise of visual sensemaking. NextD Journal; ReThinking Design, 1–12 (2009)

Kistova, A.V., Tamarovskaya, A.N.: Architectural space as a factor of regional cultural identity (2015)

Lee, J.H.: Reinterpreting sustainable architecture: what does it mean syntactically? Sustainability **12**(16), 6566 (2020)

Li, G.: The dynamics of architectural form: space, emotion and memory. Art Design Rev. **7**(4), 187–205 (2019)

Liang, X.: Regional culture expressed in modern architecture design. Cross-Cultural Commun. **10**(6), 148–151 (2014)

Mallgrave, H.F.: Architecture and Embodiment: The Implications of the New Sciences and Humanities for Design. Routledge (2013)

Manzini, E.: Design in the transition phase: a new design culture for the emerging design. Design Philos. Papers **13**(1), 57–62 (2015)

Méndez-Fajardo, S., Böni, H., Vanegas, P., Sucozhañay, D.: Improving sustainability of E-waste management through the systemic design of solutions: the cases of Colombia and Ecuador. In: Handbook of Electronic Waste Management, pp. 443–478. Butterworth-Heinemann (2020)

Muazu, A.G., Alibaba, H.Z.: The use of traditional building materials in modern methods of construction (a case study of northern Nigeria). Int. J. Eng. Sci. Technol. Res. **2**(6), 30–40 (2017)

Nettelbladt, G., Boano, C.: Infrastructures of reception: the spatial politics of refuge in Mannheim, Germany. Polit. Geogr. **71**, 78–90 (2019)

Olabi, A.G.: Developments in sustainable energy and environmental protection. Simul. Model. Pract. Theory **19**(4), 1139–1142 (2011)

Opoku, A.: The role of culture in a sustainable built environment. In: Chiarini, A. (ed.) Sustainable operations management. MOP, pp. 37–52. Springer, Cham (2015). https://doi.org/10.1007/978-3-319-14002-5_3

Pereno, A., Barbero, S.: Systemic design for territorial enhancement: an overview on design tools supporting socio-technical system innovation. Strat. Design Res. J. **13**(2), 113–136 (2020)

Ploder, A., Stadlbauer, J.: Strong reflexivity and its critics: responses to autoethnography in the German-speaking cultural and social sciences. Qual. Inq. **22**(9), 753–765 (2016)

Remizova, O.: The structure of the architectural language. Architect. Stud. (1, Num. 2), 81–86 (2015)

Ruttonsha, P.: Towards a (Socio-ecological) science of settlement: relational dynamics as a basis for place. In: Jones, P., Kijima, K. (eds.) Systemic Design. Translational Systems Sciences, vol. 8. Springer, Tokyo (2018). https://doi.org/10.1007/978-4-431-55639-8_7

Ryan, A.: A framework for systemic design. FORMakademisk **7**(4) (2014)

Ryan, C.: Eco-Acupuncture: designing and facilitating pathways for urban transformation, for a resilient low-carbon future. J. Clean. Prod. **50**, 189–199 (2013)

Sanders, E.B.N., Brandt, E., Binder, T.: A framework for organizing the tools and techniques of participatory design. In: Proceedings of the 11th Biennial Participatory Design Conference, pp. 195–198 (2010)

Sassi, P.: Strategies for Sustainable Architecture. Taylor & Francis (2006)

Sevaldson, B.: GIGA-Mapping: Visualisation for complexity and systems thinking in design. Nordes (4) (2011)

Sondhi, P.: Architecture as Communication a Study of the Role of Form, Function and Context in Evoking Meaning. Rochester Institute of Technology (2015)

Stojiljković, D., Ristić Trajković, J.: Semiotics and urban culture: architectural projections of structuralism in a socialist context. Soc. Semiot. **28**(3), 330–348 (2018)

Stokols, D., Lejano, R.P., Hipp, J.: Enhancing the resilience of human–environment systems: a social ecological perspective. Ecol. Soc. **18**(1) (2013)

Thomas, K.L.: Material Matters: Architecture and Material Practice. Routledge (2006)

Zhong, W., Schröder, T., Bekkering, J.: Biophilic design in architecture and its contributions to health, well-being, and sustainability: a critical review. Front. Architect. Res. (2021)

Author Index

© The Editor(s) (if applicable) and The Author(s), under exclusive license
to Springer Nature Switzerland AG 2023
M. Kurosu and A. Hashizume (Eds.): HCII 2023, LNCS 14014, pp. 467–468, 2023.
https://doi.org/10.1007/978-3-031-35572-1

Printed in the United States
by Baker & Taylor Publisher Services